GODDESSES OF AKRAGAS

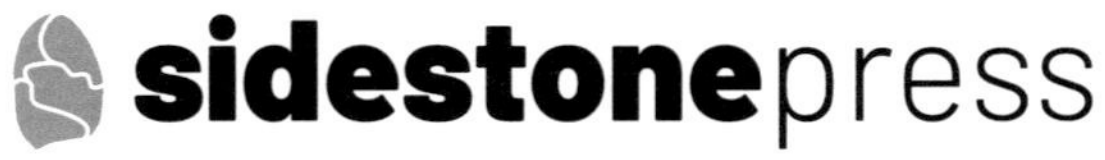

For Majid and Daniel

GODDESSES OF AKRAGAS

A STUDY OF TERRACOTTA VOTIVE FIGURINES FROM SICILY

Gerrie van Rooijen

Published by Sidestone Press, Leiden
www.sidestone.com

Imprint: Sidestone Press Dissertations

Lay-out & cover design: Sidestone Press

Photography cover: Figurine probably from Akragas, AT 3392 (713) Mus. Moscow, h.24.5cm. Photo Mus. Moscow, Scale 1:1. See Fig.14 Cat.**118**; background image: Scala dei Turchi, Sicily. Photo FP. Wing (stock.abobe.com). Back cover: Agrigento, Sicily. Photo Roberto Nencici (stock.adobe.com).

ISBN 978-90-8890-900-9 (softcover)
ISBN 978-90-8890-901-6 (hardcover)
ISBN 978-90-8890-902-3 (PDF e-book)

This book was originally written as a PhD dissertation and successfully defended at Leiden University in 2019.

This research was supported by the Netherlands Organisation for Scientific Research (NWO) under project number: 023.002.085.

Contents

List of figures with references

If not otherwise stated the photos are taken by the students involved in the Akragas Project or the author.

Chapter II:

Chapter III:

Chapter IV:

Catalogue:

These figures are below or next to the description of the related Catalogue number, in bold.

Fig.23 Cat.**170**: Very similar, but much larger head than 170. Inv. No. APM 1825. Scale 1:1 Photo Allard Pierson Museum, Universiteit van Amsterdam.

Fig.24 Cat.**171**: Scale 1:1 Head comparable with head of no. 171. Inv. no. AG9187 Mus. Agrigento.

Fig.25 Cat.**173**: Some of the content of a deposit pit at the Necropolis di Contrada Mosè. Context of no.21, 54, 83 and 173. See for other items Catalogue fig.4. Mus. Agrigento.

Fig.26 Cat.**182**: Head of a male from Akragas, S81 Mus. Agrigento; Scale 1:1.

Fig.27 Cat.**186**: The body of no. 186 resembles this complete figurine. Mus. Agrigento.

Fig.28 Cat.**198**: The front and side views of a similar figure, as exhibited in the showcase in the Louvre; Scale 1:1.

Fig.29 Cat.**198**: Figurine (h.9cm) in which a girl wears the goddess on her left shoulder, holding her with her right hand at the ankles and supporting her feet with her left hand. Mus. Randazzo. Scale 1:1.

Fig.30 Cat.**199**: A smaller figure is carried on this plaque from Carthage. Photo after Breitenstein 1941, pl. 90.

Fig.31 Cat.**202**: Part of the hair of a statue, found near the Temple of Zeus, Agrigento, AG 8611; Scale 1:1.

Fig.32 Cat.**202**: Part of a similar hairstyle, found at S. Anna, Agrigento; Scale 1:1.

Chapter I

Akragantine figurines and their context

I.1 Introduction

Akragas[1] in Sicily lies at the crossroads between different worlds, both culturally and geographically. Attracted by its fertile soil and strategic location close to the sea, successive groups of people have settled at Akragas over the centuries, shaping the distinctive material culture of the area.

In the 6th century BCE, numerous groups of people began to settle at Akragas next to its eponymous river. The Akragas river crosses the west side of the settlement and flows into the sea to the south. According to Thucydides, although the new polis established by the various settlers formed a political entity, it still lacked a shared identity. The mixture of peoples with diverging cultural identities had yet to be unified. The city, therefore, started to bridge differences by enhancing collective participation, and a new local identity was formed through social interaction, regulated by religious narratives. Whether this was an intentional process remains, however, a question.

The sharing of images in cultic expressions, involving recognisable forms, helped build social unity among people of different genders, social and cultural backgrounds. Integration and communication among people of different origins could be accomplished by the application of certain shapes and forms in the visual languages. The context in which they were used, most probably temples, makes clear that community-building was an important aspect of religion. Although we have no written records of religious narratives from Archaic Akragas, we are able to draw on evidence provided by the extensive remains of its material culture.

In order to better understand the social aspects of society at ancient Akragas, we need to examine its material culture. The material reflection of Akragantine religion is expressed on a personal level by dedications. On the basis of the hypothesis that these dedicated objects provide information on the considerations of their makers and users, this thesis provides an in depth analysis of their iconography and the technology used to create them. The choices made on specific details about the appearance of the figurines or the manner of their production give us an insight into the social structures of the society in which they were created and used. The implications of such choices are interpreted in order to reconstruct the possible geographical origin of the use of votives and their iconography by the inhabitants of Akragas, the organisation of their economy, and their religious customs.

Dedications of terracotta figurines have been found in large quantities at Akragas in sanctuaries and in fewer numbers in graves. The (approximately two hundred) figurines appear to have been produced over the course of about one hundred years, starting in the second half of the 6th century BCE. The form and development of these statuettes provide us with information both on why they were created to look as they did

1 Later the city was named Agrigentum, Girgenti and presently Agrigento, though the cities were not in precisely the same locations.

and also on the techniques employed in their production. This thesis, therefore, provides an in-depth analysis of both the iconography and the technology employed in the production of the terracotta dedicatory figurines of Akragas. The choice of Akragas for this study is not only because of its leading role among Sicilian city-states but also because of the survival of large numbers of figurines. Even when the context of these figurines is not precisely known, they can still help us to shed light on the form and production of votive material and, indirectly, on their meaning and function in society.

I.2 State of research

I.2.a Identifying the figurine and the dedicants

The first question about these figurines has always been its identity. Who is the figure depicted and what is its name? Traditionally the first reaction has been to turn to ancient texts. The result is frequently a somewhat simplistic attempt to identify the figurine or people mentioned in the literary sources using the cultural and religious background as a context. Such attempts ignore or deny the complexity of the archaeological material found on Sicily and overestimate the value of the ancient sources in providing objective, historical information.

The first section below addresses the work of archaeologists up to about 1960 in chronological order. Thereafter, more recent archaeological theory is discussed thematically rather than chronologically. This reflects the change in research methods: from a focus on textual sources to material-based investigation.

I.2.b Proving literature right by the archaeological material

Christian S. Blinkenberg, a Danish archaeologist, excavated at Lindos, Rhodes and found in 1904 the Lindian Chronicle.[2] This inscribed stele contains a list of dedications by different persons and peoples and is dated to the first century BCE. As some objects were lost in the fire at the temple centuries earlier, they are partly reconstructed in the text. With its various mythological individuals as well as other references to Homeric descriptions, the account refers to a wide range of persons over a vast period of time. The text was read by Blinkenberg as a historical account of the religious ties of the Athena cult between Lindos and Gelas. His theory implies that all female terracottas are depictions of Athena, the goddess venerated at Lindos. Her cult would have been brought by the colonists from Lindos to Gelas and from there transferred to Akragas. Therefore, the adjective 'Lindia' is added to her name and the figurines are now known as 'Athena Lindia.'

This interpretation shows that Blinkenberg was facing a well-known problem in classical archaeology: the dichotomy between literary and material sources. For a long time, it was an accepted method to try to fit together texts and materials and to refer to literary sources as proof of historical reality, even when this meant that archaeological material was selected and interpreted according to that principle. Blinkenberg's theory was convincing for so long because it combined ancient literature with archaeological material. His theory was attractive and gained popularity, even in recent archaeological literature.[3] However, the role of archaeology is not to prove literary sources right, and while it sometimes does, there are often many inconsistencies, as there are also in this case.

Blinkenberg selected the archaeological material, looking only at statuettes from Gelas and Akragas, in order to support his argument for a Rhodian origin, while ignoring numerous similar figurines found at other locations in Sicily, dating from the same period.[4] Selected elements of material culture were used as a touchstone for classical literature in order to support his aim. Despite counter-arguments, many willing accepted his thesis as it helped solve a question in the archaeology of colonisation: the relationship between the metropolis and the newly found polis.

I.2.b.i Cult transfer and a prototype reconstruction

Blinkenberg's theory not only corroborated the account of the ancient authors on the origin of the migrants but stated also the continuation of religious practices, the transfer of cult. The state of dependency on the metropolis is shaped through religious practices and the metropolis would have claimed a contribution from the colonies.[5]

In the following paragraphs, his theory will be held up to the light. A related question is whether the implementation of new cultic features took place in specific locations that were already meaningful in a religious sense to the local people. Such sacred locations may have been marked in the landscape, such as springs, caves and hills. Plato wrote in his Laws that respect should be paid to earlier sacred sites in the new settlements, that the old gods would be continued to be venerated and that a temple would be erected for the local

2 He published the text in 1912 in La Chronique du temple Lindien, Bulletin de de l'Académie royale des sciences et des lettres de Danemark, p.317 – 467. A recent translation and comments have been published by Carolyn Higbie in 2003.

3 Agreeing with Blinkenberg: Greco 2002, p.112 'Athena, although she was not called Lindia (...)'; De Miro 2000, p.101ff.; Canciani 1984, p.35f.; Orlandini 1968, p.25-8; Demargne 1984, p. 959f. nos.22-3; Byvanck-Quarles van Ufford 1940, p.54f. The information in the Archaeological Museum of Agrigento names Blinkenberg as well and suggests his interpretation.

4 Dewailly 1992, p.134ff.

5 See Shepherd 2000, p.59 on this subject regarding Brea and later Corinthian colonies.

patron.[6] The absence of earlier material of a specifically local character leaves the question unanswered archaeologically. And while the unplanned extra-urban sanctuaries[7] are an argument in favour, according to Malkin, it is generally not taken as being proven.[8] In addition, the findspots of several figurines are unknown and might have been scattered over an area or found in deposits in a single place. The majority of figurines come from cultic contexts and less frequently from burial contexts.

Another important aspect in the study of the figurines is the reconstruction of a specific prototype. The word 'prototype' means the object or objects that served as example for the patrix. Thus, the figurines could be direct representations of another object, or stand on their own, inspired by, for example, a larger sculpture. When Blinkenberg carried out research at Lindos, his argumentation lacked evidence of the old *agalma*, the cult statue of Athena Lindia. The original statue is thought to have been destroyed by a fire in 690 BCE.[9] He uses three sources of information to reconstruct the statue: depictions of Athena from the same period; other, mostly later, Athena sanctuaries; and known characteristics from literature, even second or third hand. In that way, by comparing images,[10] he reconstructed Athena Lindia, based on the assumption that the dedications were small versions of the cult statue. It is this method that led him to Sicily, where he perceived the Archaic-styled figurines as a sort of derivative of the image from Lindos. The Lindian Chronicle is, besides Thucydides, another literary key in his argumentation: both Gelas and Akragas are mentioned in this text with a dedication to Athena Lindia. It would prove the continuation of the veneration of the same goddess, Athena Lindia, after colonists went from Rhodes to Sicily. In 1917 Blinkenberg writes 'L'image d'Athana Lindia' in which he argues for similarity in the iconography between these images and the lost *agalma* from Lindos.[11]

The idea that the specific image of the terracotta figurines was inspired by a prototype is shared by several researchers.[12] They are convinced that the typical characteristics must have been features of the cult image as well. Jung writes that he is not sure that the cult image of the 8th -7th century BCE had a straight dress and no arms, but it is likely that the statue kept some traditions. It could be that the real-life dressing of the statue is reflected in the image of the terracotta figurine. The sitting position, however, he sees as not necessarily characteristics of the cult statue, because there are also standing figurines. Ritual dressing of a standing image would have been easier.[13] The discussion of the prototype for the coroplasts is in the first place one about whether the statue was standing or sitting. Blinkenberg argued for a seated pose even though the Lindian Chronicle had no mention of it. Jung and Zuntz state that the prototype must have been a standing figure.[14] Zuntz makes a distinction in her interpretation of the identity of the goddess in connection with the position: Demeter would be perhaps depicted seated and Persephone standing.[15] He sees a difference in facial expression as well: Demeter has a Ionian-styled, round and friendly face, which fits, therefore, Demeter's character, while Persephone has "that narrow and severe face which characterizes the Goddess of Death." Zuntz personal idea of a mother goddess and a chthonic one has perhaps made him ascribe a certain character to them. He admits that he has no antecedents for the identification by the facial expression of Persephone, nor does he give examples to show the differences between the faces. The heads were probably so often interchanged, because of the rather fast weathering of the expression in new generations of moulds. This repetitive use shows that there was no clear distinction between the two sorts of faces.

I.2.c Athena Lindia? Rhodian and Sicilian figurines compared

The Lindian Chronicle lists the dedications for Athena Lindia from different cities and individuals in chronological order.[16] In two parts it describes the cult statue itself and its adornment. It mentions a dedication of eight shields and a golden diadem, στεφάνη, for the cult image.[17] Another diadem[18] is mentioned together with necklaces,

6 Plat. Laws 848d.

7 In my opinion they could be planned well outside the city, because there were locations with special features.

8 Malkin 1987, p.144-63.

9 Higbie 2003, p.7 writes that the 'location of the Archaic statue base may still be possible to see.'

10 The goddess was also identified as Athena Polias, which opens the way to more comparisons. Higbie 2003, p.13: Just only late in the 3rd century BCE.

11 Kallimachos, fragm. 100, 4 (ed. Pfeiffer) was read by Blinkenberg 1917, p.8ff. for the identification of the pillar-shaped statuettes as Athana Lindia.

12 Albertocchi 2004, p.158.

13 Jung 1982, p.51.

14 Zuntz 1971, 138 n. 2. He writes that a standing wooden prototype was the original form of the Sicilian figurines. Zuntz 1971, 129. Jung 1982, 51-2 is convinced of a standing prototype because it would be easier to dress in clothes in a ritual and the various sitting/standing positions.

15 Jung criticizes the argumentation and gives examples of different exceptions. Jung 1982, p.244 n. 267.

16 The text should be seen in the light of "Greeks retrojecting later patterns into the past" Higbie 2003, p.227. It is glorifying the past and summing up the magnificence of the island inhabitants by also bringing up mythological persons, who aren't even related to Rhodes directly. For a more detailed comment on the historicity of the Lindian Chronicle by Shepherd 2000, see below.

17 Part XXII. Dedicated by "those making an expedition with Kleoboulos against Lycia", transl. by Higbie 2003, p.31. Kleoboulos was the tyrant of Lindos in the early 6th century BCE.

18 According to Blinkenberg this is the same object, but from two different traditions. Blinkenberg 1917, p.18.

ὅρμος, among other adornments.[19] The old cult image was not dressed up with the aegis and helmet or other war equipment.[20] The Sicilian terracotta statuettes were used by Blinkenberg to reconstruct the cult image of Athena Lindia.[21] The Lindian Chronicle reports that the Akragantines dedicated a *palladion* of Athena with ivory endings for their victory on Minoa.[22] Athena was given the epithet *'Patrooia'*, ancestral, by the Geloans.[23] The Sicilian terracottas would be smaller versions of the Athena Patrooia and therefore the Athena Lindia. He compares them mainly to characteristics mentioned in the Lindian Chronicle.[24] Especially the necklaces mentioned in the text remind him of the Sicilian figurines, which wear different objects on their chests.[25] Blinkenberg identifies the *stephane* as a high crown and equates it in this way with the typical headgear of the Sicilian terracottas, the polos.[26] However, he admits that there is not a single similar looking statuette from Rhodes that could argue in favour of this statement. From the Acropolis at Lindos, there are terracottas figurines of Athena from the 5th century BC, with the aegis, helmet and gorgoneion, as well as a shield with a gorgoneion.[27] An armless 31cm high female figurine with two chains on her chest with a gorgoneion on the upper one, flanked by discs and, on the second, five glandiform pendants, is presented as the key. The figurine is much older than the Lindian ones and besides the gorgoneion iconographically incomparable.[28] The gorgoneion would be very surprising, as no other is known from this period,[29] while all its other features make it a typical Akragantine figurine. The plain pectoral disc in a triple form on one cord is common. In another aspect, the figurines are very different: many Sicilian figurines are seated, while the Rhodian statuettes stand.[30] Because of the gorgoneion and the match with the description in the Lindian Chronicle, Blinkenberg identifies all Geloan and Akragantine female figurines as the main goddess of the colonies: Athena Lindia.[31] The arguments and reasoning for this identification are simply too weak. Much of the argumentation is based on the Lindian Chronicle, a text much later in date and clearly pursuing a different goal. However, he also sees the extensive pectorals with differently shaped pendants as a reflection of the real-life jewellery of the Lindian women, influenced by oriental, Cypriot and Phoenician styles.[32] The archaeological material discussed in chapter 2 supports this element of his theory.[33]

I.2.d Other views on identification and origin

Zuntz interprets the figurines as Demeter and Persephone, again with reference to the literary sources. 'Telines' he calls them, for their origin, which he finds in Herodotus, who states that Deinomenes, one of Gelas' founders had brought the first ancient images from the island of Telos. A new version would have been designed for the new sanctuary in Gelas, keeping the geometrically shaped bodies, but with Ionian faces. The cult of the chthonic deities would have become a public one after the goddesses saved the city and were linked to the ruling dynasty.[34] Hinz also sees a relation with the political situation and a role for the Deinomenids in spreading the cult of Demeter and Kore from Syrakousai and Gelas to its colony of Akragas and other parts of the Greek towns. Its introduction would have taken place in the 7th or 6th century BCE, while eventually they were turned into a pan-Sicilian symbol.[35] Hinz also states that there is no clear material of another cult previous to this one. Western Greek material dominates the archaeological records, even though there

---

19 Part XXXIV. Again it is from the spoils of a war, this time against Crete. This event is dated to the end of the 4th century BCE. Higbie 2003, p.128.

20 Blinkenberg 1917, p.18.

21 Blinkenberg 1917, p.13. Though he is the first to research the theory extensively, comparing Sicilian objects, he was not the first who thought the Athena Lindia cult had been spread to Gela by the colonisation and from there further to Akragas and Kamarina. Van Gelder 1900, p.316. This was however not based on the Lindian Chronicle or on the design of the Sicilian terracottas but on ancient authors. Polyb. 9.27.7; Diod. 13.90.20. In the same way Zeus Atabyrios was thought to have been brought by the colonists, directly from Rhodes. Van Gelder 1900, p.300; Polyb. 9.27.7.

22 From the Lindian Chronicle XXX it appears as if Akragas was a direct colony of Rhodes. According to Polybius 9.27-8 this was the case. Higbie 2003, p.119 supposes Akragas was founded by a Rhodian and Geloan together.

23 Part XXV. This title is not mentioned somewhere else, nor in Gela, nor in Rhodes Higbie 2003, p.106; Though Athena was venerated in Gela. Blinkenberg 1917, p.32 describes a pithos dedicated to Athena.

24 Blinkenberg 1917, p.32.

25 Blinkenberg 1917, 20. Blinkenberg 1917, p.35 suggests that the xoanon of Athena was decorated in this way.

26 The stephane does not necessarily need to be headgear, but could refer to a wreath, a common dedication.

27 Blinkenberg 1917, p.21ff.

28 Unfortunately this object from Akragas is lost and known only from a drawing and description. Blinkenberg's source is Kekulé von Stradonitz 1884, p.17, fig. 22. Then the object was still part of a private collection. The gorgoneion would be very suprising as no other as such is known, while all other features of its appearance make it a typical Akragantine figurine. A triple disc pectoral is common, but with plain discs.

29 There is only one object from Akragas known to me with a similar face as a pendant: AG9107(250) is probably from the first half of the 5th century BCE and marked by an Egyptian styled face with a small sun-disc flanked by snakes. Gorgoneia are, on the other hand, common in Sicily as pedimental decorations; they do not refer specifically to Athena, but are thought to be apotropaic.

30 Blinkenberg 1917, p.16f.

31 Blinkenberg 1917, p.31.

32 Blinkenberg 1917, p.32f.

33 See Section II.6.g-i.

34 Zuntz 1971, p.136-8.

35 Hinz 1998, p.21-5.

is proof of collective part celebration of the cult.[36] But she admits also that certain aspects or features of the local religious customs might have influenced the preference for a certain deity.[37]

Depending on her attributes and appearance, the figurines could be modified to depict a specific goddess. Martine Dewailly also accepts this thesis.[38] The interpretation of similar looking objects depends therefore also very much on the context[39], as Marina Albertocchi made clear in her study of the Sicilian figurines.[40] The typical features of the figurines, archaeological arguments, and the question of identity are further discussed in chapter two.

I.2.e Oikist cult and cultural identity formation

The starting date for the foundation of the colonies by the Greeks is 734 BCE, based on calculations from references to historical events by Thucydides.[41] It is probable that the island was already known and that trading posts had already been established. Early material, predating the official foundation, has been found at Gelas and Syracuse, among other cities, proving extensive contacts and probably settlement as early as the Iron Age.[42] Also, contacts with Bronze Age Greece and Phoenicians have been attested archaeologically. It is clear that when the newcomers arrived, this time with a different intention or in larger numbers, they did not find empty coasts. Because they claimed land for their colonies, their arrival caused the local inhabitants either to join them or to move further inland.

Seeking security and a stronger position on the trade routes, they formed larger settlements out of the smaller dispersed groups.[43] This development might have incited cultural exchange and hybridisation. The process of influencing took place probably in rapid form with these social organisations and its outcome, though in itself a continuous process without clear begin or end, was a culture with newly defined values and expressions of its own. Similarly, the Greeks who probably arrived from very different places and dispersed groups also joined forces to form a new society. They would have understood each other through common language and cultural traits. Such events are indeed described as conscious actions in Greek literature. A unity was constructed with the poleis-model. The multiplicity of culturally different people might have led to the idea that a certain common ground had to be established to form a unity within, in opposition to, or at least different from, the world of the 'other.' This evolution must have given a strong impulse to the institutions of the poleis.

One such example is the oikist cult, which strengthened the cohesion within the polis, distinguishing itself from others outside the polis, by means of the focus on a founder-hero. There are two opinions on the role of the oikist cult in the relations between the mother-city and the colony. The first is claimed by Dunbabin and states that the oikist cult proves the strong political ties between the metropolis and the colony since they would be a continuation of the bond between both.[44] Malkin's opinion, which seems more likely to me, is that the oikist cult was created after the foundation in order to have religious independence and self-identity, as part of the state's self-definition.[45] A religious base was thus created for polis-chauvinism.[46] This base was supported and constantly renewed by festivities at the agora, at the oikist's tomb. Not only the polis as state but also individuals could dedicate expressions of piety to the oikist. This could imply that that the oikist cult eased co-habitation and sharing values resulted in a peaceful process of shaping a new identity.[47] Dougherty gives an alternative view, a personal story of the oikist, and by doing so seems to confirm the above-described theory of the settlers as people leaving their home for personal reasons, searching for a new place to simply survive. She suggests that the oikist could have been an outcast or even a criminal in his hometown and was purified by his hero-cult. Old religious customs are replaced by completely new ones, which is a way to self-identify.[48]

Cultural distinctions may also have counted in the choice of these mythological or real leaders. Malkin claims that the strong dichotomy between Greek and others is an unnatural one, imposed by later developments of Hellenisation and projected wrongly onto an earlier period.[49] In chapter 2 and 3, this aspect of cultural identity and the expression of a harmonious society appears from the archaeological material connected with cultic expression. The politically Greek polis in Sicily, such as Akragas, certainly had a population comprised of mixed

36 Hinz 1998, p.20.

37 Hinz 1998, p.19-21.

38 Dewailly 1992, p.41. She studied the Selinuntine figurines extensively.

39 Also Hinz agrees, specifically for female deities. Hinz 1998, p.34.

40 Albertocchi 2004, p.160f. The title 'Athana Lindia' of this overview refers rather to the way these figurines are referred to, not to an interpretation as Athena.

41 The chronology and foundation dates are believed to be fairly accurate. Nijboer 2006, p.256-8. For a more extensive description of Thucyidides' account, see Section I.6.b.

42 Hodos points to the confusion on the use of the term 'Iron Age'. Here the period directly preceding the Phoenician and Greek foundations are meant, roughly from the mid ninth century BCE onwards.

43 Leighton 1999, p.238-9.

44 Dunbabin 1948, p.11.

45 Malkin 1987, p.189, 201-3; Shepherd 2000, p.57.

46 Malkin 1987, p.189. The oikist cult might also have been a strong political instrument used by the aristocracy of a city, like the Deinomenidai in Gela, who in this way sanctioned their power. Malkin 1987, p.250ff. and 259, n. 112.

47 Leschhorn 1984, p.45.

48 An example from South Italy of her theory is the veneration of Sirens as goddesses. Taylor 2014.

49 Malkin 2004.

cultural identities. While finding factual information is hard, the narratives of the Greeks give an insight into how Greeks conceptualized colonisation.[50]

The dates mentioned by Thucydides mark the start of the polis, the political entity of the city. There must have been a process of acculturation, integration, settling down, starting a life, trade and institutions, that would have taken several generations. It is even questionable whether the aim from the beginning was to start 'Greek' poleis. The number of immigrants would have been quite high and, though they would have come from different places, they would probably have gradually assumed a shared cultural identity, integrating with other peoples. The precise date of foundation or of the first settlers' arrival is not now possible to discern. There are also no contemporary inscriptions stating when exactly a certain event marked the creation of political institutions. Yet the development in technical and iconographical aspects of terracotta figurines gives a fine indication of a relative date for the process of cultural integration.

Snodgrass believes that the new settlements were strongly independent from early on, which only increased over the years and generations to follow. The groups of colonists would have had no other relationship with their birthplace in terms of power and control. The votives by some of these settlements in Olympia, for example, should not be seen as a fulfilment of a tribute to the religious ties with the homeland but were meant to show the wealth and the prosperity of the settlement.[51] The word 'colony' implies a provincial dependence, which does not do justice to the actual character of their relationship. Relations seem to have been based rather on political and *xenia* ties or newly formed bonds than by ethnic or cultural relations with their ancestors. Greekness is a concept introduced after the Archaic Period, by authors writing with the agenda of including the Sicilian settlements into a large political structure and profiting also in the east from Sicily's great wealth.

I.2.f Intermarriage and gender

The question is if intermarriage in the earlier phases of settlement on Sicily caused stronger acculturation, while later new immigrants from Greece, like the supposed group from Rhodes that co-founded Akragas, strengthened numerically ascendancy of the home-town, influencing social customs, such as burial practices. The 6th century BCE fortification of native settlements indicates a deterioration of relations.[52] The cosmopolitism of the citizens, combined with their different roots, led them to create their own identity markers and by doing so united them as citizens of the same town, rather than as individuals with different socio-cultural origins.

Bintliff argues in the case of Thessalian Neolithic villages, on the basis of chaos-complexity theory, that the underlying reason for colonisation was social pressure. The fission of villages was desirable because the face-to-face level of 150-200 people was passed.[53] An important aspect of the network of villages that came into existence in this way is the exchange of marriage partners. This means of creating social cohesion is brought up by Perlès when she states that two features eased friction: land and marriages.[54] Both social features are materialised in ceramics. Communal dining served social cohesion and pottery was made in the first place for this reason. The second argument consists of small terracottas, mostly female figurines, which showcase the role of women in reproduction, in the sense of fertility as well as the exchange between villages. The latter set the relations between the communities of the region. It is argued for that on Sicily intermarriage between settlers and locals was not uncommon.[55] Thucydides mentions a dispute on land and marriage rights between Selinous and Segesta, which shows that in the 5th century BCE this played still a very important role in society, as it was, next to land, a reason to start a war.[56]

The role that intermarriage played in social cohesion among the inhabitants could be related to the myth of Persephone. Only in the 4th century BCE, the myth was further defined by several authors with additional details such as its location.[57] The narrative of this abduction/wedding must have been created based on certain customs. Likewise, the rape of Persephone seems to have been presented as a sort of sanctioning of intermarriage.[58]

Dougherty claims that in various literature in antiquity agricultural imagery is used to describe marriage as well as colonisation. Marriage would, for example, be compared with picking flowers or fruit. Persephone is picking flowers with her friends when she is abducted by Hades, symbolising that she herself is the flower picked by Hades. The partners in marriage, when seeing each other for the first time, would represent the confrontation with local people. Also, violence would be legitimised, as it served as a model for acculturation and integration, in order to make the 'land bear fruit'. Thus she explains that in several foundation stories, both colonial or not, marriage/abduction and rape are a recurrent motif. This

50 Dougherty 1993, p.32.
51 Snodgrass 1994, p.9.
52 Leighton 1999, p.240.
53 Bintliff 2007.
54 Perlès 2007, p.293.
55 Graham 2001, p.328.
56 Thuc. 6.6.2; Hall 2004, p.41.
57 Hinz 1998, p.27.
58 One statuette of a satyr abducting the 'figurine'-goddess indicates that such a narrative of kidnapping women existed prior to the precise story of Persephone. See no. 198 in the Catalogue.

depends highly on the association of women with land and agriculture as the symbiosis of the male part with nature and earth being female. From such a perspective, the veneration of specifically female deities on the agriculturally explored island of Sicily could be explained, though in general terms. It matches the popular veneration of Demeter and Persephone in the Classical Period, whose story is so strongly connected with agriculture and the seasons but also with the transition from girl to woman and from life to death.

I.3 Aims and research questions

This research sets out to understand the terracotta figurine production in Akragas. Though Akragas is smaller then Selinous, this thesis aims to provide a similar overview of the material as Dewailly did for the figurines from Selinous.[59] As the research discussed above shows, the identification of the figurine has yet to be agreed upon. The question of her identity might depend on literary sources, but the study of her appearance could well reveal details on her attributes and function. Research into production techniques adds to this, as it helps us to understand the process of mass production and standardisation. One of the possibilities is thus that 'the devil lies in the detail,' that is that the identity might be defined by her appearance. Her identity might lie in her features, and is expressed through the specific outfit she is wearing in addition to the context of time and place. Related to this question is the modelling of figurines after a certain example. Was there a cult statue or does the appearance of the figurines reflect dress and adornment used in real life? Does the representation depict a human or a deity? Does standing or sitting, or wearing particular headgear specify her identity? Are they depicted as female and feminine?

If we turn away from the literature as the primary source of information, we must instead analyse the figurines themselves: how do they look precisely and how did this appearance come into being? With which other figurines and statuary can they be compared? In this way, a specific local Akragantine definition of the representation of the female figurine from this period (roughly the Archaic Period) can be defined. Albertocchi's work offers a good overview of the dispersal of the terracotta category.[60] While her work frames the wider, mainly Sicilian, context, this thesis concentrates on the local character of the figurines and therefore does not exclude figurines without the pectoral pendants, but places them in the development and definition of typical characteristics.

The Catalogue places the figurines into distinct groups and describes their similarities with other terracottas, from Akragas and elsewhere. From this structuring, several distinctive characteristics appear that help to answer the question of which characteristics can be seen to be local and which objects (and characteristics) are imported. These features help us to identify objects in several European museums, of which the context is no longer known, as being Sicilian or even specifically from Akragas.

By identifying the local features of the figurines, we can gain insight into the conscious decisions of the local coroplasts. We can then not only identify specific deviations from mould series and additional alterations by hand but also speculate on what such alterations imply. It is necessary to understand precisely how these figurines were created, as their material shape is the key to understanding their use and cultic value. Therefore, starting right at the beginning with the production process, practical questions need to be asked. Which material would have acted as the model, or *patrix*, for the first terracotta figurines in Akragas? How were the first moulds applied and how did the technique develop into a one of such scale and precision? The material and technical perspective is addressed in the third chapter. Where did the Akragantines find the clay? How was moulding applied? The tools and material necessary are reviewed and the quality of new generations in a mould series are scrutinised. In addition, the coroplastic work is analysed, including the investment of time, production costs, and the balance between quantity and quality. How could such large-scale production take place and what economic value did coroplastics have? Another practical question is their function and physical properties as a dedication: did they stand upright or were they hung up to be visible to passers-by? What would have been an ideal size to be carried from the workshop to the place of dedication? Where they positioned in groups or alone?

Indirectly in the same chapter, one of the methods for understanding the production technique, an archaeological experiment, is also tested in order to add to our understanding of the method of production and its wider social and economic implications.

This thesis aims not only to understand precisely what is being made (Chapter 2 and Catalogue) and how the production techniques evolved (Chapter 3) but also why the figurines were produced. It aims to reveal the political, social and religious context in which these figurines were made (Chapter 1) and, though much of that context is not easy to perceive, to gain an insight into the functioning of the society that produced and used them. By doing so, the appearance of the figurines and the techniques used to create them are placed in the wider context of Sicilian figurine production. The exchange of ideas on specific forms or tools and moulds defines Akragas in the overall development of Sicilian terracotta figurines. Akragas' local characteristics are compared to regional and Mediterranean-wide developments in order to find

59 Dewailly 1992.
60 Albertocchi 2004.

the reasons for local variations and differences from other production centres.

The political and religious structures, as far as they are known from ancient literature, are used to interpret the relationship between the polis-wide institutions and personal dedications. One of the main questions is, in this regard, whether the political institutions would have obliged the people to take part in events strengthening community building and overcoming different identities (Chapter 1 and 2). This indirect question of identity, closely relates to the-up to-now most common idea of an imported cult and a Greek culturally dominated society, after their colonisation of several poleis. This research would like to pay specific attention to the cultural traits of other groups that might have been part of the same society.

By looking at the choices made in the rendering of the figurines, religious ideas can be inferred. The intricate designs reveal a society in which several traditions merged and were absorbed into a collective object of veneration. Questions about the figurines, therefore, range from practical issues to more complex issues concerning her identity, gender and cultic role. Through comparisons with real-life objects, terracotta dedications or iconography elsewhere questions about the identity of the coroplasts and the dedicants can be answered (Chapter 2). Part of this inquiry is the analysis of the local development of the figurines and the implications of the identified changes over time.

Taken together, this thesis aims to interpret the statuettes' use and meaning within the context of a multicultural society.

I.4 Method and archaeological theory

A parallel to the method of inferring religious beliefs from their material expression, though with a different scope, can be found in Bakhuizen's horizon concept: by reviewing myths he attempts to see how the early Greeks may have experienced the unknown land of Sicily. He looks for the traces of their views as preserved in myths, topography, and onomastics.[61] 'Horizon' indicates here the line separating us from an unknown world. In the perception of Greek mythology, these far lands were both a place of danger as well as a place of agricultural plenty. The difference between the 'here' and 'there' was the unfamiliarity with the world beyond the horizon.[62] These mythological stories and rituals are known to us through non-contemporary literature and material culture.

A second method applied in this thesis attempts to reconstruct thoughts and ideas by looking at objects. This methodology might be originally based on Christopher Hawkes' 'Ladder of inference' theory, which is still found in recent literature on archaeological theory but with a remark on the supposed contrast to 'hard' and 'soft' information. Artefacts, the material objects themselves, give in a more direct way information on their physical appearance and their production, while the consequent rungs of the ladder, social-economical aspects and religious or political thoughts, are much harder inferences to make.[63] The direct information of the first rung of the ladder is gained by scrutinising research on the figurines, which indirectly reveals information on the people who made and used them. Production and techniques would be less individual from a technical perspective, as the figurines are mould-made. To what extent this applies to the Akragantine terracotta figurines, which, on the one hand, were individual dedications and, on the other, part of a collective act of votive giving, will be addressed as well. Though the implications of such material analysis remain hypothetical, the physical level of research might provide more direct, but also not always unequivocal information. The dichotomy between material and meaning is, however, a theoretical one. While anchored in material, information can be still conveyed through the use of symbols and shapes. Material expression involves several sorts of information, which are in itself cultural. This study does not deny that other sorts of information, next to the physical can be gained. On the contrary, symbols function as referant and meaning, as explained well by Robb's article 'The Archaeology of Symbols'. The symbols function as lego bricks, receiving meaning in their combination and the interaction. [64] Aspects of regional and local but as well personal aspects of figurine use return in current conceptual frameworks for studying prehistoric figurines. Many themes of analysis could be applied to the figurines from later periods as well. These approaches uncover identity, contacts and reciprocal communication. The Akragantine figurines offer an insight in local, Sicilian, contacts, in the wider Mediterranean through stylistic and material research. The personal decisions that shaped these figurines should not be overlooked. The Akragantine figurines are therefore treated here also in their application as personal expressions, votives, formed by individual choices.

The aim is to review the inhabitants' perception and conceptualisation of movement, exchange and integration. The newly formed society addressed new circumstances, from landscapes to people from diverse cultures, by means of religion. They expressed their integration into a new land and society through cultic practices. The cultic material is not just an expression of rituals, beliefs in the afterlife, and transformation, but it is also a means

61 Bakhuizen 1988.

62 The story of Odysseus' encounter with the cyclopes and their stacks of milk and cheese is exemplary. See Section I.6.

63 Hawkes 1954, p.155-168.

64 Belcher and Croucher 2016, p.43-8; Nijboer 1998, p.11; Robb 1998.

of materializing the non-physical world through the use of objects. The discussion of the materiality of objects is thus seen as directly entangled with social aspects. The physical process from collecting the raw materials to forming the objects and eventually handling the votives in its ascribed meta-physical facets, is therefore key in understanding meaning and use of these figurines. Their becoming as tactile objects gives them agency. By categorising the figurines, the conceptualisation of the body over time is related to its material form. The extent to which corporeality of these objects, their embodiment, is dictated by the material is therefore an important part of this research.

I.5 Research structure

Different aspects of the Akragantine figurines are discussed and analysed in four chapters. The second part of this chapter presents an overview of the political and social context in which Akragas developed and a review of the literature upon which we depend for much of our information. Much of the (partially mythological) information on the foundation of Akragas comes to us through ancient literature. While nineteenth-century archaeological research tried to match the material culture with Greek and Roman literary sources, more recent scientific research has provided a counterbalance, as well as additional nuance and depth, to these sources. The literature is reviewed thematically, examining the socio-economic background of what is usually called 'a colony', the political structures and connections with the metropolis, the role that religion and mythology played in the formation of a polis, and how terracotta objects functioned as an expression of devotion, and how they conveyed a reflection of the intentions of the individual dedicant.

The second chapter examines the iconography of the figurines, and how their evolving appearance reflects the changing preferences for specific forms, which can often be related to the cultural origins of the coroplasts or dedicants. The choice of a specific form tells us something about the function and meaning of these objects, as well as their role in the dedication. In order to review the implications of the appearance of the figurines, this chapter provides a thematic analysis of four distinct aspects of the figurines: the shape of the body, the face, the dress, and the furniture. This detailed investigation indirectly reveals a view of several other aspects of social-economic life in Akragas, including welfare, and allusions to metallurgy. The discussion includes comparisons with terracottas from other Sicilian towns, as well as looking at iconographic influences from additional Greek, Etruscan, and Phoenician material. To provide more context on certain details of the figurines' appearance, the chapter also discusses other archaeological finds from Akragas helping us to understand the customs of the inhabitants of Akragas. Each of the four parts of the chapter includes a discussion of overarching questions, such as the representation of real-life dress and adornment. Special attention is paid to gender: Why do the majority of representations appear to be female, and how is their gender expressed? A second, related question concerns the specific identity of the person represented and her cult. The development of the iconographic characteristics of the Akragantine figurines is explored, along with interactions with the nearby cities of Selinous and Gelas. The implications of the identified similarities and differences provide a basis for the following chapter, which looks at the organisation and development of the local coroplastic production.

The third chapter explores the technical aspects of the production of terracotta figurines at Akragas. Looking at the practical elements of production not only provides us with important information on production techniques, tools and methods but it also assists with the iconographic analysis of the figurines by enabling us to assess the meaning of specific variations and alterations. The introduction of moulds had a marked impact on several aspects of the figurines' appearance, and the use of moulds increased the options for serial production, significantly affecting the way in which objects were produced.

The technical aspects of the figurines were investigated both by carefully examining the figurines themselves, but also by using an archaeological experiment in which two moulds, created from two different figurines, were used to help reconstruct the different acts and processes required in the *chaîne d'opératoire* (operational sequence of production). The focus of this analysis was once again the local production of the objects at Akragas, although comparisons are made with Gelas and Selinous.

By analysing the raw material used to produce the figurines – clay – potential locations of production are identified. The material features of the clay found near Akragas were tested for plasticity, colour after firing, and fineness in order to identify which clays had been used for the local figurines and to assign the figurines to possible workshops. Practical questions regarding the find spots, tempering with other materials, additional hand-modelling, and reworking was also addressed by archaeological experiment.

The fourth chapter presents the results of these combined methods of inquiry. An overview is provided for the development of figurines in six distinct groups. The stylistically and technically connected groups are further categorised according to the presence of certain features: chair/throne, polos/veil, fibula shape, and pendant types. Together with the catalogue provided at the end, these results form a functional tool for interpreting the figurines in the context of daily life in the polis, and specifically their use as part of the cultic practice and religious observance.

The approximately two hundred figurines from Akragas are catalogued at the end of the thesis. Each figurine is described and ascribed a place in the coroplastic development identified in the preceding chapters, based on their place in the chronological, stylistic and technical order.

I.6 Greek historiography on Sicily – some general remarks

The different aspects of the society in which the figurines appear, as we know it from authors in antiquity, is the subject of the second part of this introductory chapter. As sources of information, the literature is divided into two groups.[65] The first category is of mythological nature, providing information of ethnographic value. This part includes Homer in Section I.6.a and Pindar in the description of the religious setting in I.6.d, who mention Sicily and Akragas' rulers in their poetry. There is special attention for Sicily in mythology for it might have been a factor in the decision- making of the settlers. The second category is one of a literary historical nature, such as Thucydides and Herodotus, whose accounts will be discussed in the following Section I.6.b-d. The discussion moves from providing a more general idea of Sicily to the political context of Gelas and Akragas to more specific questions on the social and religious setting. The discussion begins with the general perception of the Greeks through their stories about Sicily as a place far away, where the sun rises.

I.6.a Mythical past

Fitting well with Bakhuizen's[66] horizon concept is Homer's influence on the perception of Sicily by the Greeks. The island was inhabited by the Laestrygonians and Cyclopes. Thucydides[67] makes this reference to Od. 9-10.[68] He mentions these mythical figures, as they are known for their barbaric reception of Odysseus and his men. In doing so, he seems to clarify the distinction between a non-Hellenic past and the 'new order.' On the other hand, he does not refer to the culture of any of these people. Odysseus is only implicitly mentioned as it would have been obvious to his readers.[69] The whole island was probably well known for being the place of some of Odysseus' adventures. The land of the Cyclops as Odysseus comes across it, is described by Homer as very suitable for agriculture and keeping sheep. Yet its present inhabitants do not exploit it fully. This vision on 'the other world' was in this case seen as *olbia*, prosperous, the land of the plenty, specifically in the agricultural domain, but with inhabitants to be feared.[70] Odysseus' adventure forms a close parallel to the experiences of the migrants, an association probably made by those from Thucydides' time as well.[71]

Another reason for Thucydides to refer to Odysseus might be to establish the idea of a preceding Greek presence. The latter being an argument for invasion and occupation of land. This argument is more political and used as well for the story of the refugees from the destroyed Troy. One explanation of this phenomenon is to see the historical accounts of the foundation as a reflection of the time in which they were written. The stories and traditions described come from an oral tradition. They are mentioned here with a clear actual intention of justifying colonisation. In this view, it is interesting to see to what extent the parallel stretches, not only regarding the situation on Sicily but also regarding the places of origin of the newcomers.

From Homer itself, it appears that Sicily was known as *Sikanie*, an older name.[72] A female servant is mentioned as being Sicilian.[73] It is remarkable that Sicily appears in association with slavery.[74] This comment refers to Sicily as a place where slaves were kept, probably in Homer's own time, the eighth or seventh century BCE. The Sicilian origin of slaves is probable as Linear B texts refer several times to slaves. The only archaeological connection, however, between these places in this time period is a Sicilian amber bead that was found in a tholos grave in Vayenas Pylos.[75]

I.6.b Political setting

Our main sources of information on the political course of events leading to the settlements on Sicily are Greek literary sources. This colonisation is a process which is nowadays perceived in various ways but was described by the Greeks as *oikisis*. The resulting settlement is called *apoikia* which means literally: a faraway, *apo*, house/housing, *oikia*.[76] Greek authors in antiquity who

65 Antonaccio 2007, p.208-9. The third category consists of archaeological material.

66 See Section I.4.

67 Thucydides starts his description of the inhabitants of Sicily in Book 6.2 with this note.

68 And maybe to Hesiod as well, and to Euripides' play Kyklops. Pindar and Bacchylides do not situate them on Sicily. For an overview of possible references, see Hornblower 2008, p.264ff.

69 Thuc. 6.2.3.

70 Bakhuizen 1988, p.10f.

71 Dover notes that "as early as the Hesiodic poems we find indications that the peoples and places of Od. 9-10 were regarded as having existed in the central and western Mediterranean, and this was taken for granted by Thucydides' time" Dover 1965, p.5. There is some evidence that in the 5th century Odysseus' adventure was situated on Sicily in different literature. See Hornblower 1996, p.181 and 264ff.

72 Also spelled as: Sicania. Od. 24.307.

73 She assists Laertes, Odysseus' father in Od. 24.211, 366, 389.

74 When the suitors tell Telemachus to ship the guests to Sicily in Od. 20.383.

75 Leighton 1999, p.186.

76 Antonaccio 2007, p.204. 'Colony' derives from the Latin 'colonia' the verb 'colo': to cultivate land; but also to honour the gods, from which the word 'cult(us)' derives.

commented on these events and the thoughts of modern-day researchers will be examined in the light of present archaeological and historical research.

I.6.b.i The perception of ancient authors

Though the actual events preceded the written documentation by at least a hundred years, the ancient authors present an image of how the settlements of the migration waves were perceived and what they thought was important to mention. Although their information is mixed with their view on the course of history and its implications for their own time, it does not exclude them from being valuable sources. The earliest of the Greek authors on the colonisation of Sicily is Thucydides. His work from the 5th century BCE is very important for the relative dating of the several Greek foundations and our information on the political circumstances on Sicily in the 6th century BCE. His account of the events in Book 6, Herodotus Book 7 of and some information on later changes in Diodorus Siculus' Book 13 are our main sources.

Their information is discussed here extensively because they are our earliest literary sources on colonisation, specifically Thucydides, as he took a specific interest in political development. Herodotus is of interest because he comments on the cult at Akragas. He had a good knowledge of the migration as well, information he acquired from the servants of Apollo at Delphi. Those who intended to emigrate would have first come for advice to Delphi.[77] For his information on Sicily, he would have also relied on the information within the network of *poleis*, when he resided in Thurii, on the South coast of mainland Italy.[78]

The cultural baggage of these authors is to be seen as the perspective from which they wrote. An example is a specific similarity in the description of the Persian expedition to Greece and the Athenian expedition to Sicily by Herodotus and Thucydides. The subject of identity must be read in this light. Herodotus notes that Athens is seeking allies with the agenda of domination over them. Thucydides presents Euphemus, an Athenian, warning for similar ambitions from the side of Syracuse.[79] This background of the Sicilian Expedition, echoing the events of the Persian War sheds light on Sicilian identity, as it was shaped by a common enemy. Reconstructing the sociology of the period before that one, the Archaic Period is reflected from events nearer to these authors. In a similar way, Diodorus Siculus, as late as the first century BCE, relies for some of his information on Timaeus, 345-250 BCE, maybe via Ephorus, and quotes him.[80] Diodorus gives in Book 13 an extensive account of the political involvement of Athens and describes Akragas in detail, as well as the siege of the city by the Carthaginians. Though these political developments are later than our period of interest, the description of the city itself and its environment is relevant.

I.6.b.ii Sicily in the account of Thucydides

Thucydides, who lived from 460-400 BCE[81], wrote an extensive account and is seen as a relatively reliable.[82] When archaeological evidence is scanty or missing it is therefore his account that is generally believed to be true.[83] Another reason his account is perceived to be accurate is because of his source, Antiochus of Syracuse.[84] This author is known for his accuracy[85] and wrote a *History of Sicily*, which included the early years up to his own time, 424 BCE. Antiochus' work, which only survived in fragments, could have had direct sources from the Archaic period as he was from Syracuse. His detailed account for a description of the settlement on Sicily is also used by Herodotus, who lived from 485 to about 420 BCE. Whether their view on historiography and reconstruction would have been taken from Antiochus of Syracuse is a point of discussion.[86]

Thucydides' description of Sicily in Book 6.2-5 is called 'Sikelika,' the Sicilian matters. The reason for Thucydides to write so extensively on this subject seems to be to provide a background to his actual subject, political developments that took place much later in time. It is suggested that Thucydides dwells on both Attica and Sicily as the political connections between Athens and Sicily are the reason for the failure of the Athenian expedition to gain power on Sicily in 415-3 BCE.[87] Nicias, one of the Athenian generals compares the Sicilian Expedition with colonisation in his second speech to the Athenian assembly:

77 Hornblower 2002, p.378.

78 Forsdyke 2002, p.548.

79 Thuc. 6.86.

80 Diod. 13. 81.4-84.6.

81 In 424 BCE, he was banished from Athens as a *strategos*, a general, of a lost war. He might have travelled to Sicily or even lived there for a short while to seek information. His wealth gave him the chance to spend time on travelling and writing. It is difficult to trace where he travelled and stayed exactly, but he does sometimes mention the situation at his own time, which shows he had a good knowledge of the place in question, for example Amphipolis in Book 4.103. 5 Hornblower 1996, p.22.

82 This is not just what he states himself Thuc. I 1.3 but also according to modern scholars. Hornblower 2008, p.274; Morakis 2011, p.466f.; Greenwood 2006, p.3ff.; for the chronology Nijboer 2006.

83 This is the case with Thucydides' description in 6.2.6 of the Phoenicians withdrawing into three cities with the arrival of the Greeks. Leighton 1999, p.222, 227.

84 See for more bibliographical information on this theory as well as on Antiochus of Syracusa, Morakis 2011, p.463 n. 18.

85 Though not all scholars agree on that and there is discussion on what sources he used. See for a short overview of opinions and bibliography Morakis 2011, p.464ff.

86 Marincola 2007, p.191-3.

87 Alonso-Núñez 2000, p.65f.

"πόλιν τε νομίσαι χρὴ ἐν ἀλλοφύλοις καὶ πολεμίοις οἰκιοῦντας ἰέναι (...)"

"It is, in fact, as you must believe, a city that we are going forth to found amid alien and hostile peoples."[88]

Both ventures are comparable in magnitude and strength, but also imply Athens' agenda.[89] The motivation for these undertakings is described in the first book: adventure, money, and power.[90] The land hunger as a reason for migration is advocated by Thucydides but proven very unlikely by archaeologists.[91] Thucydides' perspective is a reflection on his own times.[92] The Greeks are described as if the institutions and structures of his own time already existed, while the absence of archaeological material disproves this. Culturally non-Greek people are recognized as being different, but the focus is not on their differences from each other, but in contrast to the Greeks, who did not exist yet in the 6th century BCE as a single defined cultural group. The reality was likely more culturally fused than it appears when reading literary sources. The ethnic mixture is reflected in some names of the leaders.[93] Thucydides' perspective on Hellenisation lacks the reciprocal influences among those colonists themselves but notices a difference among the Greeks. He makes a distinction between Dorians and Ionians, which is another example of Thucydides' perspective from his own time. This division is based on kinship, *syngeneia*, and plays a large role in political decisions. The rhetorics of *syngeneia* were used in order to form allies, to ask for help or even to justify the invasion.[94] Thucydides mentions sometimes the background of the founders of the cities by adding the note of 'Doric customs'[95] or the city of origin.[96] The latter would be an argument that the undertaking of the emigration would be a personal enterprise of the founders.[97]

The character of the encounter between the migrating people and those who already lived in the area of destination might not always have been as hostile as the above citation suggests. This is shown by a counterargument, an anecdote told by Thucydides in which the Sikel king, Hyblon, gave land to a group of Megarians, who honoured him with the name of the city, Hyblaia. However, from the archaeological records, it appears that local settlements were destroyed by Selinous at the end of the 7th century BCE. Cultural identity or ethnicity might not have been barriers to friendly relations.

In the case of another settlement, Thucydides mentions that the language changed because of the number of people from Syracuse who settled with the Chalcideans. Their laws, however, remained Chalcidean.[98] This example makes clear that a parallel is made between the different origins of the migrants and the social-political structures of the *poleis*. It appears from Thucydides' account that by his time local people were outnumbered by the culturally Greek, other cultures would have been overruled by the Greek expansion and land claims. This perspective might have been very different in the earlier Archaic Period and from the time of the archaeological material analysed in this thesis (Chapters 2 and 3).

I.6.b.iii The foundation of Gelas and Akragas

Akragas and Gelas are connected in ancient literature as two towns in a political setting of *metropolis* and *apoikia*. We can therefore expect this relationship to have some bearing on our interpretation and understanding of the figurines of Akragas.

I.6.b.iii.1 Gelas

Gelas was the first city to be founded on the south coast of the island, in 688 BCE.[99] Its coastline with the mouth of the river Gelas was suitable for ancient shipping. The flat-topped hill overlooking the surroundings explains the choice of site.[100] Thucydides writes in Book 6.4.3:

"Γέλαν δὲ Ἀντίφημος ἐκ Ῥόδου καὶ Ἔντιμος ἐκ Κρήτης ἐποίκους ἀγαγόντες κοινῇ ἔκτισαν, καὶ τῇ μὲν πόλει ἀπὸ τοῦ Γέλα ποταμοῦ τοὔνομα ἐγένετο, τὸ δὲ χωρίον οὗ νῦν ἡ πόλις ἐστὶ καὶ ὃ πρῶτον ἐτειχίσθη Λίνδιοι καλεῖται."

---

88 Thuc. 6.23.2, translation by C.F. Smith 1921, p.227.

89 Alonso-Núñez 2000, p.70; Avery 1973, p.8-13..

90 Thuc. 6.24. 3; Kallet 2002, p.25-7.

91 Yntema 2000, p.4.

92 Yntema 2000, p.43-4.

93 Hodos 2006, p.92f.

94 Bolmarcich 2010.

95 Thuc. 6.4.4 on Gela.

96 According to Morakis ethnic denominations like Chalcidian colonists in Thuc. 6.3.1 does not imply the polis Chalcis, but just says something about the origin of the people. Morkais 2011, p.467f.

97 Morakis 2011, p.467f.
Such a decision by the individual founders could have had very personal reasons. According to Dougherty, this was often the case. It was not the larger goals, such as a quest for arable land or political movements that were the first impulses for emigration, but rather more personal stories, like a murderer who had to start over anew. Dougherty 1993, n. 14.

98 Thuc. 6.5.1. Hornblower rightly points to the difference between this verb, 'prevailed' and the *nomima* of Gela, which are 'given.' The latter suggest a single moment, while the first implies a longer period. Hornblower 2008, p.291.

99 This is calculated as forty-five years after Syracuse, which was founded in 733 BCE. On the order of the foundation of the cities as it appears from the archaeological material, see Hall 2008, p.409. He concludes that the archaeological material is in accordance with Thucydides and it is therefore correct to say that Gela was founded some time after the earliest colonies and before Selinous.

100 Graham 1982, p.163ff.

"In the forty-fifth year after the settlement of Syracuse, Gela was founded by Antiphemus from Rhodes and Entimus from Crete, who together led out the colony. The city got its name from the river Gela, but the place where the acropolis now is and which was the first to be fortified is called Lindii."[101]

Thucydides mentions the name of a preceding settlement, Lindioi. This reference to the inhabitants of Lindos, a city on Rhodes, raises the question of how many Cretans and Rhodians were present and whether their arrival happened at the same time.[102] Gelas might have been a re-foundation of the earlier Lindioi.[103] Another possibility is that this was the second phase of the building programme. The first phase could have been just a walled citadel with extra-mural sanctuaries to the east.[104] The small sanctuary on the other side of the river Bitalemi was built before the 7th century BCE ended. The reference to a Rhodian name and the fact that archaeological material reveals a presence before the Thucydian date of 689 BCE would lend support to the two-stage view.[105] However, the predating material is not Rhodian, but Corinthian. Several other scenarios are possible: the materials could indicate a Greek trading post or the popular Corinthian vases could have been owned by local inhabitants. The older pots could have been brought by the colonists of Gelas as relics or heirlooms. In fact, neither the literary nor the archaeological sources either confirm or exclude an earlier phase of habitation at Gelas.[106] Was the name changed because Lindioi would only point to the Rhodians, while the actual situation was a populace from various origins?

The new city was named 'Gelas' after the river, as Thucydides describes it. Naming after a notable landmark is common among colonies.[107] There are two explanations for the name. The first is explained by Stephanus of Byzantium: it would derive from 'gelu,' 'ice' in the language of the Sikeloi, which is related to Latin.[108] Another etymology might be even older, as Aristophanes refers to it:[109] Gelas is derived from the verb *gelaw*, to laugh, as there is a story that Antiphemos, as well as his brother, laughed when the oracle told him he would found a city. Such an explanation is typical for the stories on foundations.[110] The first etymology, however, sounds more reasonable, as it could be linked to the river.

According to Thucydides, Gelas was founded by both Rhodians and Cretans.[111] Morakis believes that here and in some other similar cases the word ἐκ only gives the place of origin for the founders themselves. It is true that the denomination of place is specifically for the founders, without implying an initiative from the polis.[112] Also in the differing origins of the colonists, Morakis sees an argument for the private enterprises of the foundation.[113] However the relationship between *apoikia* and *metropolis* occurred from the beginning and they were aware of their identity, he claims.[114] In my opinion, the new name of the settlement, Gelas, which replaced 'Lindioi' is a counter-argument.[115]

The name-giving of settlements usually refers to the topology showing a relation to the direct environment, more often than to a cultural tie with the mother city.[116] The later connection with some other cities, if it can be proven archaeologically, could be very well based on political motives. Such a connection could be even invented with the use of mythology. As in the example above, a common aspect like Odysseus' adventures could come in handy politically. The description of the Cretans joining the foundation is only tenuously supported by some scant archaeological material.[117] The stories on Cretans like Minos and Daedalus, as well as the bronze bull of Phalaris, might have no basis in reality.[118] The interpretation of the story, mentioned by Pausanias,[119] of Antiphemos, who looted a statue, possibly a *xoanon*, made by Daedalus from Omphake, could stem from the wish to control the cult and claim the land, symbolised by the object.[120] The reason attention is paid to Gelas here is not just because it is the metropolis of Akragas, but because the figurines, that will be discussed in the following chapters, are thought to have been inspired by objects from Lindos, the city on Rhodes where the first settlers of Gelas originated. If the statue had such a strong symbolic meaning, that could imply that this affected the perception of smaller terracotta figurines, as a reflection of the cult image.

101 Thuc. 6.4.3, translation by C.F. Smith 1921, p.189.

102 See Section I.2.b and II.6.e.ii.

103 Some find a signal of the difference with other descriptions by Thucyides in his use of the verb 'to found' 'ktizein' and the substantive 'founders' 'epoikoi', instead of 'oiktizein' and 'apoikoi'. Wentker 1956, p.129-39. This opinion seems however outdated. For a short overview of the discussion, see Leschhorn 1984, p.48.

104 Boardman 1999, p.178.

105 For the specific findings dating from the Late Geometric and Early Protocorinthian see chapter 2.

106 Morakis 2011, p.471-3.

107 Bakhuizen 1988, p.19.

108 Tribulato 2012, p.135; Dover 1965, p.8.

109 Ach. 606.

110 Leschhorn 1984, p.44.

111 On the myth of simultaneous sent oikists, see Leschhorn 1984, p.44.

112 Morakis 2011, p.470.

113 Morakis 2011, p.473.

114 While some arguments would hold for the connection with Rhodes from early on, these do not include Megara Nisaea and Corinth, as Morakis does. Morakis 2011, p.473-7.

115 Nor is there agreement on his other statement regarding the cult of Athena Lindia. Morakis 2011, p.477, n.98.

116 An exception, for example, is Megara Hyblaea, founded by Megara.

117 For some heads of Cretan origin, See Section II.5.c.i.

118 Adornato 2012a, p.484.

119 Pausanias 8.46.2; 9.40.3-4.

120 Morris 1991, p.197-200.

I.6.b.iii.2 Herodotus on Gelas

Herodotus describes in Book 7.153.63 the embassy to Gelon of Syrakousai, sent by the Greek alliances in order to convince him to join against Xerxes. In this context, he digresses on the history of Gelon to describe an ancestor of Gelon, who would have joined in founding Gelas.[121] Though not explicitly mentioned by his name, we know it was Deinomenes.[122] This is a clear example of alternative history being used to praise the Deinomenides for their lineage.[123] Herodotus mentions that he was from Telos and that he became a resident. He then states that he was not left behind when the foundation took place. The order of telling of the history implies that he already lived there when Anthipehmos and the Lindians of Rhodes founded Gelas. Or, and that seems more probable, that they arrived together, implying that the official foundation took place later and involved a role for Deinomenes.[124] One of the founders from his genealogy gave Gelon, the later tyrant, certain rights. This genealogical anchoring of his power also has a religious component.[125] One of the descendants, Telines, won the office of the priesthood of the chthonic deities.[126] The latter statement, together with the interpretation of these deities as Demeter and Persephone, had a major effect on the interpretation of religion at Gelas and Akragas.

I.6.b.iii.3 Akragas

The first time that Akragas is mentioned in Thucydides is in Book 5.4.6 when Phaiax defeated the Kamarinaians and Akragantines, both Dorian cities. The same Phaiax would also have taken Lokri on the Italian mainland. This is mentioned here because the archaeological record shows an iconographic link with Lokroi/Locri as well.[127]

Akragas was founded one hundred and eight years after Gelas, by Gelas, according to Thucydides.[128] Together with Pindar's Olympian Ode 2,[129] which speaks of a round number, the year 580 BCE is usually attested. The site was certainly visited before because of pottery from the late seventh and early sixth century BCE at a cemetery in Montelusa and because S. Biagio, a rock at Akragas, is thought to have been used as a sanctuary.[130]

Thucydides mentioned two oikists. Was one Cretan and the other Rhodian, as with the foundation of Gelas?[131] Thucydides comments on the foundation of Akragas that a Geloan colony received Geloan customs. The comment on Geloan customs makes one Geloan and one Rhodian oikist possible.[132] Polybius,[133] who points to the specific topography of Akragas as well in Book 9.27, states that Akragas was founded by Rhodians. It, therefore, would have the same deities honoured with temples and the same appellation as there.[134] Also Thucydides together with later authors, names Geloans as the founders first.[135] The arguments for a Rhodian cult are weak.[136] When comparing both descriptions of the foundations of the two cities, the order differs slightly.

> "ἔτεσι δὲ ἐγγύτατα ὀκτὼ καὶ ἑκατὸν μετὰ τὴν σφετέραν οἴκισιν Γελῷοι Ἀκράγαντα ᾤκισαν, τὴν μὲν πόλιν ἀπὸ τοῦ Ἀκράγαντος ποταμοῦ ὀνομάσαντες, οἰκιστὰς δὲ ποιήσαντες Ἀριστόνουν καὶ Πυστίλον, νόμιμα δὲ τὰ Γελῴων δόντες."

> "Just about one hundred and eight years after their own foundation, the Geloans colonized Acragas; and they named the city after the river Acragas, making Aristonous and Pystilus founders, and giving it the institutions of the Geloans."[137]

In the case of Gelas, the city as object of the sentence is mentioned first, then the oikists with name and place of origin and then the date followed by the explanation of the name and the *nomina*. In the case of Akragas, the date comes first, because it is very soon,[138] followed by the Geloans as subject and Akragas as object of the sentence. It is only after the eponymy that then the founders are named. Thucydides mentions that the Aristonous and

121 Grethlein 2006.

122 Xenagoras, a 3rd century BCE author from Rhodes mentions him in his Chrónoi 240 F 15.

123 Leschhorn 1984, p.44.

124 Deinomedes is also mentioned in the Byzantine lexicon Etymologicum Magnum 225.1, Gela. Other sources mention different names, see Hall 2008, p.399 and n. 51.

125 For the Deinomenids of Gela/Syracuse and the Emmenids of Akragas, see Miller 1970, p.49ff.

126 The two goddesses, Demeter and Kore/Persephone are alluded to here, according to a scholiast on Pindar P. 2.27b. Morgan 2015, p.24 n. 1.

127 See Section II.6.h.i and II.7.b.

128 Thuc. 6.4.4.

129 Akragas is mentioned because about one hundred years after its foundation, Theron, its leader, won the chariot race in Olympia. The Olympian Ode is written in honor of him.

130 Boardman 1999, p.187-8; Dunbabin 1948, p.307.

131 Thuc. 4.4.3 stresses there fact that two different groups co-founded Gela by adding the adjective κοινῇ, 'together.' Translation by C.F. Smith 1921, p.189.

132 Dunbabin 1948, p.310.

133 A Greek historian who wrote contemporary history on the 3rd and 2nd century. BCE.

134 A temple of Athena and of Zeus Atabyrius.

135 Pol. 9.27.7.

136 See Section I.2.c.

137 Thuc. 6.4.4, translation by C.F. Smith 1921, p.189.

138 108 years after Gelas itself.

Pystilos were 'made' the founders.[139] It sounds more as if they were chosen as the leaders of the venture than that each of them had led the people from respectively Gelas and Rhodes to Akragas. It seems to have been an old custom that when a new city was founded someone from the original metropolis had to come and join the foundation.[140] This explains why a colonist from Rhodes was requested by Gelas to found Akragas. No help was needed nor is it necessary to suppose a new influx of people from Rhodes at that moment. It seems more likely that the prosperous settlements attracted people constantly from different places. Such can be read into Thucydides' account of the foundation of Zankle, directly following the description of Akragas. The city was founded by pirates, but later many joined them and lived there together. The latter is expressed by the word "ξυγκατενείμαντο," translated as "shared the land with them."[141] This is interesting but still does not make a multicultural society, as they are all from Euboea.

The question, however, is, what these *nomima* customs or institutions meant exactly and in our case whether there is an implication on religion or cult. Hornblower writes that besides a religious calendar and festivals, a legal system is meant, though it is early for that.[142] Though the word could be used more generally and applies to customs and a certain way of living/speaking/ dressing etc., like the above-mentioned case of Himera, the verb it comes with here, 'to give,' does not seem to refer to the cultural sphere. As Thucydides points out Gelas had Dorian *nomima*, and Akragas Geloan.[143] The participle of the verb 'to give' is striking, the more because in Thuc. 6.5.1. the *nomima* of Himera 'prevailed.'[144] It does not only makes a difference time-wise but implies an imposition as well. If Thucydides thinks it is worth noting that *nomima* prevailed, it is implied that other options would have been open as well. He states that the language was a mixture. This is a clear case in which Thucydides refers to acculturation. Malkin writes that there was no need for citizens of the city to take part in an unfamiliar cult for a deity-with-local-epithet with whom the citizen had nothing in common.[145] But it is argued here that migrants recognised local deities, such as for example personifications of local water resources in their polytheistic worldview, which did not limit the number nor the dwellings of deities.[146]

There is a political link between the oikist and the institutions. While Thucydides mentions them in relation to ethnic groups or birthplaces, it does not say much on the actual origins of the inhabitants. Oikists are likely to be a state-regulated matter, while the actual pluriform religion also contains 'bottom-up' personal aspects. Dedications like the terracotta figurines, as a pledge for individual wishes, seem to belong to the last category.

I.6.b.iii.4 Herodotus on Theron of Akragas

Herodotus does not comment on the foundation of Akragas but mentions Akragas' leader, Theron, cooperating with Gelon of Gelas in a military unity.[147] Carthaginians saw their chance in the west, now the Greeks were fighting with the Persians in the East.[148] Interestingly, several other peoples from Corsica, Liguria and the Iberian peninsula are mentioned as having joined forces with the Carthaginians. Theron and Gelon won the battle at Himera, according to Herodotus on the same day as the Persians were defeated at Salamis.[149]

I.6.c Social and economic setting

I.6.c.i Diversity among the inhabitants of Sicily

Researchers nowadays rightly remark that groups of people do not have a uniform identity and even individuals can have multiple identities.[150] Regarding the diversity among Greeks themselves, exposure to other cultures might have made them aware of kinship and shared values.[151] Though being from different cities and with various traditions and backgrounds, they must have realised they shared a linguistic, historical, geological and artistic common ground. Having a shared enemy, ought to help define their own cultural values. Thucydides seems to speak from that perspective in the citation above, but without a strong self-other dichotomy and the idea of Greek cultural unity. Identification in opposition and by antithesis is not yet found in Thucydides, probably because of the

139 According to Leschhorn and others, the historicity of the names of the founders is beyond doubt. For references see Leschhorn 1984, p.46 n. 2. The historicity of 'Entimos' would be proven because it appears only two times more. One is a Cretan and one a Rhodian. See Bérard 1957, p.230 n. 3. The names of the two founders are peculiar. 'Entimos' means 'honoured' or 'honourable,' while Antiphemos could mean 'he whose name is uttered (by the oracle) equally'. The names might be titular. It appears from the above literary evidence that the Cretans played a minor role in the city. The Rhodians might have outnumbered them and had already a previous settlement on the same spot. Was Antiphemos, the obvious leader, passed by the oracle, which pointed to Entimos as the founder, and therefore 'honoured'? It remains speculative, but the names do not seem coincidental.

140 Thuc. 1.24.2.

141 Thuc. 6.4.5, translation by C.F. Smith 1921, p.189.

142 Hornblower 2008, p.291.

143 Malkin 2011, p.74-5, 190.

144 Thuc. 6.5.1 ἐκράτησεν, translation by C.F. Smith 1921, p.191, on Himera, the subcolony of Zankle.

145 Malkin 2011, p.190.

146 More on the religious setting, see section I.6.d.

147 Hdt. 7.165.

148 Hdt. 7.165.

149 This was in 480 BCE.

150 Lomas 2004.

151 Antonaccio 2007, p.201.

pluriformity among the founding groups themselves. The different waves of migrants were of different origins, like for example in Gelas, which, according to Thucydides, was a cooperative effort between Rhodians and Cretans. Apparently, they could overcome differences, not as 'Greeks' at first but with a new shared identity, in this case, Geloan. The archaeological material might indicate further to what extent these roots played a role. It seems likely that these older cultural identities were maintained for a while, but for not much longer than one or two generations. The ways in which this was expressed might have varied and not always have resulted in material patterns. Among the shared social customs, which serve as markers for cultural identity, religious festivals played an important role.[152] These local events, particularly cultic expression, would serve polis community-building.[153]

The local people Thucydides mentions in 6.2 consist of Sikans, Sikels,[154] and Elymians. The Sikans, who would originally have been Iberians, would have inhabited the western part of Sicily.[155] It would have been in this period that the name of the island changed from Thrinakie[156] to Sikania. By referring to this name 'Thrinakie,' Thucydides continues to refer to the Homeric age. Later and living in the north-east part of the island are the Sikels, according to Thucydides. For both peoples, there is no clear marker of their origin. The Sikels, together with a sub-group, the Elymians, are perceived as being Italian in origin and speaking an Italic language.[157] The Elymians are described, in the 5th century BCE Greek literature, as being allied with the Phoenicians.[158] Whether they are likewise originally of eastern origin, remains unclear.[159] They would have escaped from burning Troy, just like the Phocians, who first arrived on the Libyan coast.[160] These ethnical compartments of Sicily should be treated carefully, as Thucydides' description does not recognise cultural overlap. A geographical boundary between the three groups of Thucydides description has never been established by archaeological material.[161] Archaeological traces of movement show that many inhabitants of the island are not all originally from Sicily as well and immigrants themselves from earlier migrations.[162] The wide variety of cultural traditions in the Iron Age makes it very difficult to distinguish with certainty between these groups. Partly because inscriptions dating from the time of the colonisation itself are absent.[163] The island has a history of immigrants and the first contact with 'Greeks' must have been in the Late Mycenean period. The renewed contact of settlers from the 8th century BCE would have had often both a mercantile and agrarian interest.[164] The difference with the later colonists is mostly a numerical one.

Regardless of their origins, the inhabitants of the island before and during the migration waves are nevertheless called 'locals' in this thesis, even though these 'locals' may themselves have been the children of immigrants, even of Greek or Phoenician origin, in addition to indigenous peoples. There must have been all sorts of migrants for various reasons and at several moments in time. The word 'local' distinguishes them from the newcomers who introduced another social and economic framework, possibly the same as the founders of the cities, who had more political and expansive aims then other predecessors. This adjective is understood thus to refer to the collective and probably diverse people living on Sicily when larger migration waves took place.[165]

I.6.c.ii Phoenicians

Thucydides 6.2.6 speaks of 'many Greeks'[166], arriving over the sea and forcing the Phoenicians who were spread over the whole island,[167] back into three cities, namely Panormus, Soloeis, and the island Motya. This suggests that other peoples had already been forced to move inland at an earlier stage. It also implies that the settlement of Sicily by the Phoenicians was roughly contemporary with the Greek colonisation, while it is much more likely that the Phoenicians have arrived on the island earlier.[168] Thucydides specifies in the same text the reason for the Phoenicians to choose Sicily: they traded goods with the Sikels from their *emporia*.[169] This remark does not specify the difference in habitation, but the Phoenicians have, as a result, often been seen as just traders, while Greeks were seen as more

152 Hall 1997, p.37-40.
153 See Section I.8.c for oikist cult.
154 Other spellings are Sicanians and Sicels.
155 Hornblower 2008, p.267 notices that while Thucydides might have heard of Sikans, they saw themselves as autochthones and he prefers to stick to the mythological version. On the archaeological evidence of ethnic and cultural different groups living on Sicily in this period, see chapter 2.
156 The name 'Thrinakie' is mentioned in Od. 11.107 and 12.127 and referred to in 12.261, where the cattle of Helios are located on the island as well. The name later changed to 'Trinakria' and indicates the shape of the island, with three coasts. The symbol of a three-legged wheel, which is found on coins from Syracuse, would point to this name. Hornblower2008, p.268.
157 Leighton 1999, p.221.
158 Thuc. 6.2.6.
159 Hodos 2009, p.224. Sikels seems to have been Greek-speaking people, who first lived on the mainland of Italy. The Elymians are those who escaped from burning Troy. Phokians as well, but they first arrived on the Libyan coast according to Thuc. 6.2.2-4.
160 Thuc. 6.2.2-4.
161 Hodos 2006, p.93.
162 Leighton 1999, p.220f.
163 Leighton 1999, p.215-7, 221.
164 Leighton 1999, p.224.
165 Leighton 1999, p.192 and chapter 6.
166 "οἱ Ἕλληνες πολλοί."
167 "περὶ πᾶσαν μὲν τὴν Σικελίαν."
168 Hodos 2004.
169 Thuc. 6.6.2 "ἐμπορίας ἕνεκεν τῆς πρὸς τοὺς Σικελούς."

permanent residents.[170] The role of the Phoenicians on the island has been seen as focused on trade only. According to the traditional view, based on Thucydides' note, the Phoenicians were a closed community specialised in trading goods between East and West, without much interaction with local people. This would have changed only with the arrival of the Greeks, who are presented as the bearers of culture and civilisation. Kistler, with the model of Ulf, presents a different perspective on the motives and actions of the Greeks and Phoenicians and their interaction with local people. He shows that contacts are not dominated by ethnicity, but in the first place by the motivation for such relations.[171] The motivation for the Phoenicians to head westwards was the shortage of raw material, specifically metals.[172] But in the case of Pithekoussai, it might have been shared interest that made them joint ventures in co-founding and cooperating, around 800BCE, as is suggested by both literary and archaeological sources.[173] In the traditional view, the Greeks came after the Phoenicians. Some believe that Thucydides' account of the Phoenicians' withdrawal seems to fit with the archaeological material from Motya.[174] The relation between Phoenicians and local people was according to Leighton less hostile in character than with the land-claiming Greeks. The Phoenicians concentrated on trade[175] and by these three cities kept the most important routes open. The trading network of the Phoenicians was vast and for a stopover, Sicily was well located.[176] While there is quite some material that points to Phoenician presence, the most popular Phoenician form of pottery remains scanty. The majority of the local people seemed to adopt Greek cultural traditions rather than Phoenician ones, whatever their political relations were, according to Leighton.[177] One reason might be that the Phoenicians gained less attention in the scientific records and their culture has no 'Thucydides' of its own. Yet in the last decades of research, the Phoenicians have come to be recognised as settlers as well. Unlike Spain, where metal resources attracted the Phoenicians, Sicily was mainly interesting for farming purposes.[178] It is thought that contacts with the Phoenicians were very early. The so-called 'Reshep' from Selinunte,[179] a bronze figurine depicting a smiting Syrio-Canaanite god, dates from the 13th to 12th century BCE. This object shows overseas contact but does not confirm statements on pre-colonisation.[180] Hard evidence of city-states is lacking from other places, besides the ones mentioned by Thucydides.[181] If we try to broaden the focus, we see that there are interesting parallels between Phoenician and Akragantine material culture. In the next chapter, more attention will be paid to this.

I.6.c.iii Prosperity of Akragas

Diodorus is a Roman author who wrote in Greek and originated from Sicily.[182] He mentions the prosperity of Akragas gained through the exchange of wine and olive oil with Carthage. Not only the crops are mentioned, but the trade in itself with Libya is what "accumulated fortunes of unbelievable size."[183] The last sentence of this paragraph mentions the numerous signs of this wealth, still remaining.[184] It is possible that one of the means of exchange was the silver that is mentioned elsewhere by Diodorus as being mined by the Phoenicians in Iberia and their source of prosperity. He writes that thanks to this trade the Phoenicians found colonies on Sicily and at other places (Diod. Sic. 5. 35).

I.6.d Religious setting

I.6.d.i Demeter and Persephone on Sicily

While Thucydides focusses in his description on Sicily on the political events, including the oikist cult, Herodotus pays more attention to the religion of the island. The latter names the chthonic deities in Book 7.153. It is Pindar who is the earliest literary source of a specific cult on Sicily. He mentions Demeter and Persephone in several instances and even Akragas as Persephone's seat.[185] Sicily, in general, was given to her as a wedding gift by Zeus, he recounts.[186] Very influential in the discussion of the Sicilian religion are besides Pindar, Diodorus Siculus and Plutarchus, who in their accounts stress the special relation of Sicily with the cult of Demeter and Kore/Persephone.[187] Its popularity had increased when it took on a more official, state-related

170 The Phoenicians would have been fewer in number, but the text does not indicate such a difference either. Also it has been stated that little was found near Syracuse that points to the Phoenicians. References in Hornblower 2008, p.271f. Such is not just an argumentum ex silentio, but could also indicate that Phoenician material was just not recognised as such.

171 Kistler 2014.

172 De Angelis 2003b, p.120f.

173 Brandherm 2006, p.3 and n. 11.

174 Leighton 1999, p.228.

175 See for an overview of researchers who claimed so, but opposed to his meaning of Whittaker 1974.

176 De Angelis 2003b, p.115.

177 Leighton 1999, p.232.

178 Whittaker 1974, p.64.

179 Another name is the 'Melqart of Sciacca.'

180 Aubet 1993, p.202.

181 Whittaker 1974, p.65.

182 Hence 'Siculus' is added to his name. He lived from 90-30 BCE.

183 Diod. Sic. 13.81.5, "(...) πλοῦτον οὐσίας ἀπίστους τοῖς μεγέθεσιν ἐκέκτηντο." translation by C. H. Oldfather 1950, p.351. De Angelis 2016, p.285.

184 Diod. Sic. 13.81.5: "πολλὰ δὲ τοῦ πλούτου παρ᾽ αὐτοῖς διαμένει σημεῖα", "Of this wealth there remain among them many evidences". Translation by C. H. Oldfather 1950, p.351.

185 Pind. P. 12.2-3. This ode was written on Midas for winning the flute-playing contest in 490 BCE.

186 Pind. N. I 20. Also Bacchylides mentions Demeter. B. Ep.3.1-2.

187 Friesen, Schowalter, Walters (eds.) 2010, p.223 ff.

function in the 5th century BCE.[188] Epigraphic evidence is likewise not earlier than this century and often refers only indirectly or through epitheta to the goddesses, such as Malophoros.[189] Such resulted in the interpretation of many depicted female deities on Sicily as Demeter and Kore/Persephone, in case her name was not explicitly mentioned elsewhere. Such a forced identification is problematic, because of the diversity of archaeological material and the fact that they are mother and daughter and thus two different persons. Still, there are also reasons to assume Demeter, as the goddess of agriculture, as the first to address on an island where prosperity comes forth from the fertile soils.

I.6.d.ii Temple building and politics

Phalaris was the first tyrant of Akragas, from about ten years after its foundation 570 to 554 BCE. He would have been overthrown by Telemachos, whose grandson is another famous ruler, about a century later, Theron.[190] Aenesidamus, Theron's father, is mentioned by Pindarus.[191] He defeated together with his son-in-law, Gelon of Syrakousai, the Carthaginians at the Battle of Himera in 480 BCE.[192] They formed a power block together with Selinous. There is a theory that it would have been for this victory that a Hieron built an extra-mural temple for the two goddesses in Syracuse.[193]

I.6.e Conclusions on the ancient literary sources

The literary sources provide information on mainly the political events. They are to be regarded as a secondary source of information if religious subjects are discussed. Not only were they written long after the actual events, but they also present their information from a Greek perspective. Nevertheless, they are valuable sources of information on aspects that are not directly expressed by the archaeological material and provide us with important information on the political developments in the society and organisation of several of its social aspects. It is Thucydides' account of the historical events that gives us most insight in a rather structural and factual way and his work is seen as being quite accurate. His description of the foundations of Gelas and Akragas is therefore used as the context for this research.

In addition to the Greek groups, local people were involved in the foundation and daily life of new cities, such as in the case of Megara Hyblaea. Phoenicians are also said to have been living in the same spots and were forced away by the arrival of the Greeks (Thuc. 6.2.6.). The influence of the Phoenicians on several aspects of life may have been larger then we tend to assume. Another reason for this is that the settlements of the Phoenicians have often been regarded as just trading posts, even though Thucydides described them as living there (Thuc. 6.2.6.). It is likely that the numbers of Greek migrants were higher than those of other ethnicities, and that this resulted in a culturally strong Greek influx. The 'many Greeks,' as Thucydides described them, were probably the result of migration waves that also resulted in the foundation of Akragas, just about a century after Gelas was founded. State regulated, polis-wide cults, such as the oikist veneration, might have strengthened a polis-identity.

The area was inhabited by numerous people from the migrations waves from the eastern Mediterranean. Leaders of individual groups among those migrants might have been appointed as official *oikist*, founder, in order to set up an organizational structure of such expeditions. Such a system was kept by the *nomina*, institutions, and eventually sanctioned by the *oikist* cults. These political settings would have been particularly necessary because the migrants came from different places. Cooperation between such groups is shown by the double oikist and the description of Zankle, in which different groups of settlers merged at a later moment than the original foundation (Thuc. 6.4.5). The ties between Sicilian *poleis* and their mother-cities are summed up as if they were close relations since the first settlers arrived, but the colonies might have been independent in aspects of society other than politics.

The ancient historical literature does not give much more information on religious expression for the Archaic Period but focusses on the political developments of that time. It is Pindar who connects the island at an early stage with the veneration of Demeter and Persephone (Pind. P. 12.2-3 and N. 1 20). Poetry serves a different goal and it is questionable whether archaeological material should be interpreted in the light of poetry. Herodotus mentions the chthonic deities, but this remark probably concerns the Classical Period (Hdt. 7.153).

The independence of the Sicilian cities was likely founded on their strong economies. The prosperity of Akragas specifically has become almost mythological. The fertile soil and availability of sulphur as fertilizer ensured an enormous agricultural surplus. The resulting wine and olive oil were traded with the Phoenicians, according to Diodorus Siculus (Diod. Sic. 13.81.5). The exchanged materials or luxury goods that the Akragantines were able to afford might have contained metal in raw form as well as finely worked objects. It is also Diodorus who mentions the silver trade of the Phoenicians on the Iberian peninsula. In the second chapter, the role of metal in Akragantine society, specifically in the cultic sphere, will be described along with the extensive archaeological evidence.

188 For an overview of the Roman authors, see Hinz 1998, p.19, n. 5.
189 Dewailly 1992; Hinz 1998, p.32-3.
190 His reign was 488-472/473 BCE.
191 Pind. Ol. 3. The dynasty is called the Emmenidae.
192 Hdt. 7.166.
193 But that is only part of the theory. See Bennett 2002.

Chapter II

Iconography of the figurines

II.1 Introduction

In the Archaic Period, Sicily and South Italy, along with much of the rest of the Mediterranean, has for a long time been seen as a region where a relatively homogeneous culture developed under Greek cultural and political dominance. In this period, from approximately the 7th century BCE until 480BCE (the time of the colonisation of Sicily), local culture and autonomy were thought to have swiftly been subsumed by Greek ways and culture.[194] Recently perspectives have shifted away from such binary concepts of Greek and non-Greek, West and East, civilised and savage, towards a more inclusive view, one involving mutual exchange.[195] As we have learned more about local cultural identities, it has become easier to identify the presence of hybrid cultures each with their own characteristics, borrowing from Greek culture but developed in new contexts.

II.2 Aims

This analysis is intended to place the figurines of Akragas within their proper multicultural landscape, addressing not only the appearance of the figurines but also the religious customs and behaviours of the local people that gave shape to the statuettes. The cultures of the island, including that of the inhabitants of Akragas, are no longer to be seen as culturally subordinate to a dominant Greek culture. More attention has been paid to specifically local identity and cultic formation in the material record.[196] In discussing the traits and characteristics of the Akragas figurines, it is not necessary to refer only to Greek cultural and technological influences. While they are certainly present and indeed play a major role in both iconography and technology, the figurines speak of a wide scope of stylistic heterogeneity, which ranges from East to West and which develops gradually over a period of a hundred years. These were influences on an already existing, but also not necessarily homogeneous culture. Local iconography also did not spring from a single source. Thus, the description of the figurines' development ought to scrutinise the variety in their iconographies as well as the possible reasons behind the 'adoption and adaption' of various features.

II.3 Method

In order to understand the reciprocity and exchange, often over a vast area, outside Sicily and overseas, it is important to realise that the early Mediterranean was highly interconnected. This network of connections, or réseau,[197] facilitated trade and the exchange of goods but also non-physical items. This mixture of physical and non-physical goods travelled over long distances and mixed with local materials. The figurines, therefore, stand in multiple traditions at the same time and represent the specific local material outcome of the globalisation of their time. Some of these objects, although

---

194 See Chapter 1.

195 Malkin 2004.

196 Both this topic and the connectivity and cultural hybridity of the Mediterranean are active areas of research for scholars around the world. The introduction and chapter on the Mediterranean in Hodos 2006 provide a good introduction to the topic.

197 Malkin 2004, p.358ff.

associated traditionally with the Greeks, were used and applied within the context of the existing cultural norms of the local autonomous communities.[198] This framework and the concept of globalisation is applied for the figurines discussed here.[199] This perspective includes the figurines' strong local agency within the wider context of exchange and ideas in their Mediterranean network through several aspects of their appearance and technique.[200]

In addition to providing a detailed factual description of the iconography of the figurines and comparisons with other objects, this chapter also addresses a number of questions to help interpret the identified characteristics of the figurines. One central question is whether the figurines can be ascribed a particular gender. In this light, the expression and implications of gender are also discussed. Attention is paid to the role of gender in the iconography of the figurines, and to what extent specific choices mark femininity or leave it unexpressed. A second, identity-related question is a seemingly unsolvable puzzle concerning the distinction between depictions of humans and deities. The question of whether the figurines all represent the same deity or the many dedicators is not easily answered. A related question is whether the figurines have individual identifying characteristics, despite the moulding technique. Closely related questions include whether specific details that can be found on a majority of the figurines, such as the *polos*, and whether a seated position, or pectorals, are indications of divinity. If so, could larger sculpture or even a cult statue have inspired the coroplasts to make figurines with a specific iconography, and what was the meaning of such forms, shapes, and styles in the cultic context?[201]

In order to answer these questions, several real-life objects or sculpture will be compared, in some instances because they were found nearby, in others because of their iconographic similarities. Some figurines were produced at the time of the foundation of the city by its metropolis Gela, according to ancient Greek literature. How these two developments relate to each other is also addressed. More specifically, can Greek influence be used to pinpoint a specific timing for the arrival of migrants, and did political changes affect the figurines' iconography?

The development of the iconographic scheme of the figurines is described in the light of the constant additions and alterations of the figurines. These influxes, changes, and novelties are described here and seen as a 'fashion,' a short term trend, an addition or alteration to the contemporary standard. The word 'fashion' seems suitable as it concerns the dress and physical appearance of the figurines. In common with the modern fashion industry, it may sometimes be hard to explain why a certain characteristic becomes a trend and from where it exactly originates, as well its often its short-lived nature. In this way, a distinction is made between the basic features that form the core of the cultic expression and details, and those that may have temporary significance or are just aesthetic.

On the basis of principal distinctions and their evolution over time, six groups of figurines could be distinguished.[202] Each group could be subdivided into separate sub-groups with minor differences. In brief, the groups can be summarised as follows:

Group	Period	Description/ Summarised characteristics
1	525-500	Locally produced figurines with a block-like body
2	510-470 BCE	Figurines with an increasing number of pectorals and pendants
3	500-470 BCE	Akragantine produced figurines, several with decorated polos
4	480-460 BCE	Figurines, seated or standing with elaborate hairstyle and broad polos
5	600-450 BCE	Imported objects, diverging from characteristics of the other groups
6	550-450 BCE	Others, including kourotrophoi and parts of larger terracotta figurines

In the following sections, the iconography of the figurines will be extensively discussed in four main parts: body, head, personal adornment, and furniture. Each of these subjects includes a more detailed discussion of minor parts. In the description of the body, attention is paid to the arms and feet; the head section contains a description of hairstyles, etc. The order ranges from the representation of the human figure to those depicting materials. In general, the sections start with local objects and continue to objects from other production centres, and other external influences. Object numbers are bold and refer to the Catalogue. Numbers connected with a dash indicate the same mould series.

II.4 The body

II.4.a The local tradition

The contours of the body covered by the dress – the distinction is not always clear on the figurines – differ considerably from one group to another. There are several distinctive forms for the body among the objects considered as the oldest terracotta female figurines, as found at Agrigento. One group consist of rather

198 This Greek-indigenous encounter is well explained for the case of Salento in Attema, Burgers and van Leusen 2010, p.131-3.

199 This fits the model used by Hodos in her description of globalisation in Sicily during the 7 and 6th century BCE. Hodos 2010.

200 Miguel John Versluys explains and substantiates these archaeological theories on the Mediterranean in his work, for example, Versluys 2016.

201 The question is introduced in section I.7.b.i.

202 A precise description with calculations on the percentages of certain features and tables of the groups can be found in Chapter 4.

heterogeneous, probably mostly imported, items, collected in the catalogue in group 5. The main distinction between these and the locally produced earliest figurines, as presented in group 1, is their general shape or the sort of body that characterises them. The block-like shape is characteristic and unique for Sicilian coroplastics. The clear development of the contours and shape of the body started with this shape and developed over time. This chapter begins, therefore, with a discussion of the body shape and its development and continues with a description and comparison with others. Below, each of the characteristic body shapes of imported objects will be mentioned in order to define separate traditions and characteristics that resulted in imitations and influenced local figurine forms. Several aspects that shaped the body are taken into account, like a model image or tradition, the implied pose of the figure, and the probable application.

The typical early Akragantine objects, collected in group 1, are without a doubt made locally. One of the major reasons to define this as the place of origin and fabrication is the body shape. This group is characterised by a specific sort of body and that marks the distinctive local development that continues in other, later, groups. The base of the body is formed from a rectangular block representing the lower part of the dressed human body. The geometrical shape of the block is usually taller than its width and wider than its depth. This part is usually hollow and ranges in depth from rather thin, for example, **63**, towards a considerable depth, for example, **9**. It is this shape, and mainly its depth, that keeps the figurine upright by forming a sturdy base from the lower body. On top of this block, a prism forms the upper part of the body. The back would be more or less straight with a sloping front. All sides were rectangular and the length of the upper part was usually longer than the lower part, the rectangular block. The figurines are usually hollow up to where the layers of clay join at the shoulders. The figurines differ in height from quite small, **8** (11.5cm) to almost twice as tall, **9** (20cm), and there seems to be no distinction in total length between the flatter, rectangular block and the figurines with a bending shape. The larger objects might just be the result of the desire to make larger figurines. Most figurines could stay upright without additional support because of their block-shaped bodies, but some objects were also slightly flared at the base to increase stability, **12**. This results in slightly curved contours (**11**, **12**). In such cases, the upper part often flared outwards, making the front horizontally symmetrical.

The head was placed on top of the angled upper part of the body. The upper body looks like a thick garment is draped from the shoulders, covering the front and pushed forward slightly by the knees of the seated figure. The lower part can be interpreted as the lower legs covered by a dress. On some figurines, the feet stick out from under the garment (**11**, **12**). The angle of the knees is placed more or less where they would naturally be. The knees are sometimes hardly visible, particular from the front (**12**, **63**). For those figurines, a standing pose could have been intended, in contrast to other objects that have clearly angled knees and/or even a bench (**9**, **22**, **30**). The angle can also be less sharp in some cases even when the figures are still clearly seated (**41**).

A less angled body would have been easier to take out of the mould and would have reduced the risk of cracks because the lower part is heavier. The short, bent body suggests a seated pose, **8**, though the vertical lines of the dress stress the length and tallness of the figurine. Its symmetry and near straight lines give the figure a very rigid and static pose.

In group 2, the Archaic large heads (2a), some standing figurines and those with arms (2b and c), and those figurines that retain Archaic characteristics but became increasingly detailed (2d) are introduced. With a forerunner in figurine **87**, a new body shape appears for the first time in group 2c. The body is taller, rectangular and flat, and even the face and polos are elongated (**70**, **88**). On other objects, the slight bending is not completely gone (**90**). Besides the outline of the apron along the sides of the body, the vertically outstretched arms strengthen the impression of the figurine's height.

The flat chest and flaring upper part sometimes form the shape of an inverted triangle, **98**, **99**, **107**, in group 2b. The flaring upper part depicts wide shoulders and might suggest a narrower body and a waist (**9**, **30**, in group 1, and **21** in group 2). This shape is a clear continuation of the first group, with the tendency towards stronger geometrical figures and abstractness. A rectangular shape creates a similar effect with its symmetry; the upper and lower part of the body form a same-sized rectangle, (**100**, **171**). The same tendency, but with a long rectangular form can be recognised in the figurines in group 2 that seem to have a standing pose (**70**, **176**). Regardless of the intended pose, the body of the figurine is strongly abstracted into geometrical forms.

These two body shapes are introduced at the same moment as the alternative pose, that of a standing figurine. In group 2d, a standing figurine, **176**, appears as the alternative to a similar but seated one, **171-174**. The seated pose remains definitely more prevalent. The body shape became increasingly more natural, with a more angled lap, although the contours of the body clearly bear the traces of the block-shaped predecessor. For the local tradition of the seated figurines, the knees as such might have not been so important, but rather the model that keeps the figurine up right, as well as the sitting pose that would be created in this way. The use of partial older moulds resulted in some figurines with slightly bent bodies and flaring shoulders, particularly in group 2d (**21**, **179-180**). The last mould series with the sharply angled knees is **105-106**. From about the second decade of the fifth century BCE, the body is clearly angled and the shape and contours are naturally rather than geometrically inspired. Other indications of this development are the arms, that became increasingly rounded. The general pose remains the same: stiffly seated with unnaturally long arms stretched along the body down to the knees. Some remaining standing figurines from the local tradition appear in group 4 with **185-187**. Their bodies are relatively short, particularly in comparison with their large-sized heads with a wide polos. The body of the seated figurines is rounded from the front, while that of the standing figures is flat. The sides of both remained straight. The simplicity of the shape of the bodies of these standing figurines contrasts with the contemporary seated figurines. In addition to other differences discussed below, this may indicate that they may not simply be an alternative in another pose. Although they possess similar heads, the pose could indicate a difference in the nature of the figurine. The larger, richly decorated and majestically seated figurines could well depict the deity, while the simpler objects may instead represent the dedicants. The objects in group 4 would have probably been grouped together and thus represent a miniature act, that of dedication.[203] For the earlier objects, such a setting or distinction is not clear.

I.4.a.i Arms and feet

The absence of arms in the earliest period of the local tradition might have been an iconographic aspect of aniconic objects adopted by local coroplasts, but it is also a part of the more generally abstract form of the objects. Arms and feet interrupt the geometrical shapes. The feet that appear much earlier than the arms, already in group 1, could point to a dress that covered the complete upper body including the arms. The arms developed first as very thin parallel running lines on the sides,[204] but more often out of the rim next to the dress, which resulted in rather flat upper arms. The pose remained stiff with the arms stretched out along the body. It is no coincidence that the first figurines with arms had a less bent body, and were more often standing than sitting (**70**, **87**, **88**). The arms in that pose would interrupt the geometrical form less and emphasise the length of the figurine. With the last figurines with a more triangular upper body, the arms seem to have been purposefully omitted (**103**, **21**). The next step in the development of the arms is their roundness, which is a more naturalistic rendering. The upper arms were also covered by sleeves, **100**, once they had added a dress, the coroplasts realised they needed to add arms.

A similar progression was followed by feet, from a general shape towards fully visible toes. In other words, the evolution of more realistic arms and feet reveals the tension between the wish to depict the object in abstract form and the desire to make them look more naturalistic. There is a clear development throughout group 1 to 4 from geometrical forms towards more naturalistic, but with the tendency to keep the body shapes as they had previously been portrayed (block-like), until eventually distinguishing between body shapes based on both the pose and nature of the depicted figure.

Fragments of bare feet, with detailed toes, set on a pedestal are common among the finds from S. Anna. The toes are longer than normal, the ankles are covered with a garment that reaches the floor, and the left foot is usually set slightly to the front.[205] Their characteristics match the near life-size terracotta statue of feet on a pedestal, found at S. Anna (fig. 2.1).[206] Her feet, of which the left one is a couple of centimetres to the front, have long toes. This 'step' creates a sense of motion on the large statue but is not seen on the smaller terracottas, as it was probably introduced around the mid fifth century BCE.[207]

II.4.b Imported and imitated images

In addition to local production and development, there are clear influences from other production centres beyond Sicily. Those possible influences on the shape of the body are discussed. The figurines, most of them probably imported, are collected in group 5. They are characterised by some major differences with the local tradition described above. The first difference is their general pose. Standing is more common than sitting among these objects, though in some cases (subgroup 5b) both poses are attested. As with the local tradition, the wish to create an upright and more stable figure may lead eventually to a seated figurine. This development is closely related to the increased three-dimensionality or depth of the figurines. The local tradition is one of increasing depth, eventually to create a more natural, seated pose, but in the first place to create a stable figurine. As well as the pose, the presence

203 Both the difference in pose and size between the deity and the dedicant are attested elsewhere, see Salapata 2015. Miniature pottery might also have played a role in these sets with a deity and the dedication Barfoed sums up other several interpretations of miniature vessels. Barfoed 2017, p.131-3.

204 AG1154 (see fig. 7) and 1160 seem exceptional in the way their arms are rendered. Their body is block-like, but they have thin arms with undefined hands attached to their sides reaching down to their knees. De Miro 2000, no.24 and 25.

205 This is not always the case, in particular on smaller figurines, for example the handmade base with feet in Breitenstein 1945, p.127, fig.30.

206 AGSA12505, Fiorentini 1969, tav.XXXVII.4.

207 This small 'step' may seem minor, but the protruding leg, angled hip, and the dress accentuating this, create the impression of a figure stepping towards the viewer and approaching the viewer directly. This is also visible on the Gela thymiaterion, see Pautasso 1996, tav.XIX,e.

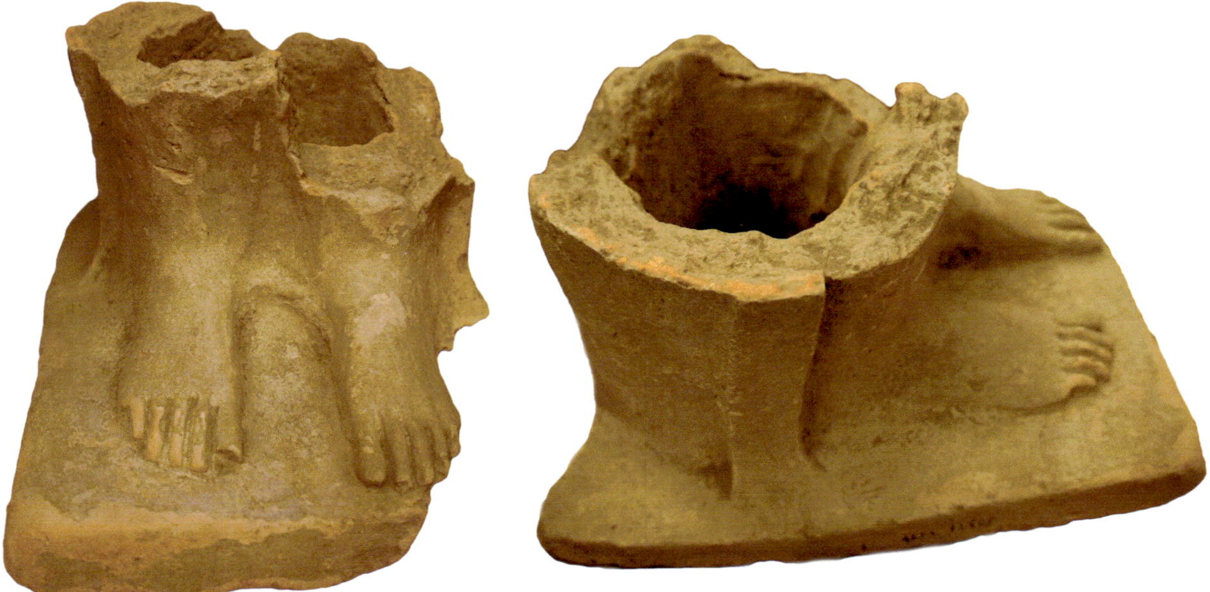

Figure 2.1: Front and side view of a terracotta base with life-sized ankles and feet from St. Anna, Akragas. The thin garment reaches the floor. Inv. no. AGSA 12.505.

of arms was a major difference. The dress was often connected with the visibility of the limbs and contours of the body. While the local objects were covered and hardly any of the shape of the body or limbs was visible, the imported objects were characterised by arms and often a belted or tight garment (**80**, **81**). This aspect is closely connected with the technical possibilities. When sticking out and free from the body, the arms were made of wood or handmade (**1**, **2** and **85**, **86**). When depicted tight along the sides of the body, the arms would not have formed an obstacle for moulding. Figurines **1** and **2** both have arms that stretch out horizontally to the front, as in a hug. These bent, rounded limbs are typical of Argive handmade objects[208] but contrast with the geometric body shapes of the local Akragantine figurines.

Group 5a shows that, at first, some of the imported figurines were hand-formed. The shapes of their bodies are therefore more rounded, but the thin waist looks intentional, particularly on **2**. Even though the transition to the head on that figurine is not defined by a neck, but forms rather a triangular shape. No. **1** has a clear neck. This kind of figurine is found in Sicilian towns, but they were originally from Argos (or were direct copies).[209] The fact that they could stay upright, supported by a stand on the back, see **2**, might have inspired the Akragantine coroplasts. Though broken off on these figurines, the front of the Argive figurines is closed because of the dress, serving as a stand at the front. The back stand or the legs of the chair were also filled in, creating a firmer base. This matches with the local tradition in Akragas, in which the back of the figurines was filled with a slab of clay. All sides would be closed as if the chair were invisible underneath the front of the dress. This does not, however, explain the absence of a waist on the Akragantine figurines. A thin waist might again have increased instability.

There is a curious example from Akragas of a hand-modelled figurine in the style of the Argive objects in combination with a possibly local 'low polos' head.[210] The waist of this object is not very thin and the lower part is, unfortunately, broken off. The arms are thinner than **1** and **2** but have the same position. The actual head of this figurine is very similar to those of **85** and **86**. Those objects were used in the same period and were combined to form new figurines. The early coroplasts showed flexibility in their adaption of the techniques and application.[211] The very thin objects in group 5d would have been unable to stay upright on their own. To solve the issue of stability for those sorts of figurines, the depth could be increased

208 See Section II.4.c on these objects and how they might have influenced Akragantine coroplastics.

209 Aurigny and Croissant 2016.

210 Marconi 1933, pl. VI.2.

211 A strikingly different application of such a thin front mould is on two handles of hand-formed pots from Monte Iato. Stamp impressions are applied on the sides of the handle, while a mould of a figurine is applied to decorate the front of the handle. The application shows the technical abilities of the craftsmen. It is possibly one of the earliest uses of a mould in an indigenous context. Russenberger 2015, p.105, 122 and Abb.6.3-6.4.

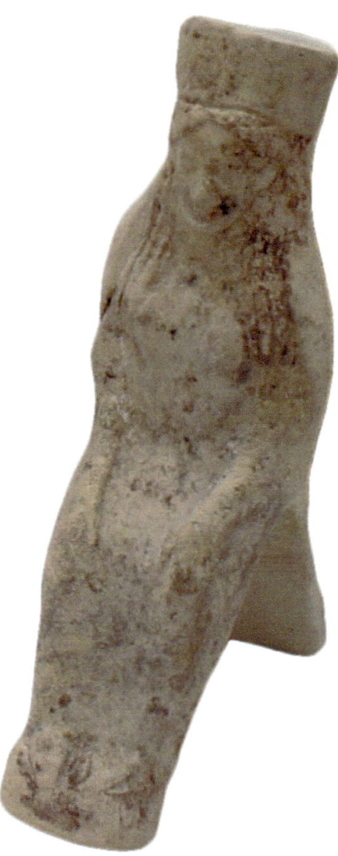

Figure 2.2: Figurine from Selinous made from a front mould, with a handmade stand to keep it upright.

or a stand could be added on the back (fig. 2.2). The mould must have been very shallow because the original wooden figurine was flat. As only a front mould has been applied, they are usually solid. Figurines **80** and **81** were probably also made from wooden patrices or *xoana*. Their arms are thin, and their chest and shoulders sizeable, contrasting with the narrow waist.[212] Mould **78** could also have been made after a wooden original. They share a rather natural rendering of the body, with rounded shoulders, long arms and a waist, often clearly visible because of the belted dress. Their femininity is indicated by the depiction of breasts. These shapes contrast to the geometrical contours of the body of the locally produced Akragantine figurines discussed above. **82**, **83** and **84** have a stiff standing pose but share the same characteristics as the original wooden figurines. In common with the group 1 figurines, their dress hides their contours and is applied to create a smoother contour, resulting in a sort of column-shaped body.

212 This can be observed in a probably contemporary 9cm tall statuette from Megara Hyblaea, from the North-West Sanctuary, temple B, even though she is seated. Gras, Tréziny, Broise 2005, p.328-9, fig.346.

No. 77 has a particular and unique appearance, as a sort of herm reminiscent of the rectangular block forming the base for other figurines but with lines drawn on it and the bust on top. The herm-body of **77** flares at the base to increase stability. It seems the object was meant to stand, but a suspension hole in the back may indicate that it could have been hung up also. Some figurines could not have stood up unaided while others used different methods of stabilization: **2** had a stand, **3** originally had a flaring dress as the lower part of the body, and **77**, **82**, **83** and **84** had widened bases. It is clear that the practical matter of its placement was of concern to the coroplast already. Possibly because he needed to display the goods for sale. The dedicant would have been concerned with the placement of the figure at the sanctuary. The different methods of placement would have been applied in order to fit more objects into the space available.

The large objects in 5b have a typical body shape that follows that of the standing, tightly-belted figurines. **3**, **4** and **5** probably had a flaring skirt. Their chest is formed as part of the dress with wide shoulders with the lower arms extending out from under it. On **6** and **7**, the body no longer consists of two parts and is bent into a seated pose. While on the first subsection, the lower arms extended to the front, on the second two objects the arms are part of the modelled body.

The round body forms in group 5c, which are seen as Rhodian influenced, are all mould-made. Figurines like **71-74** and **76** are not only particularly rounded in body shape, but show development and detail that was not common locally. Imitations of such characteristics were made, often combined with local traits, as with **75**. Figurine **71** might also demonstrate a combination of these traits with the local customs. A typical element is the rounded shoulders that run in line with the hair or veil and the thicker body. Several combinations of locally made, but clearly Rhodian inspired, figurines were found at Selinous.[213]

II.4.c Upright

As briefly mentioned above, the pose of the figurine could be problematic. The thin figurines could not stand unaided and would need to be hung or placed against a wall. One solution was to create a larger base or a stand, like **2**, another was a chair-shaped base. This solution was applied to Boeotian and north-eastern Peloponnesian terracotta figurines. These statuettes are called ‘primitives’ and do not predate the 6th century BCE in Boeotia. They are for the most part handmade, while their face is sometimes mould-made. Some seated Boeotian terracottas bear a likeness to **1** and **2** in the way the coroplast would have

213 Poma 2009, no.10-14.

had their seated position in mind.[214] Though the outcome is different than that of the block-shaped figurines from Akragas, because the Boeotian figurines are handmade, there are a striking number of similarities. The thin body of these so-called 'pappades,'[215] could be easily bent at the waist to shape them into a seated posture. The waist is usually rather narrow. In order to keep their balance, a stand or 'legs of a chair' were placed at the rear of the figurine to support it. An object from Tanagra leans backwards with her upper body. [216] The front part of the 'chair' is not visible because it is covered by the figurine's garment. Unlike most other figurines, she has arms, which are placed on low armrests of the chair. Most of the Argive figurines have just small stumps as arms, even though they are sometimes functional.[217] Szabó calls the more natural depiction of longer, more realistic arms 'functional naturalism', as the indication of arms is usually referred to by the stumps, while for carrying an object longer arms are necessary.[218] Some seated figurines show a likeness to the block-like terracottas of Akragas. A 20.5cm tall Boeotian figurine, presently in the National Museum of Athens, makes a very block-like impression frontally.[219] The frontal view does not show that the body is made out of a thin plank of clay, which is bent. The lower part of the object is therefore very square, uninterrupted by feet, and not painted like other figurines.[220] It is this frontal view and dress attached to the stand, which are reminiscent of the block-like group of figurines from Akragas. If a mould were to be made after such a figurine, the frontal part could be connected to side walls in order to create a mould with some depth. The slab of clay that forms the back would keep the figurine hollow and adds stability. Precisely this combination of techniques is found in a handmade figurine from the Sanctuary of Malophoros, Selinous. The facial features, pellet eyes and absence of the mouth are reminiscent of the Boeotian figurines. Her arms are bent forward in a similar way. The body is plank-like but with a sloping upper part.[221] The other solution is to place a stand at the rear, common for Boeotian figurines, and also seen on a figurine from the same sanctuary. The thin mould-made front shows a combination of characteristics that does not exclude the possibility of an imported object. She wears a large polos and has long strands of hair that might have been coloured (fig. 2.2). Another female figurine with a stand on the rear from Selinous has a similar body but a different head.[222] An example with a very thin body from Catania is strongly bent at the narrow waist.[223]

II.4.d From wood to terracotta

Terracotta figurines with the arms inset are called *xoana*.[224] The 14.5cm tall terracotta figurine **86** and an upper part **87** from Agrigento are very similar to one of the three wooden objects that appeared in surprisingly good condition from a well about 25km from Akragas, no. 47136 (fig. 6 in the Catalogue on the right).[225] It is clear that a mould for terracotta figurine production was made after this wooden statuette, without much modification.[226] The wooden statuette measures 17.2cm and thus the terracotta figurines are from the first generation.[227] The object's size matches because both the clay for the mould and for the figurine would have shrunk.[228] The lower arms needed to be attached later, and also in the case of the terracotta figurines were probably made of wood. The question remains whether these arms were functional and originally held something. Though not very common, there are some other figurines from Akragas that were supposed to have inset wooden arms.[229] A remarkable detail is that the pin on the right arm inset was already missing when the terracotta mould was made. This part was smoothed on **86**, while on the left side the pin created a hole. This would be an argument that it is an exact copy of this wooden statuette, though it was made when the wood was still in a good condition, and not yet cracked. The terracotta figurine is not placed on a podium as high as the original wooden one.

214 Szabó 1994, p.106, n.157 mentions that besides similar Corinthian objects several are known from Southern Italy and the Sicilian towns of Syracuse, Selinous, and Megara Hyblaea.

215 These figurines are known under several different names such as 'idol' in English, 'Brettidole' in German, and 'pappas' in Greek, referring to their polos, which resembles the headdress of Orthodox priests.

216 British Museum number 1879,0624.2. The object is dated to 580 BCE; Szabó 1994, fig.36.

217 Szabó 1994, fig.84 and 85.

218 Szabó 1994, p.78 on kourotrophoi.

219 Szabó 1994 no.85.

220 Cf. Szabó 1994, no.84; Athens National Museum number 17426.

221 She wears pendants around her neck and a low polos on her head. Gabrici 1927, tav.XLIII.9. Other figurines from there seem to be a combination as well, with a moulded head in the style of the xoana. Gabrici 1927, tav.XLIII. 1 and 7.

222 Gabrici 1927, tav.LXXVI.8; also different but with a similar body and support on the rear is Gabrici 1927, tav.LXXV.1.

223 As they look plank-like, their name is 'a sanìs' in Italian. Pautasso 1996, p.41, no.48, tav.V.48.

224 Böhm 2007, p.15.

225 They were found at Contrada Tumazzu, Palma di Montechiaro, province of Agrignto and are presently exhibited at Museo Archeologico Regionale P. Orsi, Syracuse, no.47134, 47135 and 47136. See Holloway 2000, p.65; Donahue 1988, p.215ff.; Caputo 1938.

226 In Zuntz' opinion the Sicilian terracottas are developed after xoana. Zuntz 1971, p.135.

227 Richter and Frantz 1968, no.53 p.43, fig.175-8. The wood might have shrunk slightly over time in dry circumstances.

228 Tests on the shrinkage of local clays are discussed in the following chapter.

229 Inv. no.AG 9107 (250) Mus. Arch. Agrigento. has holes for the inset of wooden arms. The left one is placed much higher. Another example of later date, see De Miro 2000, no.1482.

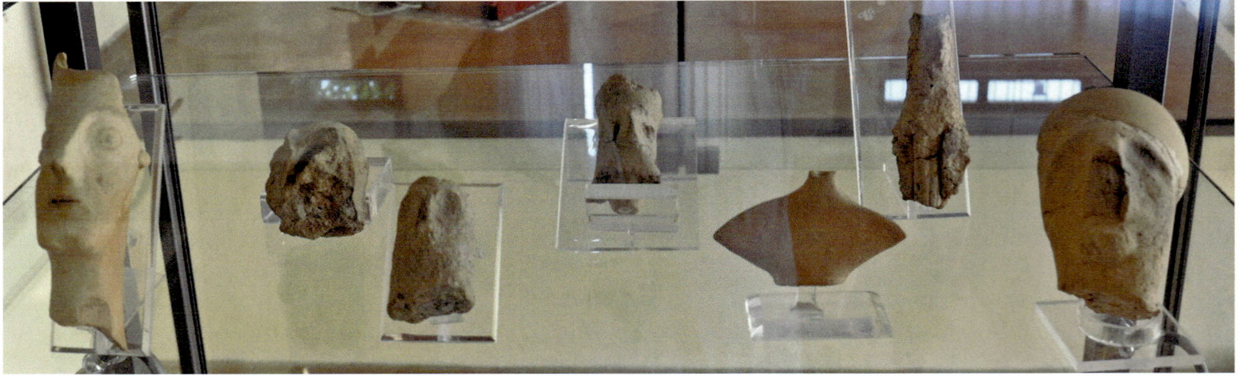

Figure 2.3: Several long shaped heads and pinched faces, dated to the 7th century to the first quarter of the 6th century BCE. Particular the nose marks the face. Arch. Mus. Agrigento, showcase 10, head on the left, Inv. no. 19896.

This unique example is a strong argument that terracotta figurines were inspired by, or even, as here, copied from wooden figurines. Yet there is no clear indication of a one-way development from wood to clay as the preferred material. The two traditions might well have existed alongside each other. The three wooden figurines, which differ from each other, have many features in common with statuary from the same period made of other material. The two larger ones, in particular, are reminiscent of the late 6th century statuary (fig. 6 in the Catalogue middle and right).[230] Similar traits are unmistakably visible on several figurines from the Sanctuary of Malophoros, Selinous, such as dress, hair arrangement, low polos and facial features, making it very likely that preceding wooden originals inspired the terracottas or were even copied.[231]

II.4.e An aniconic tradition

This reconstruction explained only partly the block-like body with its plank-shaped front. It raises the question of whether another source of inspiration for the nearly aniconic shape of the body would have been available.[232] Rectangular stone columns, *cippi*, sometimes with a spherical shape on top were often placed as grave markers and were popular in the Etruscan area in the 6th century BCE.[233] *Cippi* are known from other places, among which are 7th century BCE Metaponto[234] and Kamarina.[235] On some indigenous sites in Sicily, aniconic objects have also been found, such as two stone spheres from the Contrada Tumazza spring.[236] Both the shape as well as the sepulchral sphere are shared with the characteristics of the block-like figurines. Cippi were probably seen as seats for the soul of the deceased or the deity.[237] Similar looking objects are stone Carthaginian *tofet stelai*. Such stelai, rectangular blocks, sometimes with a small protruding base and a rectangular shaped part on the front are known from Mozia.[238] A third comparable sort of object is the Phoenician *baetylus*. These aniconic stones with shapes ranging from conical to rectangular were probably seen as the seat or house of the deity, the latter is the literal meaning of the word 'bethel'. Aniconic representations are also applied in Greek areas.[239] These analogue aspects would make it less coincidental that this shape, the block-like base with sloping body, was the outcome of the iconographic transformations that took place under influence of several different sorts of anthropomorphic statuary. Even though there is no direct evidence of such *cippi* or *tofet stelai* from Akragas, the popular block-like bodies seem at least partly aniconic. Rectangular stone objects might have been in use till the end of the 6th century BCE. The pillar shape could have inspired coroplasts to form a different shape than the narrow-waisted examples of Greek origin. Such a 'pillar body' might have also supported busts, another category of

230 Donahue 1988, p.215.

231 Surprisingly among them is also a bust. Gabrici 1927, tav.XXXVII 1-5.

232 A good discussion of Greek aniconic images as well as many references to both objects and literature can be found at Donahue 1988, p.219ff.

233 Neudecker 2006a.

234 For more on Sicilian cippi, horoi stones, and stelai and their development, see Doak 2015.

235 Lanza 1975.

236 Urquhart 2010, p.133.

237 Steingräber 2009, p.130.

238 D'Andrea 2014.

239 For a proper description of the idea see: V. Platt, *Facing the Gods: Epiphany and Representation in Graeco-Roman Art, Literature and Religion*. Cambridge, Cambridge University Press, 2011, p.100-1. Zeus Meilichios had a pyramid stone in Sikyon, according to Pausanias 2.9.6.

objects from Akragas, but from the 5th century BCE.[240] The image of an aniconic body would have appealed due to its resemblance to familiar images, and was then transformed the small statuettes into a seated body, by turning the upper part into a slope. The outline of the apron is marked in a rather similar way as on some *stelai* with a protruding rectangular part. The protruding footstool, which on some figurines does not show feet, shows a striking similarity with the protruding base of some stelai, increasing the stability of the object.[241] A flat figurine from Licata has a semi-iconic body. The thin rectangular model not only has a head on top, but also arm stumps stretched out on each side. Its head is column-shaped with only a pinched nose as a face.[242] A figurine from Akragas (fig. 2.3, third from the right) of which the head is missing has a flat body with on each side triangular arms shaped like wings. Besides 77, the figurines are quite different from the Attic tradition of herms.[243] It is likely that the shape of the figures derives from or was inspired by column-shaped imagery on the one hand and technical advantages on the other. This would explain the geometric shape as well as the absence of arms and other defined curves of the body. It was clearly a conscious choice to depict the body like this,[244] because other items are added as well, such as fine jewellery, details on the head, etc.

A particular example of a continuation of the supposed tradition as late as the Hellenistic Period can be found on the block-bodied *pinakes* of three female figures. These objects (fig. 2.4), dated to the end of 4th-3rd century BCE and found in large numbers at the extramural sanctuary of Grotta Caruso, Locri, are thought to be connected with a fountain cult. The female figures are interpreted as nymphs.[245] There are variations on similar objects with a bull/Acheloos or a table with three bowls on the lower part of the block or the side. Numerous terracotta nude female figures in a kneeling pose, wearing a *polos*, are found together with articulated limbs and thrones in the same size at this nymphaeum. They are seen as dolls representing the goddess.[246] It is tempting to interpret similar features in iconographies, such as the polos and throne, as well as the possible dressing as a sign of identification with the goddess for figurines from an earlier period. That does still not explain the block-shaped body, nor the triple form of the nymphs. Their shape is reminiscent of the double figures, male and female, usually from the Sanctuary of Malophoros, Selinous. They are also block-shaped with a head or two heads on top.[247] They are made of tufa and dated to the end of the fifth and fourth century BCE.

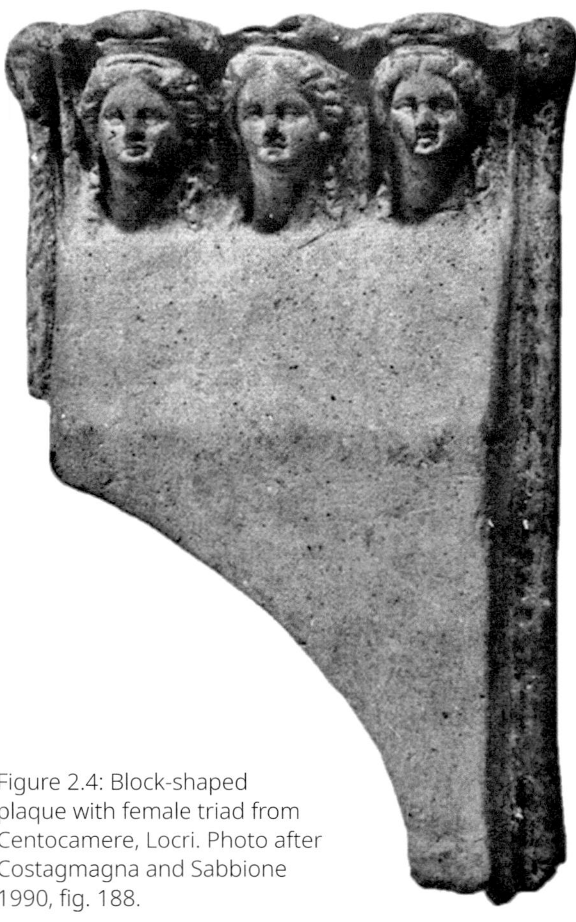

Figure 2.4: Block-shaped plaque with female triad from Centocamere, Locri. Photo after Costagmagna and Sabbione 1990, fig. 188.

II.4.f Gender

The block-like bodies of most Akragantine figurines lack distinctive indications of gender. Gender is defined by the head, not by the body, and the facial features are the

240 Marconi 1929, p.182-7. Probably from the 4th century BC are some stelae with a double head, one male and one female, from the Meilichios Sanctuary precinct in Selinous. Ferri 1929, p.70, fig.30; Moscati 2001, p.314-5. Earlier, in the 6th and 5th century BCE, this area, the 'campo di stele' was in use as well. Grotta 2010. The majority of the finds at this sanctuary dates from the 6th century BCE, see Parisi 2017, p.63-4.

241 See D'Andrea 2014, p.124-6 fig. 3, 4 and 5.

242 De Miro 1962, tav.XXXIX, fig.1.

243 Zuntz 1971, p.130, n.4.

244 Donahue points out that the use of aniconic images is often a deliberate choice, not a technical matter. Donahue 1988, p.226.

245 Arias 1940, p. 177-80, fig.3-5. Pausanias mentions in a description of a temple called Nymphon near Sycyon depictions of Dionysos, Demeter and Kore, who have their face revealed. Hence their bodies might have been concealed. Paus. 2.11.3. See Bell 2014, p. 105, n.47.

246 An anonymous epigram from roughly the same period suggests that girls would bring their toys, among which are the dolls and their dresses, before the wedding to the sanctuary. The wordplay is striking; the girl, the goddess and the doll are all referred to as 'kore', Palatine Anthology 6.280. In the same way, the word 'nymph' is the Greek word for 'bride'. The goddess is thought to be Artemis or Persephone. MacLachlan 2009.

247 Gabrici 1927, tav.XXVII2-4, tav.XXVIII-XXIX.

clearest indicator of gender.[248] If the head is of Greek origin and so specifically defined as female, why does the body lack any indications of gender? Was the gender thought to be unimportant? Was it assumed to be known already? Or was the face in itself sufficient? If the coroplast did not care to define the arms, why would he be concerned about making the body feminine with the addition of breasts? The answer may lie in the dress of the depicted figure. In comparison, figurines of Tarentine male banqueters have detailed bodies that show their muscular chests, partly covered with a himation. Though their faces do not differ much from the Akragantine female figurines, their body, pose and dress do.[249] The coroplasts might have known how to render female bodies, but expressing the gender more explicitly might have been considered either superfluous or inappropriate. In general, the number of female figurines from this period from Sicily is much higher than that of male ones.[250] In Paestum and Santa Venera, moulds of kouroi were altered to be used for naked goddess figurines.[251] Similar figurines are not known from Akragas, and there are no clearly male predecessors. If the standard figurines were generally perceived to be female, there was perhaps no need to add additional indicators of gender. The female gender might have been considered inherent to objects bearing this dress and adornments, making it unnecessary to express the gender explicitly by depicting sexual characteristics. The coroplasts created several examples, such as the belted figurines discussed above, who also clearly represented females. Another possibility might be that local customs meant that more explicit depictions of the female body were considered improper as feminine shapes were supposed to be covered or even concealed. The characteristic ankle-length dress topped with a straight apron is the most common garment for Akragantine figurines. This garment almost entirely covered the front of the body, leaving just the edges of the neck and the feet uncovered, as if it were just a thick rectangular piece of cloth. This dress is most likely an indication of gender, in addition to the jewellery, as opposed to the unadorned and sometimes naked male figures. Social acceptance of the female body could have been the reason for depicting a female goddess without depicting or even hinting at any of her sexual characteristics. There is just a very light development notable in this regard. When the body is depicted more naturally and has round arms, bending independently from the body. Just one figurine from the locally made objects, **103**, has a slight elevation of the chest that seems to indicate breasts. However, this object has a smoothened chest as the pectoral jewellery seems to have been erased (Catalogue fig. 9). Until the last group 4 with locally made objects, the chest stays flat, usually covered by pendants. Other sexual indications on the body are absent.

248 See section II.5.d.

249 Bencze 2010. See also n.366.

250 Ammerman 2002, p.35; Holloway 2000, p.85.

251 Ammerman 1992, p.212.

II.4.g Practical implications of the figurines' form

Employing the local production technique, the use of a front mould with a slab of clay for the back, resulted in hollow rather three-dimensional objects. However, the image is still flat and the back remains unworked. In addition, the sides are usually not detailed; only the seam between the two halves is smoothed. Some of the imported figurines are solid (**71**, the upper part of **75**, **80**, **81**, **85**, **86**, **200**) but almost all share the frontality. The increased depth might have functioned well in creating a better impression when the figurines were in situ, mainly because the objects could stand upright facing the viewer. The protruding lower arms originally attached to figurines **3-5** and **85-86** would have made an upright position necessary. The reason arms, or specifically underarms, are represented only later, may have been because the upper arms were usually not represented in these earlier figurines. If these were the predecessors of the locally made figurines, the very different body shape and dress would be surprising (table 2.1). There is not only a large difference in technique, but also in iconography.

With this overview of figurines and the developments involved, it must be concluded that the overall shape of the body is one aspect that largely depended on technical practicalities. Of course, there may have been a preference for a simple shape and no desire to create a more detailed or naturalistic body, yet the fact that straight contours are much more practical and easier to unload from a mould would make it a logical step for the coroplast to omit protruding limbs of any kind.[252] Nevertheless, we can safely conclude that such a body shape was sufficient to meet the needs of the dedicants. Technical matters were decisive in determining the body shape of the majority of figurines. On the other hand, hand-modelled figurines had different technical constraints and would have been produced with more attention and flexibility for alterations. Eventually, their shape had consequences for the way in which they were applied and handled – and their use had consequences for their iconography. There would have been a constant tense relationship between the three key elements of iconography, technique, and practical use. Coroplasts seem to have shown much more interest in the more rapidly produced moulded objects. The ease and speed of production must have outweighed artistic concerns for hand-modelled figurines or more complex body shapes for some decades. This does not explain,

252 An extensive discussion of these and other technical aspects can be found in Chapter III.

Characteristics of body	Daedalic/Early figurines	Block-like figurines
Body shape	abstracted naturalistic	geometric
Pose	standing	standing and seated
Legs and feet	usually indicated	usually indicated, bent knees indicated
Arms and hands	short arms or wooden, inset arms	no arms or flat along the body
Waist	tight waist	no indication of a waist
Breasts	yes	no
Dress	dress with a belt at waist, bulging upper part	apron, straight rectangular garment, covering the front of the body

Table 2.1: Summary of the iconographic characteristics of the two oldest groups of figurines.

however, why the addition of a chair, a hand-modelled addition, prevailed most of the time over the creation of a more naturalistic body (for example, by adding arms). Nor is it clear why the female body was not made more explicit with the addition of breasts or a rounded bosom. It seems there was no interest in depicting the specific female body, as the decoration, by contrast, was treated with surprising attention for the detail.

Another argument for explaining the variation in the pose that was discussed in relation to group 2 is also closely linked to the shape and size of the body. The generally small figurines in group 1 would have been easy to handle: one figurine would fit in the hand. If the figurine were larger, it could be held in the middle around the waist. In the latter case, a flat body would have been easier to hold than the strongly curved one, not only because of the curvature but also because of the uneven weight distribution. Heavier figurines would have been more stable. In addition, a bench would have increased weight and stability but made handling more difficult. When figurines from group 1 are compared, it is clear that **8**, **12**, **63** and **57** would have been much easier to hold than **22**, **30** or **36**. The taller, wider and heavier figurines would also have taken up more space when dedicated. Though it may sound an odd argument in view of the minor size of the figurines in general, it is not when we consider the enormous number of objects[253] and the rather modest size of some sanctuaries.[254] Stacking the figurines at the place of dedication would have been easier if the figurines were flatter, without protruding parts.

There might be several reasons for the different body design developments described above. One reason is probably that their predecessors were made from different materials. For quite a number of small and flat figurines, it seems clear that the original objects were made from wood or bone which were then used as a patrix.[255] For small statuary, rounder shapes would have been much easier to carve in wood than in stone. Even though the local sandstone is not hard, sculpting it with fine details is not so easy. The newly introduced technique made it possible to create similar figurines more rapidly in terracotta. Terracotta objects of the plank-shaped model, often with inset holes for arms, are much less frequent than the block-shaped models with a sloping upper body but without arms.

II.4.h The form of the figurines and their role as votives

Another reason for the absence of local predecessors might be that there was no local tradition of statuette making before it was introduced as part of a cult. It may have been that no local population or religious observance had previously required the mass production of figurines. It may be that a different tradition may have been the origin of the special appearance of the figurines. The original model of the figurine was block-shaped, and the geometrical shape was transformed from being aniconic into a human being by the addition of a head and a dress. The still abstract body of the earliest locally produced figurines gradually became more naturalistic but remained flat-chested, remaining simply a bearer of adornment. The apron that created the typical block-like shape was distinctly present in the locally produced objects over a long period. The dress of the figurines is reminiscent of rituals in which such a garment was applied to a statue or even a living woman in order to represent the goddess. It is possible that dressing up the body of the figure, a ritual known from other places, would have concealed the

253 Even though calculations are not easy to make, the different moulds, series and generations make clear that production was on a large scale, and estimates of the total number must be into the hundreds per mould series.

254 For example, the S. Anna Sanctuary in Akragas would have consisted of several relatively small buildings. It is likely that the figurines, in addition to other votive objects were placed in a specifically dedicated area: a sort of bench, shelf or table. Of course, these places would have been quickly filled with all sorts of items, as is the case with modern dedications and votives. They were afterwards deposited in burial pits.

255 A female figurine in bone from Megara Hyblaea has similar traits and is also very thin. Parisi 2017, p.189, fig.82.

seated figure, forming the distinctive block-shape.[256] It may be therefore that a shape or object that was already in use for cultic purposes was then humanised in the terracotta figurines with the addition of a head and feet, as those parts would have been visible on the statue itself. Such a figure is likely to have formed a stable model, which could then be adorned with various items. Even though in the first group some exceptional figurines had no indication of a dress (**8**, **22**), the majority does.[257] This suggestion is not conclusive and the ex-planation remains speculative.

II.5 Head and face

Having discussed the possible sources of inspiration for the overall shapes of the body, it is time to focus on the head and faces of the Akragantine figurines. The heads, and the moulding technique used to make them, are a characteristic feature of the figurines. The heads were interchanged and do not always match the style and size of the attached body. The faces of local Akragantine figurines are distinct from imported items. A clear development in facial shape among the Akragantine figurines is discussed with reference to the individual aspects that influenced the appearance of the face in the specified groups. After that, some individual traits are discussed separately in order to trace specific cultural influences. A short summary and table are followed by a discussion of facial features and gender. Hairstyle is discussed separately, as it is a more complex and more rapidly changing feature than others.

II.5.a General shape and expression of the face

On some early and large figures, the face is moulded and the body is handmade (**3-7**). The use of a mould for a part of the figurine, while the rest was handmade, would have been one of the first steps in the application of the new moulding technique. A detailed face was apparently the most difficult part to render, and producing multiple copies of a detailed face using a mould would have been a quick and efficient solution. The head was an area of focus for the coroplasts.[258] Not only were faces often relatively large, but they were also more detailed in comparison with the smaller and roughly shaped block-like bodies on objects in group 1, such as **8**, and **21**, (**12**, and **57** were better in proportion). One series was exceptional with its relatively small and more roughly shaped: **9**, **36** and **41**. The larger size of the head could be ascribed to the practice of interchanging moulds. Heads from older moulds that retained the sharpness of their facial expression could be attached to (differently proportioned) bodies made in newer moulds.

The face was often rounded, **12**, **15-17** or at least gives the impression, because of the frequent presence of a heavy jaw.[259] The length of the face is usually still greater than its width, but a low polos, veil or the absence of headgear strengthens the impression of a round face, while a taller polos lengthens the face. In addition, the rendering of the hair also affects the overall impression. The heads in group 4, for example, with their bulging hair and wide low polos give the impression of a small, round face. The face can also appear triangular, wider, and broad at the top with a pointed chin, as on **16**, **21**, **53**. In such cases, the jaws are not wide. Some faces are particularly chubby and have fleshy cheeks, **9**, **11**, and a sizeable nose. The effect is strengthened by dimples next to the mouth, **9**, **11**, **48**. These dimples on the corners of the mouth are typical of Akragantine coroplastics.[260] Because of this chubbiness, the details and depth, combined with the Archaic smile, many faces have a naturalistic expression, even though the eyes are not very detailed.[261] This contrasts with a few exceptional faces, for example, **63**, with a flat face and lacking the curled lips, resulting in an empty, blank expression. This could also be the effect of weathering after intense use of the mould, as a comparable face, **71**, clearly from a newer mould, is much more detailed. It is very likely that these two were made in the same workshop.[262]

---

256 The high number of loom weights and other instruments for weaving, which are dedicated in votive deposits and even in foundation deposits for buildings on Sicily, might point to the importance of textile production. The weaving might have been a ritual, taking place on the site. In Franacvilla Maritima, a specific building dating from the 8th century BCE was used for weaving and it is suggested that a special robe played an important role in the veneration of the goddess. Gleba 2008, p.74ff, 77ff.

257 On figurine AG1155, where the hem of the dress is marked above the feet, the body suddenly turns out to be dressed. De Miro 2000, p.128 no.8, tav.LXI.

258 A comparable attention for the head is visible in the terracotta figurines found at Es Cuieram, Eivissa on Ibiza.

259 This contrasts with earlier wooden examples and their terracotta counterparts. The forehead in particular seems thick at the front and flattened on top, no.86. No. 202 has a similarly shaped head. Earlier faces from figurines made from other materials had a more triangular shape with flat cheeks. See, for example, the face on the marble lamp from Selinous. Parisi 2017, p.55, fig.13; Dewailly 1992, p.17, n.58 dated to the end of the 7th century BCE; the Laganello head and the sphinx from the Ionic temple of Syracuse. The latter is dated to the first half of the sixth century BCE. The tendency towards rounder faces with a heavier jaw and higher cheekbones is clear from the Sphinx head from Akragas and appear in the last quarter of that century. Inv. no.1316 Arch. Mus. Agrigento. Adornato 2012b, fig.24.

260 Wiederkehr Schuler 2004, p.211, n.17.

261 This face is reminiscent of the Full Face Type from Geloan *protomai*. The faces with more volume are nicknamed the Fat Face Type and are similar in chubbiness to the types described here, and are dated to the last quarter of the 6th century BCE. Uhlenbrock 1988, p.41ff.

262 There are some other arguments, such as technical specifications that make it likely they are made by the same workshop. Both were found at the Pezzino Necropolis, Agrigento.

In group 2, the subgroups are mainly based on the heads, on the basis of both their facial features and hairstyle. The shape of the head in group 2a is oval, **154** has flatter cheeks, and **155** is chubbier. The faces remain fleshy, but a flatter face reminiscent of **63** in the previous group, also appears here: **70**. This is possibly an example of the replacement of heads.[263] The heads of **66-68** and **34** are also very similar. Hair and polos are differently shaped. Another example of a head of which the facial features are repeated in different groups and applied on different bodies is that of **20**, **100** and **107**. The last two are very likely to be from the same mould series. The face is very chubby, with a large nose and fleshy cheeks. It shares these characteristics with the other faces in group 2d. This extreme chubbiness is considered to be Ionian influence.[264] An object that raises the question of whether this influence indeed came from somewhere else is **181**. The figurine is very different in its pose and with the presence of snakes, but shares the same characteristic facial features. The chubbiness of the face continues in group 3a with some objects, but in less extreme form, **124**. The heads become more oval, or so give that impression with the tall polos. The lips are sometimes thick, but not so small and rather a result of the overall chubbiness: **168-169.** Also in 3b, the oval shape of the head continues, but with some more rounded and plump-cheeked faces as exceptions, where the absence of headgear or a low polos strengthens the impression of a round face: **114, 111, 110. 112** possibly had a polos. They seem to have been made after a Selinuntine example. One of the largest and finest faces from Akragas is **95**. In group 4, the faces did not receive the same detailed attention as earlier groups. The faces are flat and less expressive. Under the large polos and hair, the faces look small. They have an Archaic smile.

II.5.b A personal expression

For many figurines, it is as if the eyes are gazing at the ground, with most of the eyeball covered with an eyelid. The impression is in some cases lofty and august. The smile makes the face again open and personally accessible. At the same time, the slightly curled up lips and the gaze of the eyes create distance. It is not an arrogance, but certainly a distinction, and air of grandness and sublimity. The chubbiness of the faces gives them a friendlier expression. The bulging cheeks strengthen the impression of a happy expression in the case of **15-17**. These are personal impressions and others may view the expressions in different ways, expressing different emotions.

While the body was not as anthropomorphic as the head, the interpretation of realism, that the heads were sculpted to have similar facial features to the people who made or used these figurines, is unlikely.[265] The face should rather be seen as an idealistic image. In the same way that prosperity is revealed by the adornments, health and an abundance of food are shown by the chubby faces. The good life and wealth are certainly elements expressed by the faces. In their idealistic form, the figurines express the wishes and endeavours of the dedicants.

The variation in facial features and expression creates individuality and, to some extent, expresses similarity with the dedicant. This approachability creates a certain interaction, a dialogue with the viewer. The appearance given to the object creates not only a human being the dedicant can relate to, but the personality expressed by the face gives it a character. This personal gaze of an object is a Greek way of thinking about the interaction between object and user. It is reminiscent of the direct manner of address seen in written texts, often in the first person singular, on all sorts of Greek dedications. The facial expression also comes close to those of kouroi and korai, on the bases of which such personal addresses are also common when used as grave monuments.[266] The strength of the facial expression is greater for the earlier groups, 1 and 2, more idealistic in the third, and less distinct in the last group.

II.5.c Cultural influences

II.5.c.i Noses

Group 5 comprises objects found at Akragas, but the majority was produced elsewhere. In the following paragraphs, the potential cultural influences on Akragantine coroplastics of figurines from this group are discussed with respect to their facial features, comparing their shape, size and expressiveness.

The Argive figurines, group 5a, **1** and **2**, have hand-formed pinched faces, on which large clay bullets form the eyes. The main characteristic of this 'bird-face' is its nose, formed by squeezing the clay between forefinger

263 Apparently, this was a commonly applied technique. Huysecom-Haxhi writes in the summary of her article on objects from Thasos: "The technical process that combines a facial type with different types of bodies belongs to a set of solutions adopted by Ionians to multiply the images and to enrich the typological repertory with minimal effort. Huysecom-Haxhi 2016, p.65.

264 Pautasso 1996, p.115. Barletta, however, writes that characteristics like the high cheekbones, bulging and shaped eyes, the wide jaw and deeper parts around the mouth on the Leontini kouros head, which indeed shows very similar traits with the chubbiness discussed here, is indirectly influenced by Ionian sculpture, through an Attic interpretation. Barleta 1983, p.42-5.

265 Probably of a later date, objects that depict African faces obviously combine naturalism and idealism. Protome S83 is an example, and the head S36 could be also be an older man of African descent (Arch. Mus. Agrigento, found at the round altar of S. Biagio). Like the other objects S36 would be Hellenistic. Marconi Bovio 1930, p.99, fig.33.

266 For example, Phrasikleia or Kroisos.

and thumb. On some hand-formed heads found near Temple A, but probably predating it, the nose is what makes the face recognizable as human (fig. 2.3 right).[267] Its mouth with thin lips and a pronounced chin is very narrow and does not exceed the width of the nasal alae. These features are very similar to some heads from Akragas.[268] The nose occupies a substantial part of the face and might have been considered as one of the basic elements of the human face.[269] The smaller head (fig. 2.3 third from the left) has no mouth.[270] In some of these instances, the eyes are marked only by indentations in the clay, suggested by the edge of the eyebrow edge and the deeper eye sockets. The Argive figurines, **1-2**, have clay pellet eyes, like another bird-face from Akragas (fig. 2.3 middle). The chin and mouth are absent. On another sort of head from Licata, it is the nose and mouth that are both pronounced.[271] The vertical placement and the narrowness create the impression of a long head. The larger head (fig. 2.3 right) is elongated by the addition of a polos, which widens slightly and seems to continue directly upwards from the forehead. The suggestion of Dewailly that the polos actually developed out of the head is very plausible. These elongated heads would have been the predecessors or examples for the Akragantine coroplasts.[272] The eyes are particularly large and the protruding nose, though broken off, dominated the face. These features are also seen in a finely executed head (fig. 2.3 left), found near the City sanctuary, in the western sector and may be dated earlier than its context. The head resembles faces from Crete.[273] This head shows a similarity with the heads discussed above, but also with some Archaic figurine faces. The ear studs, made of a round, separately pressed-on, pieces of clay could mark the ear or just the earlobe. The eyes are round with a point in the middle.[274] The arching eyebrows create another circular form above the eyes, which appear wide open as if in amazement or surprise. They are connected to the long straight nose that runs parallel to the jaw and flat cheeks. The nose runs in one line from the forehead down. This is a characteristic of Greek sculpture and returns in the later figurines. From group 1 onward this is the case, but the sharpness or geometrical shape shifts to a much more naturalistic shape, often with wider alae and a rounder tip. The tip of the nose sometimes becomes thicker (**17**, **19**, **23**). A face with a long thin nose might have been more difficult to remove from the mould. However, the coroplasts would have been skilled by the time they had produced hundreds of figurines and the nose became thinner and longer again, keeping the rounded tip. Compare, for example, the very similar faces of **34** and **70**.[275] The general development among the Akragantine figurines was that the nose became thinner, with the exception of the wide fleshy faces in which a chubby nose was more suitable (**107** and **100** in group 2). The tip of the nose generally remained rounded with exceptions on both sides: a pointed tip (**133**) or a round almost drooping tip (**95**). The nose is very thin in the variation on this series, **131**, but thicker on others, **168**, depending on the overall chubbiness of the face.

II.5.c.ii Mouth and chin

The shape of the chin is particularly pronounced on figurines in group 1 and 2. The chin is often pronounced and this seems to originate from early statuary. On the very early heads (fig. 2.3, right and left) the chin is large. One of them (fig. 2.3 right) has an indented area in the middle to create a cleft chin. Such a cleft chin appears on figurines **4-7** which have a pointed chin. A vertical dimple, roughly in the middle, marks the protruding chin. The cleft would be made with a sharp tool after moulding the face, and was not always perfectly vertical. This peculiarity draws the viewer's attention and is not seen in other Akragantine figurines. It could be a rendering based on reality, a development of the muscle in the chin in adulthood, but such a deep groove is not prominent in many women, and

267 The Temple of Heracles. De Miro refers to similar objects from Greek mainland, Rhodes and Crete. De Miro 1962, p.141-2, tav.LIII fig.2 right.

268 See n.273 below.

269 The nose as the main characteristic of the face itself appears on the 'pinched-face' figures, such as the Licata figurine mentioned above in section II.4.e and no.49.

270 De Miro 1962, p.141-2, tav.LIII, fig.2 left.

271 De Miro 1962, tav.XXXVI, fig.2-3.

272 The libation tube, modelled as a head with the addition of hair and ears suggests with its long and narrow shape the same hypothesis that the polos reflects the aniconic tradition of the shape of the head, see section II.5.c.iv. Dewailly 1983, p.8.

273 Another terracotta head, Mus. Arch. Agrigento Inv. no.10865, discussed by Adornato 2017, has very similar traits: mouth and chin. He refers to a Geloan head, Mus. Arch. Inv. no.7817 to state that similarities are due to Geloan influence. In my opinion, the eyes on all three of these heads are differently rendered. The mouth, created by just an incision is further marked only on the Akragantine heads. In addition, the broad chin with the soft groove is characteristic of just these two, differing from the very pointed chin on the Geloan head. However, that is no reason to deny Cretan influences. I agree with Adornato that it is no proof of Cretan presence either. See discussion on its polos no.167. See also Perna 2015, p.35, fig.7; see also two others from Prinias, Pautasso 2015, no.16 and 17, p.75, fig.20.

274 These sort of concentric circles appear regularly on local pottery. This might be an indication that the human eye was an important concept in the iconography, also for pottery decoration.

275 This is another example of a head, probably from the same mould, with a different body.

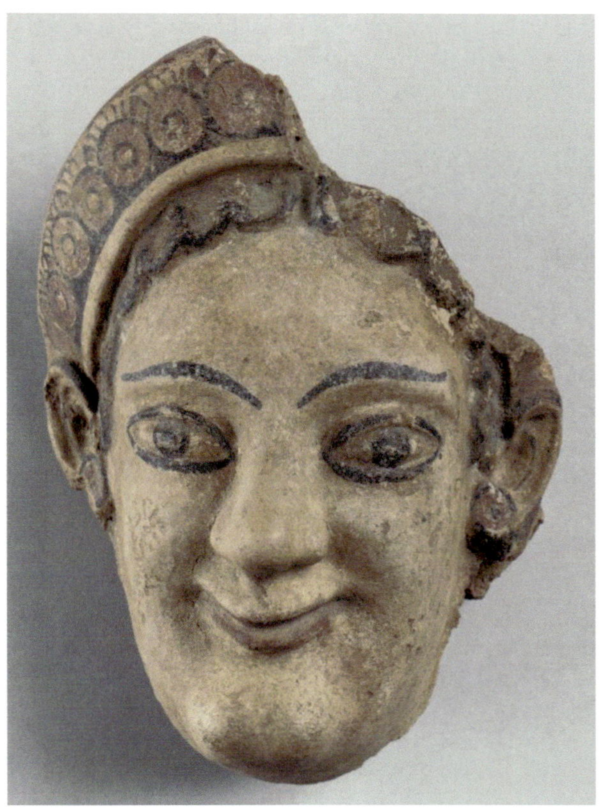
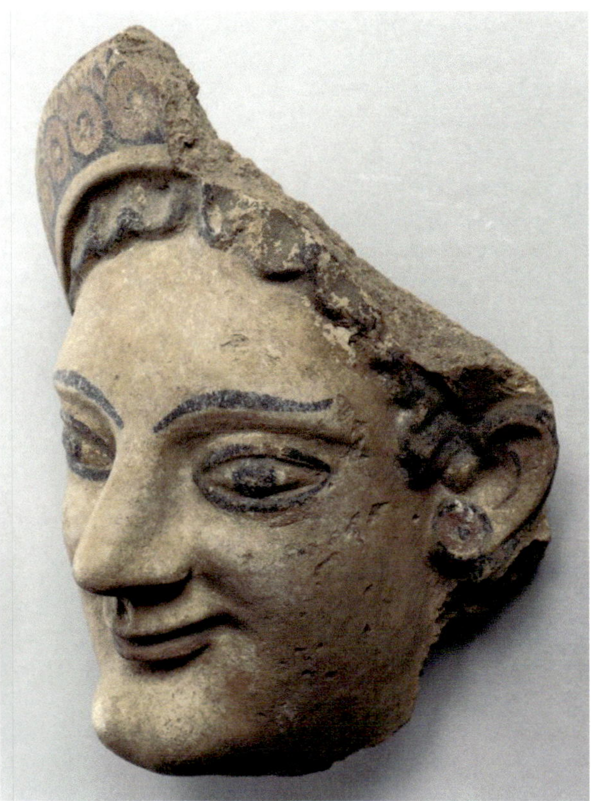

Figure 2.5: Etruscan female head antefix from different angles, sixth century BCE. Photo after digital collection of the Frances Lehman Loeb Art Center.

is exceptional in general. On figurine **7**, the philtrum is marked also with a groove. Though not straight, it clearly marks a continuation of the chin cleft.

The mouth was not very pronounced, or even absent, on the very early heads (fig. 2.3), but it is prominent on **3-6**. It is unsmiling, small, and narrow, but the lips are very thick. Its placement is directly under the nose, in line with the chin. Again **7** is exceptional as the mouth has been altered by hand to be wider, diverging from the mould. The mouth is slightly opened and curving up with dimples on the sides. It might have been made when the Archaic smile became the preferred fashion. These two sorts of mouths also appear among the locally produced figurines, while small mouths and relatively thick lips are less frequently attested **(20, 24)**.[276] The placement of the nose, mouth, and chin creates a vertical line, **184**. Notable in group 2d is the large nose, particularly compared with the mouth, which is narrow, **182**. The alae of the nose are in line with the width of the mouth. The same feature, but less extreme can be seen at **90-92**, from group 2c. The same development, from a small mouth with thick lips to a wider one with thinner lips, can be seen on figurines in group 1 and 2, compare, for example, **20** and **100**. The wider mouth, not fully smiling, but with dimples and protruding cheeks becomes the standard (**15-17**). The protruding chin adds to the cheerful expression because it makes the mouth seem deeper between the bulging parts around.

The small mouth with thick lips, pronounced cheekbones and chin are characteristics that appear on larger stone Phoenician statuary from as early as the 7th century BCE.[277] The development of the facial features, particularly visible in the shape of the lips, seems to parallel that of Akragantine terracottas **3-6**. Even when the different character of the material is taken into account, the objects or similarly styled ones, might have inspired coroplasts. The head of the early Phoenician image is square. Influence from this direction was certainly possible, but in the course of the sixth century BCE, there are other objects with comparable facial features from different cultural centres. One of them is an Etruscan antefix of a female head (fig. 2.5)[278] that is reminiscent of Akragantine figurine

276 The three heads, mentioned in the second part of note 34 above, (the lamp, the Laganello head and the Sphinx) also provide insight into the development of the lips. Where the first two faces have the small mouth with thick lips, the third, the sphinx, has a wider mouth with Archaic smile and dimples.

277 Moscati 2001, p.286.

278 The Frances Lehman Loeb Art Center, Inv. no. 2003.18, h. 20.3cm.

faces from group 2d. Its mouth with thin lips, curling up, with dimples on the sides and pushing the cheeks up are similar to the Akragantine figurines **99**, **156**, **107**. The overall shape of the face, however, differs. The face of the antefix is oval and almost pointed at the chin. The placement of the ears, their shape, and ear studs are comparable to the Akragantine objects **99** and **107**.[279] Though the impression of these painted elements is different, their form in terracotta is similar. Most of the chubby faces among the Akragantine objects have a broader or roundish face, but a similar impression of a wide and low jaw.[280] The facial features of the Etruscan antefix, particularly the smile and the expressive eyes, also strongly engage the viewer. The detailed rendering together with the fine painting draws the attention of the viewer.

II.5.c.iii Eyes

One of the most important parts of the attraction of the figurines is the expressiveness of the eyes. The eyes vary in shape from rounded to almond-shaped. The eyes are sometimes very large and bulging, as on **3-7**. The lack of details on the eyes, as if fully opened, creates more distance and detracts from their vivacity. When the eyelids are just visible, there is a determined expression, as with the almond-shaped eyes of **95**. The impression given by eyes with eyelids and those without is quite different. It is possible that eyelids, the eyes themselves, or the eyebrows were drawn in with fine lines. Though this is not unlikely, and was not uncommon in the region at the time, none of the figurines from Akragas has traces of paint left on their eyes.[281] However, particularly early faces, in group 1, continuing in group 2, have large plain and slightly bulging eyes. These three examples are rather different from each other, but share the large, bulging eyes without eyelids, which gives them a blank expression (**154**, **163**, **155**). On some faces, the eyes tend to be more diagonal and slightly slanting. Eyelids or lines sometimes sharpen the effect, **107** and **99**. The eyes themselves bulge a bit between the eyelids. These sort of eyes are of East Greek influence and also appear on Geloan *protomai*, dated after 540 BCE.[282] On many figurines, likely from later generations, the eyes became vaguer, leaving just the contours visible, **74**. In some cases, the eyebrow is absent (**87**, **100**), but more usually the curve of the eyebrow follows the line from the nose up, arches high and round. On **58**, for example, the eyebrows are actually shaped almost into a semicircle around the large eyes. With other figurines, the eyebrows are only slightly arched; on **95**, the eyebrows curve downwards at a clear angle.

II.5.c.iv Ears

Some figurines have particularly large and striking ears. They are placed where the two parts of the hair, the fringe and the hair on the sides, come together. Sometimes this is high and not very naturalistic. The ears of **21** stand out from the head. They often have a large round lobe, for aesthetic purposes. A nearly complete 40cm tall terracotta tube (fig. 2.6), dated to the second half of the 6th century BCE has separately applied pierced ears on both sides and a thick round fringe of hair with vertically incised lines curving slightly down, as on a forehead running from one ear to the other. It is reminiscent of the aniconic tradition[283] although it might have had painted eyes, nose and mouth.[284] The upper part of the tube, above the hair, is slightly smaller and appears to be headgear, with the ratio of a medium-height polos. The 'face' is slightly flaring, increasing the suggestion of a human head. The ears are plain, oval and concave-shaped with holes in the ear lobes. The ears are placed as endings of the fringe of hair that bends down towards the ears. The pierced ears and the beaded hair suggest a female head. The ears might have been embellished with metal earrings and the hairstyle in a beaded strand is very similar to that of some figurines, for example, **179**.[285] The tube may have been painted with other parts of the human face, but no traces of this are left and the contrast with the finely shaped fringe and ears make it also unlikely. Ears and hair are not considered the most essential parts, given that many, and particular early, figurines lack ears. It seems that rather the jewellery, in this case, the earrings are the reason for adding ears so that earrings could be applied to the tube. On the figurines, the body is the part that is aniconic to a certain degree, while the head receives the attention in detail.[286] The tube is interpreted as being intended to facilitate libations.[287] Its length suggests that it was partly put in the ground. Together with the masks with similar hairstyles and

279 For more on the ears specifically, see section II.5.c.iii.

280 The jaw is discussed below.

281 For an impression of how such a painted face looks on a terracotta statuette, see Taranto figurines MNB 2671, CA 214, on which eyes and eyebrows are marked with dark paint, dated circa 510-490 BCE. See museum website: http://cartelen.louvre.fr/cartelen/visite?srv=car_not_frame&idNotice=6700&langue=en. The chubbiness and large nose with a rounded tip are very similar to Akragantine examples.

282 See different comparisons. Uhlenbrock 1988, p.42

283 See section II.4.e and II.4.h.

284 S 67. There are several fragments of four such objects from Akragas. One of them is AG 8610, middle-right part h. 9.2cm from the hair up, found at the Temple of Zeus and the City Sanctuary. Hinz 1998, p.86. Similar objects have been found on Sicily in Kamarina and in Southern Italy at Lokroi (Locri Manella) and Monticchio. Marconi 1933, p. 45-7, tav.XV.3. Some aniconic limestone heads are compared with it. Surgeon 2017. For the one in Lokroi, which is smaller and has a simpler rendering, see Ferri 1929, p.15ff.

285 As well as many in group 3a, which wear their polos directly on top.

286 Several busts from S. Biagio, dated to the beginning of the 4th century confirm a continuation of such ideas.

287 Zuntz 1971, p.80. See also the note above on busts that were probably applied in the same way.

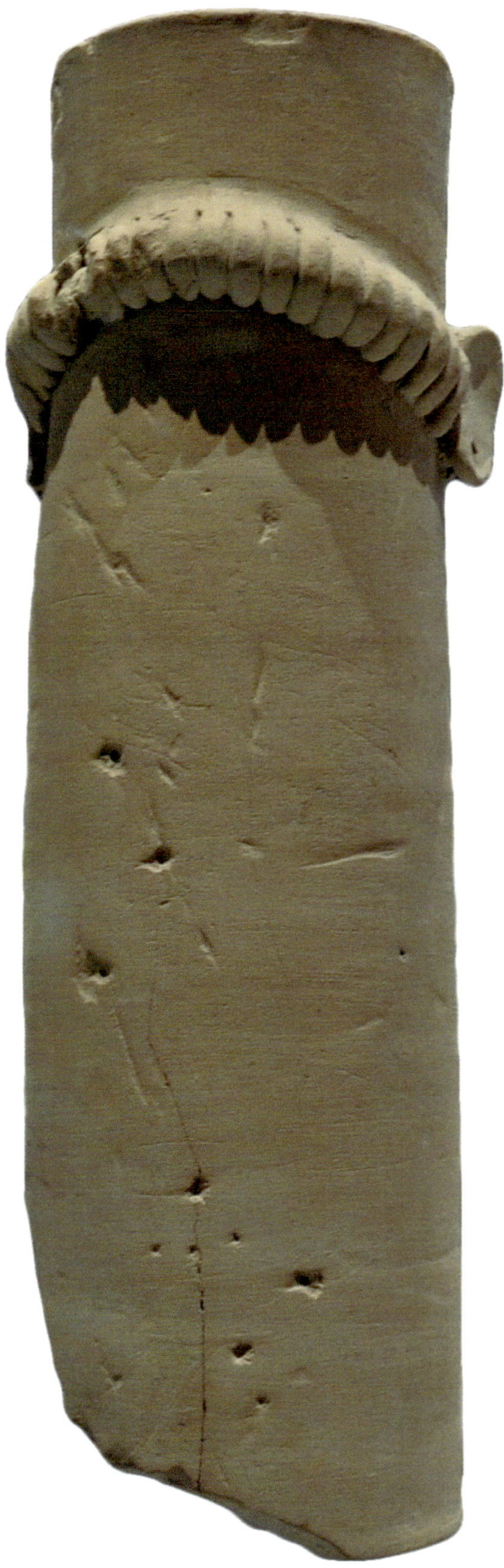

Figure 2.6: Terracotta tube-shaped head with ears, fringe and polos.

several busts, it shows that there was specific attention for the head.[288] Placed on the ground, these objects would have been seen as emerging from a world below. In this way, a connection was made with the so-called chthonic deities.[289] The tube is a sort of aniconic head, on which the face is left to be filled in by the imagination of the viewer. It creates a mysterious object.[290]

It seems that ears are added in early examples to make the figurine more naturalistic, while later they act more as decoration, and a place from which to hang large earrings. Sometimes the coroplasts might have added them after moulding, by just pressing a round or oval shape onto the hair, **154**, without paying attention to the size or shape. The round hollow shapes on AG 1154 (fig. 2.10 below) are an example. These are among the first examples as they do not appear in group 1, except for **14**.[291] **14** has indented ears very similar to **154**. The ear did not always have a specific function and might have been applied in some instances just because that was the norm (**163**). The part around the ear is often messy, a result of the addition at a certain point in time, possibly around 600 BCE. Such ears, formed by an impression, seem to suggest that the hair was kept behind it. In this way, the earring stands out better. This technique is applied to figurines **3-7**. However, the earrings were not always the motivation as a similar outline for the ear is seen on **14**. Soon afterwards the ears became slightly more naturalistic with an edge, and they are no longer flat, but three-dimensional: **34**, **21**, **70**, **90**, **99**. The last, **99**, has particularly large earlobes. In some cases, ear studs alone represent the ears (**84**). Large, round or thick earlobes might have been seen as a sign of beauty because they would be perfectly round. The difference between a large earlobe and an ear stud in the same round shape is not always very clear (**107** and **118**). On larger figurines, the earlobes are thick (**202**). From the second group onward, it became standard to depict the ears. There are only a few exceptions and lack of detail may be to blame for this (**62**, **87**, **92**). The ears were at first small and geometrically shaped (**154**). The ears of **171**, for example, are very similar to the ears on the tube. After a while, they become more naturalistic and more details are added: compare, for

288 Similar objects with a hairstyle and polos were found at Cyrene. The long head is however similar to the Akrantine tubes.

289 There are similar busts and stelae from Cyrene, which are interpreted as aniconic depictions of Persephone. These are not tube-shaped and not meant for libations. According to Zuntz, these two different things should not be related to each other. Zuntz 1971, p.80.

290 Some terracotta busts from the cave sanctuary at Grotta Caruso, Locri, have an open polos and would have probably served in libations. They are dated to the same period as the above-mentioned triple nymph from the Hellenistic Period. See section II.4.e.

291 Except for **34**, whose ears are more natural. This head, however, is later in date, and from the same series as **70**.

example, **155** and **156**, different figurines from the same mould series.

In group 2d and continuing into group 3, the ears seem functional. The earrings, included in the mould, have often much more detail than the ear itself. Both the seated counterpart[292] and the standing figurine, **176** have large ears and the earring pierces the middle of the lobe. On **179** also the ears seem to be made for hanging earrings; the left ear is hardly visible and the right one is merely an impression on the head, and thus likely to have been added after moulding. The finely detailed example of a naturalistic ear is the one on **95**. Its size has been reduced to a more natural ratio, but its placement is more diagonal than straight. The ears in general, are rather deep and flat, not standing out as much as on others. The shape and placement of ear is rather a matter of aesthetic preferences of the coroplasts, hence the wide variety. The ears of **103**, for example, are very stretched out and the ears on **130** and **131** are particularly small. It is often even unclear whether ears were indicated or not. The frontal nature of most figurines would explain this.

II.5.c.v Hair

The hair of most figurines comprises two parts. An abstract part, placed in a band on the forehead, framing the face in an arc. This solid mass represents a fringe, running from one ear to the other. Its form varies from smooth to protruding, indicated by vertical lines.[293] These bulbs, puffs or elongated pearls (or 'tongues' as they are called when more flattened)[294] vary in size and roundness.[295] The curls or strands of hair vary from geometrical shapes and precise waves to forms that are more irregular. On one occasion, the protruding part appears with some similarly stylized bundles across the forehead (**58**). The hair is sometimes also parted in the middle, creating a triangular forehead,[296] but it is less common than the arching one, which that makes the face more rounded. The rim of hair is visible from under the polos or veil and frames the face like a halo. The second part of the hair is visible along the sides of the neck. From behind the ears, if shown, or starting off under the fringe. Usually, a polos or veil covers this part, but in the case of **21**, a hairband makes clear that the hair is kept together and pushed forward to create the fringe. The back of the hair is usually left hanging down and slightly protruding, almost reaching the shoulder. The protruding effect could be created by the fashion of tying the hair up at the back of the head into a *krobylos*, a hairstyle that became common at the end of the Archaic and the beginning of the Classical Period in mainland Greece. The hair in the neck was folded up and bound by a hairband or kept in place by the polos. A smaller amount of protrusion than the *krobylos* could also have been created by tying up the hair lower down. Many Syracusan coins with a female head in profile display this *krobylos* or tied hairstyle. They show that the hairstyle was common and popular in the first half of the fifth century BCE in this region.[297] This part of the hair is not reworked and its simplicity contrasts with the often finely decorated fringe, as if they do not belong together. On the back of the figurines, nothing is depicted, with the exception of **1**, which has strands of hair on the back, and the 'Locrian' standing figurines **3-5**, which have hair marked on their back by a layer incised with horizontal lines. On the seated figurines, **6-7**, the hair is covered by the back of the throne. A particular difference between the hair arrangement of the standing and seated figures is the strands of hair, two on each side, that are draped over the chest, while the hair on the front is omitted from **6** and **7**, the seated figures.

In general, hair is more frequently applied to the back of figurines when they were handmade. The moulded figurines do not depict hair at the back, because a mould for the back would have been needed. The fully handmade figurines therefore have more details on the back because this was easier to do. The fact that the coroplast applied hair also indicates that the rear was potentially visible and could not be left unattended. The hair is thus not only an indication of the technical and practical side of figurine

292 Standing counterpart of **171**, which is seated. Because of the veil, the ears are hardly visible. This part was clearly reworked.

293 Earlier large sculpture has a rim with flat stylized curls that are typical for Sicily, for example, the Laganello Head. Albertocchi 1992, p.44. See also Ridgway 1977, p.42; Wallenstein 1971; Richter and Frantz 1968, p.no.41; Cf. Inv. no. 754, Mus. Arch. Syracuse.

294 Uhlenbrock 1988, p.36 calls them 'vertical bundles or "puffs"' when discussing *protomai* from Gela. It appears frequently on these *protomai*, but the Geloan hair arrangement described as 'standard' is a different one than the Akragantine one. It appears infrequently at Akragas, for example, no.95.

295 The inspiration for these protruding parts probably came from earlier statuary that has the hair on the side divided into bulbs, arranged tightly in rows with several strands on each side of the head. The fringe on these objects also consists of bulging curls, arranged in a row. The hair seems to reach the shoulder or to continue on the back.

296 This is usually the case, for example no.124, but depends on the hairline. When the hair is parted, the hairline on the sides of the forehead becomes lower than in the middle. In that respect no.3-7 are exceptional.

297 Boehringer 1929.

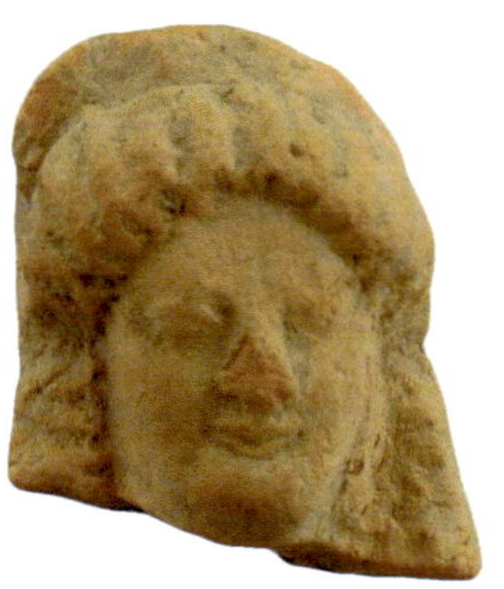
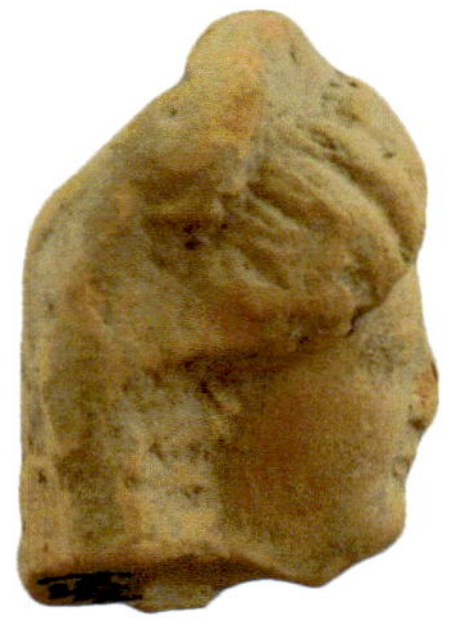
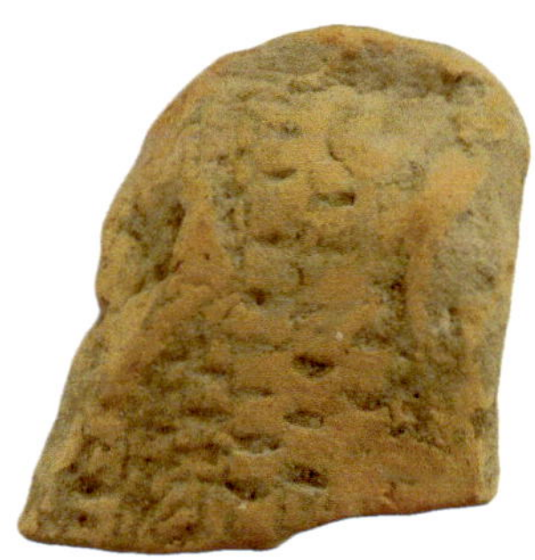

Figure 2.7: Head with indications of the hairstyle on the back. Arch. Mus. Agrigento Inv. no. 20540bis, h. 4.2cm.

production but also the iconographic side.[298] There is one exception with a moulded figurine, whose facial features fit the local forms, except for the rendering of her hair. On the back of the head (fig. 2.7), the coroplast has indicated the hair falling down loose and applied some marks with a sharp tool. The small notches could indicate stylised curls positioned on the strands of hair. Though reworked roughly, it is an important detail because it shows that, while she is wearing a sort of diadem, the hair on the back was visible and not covered by a veil. For the majority of figurines, the rear was left undetailed. They might have been dedicated at a spot where the rear was not so visible or was simply not considered to be as important.

The earliest figurines from moulds seem to have a round face accentuated by a smooth thick fringe running around their forehead. Later the band is then divided into vertical ridges, tightly aligned. These 'bulbs' could indicate stylised curls or pushed-forward hair. This band was at first rather flat and can be seen with the vertical division of the fringe and usually with the horizontal lining on the sides on early figurines like **86**. Figurines from Selinous are comparable.[299] Their hairstyle points to their wooden originals. In comparison with the other two wooden figurines (fig. 6 in the Catalogue), the figurine on the right has the same hairstyle as **86**, while the one on the left has geometric curls in a row. The block-shaped hair derived from wooden objects, **81**, and larger statuary are also geometric.[300] This is also visible on **181**, whose hair is divided into different strands, falling separately over her shoulder to the front in slight waves. In general, it seems that the larger the bulbs, the older the figurine. An example of such a development is figurine **12** and **13**. That is, however not always the case as with **14** and **138**, and as a single characteristic, it is not sufficiently reliable to establish the date of a figurine, as there are many exceptions. The preference for a hairstyle with bulbs could be seen as an Archaistic one, representing a tendency for old-fashioned characteristics. The hair rendering in group 3a is a clear example. Even in group 4, some continue this sort of fringe, sometimes flattened. Usually, the horizontal lines on the sides are an indication of early figurines, but some figurines maintained the lines, possibly as part of an intentional conservative element (**113**, **136**, **155** and **165**). On the latter and on **97**, the lines continue slightly like a fringe.

There are variations on this fringe with a very thick, slightly square form, **20**, **100**, **107**, and with a less round and more angled form (**163** and **164**). The parted fringe can look a bit curtain-like (**21**). As a result of the fringe, the forehead on **14** was shortened, but on others, it remained high (**56**). The parted hair is often smooth, but sometimes has vertical lining (**124**). A different effect is created by giving the shortened bulbs the same length or by dividing them unequally.[301]

Another extraordinary variant in group 3 is the pearl-rim that appears above the fringe and could be part of the polos (**115-118**, **126-129**, **133**, **166**). These 'pearls' are very similar to the fringe ridges but are round. There is a reason to see them as part of the hair rendering because they also appear on a *protome* from Gela with a similar hair arrangement, but with the pearl rim below the fringe and

298 Both the 'fringe' and the hair along the sides differ from most of the Attic korai. On almost all of them, the fringe is flat, while the hair on the sides is draped in three or four strands over the chest. The latter is visible on only a few objects from Akragas, all very likely to have been inspired from elsewhere: Locrian 3-5, wooden patrix 81. A mould, 181, has a hair arrangement typical for a kore: the strands, six in total are draped in groups of three on each side over her chest. There is just one kore known to me with a very thick fringe of hair around the forehead, while the rest fall over the shoulders on the back in a mass: Kore Akropolis 683, known for her red slippers. Ridgway 1977, p.107, fig.19.

299 Albertocchi 2012, p.93-4, fig.12.

300 The horizontal lining imitates the previous arrangement of bulbs on the hair on the sides of the head. See also a terracotta head from Gela, Inv. no. 21429 Mus. Arch. Gela, Adornato 2012b, fig.25.

301 Because the differences between the parted bulbs and the shorter bulbs in the middle are very small, it is the question whether this was intentional. The shortened middle part is clear on figurines from Taras, see Bencze 2008. A large protome from Akragas also features four shorter segments of hair in the middle. This object, AG 20510 was probably imported from Taras.

only on the sides.[302] A different way to create a variation on the fringe is the zigzag band. On **133**, **134**, **161** and **162** this particularly shaped fringe has a zigzag form. The perfectly circular endings, the repetition, and symmetry are highly aesthetic and have nothing to do with a realistic hair-arrangement, while that of the band-like fringe could be an imitation or stylization of real hair.

Sometimes large earrings hang in front of the hair, as on **124**, **125**, **133** and **134**. The horizontal double incision on the hair on each of the sides of the neck of **179** is exceptional. A very specific type of hair, very fine and not always easy to distinguish if the figurine is from a worn mould, is a wavy layer, like a thin piece of cloth with sharp folds in a triangular shape. This is clear from the front part, where the 'tubes' are open **95**, **99** and another figurine from Akragas, now in the National Museum of Denmark.[303] The hairstyle is common on *protomai* and may have been inspired by them, for example, three *protomai* fragments from Morgantina[304] and Gela.[305] The hairstyle of **168** looks similar, forming a sort of layer. The hairstyle is comparable to that of the Kore of Lyons, which is scalloped to the front because it is waving.[306] An exceptional hair rendering of the fringe appears on **171** and **176**. The bulging parts are replaced with fine vertically-stretched flat loops. It is once again this particular group of terracottas that stands out in artistic craftsmanship with an original design (**171-178**).

The hairstyle in a double waving row, nicknamed 'dogtooth', appears quite frequently with veil (**107**, **109-114**), or polos (**156-158**). The figurines with three rows (**159** and **160**) follow this style. These might have been inspired by larger objects, such as a protome from S. Anna with a similar hairstyle in three rows.[307] This hairstyle is Greek inspired, as evidenced, for example, by the wavy bands on the forehead of the Peplos Kore.

One figurine has scalloped hair, impressed with a stick after moulding (**99**). The finely lined scalloped impressions might indicate that the coroplast used a shell to create these shapes. The hairstyle of the figurines with the broad polos, group 4, is very distinctive with a broad band around the forehead, and small details indicating an elaborate and intricate hairstyle. The hair is wavy, regular at the fringe, but more irregular on each side of the neck. **189** has a very thick round fringe with about 4-5 wavy rows, while on **191-192** the fringe becomes thinner, and on **190** it is divided in the middle. The hair at the sides continues to protrude, which is clear in **185-188** and sometimes indicated by fine lines. The trend towards naturalism only starts in this last group. In general, the hairstyle of the Akragantine figurines became less geometric over time. The variety is wide and the eye for detail remarkable.

II.5.d Gender

The particular Sicilian face is not restricted to women. Some characteristics, such as a protruding chin and fleshy cheeks, the large almond-shaped eyes, and the short but wide nose are genderless. This is demonstrated by comparison with male banqueter terracottas.[308] In addition, within Agrigento itself, the faces of some female are comparable with male ones, for example, S81 and AG9187 (Catalogue fig.22 and 23). They share many features, such as chubbiness, the shape of the nose and mouth, the bulging eyes with eyelids, and the oval shape of the large ears formed by shaping them onto the hair at the end of the fringe. While thick lips may today be seen as feminine, it was apparently a sign of beauty in both men and women. The same is true of long hair and the band used to hold it in place.[309] An anatomical difference between men and women should have been the jaw. However, the coroplasts did not pay much attention to that aspect, probably because the figurines were meant to be seen from the front. A lower and wider jaw would have been more masculine, but there is no difference visible between the male and female jaws. On a kouros head from Akragas, the jaw is quite similar but the face is clearly less chubby and flatter with a sturdy forehead.[310] When comparing the jaw of the otherwise similar **154** and **163**, there is a large difference. The first runs much higher and looks much more female, while the second is lower, resulting in a squat face. Most of the figurine faces would still be immediately recognisable as female, even with a wider jaw. The distinction between the gender is more than the jaw and depended on an interplay between the facial features.

Hairstyle was not always an indication of gender either. Tarentine male banqueters wear their long hair in separate strands over their shoulders and have a fringe on the forehead, just slightly shorter and flatter, but otherwise similar to the fringe of female Akragantine figurines from the same period.[311] Yet the hairstyle of most of the figurines from Akragas received specific attention from the coroplast, in its detail and variation. In the first three groups, the fringe in particular is often finely reworked and could be seen as a feminine characteristic. The fringe

302 Uhlenbrock 1988, p.52-3, pl.8a, b. See also n.366 and section II.6.e.ii.

303 Breitenstein 1945, fig.21.

304 Raffiota 2007a, no.119 -121, tav.23.

305 Uhlenbrock 1988.

306 Athens, Acropolis 269.

307 Fiorentini 1969, p.79 tav.XXXIX.1.

308 Bencze 2010, p.26.

309 Bencze 2010, p.26.

310 Arch. Mus. Agrigento Inv. no.C 1837, Adornato 2012b, fig.33.

311 Bencze 2010, p.26f, fig.1-4.

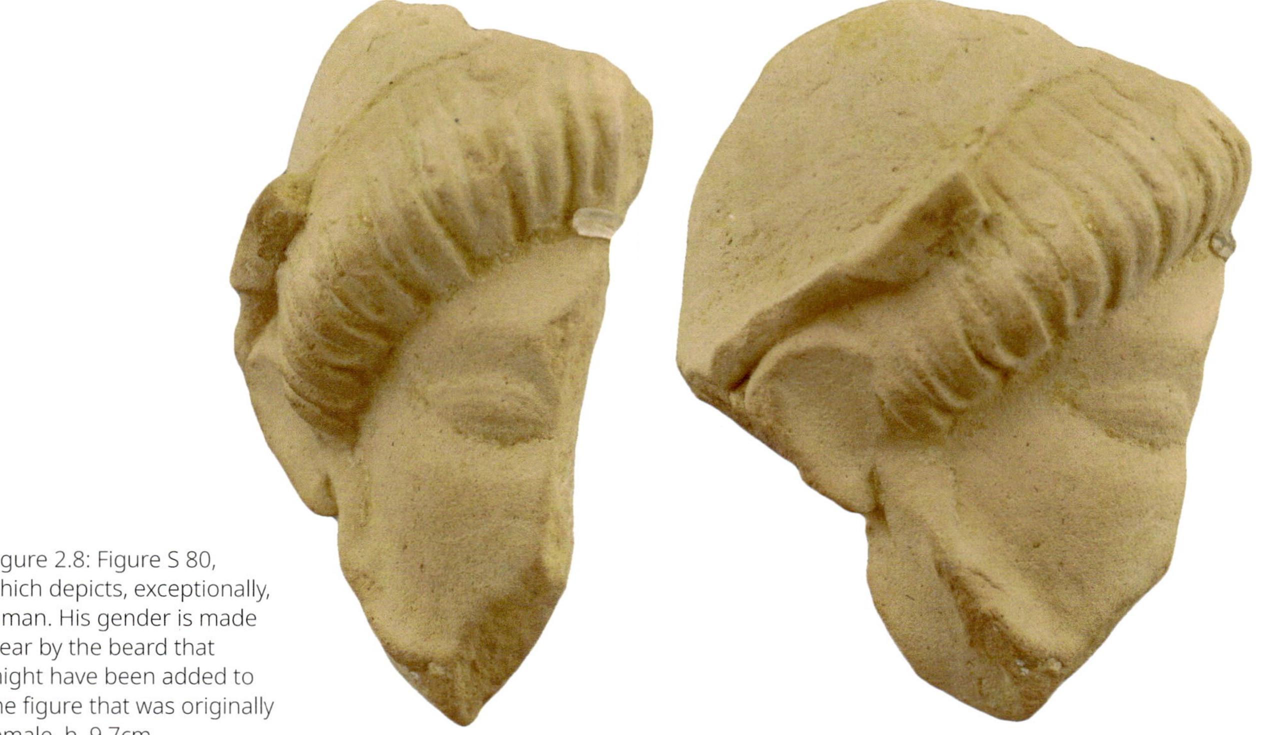

Figure 2.8: Figure S 80, which depicts, exceptionally, a man. His gender is made clear by the beard that might have been added to the figure that was originally female. h. 9.7cm.

of the kouros head from Akragas is much shorter.[312] By framing the face with a large fringe, the forehead was often made smaller, resulting in a rounder shape of the head. The hair on the sides of the neck often functions as a background, technically necessary, for earrings. In group 4, the large and detailed hairstyles are one of the main ways of identifying the figurines as female.

One particular head from Akragas must depict a male figure, as it has a beard (fig. 2.8).[313] The beard seems to have been added after the figure was moulded and the face could originally have been female. The fringe of hair in long loops, slanting eyes and plain ears are common on other female heads. There is, however, no example of a female head from the same mould or series at Akragas. The thin beard that runs along the jawline identifies him as a young adult. In addition, a string of clay was added to the fringe, after the head was moulded. This seems to indicate a fillet on the crown of the head in the hair, but it is not flat and therefore possibly a part of his headgear. The crown of the head is smooth with no indication of hair.[314] Originally, therefore, a female figurine may have been depicted wearing a veil comparable to that of **58**, but the headgear was then altered to form a rounded flat hat in order to suit the now male gender of the figure.

A table below summarises the principal findings and comparisons above (table 2.2). A short description of the main aspects of the facial features in Akragantine coroplastics follows. Special attention was paid to the face, compared with the details of the body. If a face was too faded, the coroplasts often replaced it with a new one. This was probably not only to follow the latest fashion, such as the hairstyle, but primarily to ensure that the facial expression was visible. The use of moulds from old bodies with newer faces sometimes results in odd combinations. One example is figurine AG 20175 (Catalogue fig. 10) and a figurine with a local face placed on the body of a 'Rhodian' figurine.[315] The shape of the head varies from round to oval. The jaw on some figurines is particularly wide and low, but this does not indicate a different gender. Chubby faces with high cheekbones are a characteristic of Akragantine figurines and appear more female. The nose varies from thick with a particular round tip to thinner at the dorsum and stretched longer. The nose is sizeable,

312 His hair is held with a ribbon that runs around his head, above the fringe and holds the long hair together on his back. He seems to have less bulging hair on the sides of his neck, though this part is broken. The small extension from the fringe in front of his ear could be interpreted as sideburns. This does not appear on the female iconography. Arch. Mus. Agrigento Inv. no.C 1837, Adornato 2012b, fig.33.

313 Arch. Mus. Agrigento Inv. no. S80, h. 9.7cm. The head is from a first generation mould.

314 A bronze head from Olympia, dated not later than 500 BCE and usually interpreted as Zeus wears a very similar fillet, which is reason to interpret it as a deity, by Mattusch 1989, p.64-5. Nat. Mus. Athens Inv. no.6440, h. 17cm.

315 De Miro 1989, Tomb 1254, tav.XVII middle.

Part of the face	Group 1 and 2	Group 3	Group 4
Shape of the head	Mainly round	Mainly oval	Mainly oval
Eyes	Large, sometimes with eyelids; more almond- shaped	Usually with eyelids, slightly bulging	Smaller eyes, diagonally rising towards the nose
Nose	Large with rounded tip	Narrower sometimes long and with a pointed tip	Less prominent, average size
Cheeks	Most have fleshy cheeks, high cheekbones	Less fat with high cheekbones.	Flatter cheeks
Mouth and lips	Smiling, sometimes with dimples	Smiling, prominent mouth, of various shapes and thickness	Straight or Archaic smile, average-sized mouth
Ears	Absent from group 1; geometric or partly visible	Tendency towards naturalistic rendering	Invisible because of voluminous hairstyle
Hair	Fringe and hair hanging down on the sides; abstract shapes	Large variation in hair, including more often details on the hair next to the neck.	Thick large fringe, more like wearing hair partly raised; naturalistic, voluminous.

Table 2.2: Comparison of facial features between the earlier objects in group 1 /2, with the later ones in group 3 and 4.

sometimes with wide alae in the case of the fatter faces. The mouth appears in two forms, either thick or very narrow lips, with the same width nose. This is possibly the result of Phoenician influence. The second form is a smile with a wide mouth, and often with dimples. This could reflect Etruscan/ Greek influence. The eyes are very large and plain, until the addition of eyelids from the end of the sixth century BCE. The ears were at first not depicted, but became more important, first with a geometric shape, and later a more natural form, in particular as a carrier of jewellery. Their placement at the edge of the fringe is not always natural. Paint might have been used to add detail to the face and strengthen the expression, which is already quite strong. Figurines **3-7** might had an influence on the shape of facial features. The Akragantine figurines have an outspoken face that is idealistic and modelled according to the latest trends, but at the same time were approachable for the common dedicant. In this way, the dedicant or viewer would have felt included in the dedication because of personal involvement. The object seems lively and engages the viewer with just a slight feeling of distance, as befits divinity.

Anthropomorphism increased over time and there is even the sense of realism in some typical facial features of Akragantine production. However, some Archaist trends in the style of the ears and hair interrupt this development. The balance between human and divine fades and the dedicator and viewer are presented with an image that was recognisable as a supernatural ideal beauty. The focus appeared to shift so that by the third decade of the fifth century BCE in group 4 in particular the hair was depicted more naturally marking perhaps a transformation from a deity-central to a dedicant-central view, including images in which the deity seems to be interchangeable with the dedicant.[316]

The skin colour of the figurines, male and female, was that of the clay. It is unlikely in this period that skin colour was gendered and skin tone would rather have represented a distinction in social class, similar to other parts of the Mediterranean world.[317] The skin of aristocratic women would have been pale, as they did not have to work outdoors. The Akragantine figurines' faces were not painted white. Make-up in the form of red paint was added to some figurines and is clearly visible on **3**, red lips and cheeks, and **176,** red lips.

Several aspects combine to reveal the gender of the face. The female face must have been the standard, given the example above of an object altered by the addition of a beard to change the gender. The majority of figurines were female.

II.6 Dress and personal adornment

The bodies of the Akragantine figurines were not intended to be naturalistic. The faces, by contrast, were executed with considerable attention to detail. The rich adornment and dress seem at first sight also to contrast with the simple rendering of the body. Dress and jewellery could be considered to adorn the body, increasing its aesthetic appeal. This was certainly the case with some imported figurines discussed below on which the dress creates a distinction between the upper and lower part of the body, creating geometrical forms and expressing contrasting shapes. For the majority of locally made figurines in group 1 and 2, however, the decorative aspect of the dress seems unimportant. Even when a finely folded undergarment is depicted, a plain rectangular apron remains the main cover for the figurine. The apron itself seems to have been included as a form of identification, as it is a specific garment, unique to these figurines. The attire and personal adornment play a distinct role, independent of

316 The facial features, hairstyle or dress do not reveal such a difference directly and are probably left ambiguous on purpose.

317 For example, on Attic Black Figure ware, see Eaverly 2013.

the form of the body. They are items with intrinsic value, not only because what the figurines are wearing often lacks a practical application, but primarily because they are additional elements with a message to convey.

In contrast to the body that, particularly at the end of the 6th century BCE, appeared to be primarily functional in its shape, some of the personal adornment had a meaningful form. The body is a bearer of, and subordinate to, its adornment, particularly the jewellery. The rectangular apron might in this regard even be appointed to a third category. In itself, its form is not specific or meaningful, while at the same time its presence is required. On the other hand, it forms by itself the shape of the sloping upper body. Even as the shape of the figurines changed over time, the apron remained in the same form. Naturalism was not the goal for most of the time. Precise imitations in clay of existing decorative objects were applied to the figurines right from the beginning. Precisely shaped earrings were hung from smaller, less detailed and sometimes hardly visible ears. In the discussion of the dress and jewellery below, one of the aims is to find out how much of this 'realism' was based on real actions adorning a deity or whether it instead provides us with an accurate image of the changing attire and adornment of the people of Akragas, or both.

II.6.a The apron

The very early figurines are not always clearly dressed (**8** and **22**). Most figurines from group 1, the block-like type, have a kind of rectangular apron, indicated by a protruding part that is smaller than the front of the body. The garment follows the contours of the body, also when flaring or seated. A small rim along the edge of the front of the body is left open on each side. This is visible on the left and right of the front of the body in **9** and **11**, but sometimes it is visible draped over the feet (**12**), or has a neckline (**63** and **30**). The outline of the apron was drawn on the lower part of the body of **135**.

These increasing details seem more or less chronological. Over time, the dress becomes more distinct while remaining a plain rectangular garment. Other objects, such as the clasps on each side at the upper corner,[318] or the garments underneath emphasize the simplicity of the upper garment. It remains almost part of the body, with which it shares its unnatural and unpretentious form. This appears from details that seem to lack a link with the supposed reality of a cult statue or even human being. Between the clasps depicted holding the garment at the shoulders, a line could be interpreted often as both the neckline and a cord for pendants. The neckline, therefore, does not run around the neck but is instead wide, reaching the shoulders. The apparently straight apron falls as a rectangular piece of fabric following the contours and angle of the body. It is a thick garment, as if it was felted, which is apparent from the edge it forms with the body below, **30** and **48**. The garment, reminiscent of a traditional chasuble,[319] continues to be applied in the other groups without any alterations. While all other iconographic aspects of the figurine developed over time, the apron remained the same. Even though there was not much to change in its plainness, it is remarkable that this element remained unchanged through the decades of production. It is applied on almost all figurines and serves well as an indicator of local production. It is therefore even more unfortunate that we can only speculate as to its function.

From the folds in the undergarment that appear in group 2, it becomes clear that the apron is an upper garment that was not intended to cover the body in the round, but just most of the front. As a garment below is in many cases not visible, a protecting function of the apron is not clear. An aesthetic reason is hard to prove as the design is straightforward and unchanging. This part of the clothing was some form of identifying garment.

In other instances, the feet make clear that the figure is wearing an undergarment. Where a distinction is visible between upper and undergarment, the apron falls to the ankles or just above, while the undergarment is draped over the feet, reaching the ground. This forms a rounded shape as if the garment continues to the sides of the pedestal. Such partially visible feet under an often arched and apparently thick dress fabric are depicted in **12, 19, 28, 29, 32, 70, 90, 102, 136** and **180**. On **180** the feet were added later and were not part of the mould. The particular placement of the feet and the draping of the garment over it are reminiscent of the Kore of Anaximandros,[320] and also of a *xoanon* from Megara Hyblaea.[321]

The identification of this particular upper garment has been discussed extensively and is usually called an *ependytes*.[322] This upper garment would be of eastern origin and appears in different forms in various depictions.[323] In the case of Akragas, it seems unlikely the influence came from afar and was therefore probably ubiquitous at the time. It is much more likely that the apron had a real-life equivalent, even if it were only used for the cult statue. This contrasts with the undergarment that is clearly of

318 See section II.6.f for a description of the function and form of these fibulae.

319 'Pianeta' writes Albertocchi 2004, p.110. The chasuble does not need clasps, as the part of the back balances that on the front. A neckline would have been much more round. But it is comparable in a cultic sense.

320 Inv. no.109894, Berlin; See website: https://arachne.uni-koeln.de/arachne/index.php?view[layout]=objekt_item&search[constraints][objekt][searchSeriennummer]=109894.

321 Gras, Tréziny, Broise 2005, p.308-9, fig.328, Inv. no. 50717.

322 Zuntz 1971, p.126-7.

323 Lee 2015, p.123-4.

Greek influence as soon as it appears with fine folds and a specific form, usually called a *chiton*. Because of the partial covering, the apron does not seem directly functional.[324] The thick layer and the sloping upper part even seem impractical. Its shape and use have therefore long been interpreted as cultic.[325]

The question arises whether the apron of the figurines was painted and possibly divided into several horizontal sections. The dress of a statuette from Megara Hyblaea, though similar to a peplos, has such a division.[326] There are no traces of paint visible on any of the Akragantine aprons however and the jewellery that falls over the apron would have made such painting less likely.

II.6.b Non-Sicilian garments

The shape of the body is closely connected to that of the dress. The general rendering of the different sorts of dresses might be thus explained by the use of the original material, wood, as opposed to the wheel-turned figurines with a flaring dress.[327] Figurines, directly made after a wooden patrix, are very differently dressed (**85-86**). They wear a *peplos* folded over to form an *apoptygma* over the belted waist. Other figurines in group 5 also appear to have Greek inspired dress, such as the similarly dressed **80** (peplos?) or the long cloak, open to the front worn by several standing figurines (**82-84**). Such a garment is known from other figurines on Sicily as well.[328] Possibly **78** wears this large garment, by stretching out her arms, the size is revealed. Such a long mantle, called an *epiblema*, is not uncommon on korai and probably functioned as a coat.[329] The East Greek figurines seem to wear this mantle on top of an undergarment. The parts of the mantle are depicted below their hands (**72**). The lower part of the body, **75**, that is inspired by them, lacks this mantle and was probably produced locally. In contrast to the apron, these dresses serve to enhance the body. The belt not only holds the garment together and shortens it but it also stresses the thinner waist, marking a distinction between the shorter, wider upper body and the longer lower body, suggesting long legs.

II.6.b.i The undergarment

The undergarment that appears from group 2c onwards is probably Greek in origin. It is depicted for the first time on the figurines in the second decade of the 5th century BCE, possibly because the Greek dress was worn by local people at that time. The folded undergarment could be a *peplos*, instead of a chiton, as the sleeves are sewn and it does not have a *kolpos*, the part overlapping a belt.[330] The folds indicated on it, however, seem rather an indication of a thinner fabric and point to a *chiton*. As an undergarment, the *chiton* is more likely, as the peplos is a much heavier and thicker garment. On the life-size statue (fig. 2.1) of the feet the very thin garment, visible only on the ground between the feet, is so thin that it appears translucent.

The first folds depicted on the garment are straight and run next to the apron on the small edge on each side. The vertical folds stress the length of the figurine and give the impression of standing figures, **90**. This is why some figurines, like **62**, are described in the literature as standing, even though the bend in the body is clear.[331] Sometimes, thin folds are marked at the ankles. In the case of **88,** this is just between the feet while the chiton even has a thin line along its hem. **89** also depicts the chiton as made of very thin fabric and draped gracefully over the feet. The third area where the folds are visible beneath the apron is at the arms and neck. The arms of **115**, formed by using the edge of the body and apron, have three vertical lines that indicate the sleeves, ending in loops. The absence of the apron on this mould series is remedied later as it was added once again (**135**). Similar loop-shaped endings are depicted at the hem of the *chiton* on **176**.

The depiction of the folds at the neck is less common and starts later. On **94**, **97**, **113**, the thin lines continue to the neck and the upper hem is raised showing fine folds in a parallel manner. The seam in the middle creates a triangular shape on the arm and a pleated sleeve. The fine details are often depicted in the same way as horizontal or diagonal lining on the hair next to the neck (**152**). This creates a repetition of forms that must have appealed to the viewer. The folds are sometimes also indicated by wavy lines, arranged in order (**114**). On **97**, the width of the sleeve is clear. It is as if the figurine is holding the chiton up slightly with both hands, a gesture that implies taking a step forwards. It gives the figurine a sense of motion and vivacity. More crude forms of the folds on the arms appear on **101-102** and are just diagonal. The apron on these figurines is remarkably small. This is, however, not a general tendency. When the

324 Though Richter notes that it could have functioned as extra clothing against coldness. Richter and Frantz 1968, p.9. This would be reflected the name of the garment, because 'ependytes' literary means 'garment on top'. Lee 2015, p.123. Also spelled as 'ependytis' Pautasso 1996, p.56.

325 Orlandini 1956, p.369. For an extensive discussion on the different interpretations, see Albertocchi 2004, p.110-2.

326 Gras, Tréziny, Broise 2005, p.329, fig.346.

327 Ridgeway 1977, p.24.

328 Poma 2009, no.36.

329 Korai Acr. 593 and 671. A similarly long garment is worn by several figurines from Selinous, for example Arch. Mus. Bonn Inv. no.D 189. 30; Garbrici 1927 254 tav.L.3 (possibly from the same mould as **82**). A female terracotta figurine from Bitalemi, Gela wears this mantle on top of the belted garment Mus. Arch. Syracuse Inv. no.21294. Bennett and Paul 2002, p.228-9.

330 These are the two indications of distinction between the two given by Ridgway 1977, p.91.

331 Albertocchi 2004, p.96, no.1710.

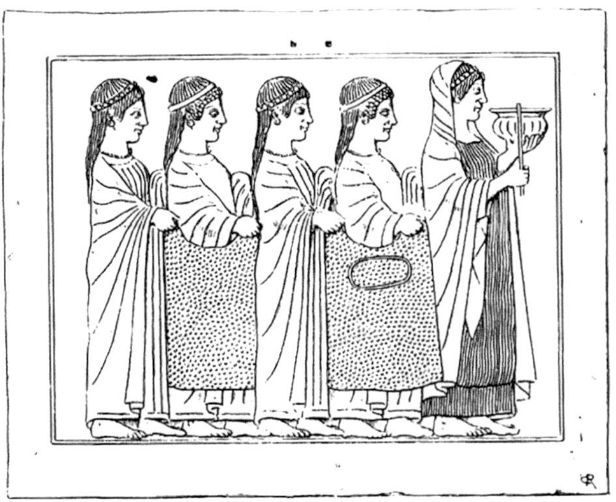

Figure 2.9: Drawing of pinax 21 from Locri Epizefirii. Drawing after Orsi 1909, fig. 25.

arms have folds, the apron apparently covers the whole upper part of the body, including the lap, while on the legs the apron is smaller and reaches above the ankles, leaving parts of the chiton on the right and left visible. The coroplasts never continued this on the side parts, **144**, which confirms again the frontality of the figurines. A dress with decorative folds, shorter in the middle, is worn by the also otherwise exceptional **181**. In group 4, the last in local production of this sort of figurines, the folds of the dress are no longer regular (**195**). Again this development is in step with how the hair is rendered and is a further development in the direction of naturalism.

II.6.c Cultic dress

There might have been a specific ritual around the dress as a specific item depicted on the figurines. There are similar cultic dresses known. In the same cultural region, some *pinakes* seem to depict such a ritual. On several plaques from Locri Epizefirii, there is a large-scale piece of fabric depicted. On *pinax* 21 (fig. 2.9),[332] it is carried in a procession. One veiled lady at the front leads the procession with a sceptre and a bowl, which she is holding up. She is followed by four girls, walking two-by-two, holding a large garment between them. This garment must be of a different nature from what they are wearing. Their Greek-styled clothes are a *chiton* for the woman at front and probably a *peplos* for the girls. Their age difference is marked by a slight difference in height. The garment they carry carefully so that it does not touch the ground, is spread out, unfolded, with a spotted pattern or structure and an oval shape marked on it. The oval could indicate the space for the head. The same garment is folded and placed on a table in another depiction, *pinax* 2. In another scene,[333] older girls are followed by the leading woman.[334] They are lifting the garment while walking in a row. The scenes depict a dressing ritual. It is reminiscent of the Panathenaic procession in which a *peplos* for Pallas Athena was carried to the Parthenon. A local version of such a cultic ritual might be imagined for Akragas as well, considering the presence of the special apron and its depiction on almost all figurines. There are, however, no clear indications, such as the *pinakes* from Locri depicting this in an Akragantine context. Weaving as a ritual act is possible and known also for Sicily, but the presence of loom weights at the sanctuary alone cannot serve as sufficient proof that a garment was woven for the goddess.[335]

II.6.d Footwear

Because the feet of figurines are often indistinguishable, we cannot expect to be able to say anything about their footwear. If a coroplast showed no concern even to depict the hands of a figurine (**102**, for example), we cannot expect him to pay attention to the finer details of footwear. Yet there are some instances in which it seems that attention was paid to the details of the feet or shoes. The footwear of **180** is reminiscent of the Kore of Anaximandros and similar footwear to the Red-Slippers Kore (Kore Akropolis 683). They wear a pointed shoe that covers the whole foot. A similar shoe, but with a rounder nose is worn by **176**. Both shoes seem to follow the shape of the feet and have a more protruding part at the big toe. **70** and **88** are also wearing a similarly shaped shoe, while those in mould **90** have square toes. The feet of **141** seem to be wrapped with a pointed end. **176** is interesting, because it is likely that her feet are dressed in closed shoes, while the otherwise very similarly dressed **171** and **173** have visible toes, wearing sandals. The soles of the sandals are visible but the straps are not. They must have been thin and the dress covers the upper part of the feet. More extensively adorned figurines wear sandals (**115**). It is probable that footwear, like the dress and jewellery, were a typical part of the attire and are presented as costly items, but were not omnipresent.[336] It seems that visibility of the bare feet itself was not inappropriate and the depictions might reflect that many people in daily life were not always wearing footwear, as it would have been too costly (fig. 2.1).

332 Type 21 from group III, dimensions: 28x22.5cm, see Orsi 1909, p.426-8.

333 Type 22 from group III, dimensions 25.5 x 20cm, see Orsi 1909, p.427-8.

334 The taller lady is similarly dressed and holds up her bowl and stick. The girls are now dressed in a chiton and have their hair styled.

335 Agostiniani, de Cesare, Landenius Enegren 2014.

336 The more than lifesize sculptures from Morgantina, whose extremities were made of marble, wear red painted sandals. Maniscalco 2018, p.6.

II.6.e Headgear

Headgear, in particular, a cylindrical hat, appears as one of the main characteristics of Sicilian figurines. It is a notable characteristic of many Akragantine figurines from the earliest, the so-called Daedalic figurines, as well as one of the Boeotian figurines, and up to the late Archaic terracottas. The cylindrical hat, usually called a *polos*, varies in shape, size, and decoration. Its general shape is cylindrical, and it is usually closed at the top. Though it sometimes rises to a point like a basket or *kalathos*, it differs from a *kalathos* in being closed and as such does not seem to have been used to carry or contain objects.[337] The difference is that the latter is usually a functional headgear, though not always[338], while the *polos* is seen as ceremonial. The *polos* looks somewhat similar to the *modius*, which usually has a closed flat top and also does not seem particularly functional, though originally it was a grain measurement. The *polos* is of eastern origin, while the *kalathos*, also mainly related to the female sphere, is Greek.[339] Male deities also wear the eastern *polos*, while the Greek counterpart seems to have been specifically used by women. The origin of the headgear would have been a characteristic part of the dress of the eastern fertility goddesses. Astarte, as depicted by the Assyrians, wears a *polos*.[340] From the east, its use spread in the early Iron Age, gaining wide popularity in Greece.[341] It is likely that the Phoenicians had a share in this spread of a divine dress code. One of the possible means of transfer might have been the *potnia theron*-model.[342] Comparable as well in the iconography is the goddess Kubaba/Kybele. She is shown enthroned and wearing the *polos*, both elements indicating her status, similar to the Sicilian figurines. Her throne was also typically supported by lions, a theme that reoccurs in the furniture[343] of Sicilian depictions.

Though these iconographic similarities might be striking, we cannot use them to reach any firm conclusions on the identification of the Sicilian figurines. We can state that the images travelled over a vast area, and could have inspired Sicilian coroplasts. Distinct elements were adopted and applied in the new context, in different combinations. For this reason, it is important to realise that not every detail is in itself meaningful or symbolic, but may have held meaning in its context. Other elements may have simply been used for aesthetic reasons. Distinguishing the difference in interpretation and revealing those forms that may have been symbolic can only be deduced from the context in which they appear.

In addition to the apron, garment pins and chest decoration, the *polos* entered the standard outfit of the local figurine tradition. There is no fixed combination of these parts of the dress nor order in which they are introduced. The majority of the objects in group 1, 68 per cent, wears a *polos* and this percentage rises in the other groups of locally produced figurines. It seems that around 580 BCE the *polos* gains in popularity and from that moment, almost all the figurines wear one.[344] Some figurines were updated with a new head that included a *polos* in the prevailing fashion of the time (**54**).

II.6.e.i Veil

Besides the *polos*, sometimes a sort of flat hat or thick veil was used to cover the head (**8**, **9**, **11** and **12**). As the back of the figurines is usually cut off straight, it remains rather unclear how it precisely looked. Similarly to the *polos*, the veil, does not cover all of the hair but leaves a considerable band of hair visible across the forehead. On both sides of the neck, a bulging part of hair or veil runs down and seems to end just at the shoulder or slightly lower on the back.[345] The frontality of the figurines usually leaves the back and sides undetailed (**58**). On early Daedalic figurines, the veil also appears in combination with the low *polos*.[346] Ears are sometimes visible in front of the veil (**109** and **179**). It is likely that the veil was attached to the hair, just above the ears. This seems to be suggested at **58**.[347] Even more clear examples of the veil are figurines AG 1154 (fig. 2.10) and AG 1160,[348] which have a very thick veil running around their face and down behind their bulging hair. On those figurines, it is as if the veil is attached behind the ears.[349] The veil is aesthetic rather than that functional (for covering the hair). The way of wearing the veil, very much on the

337 Exceptions among the larger statuary are described below. The libation tube discussed above is also exceptional in this regard. See section II.5.c.iv.

338 Papantoniou 2012, p.243-4.

339 Dewailly 1983, p. 7 and Nunn 2000, p.74.

340 This high polos on ivories is sometimes decorated with rosette panels, see description of decorated poloi below. Simpson 2011, p.89-90.

341 Müller 1915, p.51.

342 Schuhmann 2009, p.64 writes that the polos gains in popularity in this period, specifically on depictions of the 'mistress of animals'.

343 See section II.7.

344 There are examples that can be dated around the mid of the century or later which do not wear the polos, no. 107 and 109.

345 The protomai from Gela wear the veil in the same way, mostly under the polos. Sometimes a small rim is visible on the forehead. Uhlenbrock 1988, p.36

346 Inv. no.91/85 from the Asklepion, Akragas. Mus. Arch. Agrigento. De Miro 2003, p.183. pl. 89.1.

347 AG 1153 is from the same mould as 58, but because of the crack is not visible in the picture. De Miro 2000, no.13, tav.LIX.

348 These are very similar to another head originally from Akragas, Breitenstein 1945, p.125, fig.13.
Other block-like figurines with a veil are AG 22587, See Albertocchi 2004, no.1696, Veder Greco 1988, p.332, n.15, De Miro 1989, p.43-46, tav.XXXIV, complete 23.3cm; AG 1151, See Albertocchi 2004, no.1697, De Miro 2000, p.129, tav.LX n.20, missing left shoulder 21.7cm; AG 1166, See Albertocchi 2004, no.1698, De Miro 2000, p.129, n.21. These three are from the same mould. 2 fragm. 16.7cm.

349 The round shape, however, does not resemble a natural ear.

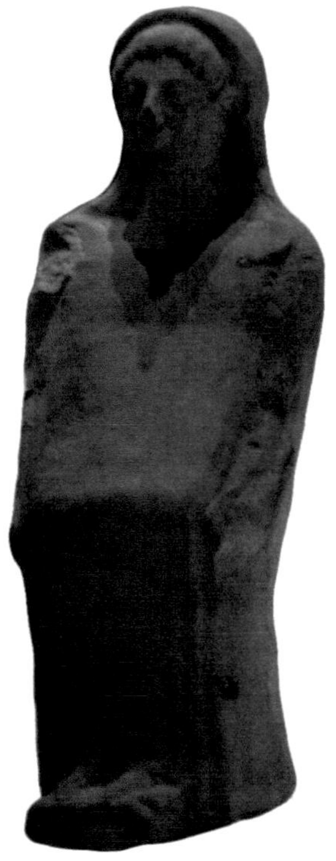

Figure 2.10: Figurine with a block-like body shape, wearing a thick veil. Inv. no. AG 1154 Mus. Arch. Agrigento.

back of the head, leaving hair on the sides and forehead visible, does not seem very practical or convenient, unless it were somehow attached. Like the hairstyle itself, the veil frames the head. Numerous *protomai* from Gela have comparable veiled depictions.[350] On the *protomai* from Selinous, the *polos* is more common, with a close majority of 52 per cent;[351] the *polos* also seems to be the preferred head covering for the figurines too.

II.6.e.ii Polos

The *polos* became a rather common feature of dress over a vast area in the 7th century BCE. Uhlenbrock notices that all of the figurine heads from the Extramural Sanctuary in Cyrene, dated to the seventh century BCE, wear the *polos*. She concludes that it would have been a standard feature of figurines meant for votive purposes, though their origin remains mysterious.[352] In the other direction, around Paestum, figurines wearing the *polos* are also a common feature in this period.[353] The very low polos, often placed further up the head is also known from ivories, such as the fibula, shaped like a woman, from the second half of the seventh century BCE from Megara Hyblaia, shown wearing a low *polos* with tongue-pattern.[354] The three wooden figurines from Palma di Montechiaro all wear a *polos*, of different size and shape. The smaller one, dated to the last quarter of the seventh century BCE, has its *polos* placed a little higher on the head, further to the back and is smaller than the width of the head. The two others, dated to the first quarter of the sixth century BCE,[355] are placed lower on the head and seem to lengthen the head, as they are the same width. They are smooth and straight and clearly visible from the sides.[356] The hat that appears on depictions of larger sculpture from the same period is similar to the *poloi* of the wooden figurines. The Laganello head, a nearly 56cm high stucco-layered limestone head, found near Syracuse and dated to 580-570 BCE,[357] wears a *polos* on top of her typically flat stylized curls on the forehead.[358] This *polos* is somewhat taller, but still appears narrower than the actual width of the head, resulting in a placement higher up the head. In the catalogue, this is described as high up the head, and it seems this placement was common on early figurines (**64**). The low *polos*, almost like a ring or band, placed on top of the head, is a characteristic of very early figurines from Akragas. The different styles of headgear must have been developed in this period. Several large archaic korai wear a *polos* in the same way, such as the Kore of Lyon and the Berlin Goddess. While on the first, the tapering model gives a very different impression, while the small straight model of the Berlin Goddess seems to lengthen the face. The taller straight poloi of some Daedalic figurines from Sicily are also comparable.[359] The following fashion, the wider and somewhat tapering *polos* truly crowns the head. It has more volume, fits better on the head and therefore gives the head a more majestic look. Both effects are applied to Akragantine figurines.

Probably the oldest depiction of a *polos* in the records of terracottas from Akragas is a handmade 15cm high female head, probably originally from Crete (fig. 2.3 left).[360]

350 Uhlenbrock 1988.

351 Wiederkehr Schuler 2004, p.61, Diagramme 4.

352 Uhlenbrock 2016, p.150.

353 Ammerman 2002, p.77-80.

354 Böhm 2007, p.25ff.; fig.13.

355 Richter and Frantz 1968, no.53 and 54. No. 31 from the same collection is dated to the late 7th century BCE.

356 Ross Holloway 2000, fig.65 and fig.67.

357 Comparable heads from Corinth make an earlier date possible. The Corinthian style does not exclude the possibility that the head was made by a skilled artisan from Syracuse. Böhm 2007, p.14-15.

358 Another example is the large limestone head of Hera from the Heraeum, Olympia, dated around 560 BCE. She wears on top of her fringe of stylized curls a cap of thin fabric with a rim, a very low polos standing upright with a thin rim and slightly curved tongues. The placement is high. The part behind her ear may have been part of the throne upon which she was originally seated.

359 Albertocchi 2009, p.15, fig.1-2.

360 It is dated to the end of the second millennium BCE, Anzalone 2015. He interprets its use with Boardman's expression of nostalgia. The head was found in a sixth century BCE sanctuary context and is therefore explained as re-use. It could have been part of the recreation of a mythical past. Its looks were supposed to represent a history. Such a use as *keimelion* is based on specific characteristics, recognizable and with an embedded message. The *polos*, worn by a female figurine, as well as the large ear studs could be such characteristics. Boardman 2002, p.79-103.

There is no real distinction between forehead and polos. It differs in style from the Archaic figurines. The polos-wearing figurines from the end of the sixth century BCE appear to form a continuum. As stated above, it is possible that the *polos* was added to the figurines locally to create an extension of the head.[361] The foreheads on some very early figurines (see fig. 2.3) are partly hollow, which also supports this. It looks as if something could be placed into the polos. Some larger objects, **3-7**, have a hollow *polos*, and it looks as if they could have functioned to hold small objects or as a censer.[362] This hollow *polos* appeared on larger statuary, and people passing the statuary would have been easily able to reach the hollow *polos*. The statue from Megara Hyblaea mentioned above also had a hollow upper part to its head.[363] For **3-7**, one could imagine that the viewer would have looked directly into the polos when passing these figurines, which are about sixty cm tall, unless they were placed on a base, which may have been the case for the seated version. The *polos* as a container could be compared with the numerous miniature vessels that have been found in the same contexts as some of the figurines. The small volumes that such vessels contained are comparable to the volume of the figurines' *polos*.

Among the Akragantine figurines, there are five *polos* sorts that were common on the Akragantine figurines (table 2.3). There is variation in size, straightness, rim, and decoration. The most common shape both at Akragas as well as in Sicily is slightly tapering, medium-high, and with a rim. The rim varies in thickness and is sometimes round, **103**, and sometimes more edged, **154**. Over time, the frequency of the rim increases.[364] Several figurines from the Mould II series, the decorated *polos*, have a pearl-rim.[365] There is another instance of such a pearl-rim, combined with a normal rim, but placed higher, not directly above the pearls, on a relatively large sized head.[366] Metal ornaments for the polos are not very common, unlike on *protomai*.[367]

The polos and hairstyle may have provided additional reasons for interchanging the heads of figurines.[368] The size of the polos increases in width and height from low to medium-high in group 1 (**36**). In group 2, the polos is elongated (**154** and **163**), or even stretched, together with the body and face (**70**). Several figurines in group 3 have a decorated polos. There is only one variation in this decoration, the square and disc pattern.[369] These decorated polos figurines could only have been locally made, from patrix and matrix to final production. They appear elsewhere on the island, and this specific decoration became more popular over time. As the figurines found elsewhere are smaller, they would have been traded or imitations and should be dated later than the Akragantine figurines. The polos was decorated by being divided into squares, each filled with a disc. The size of the discs vary, but they are generally large, sometimes with a flaring upper part. A flared example is found on the upper fragment of a figurine that probably came from Agrigento.[370] The squares cover the polos usually in two rows and not more than four squares horizontally. The decoration is reminiscent of the decorated polos of Kubaba on a neo-Hittite sculpture. Her polos is decorated in the same way, but with rosettes as well as discs in the squares.[371] Whether or not the inspiration came from that far, the hand of a truly creative coroplast is clear. The coroplast is recognisable by the detailed work on various decoration items.[372] One of them is a polos with a unique pattern and, on another, with a

361 See section II.5.c.i.

362 In particular no.3, which has a large crack inside and some ash residues. The Geloan *thymiaterion*, dated to 530-520 BCE, does not wear a *polos*, but a sort of band or cushion on her hair. Pautasso 1996, p.115, tav.XIX,e; Uhlenbrock 1988, p.66. Another Sicilian *thymiaterion* from the first quarter of the 5th century BCE and interpreted as Nike, does not wear a *polos*, but a sort of diadem instead. The incense burner is placed further up on a stand supported in the middle of her head. J. Paul Getty Mus. Inv. no.86. AD.681. Both are very different from the relatively straight and deep *polos* on the objects from Akragas.

363 See n.212 above. Parisi 2017, p.180, fig.79.

364 Though Hurschmann describes the polos as always without a rim. Hurschmann 2016.

365 Clearly visible on AT 3392 (713) Pushkin Museum, Moscow. fig. 14 in the Catalogue; such a pearl-rim appears also on a *protome* of a female figure wearing a low *polos*, dated to the beginning of the fifth century BCE and thought to be of Greek fabrication, Inv. no.M2893 Mozia, Arch. Mus. Whitaker.

366 Inv. No. S111 Mus. Arch. Agrigento. Marconi 1933, pl. X.4. The pearl rim appears on a polos, just above the hair with *protomai* from Selinous. Wiederkehr Schuler 2004, p.61, pl. 37 and 39; a similar decoration of the *polos* with large beads, not necessarily as the rim on the lower part of the *polos*, is seen on figurines from Taranto. For example, a terracotta female head from the last quarter of the sixth century BCE, but also male ones. Respectively Inv. no.APM01244 and APM01203 Allard Pierson Museum Amsterdam. A large banqueter from Akragas, probably imported from Taranto is AG 201515.

367 AG 9204 is the only example known to me. It has two holes just above the fringe in the middle. De Miro 2000 no.1184, tav.XCIV.

368 Marconi 1933, pl. VI.2 is an example of such a figurine.

369 On an amphora fragment from the sixth century BCE, a woman, in front of Herakles, is wearing a polos with a decoration of squares on the upper rim. Round items are placed on top of the hat, at the rim, Inv. no. 302095 Mus. Arch. Etrusco, Florence. See website digital Beazley Archive. http://www.beazley.ox.ac.uk/XDB/ASP/recordDetails.asp?id=2A7BA9D4-F681-47A5-80A0-737FA17ABC52&noResults=&recordCount=&databaseID=&search=.

370 Inv. no.2673, h. 14.6cm Pushkin Museum, Moscow. See Catalogue fig. 13, p.285.

371 The orthostat stele dates from the 9th century BCE and was found at Carchemish; Museum of Anatolian Civilizations, Ankara, Turkey. The dress may have been influenced by depictions of Kybele. A veil is often present in these depictions as well. Brijder 2014, p.92-3.

372 For example, the short necklace with pendant, and the detailed toes. See section III.10.d.

Description of polos form	Examples from the groups
The very low polos	Figurines with wooden patrix: 86
The low or medium height polos, slightly tapering [a]	Group 1, 2 and 3
The high polos [b]	Group 3
The very wide low polos	Group 4
The narrow and high polos [c]	Several in group 5: 63, 71, 72, 73, 74

Table 2.3: Overview with the most common polos shapes on Akragantine figurines per group. (a) Müller 1915 Formentafel A 52, B74, B 87; (b) Müller 1915 Formentafel A 44; (c) The tapering polos figurine, Müller 1915 Formentafel B 95) 'Rhodian', has a smooth outline.

completely different form, shorter and somewhat rounded at the top with a veil draped over the polos.[373] This addition to the mould, an invention of the coroplast, is clear from the somewhat messy reworking on the sides of the face. It is very possible that the veil was placed by hand on **171**. In both cases, the figurines are highly original and stand out because of the variations produced with mould combinations or handmade editions. The coroplast was both a skilled craftsman and an artisan.

The 'Rhodian' type of polos, dated to 570-500 BCE is a specific, very tall and stretched polos that is usually either straight or slightly tapering towards the top. The name is deceptive, however, as the origin of the figurines or the original model has never been proven to be Rhodian.[374] These figurines are widespread and come in two sorts, without a polos or with a high narrow one, with the same width as the face. All of these figurines share a rounded outline of the body. The face and the headdress also form one smooth line. The polos for the most part covers the forehead rather than standing on top of the head as with other polos types. Unlike most other figurines in Akragas, the hair is covered completely. The polos frames the faces and the sides are covered by what seems to be a kind of veil. The figurines with this high polos are dated by De Miro as being earlier than the ones with a veil, from around the middle of the 6th century BCE.[375] Though there are some cases of imitation, most of the local figurines from the same period are very different. Fundamental differences such as the depiction of the body, and details such as the polos, show that this type was not part of the mainstream development of terracotta figurines in Akragas. The figurines should be seen as an external element.[376]

II.6.e.iii The meaning of the polos and veil

At first sight, the polos appears to have been an honorific headgear reserved for deities.[377] Müller shows that in a cultic context the polos is also worn by the worshippers, in which case the distinction between divine and human is less clear.[378] Most of the depictions of straight-forward worshippers from Akragas, who are carrying a dedication such as a wreath or a piglet, do not wear a *polos*, though their act is a cultic one. They are more likely to portray humans. As most of the figurines from the second half of the sixth to the first quarter of the fifth century BCE in Akragas wear a *polos*, the initial question at the start of this chapter remains unanswered. Some figurines without the typical headgear are so similar to other figurines wearing the *polos* that it is not very probable that the *polos* or veil marks a clear distinction between human and divine. Unlike the apron, which in its omnipresence on the figurines of this time, remains a constant in both presence and iconography, the polos often changes in model. This susceptibility to fashion would tend to indicate that it was part of the dress of humans as well as the deity. By the same token, the apron, which remained unchanged over a long period of time, may not have had a real life counterpart.

But if the *polos* was a common part of the dress, should it not appear more often in the archaeological records? There are a few instances in which the *polos* is used for humans, but they seem to refer to a semi-divine state. The person in question would be heroised, like the deceased wearing one as a reference to the afterlife.[379] The *polos* has been found made of terracotta or gold, but not as an object of daily use.[380] The polos is an object that belongs in another world, that of the divinities or the afterlife. The *polos*, Bell concludes, is "a sign of a godhead" and therefore "a majority of the terracottas from the sanctuaries must have divine subjects." That does not solve either of the two problems and risks even circular reasoning. The opinion that the *polos* is divine headgear is shared by Albertocchi, based on discussion with Bell. In her discussion of a seated

373 The veil draped over the polos, running down each side of the headgear and face, is seen as a typical Ionian fashion. Langlotz and Hirmer 1963, p.72 no.68. This fits well with the Ionian facial features of this group, who wear the veil on top of a low polos.

374 White and Reynolds 2012, p.103, no.105.

375 De Miro 2000, p.101.

376 De Miro 2000, p.106.

377 The polos as exclusively divine headgear has been used as an argument that the figurines depict a goddess. Uhlenbrock 2016 warns against circular argumentation. Merker is only convinced of divine representation when the two status characteristics of being seated and wearing a polos are combine,. She recognizes a vagueness between the identities of the worshipper and the deity when represented in terracotta. A similarity of dress would have certainly made it possible for the worshipper to identify with the goddess. The anthropomorphism is strengthened by the fashionable dress, part of which was likely the polos; Merker 2000.

378 Müller 1915, p.84.

379 Bell 1981, p.82.

380 Bell 1981, p.103, no.6.

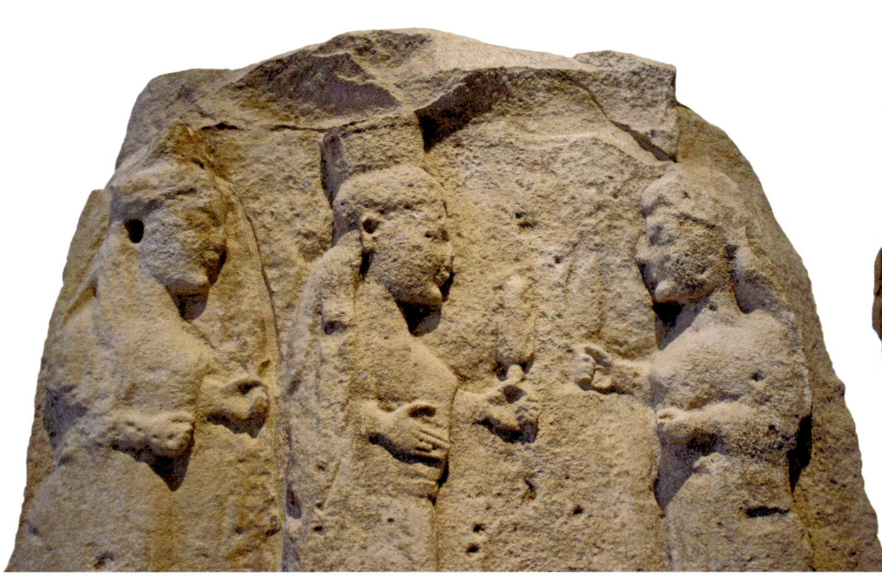

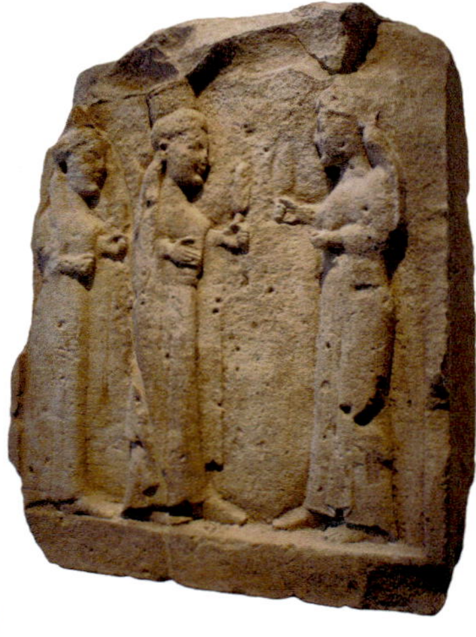

Figure 2.11: Metope Y7 of Temple Y in Selinous depicting three females, one wearing a polos.

figurine without a *polos*, she argues that “the absence of the polos is making the xoanizing and hieratic effect less evident.”[381] The *polos* is thus regarded as an old element. She does not broaden these conclusions to the category of statuettes that follow the Archaic Period nor does she consider whether the figurines with piglets and torches,[382] should also be regarded as divine when wearing a *polos*.[383] For the categories and period discussed here, the presence or absence of the *polos* is not sufficient for distinguishing the nature of the figurine. As such, it is comparable to the presence of arms or variations in pose.[384]

There are simply too many depictions, heights, shapes and sorts to assume that the polos was an imaginary item of dress. Its widespread use over a long period of time makes it impossible here to do more than address its particular application on Akragantine figurines. The rapid changes in fashion on the figurines gives reason to assume that the divine dress was created after human dress. It is likely that the deities were dressed up similarly to aristocratic dress, which expressed wealth and status. The omission of real life *poloi* might indicate that the *polos* was used only in a few instances and in special setting. The transition theory, as Bell explains, is a very interesting one. Specifically, for the case in Akragas where several statuettes where found in graves, both with and without a *polos*. The connection with the underworld seems of particular importance and from this point of view the *polos* could be interpreted as a symbol of transition.[385] It may also indicate both the transition made by Persephone herself, like the deceased, on her way to the underworld, but also her transition into becoming a goddess. The connection with the myth of Persephone could very well have been a Greek association with the locally existing customs and rituals. The *polos*, however, is not an argument for the Persephone-Kore cult, often associated with Sicily, as the distinction between her and Demeter is not clear from the iconography. It is usually interpreted as the standard headgear for Demeter, while her daughter would be wearing a veil.[386] Neither this distinction nor the appearance of the two divinities can be observed with the Akragantine figurines. There is only one instance, **179-180**, in which the polos seems to be omitted, even removed, on purpose. The figurine is similar to **171**, but it seems unlikely that they formed a pair because of their large difference in size, respectively about 30cm and 23 cm. The alteration of the headgear would have been for other reasons for **179**, and it should be noted that the combination of *polos* and veil, as on **171**, is also unusual. There is already a counter figurine in the form of a standing figure, **176**, and the coroplast of these objects was keen on variation. If the figurines were set up in groups, a difference between deity and worshippers carrying votives and possible other items would have been more likely. In other instances and on objects from a different category, time or context, a difference between Demeter and Persephone/Kore is quite clear. This can be observed, for example, on a *kalathos* depicting two figures, both wearing a tall *polos*. They are offering each other items,

381 Albertocchi 2004, p.35.

382 On the latter sort of figurines, Bell states that the piglet is held by the deity, not necessarily the dedicant. The receiver holds it and the act of dedication is depicted in this way; Bell 1981, p.82ff.

383 Bell 1981, p.117.

384 However, the selection of figurines for Albertocchi's research is based on the presence of pectoral pendants. Albertocchi 2004, p.7, while I think that this is another of the variations.

385 For the instances of the polos, as worn in grave context, see also Bell 1981, p.103, no.5. As the majority of figurines is found in sanctuary context, this study focusses in its results on those objects as votives.

386 Maniscalco 2018, p.6.

while one of them is seated on a throne, the other standing in front of her.[387] The *polos* is thus not only common for Demeter but appears as the headgear of Persephone as well.[388] On the Akragantine figurines of this sort, such a distinction is not clear. The headgear does not identify her as Demeter or Kore, because there are no indications from the same period from Akragas pointing in that direction.

On metope Y 7 of Temple Y from Selinous, dated to the early sixth century BCE, one of the two women facing a third wears a polos. Each of the three is holding a spindle in the hand furthest from the viewer (fig. 2.11). While they are otherwise similarly dressed and holding their arms at an angle to the front, the polos-wearing woman holds her right hand open, in contrast to the other two who hold their hands closed in a fist with the thumb on top. It is as if they are holding something and they are reminiscent of figurines holding a wreath. Perhaps a metal ornament was once attached. The single, small, vertically-lined polos identifies the middle figure as the deity, and her open hand might be interpreted as a gesture of receiving the gifts from the two female dedicants.[389] This is a different interpretation from the usual triad of goddesses, and the differences between goddess and mortals are minimal.[390]

II.6.e.iii The headdress as an indication of marital status

Ridgway writes on the korai of the Acropolis that the *polos* and the diadem are interchangeable headgear, and as such do not have a specific meaning. But at the same time, she seems to agree with Müller, to whom she refers, in his judgement that the *polos* is never worn by a regular woman, but fits semi-divine creatures and heroic images.[391] This does fit with the depicted use of the *polos* at Akragas, as noted above. In a footnote, Ridgway also refers to the interpretation of the *polos* as a bridal crown, which would explain its appearance on funerary korai.[392] Simon writes in her article on the Boeotian life-size terracotta polos that the polos functioned as a bridal crown .[393] Schipporeit states that the *polos* could have been part of the wedding attire, but does not mention a specific interpretation on the veil.[394] The *polos* used in a transition ritual from virgin to married woman seems a reasonable solution for the interpretation of the polos, which, on the one hand, is not a very common part of the dress and, on the other hand, appears in various shapes and sizes. The eventual narrative of Kore/Persephone would fit such an interpretation. The seated position of many figurines is often used as another argument and would confirm their status. Thus, also Schipporeit concludes that the enthroned figurines should be interpreted as married women or goddesses.[395] From the objects of Akragas, there are some examples of a figurine seated without *polos*, as well as the other way around. Both are therefore not necessary to indicate the same status. They could add to recognisability of the goddess.

For some authors, the veil rather than the *polos* is a clearer indication of the marital status of the depicted. Zuntz gets the impression of a *matrona* from the seated position and the veil of some figurines.[396] An application of the veil in bridal ceremonies, as is the case in many cultures is certainly possible, also in combination with the *polos*. Bell goes a step further and interprets the veil as a symbol of the bride, whom he interprets as being Persephone, the bride of Hades. For Zuntz, it is problematic to interpret every veil-wearing figurine as a bride and every bride as Persephone.[397] The lack of other attributes that point in the direction of a wedding celebration is also pointed out. It seems likely that the veil indeed represents marital status, while the polos might have been a hat worn at specific cultic occasions, such as the religious sanctioning of marriage. Whether the goddess is depicted as a bride herself, cannot be concluded from the Akragantine figurines.

II.6.f Fibulae

A vast majority of Akragantine figurines wear clasps on their shoulders. In group 1 only, they are absent from most of the group, **9**, **11**, **12**, although the rounded shoulders of some suggest them (**8**, **22**). These clasps are identical on each side, and are often rendered as large discs placed on the shoulders. They seem to keep the apron in place and therefore the most common interpretation is that they are fibulae. Such a function is to be expected, but at the same time, it is not entirely clear how the dress was fastened and

387 Inv. no. 5787, National Museum Athens, dated 575-525 BCE. http://www.beazley.ox.ac.uk/record/7C920184-60AE-4572-A16D-3FC0AF80D092.

388 On another, also Athenian, amphora from the same period, Persephone, in a scene where Herakles asks Hades for permission to bring Kerberos out of the Underworld, wears a polos with a hatched pattern and dotted inside. Inv. no. 302102 Mus. Gregoriano Etrusco, Vatican City. http://www.beazley.ox.ac.uk/record/F6FA2648-330F-462E-91E2-2240AD37B482.

389 Another distinction are the shoes. The two others have bare feet. He states that probably all three wore a polos. The middle figure's attribute is more carefully rendered and interpreted as a torch, flower buds or spindles. Giuliani 1979, p.63-6.

390 Giuliani sees them as vegetation goddesses or Moirai. Giuliani 1979, p.66. Bennet 2002, p.89 as Demeter and Kore with Hekate.

391 Out of the Akropolis korai, there are only three with a *polos*, of which one is identified as a sphinx by Ridgway, while the two others might have served as caryatids. Ridgway 1977, p.108-9.

392 Ridgway 1977, p.109, no.32.

393 Based on its yellow colour, it cannot be dated earlier than the third quarter of the 6th century BC. Simon 1972/1997, p.51.

394 Schipporeit 2014, p.327. But Müller, though he says that they could have been part of the wedding attire, does not recognize the poloi as bridal crowns on South-Italien vases. Müller 1915, p.86.

395 Schipporeit 2014, p.326-7.

396 Zuntz 1971, p.35.

397 Zuntz 1971, p.41.

in what way the applique, as that is the shape we see, was attached to it. When arms are present, the fibulae appears on top of the dress, covering the upper part of the arms as well. It seems the apron is attached by a pin or clasp to the undergarment but covered by an applique shaped most commonly as a disc. These fibulae have a second function to hold one or several pectoral bands.[398] Usually the upper one is connected to the fibulae, while lower bands run under the fibulae in their depiction on the figurines.[399]

The discs shapes, starting in group 1 and continuing to the first part of group 2, are, particularly in the early phase, relatively large (**36**) and, exceptionally, feature a knob in the middle (**30**), which makes it likely they were attached to the pin in the middle. They cover the corner of the triangular or rectangular shaped body and interrupt the rigid lines of these shapes.[400] They form the first decorative element of the figurines and so the pectoral band attachment is a secondary function. The choice of a disc is aesthetic: its geometrical shape, regularly appearing as decoration on locally produced pottery, contrasts with the rectangular form. Their form sometimes repeats that of the discs on the pectoral bands (**100**). When exceptionally omitted, the discs appear to be imitated by the shape of the shoulders (**57**).

In group 2, with just one exception, all figurines wear fibulae.[401] The discs are replaced by other forms around the transition to the fifth century BCE. Symmetrical long shapes are the most common, appearing even on figurines without arms. On **62**, the fibula is longer and placed at the side of the apron. On **87**, this form is hardly visible but the upper chest appears to have been broadened to make space for the arms. By looking at mould **90**, it becomes clear that the vague outline seems to refer to or was originally the outline of a double palmette. The outline was probably recognized by the people using the figurine.

In the mould, the palmette motif is clear and finely detailed. The palmette is mirror symmetrical both horizontally and vertically. Each part comprises a rhombus connected by a narrow rectangle. On each side, volutes flank and support the petals. The palmette springs around the rhombus, creating a triangular outline with the seven round topped petals that repeats the upper part of the rhombus. The unequal number of petals create a more pointed shape. The palmette is intricate and fine, and was apparently applied separately with a mould for just the fibulae. The cavity on the rear of **175** suggests that the clay was pressed with a thumb here in order to create a clear impression.

The shapes of the palmettes on the Mould I group is slightly different from those described above. The rhombus is reduced to a small knob, while the volutes are larger. The petals together appear rounder recalling an earlier rosette shape, but are the same in number as the first palmette.[402] Their large size means they often rise from the shoulders. Their appearance on some of the slightly bent figurines increases the impression of length and in some cases a standing pose (**88**). The double palmette is typical for Akragantine production.[403] This form is less common than the usual round fibulae and must have been a local invention and imitation of the same motif from architectural terracottas or metal ornaments. The sometimes simply shaped outlines suggest that a similar pattern could have been painted onto it (**97, 103**). The palmette fibulae seem to have sometimes been made separately. Such a moulded fibula has clearly fallen off on an extensively decorated figurine.[404] Surprisingly, the figurines from the same mould series, **115**, **118**, wear rectangular, but often rather irregularly shaped fibulae. Such coarseness does not fit with the fine reworking of other parts. It is likely that something was placed on top, as this part of the fibulae is particularly smooth. Another example of such irregular shapes is a figurine with particular large empty spots on her shoulders.[405] On other later figurines, the oval shape was not very defined and the suggestion of fibulae might have been enough (**143**). Whether a different model than the double palmette was intended is not clear.

Rosette-shaped fibulae also appear in two mould series. First, in group 1, **49-51**, with seven(?) petalled flower fibulae. Besides the original fibulae, the crescents flanking a disc are not common among Akragantine figurines. The second instance is again in the group of figurines thought to be made by a creative coroplast (**179-180**). The eight petals it consists of are loop-shaped and placed in the round, leaving the middle empty. They attract attention on the shoulders of a figurine from whom the arms seem

398 Barfoed 2013, p.100, no.3.

399 Albertocchi 2004, p.112. The figurines without pectorals, wear fibulae. It is very likely they served both purposes, attaching the apron and the pectoral bands.

400 In one case, they are incorporated into the dress and only the outline of the round clasps distinguishes them. Mus. Agr. Inv. no.AG 1161 and Kinský Palace, Prague Inv. no.NM-HM10 1751, both from the same mould series.

401 For a precise account of the numbers and percentages of each fibula category, see calculations in Chapter 4, Group 2.

402 Among the figurines of this series the number varies, sometimes even between the upper part with (usually) five petals, and the lower with seven. Because the space available is similar, the leaves are narrower. **177** also has seven flower petals on both parts of the fibula. It is likely that this belongs to another generation in which this part was reworked.

403 Albertocchi 2004, p.96, no.1710.

404 Figurine AT 3392 (713) Pushkin Museum, Moscow. See Catalogue fig. 14, p.285.

405 Inv. No. C 5122 Louvre, Paris. Not only is the head of this figurine very similar to **104**. The facial features and body resembles **179-180**. See Catalogue fig. 9, p.272.

to have been removed on purpose, and contrast with the coarser pectoral pendants, **179**.[406] Rosette-shaped fibulae of the first sort are applied to a figurine, 20175, now lost, (Catalogue fig. 10).

A third special fibula applique shape recalls a wheat sheaf. On **105** and **106**, the original fine-lined wheat sheaf is visible. The upper and lower part have a rounded outline and are symmetrical. They composed of five bundles, bound together in the middle. The details are often faded, but the outline would have been sufficient. Sheaves of wheat are not a commonly known motif from any of the nearby cultures and may represent to an exceptional form or a variation on the double palmette, which has a similar outline.[407] It might have been the result of the creativity of the coroplast, drawing precise new lines over an older fibulae outline, as these two objects are very sharp, and clearly of the first generation. They are distinctively original in their iconography in other aspects as well.[408]

Following the rectangular fibulae, which form half of the fibulae in group 3, and the oval outline in 3b, which forms about one third of the fibulae in group 3, and some disc-shaped fibulae, interest in fibulae declined. While there is attention to the fine folds in the garment in the same period, the fibulae in group 4 are just very small knob or disc-shaped items that are hardly visible or completely absent; the pectoral pendants remain (**189**).

II.6.f.i Interpretation and comparison with real-life objects

In this subchapter, the fibulae will be compared with real-life objects, and their motifs with similar figures appearing on terracottas in other cultures.

Disc-shaped fibulae appear on terracotta figurines already in the early 6th century BCE in Southern Italy, in particular from Tarente. Their form is usually a large disc, sometimes with a knob or smaller disc on top, as on a figurine from Tarente.[409] The fibulae on this figurine are placed close to the neck, and unlike those on the Akragantine figurines, it does not cover the 'corner' of the shoulder. On the Argive figurines, found at Akragas (**1** and **2**), the disc shapes are placed further on the stretched out upper arms. Here, their function is to hold the pectoral bands, while on the Tarente figurine they probably serve as fibulae proper. Also, on other Boeotian statuettes, some wear two attached pectoral bands between a double set of clasps at different heights on their chest.[410] This can be explained by the several pectoral bands. There are no Akragantine figurines with more than one clasp on each shoulder or as many as seven bands.[411] The number of pectoral chains and pendants increased over time from one up to three.

Both functions of the fibulae as depicted on the figurines, as a clasp for pendants and as cloth pin, as well as both parts of the fibulae, pin and applique, existed in real life, and were combined at some point. They would have served as models for the clay versions. Applique in which only the disc is visible are found on Crete and Rhodes; the disc is simply fixed on top of the fibula.[412] Sometimes the knob in the middle makes the joint visible where they are put together. While Akragantine discs on figurines are usually smooth, except **30**,[413] the Selinuntine ones occasionally feature a knob or hole in the middle.[414] These objects are an argument for the traditional function of fibula, as they are found also in the region. An example of such a disc, together with a possible attachment ring for the pectorals is found in an Akragantine grave context.[415] The disc might have been made from various materials, as some bone discs from a grave context at Monte Bubbonia, further inland, reveal (fig. 2.12).[416] The attachment to the fibulae would have been by a metal pin through the hole with a knob to prevent it from detachment. Such appliques of bone and ivory are also known from Megara Hyblaea, dated to the 7th century BCE, [417] and a fibula with a bone disc was found at the Malophoros Sanctuary in Selinous.[418] Such a fibula has also been discovered at Akragas, found

406 The rosette shape reappears on the endings or the high winged throne, as well as on an earring stud. See section II.7 on furniture and II.6.h.i on earrings.

407 As this instance is unique, it is not reasonable to infer from it that all votive dedications refer to the fertility of the land and prosperity from good harvests. Also a connection to Demeter also seems far-fetched, even though she is frequently depicted on Greek vases with sheaves of corn.

408 See the description of the exceptional combination of pendants below.

409 Upper part of a figurine, Allard Pierson Inv. No. APM01656. See museum website: https://www.uvaerfgoed.nl/beeldbank/en/allardpiersonmuseum/xview/?identifier=hdl:11245/3.1359;metadata=APM01656.

410 Pautasso 1996, tav.XXI, c. A figurine from Catania also seems to have two partly overlapping discs on her upper arm. Pautasso 1996, tav.IX, 75.

411 Some attachments discussed below feature seven small rings for pectoral bands or chains.

412 Sapouna-Sakellarakē et al. 1978, p.113-4, Type XAh, tav.47 no.1544-1549.

413 Also a mould, AG 8944 from Akragas. De Miro 2000, p.251 no.1530, tav.CVIII.

414 Mould AG8944 also features such a small hole. De Miro 2000, no.1530, tav.CVIII.

415 Necropoli Contrada Pezzino, Akragas, tomb 1116. Mus. Arch. Agrigento. It is described as a brooch. The same grave also contained a 'Rhodian' figurine. Veder Greco 1988, p.293.

416 See other references to publications on the Eastern necropolis in Urquhart 2010, p.109.

417 As well as from other places outside Sicily. See for these examples Albertocchi 2004, p.121, n.55.

418 Trombi 2003, p.105 tav.XXIII 66g.

together with a partial bronze ring,[419] which could have come from Calabria, where they are known from the ninth or eighth century BCE onwards. It is an interesting object, as its decoration of circles with a point in the middle along the rim is a motif known from the acropolis of Polizzello.[420] Several disc-shaped fibulae appliques with circular decorations and symmetrical motifs, and one with a female figurine, were also found in a deposit in a building on the agora of Megara Hyblaea.[421] The figurine fibula applique, dated between 650-40 BCE, is belted and wears a low *polos*, reminiscent of the thin wooden *xoana*.[422] The frequently depicted disc shape fibulae on the Akragantine figurines could very well represent these sorts of fibulae. The valuable material fits with the overall richness of the decoration and the display of wealth and status on the terracottas (fig. 2.13a).

The fibulae were attached to the pectoral bands and would have been used to secure them and to hold the garments together.[423] The arguments for this are stronger as several Argive figurines have been found at Akragas, **1** and **2**, as well as in other Sicilian towns such as Catania, Gela and Syracuse.[424] However, fibulae and pectorals are absent from most of the figurines in group 1, and there are figurines on which the pectoral band appears without fibulae **(54-57)**. The Argive objects however, might look much older than they actually are as fabrication by hand continued for a long time, up to the first quarter of the fifth century BCE.[425] It is thus possible that the clasps were applied in a new function, possibly inspired by Sicilian figurines.[426] In addition to holding the garment, they would also keep the pectoral bands in place. The appearance of these Argive figurines over such a large geographical area, shows that they became a generic type.

Several finds suggest that metal chains, possibly worn on the chest, were probably decorative. Such metal rings and chains, found in grave contexts could have served as pectorals and were probably the traditional and local way to display a particular status. The amount of metal, bronze in this case, and also its very fine reworking would have indicated the status and wealth of the

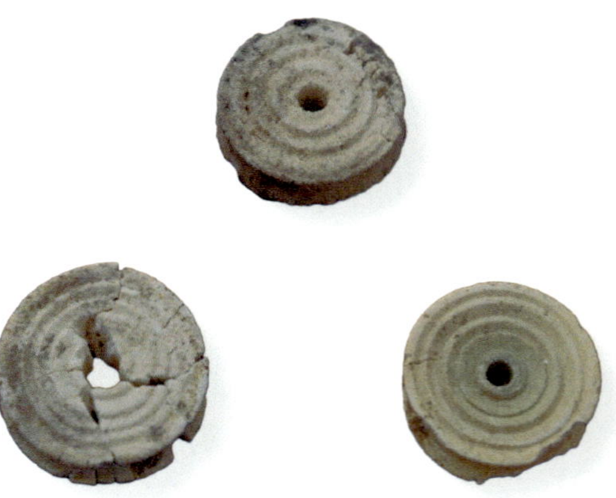

Figure 2.12: Bone decorations of fibulae from a grave context, tomb 16/72 of the necropolis of Monte Bubbonia, sixth century BCE, Mus. Caltanisetta without inv. no.

wearer. These chains, consisting of small links, were fastened onto a larger ring with on one side a row of small eyes to which the chains could be linked. Bronze pectoral chains, combined with the clasps and other items of jewellery were found in a rock-grave in Butera.[427] To keep jewellery in place the clasps would have been fastened on the shoulders. These sorts of attachments are probably Sicilian in origin and are interpreted as finial pieces of the pectoral (fig. 2.13b). They are spread over the whole island of Sicily, but particularly found in eastern Sicily in inland grave contexts and are therefore called 'Siculian.' There is another example of a dedicated clasp from the Bitalemi Sanctuary in Gela. They all date from the late 7th – early 6th century BCE and one of the clasps has been found at Agrigento.[428] Interestingly, some are also dedicated at Olympia, together with the chains and differently shaped beads.

Double fibulae, sometimes spiral in form, or 'Brillenfibeln' in German, with several chains attached, have been found in southern Italian graves.[429] The chains of these, however, are shorter and end with the attachment of several small pendants. These small pendants on the chains might be interpreted as pectoral pendants with the function of producing sound. This would be similar to a bronze *calcofon* from Sabucina (fig. 2.13b), which is thought to have also been used to produce noise.[430] Also, at the sacred area south of the fortification wall in Sabucina, several chains have been found dated from the sixth century BCE. In some Etruscan grave contexts too,

419 Necropoli di Contrada Pezzino tomb 572 together with miniature jars and other ivory objects. They are dated to the second half of the sixth century BCE. AG22244 and AG22245 Mus. Arch. Agrigento. Veder Greco 1988, p.385.

420 Trombi 2003, p.105-6 tav.XXIII 66g.

421 At a votive depot of temple G. Gras, Tréziny, Broise 2005, p.441-2, fig.422.

422 Parisi 2017, p.189.

423 See Zuntz 1971, p.129-30.

424 For literature on these findings Ammerman 2002, p.84, n.5.

425 Barfoed 2013, p.85; Muller 2010, p.100.

426 They were spread across the northeastern Peloponnese, the oldest probably from Argos. Barfoed 2013, p.85-7. The ones from Argos, Corinth and Perchora were produced in the 6th century BCE, as well as the ones found in Catania. Barfoed 2013, p.97 and 102, n.59.

427 It will be more extensively discussed below in section II.6.h.ii. Admesteanu has found and described its content. Adamesteanu 1958, p.472.

428 According to the map by Baitinger 2013, p.199ff., Abb.69, but I have not seen this object.

429 They were, however, much more common in Eastern Europe. Pabst 2012 33 Taf. 3, 1 and 3.

430 See section II.6.h.viii.

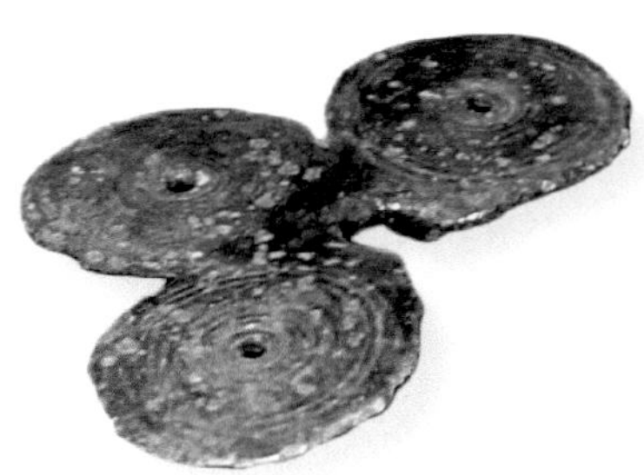

Figure 2.13a: A bronze disc fibula applique with concentric circles from tomb C 69, indigenous necropolis of Vassalagi, dated to the sixth century BCE. Mus. Caltanisetta without inv. no.

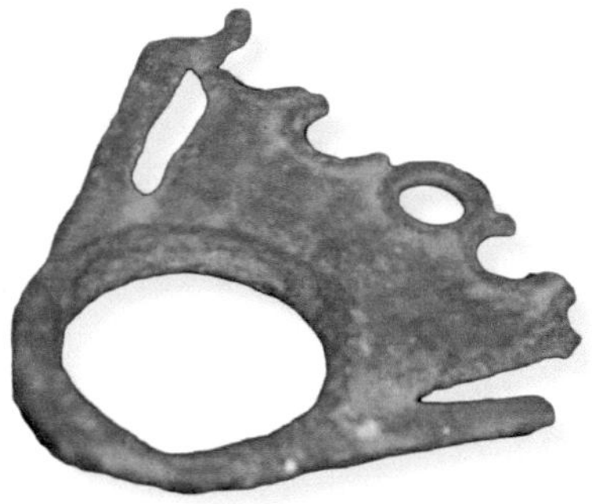

Figure 2.13b: A bronze finial, shaped as a large ring with smaller rings for attachment, found at the fortification wall of Sabucina. Mus. Caltanisetta Inv. no. 54062

a number of fibulae have been found featuring the large disc as an applique, as well as a ring to which something could have been attached.[431]

Among the bronze objects found in the large jar with local decoration, from S. Anna Sanctuary at Akragas, there is also one object likely to be a part of a fibula. It is interpreted as a fibula decorated with a stylised animal head.[432] From the same context, there is also a large somewhat conically shaped disc, which could have covered the fibula itself. Such a bronze disc is also found in a Butera grave.[433] The latter shape resembles the round shape of the discs on the figurines. These sort of objects – others are found in Selinous and Monte Bubbonia – are interpreted as cymbals.[434] Their concave form makes this possible, though its application is not immediately clear.[435] It has also been suggested that several other disc shaped bronze objects with a knob in the middle found at Akragas, with parts sticking out on one or two sides, were used as musical instruments.[436]

Large fibulae appliques in disc form are known from the Etruscans. As they often appear in pairs they are sometimes interpreted as earrings. Some would be very large for such an application, with a diameter of 6.1cm. The latter example is part of a grave context dated to the fifth century BCE in which several items in gold show the importance of jewellery as a status marker. These fibulae have a very fine reworked decoration.[437] Two gold finely reworked discs, 4.6cm in diameter, could also have been appliques.[438] The gold 'Prunkfibel' from Vulci is even larger still, and its height of 18.5cm would have precluded it from ever having a practical purpose. Its role must have been purely aesthetic.[439]

In addition to the disc shaped objects discussed above, there are several other fibula applique shapes known from Akragas' figurines. It is likely that these were developed locally, but the forms might have been inspired by other cultures. Some of the Akragantine as well as the Argive figurines have flower decorations reminiscent of the rosette.[440] The rosette is a widespread motif that

431 Rutishauser 2017, no.157-8. More on Etruscan pectorals and other jewellery below.

432 Trombi 2003, p.92; Fiorentini 1967, p.73, tav.XXXV, fig.2.9. Baitinger 2017, p.115, fig.16 describes it as an elbow fibula with horns of Elymian type.

433 See Adamesteanu 1958, p.465-6, fig.167.

434 Musical instruments might have played a role in gatherings at specific occasions. In a grave at Akragas, a small bronze bell was discovered. Necropoli Contrada Pezzino, Akragas, tomb 1253. Mus. Arch. Inv. no.S15 Mus. Agrigento h. 5.5 cm Veder Greco 1988, p.322.

435 Bellia 2014, p 16 and Bellia 2012, p.258 fig.6.

436 As timpani. They are finely worked and measure in diameter of the disc between 2.7-8.3 cm, see De Miro 2000, p.279-280, cat. no.883-1886. The latter have on one of the 'wings' small holes to be hung upon or fixed to something. De Miro 2000, p.296-297, cat. no.2098-2104.

437 Inv. no.40.11.7-.18 Metropolitan Museum of Arts, New York. See museum website: https://www.metmuseum.org/art/collection/search/256976.

438 Etruskische große Goldscheiben. Ende des 6. Jh.v.Chr. Antik. Staatl. Mus. Berlin. http://library.artstor.org/asset/BERLIN_DB_10313801728. Web. 17 Jul 2018.

439 An oval shield forms the lower part, which is connected to a large, rounded triangular leaf-shaped disc on top of a double tube. These and the lower part are decorated with fine granulation in parallel triangles; while on the upper part, a battle seems to be engraved between two men, wearing a weapon, a shield and an impressive helmet, each accompanied by a roaring dog/lion and a bird. In the air, seven more birds fly in different directions and the space left in the middle is filled by a Greek cross. Staatl. Ant. Munich. Wünsche and Steinhart 2010, p.84-5 no.45, dated to around 650 BCE. Five lions and several griffins are depicted on a similar golden fibula, 30cm high, from the main tomb in Cerveteri. Vatican Museum Inv. no.20552. See museum website: http://www.museivaticani.va/content/museivaticani/en/collezioni/musei/museo-gregoriano-etrusco/sala-ii--tomba-regolini-galassi/grande-fibula-da-parata.html.

440 Barfoed 2013, p.98.

also appears on a convex disc fibula applique from the Artemision at Ephesos.[441] The palmette was also a general Greek architectural ornamentation and decorative motif on pottery, but was originally from the East and introduced by the Phoenicians. The Cypro-Phoenocian metal bowl ornamentation[442] seems to have also influenced jewellery forms.[443] The rosette often appears as the centrepiece of bowls, including a bronze one from Akragas.[444] The round palmette is Phoenician in origin, while the more elongated palmette, particularly the middle, is Greek.[445] The Greek-style palmette seems mostly to have been applied in Akragas as a fibulae applique on the statuettes. The single palmette appears as a repeated motif on the diadem of a multi-coloured Etruscan terracotta antefix of a female head. The palmette appears six times on the bordeaux-red diadem with seven petals alternating between bright red and bluish grey, and the curls, in white, on top of a small grey rhombus running in a semi-circle around it, forming alternating lotus-plants. The female head wears disc earrings, again with a seven petalled rosette.[446] The application of the architectural motif is an original way of decorating the diadem.

Coroplasts in Akragas might have been inspired by these motifs applied originally in a setting of architectural terracottas and used it as a fibula applique. Whether the influence came directly from Phoenician, Greek or possibly even Etruscan works is not possible to ascertain. Rosettes became a very general ornamental motif in Greek decoration. The palmette in several forms is also applied to decorate furniture, for example, painted on the lower front part of the chair of Attic seated female figurines. The way they stick out from the seat is reminiscent of the palmettes sticking out from the shoulders.[447]

Some objects featuring the palmette were also found at the Akragantine S. Anna Sanctuary. A handle decoration is shaped into a rounded palmette, incised with (9?) fine leaves. On top of each of the leaves, there is a small knob. The middle, raised by a thin disc, is again decorated with petals and knobs.[448] Another object, a handle attachment from a Greek bronze cauldron, is also decorated with a palmette. This one, although on its own, is very similar to the palmette on the figurines' fibula, including the rhombus, volutes and five petals (**171**). The other side features a lion protome on each thicker part.[449] These objects make clear that the rosette and palmette were ornamental motifs over a vast area and were not specifically Akragantine.

The palmette and rosette were common motifs in temple architecture too. Interestingly, the most common palmettes have five petals, for example, those painted on the Temple of Hercules. On the figurines there are fibulae palmettes with seven petals, for example, AG 9589, which includes larges volutes beneath.

The rectangular fibulae seem anomalous, as other parts of the figurine were so carefully detailed. One reason for this anomaly, may be suggested by gold sheet jewellery, *Schmuckblech* in German, of the seventh century BCE, moulded or hand-reworked from the islands of Rhodes, Melos, Thera, Delos, Naxos, Crete and Cyprus. These could have served as a pectoral. They were possibly fastened to a garment on the upper seam using a pin or fibula behind the sheet.[450] The rectangular form of figurines' fibulae, though from another period, are reminiscent of these.[451] An example of such a very finely reworked rectangular (17.3 x 10.3cm) golden shoulder pin is probably of eastern origin, but found in an Etruscan grave and dated to the seventh century BCE.[452] It is possible that the original rectangular objects were finely reworked but that such detail was not possible to depict on the smaller figurines. Some details may, therefore, have been painted onto the rectangular fibulae but no visible traces of this survive.

The primarily practical fibula was quickly covered with an applique and applied as a decorative item. On the figurines, the decorative discs or ovals seem to refer to the metal or bone appliques used to diguise functional fibula below. There are indications of influences from living local traditions, visible in the use of such extensive jewellery. This is particularly clear for the grave contexts, but also apparent

441 Diam. 2.28 cm Pülz and Bühler 2009 cat. no.409 Farbtaf. 27. It is also common on the dress appliques found at the same place: cat. no.376-379, 382 Farbtaf. 22-23.

442 This sort of bowls, of different metals, were also found at Akragas. An example of a silver bowl with a rosette in the middle is 1931, 0819.1 at the British Museum. See museum website: https://www.britishmuseum.org/research/collection_online/collection_object_details.aspx?objectId=282690&partId=1.

443 See Section II.6.g.

444 A large bronze bowl from Akragas also features a fine rosette in the middle. Mus. Arch. Agrigento, presently in showcase 52.

445 Willers, D. B. 'Ornaments'. Brill's New Pauly. Ed. Hubert Cancik and et al. Brill Reference Online. Web. 22 June 2018.

446 Inv. No. 1997.145.2a Metropolitan Museum of Arts, New York. See museum website: https://www.metmuseum.org/art/collection/search/256571.

447 Inv. no.1980.303.5 Metropolitan Museum of Arts, New York. See museum website: https://www.metmuseum.org/art/collection/search/255697.

448 AG 126666 Arch. Mus. Agrigento. The handle of a bronze basin dated to the third quarter of the sixth century BCE. Baitinger 2017, p.112, fig.6; Trombi 2003, p.92; Fiorentini 1967, p.73 tav.XXXV, fig.2.7.

449 AG 12650 Arch. Mus. Agrigento. It was deposited near the pavement of building A of the S. Anna Sanctuary, Akragas. Baitinger 2017, p.110, fig.3; Fiorentini 1967, p.73 tav.XXXVI, fig.1-2.

450 Deppert-Lippitz 1985, p.98-101.

451 There are also fibulae with a square part suitable for engraving known from the end of the ninth century BCE onwards. The fibula pin however is never visible on the figurines and the shape is rectangular. Deppert-Lippitz 1985, p.58.

452 It is reminiscent of the rectangular objects in the Treasure of El Carambolo. Rutishauser 2017, p.137.

from the figurines. It might indicate the more traditional image they had of the goddess and may have been a deliberate archaism. The contemporary, 'indigenous' inland sites continued to engage in practices that emphasized the material value of metal. In Akragas, one example of such a practice is a large jar with a random collection of bronze items left as a dedication in the S. Anna Sanctuary. As elsewhere, metal could be traded and functioned in the same way as coinage.[453] The supposed application of valuable metal items in a cultic context, as depictions in terracotta show, could have also included fibulae and their appliques. Their original purpose as jewellery and decoration for distinguished women was expanded to highlight the status of the goddess. These jewellery items were re-interpreted and placed in a new setting, adapted to the mixed cultural context of Akragas and extended with various motifs from other cultures, such as the rosette and palmette. These motifs were re-interpreted, and the doubling of the palmette reflects the doubling of the discs and the oval outline. For now, it remains a question to what extent these motifs were meaningful, whether they were chosen for their iconography alone or for their meaning in their original context.

II.6.g Pectoral bands and pendants

II.6.g.i Akragantine pendants

One of the most significant characteristics of the Akragantine figurines are their pectoral bands and various pendants. Most of the figurines with a line across their chest between the clasps possessed pendants. The upper or single pectoral band, coincides in shape and place with the upper hem of the dress. In some cases, it runs closely parallel to it (fig. 2.14).[454] This sometimes creates the impression that one or several bands are depicted, even without pendants (**40-47**). In some cases, the pectoral band is left empty, for example, the Argive objects, **1** and **2**. This occurs only with a single band, which is then depicted as being thick. The opposite occurs more frequently, where the cord itself or the clasps are not depicted, but the pendants are displayed. The absence of clasps could have been caused by the formation of arms next to the apron, for example, AG8982 (fig. 2.14). Surprisingly, the cords are clearly depicted but hang differently than on most figurines. While the upper one seems to have been fixed on the shoulder, the lower band makes smaller curves as if it is attached to the dress as well. On Boeotian statuettes, the pectoral band sometimes seems to be fixed in the middle as well, creating

453 Baitinger 2017.

454 AG8982 h. 8.2cm dated to the end of the sixth century De Miro 2000, p.240, no.1413.

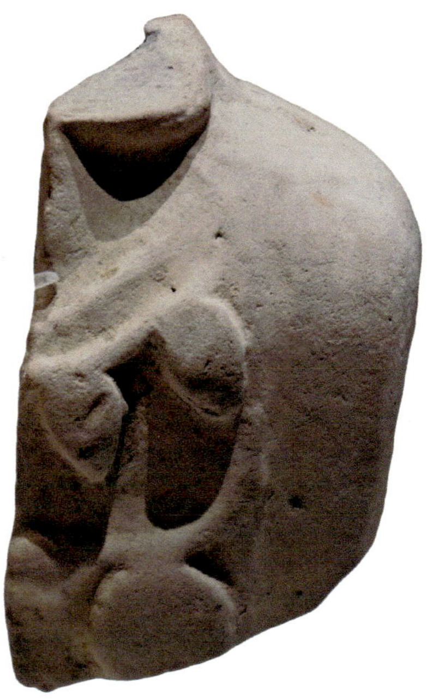

Figure 2.14: The upper hem of the dress, just above the line with the pendants is clear. The second cord seems to be fixed to the dress. The tube- shaped attachment of the disc, which hangs exceptionally from the second cord, is clearly visible. Her left shoulder is round and the wider part next to the dress might have indicated her arm. H. 8.2cm, Inv. no. AG8982 Mus. Agrigento.

two hanging parts.[455] Zuntz believes pendants would have been attached to the dress: "sewn on to it, presumably."[456] Such a practical attachment suggests that the pectorals were applied in real-life. If so, what was their function and meaning? Their role is presumably larger than that of the solely decorative jewellery items. Their presence in such high numbers on the figurines and their relative large size reveals their importance. Figurines with pendants are the main characteristic of Sicilian coroplastics,[457] and, apart from at Akragas, were produced in large number at Selinous[458] and Gela.[459] Figurines with pectorals are nicknamed Athana Lindia, a misleading name.[460] Probably the oldest figurine with such a pectoral band and pendant is a polos-wearing figurine with two pectoral bands, one painted and one with a double disc pendant. It was found at Gela and dated to the end of the seventh to the first half of the sixth century BCE, but possibly of Corinthian

455 Nat. Arch. Mus. Athens Inv. No. 17426 Szabó 1994 no.85. The technique of applying items separately by hand, as is the case here and also for no.1 and 2, is called 'barborine' or 'barbotine'. Muller 2010, p.100.

456 Zuntz 1971, p.120.

457 Albertocchi 2004.

458 Dewailly 1992.

459 Panvini 1998.

460 See chapter 1.

origin.[461] At the same time, it is questionable whether it can be compared, as its pendant is not directly comparable with the later figurines from Sicily. A double disc, placed on top of each other is exceptional. Such a pendant is not found at Akragas, but there are two other examples of figurines from the acropolis of Gela.[462] Even a figurine with a single pendant on her pectoral band is not known from Akragas and considering the occurrence of empty ones, the pectoral, the shape and number of pendants seems a local development. Rather than inspired from these Corinthian figurines, the Argive figurines might have been the direct inspiration at Akragas. As a feature of Sicilian coroplastics that might have been inspired by other cultures, it developed its own characteristics on Sicily.

Looking at the Akragas figurines, we can see how the the pectoral forms developed. Figurines from Akragas group 1 share a characteristic blockish body and do not always have pendants. The pectoral became common from group 1d onwards.[463] Over time, the number of pendants increased, while their individual size decreased. In the table below, the most common forms of pendants on the figurines are listed, summarised and distinguished by variation. The identification numbers of figurines with each variation are not all mentioned individually (table 2.4). The variation is wide and the high number of special forms, in particular in group 2, led to creating a subdivision in Variation C. Some smaller variations or exceptional figurines have not been included, such as **114** and **141**.

At first, the number of pendants was three. These were usually relatively large, filling the space available on the chest. In the first group still, the number was expanded to five. Discs and crescents were alternated, and an inversed droplet or pear-shape occurs just once (**48**). The variation is limited to symmetrical compositions, while the total number of pendants is always odd, three or five per line. The last figurine of this group shows a continuation of the symmetrical pendants on the first row, as well as an additional second row. The disc shape turned more ovoid and three dimensional. The resulting egg shape was less regular than the disc. In group 2, the number of pendants is no longer always odd. The egg shape is sometimes rounded, sometimes pointed, but clearly distinguishable from the disc. The total number of pendants increased, up to seven pendants per line, and the pendants become relatively smaller. Some pectorals still display alternating pendant sorts. Together with the appearance of the pendant in triple form, it gives the impression of an older model. The use of the crescent is also a recurring element, even applied on the bands with multiple pendants. The pectorals refer in this way to an earlier style, though from no more than a couple of decades before. On the one hand, it could be seen as an Archaistic trend; on the other, it is likely that its symbolism remained appreciated and that both the earlier and newer versions had the same meaning and value. Two figurines from the same mould, **105-106**, are remarkable for their combination of pectorals. It is as if the coroplast could not decide between an older and newer style in chronological order from the upper cord to the lower. The upper band with the crescent, and the second band with the three discs are very traditional and figurines with just these three are datable to the end of the sixth century. The lower band, however, has the stylistic character of a later period with thin pendants, similar to each other, attached to a sort of knob or bead on top. Their form possibly imitates a flower bud and are reminiscent of a similar looking object held by *korai*.[464]

The pendants can thus be divided into two sorts based on both form and number. The depicted objects and the multiple similar, usually ovoid or somewhat pointier, pendants that followed later. The first category is introduced in group 2. Some are clearly recognizable, such as the bovine and satyr *protomai* and acorns. Others, on the same figurines, are reminiscent of pottery containers, such as aryballoi, with a rim on top, but it is not completely clear what they represent. They could have been shaped like this because the pendant in real it represents contained small amounts of valuable perfume oil. Because the pendants in the first category depict real objects, it is likely that the second line of pendants were also copying real-life pendants (**171-177**). The discs are reminiscent of coins. Silver coins were introduced in the same period, while gold followed a few years later. With their intrinsic value, real coins could have been applied as pendants, but reworked coins hung on a cord are not known from the area. The lack of detail on **172** suggests that a plain disc is represented. The ovoids, as they appear on **179-180**, could represent an object or could have been a symbolic shape, perhaps referring to the sun, as the crescent refers to the moon. The latter seems more likely as they are at first a neat, thick ovoid but become thinner and more irregular as the moulds deteriorated. They would nevertheless still have been recognised as symbols. It seems that in the later stages of pectoral development the number of pendants was more important than the detail. The pendants may

461 Panvini 1998, p.18, I.16; p.20 I.19 A, D.

462 Panvini and Sole 2005, p.38 tav.II.e, III a Mus. Arch. Gela inv. nos. 10387, 8324.

463 Albertocchi did not include the figurines without pendants in her study of the collection of this Sicilian figurine type.

464 This figurine combines the older conventions and newer models in several ways. The figurine as a whole combines the rectangular outline with ependytes with a newer body shape for the arms with smooth, rounded lines from the shoulders down. The earrings, which combine the ear stud with a ring and pendant, are newly introduced here.

Letter of variation	Short description pendant form	Group 1	Group 2	Group 3	Group 4
	no pendants	**12, 30, 41**	**103-104, 21**	-	-
A	Variants on one row with usually three objects: discs and crescents	**54, 55, 56-57, 49-51, 59**	-	-	-
B	Variants on two rows with an increasing total number: mainly ovoid, sometimes combined on the first row with pointed shapes, discs, and a crescent	**61**	**62, 70, 87, 88?, 90-92, 98, 99, 100; 107-109**	-	**185-186, 188**
C a-c	Large pendants in two or three rows a: 1: crescent flanked by discs 2: three discs 3: four thin pointed b: 1: five pointed ovoid 2: seven pointed ovoid from round bead c: 1: five bovine protomai 2: two discs alternated with three bottles? 3: three satyr heads alternate with two acorns/ two satyr heads alternate with three acorns	-	a: **105-106,** b: **179-180** c: **171-177**	-	-
D	A large number, 5-9, pointed or ovoid pendants on two or three rows	-	**115-120, 135-137**	**97, 113, 139, 142-151**	**189**

Table 2.4: Overview of the most common sorts of pendants, in the different groups with examples of the figurines and catalogue numbers. Numbers connected with a dash imply that they belong to the same mould series. The '1:', '2:' and '3:' stand for respectively the upper, second and lower pectoral band. In general, the table shows that at first there is a lower number of pendants as well as bands. In general, there are two sorts of pendants: one larger more detailed one, sometimes with a depiction and alternating with others; and the small ovoid or pointed variant that is less carefully rendered and occurs in a larger number in each row.

have been linked to distinct wishes and prayers, and a large number of pendants would therefore represent a desire for welfare in all aspects of life. Some pendants were connected to the cord by a bead on top.

In group 3, only the multiple pendants continue, often covering the complete upper body of the figurine. They are small and often irregular in size. The ones on the third row of **115-117** are more elongated. As with the ovoid pendants, the novelty was applied in an additional, lower row under the existing ones.[465] The reappearance of the crescent pendant in group 3, **94** and **152**, shows the strength of this symbol through time. It is an otherwise unusual setting on Akragantine pectorals with a double flanking pendant. The number of pendants on these two figurines compared with others still increased per row over time, but they were not necessarily divided over three rows. In general, the multiple pendants are similar in shape and neatly hang at a similar distance from each other, except for **141**, on which the bands runs very straight but the pendants are unequal in size and shape.[466]

In the last group, 4, the return to the previously common lower number of pendants and the combination of discs on the upper row with thin, pointed shapes on the second row seems to be a return to an earlier style. This is both an Archaism as well as a simplification, because the discs are considerably smaller. For the more detailed seated figurines in this group, an unknown number of fine pointed pendants in three rows continues on the multiple pectoral. The distinction between the smaller, less numerous pendants on the standing figurines and the fine multiple pendants on the taller, seated figurine could point to a difference in status.

In the table, four groups summarise the combinations and arrangement of the pendants (table 2.4). In the first place, they show the increasing number of pectoral bands as well as the number of pendants per band. It is noteworthy that single pendants are so uncommon.[467] Variation A consists of variants of pendants on one row. The total number is three, with just one exception, **60**, that has five, but still on one row. The odd number maintains symmetry and the large pendants usually fill the available space. The odd numbers are often combined with a different pendant in the middle. The high number of the later and more common small pendants is relevant as the number and fineness of the pendants would have made more of an impression.

The pectoral bands themselves are sometimes rather thick, but seldom detailed, as on **172**, on which the

465 With the exception of **94** and **152** which probably have another source of inspiration from beyond Akragas. On the first row nine/? pointed ovoid pendants and on the second row a crescent flanked by two/three small discs. As these two are exceptional on Variation B in the table, which shows the disc/crescent pendants on the upper row, they are not shown in the table. The figurine of fig. 14 is also an exception to this rule.

466 The different sizes and forms are reminiscent of the irregularly shaped amber pendants. See section II.6.h.v.

467 There is one example from Selinous exhibited in the arch. Mus. Palermo with a small vase-shaped pendant on a thin cord between round fibulae.

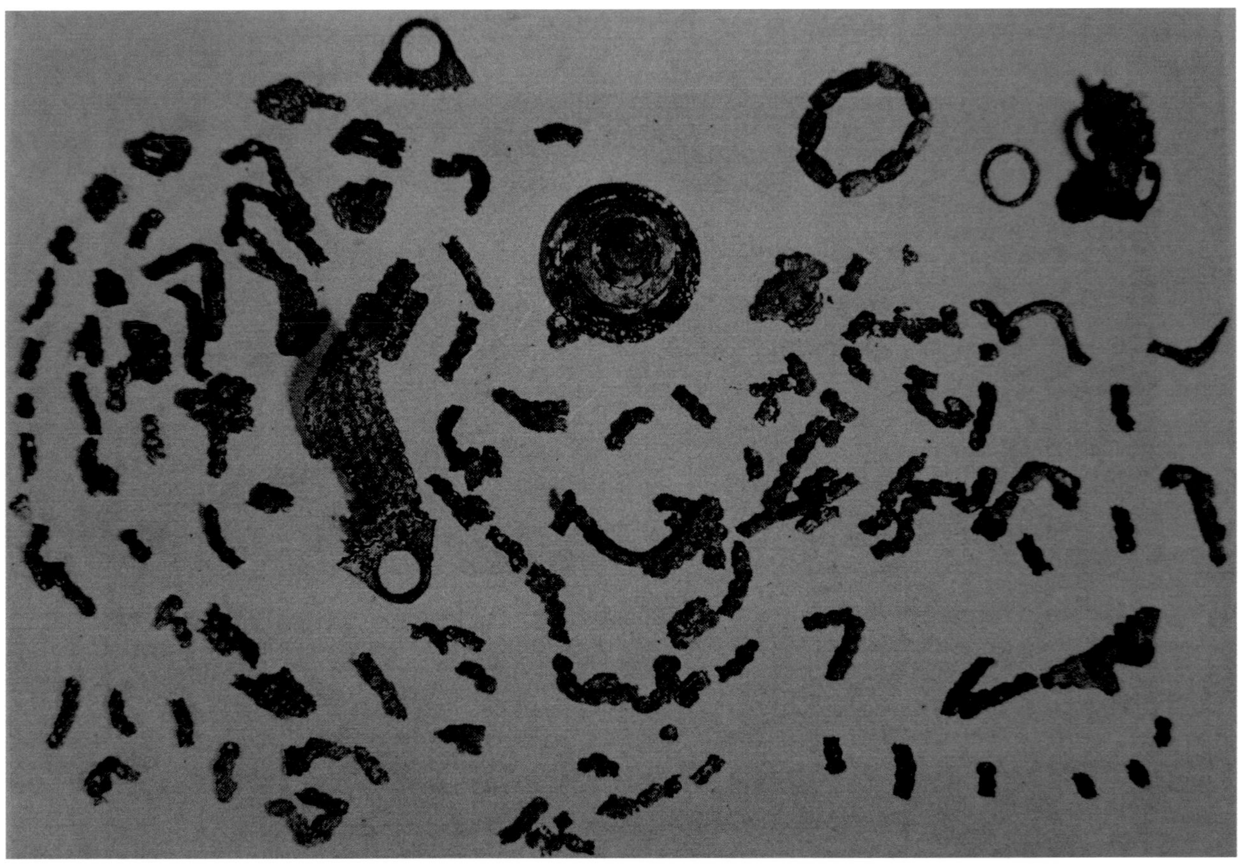

Figure 2.15: Content of grave 165 with the two attachments, pieces of chain, parts of fibulae, a conical object, a large ring and a bracelet. There is something undefined in the upper right corner. After Adamesteanu 1958b, fig. 167.

larger, round beads are alternated with smaller beads.[468] The connection between pendants, in this case the satyr *protomai* and acorns, is also clear. On top of this attachment, there is a tube, only clearly visible on the left side, that seems to be connected with the bigger bead. Such a tubular suspension can be recognised on other disc pendants (fig. 2.14). It is also this particular group of Mould I figurines that reveals most clearly the possible function of the pectorals. The depictions of certain images is used to convey specific aims for the dedication. The figurine is a bearer of these symbols that would have been recognised by the passer-by. They encapsulate the words of a vow and replace an inscription with a single – or in this case repeated – image. The repetition and large size makes the message stronger. This visual language was understood over a very wide area, all around the Mediterranean, even though some of the symbols have clear Greek or Phoenician origins or are derivatives of specific items used in daily life. The later fading of detailed images and increasing number makes the messages more inclusive and general.

The use of visual vows is comparable with the use of images and emoticons on modern day social media platforms. Emoticons have a general message representing a specific feeling, event, or object, but may be used to convey a more personal message in a specific context. Size and number magnify the message. The reason for using a visual language need not be illiteracy. The tangibility and durability of the message may have been a reason for embodying the vows in this way. Their appealing shape and impressive number may have been thought to help convince the deity to whom they were addressed.

II.6.h.ii Linked to the locals: pectoral bands

The pectorals are more complex than regular jewellery and more meaningful. The pectorals have a symbolic value originating in earlier local practices in which magical powers would have been ascribed to objects. The fibulae and pins, as described above, probably held a number of chains attached to the dress. It could be that originally it was the chains themselves that served as a pectoral in local traditions during the early Iron Age. Such is the case

468 The beaded cord has been replaced on the other objects from the same mould series **171-176** by a plain cord.

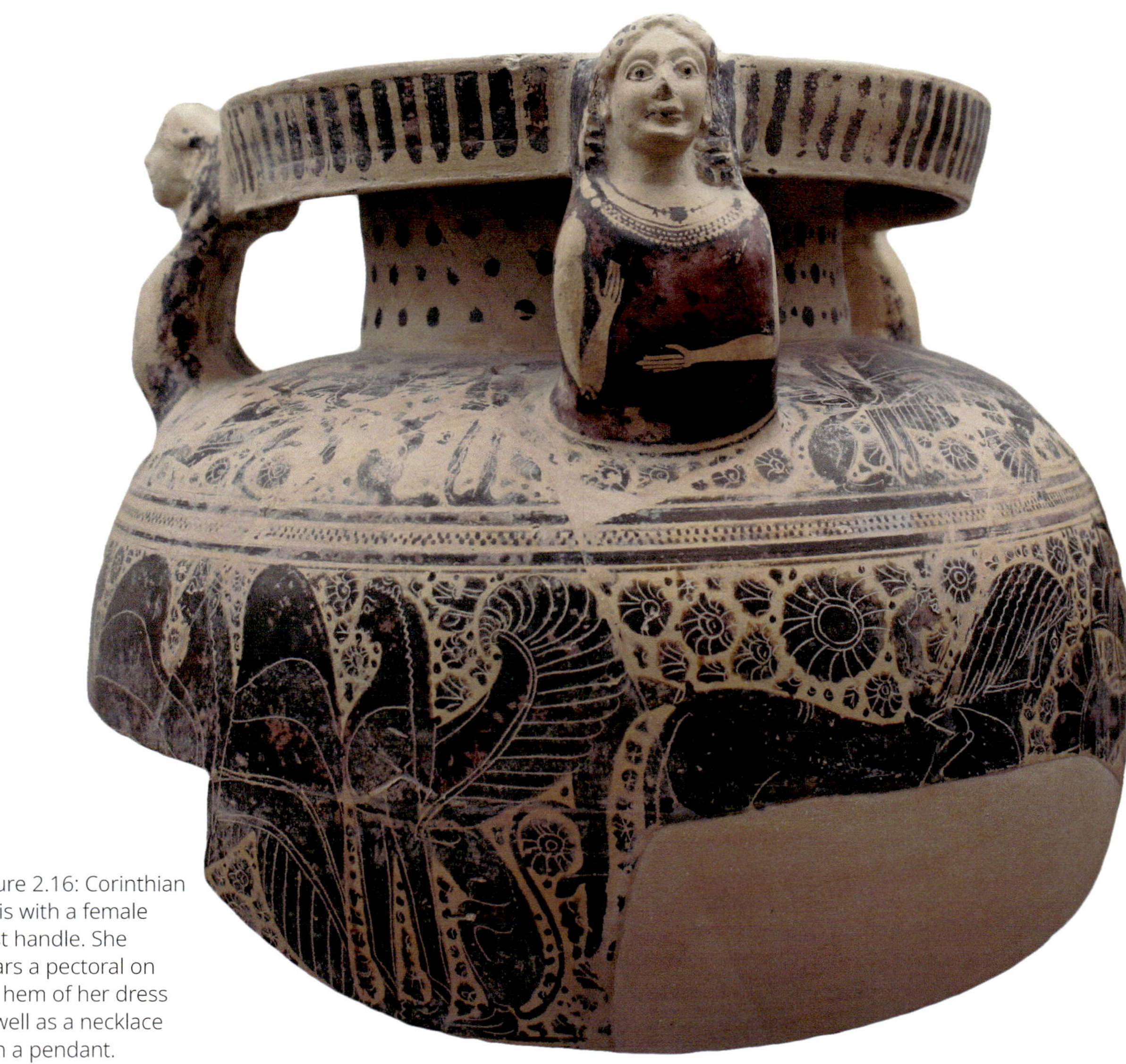

Figure 2.16: Corinthian pyxis with a female bust handle. She wears a pectoral on the hem of her dress as well as a necklace with a pendant.

of the pectoral found in grave 165 at Butera, which consist of at least seven fine-linked, braided, chains, as well as a large stud consisting of four rings that could be closed. In addition, nine biconical beads, a bronze ring and three iron fibulae (fig. 2.15) were found in the grave.[469] Sometimes the chains were short, and small pendants were attached to its finials. Such an item is found for example in grave 57 at Butera.[470] A bronze ring with six chains, each bearing a pendant of the lantern/biconical type, was found in the necropolis of Porrazzelle, Monte Catal-faro.[471] Similar chains, as well as a lantern pendant have also been found at Syracuse[472] as well as in many other early Iron Age tombs.[473] The two sorts of locally common pectorals, even though different from the one depicted on the figurines might have inspired the depiction of pectoral chains. The chloroplasts would have known of these traditional grave gifts and may have extended their application to the figurines.[474]

Empty pectoral bands also appear on the terracottas in Akragas and may simply represent their intrinsic metal value. There are no direct role models for the pectorals known to have existed in real life or in other images, before the Sicilian tradition started. However, there are

469 Necropolis Piano della Fiera: a low burial chamber in the rocks with two skeletons. Adamesteanu 1958b, p.472.

470 Adamesteanu 1958b, p.340.

471 See Adamesteanu 1958b, fig.13c. The small rings of the chains each consist of three parallel links. The approximately 50 tombs here are dated to between the ninth and seventh century BCE. The object is presently exhibited at Museo Civico "Corrado Tamburino Merlini" di Mineo, Sicily.

472 Other beads, pins and fibulae were also found, Syracuse, Fusco necropolis. Leighton 1999, p.235, fig.124.

473 Leighthon 2014, p.104, n.18.

474 Cf. Leighton 1999, p.250-1.

real-life pendants reminiscent of the ones depicted on the figurines' pectorals. They are likely to have functioned in a similar symbolic way in real life as on the figurines, but we lack directly comparable pendants with pectorals. This does not mean that such pectorals did not exist. Indeed, it is likely that the pectorals on the figurines represented real objects but that they were more exclusive than their near-omnipresence on the terracotta figurines may suggest.

A difference between the two sorts of pendants is their three dimensionality. While the similarly shaped objects are often in the round, the earlier large pendants are flatter. Some are also flat, but three-dimensional, like plaques, as if they are made from a thin layer of metal that was embossed or pressed into a mould, **172**. The first technique causes them to have, like our figurines, a front and a rear, while for the second the halves were placed together. It seems that this change in technique of metal reworking is visible on the pendants of the figurines.[475] The pendants have in their most usual form, the disc and ovoid shapes, many similarly shaped counterparts on Geloan and Selinuntine terracotta figurines. Contemporary objects in real life from Sicily itself are not that common however. Below, the different pendant types will be summed up chronologically and as they appear on the figurines together with comparative objects, from a wide variety of periods and places.

There are not so many representations of pectorals other than terracotta figurines. One of them is the depiction of the Moirai on the third frieze of the François vase. The second Moira from the right wears such a cord with six round pendants. The cord is fixed to the peplos by two horizontal pins that are placed on the chest below the shoulder. As mentioned above, the pectoral on the figurines often coincides in form and location with the upper hem of the dress. This seems also the case with a female bust-shaped handle on a Corinthian vase (fig. 2.16).[476] The figure painted in detail wears a triple chain with small links or cords with beads between small discs, attached to her dress on her shoulders. She wears the pectoral on the upper hem of her dress, which is indicated possibly by the fine black line just above it. The pectoral is coloured like her skin, contrasting with the darker coloured dress, and might indicate for the real object a light or shiny coloured material, like metal.[477] In contrast to the pectoral on the François vase, this one does not feature large pendants. It therefore comes closer to the local chain pectorals discussed above. The one on the François vase, with disc-shaped pendants is comparable with the depiction of discs on the figurines. Similar to the handle figurines are some flat female figures found in the terracotta industrial quarter in Selinunte.[478] Their pose, but also the pectoral is comparable. It consists of several rows with fine pendants and a larger one on a separate strand, in the middle. These are dated to the third quarter of the sixth century BCE and could have been made with an imported mould. Such images could have inspired the local coroplasts and appealed to the dedicants who recognised such fine jewellery from their own traditions.

II.6.h.iii Discs and crescents

The disc-shaped pendant is the most commonly used pendant shape in group 1 and remains until the last group. Its form and attachment with a loop is reminiscent of the Etruscan bulla, which had a long history.[479] As early as the Villanovan culture, gold disc pendants were made. Their size is striking and matches the relatively large size of the terracotta figurines. The disc has a tubular suspension attachment.[480] It is this suspension that is common for disc pendants over a wide area and different cultures. In some cases, this type of suspension if clearly visible on the Akragantine figurines (**48**). A later example is also Etruscan. It appears in this case again as the centrepiece, but now combined on a cord with smaller beads.[481] Whether the discs are comparable in their three-dimensionality this early, is not clear. On the figurines, they appear rather flat. A thin sheet with a longer upper part that could be rolled

---

475 Such a bronze mould for the production of earrings, beads and pendants exists, even though it is from the fourth century BCE and of unknown origin. Among them is an acorn. The rosette and possibly the shell would have remained probably single and two-sided, flat, while the other would have been constructed from the two halves. Staatl. Ant. Munich. Wünsche and Steinhart 2010, p.19.

476 Arch. Mus. Palermo. The vase is decorated in horizontal bands with sirens, sphynxes, panthers, roosters and horse riders. It is ascribed to the Painter of Athens 931 and dated 600-570 BCE.

477 She wears a necklace, a fine cord, and a pottery or pomegranate shaped pendant in the middle flanked by a bead and a small delta-shaped pendant. Other female bust-handles of Corinthian pyxides wear a similar necklace with a vase shaped middle pendant or a tight necklace without pendants.

478 Bentz 2014, p.69-70, fig.4.

479 There is a silver 4.5cm high bulla with a depiction in gold of a women on it from the seventh century BCE. Rutishauser 2017, p.141, no.32. From the Hellenistic Period onwards children would wear a bulla as protection. The Romans took over this custom.

480 Found close to Bologna the 7.1cm high disc is dated to the ninth to eight century BCE and consists of two thin discs held together by thread in gold, decorated in the same way with five half globes in a cross and four swastikas. Staatl. Ant. Munich. Wünsche and Steinhart 2010, p.75, no.37. The pendant could have served as a middle piece on a necklace like Wünsche and Steinhart 2010, p.76-7, no.38.

481 This is an example of a finely worked one with a smaller disc suspended from it. Necklace with bulla and gold beads. 7th-5th Century B.C. The Metropolitan Mus. New York, See museum website: https://www.metmuseum.org/art/collection/search/246005.

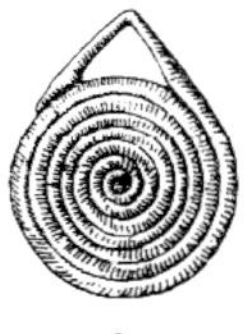
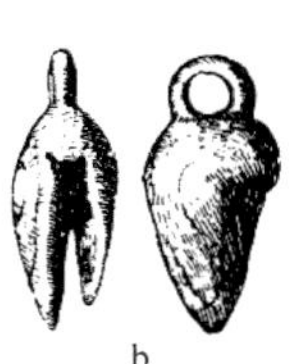
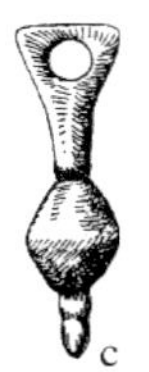
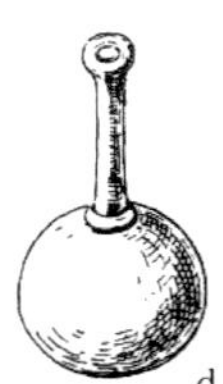

Figure 2.17: Drawing of pendants found in grave contexts in Selinous. The second from left is a particularly common shape. After Trombi 2003, tav. XXIII 69a-d, after Gabrici 1927, p. 362, fig. 155g, m, n, q.

to create a suspension tube is also very possible.[482] The method of hanging something made of metal with such a folded suspension tube is know from phialai. They might have been hung on the walls of the temenos or temple.[483]

The crescent is a motif featuring regularly as a pendant on the figurines, always pointing down and most commonly as the centrepiece. Exceptionally it flanks a disc (**49-50**). It is known as an eastern symbol for the moon, often found together with a disc shape, also seen on the Akragantine figurines. The disc symbolise the sun and is often placed in the crescent in eastern depictions.[484] The Phoenicians took it from the Ancient Near East,[485] where both disc and crescent were applied as a talisman. Their presence in the West would make a transfer of such symbols to Sicily possible.[486] There is one example of a Geloan handmade figurine with an upwards pointing crescent containing the sun in the middle – the most commonly used Phoenician form of the symbol.[487] It is striking that in all four groups of Akragantine figurines, except for the last, the crescent appears prominently. A figurine from the acropolis of Gela, dated as late as the end of the fifth century BCE, still wears a crescent[488] It indicates the remaining symbolic or artistic value of the originally eastern symbol in the mixed culture that these figurines represent.[489]

Several bronze pendants are known from the early Iron Age from the sanctuary of Malophoros, Selinous. Some of these bronze pendants of various shapes show similarities with their depictions on the terracottas: a disc with a spiral form could be made from a fibula, but applied as a pendant. Several other forms are more spherical or almond-shaped. In particular, the second shape (fig. 2.17) is reminiscent of pointed pendant that appeared for the first in group 2, for example, **70**, **100** or very clearly on **179**. They are found in graves at Selinous, as well as in Montagna di Noto and Polizzello dated to the eight century BCE.[490] Bronze pendants, very similar to the other two (fig. 2.17c-d), are also found on the acropolis of Gela. One of them is similar to the biconical shape that was common on the short chains of local early Iron Age pectorals (fig. 2.17c).[491] Similar to this pendant (fig. 2.17c) is a 5.5cm pendant and another is similar to the spherical pendant (fig. 2.17d), both from Macedonia and dated to 750-600 BCE. These sorts of pendants were found in graves in Northern Greece. In central and southern Greece, they are also found at sanctuaries. The similarities are striking, though the Macedonian ones seem slightly more elaborate.[492] These objects make clear that pendants as such are widespread and local variations indicate a specific preference for the form or its symbolic value. The exchange over such a distance shows the intensive contacts with settlements in all directions. The symbolic value or magical power ascribed to such pendants must have been recognised by people living in the Mediterranean area.

II.6.h.iv Figurative pendants

In addition to the possible influence of Boeotian and Corinthian terracotta figurines mentioned above, the pectoral tradition at Akragas may also have been started by an influx of Greeks. After the discs and crescents of the first group, new forms were added. New and differently shaped pendants could have been used to represent other aspects of life to the deities. The pendants discussed

482 Examples of such a suspension method are known from the Artemision in Ephesos. Pülz and Bühler 2009, cat. no.155-160, Farbtaf. 10.

483 Their round shape is reminiscent of the discs, and they possess two tube suspensions; for example, a phiale from Akragas from the same date as the figurines. De Miro 2000, p.295, no.2067, tav.CLIX.

484 In Phoenician art, they are the symbols of Astarte. Likewise, the amphoriskos is a symbol of Tanit. Moscati 2001, p.195, p.424-425.

485 Already in the first half of the second millennium BCE. Metropolitan Mus., New York. Inv. no.47.1a-h. See museum website: https://www.metmuseum.org/art/collection/search/30009049?rpp=20&pg=1&ft=mesopotamia&pos=17.

486 Pendants with Phoenician symbols could very well have reached Akragas, through connections on Sicily, for example, at Panorma (Palermo). Phoenician influence might have also come from Sardinia.

487 Panvini 1998, p.254 VI.48.

488 Panvini and Sole 2005, p.175, tav.LXXVIIId Mus. Arch. Gela inv. no.8478, h. 23.8cm complete, Dewailly 1992, p.100; Albertocchi 2004, p.42 no.627.

489 The symbol become widespread. On an Etruscan gold disc attached with a tube, the downward pointing crescent and disc are surrounded by a granulated Greek meander. Staatl. Ant. Munich. Wünsche and Steinhart 2010, p.78 no.43 from Vulci, dated to the early seventh century BCE.

490 Trombi 2003, p.106.

491 Panvini and Sole 2005, p.53-4 tav.XVIIb-c. Mus. Arch. Gela inv. no.39386 and without number, h. 4.3cm and 2.9cm.

492 Benaki Museum, Athens inv. no.resp.ΓΕ7886 h. 5.3 cm and ΓΕ7871. See museum website: https://www.benaki.org/index.php? option=com_collectionitems&view=collectionitem&Itemid=540&id=140447&lang=en and a second object: https://www.benaki.org/index.php?option=com_collectionitems&view=collectionitem&Itemid=540&id=140528&lang=en.

below are depictions, often *protomai*. Some of them have a known symbolic value and, as such, would have been applied by an Akragantine coroplast who was aware of their significance. The choice of these objects, combined with the earlier disc, gives reason to believe in a parallel application: pectoral pendants expressing the specific vows and wishes of the dedicant.

Series **171**-**177**, an exceptional series in many ways, depicts a number of unconventional pendants. With just some minor variations, the pendants are large, alternating in three rows, and depicting specific items. The first row consists of five bovine *protomai*.[493] The second row consists of at first slightly flat pendants with three aryballoi-shaped pendants alternating with two large discs .[494] On **172**, earlier in the mould series, the aryballoi are not flat but represented in the round, with a clear rim. On the third line of **171**, **172**, **173**, **174** three satyr heads alternate with two acorns. In one instance, the standing figure **176**, the last row contains the objects in reverse order. There are just two satyr heads and three acorns. The pendants are flat but with relief, like pinakes. It could indicate that the pendants were moulded separately and attached to the patrix. The same is true of the fine impression of the beads on **172**. These pendants on **172** have a clear attachment to their beaded cord, a small part in the middle is attached to a suspension tube with the same width as the pendant. The impression is so clear that it looks like a complete, real-life pectoral was used to make this representation in clay, by pressing the real pendants and cord directly into an unfired mould. The size of **172** is rather small for a real-life object, as the disc measures 23mm in diameter.[495]

The difference with the objects described above is that the coroplast decided to 'modernise' the choice of pendants in a style partly influenced by Greek models. While the crescent and disc might have only existed still as heirlooms, contemporary pendants were more likely to be more in a Greek style. The bovine *protomai* or bucranea are depicted as pectorals on a terracotta mask of more than 50cm high from the extramural sanctuary of Predio Sola, Gela.[496] While earrings and other metal adornments are not uncommon on masks, a pectoral adornment is exceptional.[497] This mask seems to suggest once again that moulds for pectorals could have been made after real objects. The five calves depicted on the upper row are very similar, also in number, to the ones on **171, 173-174**. They lack a cord on the mask, while on **172** the cords are even detailed with beads. The second line consists of five elongated pendants alternating with a bead. These objects are interpreted as *alabastra*. Such an elongated shape is common on the Akragantine figurines as well, as on **105-106** on the third cord, with a clear knob on **189** as an earring. Both bulls[498] and a crescent occur on a golden bowl from a tomb at Sant' Angelo Muxaro, about thirty km inland from Akragas. The bowl, once inlaid with a gem, depicts six bulls with remarkable big hooves and four ribs each.[499] A thin dotted crescent is hammered in on one side. Gold-work as well as the technique of dotted lines and the depiction of bulls and a crescent make the object Phoenician in style. It is thought that it was made locally but influenced by Phoenician contact.[500]

There are no depictions on the figurines of female head *protomai*, but female head lead pendants were discovered at S. Anna at Akragas: two different female head pendants, one longer pendant showing part of the neck and hair, the other with a broader face and an open mouth (fig. 2.18).[501] A satyr protome that was also discovered with a thick nose and raised ears. It is very similar to the satyr depicted on figures **171**-**177**.[502] Several female, male and Bes(?) pendants were found in Cuma.[503] The similarity of the lead pendants, their possible original alternating order and the similar suspension attachment make it very likely that the pectorals on the figurines had a counterpart in reality.

---

493 A figurine from Necropoli di Contrada Pezzino, tomb 936, has two pectorals. The lower one features a bovine protome between discs. The figurine is of the block-like model. h. 24 Mus. Arch. Agrigento Inv. no.22587.

494 On other figurines than **172**, the pendants are flatter and have a smoothed surface. The aryballoi are reminiscent of the container-shape discussed above. Gabrici 1927, p.357, fig.154b.

495 The depth of the impression is another argument for this. **172** is surely of the first generation.

496 Panvini 1998, p.182, V.23.

497 Busts or masks might have been usually adorned with real pendants, pectorals and necklaces, as they often feature holes in their ears for earrings.
A bronze pendant from Wadi Bel Gadir represents a cow's head, very similar to the ones depicted on the figurines. White 1975, p.14, fig.1.

498 In mythology, the bull appears in one of the labours of Heracles, the Cretan bull and in the story of Zeus in disguise bringing Europa to the eponymous continent. The story of Europa was very suitable for the colonizers depicted on a metope of temple Y at Selinous and soon became a motif in itself, depicted on plaques and figurines on Sicily, as well at Akragas.

499 Three other bowls from the same tomb are lost. This bowl is held by the British Museum, Inv. no.1772,0314.70 See museum website: https://www.britishmuseum.org/research/collection_online/collection_object_details.aspx?objectId=463325&partId=1&searchText=1772,0314.70&page=1.

500 Jenkins and Sloan 1996, p.237, no.140. Granulation is a very common feature in Phoenician gold workmanship.Others state that the bowl is a Greek colonial product, perhaps from Gela, Vagnetti 1972; Falcone 1988.

501 They have been found together in S. Anna, Akragas: Schnitt A, Sekt. O, US 2 in the context of wall parts with fragmented roof-tiles, stones and pebbles.

502 Cf. AG8941 De Miro 2000, no.1539, tav.CXI.

503 Gabrici 1927.

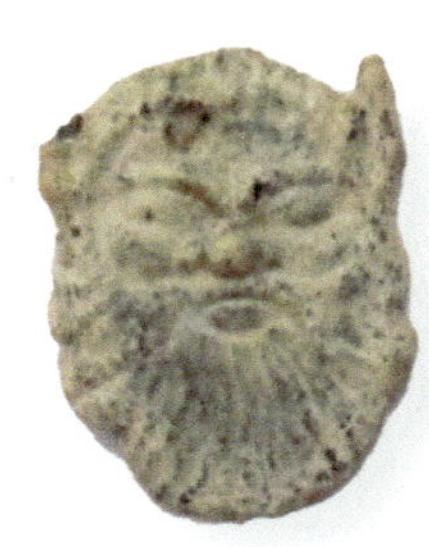
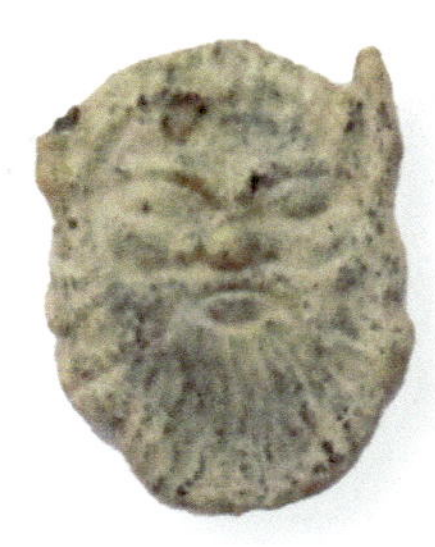
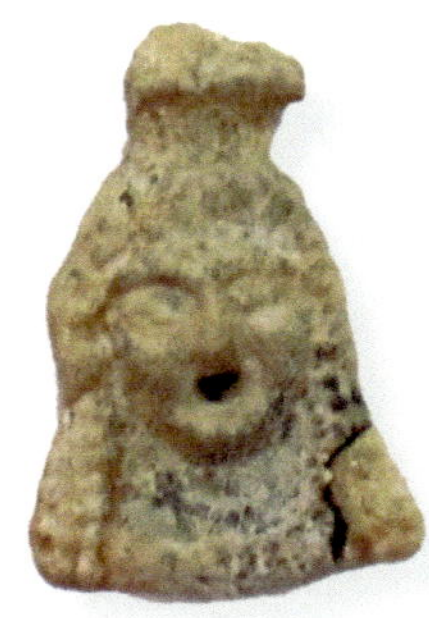

Figure 2.18: Lead pendants of a satyr and two female head protomai, found at the extra-mural sanctuary of S. Anna, Akragas; scale 2:1.

A golden necklace with six female *protomai* with tube attachments alternating with six small golden beads was found in a grave at Ruvo di Puglia. The chubby faces with the wide nose and smiling mouth are reminiscent of the faces of the figurines. Their tube attachment is similar to the lead pendants.[504] The function of this broad tube attachment and the numerous bronze biconical beads might be to keep the object in a certain position on the necklace, so they did not touch one another. A similarly regular spread of pendants on the cord is visible on the figurines.[505] Several pendants have also been found at the Sanctuary of Demeter and Kore at Cyrenaica: an ivory pendant with a female protome predates the foundation of Cyrenaica and an almost 4cm high satyr protome of silver is dated to the late sixth century BCE.[506]

A throned figurine from Taranto wears a pectoral band with alternating female and monkey *protomai.*[507] Another protome, absent from Akragas, but appearing on Selinuntine figurines is the lion. The lion *protome* appears as the central pendant on the upper pectoral band.[508] From a grave at Pezzino, Akragas, a lion or dog *protome* stone pendant came to light.[509] These variations might indicate that the specific depicted figure has a special meaning and might symbolise a certain value, such as health or prosperity. The monkey for example, though not depicted on pendants, frequently appears in Akragantine terracotta objects caring for a baby. The grateful dedicant or the person in need could have used such a pendant and dedicated it to the benevolent deity.

The pottery pendants on the second line, alternating with discs are reminiscent of Etruscan aryballoi-shaped pendants. The tube-attached pendants are spherical with a slightly conical bottom, and date from the seventh century BCE. They could have been used as a small container and are thought to have been inspired or even invented by the Phoenicians.[510] Another possibility is their function as perfume holder shaped like Etruscan bullae. The representation on **172** is three-dimensional and makes their use as small containers very possible.

Another form on the third row, alternating with the satyr *protomai*, is the acorn. The acorn is very common in metalwork and as a jewellery pendant. Some terracotta biconical objects from Akragas, eleven in total, have been interpreted as acorns as well. They must have had a full length of about 8-10cm.[511] Acorns appear as pendants on Etruscan jewellery from the end of the sixth century BCE. The very finely worked golden pendants are made in the round with a smooth lower part and lozenge- shaped and patterned upper part with a loop, hanging from mirroring

504 Mus. Arch. Naz. Taranto Inv. no.6429; Langlotz and Hirmer 1963, p.64, pl. VII, Lippolis 1996, p.147 dated 520-500 BCE. Each pendant is about 2 cm, which is slightly larger than the Akragantine lead pendants.

505 These long biconical beads are also known from Rhodes and found as well in Etruria, dated to the second quarter of the seventh century BCE. In the latter case, they are alternated with spherical beads and decorated with fine lines. Many bronze examples are also known from Etruria. Rutishauser 2017, p.140, no.30. Verger believes the longer biconical beads are later than the small ones. Verger 2011, p.34-5.

506 Seventeen small bronze shells with a hole or a suspension loop were also found at Cyrenaica. Warden 1992 p.51. The shell might have been connected with seafaring.

507 Mus. Arch. Naz. Taranto Inv. no.1791. Lippolis 1996, cat. no. 135 dated to the second half of the sixth century BCE, h. 21.1cm.

508 Dewailly 1992, p.110-4, type B XIX.

509 Together with stone bobbins and bronze earrings? from Necropoli Contrada Pezzino, Akragas, tomb F/398. Mus. Arch. Agrigento. Veder Greco 1988, p.334.
A bull combined with a lion protome in gold on the upper side from the Artemision at Ephesos. Pülz and Bühler 2009 cat., no.42., Taf. 11/ Farbtaf. 7.

510 Die Etrusker: Weltkultur im antiken Italien 2017, p.125 no.12a. That is very possible as it is reminiscent of a Phoenician pendant from Palermo, which is also described as an alabastron shape. Spanò Giammellaro 1995, p.33-56, p.35 n.24.

511 AGS10941, AGS10938 and AGS10935; Fiorentini, Calì and Trombi 2010, cat. nos. 26, 77, 78 tav.XXXV.3.

ducks.[512] Flat acorns were applied as thin silver appliques, as found at Taranto from the second half of the sixth century BCE.[513] The combination of acorns with satyrs, as on this pectoral band, provides the context for an interpretation of the third row of pendants as a reference to sexuality. The acorn refers to the physical appearance of a penis. Aristophanes mentions the acorn in this sense in the *Lysistrata* in connection with a golden necklace/ pectoral (*hormos*).[514]

The satyr head is a very common motif and appears in often in different materials. The ridiculous image protects the wearer from harm, an apotropaic function. Also in gold, they appear to be a common depiction on necklaces. On a necklace from Palestrina, dated to the second half of the sixth century BCE the bearded figurine in the middle is flanked by three palmette pendants. Small beads hold the tube-attached pendants in place.[515] The satyr or silenos in general might have been seen as a contrasting gender to the female figurine. These opposite associations, female virginity and male sexuality, appear from a particular figurine (**198**) that could be reconstructed with the help of another example from the same mould series:[516] an ithyphallic satyr runs away with a block-shaped female figure. In contrast to the satyr, she is very static, defenceless and without arms. The polos, the block-shaped body, and the pectoral pendants make her very similar to the terracotta figurines, specifically those in group 1. Comparing the size of the satyr with that of the women, this might be considered a depiction of the cult statue. The muscled satyr has a large head with beard and big ears. He holds the statue with his left hand and his tail with his right. The pinax like figure depicts a satyr in an act that is reminiscent of the abduction of a bride/nymh, a known theme.[517] Framed in this depiction, the goddess is depicted here as the representative of the future bride, characteristic of chastity. His phallus reveals his intentions and strongly marks not just their opposite gender, but their opposite roles also. The satyr *protomai* on the terracotta figurines might similarly symbolise male fertility and sexuality,[518] like the acorns.

II.6.h.v Other beads and pendants with their real-life counterparts from other sites

Polychrome glass paste beads of Phoenician origin and style are contemporary with the figurines. Several small rings and human *protomai* that served as pendants in the middle of a necklace were also discovered at S. Anna at Akragas. A light blue head, possibly Horus, with white eyes and a suspension hole was found among the sporadic finds at the Pezzino Necopolis.[519] These objects date from between the sixth and the fourth century BCE, and though not directly represented, except for possibly the beads on **172**, were commonly used jewellery, as well as being used as votives.

Biconical bronze beads from the sixth century BCE were also found in several places at Akragas. Their size and form meant that they could have been applied as spacers to hold the larger pendants apart.[520] There are several other sorts of beads found on Sicily, as well as similar items in other regions.[521] A copper necklace or pectoral dated to the eight to seventh century BCE was found in Macedonia. It was made of very similar biconical beads, ranging from larger in the middle and smaller towards the finials.[522] Though they are much larger and slightly stretched in shape, Sicilian objects could have influenced the Macedonian beads or vice versa.[523] Similar beads, biconical and spherical, from the same period are found in the Artemision at Ephesos.[524]

Some late figurines, from the second half of the fifth century BCE depict the typical gorgoneion as a breast decoration. On one Classical figurine from Akragas, such a protome is placed in an Egyptian manner, hanging low on the chest on a chain: a snake at each side, a disk

512 The necklace pendants feature a very small knob, and are reminiscent of the amphoriskoi shape. Staatl. Ant. Munich. Wünsche and Steinhart 2010, p.98-9, no.55.

513 Six appliques of an acorn and one of a disc with a griffin on it. Mus. Arch. Naz. Taranto Inv. no.51.618. Lippolis 1996, cat. n.107.

514 Aristoph. Lys. 407-13 mentions the acorn twice: ἡ βάλανος. It fell out of its opening and the goldsmith is asked to fit it back in. The acorn refers at the same time to the necklace and to the sexual organs in a sexist joke.

515 Ant. Staatl. Mus. Berlin http://library.artstor.org/asset/BERLIN_DB_10313801726. Web. 17 Jul 2018.

516 One example is in the Louvre, another one was in a private collection in the Netherlands, but is now lost. For a description, photographs and references see Catalogue no.198.

517 There are examples from fifth-century BCE Tarento: Arch. Mus. Amsterdam APM01173. On a fourth century BCE example the satyr is accompanied by a rooster: APM01174.

518 Such abduction scenes of a satyr with a maenad appear on vase painting from the same period. It is also reminiscent of Thasian silver tetradrachmai with a depiction of a satyr abducting a nymph.

519 Arch. Mus. Agrigento inv. no.23163.

520 Four of them are found together with a glass paste amphoriskos in grave 9 A of the necropolis di Contrada Mosè. De Miro 1980-1, p.568 tav.XL fig.2: AG 2308.7.

521 For a detailed account of these metal objects, see Verger 2011, p.34-5. A biconical bead from the Malophoros sanctuary, Selinous: Gabrici 1927 358 fig.154.e.

522 Benaki Museum, Athens inv. no.ΓΕ 20677 See museum website: https://www.benaki.org/index.php?option=com_collectionitems&view=collectionitem&id=140719& lang=en&Itemid=162&lang=el.

523 Also spherical beads and a longer one from the sixth century BCE are reminiscent of Sicilian necklaces/pectoral bands. Benaki Museum, Athens inv. no.ΓΕ 1525 See museum website: https://www.benaki.org/index.php?option=com_collectionitems&view=collectionitem&id=140113& lang=en&Itemid=162&lang=el.

524 Pülz and Bühler 2009, cat. no.180-181 (biconical); 191-193 (sphere with lines), Farbtaf. 12.

on top of its head.[525] A probably Archaic figurine wore a gorgoneion on the upper pectoral band, but is now lost.[526] On a statuette from Gela the gorgoneion is finely detailed and placed on top of a small triple pectoral. The figurine also wore a lophos, making it more likely that she was indeed meant to depict Athena.[527] Another example from Selinous even has gorgoneia in triple form, applied possibly by a separate mould on top of a pectoral with probably three rows of multiple pendants.[528] A bust from Himera appears with several gorgoneia, three on the fragment of the right part on the second row of the pectorals.[529] The late date and the different iconographic features of those examples exclude an interpretation of all gorgoneia depictions as representations of Athena's aegis. It seems the use of such symbolic *protomai* gained terrain when parallel Athena figurines became known, and eventually replaced the earlier pectorals. The gorgoneion as an apotropaic object stands by itself and confirms the protective function of the pendants. Again, this parallel in the choice of the pectoral, reveals that the Sicilian pectoral pendants were not chosen randomly nor simply to be decorative, but were selected as specific and strongly symbolic items that could convey an embodied wish.

Simetite, a darker red variation of amber, was found in south-eastern Sicily and was exported from there since the Bronze Age.[530] The Etruscans used simetite in pendants and beads for making necklaces. On such a necklace from the sixth century BCE, the middle pendant is bright red, in the form of a disc with a tube shape attachment. Two other pendants seem female *protomai*.[531] Also striking is the combination of gold and amber necklaces and pectorals of a young girl at the Braida necroplis in Serra di Vaglio, southern Italy.[532] Among the many different shapes and sizes of amber pendants, there are several that are reminiscent of the numerous 'fruit' or 'pointed' (irregular) pendants on the Akragantine figurines. Some have a tube-shaped attachment and there is a somewhat inconsistent alteration between larger and smaller pendants.[533] One other object worth mentioning is a 6.7cm amber bead shaped likee a standing female figure or kore. She has detailed clothes and wears an empty pectoral band between large round clasps.[534] It is very likely that magical powers were ascribed to amber pendants and possible that the second, more numerous type of pendants on the figurines represent amber beads.[535]

In total, the number of pendants found at Akragas itself is rather scarce. There are, however, many indications that such pendants and beads existed in real life, as their forms and iconography are recognisable from real objects found and used in the wider area. The question remains of whether they were worn in daily life or created only for very specific occasions, such as dedications, grave gifts or possibly the adornment of the bride.[536]

II.6.h.vi Comparison with other cultures

Terracotta figurines in several other cultures are also adorned with a multitude of pectorals. The Etruscans, who have appeared above already several times in comparisons, were well known for their metal mining, and their jewellery is often strikingly similar to what appears on the Akragantine and other Sicilian figurines. Etruscan dedications consisted mainly of metal and jewellery, as a way of demonstrating status. Pendants as amulets seem to have been used by the Etruscans in a similar way as on Sicily, as is apparent from the Akragantine figurines. The bulla shape in particular was a special pendant, serving as an amulet for children. This small round or flattened metal container probably had an apotropaic function. It may also have had a protective

525 Inv. no.AG 9107 (250) Mus. Arch. Agrigento. She wears a chiton, indicated with vertical thin lines, and a draped himation, small round fibulae, and a tight, rather thick, necklace. Head and lower body not preserved. De Miro 2000, p.246, no.1482, tav.LXXI and dated by him to the first half of the fifth century BCE. Dress and jewellery suggest rather the second half of the fifth century.

526 As just a drawing and no photograph has been left and the object was already missing at the time of Blinkenberg, it cannot be excluded that a disc was mistaken for a gorgoneion head. The figurine would have been 31cm high and was part of a private collection on Sicily. Blinkenberg 1917, p.27 fig.3; Winter 1903, p.127 no.1. See also the discussion in section I.7.c on the gorgoneion.

527 Panvini 1998, p.54, I.60.

528 From Selinous: Gabrici 1927, p.272, tav.LIX.7. On this figurine a gorgoneion features on the frontal part of the seat, just below the cushion on each side. It is dated to around the middle of the fifth century BCE.

529 The bust was found at Temple B in Himera and dated to the second half of the fifth century BCE. The first row of pendants seems to depict acorns. A head with paint residues is thought to have belonged to the same object. S. Vassallo, Himera, Città greca, Guida alla storia e ai monumenti. 2005, p.87, fig.147.

530 Leighton 1999, p.144. For the earlier use and ascribed value of amber in funerary context and applied as jewellery, see Dewailly 2010.

531 Staatl. Ant. Munich Inv. no.342-6.

532 Photograph and explanation: See museum website: fig.3, http://museumcatalogues.getty.edu/amber/intro/2/.

533 A 4.6cm long prone sphinx looking backwards is the largest pendant in the middle. There is a shell-shaped pendant next to it. Some of the shapes, in particular the long ones, are reminiscent of the amulets of the small boys.

534 J. Paul Getty Mus. Malibu Inv. no.76.AO.77 See museum website: http://museumcatalogues.getty.edu/amber/objects/8/ and: http://www.getty.edu/art/collection/objects/7385/unknown-maker-pendant-standing-female-figure-kore-etruscan-or-south-italian-600-500-bc/.

535 The irregularity in forms of the pendants on the figurines could point to worked stone of different sorts.

536 For its relative rarity in mainland Greece, Lee suggests objects might have been purpose-made as dedications or grave gifts in the Archaic and Classical Period. Lee 2015, p.142.

function for adults.[537] This object has a very long history of use, as the earliest were found in graves from the eight century BCE. According to Culican, the Etruscan bulla, found in large numbers as pendants in Etruscan jewellery, was introduced by the Phoenicians. At Punic sites, the bulla is more vase-shaped, while the Etruscan bulla is stubbier and heart-shaped. Italic jewellers copied different shapes. The Punic origin seems to be supported by the disc and crescent shapes also found in early Etruscan jewellery. The disc and crescent is known as a cultic symbol of the Phoenicians, while for the Etruscans it might have had no specific religious connotation.[538] The Italic artisans were inspired by its form and might have taken over its shape, but not necessarily with the same religious meaning.

The second comparable figurines are Cyprian. Female statuary in stone and terracotta wear large, striking necklaces with beads and pendants. In addition, earrings are common. The figurines and adornments are different from the Sicilian objects, although they date to roughly the same period, during the sixth and fifth century BCE.[539] The jewellery is abundant, particularly the necklaces that hang in several strings around the neck, sometimes with a triangular pendant between the breasts. Some of them carry a dedication and are therefore interpreted as worshippers or priestesses while the similarly adorned figurines holding their breasts are interpreted as deities. What they have in common is thus that any difference in dress between deity and worshipper is not particularly striking. The difference, if there is one, is in the actions or gestures of the figurines, and the distinction may deliberately have been vague.[540] The Phoenicians too appear to have provided the inspiration for these Cyprian objects. Examples demonstrating a Phoenician origin are three golden pendants in the round from Marion, Cyprus, dated to the fifth century BCE. Two are amphoriskos-shaped and one had a pomegranate/aryballos shape. They might have form a similar triple alternating arrangement, as on the figurines.[541] Numerous pointed pendants are also common on fine jewellery from Cyprus. Due to their finess and pointed shape, they are often interpreted as seeds. Seeds represent the unblossomed flower, which symbolises the unmarried bride. At the same time, they are reminiscent of the amphoriskoi, [542] which seems to have been the most common shape for pendants from the Classical Period in the Mediterranean world.[543] Another striking example from Cyprus that combines several of the pendant sorts mentioned above on the figurines is a Phoenician-style necklace dated from the end of the eight century BCE. Among other sorts of beads, it also displays acorns, a disc, and a bull protome. It is similarity in the alternation between pendants and beads as well as the means of suspension: a small tube for the pendants and a gold setting for the bull's head.[544]

The third group of comparably adorned figures on which large jewellery plays a role is Iberian. Again the distinction between deities and aristocratic humans is hard to make. The bulla shape is also common in this culture.[545] A pectoral with pendants in one short and three longer strands is dated to the fifth to fourth century BCE.[546] The influence of Phoenician culture is apparent in some of the disc-shaped pendants and in terracottas with a nose-ring.[547] The trading of mined metals was the cause of intensive contact and exchange with the Iberian peninsula, resulting in Phoenician/Punic

537 A terracotta female figurine lying down on a bench and putting oil on her hand wears very large pendants: an elongated shape is flanked by seeds with lines and smaller pointed or fruit-shaped pendants. The first two sorts and larger ones have the typical tube suspension. From the necropolis of Monte Abatone, second half of the sixth century BCE, now in Mus. Naz. Etr. Villa Giulia. Rutishauser 2017, p.185; still in the fouth to third century BCE, the Etruscans depict women of high class with large pendants. A terracotta bust from Cerveteri wears a palmette-topped half disc, flanked by elongated shapes and bullae. Rutishauser 2017, p.278 no.94. Eventually the use of the bulla was adopted by the Romans. K. Hladíková 2018. Protection of Children? A Case Study from the Early Iron Age Cemetery of Quattro Fontanili, Veii. Studia Hercynia XXII/1 56-76.

538 Culican 1973, p.37-3. The bulla as amulet seems to have become the variant for boys, while the crescent or lunula would have been hung around the neck of a girl. This distinction is clearly from later centuries and not of concern here. Glinister F. 2017,Ch. 7: Ritual and Meaning: Contextualising Votive Terracotta Infants in Hellenistic Italy. J. Draycott, E. Graham (eds.) Bodies of Evidence: Ancient Anatomical Votives Past, Present and Future.

539 The Cyprian figurines are inspired in form by the eastern Astarte figure, standing, naked and supporting her breasts with her hands, as a fecundity goddess. Figurines giving birth confirm this interpretation. See Dewailly 2010.

540 Karageorghis, J. 1977 La grande déesse de Chypre et son culte : à travers l'iconographie, de l'époque. néolithique au VIème s.a.C. Lyon: Maison de l'Orient. p.206ff. Pl. 34a, c, d (terracottas) p.215 Pl. 36a-c.

541 From tomb 10. They have a suspension loop and a decoration of palmettes made with wire. They are dated to 450-400 BCE. Williams and Ogden 1994,p.246 no.181.

542 They are dated from 450-400 BCE and the small beads inbetween show much variation. Williams and Ogden 1994, p.251 no.179, p.245.

543 A gold amphoriskos pendant with suspension hole said to be from Melos and dated to 500-450 BCE. Williams and Ogden 1994.

544 It was found among twenty-two other pieces of gold ornaments in the tomb MLA 1742 at Larnaka Town, Cyprus and probably belonged to a member of the upper class. Pavlos Flourentzos et Maria Luisa Vitobello, « The Phoenician gold jewellery from Kition, Cyprus », ArcheoSciences, 33 | 2009, p.143-149, fig.5.

545 A life-size enthroned statue found in a grave context wearing a necklace with large bullae pendants is interpreted as the deceased. The so-called 'Dama del Llano de la Consolación' Inv. no.38431 Mus. Arch. Nat. Madrid. It is dated to the end of the fifth century BCE.

546 Metropolitan Mus., New York. Inv. no.1995.403.1 See museum website: https://www.metmuseum.org/art/collection/search/327510.

547 Harden 1963, p.199 pl. 77.

styled objects. Silver in particular is likely to have been imported from Iberia, at least in the case of Selinous.[548]

All of these cultures, Etruscan, Cyprian, Iberian and Argive were heavily influenced by the Phoenicians in the way they applied and shaped jewellery. The Phoenicians themselves adopted Egyptian and Ancient Near Eastern symbols. The crescent with sun disc would have been an ornamentation copied from Egyptian amulets.[549] Phoenician customs too are very likely to have influenced local cultures on Sicily. As mentioned, the metal trade was probably the basis for such an exchange.

The influence of Phoenician jewellery and its diffusion into neighbouring cultures might also have reached Akragas. Disc pendants with a tubular shape and a granule in the middle are known from Tharros, Sardinia to Cyprus. The necklaces from Tharros in the British Museum are striking because they are very similar to the two upper long necklaces depicted on the limestone goddess/priestess from Cyprus: the thick necklaces with beads each have a large pendant in the middle.[550] On the real necklaces, it is clear that the pendants are of metal and contain symbols. The necklaces also have smaller metal pendants in the shape of discs, [551] sometimes with a crescent depicted on them. As solar symbols, they could refer to the different phases of the moon.[552] There is, however, an Archaism in these depictions that date mostly from the sixth to the beginning of the fifth century BCE, while the necklaces are dated from the eight or seventh century BCE. A similar Archaism (but for the most part dated to an earlier time) as is visible in the jewellery of the Akragantine terracottas and the real jewellery that served as its model.

II.6.h.vii Cultural exchange

The Punic settlements themselves adopted the iconography of Sicilian figurines, probably under the influence of Akragantine figurines. Some figurines found at Mozia are thought to have come from Akragas.[553] Later, a figurine was developed with a large round shape like a billowing mantle behind the upper body. The fine details and high number of pendants on these figurines reveals a fifth century BCE date. Also on the Iberian Peninsula, a long tradition of bust figurines bears the traces of Sicilian influence. Bell-shaped figurines with a polos and a pectoral with one or more flowers are found in high number at the shrine of Es Culleram, Ibiza. These winged figures, painted and decorated with gold foil, were dedications to Tanit. Their bodies, with their abstract form and absence of arms, are comparable to the Sicilian figurines. Busts do appear sometimes with separately made arms. Their ears and nose are sometimes pierced in order to add jewellery. The terracotta grave gifts, both male and female, wear extensive jewellery: pectorals and necklaces with pendants, earrings and nose rings of metal or in terracotta.[554] Both the Punic jewellery, such as boat-earrings, and the depictions on the figurines show great similarity with the Sicilian objects.

Greek coroplastics could have influenced the typical Sicilian pectoral, but besides the Argive objects, it is less evident for an early date. Perhaps it was rather the reverse a century later. A terracotta polos-wearing female figurine, thought to be from the Peloponnese, wears both a tight necklace and a pectoral with amphoriskoi.[555]

The influence of pendants in connection with the kourotrophoi might be seen in the southern Italian figurines of toddlers with chains of amulets, found at the southern urban sanctuary near the Italic Temple, Paestum. These swaddled infants wear a diagonal cord across their body with objects like the crescent and the disc, among other pendants.[556] The 'temple boy' figurines are comparable. These terracotta figurines of young boys in a specific pose are dated from 450 BCE onwards and found mainly in Cyprus, but also in Carthage. Some wear diagonally over their body a string with small pendants in the form of various objects, such as crescents, discs and

548 De Angelis 2016, p.252.

549 Culican 1973, p.38, n.28.

550 The third and lowest necklace is often very different. It contains just one object on a thin cord. A tight necklace is often worn high around the neck and seems to consist of three beaded necklaces. Some more examples of necklaces have smaller metal pendants in the shape of discs, sometimes with a crescent depicted on them. British Museum: Inv. no.1856,1223.719 (sixth century BCE), 1856,1223.856 (seventh to sixth century BCE).

551 The discs of the Phoenician jewellery usually have a granule in the middle. This is omitted on the discs of the Akragantine figurines. It might have been painted, but traces of such additions are not found. It might also be that the Phoenicians indicated a sort of seed, as the shape is not always completely round either.

552 For example, British Museum: Inv. no.1856,1223.719 from the sixth century BCE, 1856,1223.629 from the seventh to fifth century BCE, 1856,1223.856 from the seventh to sixth century BCE.

553 Albertocchi 1999, p.355-6 fig.1 and Albertocchi 1999.

554 Necroplis of Puig des Molins, Ibiza. Dated to the fourth-third century BCE. They hold their arms, interpreted as a prayer gesture. The most famous one is probably the Dama de Ibiza, Mus. Arq. Nac. Madrid. Inv. no.1923/60/541. See museum website: http://ceres.mcu.es/pages/Main?idt=62108&inventary=1923%2F60%2F541&table=FMUS&museum= MANT#.XOamQoncNHo.

555 Benaki Museum, Athens inv. no.ΓΕ 30914. The website states that it is perhaps from Mantineia, Peloponnese, 550-500 BCE. See museum website: https://www.benaki.org/index.php?option=com_collectionitems&view=collectionitem&id=140837&Itemid=540&lang=en.

556 Besides these figurines of swaddled infants, there were also terracotta uteri and figurines of pregnant women found. Miller Ammerman 2007, p.142-3.

elongated objects.[557] Three of the temple boys – without amulets, but seated in the same pose – are thought to be from Gela and dated to around 450 BCE.[558] There is also one from Selinous.[559]

II.6.h.viii Function and meaning

As a gift to the deity, jewellery was a very common choice in Greek culture. It would function as a votive for the gods, and at the same time served as a status marker of the dedicant. From lists with dedications, we know, for example, that in exchange for a cure several jewellery items were dedicated in Asklepios' sanctuary in Athens. The items donated – like the illness cured – were personal and – like health – very valuable. For male deities, wreaths were a common gift, for the goddesses, jewellery, such as for Athena Polias.[560] On Sicily itself and in southern Italy, the amount of pendants and other jewellery objects is high, as is their variety both in material and form: amber, metal, bone, and glass paste. There was an established network of metal exchange, including jewellery.[561] It is probably through the trading networks, ports, and settlements of the Phoenicians that the inhabitants of Akragas – who themselves were probably from different origins – came into contact with finely worked gold and silver items. With the exchange of jewellery, came new forms that were appreciated for their aesthetic or semiotic value and were adopted and applied in a similar or different way. Bronze Age Sicily already had a living tradition of the application of beads into which the new forms could be taken over.

It would have been the forms and shapes of the new items that appealed. Unlike the collection of bronze items in the large jar at the S. Anna Sanctuary, most of the pendant forms were meaningful because of their shape. Their function as a marker of status would have certainly played a role, but the imitation of similar forms in baser metals like bronze or lead, and other depictions of the forms on the figurines indicate that some of the pendants were, like their Phoenician originals, applied as amulets. The pendant in the form of a small container might have held something to which a special power was ascribed. To what extent they were seen as magical objects is difficult to say, but it would have fitted with Greek customs too, as the Greeks also used phylacteries or apotropaic talismans. The locally common custom of protecting temples with a large Medusa head signifies similar beliefs and shows that images from other cultures – in this case the Greek Medusa – could be applied as apotropaic objects. Magical powers were traditionally ascribed to gemstones in particular.[562] Whether the small pendants and beads could also be interpreted in this way, is questionable.[563]

Application as a musical or percussive instrument has already been discussed above. Certain chains or pendants could have been used in a cultic context to produce a rhythmic sound, adding to the sphere of the supernatural. The losely hanging chains in particular might have produced a noise when the wearer moved. For the beads and pendants such an application is not so obvious. The pectoral on the figurines contains one to three cords and sometimes the attachment to the pendants or the beads in between can be recognised. It seems that the carefully placed and designed smaller number of pendants may have functioned differently from the larger number of similar pendants, usually seven or eight per cord, which may have been used to produce a noise. Three-dimensionality plays a role in this as well. The thicker pendants, from group 2 onwards, could have hold a small ball or clapper, functioning like a bell.

The large flat discs, appearing on figurines in combination with the crescent, are probably symbolic. Their form was probably adopted from the Phoenicians, and may still have referred to the sun, moon, and the concept of time in general. The upper line of pendants often seems to be the one with the more traditional objects, the disc or crescent. Additional bands could have had not only pendants in new forms, but also with new functions. The sound-producing small chains predate the pectoral pendants as depicted on the figurines, but the smaller pendants could have revived the idea of musical pectorals.

The chains with beads are found locally as pectorals in graves. Their form and function are in some sense modified through the presence of other cultural groups. This starts clearly with the Phoenicians who applied pendants in the form of discs and crescents. This form transference might be explained by the recognition of an Ashtarte-like goddess. Pendants would have been added to the existing custom of a pectoral chain. Metal became the marker of wealth and the pendants reflected the prosperity of the settlement. The migrating Greeks, bringing their own mythology, added their own symbols and charms, which were probably apotropaic. It could be that a bride's jewellery is connected with these applications. The figurines are offered to the mythological bride-goddess Persephone, connecting both the underworld and marriage as a transitional goddess. These different identities are not distinguished that clearly and remain a hypothetical interpretation for this period.

557 Louvre Museum Inv. no AM 2828, AM 2927 (fifth century BCE); Metropolitan Mus. New York Inv. no.74.51.2756 (begin fourth century BCE), 74.51.2767 (fourth century BCE). https://britishmuseum.withgoogle.com/object/limestone-temple-boy.

558 British Museum Inv. no.1863,0728.284, 1863,0728.283 and 1863,0728.282.

559 This one also lacks the amulets, but is seated in the same pose and is similarly chubby. Gabrici 1927, tav.XXIII.6.

560 Williams and Ogden 1994, p.32.

561 Lippolis 2009, p.39.

562 Lee 2015, p.140.

563 Verger 2011, p.34-5.

Persistence in the iconography of some pendant forms even in the fifth century BCE is seen in the form of discs and crescents. The form might have continued to have been appealing, but a shift in symbolic value could also have occurred. Figurines as grave gifts might have still served in the old function of the amber pectorals, as protection for the deceased. The pectorals may have undergone a transformation to being used daily as a form of amulet. Similarly, gorgoneia, satyrs and monkeys may also have been adopted and added to the apotropaic repertoire following interactions with (or the settlement of) people from different cultures. This cultural hybridity may have aided contact and interaction between different cultures and ethnicities. Such contact made political unity easier, through shared cross-cultural forms and cultic practices.

II.6.h Other jewellery

Jewellery is personal adornment worn on the body, primarily as decoration. In addition to their aesthetic aspect, the fibulae and pectorals discussed above also have a functional role. The jewellery is concentrated on the upper body and around the head, and, over time, the quantity increases. The addition of jewellery only emphasises the fact that the head of the figurines receieved the most attention, while the body was almost abstract.

The items commonly depicted on the figurines will be discussed below in relation to their counterparts in real life, in order of appearance: earrings, bracelets, the tight necklace or choker, and the hairband. The analysis will conclude with a general discussion of the application of jewellery to the figurines in comparison with larger sculpture and its interpretation, looking once again at the identity and gender of the figurines.

II.6.h.i Ear studs and earrings

The very earliest earrings on terracotta figurine heads found at Agrigento are the ear studs or disc earrings. These early heads, 1200-600 BCE, probably imported from Crete, have remarkable ear studs, made of a disc of clay applied separately, as for their eyes.[564] These, as well as those on the Argive and Locrian objects, seem to be the most common form of early ear adornment (for example, **2** and **3**). The Locrian figurines have a moulded face, but the large discs were applied later by hand. The locally produced figurines often wear strikingly large ear adornments and the number of figurines with earrings increased over time. Before 500 BCE, they often take the form of a disc and sometimes the distinction between the earlobe and the stud is not clear (**99**). In this period, abstract geometrical shapes might have been preferred over the naturalistic shape of the ear. Sometimes the ear stud is just a little larger than the globule of the ear itself, **107**, while in other cases, the ear itself is not visible at all, just the knob (**84**). The disc-shape that is common for the shoulder pins and pectoral might have appealed, as the globule of the ear has a similar shape. A disc ear stud repeats the form and is usually just slightly smaller than the fibulae.[565] Such an ear stud in the shape of flower with six petals can also be seen on Locrian pinakes.[566] The disc stud was common in Etruscan jewellery in the sixth century BCE.[567] Etruscan antefixes might have influenced the shape of the ear stud, as it did for the facial features, like the antefix named above that wears an ear stud with a knob in the middle (fig. 2.5). It is possible that the locally produced figurines were inspired by the earlier imported Cretan, Argive and Locrian[568] examples, but also by examples from contemporary representations from the Italian mainland.[569]

Earrings appeared later than ear studs, on the figurines in group 2, probably around 500-490 BCE, when the pectorals were already part of the standard adornment.[570] As the ears on some figurines became relatively large,[571] the new ear ring form was introduced. The ears were pieced by a ring on which a pendant was attached. On **21**, for example, the ears, earrings, and the triangular pendant are all large. **21**, **100**, and **105-106**, mark the introduction of this new model. Sometimes it still features the ear stud from which the ring hangs (**105-106**). The ring itself can be boat-shaped, becoming thicker as it descends, for example, AG9187 (Catalogue fig. 22). The ring was also sometimes thicker in its entirety. This can be seen on some of the group with the decorated polos (**134**). In this group, the pendant is sometimes more triangular, while in other instances it is conical.[572] This is a repeated shape, as the pectoral pendants are not completely ovoid, but pointing downwards underneath. The shape of the objects on the chest and the pendant on the earring form a set. More

564 Mus. Arch. Agrigento Inv. no.79876. See fig. 2.3 on the left.

565 These Etruscan 6cm diam. discs from the sixth century BCE seem large for earrings. They are extremely finely decorated. Staatl. Ant. Munich. Wünsche and Steinhart 2010, p.94-5, no.52.

566 Typus 5/20 and 2/25 Mertens- Horn 200/2006, Abb.6, 48 and 49, p.66-67. For both Demeter herself and the dedicant.

567 It is thought to be of Lydian origin. Haynes 2000, p.158.

568 On a Locrian pinax two women, both the goddess and the worshipper apparently wear rosette-shaped ear studs. Orsi 1909, p.413, fig. 5 and 6. Whether they are wearing a sort of pendant earring on another pinax is not entirely clear. Orsi 1909, p.421, fig.17.

569 One of the most popular types was the disc, even though not so many real ones have been found. Higgins 1961, p.127.

570 An exception is figurine **103** that has just earrings and no pectorals. It is the body that is exceptional here, not the head or earrings.

571 On other figurines, the ear itself is not depicted. The ring with pendant is placed unnaturally high on **105-106**.

572 As seen on the pendants, the difference between in the round and flat, here conical and triangular, can be the result of smoothing the surface of the moulded figurine and new generations.

Coins	Short description earrings	Figurine example	Differences
Siracusan tetradrachm 485-480 BCE[a]	Knob-like ear studs	84, 107	knob seems fairly small on the coins
Siracusan tetradrachm 485-479 BCE Siracusan litra 474-450 BCE	boat-shaped ring with pointed pendant	100 133	pendant on figurines are larger, pendant is reworked and coarse in shape
Siracusan tetradrachm 450-439 BCE	spiral earring	-	not appearing on Akragantine figurines
Siracusan dekadrachm 405-400 BCE Siracusan tetradrachm 310-304 BCE[b]	single alabastron- shaped pendant	-	appearing on Greek objects, like korai, not on Akragantine figurines
Siracusan dekadrachm 400-370 BCE[c]	triple pendant	201	mould features also knob and ring; middle pendant on coin thicker.

Table *2*.5: Table with comparisons of representations of earrings on Siracusan coins and Akragantine figurines. (a); Boehringer 1929 series IV, 41 (V26/R25), 42 (V26/R26), 48 (V27/R31). Struck under Gelon; (b) With inscription 'Koras'. See university website: http://thor.lawrence.edu/omeka/buerger/items/show/354; (c) For photographs and dating of these coins: Boehringer 1929; See Swett 1993.

elongated pointed pendants on both earrings and chest are visible on **179**. **105-106** are an exception, as the pendants are of great variety and the earrings with the knob, ring and triangle pendant do not directly match with the shapes on the pectoral pendants. The large earring is often placed on top of the hair. A figurine of the patterned polos sort, with horizontally lined hair, **124**, but without earring suggests that the earrings are a later addition in this series, taken up in new generations and possibly applied with another mould. In one instance, **133**, both the ring and pendant are decorated with notches arranged in irregular lines. Is granulation or another sort of fine metal working suggested here? On figurines from the latest group, the earrings are still of this model and rather large. The pendant is similar in shape to the pectoral pendants, but more elongated, **189**. The jewellery, like the earlier examples, is therefore matching. This may show that pectoral pendants from this time were also seen as jewellery.

The representations of the shape of the ears and earrings follows a similar development, parallel to the depictions on Siracusan coins with a female head. There is no consensus on the identity of the depicted woman and she has been seen as a goddess or nymph, representing the town. In the table below, the different forms of jewellery, as seen on the figurines, are compared with those depicted on the coins from parallel periods in time (table 2.5). The order of models on the figurines corresponds with that on the coins: the earliest form is a simple knob, with often the same uncertainty over whether it is the earlobe or a stud represented. The following form is the ring with a pointed pendant. The relative size on the figurines is larger, which could be explained by the technical limitations of the terracotta moulding. A more realistic size would have been too small to make a clear impression in clay. The coins confirm the relative date and the development in earrings for the figurines, but point out that the exceptional earing mould, **201**, with its triple form – a model that does not appear on the figurines – is likely from the beginning of the fourth century BCE. The adornment of terracotta representations with fine jewellery continued in the fourth century BCE, when the production of fine gold jewellery was intensified.

This mould for just an earring, **201**, was probably meant for larger statuary. Though it follows the same schedule of disc, ring and pendant it is clearly much more refined than the examples on hand-sized figurines. It has a knob decorated with a rosette. A boat/crescent-shaped ring, curling slightly inward and outward like a lyre, slightly thicker on the underside and curling outward at the top hanging from the disc. Three thin pendants are hung from this ring. The earrings made out of it would have been about 4.5cm, which is larger than would fit most figurines, but smaller than would be expected for a life-size statue. It could have been meant for large busts or masks. The holes in the ears of such objects show that these could be adorned with real metal earrings.[573] When we compare the larger statuary from Akragas, the earrings also appear and are significantly larger. On the fragment with hair of what was once a near life-size statue, **202**, a thick boat-shape earring hangs from a small knob that is placed on the earlobe. Surprisingly, a pendant is absent. The earrings of the large terracotta mask from Gela mentioned above, consist of a ring with a vase-shape, which she wears on the second row.[574] This indicates that matching jewellery was usual in this period.[575]

Boat-shape earrings were common in South Italy and remained fashionable for a long time. Partial bronze earrings from Akragas could have belonged to this model. They have been found in a grave-context dated to the end of the sixth century BCE.[576] A gold example with acorns as pendants is dated to around 350 BCE and decorated with

573 Such as AG16085 (bust, h. 37cm) found at the sanctuary at S. Biagio. Bennett and Paul 2002, p.243.

574 Bennett and Paul 2002, p.255, no.59.

575 See Section II.6.h.iv.

576 As the parts are very small, it is unclear whether they belonged to these model earrings. Together with stone bobbins and a dog/lion stone protome from Necropoli Contrada Pezzino, Akragas, tomb F/398. Presently the finds are in showcase 77 at Mus. Arch. Agrigento.

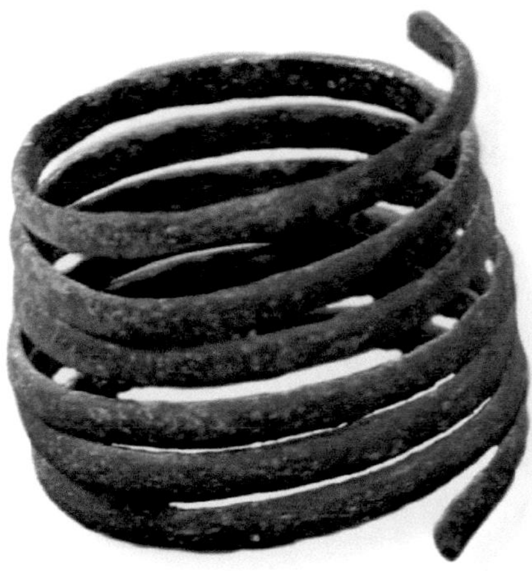

Figure 2.19: Bronze bracelet from Monte Bubbonia. Mus. Caltanisetta Inv. no. MR 34911.

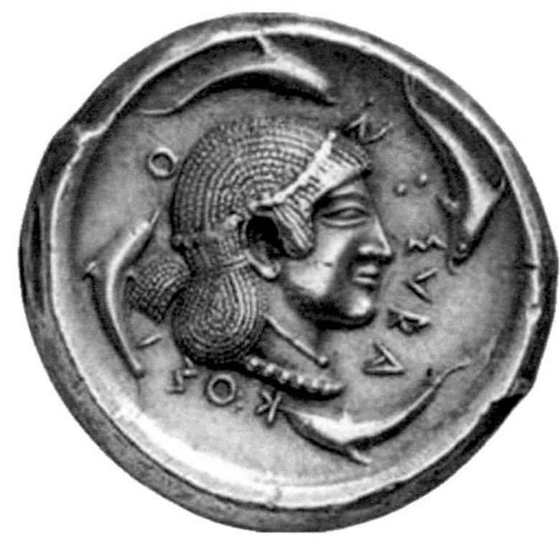

Figure 2.20: Syracusan tetradrachm. Photo after Boehringer 1929, p. 45 (R 29).

very fine granulation.[577] This shape is oriental in origin[578] and could be Phoenician in this case. They might have had matching pendants. Earlier metal examples are known from Akragas, Gela and Megara Hyblaea, but have a granular addition, smaller than a pendant.[579] The conical pendant on some figurines' earrings is more similar to examples with just this sort of pendant, finely granulated from the fifth and fourth century BCE, but of unknown origin.[580] Clearly similar objects in real life, however, are not available, and it remains unclear whether combining the boat-shape ring with a pendant influenced by another culture.

II.6.h.ii Bracelets

Among the figurines, only a small number wears bracelets. In these cases, it is not entirely clear whether several bracelets or a single spiral bracelet is depicted. The series of the decorated polos, **115**, **135**, **136**, wears a four-ringed bracelet at the end of her sleeves, around both her wrists. Also **144**, **149-151**, the fine folded sleeves series, might wear the same sort of bracelets, a development that fits with the increasing adornment of the body and fineness of jewellery. The bracelets are sizeable compared to the hand, but are not large in diameter, as they are tighter than the sleeve. On a figurine from Selinous, a spiral bracelet is very clearly shown, but worn somewhat higher on the lower arm.[581] Very similar bracelets are depicted on a life-sized terracotta figurine from Katane (Catania), dated to the first half of the fifth century BCE.[582] Such bronze bracelets are known from the sixth to early fifth century BCE from Northern Greece, Corinth and Sicily.[583]

A bracelet in bronze with spiral form, circling six times around the arm, was found at Necropolis Monte Bubbonia tomb 11/71, dated to the sixth century BCE (fig. 2.19).[584] It is very likely these bracelets, in particular spiral ones, were fashionable at the time and were therefore added to the terracotta figurines as a sign of up-to-date luxury.[585]

II.6.h.iii Necklaces and hairbands

The pectoral is sometimes taken for a necklace. Dewailly distinguishes two forms of colliers, which are mentioned by Homer in Od. 18, 295. The first is the *hormos*, which contains several strings of pearls, interpreted here as a pectoral. The second form is the *isthmion*, which hangs around the neck, a necklace proper. There are two composition possibilities, with one larger pendant in the middle or with several objects of similar size.[586]

On some figurines, a tight necklace appears, placed high on the neck, some without pendant, **125**, **152**?,[587] but most with, **115**, **140**, **189**.[588] An originally Selinuntine series omits the pendant and is usually more pronounced

577 Hamdorf 1996, p.211, no.144.

578 Deppert-Lippitz 1985, p.93.

579 Akragas: lead earrings, bronze beads(?) and a silver fibula. Necropoli Contrada Pezzino, Akragas, tomb 1002. Mus. Arch. Agrigento. Veder Greco 1988, p.298. Other bronze jewellery from tomb 1502. Veder Greco 1988, p.316. For other places see Higgins 1961, p.127.

580 Deppert-Lippitz 1985, p.126-7, no.74-75.

581 Mus. Louvre, Paris Inv. no.Cp5137. See museum website: http://cartelen.louvre.fr/cartelen/visite?srv=car_not_frame&idNotice=6730&langue=en.

582 Pautasso 1996, p.109, no.168, tav.XVII.

583 Deppert-Lippitz 1985, p.131.

584 Now exhibited in the Mus. Arch. Caltanisetta.

585 Bracelets as a jewellery might have become more common in this period. Other examples, not spiral, are two bracelets found at the Sanctuary of Malophoros in Selinous. Trombi 2003, p.99 no.67-8; Gabrici 1927, p.362, fig.155.i.

586 Dewailly 2010.

587 Also a head, which is probably from Akragas. See Catalogue fig. 28.**160**.

588 On two figurines from the same mould, **179-180**, the necklace with pendant was impressed after moulding.

(**94**). Unlike some pendants, and comparable to the addition of bracelets and earrings, this jewellery item is more likely to be contemporary. It does not belong to the tradition of the pectorals and has no other value than an aesthetic one. It should be seen as bringing the appearance of the goddess up-to-date with that of contemporary fashion for women. Though it reflects fashion, it could also highlight the status of the goddess, as it fits in the tradition of adornment, emphasising the female gender of the figure. It presents her in this way as an ideal woman. In depictions of women in other sculpture and coins, this tight necklace appears from the sixth century BCE onwards, as on a Cypro-Archaic II terracotta head,[589] but gains popularity in the first half of the fifth century BCE. It has a long use afterwards, for example on a gold pendant of a female head, dated to between 350-330 BCE.[590]

Several of the Siracusan coins feature a female head with tight, beaded or plain necklace. The depiction of the head alone did not leave space for pectorals. On a demareteion, a silver dekadrachm from Syracuse, multiple beads or pendants on two necklaces, as well as an earring with pendant, are depicted.[591] On another coin, a rare silver tetradrachm from Syracuse, one necklace with a small pendant in front is placed high on the neck, while another larger beaded necklace is depicted just on the edge of the neck (fig. 2.20).[592] This combination of a thin, high necklace and a lower, larger one is seen on other coins from Syracuse. Some can be precisely dated as being minted under the authority of Gelon.[593] The lower necklace might replace the pectoral with pendants, as that could not be fitted onto the standard depiction of a head on the coin. The beaded form, the size and placement distinguish these necklaces from the pectorals on the terracottas.

The pearl-rim in the hair may have been part of the jewellery and not of the polos, as seen on **115-118**, **126-129, 133, 166**?, as it is not clear whether the rim is part of the polos. Siracusan coins could shed light on the matter as the female head depicted on some wears such a pearl-band in her hair. On some coins, it is merely decorative, placed around the head (fig. 2.20), on others it functions to keep the hair up from the neck. On the figurines and on some coins, it marks a distinction between the fringe and the hair on top of the head. Some of the girls depicted on a pinax from Locri Epizefyrii also wear a pearl hairband (fig. 2.9).[594] It might be one of those jewellery items that became fashionable at a certain moment. The pearl-rim appeared somewhat later than the tight necklace on the Akragantine figurines, and it is only once that a hair band without polos appears on the Akragantine figurines, **21**.[595]

Other jewellery is found often among the contemporary grave goods at Akragas. Six rings, for example, were found in grave 1477 at Akragas next to pottery of normal and miniature size, as well as a terracotta figurine holding a dove.[596] Rings might not have been depicted on the figurines for the practical reason of their fineness, which does not fit well with the technique of moulding used.

II.6.h.iv Comparison with korai jewellery

In the case of larger statuary, the korai, jewellery in stone is often ommitted.[597] There are two noteworthy exceptions, however, Phrasikleia and the Berlin Goddess, who wear jewellery as well as a sort of polos or crown. Phrasikleia's necklace, earrings and possibly the bracelet have been reconstructed as gold-coloured. The flower bud she holds up with her left hand in front of her is repeated on her crown in two stages: completely closed and about to open. They clearly symbolize, underlined by the epigram that she would remain unmarried, that she is like a flower bud that would never bloom. The Berlin Goddess wears an even tighter necklace, a thin string with three amphoriskoi/ small vase-like objects, placed away from each other. They are not really hanging from the string, but rather seem perforated in the middle.[598] This sort of pendant is reminiscent of pendants on the Sicilian figurines and might have been inspired by them. Direct imitation however is difficult to prove. The Berlin Goddess wears a spiral or double bracelet on her left wrist. Matching jewellery can be seen in in both cases: the Berlin Goddess, which has earrings with a small vase/ amphoriskos-like pendant and a necklace with similarly shaped pendants. Phrasikleia matches the flower bud she holds in her hand with the same motif on her earrings and in her crown.

589 Met. Museum, New York Inv. no.35.11.20, dated to the sixth century BCE. See museum website: https://www.metmuseum.org/art/collection/search/253497.

590 The thin tight necklace with one small pendant is worn high on the neck and its depiction is precisely like on the figurines. It is thought to be from Taranto. Hamdorf 1996, p.204-5, no.135.

591 Boehringer 1929, Group III, series 12e. Boston, Museum of Fine Arts Inv.no.35.21.See museum website: https://www.mfa.org/collections/object/dekadrachm-demareteion-of-syracuse-with-quadriga-1205.

592 Boehringer 1929, p.45 (R 29) without earring.

593 Boehringer 48 (V27/R31) is dated to about 484-483 BCE.

594 Orsi 1909, p.426, fig.25.

595 On some others, it remains unclear, **179**.

596 Necropoli di Contrada Pezzino S90bis, dated to the second half of the sixth century BCE. Veder Greco 1988, p.296.

597 They were often painted, or had real metal adornments. Lee 2015, p.141-2.

598 For a discussion on the pectoral depicted on Corinthian vases, see section II.6.h.ii and fig. 16.

II.6.i Gender, identity and the display of wealth

The main difference between the pectorals and the other forms of jewellery is its application and meaning. In accordance with Zuntz, the pectoral, whether attached to fibulae or directly to the garment, should be interpreted as 'a cultic ornament.'[599] Together with the polos and the seated position of most of the figurines, the particularly fine or multiple pectorals, of which the fibulae or clasps in its double function are part, form an indication that a female deity is depicted. Like the Argive figurines, the iconography of the Akragantine statuettes might have become a generic type. The pectoral, though changing in form and size, becomes part of the standard. The other jewellery is just additional, appears infrequently, and simply has the aim of beautification, combined with the recognisability of contemporary fashion.

The hairstyle, polos, and rich adornments clearly indicate a female figurine. For the Greeks, jewellery was feminine, but in the east, it was not so gendered. Wearing very elaborate gold jewellery was socially and sometimes legally restricted to specific occasions, such as weddings. Jewellery is therefore often depicted, for example, on Greek vase painting, on the occasion of dressing the bride.[600] The attention paid to these details, however not only emphasises gender and status, but also her divine identity. The similarities in jewellery and hairstyle between Siracusan coins and figurines from Akragas make the depiction of a goddess, rather than a mortal, more likely. The identification of a specific goddess remains difficult. On Siracusan coins, Arethusa, a locally venerated fountain nymph, who seems to have been the patron and symbol of the town, is often thought to have been depicted.[601] Persephone also features sometimes on these coins and their mythologies as unwilling brides are comparable. It is possible that bride's jewellery is depicted on the figurine.

Several female deities could be depicted by applying this general standard form. Only in a few exceptional and later fifth century BCE figurines, does there appear to have sometimes been a desire to express a specific identity. In the case of Athena, the depiction of a lophos and gorgoneion, her Greek attributes, leave no ambiguity about her identity. However, this does not imply that all figurines should be interpreted as Athena. The considerable variation in details is a strong argument against this. Depending on the context and appearance, the figurines may have been identified as specific, but different, goddesses.[602]

The adornments and quantity of jewellery represented on the figurines speaks of the wealth of individuals and prosperity of the town. From literary sources, the building program of Phalaris in the first half of the sixth century BCE suggests a prosperous town. Economic growth would have continued in the second half of the century, fuelled by the export of grain, olives and livestock, but possibly also by the transport passing from the sea over land.[603] The port of Akragas, present day Porto Empedocle, is close to the town and there must have been transportation of different goods from the East and northern Africa. From Cyrenaica, a similarly flourishing city, the sylphium plant, whose application is still surrounded with mystery, would have found its way to Sicily, South Italy and further north. Theron, Phalaris' successor, also expanded Akragas geopolitically, and it is in this period that the first silver coins were minted.

During this time, Sicilian towns probably experienced several social changes, reflected in their architecture with the creation of monumental city centres and spaces for the communal consumption of food. Both developments point to the creation of civic identity. This also seems to have been the case with cults, which may have been used to create a sense of unified identity, overriding cultural differences. A cultic symbiosis could have provided religious validation for marriages between local women and immigrant men (or vice versa). This symbiosis may have been reflected in the hybrid figurines, which rapidly changed over time, becoming more Greek in style and detail, but not losing their link to their past, retaining the symbolic pectoral. It is not surprising that the Greeks set the myth of Persephone within this cultural and religious background.

The shift from aristocratic grave goods to the dedication of figurines with the same adornments at temples might also indicate a social shift with an increasingly prosperous (and visible) middle-class. The communal life may have also moderated the demonstrative display of wealth by individuals. The terracotta figurines with their relative uniformity and affordability would not only serve to integrate different cultures but also to create harmony between people of different social status.[604]

II.7 Furniture

As discussed above, the figurines were usually intended to be seen as seated. It is therefore not surprising that the chair, bench or throne stresses this seated pose.

599 Zuntz 1971, p.129-30.

600 Lee 2015, p.140-1.

601 The four dolphins that surround her make this identification likely. On some coins of Kimon from the early fourth century BCE, her name is added on the coin.

602 Dewailly, who researched the terracottas of the Selinunte Malophoros Sanctuary, also argues for an interpretation with a multiple identity. Dewailly 1992, p.156.

603 On the reverse of the Taleides amphora from Akragas, dated 540-530 BCE, a scene with a large scale and packed goods indicates trade and transport.

604 Bintliff interprets the shift from the rich grave goods to cultic dedications as a social and political change for the polis of Azoria, Crete from the Archaic to the Classical period. Bintliff 2010, p.20.

The different sorts of chairs will be discussed here and compared with other representations and real objects.

There are several examples of figurines that are clearly seated, with a block-shaped seat clearly visible from the side. With some figurines, the seat is not specifically indicated (**71**, **75**). Other features make clear that the East Greek model, for example **72**, might have inspired this seat shape.[605] Such a simple block is not very common and only on one figurine, **21**, is it visible from the front. Another exceptional, rather block-shaped chair with round armrests is visible on figurines and mould **31-32**.[606] Armrests are rare on the chairs of Akragantine figurines.

II.7.a From bench to throne

If the chair had to be made explicit, the coroplasts opted for a large, finely modelled version, as if to express the importance of the figure seated upon it. The object was also physically enlarged by the addition of the chair, varying from a small bench (**22**) to wider versions (**36**). They consist of a seat and frontal part that slopes inwards (**23**) often curving elegantly (**25**). The increased width makes the object as a whole more substantial (**27**). The wide bench, as well as other seats, are usually not straight but placed at an angle. The older figurines usually have a steeply sloping seat (**37**), while the later ones are less steep and straighter. The figurine appears to lean against the steep seats rather than sitting (**30**). The slope of the body coincides with the slope of the seat. The angle of the bent body is repeated by the angle of the bench. This pattern of geometrical forms and symmetry is aesthetic and creates a balanced form that leads the attention to the more detailed head.

Some of these benches curve up at the sides, creating a hollow seat. Examples of these are mostly figurines with a simple body, for example, **27** and **28**. A simultaneous step in the development of this bench is the high-winged back or 'ears' that form the backrest of the chair, visible by small rim features with semi-circular extensions on top. These parts sometimes protrude halfway along the back or at the height of the shoulders, and are sometimes decorated with a disc repeating the form of the fibulae (**39**). When placed lower, they create a triangular outline on the upper part of the figurine (**48**). The aesthetic form of the bench in itself seems to have been appreciated, such as the curving ending and the wide back of **34**. The addition of a cushion is a next step (**34**). All of these variations of the bench are mainly common in group 1, and often hardly visible in group 2,for example, **100**, when the height of the figurine is stressed often by a standing position. In group 3, there is a return to the bench, without backrest, but with a cushion on it usually reaching close to the edges of the seat at the front and back (**109**) or even completely covering the seat (**135**). The cushion is mattress-shaped and rounded at the corners. Sicilian figurines can be recognised by their sloping body and the chair with pillow. One example is a figurine in the Metropolitan Museum thought to be from Soli, Cyprus, which was probably made with a mould from Sicily. Her pillow partly overlaps the front of the chair, while usually it remains on top. The model of the chair with its widening shape and sloping seat is also common in Akragas.[607]

The wide benches and winged back were often handmade and the sides are therefore not always equal or placed at the same height. As this also meant additional work for the coroplast there are variations of figurines from the same mould series both with and without a chair: for example, **118** and AT 3392 (713) from the Pushkin Museum, Moscow (Catalogue fig. 14). The latter was made with attention to detail; the seat has curved sides and the lower part of the front is worked by hand with small lines depicting a lion paw.

In the last group of Akragantine figurines, we can truly speak of an enthroned figure. The chair has been very elaborately and detailed rendered with clearly defined chair legs. The animal-like shape of the leg, with a knee in the middle, and a thicker part at its base, like a hoof, could be imitating a horse leg (**194**). The construction with a horizontal stretcher at the front is made clear by the bas-relief on the figurine. On another part of a figurine (**197**), the decoration with a lion protome is represented, holding a ring in his mouth fastened with a high number of thin cords to the leg of the throne (**197**). The detail is striking.

II.7.a.i The footstool

In addition to the throne, a footstool is also commonly depicted. In its development, it follows the same steps as the chair, from very simple to detailed and elaborate. It might have functioned at first simply to increase stability, as it protrudes to the front it would prevent the figurine from toppling over. Sometimes it is not clear whether the feet or a footstool is indicated by the protruding part at the front (**11**). The footstool in the first three groups was usually part of the base, closed on the sides and lacking other details (**100**, **102** and **150**). It sometimes retains the width of the body, but varies in height, for example,

605 Standing, for example with a flaring lower part or a wider base as with 77, **82**, **83**, **84** – **85**, **92** and **93** would have been an option as well, but the seated version seems to be preferred or the first known option. The seated version is much more stable with its larger base.

606 There are no figurines with this sort of chair from Akragas and the mould might come from somewhere else.

607 Both technical and iconographic details make clear that it is probably not from Akragas. Inv. no.74.51.1587 Metropolitan Museum of Arts, New York. See museum website: https://www.metmuseum.org/art/collection/search/241143.

141.[608] The base or footstool may look unrealistically high (**144**). Only a few examples show a footstool with legs and a stretcher, vertically and horizontal (**171**, **173-174**). From group 4 onwards, this becomes the standard, fitting with the detailed throne. The legs of the footstool are decorated with semi-circular forms on **195-196**; a stretcher is analogous to the model of throne. Its legs, though hard to see might well imitate the bent legs of an animal and its hoofs. The footstool has thus become not only a place for the feet, but increasingly presents the chair as a real throne, as the seated person would be completely lifted from ground level.

It is possible that the furniture depicted represents real footstools, as they have been found at the Malophoros sanctuary at Selinous. The footstools, sometimes made from volcanic tufa, measure about 20-25cm high and about 45-50cm wide, and are thus life-size.[609] They have different shapes, such as rounded legs or lion paws, but some are also straight-legged and decorated with hatches. On an Akragantine krater, Zeus is depicted seated on a finely worked stool with a simple solid footstool and pearl-rim decoration.[610] Footstools are common in depictions on Greek vases and monuments, as well as on the Locrian pinakes.[611] Feline paws are known from footstools as well.[612]

II.7.b The origin of the represented chair shapes

Some of the earliest figurines with a chair might be the Argive objects that have a stand at the back or legs (**2**). The whole body is in some cases shaped like a chair, but not on figurines from Akragas. Yet the idea of placing the figure on a chair might have influenced Akragantine coroplastics. As pointed out above there are a couple of 'sets,' figurines with a standing and a seated counterpart. The earliest of these are the Locrian figurines. The seated ones (**6-7**), have a clear throne with armrests with a disc-shaped frontal decoration and a backrest, visible on the sides and above their shoulders. Such a chair with armrests ending in a knob is depicted on one of the Locrian pinakes, in this case decorated with a rosette.[613] Such a chair is not common on other Akragantine figurines, except for on **31-32**. Another clear 'set' of seated and standing alternatives is the Mould I group (**171-175** seated, **176-177** standing). This model of nearly identical objects, except for their pose, starts changing in the last group with more distinction between the two in the dress. The standing figurine then led to the popular figurine type of the worshipper carrying a piglet.

A 74cm high terracotta hand-modelled female figure on a bench with sides bending upwards sharply, almost like a saddle, are reminiscent of the wide upwardly curved seats of the Akragantine figurines. A possible cult statue was found in a deposit at Poggio dell'Aquila, Grammichele and dated to the second half of the sixth century BCE.[614] It might be that the seated pose of female figure, probably a goddess, inspired the coroplasts of sixth century BCE Akragas to place their female figures also on benches with upwardly curved sides. It is as if the bench not only raises the figure above the ground but also protects her by literally surrounding her. While the seated pose might have been inspired by such local representations of deities, it could also have been developed from some aniconic objects, seen as the seats of the gods, for example, cippi.

Another source of inspiration for the figurines could be Near Eastern models taken over by the Phoenicians. Goddesses like Ishtar and Isis in their respective depictions are often seated, as with the Kubaba depictions discussed above.[615] The female deity in these images is often flanked by wild animals. Lions or sphinxes on each side seem to carry the throne and protect the goddess. The Phoenicians took over this model. Their large stone sculpture would have probably been a source of inspiration for the Akragantine coroplasts, as they would have come across it on Sicily. An example of such a sculpture is the enthroned deity between sphinxes from Solunto.[616] It resembles the wide seat of many Akragantine figurines. The sides are not upwardly curved but are instead formed by the wings of the sphinxes.

II.7.b.i Greek chairs: thronos and klismos

The shape of the other furniture was already introduced by the end of the sixth century BCE clearly showed the influence of East Greek chair models. Two Greek seat types seem to have been combined on representations in Akragantine coroplastics.

As the figurines have a frontal focus, the picture of how the furniture might have looked in real life can be completed with those represented on vases and pinakes, often shown in side view. These representations are however not available on locally produced objects and thus it remains often a guess as to how the three-dimensional object would have looked from other angles than the front.

The chair with the 'ears' or winged back is probably the *klismos*, combined with a *thronos* related type with solid sides, as Richter distinguishes them.[617] The Greek *klismos* has outward-curving legs and a rounded back. None of

608 A higher base was a way to increase the overall size of the figurine and reduce the effect of shrinkage in the new generation.

609 Gabrici 1927, p.202-3.

610 Veder Greco 1988, p.208. A similar footstool is used by two deities, a female one and Poseidon on a calyx krater from Akragas, presently in the National Library, Paris Inv. no.418, dated 480-460 BCE.

611 Richter 1966, p.51.

612 Maniscalco 2018, p.5.

613 Orsi 1909, p.413, fig.5.

614 Orsi 1897, p.217 tav.III. Mus. Arch. Syracuse Inv. no.14336.

615 See section II.6.e. For more examples of the models, see Dewailly 2010.

616 Panvini and Sole 2009, p.205. It is dated to the sixth century BCE.

617 Richter 1966, p.29.

this is visible on the figurines. It is the large horizontal top part of the back, stretching further than the seated person, which makes it possible to recognise it on statuettes. This is a wing-back with 'ears' sticking out horizontally. The rounded endings are often the only parts visible on the terracottas. While the relative height of the backrest on the figurines varies, it seems a combination of the *klismos* and the *thronos*, as the latter has straight legs and sometimes closed sides. The appearance of this chair among Akragantine figurines is likely to have been influenced by the high number of imported East Greek figurines (**72**), which have a clearly seated pose, often with a back.[618] The typical 'ears' are sometimes lacking and appear frequently on Attic terracotta figurines.[619] These parts are sometimes decorated with rosettes or palmettes and painted in mainly reddish colours, like the above mentioned decorated throne of an Attic figurine.[620] Their shape is comparable to the 'ears' of the Akragantine chairs, though on the latter they are often slightly more stretched and oval (**103**). These forms do not explain the wide seat, turning it into a bench, nor the sometimes upwardly curved shape.

Both the *thronos* and *klismos* are, in particular, chairs for kings and deities in Archaic Greek representations. It is the *thronos* that endows the seated person with dignity.[621] That is how the guest is honoured in Homer, by being invited to sit down on a beautiful *thronos*.[622] It is a royal or divine seat. It therefore is also often accompanied by a footstool.[623] Thrones were found frequently in Greek temples as the seat of the cult statue.[624] In larger sculpture, a headless and badly worn marble statue from Asea, Arcadia is reminiscent in its form of the terracotta figurines, and its throne is similar to the Selinuntine figurine thrones. A female figure, dressed in a plain ankle-long dress, sits with her hands reaching her knees on a throne with lion paws. The figure is interpreted as Artemis or the Mother of the gods, as an inscription mentions Agemo, for Hegemone.[625] As head and attributes or other details are absent, the figure could not be securely identified.

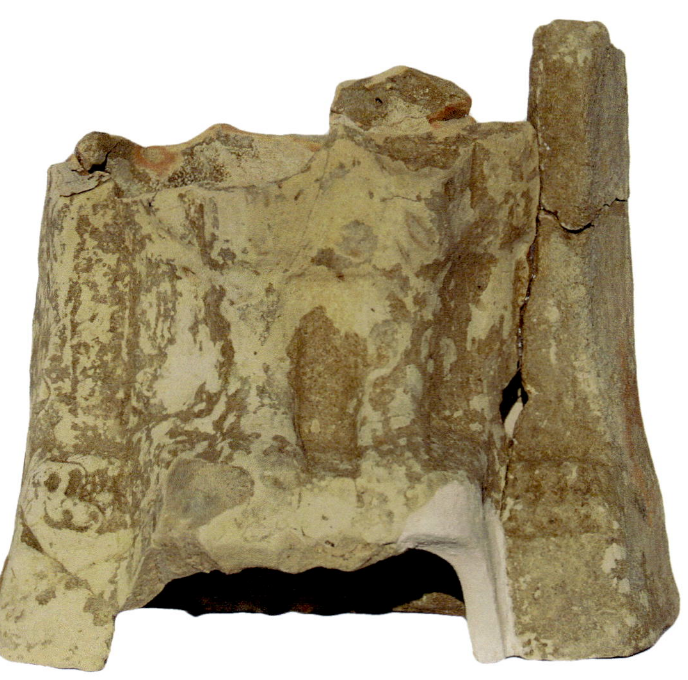

Figure 2.21: Figurine part on a throne with lion pawns from Selinous. h. 17.2cm, Inv. no. SL31791 Selinunte; scale 1:2.

II.7.b.ii Thrones and lions

The eastern model of wild animals carrying or flanking the throne influenced Greek iconography and resulted in chairs partly shaped as animals. This corresponded with the protective function of the throne. Absent from the other Akragantine figurines from the same series, lion paws mark a specific type of throne.[626] Lion legs and large paws also characterise the final developments of some thrones of Selinuntine figurines. There are more references in terracotta to lions,[627] but in furniture it seems of eastern

618 There are also examples from Attica, Boeotia, Capua, and other sites at the British Museum. See Richter 1966, p.29 n.3.

619 Two examples from South Italy are a stone figurine from Garaguso and a terracotta figurine from Medma. The latter has 'ears' with rosettes and the throne has lion paws. It is set on a base that includes a protruding part for the feet. Bennett and Paul 2002, p.190-1; Richter 1966, p.28-9, fig.124, p.391.

620 Inv. no.1980.303.5 Metropolitan Museum of Arts, New York. See museum website: https://www.metmuseum.org/art/collection/search/255697; Karoglou 2016, p.2 fig.2.

621 Richter 1966, p.13-4.

622 Il. 24. 552, Od. 8.162.

623 For example, Od. 1.131 'θρῆνυς.'

624 Richter 1966, p.14-5.

625 Richter 1966, p.16, fig.45. The statue is in the Nat. Mus. Athens. Inv. no.6 h. 98cm It is dated to 640 BCE. There was an animal next to her right thigh, which had its head, now lost, on her knee. Kaltsas 2002, p.36, no.8

626 Figurine AT 3392 (713) Pushkin Museum, Moscow. See Catalogue fig. 14, p.285 .

627 One figurine from Bitalemi Gela, Inv. 18092 Panvini 1998, p.172, V.8 and a similar one from the Malophoros Sanctuary, Selinous has a lion on her lap.Mus. Arch. Palermo Inv. no.10302. Such figurines are likely Eastern Greek imports. Bennett and Paul 2002, p.296-7; Gabrici 1927, tav.XXXIX.8. The typical figurine type is described by Gabrici as Ionian and characterized by a broad face and smooth lines. She wears a veil. In her right arm she holds a lion and in her left hand a pomegranate. A very similar lion vase form was found in Akragas, Necropoli di Contrada Pezzino tomb 1119. Mus. Arch. Agrigento Inv. no.22568 h. 9cm presently in showcase 76. Veder Greco 1988, p.309, no.1. Another terracotta lion, lying down with a turned head, possibly from the same mould series: de Miro 2000, p.249, no.1508, tav.CV dated to the fifth century BCE.

origin[628] adopted by western cultures and appearing frequently on vases and sculpture from the sixth century to the first half of the fifth century BCE.[629] The lion head appears as a protome on one elaborate throne (**197**), and Selinuntine figurines, both relatively late. Lion legs and paws appear on the thrones of the female figures from the second and third quarter of the fifth century BCE.[630] The style of those figurines is very elaborate with fine details.[631] The lion paw is very naturalistically rendered, with four fingers and attention to the detailed structure of the phalanx bones. Such large lion paws are also represented on Locrian pinakes. One famous example depicts Hades and Persephone on a throne with both lion paws and protome. Similarly to the Akragantine figurine thrones, it has a horizontal stretcher and a cushion. Like the Selinuntine figurine (fig. 2.21), the throne is set on a base, though on the pinax they are individual blocks. There is a footstool with lion paws as well. The backrest finial is bended and shaped like a goose or duck's head, as is commonly seen on vase paintings (Richter 1966, p. 17, fig. 49). It is likely that such chairs existed as they appear on these different materials. Large ones might have been made for the cult statue. A large terracotta lion paw from Akragas might have been part of such a throne.[632] A terracotta statue of nearly one meter from Grammichele represents a kore seated on a throne with lion paws, cushion and footstool.[633] The throne might be a combination with a *klismos*, as the 'ears', though rectangular, stick out.[634] A sixth-century BCE terracotta throne from Sicily has lion paws as well. This intruiging object is decorated on the lower sides with front-moulded appliques of female and male figures.[635] Maniscalco suggests that it served in the thesmophorion of San Francesco Bisconti, Morgantina as the seat of an acrolithic statue.[636]

The lion became a symbol applied in different instances as the symbol of power and strength combined with a graceful body. It might have stood for power but most likely had an apotropaic function as well.[637] On a terracotta throne for the life-size statue of the deity, a protome could also have featured. An approximately 6cm mould for such a protome was found at the southern fortification walls of Akragas.[638] These sorts of powerful but graceful references to the lion awe the onlooker and give status to the enthroned.

II.7.b.iii An enthroned couple

On the figurines from Akragas a single female figure is usually seated with one exception: the couple figurine. On top of a handmade, horse-shaped vase, a mould-made figurine couple is placed (fig. 2.22).[639] They are seated next to each other on a wide throne, sharing the footstool or base of their bench. Both figures are seated in the same position, straight, with their arms placed in their laps, their hands reaching all the way to their knees. They are dressed in a long garment ending at their ankles. The woman, seated on the right of the man, wears a veil tightly around her fine face.[640] Her head is round and small, while her shoulders are large. Details such as the hands are faded. She is reminiscent of the similar **76**, though her veil and hairstyle, as well as the throne are different. The man has a beard and larger head, which makes him slightly taller than the woman. His chest and shoulders are bigger, leaving no doubt of the distinction between man and woman, though his chest is more clearly indicated than on the female figure and his long hair falls in tresses to the front, two on each side of his neck.[641] His nose is remarkably broad. Both seem to have an Archaic smile, but the impression is not that sharp. As on East Greek

628 The lion in its eastern form appears as well frequently on arulae, small altars. In these depictions, the lion is fighting another animal.

629 Richter 1966, p.15-8.

630 From Selinunte Cotone: SL 31791+ 31792 (unpubl.) Lower part of a female figure on a lion paw throne and a fragment of the left breast and upper arm; right knee (fitting on the first fragment); three other parts of the back? h. 17.2cm; Another small part of just this paw, likely from the same mould series Inv. no.23132. Its findspot R 2000 US 003 h. 6.1cm present location: Terrakotten box IV, as well as inv. no.23134 with possibly a lion throne.

631 Cf. Dewailly 1992, p.84 Type B XV.

632 Lion paw from Akragas presently in showcase 58 Mus. Arch. Agrigento. A lion paw was also found in the Thesmophorion at San Francesco Bisconti. Maniscalco suggests that it could have been part of a footstool, though its size is larger than that of the throne now in Vienna. Maniscalco 2018, p.4-5; Raffiotta 2007, cat.152.

633 Mus. Arch. Syracuse Inv. no.23166. Richter 1966, p.18 fig.60. It is dated around 470 BCE. Langlotz and Hirmer 1963, p.66 no.39.

634 It even features the knob towards the front. And thus seems to combine different shapes and forms.

635 It is tempting to interpret it as a throne for a deity and the figurines as her worshippers. Kunsthist. Mus. Vienna Antikensammlung Inv. no. V 3299a; dated to the third quarter of the sixth century BCE See museum website: https://www.khm.at/objektdb/detail/63826/

636 Maniscalco 2018.

637 Besides this stone lion protome from Akragas, dated to around 490-480 BCE. Marconi 1933, p.43, tav.V,3-4. There is another one from the Hellenistic Period and seven very small *protomai* from a fourth century BCE burial. Sottogras Cemetery, Agrigento: tomb 1 deposit XII. Presently in showcase 84 Mus. Arch. Agrigento.

638 AGS 7244, De Miro 2000, p.173, no.510, tav.CXV.

639 Mus. Arch. Agrigento R221 unpublished h. 19cm.The couple measures 8 x 6.4cm. The object is now stored in the archives of the Mus. Arch. Agrigento, but might be originally from Locri. The inventory number is similar to that of no. **3-6** and the clay different from the other figurines.

640 See the veil of the figurine with a lion on her lap from Selinous. Bennett and Paul 2002, p.296-7.

641 His body, hairstyle, seated pose, dress and beard are similar to the 90cm tall terracotta from Paestum, usually interpreted as an enthroned Zeus. He had a metal stephane. The addition of such headgear, but also the hat he is wearing, might explain the somewhat odd shape of the upper part of the male figure. Bennett and Paul 2002, p.131.

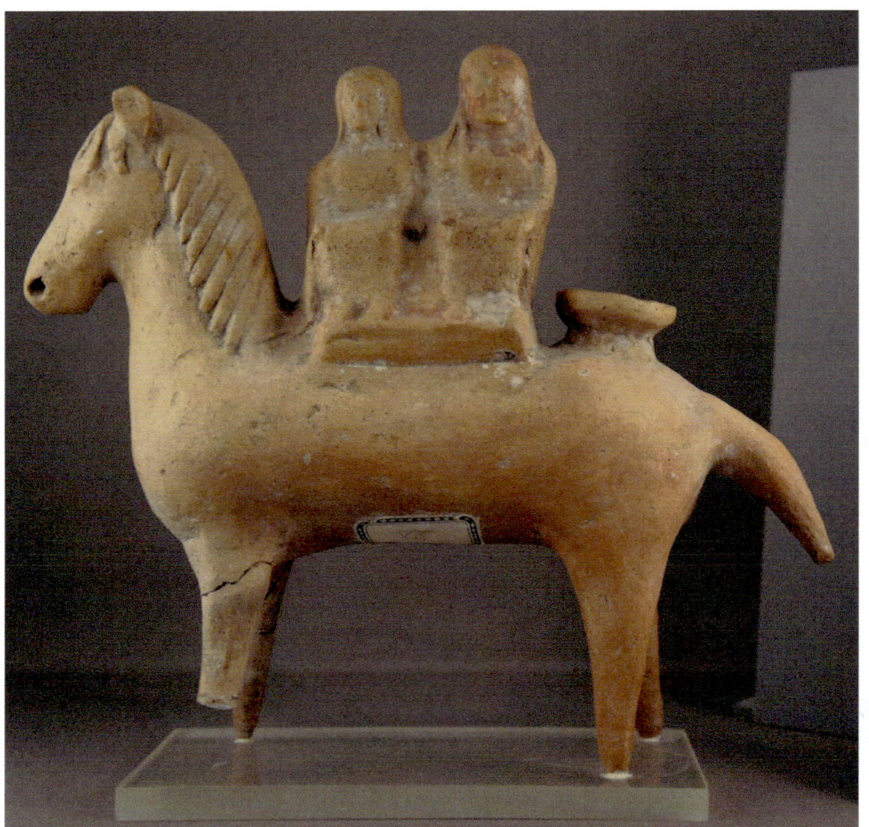

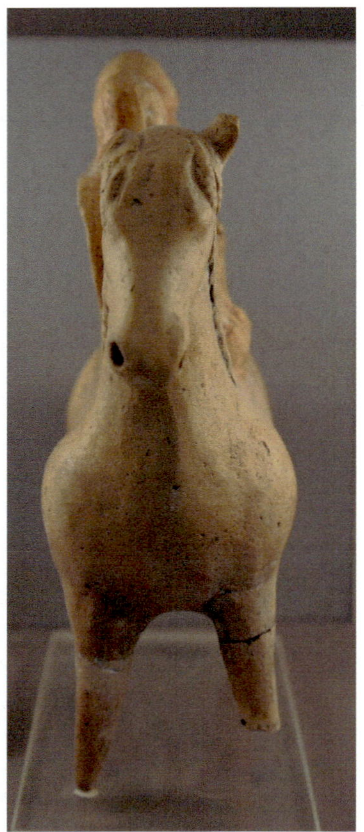

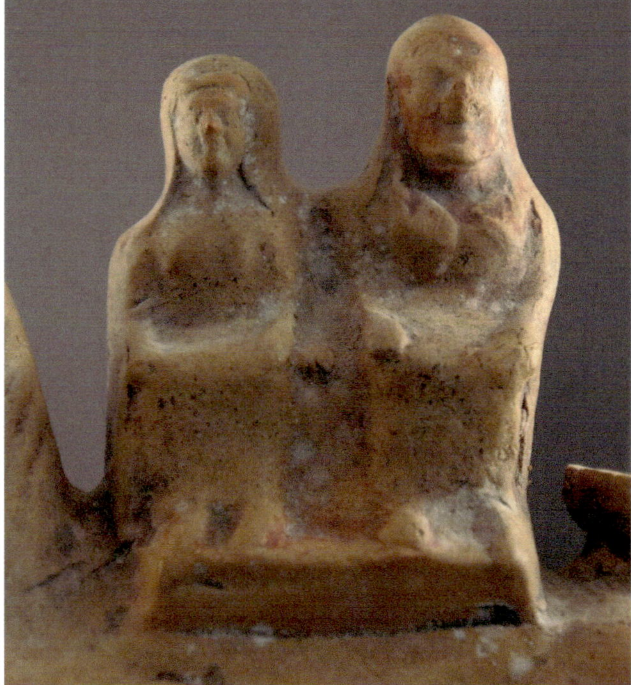

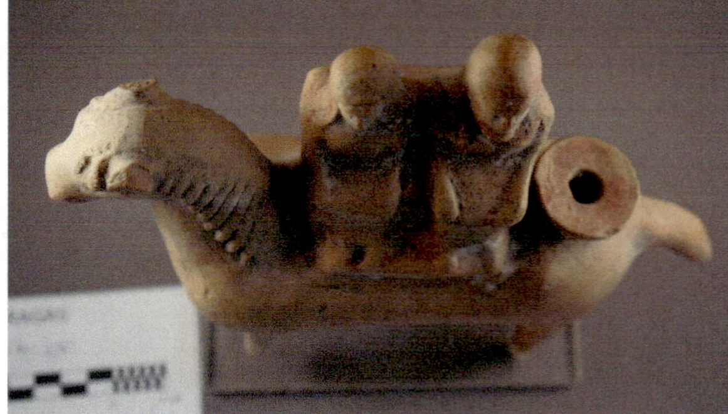

Figure 2.22: Terracotta horse-shaped vase with an enthroned couple on its back. h. 19cm, couple, h. 8cm, Inv. no. R221; top left and right scale 1:2, bottom, left scale 1:1, bottom right: scale 1:3.

figurines, the outline of their posture from the head runs down to the large shoulders in a fluid line. The moulded couple is very likely of East Greek origin. The mould or figurines travelled and were appreciated and used in other places as well.[642]

On the Locrian pinax discussed above, a couple, usually interpreted as Persephone and Hades, are sitting next to each other on a wide throne, their feet placed next to each other on a footstool. The scene could be seen as their wedding. This interpretation of the female figure as the main goddess for soon-to-be brides, but also as kourotrophos, has been extended to representations in which she is depicted alone. She is thus identified in all cases as Persephone by default, while details and context are overlooked. The bride, preparing for her wedding, or a mother as a dedicant-figurine, are common subjects as well.[643] From this perspective, the Akragantine figurative vase could be interpreted as a container for specific perfume for the bride, depicting the marrying couple or their divine prototype on top.

II.7.c Gender and identity

The chairs themselves are not gendered, though it seems that the winged-back chair is not used by men, either mortal or divine. Typical status-marking furniture for men is the couch, on which they recline in several representations.[644] When represented as a couple the woman and man are usually seated next to each other on a bench/wide throne. Reclining seems specifically reserved for dining or feasting men.[645]

It is the seat, klismos or throne, which grants the seated person power and dignity, and distinguishes its nature from that of others. It is very likely that this in origin eastern view was passed on by figurines or via worshippers of East Greek descent to the Akragantine fabrication of figurines. This might be the reason that the handmade addition of a visible chair is rather frequent and so much attention is paid to the details on elaborate thrones in group 4, while others remain standing. It would have presented the seated person as distinctively divine. The application of the footstool is the same. As the throne would have been high, a footstool may have been convenient, but a figuratively higher position is also intended. While the chair or throne is not necessary for identifying the deity, it functions well as a status marker. This application is clear from other material such as the Locrian pinakes, large statues and small terracottas from Sicily and southern Italy. The new inhabitants of the region influenced the model of the chair, in particular with the characteristic 'ears' inspired by East Greek models. The results are hybrid forms that still bear traces of early local models, like the upcurving sides of the wide seat. The use of lion-shaped legs, feet and heads bears traces of the eastern origin of the lions[646] and sphinxes bearing the throne. Its representation displays a high status that is protected by power. The horse leg, like the lion counterpart, would have been a valued shape, for its own elegance and for its indirect display of wealth. There are however not many parallel examples and it could be an invention of the Akragantine coroplasts. Sitting in itself would be also sign of wealth. The resting position implies not working, having others to do the work, while at the same time the furniture itself would have been a costly object, particularly the thrones of group 4.

II.8 Conclusions

The most common figurine category from Sicily is that of a female polos-wearing figure, often seated, and adorned with a rectangular upper dress, shoulder clasps and pectoral. Within this general grouping, the iconography of the individual objects varies. These variations and alterations, show how its form developed and was influenced over time by several cultures. The impact of these influences has been described along with the development of four specific aspects of its iconography: the shape of the body, facial features, dress and adornment, and furniture. Each has characteristic features and some can be said to be typical for Akragantine figurines. Following a summary of these features, further conclusions on gender and identity will be discussed below.

The abstracted form of body that marks the first group of Akragantine produced examples of these figurines was block-shaped, and relatively deep in order to be able to stand unsupported. With its sloping upper part, it appears to represent an armless seated figure. Earlier figurines depict a thin standing female figure with a plank-shaped body. Wooden figurines that were found near Gela were

642 There are several similar objects, with some variation in order (for example, Mus. Louvre MNB 542), gender, pose of the hands, folds, and other details. They are seen as being from East Greece or Samos. They were copied in particular in Magna Graecia. See for an overview, Sinn 1977, p.33, no.42.

643 Bennett and Paul 2002, p.84.

644 An inevitable comparison when speaking about the furniture, gender and enthroned figures, is the Samian Geneleos Group. This group of large marble statues is usually interpreted as a nuclear family. The enthroned female is named in an inscription as Phileia and is seen as the wife of the reclining man and mother of the four children. The chair pays tribute to this status of married woman, as well as mother. The children are standing, while their parents use furniture to sit and recline. Phileia's chair has a high stretcher and armrests with a rounded knob. The part down at the floor of the front leg widens and has a hoof-like foot. It resembles the general construction of the chairs on the Akragantine figurines. Phileia has her arms placed on her lap, not reaching her knees in a very similar position to the East Greek figurines.

645 Examples from Akragas of reclining men: De Miro 2000, p.246.

646 In general, the lion was sometimes connected with the female deity. See n.627 and 640 on the lion held by the female figure on her lap from Selinous. Later the lion is associated with Kybele.

applied as a patrix for terracotta figurines in at least one case at Akragas. Similar shallow, solid figurines show a female figure, but of different shape and dress, and probably predate the category discussed here.

The new category commonly differs in pose and appears in larger numbers. The angle of the trapezoidal, almost prism-shaped upper body with cube-shaped lower body of the first group seems to suggest the knees, while later the lap becomes more angled. The early block-shaped body and absence of arms is not directly developed from the imported figurines but might have a predecessor in aniconic objects, which are locally attested. This fitted well with Phoenician customs of *cippi* and *tophet stelai*. At the same time, geometrical forms dominated larger sculpture as well, but tend to become more anthropomorphic over time, like the Akragantine terracottas. This is visible with the development of the arms, that were introduced even later than the feet, while earlier figurines had inset-arms. The differing iconography between these two sorts supports the theory that the block-shaped figurines are not a derivative of small wooden or metal figurines, but more likely miniature versions of larger stone or wooden statuary. Their size and possibly their function, however, are comparable with the first category. They are small and light enough to be carried over a distance. The new design of seated figurines is larger and able to stand upright and make an impression at the place of dedication.

The attached head humanises the figurine from an early stage onwards. The difference between the attention paid to the detailed facial expression in contrast with the simple body is striking. The same counts for the adornments, armless figurines are sometimes adorned with large pectorals and shoulder clasps. This indicated the importance of such adornments. The bodies, on the other hand, remains abstract for a long time and merely seem to act as the carrier of the adornments that needed to remain stable and upright. Over time the seated position is made more clear by the addition of a chair. It is in then that similar figurines were produced, both standing and seated, as if they belong to a set with a seated deity and standing worshipper. A special category, the Locrian objects, was also produced in a set with similar seated and standing figures. For other Akragantine objects, this distinction of pose is not a clue to identity. The division in some studies between standing and seated figurines is rather artificial.[647] Only in the final stage of this category does standing seem to be an indication of a difference with the more richly adorned seated figurines. The standing figurines with simple pectorals in this group might indicate mortals, as opposed to the finely dressed enthroned goddesses.

In the early phases of local coroplastics, the inspiration for the techniques and, in part, appearance was probably the handmade Argive/Boeotian figurines. In order to stay upright, a stand was included on the rear of the figurine. Transitional objects are known from Selinous. The idea of creating a hollow figurine by covering the stand or the legs of the chair might have come from Selinuntine coroplastics. By applying a slab of clay to the back, the figurine could be kept upright and makes a more three-dimensional impression. There are, on the other hand, several iconographic differences with the mould-made figurines. The outreaching limbs of the Argive objects contrast with the geometrical, abstracted body of the Akragantine figurines. The back was unworked and a mould only applied for the front. Predating this novelty was the introduction of the mould itself, possibly from Locri. The face would be moulded on an otherwise hand-modelled figurine. Smaller, easily movable figurines could be moulded completely. The development in the shape of the mouth shows influence from Phoenician objects at first, a small mouth with thick lips, followed swiftly by the 'Archaic smile.'

Production influenced form, in particular in the case of the application of moulds. The polos might have been introduced in this way as it also had technical advantages. Earlier 'Cretan' heads that are found near Akragas have a hollow flaring forehead that could indicate familiarity with this shape. The polos is sometimes replaced by or, exceptionally combined with, a veil. Over time, it became taller and even decorated in a way unique to Akragas: a pattern of open squares, filled with a disc. The transition to a new category of figurines is, in group four, marked by a widened and lower polos. In the same group, the hair was depicted in a large updo hairstyle, following Greek fashion. The earlier hairstyle was probably the *krobylos*, but the fringe around the forehead is the clearest part of the hair and appears in different styles, divided into two or several parts. These hairstyles, as well as jewellery, are similarly depicted on Syracusan coins and follow the chronological development.

The different facial features, as well as hairstyles, are influenced by east Mediterranean standards. The chubby or fleshy faces show Ionian influence. Heads were also exchanged, in particular with Selinous and Gela, and partial moulds applied to create a face with a fine expression, on which the lips were sometimes painted red. The need for well-shaped and sharp faces, which are hard to make by hand, might explain the intensive exchange with Selinous. The development of facial features are part of an increasing naturalism, and often reached Sicily through Etruscan sources.

A thick upper-dress or apron covers the body of the figurine and follows its rectangular outline. This rectangular apron is fastened by fibulae covered by appliques in several shapes, but most commonly round.

647 Albertocchi 2004; Fiertler 2001; Dewailly 1992.

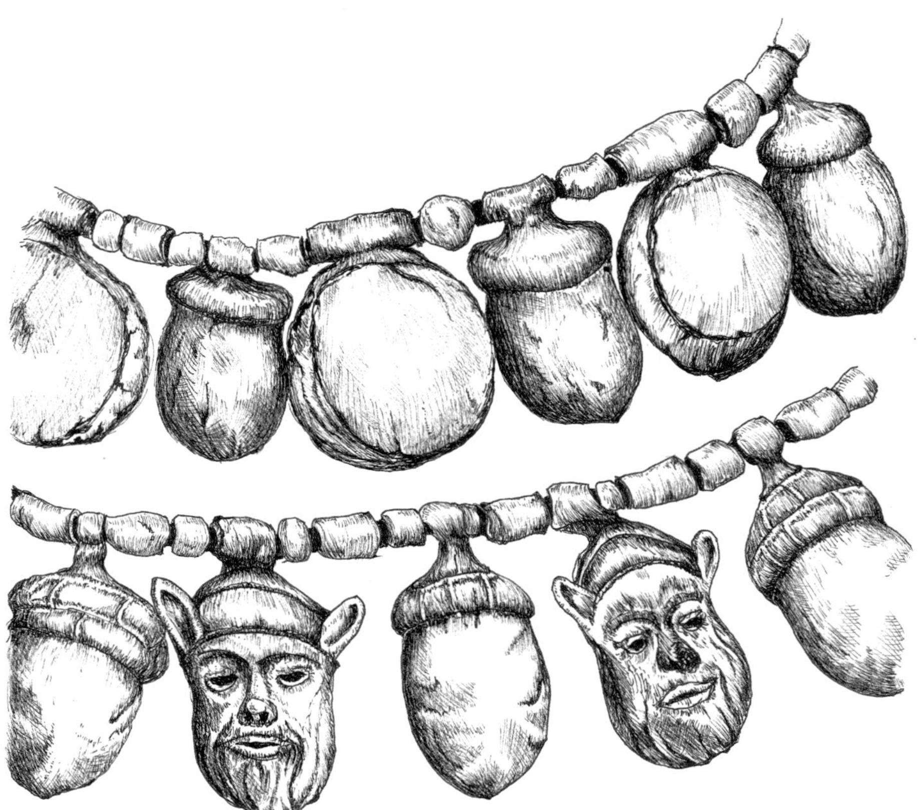

Figure 2.23: Drawing of the pectoral pendants with satyr protomai and acorns on figurine fragment no. **172**, partly reconstructed. Drawing by E. van Rooijen.

They are probably shaped after real-life bone appliques of the same shape, fixed in the middle to a dressing pin. This is the first jewellery to appear on the terracottas and maybe the only clearly functional one. Several metal rings with up to seven smaller eyes found on Sicily and in Olympia, make clear how the pectoral bands were attached to the fibulae. The disc-shaped shoulder clasps could have been inspired by Boeotian/Argive figurines, that also wear pectoral bands.

The pectoral or *hormos* is to be distinguished from a necklace. The François vase depicts a single pectoral band with discs, and some Corinthian vases show numerous pectoral bands, along with a tight necklace or choker that also appears on some figurines. Sicilian grave goods prove the existence of metal chain pectoral jewellery. The use of amber pendants, both shaped and irregular, is also comparable with the jewellery displayed on many figurines. The larger number and variation of the pectoral jewellery is unique to the Sicilian terracotta figurines and was developed locally.

For Akragantine coroplastics, several pendant forms must have been meaningful and might have served as amulets. The first pendants are larger, odd in number, usually three, sometimes five, with specific shapes. They develop towards multiple similarly shaped small pendants on more bands. The latter might have had a more general or standardised meaning. The earlier pendants of discs and crescents are eastern in origin and could have been brought to Sicily by the Phoenicians. Some other *protomai* and pendant forms are Greek and might refer to the specific cult involved. Small vase shapes and calf *protomai* are depicted on a special group of figurines. It is, in this case, the Greek migrants who took up the local custom of adorning the figurine with symbolic objects. Their influence permits an interpretation of satyrs and acorns as a reference to fertility (fig. 2.23). It marks the progression towards more Greek-inspired figurines (Catalogue fig. 28).

It is very likely that pectorals were worn in real life and that the figurines wore direct copies of real items. They might, however, have been reserved for specific occasions. The find of lead pendants at the sanctuary of S. Anna in Akragas shows that they also could have been dedicated as votives. The pendants may have adorned a life-sized statue or they may simply have been dedicated as gifts to the goddess. In addition, masks and busts with small holes in their ears could have worn jewellery items, representing the goddess herself. The deduced protective function of the pectorals matches with their application as amulets, a ritual practice that continued in this area with other objects.

Once earrings were added to the figurines, it can be proven that the terracotta figurines were imitating contemporary real-life jewellery. This later extended to the dress with fine folds and furniture details, which were very much in Greek fashion. For the earlier objects, figurines from group 1, the aim does not appear to have been to present an imitation of daily life. Unlike some of the jewellery items, the large shoulder clasps and polos were probably not regular items of adornment for all women. The exceptionally large Etruscan fibulae might mark a connection with the cultic sphere, as does the polos. Though jewellery plays a role in other cultures as well and could have inspired the Sicilian forms, the large size and number of pectoral pendants on small figurines are typical for Sicilian coroplastics. They influenced in their turn the Cyrenaican, Southern Italian and Punic coroplastics. The use of the amulets are probably inspired by similar pendants or directly by the Sicilian customs.

The seated pose and the more naturalistic rendering of the body over time could well have been influenced by contemporary terracotta 'enthroned' figurines from the east Mediterrean. Several of these objects, characterised by their rounded shapes, are found on Sicily, including Akragas. The chair received specific attention from the coroplast, from being handmade in the early stages with 'ears' on the sides like the East Greek examples to very elaborate thrones that refer to real furniture. The attention paid to the chair and the later more clear distinction between sitting and standing marks the importance of the seated pose and confirms the status and nature of the figure: a deity. The variation and spread of the type are too large to identify all of them as one specific goddess. It is rather the appearance with details like the dress and adornments that specifies a certain identity. The adornment and dressing of the goddess was probably part of a ritual performed by the women of Akragas, one that was familiar to the Greek migrants, and helped to create a shared identity.

Chapter III

The technology of Akragantine figurines

III.1 Introduction

The focus of this research is the terracotta figurine, the object itself in all its aspects. Having analysed the physiognomy of these objects, I will provide a detailed investigation of their technical aspects. In examining the figurines, we need to consider the juxtaposition of materiality, technique and iconography, and some of the questions posed in this research cannot be answered without incorporating all of these aspects. For example, was the typical block-shaped base chosen for aesthetic reasons or were there material or practical considerations for choosing this shape? Were specific forms or details intentional or were they a result of the moulding technique employed? There are also overarching questions, such as how does the function and production method relate to the intended form of the final result? Was form adapted to function or did it depend on the production method? These questions can only be answered if we analyse both the materials and production methods used. Only then can we address questions concerning both materiality and iconography: why did the Akragantine figurines become larger over time? How did the coroplasts respond to decreases in figurine size and detail? What effect did changes in fashion have on mould- produced objects?

The process of modelling clay into figurines can be seen as a transformation from nature to culture, from natural material to objects. The outcome of these processes and human actions is often called material culture. The research on these figurines should include the study of the material as the products of a specific *chaîne opératoire*. Material culture has a long tradition of research and debate. Specifically, ceramics have long been valuable indicators of culture for archaeologists. From this perspective, the outcomes of this investigation may shape our view on the interpretation of the materiality and iconography of the figurines themselves, but also affect our view of the social, cultic and economic significance of these figurines. The investigation of the material and the production method is not secondary to the interpretation of the cultural environment, but part of it and one of the methods that provide an insight into the lives and practices of the coroplasts and their customers.[648]

Production by mould was an invention from the Middle East dating back to the third millennium BCE but was only applied for the first time on Cyprus and Crete in the seventh century BCE. Though it did not always immediately change existing manufacturing practices, the technique spread from there across the Mediterranean. As a result, the moulding method created more uniformity among terracotta objects and resulted in the diffusion of popular models. On Sicily too, the assortment of imported moulds, objects, and their copies created a new form of votive objects that was relatively easy to produce around the mid of the sixth century BCE. These objects were then copied and combined, altered over time and changed locally, resulting in a wide variation of what could be

648 Preliminary results have been published in Van Rooijen et al. 2017.

called the Sicilian style. The original cause of this chain of events was a technical one: the application of a mould. Although the form of the terracotta objects depends to some extent on the technique used to produce them, their numerical success can be wholly ascribed to the adoption of mould production.[649]

The process of production, from material to final product, is described in this chapter in detail. This *chaîne opératoire* was investigated by means of an archaeological experiment in which two series of figurines from Akragas were recreated. Although this research primarily reveals technical aspects, it also provides information on related social aspects of production, such as division of labour or investment of time. In some cases, it supports existing theories based previously on iconographical arguments, in other instances, it helps provide an alternative view on the objects. Over the last decades, there has been an increasing interest in researching manufacturing processes as a primary aim, often reinforced by experiments. Part of this method is to have the same experiences as manufacturers from the past in order to understand their choices.[650] The experiment is carried out not just for the aspect of 'experiencing', nor to personally learn the same techniques, but rather to fully understand the craftsmanship and choices involved. The coroplasts in the sixth century BCE might have experimented with the new method of moulding as well, experiencing similar choices and consequences, and may have run into the same difficulties and questions. The results of their experiments are visible in the archaeological record. This chapter therefore also engages with the discipline of anthropology: in the projection of the choices of present-day potters and artists to coroplasts in antiquity and considering known techniques, tools, etc., from other periods and places as possibly applied in the production of these figurines.

Both the theoretical framework and scientific execution of experiments in archaeology have become well developed in recent years.[651] From as early as the 1940s and '50s, the advanced technological development of moulding figurines in antiquity was acknowledged and investigated by the appliance of practical experiments.[652] Archaeological experiments have often been applied to gain a better understanding of ceramics.[653] At the end of the twentieth century, the research of terracotta figurines and specifically its technical aspect were the subject of seminars organized by the University of Lille, France. This research was intensified by the foundation of the Association for Coroplastic Studies.[654] The very recent excavation of the large terracotta industrial quarter of Selinous, in which several workshops were dedicated to the production of figurines will likely contribute to renewed attention to the production of figurines. The role this production had in the economy has been investigated by researchers at Bonn University.[655] The importance of technical details for understanding the figurines in all aspects are nowadays well understood,[656] but the methods for investigating them are various. Experimental archaeology as such has gained respect as a scientific method, although it is still warned that without the application of archaeological theory, such experiments are scientifically useless.[657]

Production using a mechanical method like moulding employs a general sequence of the same steps and with similar outcomes. This naturally leads to an increased uniformity, compared to hand-made objects. Objects **3**, **4**, **5** and **6**, **7** are examples of hand-made figurines, except for their faces. The aim of the coroplast was probably to make the same figurine, but there are differences in the details. Surprisingly, however, it is in the moulded part that a clear change is made: the mouth of **7** is shaped considerably differently from the lips of the others. In addition to this intentional change, there are other unintended differences: material conditions and treatment led to minor deviations from the standard in moulded objects. Some of these distinctive features mark the technical actions that are typical of the coroplastic art at a specific period of time and place. The *chaîne opératoire* of the objects and the different actions and processes that resulted in the typical Akragantine mould-series are central here. The challenge lies in ascertaining whether the characteristics are intentional or a side-effect of the applied technique. Materiality is thus an aspect that is essential for the complete investigation of these figurines: the process, the human activity, all actions and circumstances that shaped and formed the material from the beginning to the final result.

The main part of this chapter consists of the description of the production method and the outcomes of the recreation of the figurines. The numerous objects from Akragas reveal, when carefully analysed, the processes of their production and use. By this approach, the figurines

649 Van Rooijen et al. 2017, p.153.

650 Blondé and Muller 2000; Caubet 2009.

651 Ferguson 2010.

652 Jastrow 1938; Neutsch 1952.

653 Orton and Hughes 2013, p.140ff.

654 Figurines in themselves were largely ignored in the past for their low intrinsic value, but are now more highly valued for their role in assisting our understanding of ancient religions and daily life. Today, a worldwide group of researchers dedicated to terracotta figurines is united in the Association for Coroplastic Studies, headed by J. Uhlenbrock. The Association also publishes regularly on technical aspects of coroplastics. http://coroplasticstudies.univ-lille3.fr. For an extensive review of the present state of research, see Caubet 2009.

655 For a description of these workshops see further Section III.10.

656 Burn 2011.

657 Orton and Hughes 2013, p.140.

are no longer seen as a static set of data but regarded as the outcomes of these processes, a set of actions, a series of events in time and place.

III.2 Aims of technical research

The first aim of this chapter is to identify the material used to produce the figurines and the reasons for this choice. By identifying the local source of the clay and other materials used, the local production of the figurines is confirmed. Clay samples were collected from nearby sources and tested for the characteristics that would make them suitable for application in the production of figurines: composition, workability and shrinkage. The characteristics of the clays have a high impact on both the coroplastic production and the final result. Clay shrinkage, for example, adversely affects new generations of figurines considerably, as figurines become smaller, and detail is lost. This seems to have been an undesired side-effect of working with moulds. Different clay combinations were tested and the results compared with the original objects.

The second aim is to reveal coroplastic techniques and methods as they were applied in Akragas in the roughly hundred years of the second half of the sixth and first half of the fifth century BCE. The available clay, moulds, coroplastic skills, and knowledge determine the possibilities for production.

A third objective is to identify the individual coroplasts of Akragas, their methods, techniques, and tools, but also their choices and preferences. The final aim of the coroplastic experiment was to understand the terracotta moulding business, and its social and economic implications. These questions range from practical issues such as time management and the preferred size of objects to larger implications on the exchange of objects and skills with other Sicilian towns. These perspectives might reveal how the coroplastic art became such a flourishing business in Akragas. This overarching question concerns the coroplastic craft of Sicily, and more specifically Akragas, as well as individual workshops: what marks local production? Questions related to this topic concern individual workshops and specific coroplastic techniques that might have originated in Akragas. Besides figurines, other terracotta objects are mentioned, made with the same or similar techniques and comparisons are made with Selinuntine coroplastics. Specific features of the clay might have resulted in adjustments to the methods followed. The interaction between material possibilities, technical skills and the wish for variation in design determined the final morphology of the figurines. The outcomes are implemented in the interpretation of their application, use and meaning.

III.3 Method: An archaeological experiment with analogue reconstruction

There are no written records of the production of Sicilian figurines, let alone as early as the sixth and fifth century BCE, or specifically from Akragas. In general, the role of literary resources on studying the production and use of terracotta objects is marginal. The lowly valued artisanship could be the reason for that. Aesopos' fable of Hermes and the *agalmatopoios*, statues-maker, makes exactly that point.[658] Votive figurines were a common practice in the Mediterranean world and there are no authors paying specific attention to their production. Inscriptions referring to figurines in Akragas have not been found and the majority of people were probably illiterate. The votives from Akragas are not textual, but visual.

A true understanding of the coroplasts' work is possible by experimentally reconstructing the production process according to the sequential steps of figurine making. This process is the general way in which figurines were produced using moulds from the seventh century BC onwards around the Mediterranean.[659] Though the general activities of such a production process are well described by different authors,[660] a detailed revision is necessary in order to understand the figurines' specific features at Akragas. The applied techniques and the development of the mechanical method have so far not been connected with the iconographic characteristics of Sicilian figurines. The experimental approach reveals technological features that otherwise might have been contributed to the iconography of the statues. Certain characteristics could now better be explained by the technical aspects of the moulding method. The method of research is, therefore, a practical approach: an archaeological experiment in which several generations of figurines were re-created.

The production process could be reconstructed based on finds exhibited in the archaeological museum of Agrigento, including moulds and figurines of various sorts and shapes. The experiment was carried out partly with clays collected from nearby Akragas. The availability of similar clay and the relatively small size of the figurines, between 5-30cm from head to toe, made such a reconstruction experiment possible. Even though not all conditions are known or possible to replicate, the coroplastic process could to a large extent be followed.

In this experiment, there were two ways to gain information on the sequential *chaîne opératoire* of the production process. The first was based on the probable operational sequence of materials and actions: the *chaîne opératoire*. The second way is by copying details of the figurines in order to reconstruct how and why they were

658 For a discussion of Sophokles' comments, see Neutch 1952.

659 Caubet 2009; Muller 2000.

660 Neutsch 1952; Nicholls 1952.

applied. This method can be described as a 'reconstruction'. Caroline Jeffra splits it up in 'construct' and 'simulation'.[661] In this case, 'construct' means that the different steps in the experiment were founded on archaeological evidence, for example, the moulds, while the simulation was carried out based on the information about probable actions in the past, deduced from the archaeological record. Our experiments could not be based on functionality alone, unlike many other archaeological experiments on utilitarian objects, in particular, pottery,[662] because the objects had a different extrinsic value and their decoration was not only aesthetic.

The method of experimental reconstruction is based on hypothetical production techniques. The hypothesis was tested and compared with the original objects. The experiment is, therefore, a process of trial and error, and involved constant comparison with the original figurines. This method functions according to the principle of analogy: the hypothesized production method is analogous to the experimental one creating the possibility of seeing the options available to the coroplasts. The method or tools could be adjusted in order to achieve closest reconstruction within the limitations of the possibilities of that period. By making replicas of the museum pieces as a starting point, mould-series were then created. Clay with a similar consistency and characteristics to the local clay was used in order to test whether certain features of the figurines were the result of the production method and the materials used. The use of certain tools was also reconstructed. The imitation of the coroplasts' actions led to new insights into their work, difficulties, and solutions, and the tools they used. This part of the experiment is, therefore, more human-centric and leaves room for individual characteristics of figurines as a result of a specific workshop or coroplast. By simulating the production process, we can better understand human actions of the past. This method does not provide certainty on all aspects but provides us with plausible explanations and the possibility to exclude processes.[663] While context and conditions were certainly different in the past, certain practices can be tested and evaluated on their applicability.

III.4 Interpretation and the *chaîne opératoire* approach

Production techniques are transmitted from one craftsman to the other. The long period over which coroplastics existed and thrived, and their wide dispersal across Sicily could, therefore, shed light on anthropological questions, for example, the transmission of knowledge and skills. This *chaîne opératoire* approach helps to minimise the dichotomy that seems to exist between the study of the technical aspects of production and interpretation in a social context.[664] By tracing specific technical aspects of figurine production, some social and economic connections between the coroplastic workshops of towns on Sicily could be understood. This directly relates to the typical physiognomy and dispersal of figurines. The application of techniques and the use of local materials give insight into the transmission and exchange of knowledge on the production methods, for example, between Selinous and Akragas. The objects and their production should be seen in the light of their social, religious and artistic context.

In the description of the *chaîne opératoire*, there are three aspects to be distinguished:

- Acquisition and preparation of the raw material
- Methods and techniques: modelling the clay in the steps of the production process
- Tools: the different sorts of instruments applied.

Considering these aspects, the overlap between iconographically defined groups[665] and workshops can be distinguished.

III.5 The general production process

III.5.a Object categories

Six varieties of coroplastic object categories can be distinguished in Akragas, of which five applied a mould in production for at least a part of the object.[666]

- Completely hand-modelled objects (probably not local): **1** and **2**.[667]
- Partly mould-made figurines (the face is mould-made, whereas other parts are hand-modelled in a specific group of figurines): **3**-**7**.
- Plaques: the shallow mould was filled with a slab of clay paste. The object remains two-dimensional, with a small amount of depth: **198** (though not solid).
- A small, completely solid object made in a mould, which was filled with a clay body: **7, 77**. One object that remains very thin and more like a plaque: **200**.

661 Jeffra 2014, p.142.
662 Jeffra 2014.
663 Orton and Hughes 2013, p.143.
664 Jeffra 2014, p.141.
665 See chapter 4 for the defined groups.
666 Not included in this list, as they belong to different categories, are pottery and roof terracotta, as well as larger statues. For those partly mould-made, the production of their parts is the same as described in the general production process.
667 Even though based on the clay colour, Pink 7.5 YR 7/4 and 7.5 YR 8/4 it would be possible, the iconographic differences seem to indicate otherwise.

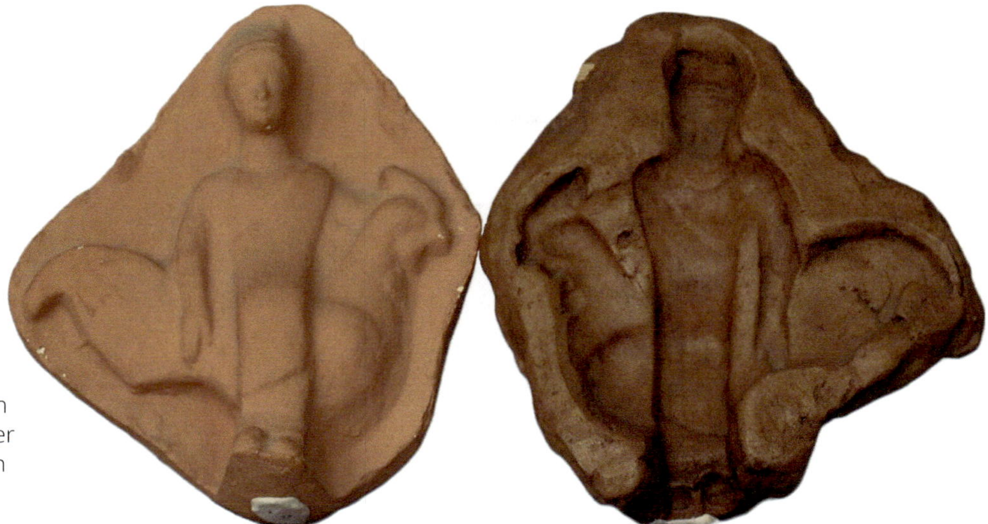

Figure 3.1: A near 13 cm high mould of a figure on a rooster with modern gypsum cast on the left. Mus. Agrigento Inv. no. S4; scale 1:2.

- Modelled figurines may appear as decorative additions to wheel-made pottery.[668]
- *Protome* or masks: the deep mould was filled with a slab of clay paste, covering all sides, except for the back. It was meant to hang with the hollow side to the wall and therefore was commonly pierced to be hung.[669]
- Figurines in the round, hollow: a mould is filled with a slab of clay paste and the back is formed from an unworked slab. The smaller parts, like the head or limbs, particularly in earlier and smaller objects remained solid: **18**, **24**, **28**. Some objects had wooden attachments, such as arms, that were sticking out: **3-7**, **85,** and **86**. Eventually, a mould could be used to shape the back. The latter is never the case in this period.[670] Protruding additions, such as chairs, are sometimes hand-formed.

III.5.b Solid objects and plaques

The seated figurines depicting a goddess are never solid, while a few standing figurines are. The latter are then relatively small, about up to 10 cm in height. There is a group of four very small busts, depicting a female head with a veil or long hair, but with weathered or broken faces. One of them, AG23118 has only three sides, like a miniature *protome*, but the rim shows that it is probably mould made. Other small objects have a head that remained solid, while the body is hollow, like **74**. The width of the head is only 14mm. At **69**, with a width of 17mm, the neck is still hollow.

The much deeper *protomes* might have inspired coroplasts to make figurine moulds deeper and in that way create the possibility of proper sitting along with a more balanced figurine. Figurines with a large clay-rim might have given the coroplast the idea of creating objects with multiple figures in a scene. Such a thin slab of clay lends itself well to fine details and figures in motion, but are on the other hand less three-dimensional. A plaque, such as **198,** is distinguishable by the scene in relief that would not have been possible to make with freestanding objects. In this case, the combined freestanding objects could have been used as a *patrix* to create the depicted action, while clay overlapping the moulds functions to hold the figures in position. The technique for filling the open space between parts with clay in order to depict a detail as three-dimensional can be seen on **194-5**, which suggests by its depth a void between the chair parts. The advantages of each of the categories are applied by the coroplast in **181**: filling the background gave the coroplast the freedom to have a figurine with her arms raised and a snake curling around it. The space between arm and head would support the different parts. The line is thin between freestanding object and plaque. An example is a mould of a figure seated on a rooster. Whether the original cast was a plaque, like the modern cast exhibited in the museum, is not known. The seated figure would not have needed support between the bird and the person, but the object as a whole was probably not able to stand straight-up either. If the aim were to produce a plaque, a

668 The libation tube and the Corinthian vase mentioned in Section II.5.c.iv and II.6.h.ii are examples.

669 This category, of which there are many from Akragas was not part of this research. An example is AG2167, a mould of a large *protome*, see fig. 15 in the Catalogue.

670 Object 20398 from Mus. Agrigento is probably such a mould. It has indications of where the front-mould should be attached.

Clay	Consistency	Shrinking percentage	Munsell colour (fired)	Workability
Macalube di Aragona	homogenous	7%	5YR 6/6 Reddish yellow	Highly suitable for making moulds; not very suitable for making figurines.
Scala dei Turchi	homogenous	2.5%	5Y 8/2 Light grey (unfired)	Lacking plasticity; not suitable to use as the basic clay to make a figurine or mould. Preparing process: grinding dried pieces of clay and add to another sort of clay or add water to the dry clay.
Macalube di Aragona / scala dei turchi / silt	45% Macalube di Aragona /45% Scala dei Turchi / 10% silt	5%	7.5YR 8/4 Pink	Highly suitable for making figurines.
Sicilian (commercial)	Macalube natural with inclusions	6.5%	7.5YR 6/4	Simulation of the original clay used in the original figurines in Agrigento. Highly suitable for making figurines, less suitable for moulds.
Dutch mixture (commercial)	42.5% VeKa red-firing/42.5% VeKa white-firing/15% river sand (250μ)	5%	2.5YR 5/8	Simulation of the original clay used in the original figurines in Agrigento. Highly suitable for making figurines, not suitable for moulds.

Table 3.1: The different clays and their consistency as applied in the experiment, their shrinkage, colour after firing and workability (after Van Rooijen et al. 2017).

rectangular outline of the mould would have been more suitable.[671] (fig. 3.1)

The objects in this research are mainly from the last category mentioned, figurines in the round. The production of figurines in a mould is a technical development that could be characterised as hand modelling, in which the mould functions as a support tool. The wheel technique was less suitable for the production of anthropomorphic figurines with rather rectangular shaped bodies. This archaeo-logical experiment focuses on the moulded figurines originating from the final quarter of the sixth century BCE, when the production of mould-made figurines started in Akragas.

The method of moulding hollow objects gave the coroplast the possibility of producing figurines of increased three-dimensionality. There is a certain gradation in the above list in this regard: deeper moulds mean deeper relief and increased three-dimensionality. Another important aspect is the intended method of display. Some objects were pierced in order to be hung, for example, **77,** while the figurines in the round, open at the base, were usually intended to stand. Moulds might have been kept hanging as well, as they often feature a small suspension hole in the middle of the back side, for example, **90**.

Some objects, though in general it is not a common characteristic of Akragantine figurines, feature a larger opening on the back, usually a couple of centimetres, which might have increased air circulation, even though it was not necessary with an open base, for example, **23**, **25**, **60**, **152**.

671 The mould, S4, h. 12.9cm, is on permanent exhibition in the Mus. Arch. Agrigento with a modern cast that suggests a plaque. The left arm of the figurine, held around the neck of the rooster, indicates at least combined features. On the other hand, the mould is relatively deep, open at the bottom and leaving little space above the head of the figure, which is comparable with moulds for seated figurines.

In Akragas, the most produced moulded figurines were figures in the round. The description below and the experiment focuses therefore on the production of these objects, produced by using a front-mould. Sides and back were left unworked, and the figurine was left open at its base. The mechanical method produces fast semi-identical objects that could be called 'industrial'.[672] The scale on which they were produced in Akragas could certainly be called serial, as the disappearance of real artistic and creative values, implied by the word 'industrial' is not really applicable in this case. The artistic and technical aspects both developed swiftly.[673] The methodological aspect should and cannot be seen separately from the physiognomy and design of the objects.

III.5.c Description of the steps in the production process

To fully comprehend the salience of the manufacture of the figurines by moulding, the different steps of the production process are first described shortly. These are the general steps, which are thought to have been taken by Akragantine coroplasts.[674] The steps are abbreviated in table 3.1 and the development of a series is schematically drawn in fig. 3.3. The mechanical method for moulding

672 Muller 2000, p.93.

673 Neutsch 1952, p.1.

674 Reference for the terminology used is Muller 1997. Because of the confusion in some works on terracotta objects, the distinction between the two sorts of application of 'type' should be specified: the first 'type' is derived from the Greek word *tupos* and used to describe objects produced using a similar production method, for example, from the same mould series. Muller 1997, p.451 'type'. The second use is more general, for example, 'iconographic type' means different sorts of figurines. Muller 1997, p.449-50 'type iconographique'.

figurines has hardly changed to this day.[675] The methods and features specifically applied in Akragas, and used in the experiment, are described below.

General steps in the production process for moulding figurines in series:

1. *The gathering and preparation of the clay*
   Different clay sorts could be combined for their specific properties in order to compose the desired mixture of clay. In addition to the clay and water, other components were added as temper, for example, several sorts of sand, silt, grit, or grains of broken terracotta, shell, etc.

2. *The patrix*
   In order to produce a mould, it is necessary to have a figurine. This could be a figurine from elsewhere or one made by the coroplast himself. Different parts of figurines could be combined, such as the head and body, in order to create the desired design. The coroplast could not alternate or add features easily at this part of the process, as he was dependent on the availability of an existing object, unless he were to create it himself. This object, which stands at the start of the genealogy, is called the archetype or patrix. The patrix could be made by the coroplast and, in that case, would have been created according to his insights and skills, probably influenced by the demands of its function: the requirements for a votive figurine. Apart from terracotta, the patrix could have been made of other materials, such as soft stone or wood. The choice of material would naturally influence the details of the physiognomy of the figurine, as harder materials like stone or wood are processed in a different way from clay.

3. *The matrix*
   The mould made from the patrix is called the matrix.[676] The matrix is formed as a print-off from the patrix, and required a plastic material like clay. In order to obtain a sharp print-off, comparatively fine clay was used for the moulds. Details of the execution are influenced by clay properties, like plasticity, resistance to deformation, and shrinkage. At this stage of production, changes in the design have to be considered as conscious alterations. After its production, the matrix is dried and transformed into terracotta by firing.

4. *Figurines from the matrix*
   The matrix can now be put to use for the production of multiple identical figurines. To do so, a sequence of actions is taken as summarised below (table 3.2 on the right).
   a. *Preparation of the clay*
      The general procedure in this step is similar to the procedure described above. The clay used for the production of series of figurines is tempered with slightly coarser grains compared with the clay used for the moulds. The function of these tempers is to improve the workability of the clay and to reduce shrinkage.
   b. *Forming the figurine*
      The mould is filled with moist clay, soft enough to obtain the details of the mould. Clay lacking in flexibility would result in figurines with cracks (fig. 3.2). The result of good flexibility is clear on the back of **146**.[677] The statuette should remain hollow in order to dry evenly. Only for the production of small objects an entirely solid construction is possible. For the back of the figurine, a slab of clay is applied. By this method, the circulation of air during drying is assured, due to the thin-walled construction.
   c. *Drying the moulded figurines in two steps*
      In the first step, the cast is dried to a leather-hard condition. Due to shrinkage, the figurine can now be released from the mould relatively easily. The main shrinkage occurs during this first stage of drying. As a second step, the statuettes' details and surface, which is now just dry enough, can be reworked. In this stage, small parts are added or removed. Hereafter the figurine is removed from the mould. The cast is left to dry thoroughly for a longer period. The joining of the two halves, the front and back, is the most important part. Reworking is not only done for aesthetic reasons. The seam on the front and back should be strengthened with extra clay in order to prevent the vulnerable connection from breaking. Before the final touch of smoothing, alterations could be carried out, for example, the addition of a chair. After reworking, the figurine is left to dry again.

675 For example, Muller 1996, p.27-47 on Classical and Hellenistic figurines from Thasos. Up to today, many objects used daily are produced in a double mould. On those glass and plastic objects, the seam of the two halves can be recognised.

676 It can be confusing that in Italian the word 'matrice' is used for 'mould' in general. Here a distinction is made between the matrix and a derivative mould, which is a mould further on in the genealogy. The matrix is therefore crucial in understanding the design of the figurines. The word 'mould-series' refers to a certain group of figurines, which is almost identical in physical appearance and therefore appointed to the same genealogy.

677 See photo Catalogue **146**.

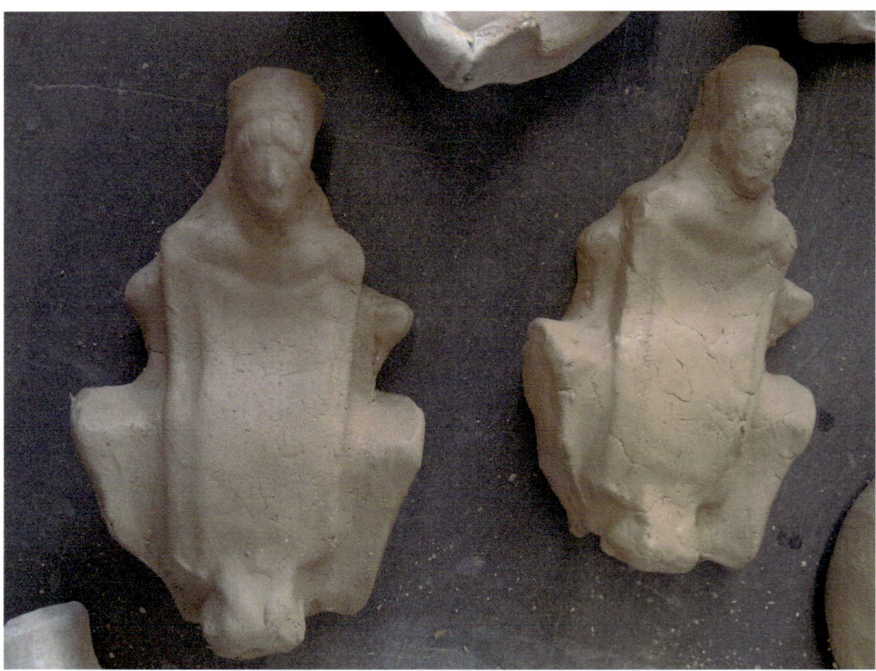

Figure 3.2: If the clay is too dry, this may result in cracks on the surface after being pressed into the mould.

d. *Firing*
Dried thoroughly, the object can be fired. During this firing process, chemically bound water should be able to escape from the clay. In order to avoid damage caused by the thermal expansion of the water, steam, and to allow the ceramics to shrink gradually, the firing process should not be speeded up. After firing, the object could be *painted*.

5. *Use and application*
The figurines were used as a votive object and also had an economic value. If the matrix was not available or suitable anymore because it was worn or damaged, it had to be replaced. Now the figurine had a practical value because it could serve as a patrix for the second generation of figurines. In that case, the sequence of actions was repeated. The derivative mould is thus made from a figurine from a previous generation (fig. 3.3). The result, however, is a smaller figurine of the second generation and often with a decline in quality (fig. 3.4).

The described production method results in a series of moulds and figurines and will be experimentally verified as is shown in fig. 3.3.

III.6 The coroplastic experiment

An experimental reconstruction was set up according to the hypothesised sequential steps of the production process. The experiment was carried out in the Ceramic Laboratory at Leiden University, with the availability of modern utilities for terracotta production, such as furniture, ovens and different sorts of wooden and metal tools. A woorden or hard stone worktop was required for the work. If moisture had to be extracted from the clay, a chalk plate was used. For the practicalities, Loe Jacobs, a potter and ceramic specialist, and Bibi Beekman, a student with knowledge of pottery production, provided assistance. The numbers correspond to the steps in the general production method described above.

Three samples of local clays were collected around Agrigento and transported to the *Museo Archeologico Regionale di Agrigento*. The first sample was collected at the national park of Macalube di Aragona, since this was the nearest source of clay, within a range of 12km of Agrigento. This information was obtained by asking local people involved in the production of modern terracotta. The second sample was collected at the white 'rock formation' of Scala dei Turchi, situated at the coast at a distance of about 12km from Agrigento. Both places are relatively nearby, but there is a considerable variation in height above sea level.[678] The third clay sample was collected at the beach of Giallonardo, around 18km walking distance from Agrigento, at a place mentioned by a local geologist.[679]

678 Macalube di Aragona, (37° 22' 31.68" n 13° 36' 2.37" e) and Scala dei Turchi (37° 17' 23.88" n 13° 28' 21.58" e) are about 12 km walking distance from Akragas, respectively to the north and west. Van Rooijen et al. 2017.

679 Giallonardo beach (37° 19' 1.388" n 13° 25' 2.975" e) is much further than the other sources and the road to the beach varies considerably in altitude. Only one figurine was made with this sample because suitable clay was found much nearer to Agrigento.

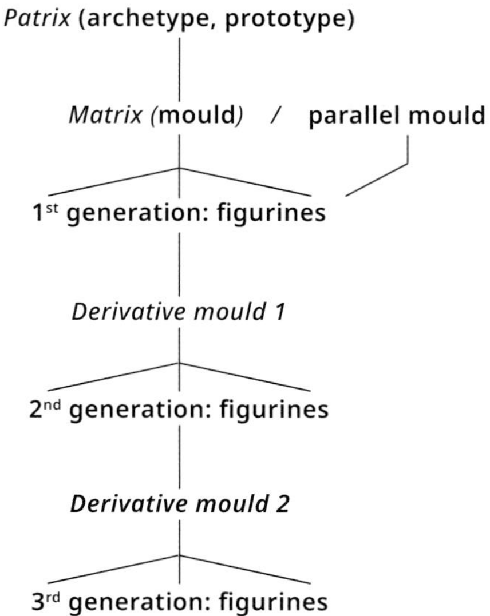

Figure 3.3: Schematic development of a series with the terminology as used here.

Because of the limited amounts we were able to carry, we also used some commercial local clay from Agrigento, which has similar properties to the Macalube di Aragona clay. The rich supply of clay at Macalube di Aragona is still used today as a source for commercial clay. In colour and workability, it is similar to modern commercial clays. Because the samples were not sufficient to make all the figurines, two commercial clays, one from Agrigento and one from the Netherlands with similar characteristics were used as well.[680]

The preparation of the clay consisted of moistening, kneading, and adding tempering material. The mould was filled with a slab of clay paste around 5mm thick.

To make a similar series of figurines, a patrix and matrix were required. Originals provided by the *Museo Archeologico Regionale di Agrigento* were used as patrix: S901 and S273.[681] They were chosen for their difference in size, fineness and because they each represent a larger group of figurines. In the museum, matrices were made from these two figurines. In a leather-dry condition, they were transported to Leiden University and fired in a modern oven. [682] The moulds thus obtained were used throughout the experiment as matrices of the respective series. A total of eighteen objects were made from different moulds in the two series. The tests with the clays from nearby Agrigento were all done with the mould of S273 for the smaller amount of clay needed. The moulds themselves were made of pure Macalube di Aragona clay for its fine results.

The actions from clay to figurine:

a. *Mixing and kneading the clays*
In this experiment, different sorts of clay were mixed to utilise all the properties and optimise functionality. To improve the workability of the clay body, finely ground marl from Scala dei Turchi and some silt material were added during kneading. This step did not take more than ten minutes, considering that the clays were already prepared in that they. contained the right amount of moisture and were purged of impurities such as stone particles and plant remains.

b. *Moulding*
A front- and rear-mould were made of the patrix in the Archaeological Museum of Agrigento.[683] The frontal mould was filled with a layer of clay. The inside was pressed and smoothed by hand. Before making the rear part, the front was dried a bit. The hollow space in the inside was temporarily kept open with cloths. The pieces of clay that overlapped the edges of the mould were cut-off neatly or smoothed to create an extra rim. In fact, this part of the process consisted alternatively of moulding, drying and retouching and was generally done in 10 to 15 minutes.[684]

c. *Drying, unloading and retouching*
To dry evenly and prevent deformation, the right conditions are necessary. Drying the rough-out to a leather-hard state took around 40 minutes after which the figurine could be removed from the mould. After retouching and eventual additions, there is a second period of drying in order to remove almost all moisture from the figurine. Depending on air humidity and temperature, this took at least a couple of days. We assume that potters had to make sure that they were completely dried in order to avoid a steam explosion.

The addition of a bench or chair, and adding specific decoration or removing unnecessary pieces of clay, refining edges and smoothening are all done at

680 This sample, acquired in a local shop, was also insufficient. The Dutch commercial clay is a composition of clays from the Netherlands, very different in colour but close in workability. These clays were used to try the different techniques and working on the figurines, not to test the properties of the clay.

681 These are respectively **118** and **42** in the catalogue.

682 The matrices from the experiment have been returned to the museum.

683 The rear mould was only made in order to have a good impression of how the rear was shaped. The assumption is that in Akragas in this period only frontal moulds were used.

684 The moulding process for the objects in bas-relief is roughly similar to the process described for the figurines. These plaques and small solid figurines were not imitated in this experiment, because the process does not diverge much.

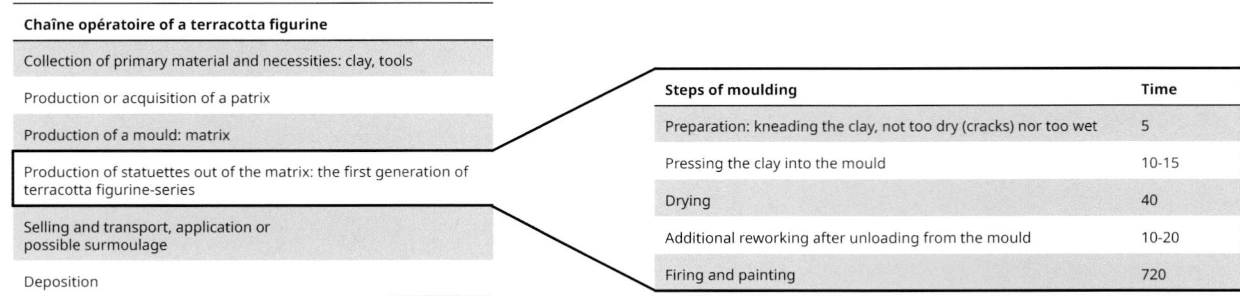

Chaîne opératoire of a terracotta figurine
Collection of primary material and necessities: clay, tools
Production or acquisition of a patrix
Production of a mould: matrix
Production of statuettes out of the matrix: the first generation of terracotta figurine-series
Selling and transport, application or possible surmoulage
Deposition

Steps of moulding	Time
Preparation: kneading the clay, not too dry (cracks) nor too wet	5
Pressing the clay into the mould	10-15
Drying	40
Additional reworking after unloading from the mould	10-20
Firing and painting	720

Table 3.2: Summarised overview of the steps of the chaîne opératoire on the left and the specified steps in the moulding, step 4, with an indication of the duration of each step in minutes on the right (after Van Rooijen et al. 2017).

this stage. Some of the retouchings are essential for the strength and stability of the figurine.

The hand-modelled chair results in a change in the appearance of the figurine. This step of the production process depends partly on the demands of the coroplast or the client who commissioned the object. The time involved depends on the requirements, but also on the experience of the coroplast. In general unloading and retouching took us 10 minutes, the addition of the chair excluded. The latter took up to about 20 minutes more.

Because a slip layer covering the surface is not very common on the figurines from this period, the addition was not been part of the experiment. In order to cover the figurine with a slip layer, usually in a light colour, the object would be submerged into a suspension of clay and water. A resulting slip layer had to dry before firing.

d. *Firing and painting*
This experiment did not involve specific firing techniques. All objects were fired to 750˚C, in an oxidizing atmosphere. Painting was not included as part of the experiment.

Use-wear of the completely finished and fired figurines during their application as votives was not part of the experiment. They were restricted to the causes of change in the production process, the wearing of the mould, influences of shrinkage, workability properties of the material on the sharpness of the print-offs, etc. The use of the figurine was limited to its use as a patrix and the effect of generating new figurines by this method.

III.7 Results of the experiment and comparison with features of the original objects

III.7.a Step 1: The clays used in Akragas

Terracotta as a material for statuettes offered a great alternative to metal and marble. The lower sustainability impact of terracotta, compared to metal, might have been considered as an advantage, as these votives of sanctuaries were meant to be temporarily displayed, after which they were likely ritually discarded. Also, the local sandstone outcrops and associated clay-rich resources found near Agrigento are rather porous and therefore not suitable for fine statuettes. The nearby availability of other clays in huge quantities provided the necessary material. The motivation to opt for this material was probably also cost-effective, as it was inexpensive and easy to shape.

Earlier pXRF tests in the field and museum indicated that the figurines were probably made of local clay mineral resources. For experimental results comparable to the original objects, two sorts of clay from nearby Agrigento were used. The first clay is from a natural park, Macalube di Aragona, where hot volcanic sulphuric gasses bring up melted clay. This clay is very fat, plastic or fine, and dark grey in colour, turning light red by firing. The clay works well, even non-purified.[685]

The second source is a spectacular natural phenomenon, the white coastline of Scala dei Turchi.[686] This fine, very white marlstone, a natural combination of clay and chalk, is as a lean material, scarcely suitable for modelling, but very useful to temper the first clay.[687] The material of Scala dei Turchi has a shrinkage rate of 2.5% and the clay of Macalube di Aragona has a shrinkage rate of 7%.[688] The last material

685 The clay is already very pure naturally. The sulphuric gasses prevent vegetation in the clay deposit. Yet other inclusions might leave cavities in the surface of the figurine when fired.

686 The Munsell-colour of the Macalube is 5YR 6/6, Scala dei Turchi: 5Y 8/2 (unfired) and the mixture is 7.5YR 7/4.

687 The difference between a highly plastic and a low plastic clay is made visible by twisting rolls of the material. While a coil made of plastic clay bends well and does not crack, a coil made of lean clay almost immediately cracks. The degree of fineness of a clay is also visible by comparing the break structure of fired objects; the finer the clay the more straight the break and the smoother its surface.

688 In comparison, the shrinkage of the Taranto made objects is 9-10%. Jastrow 1938, p.3.

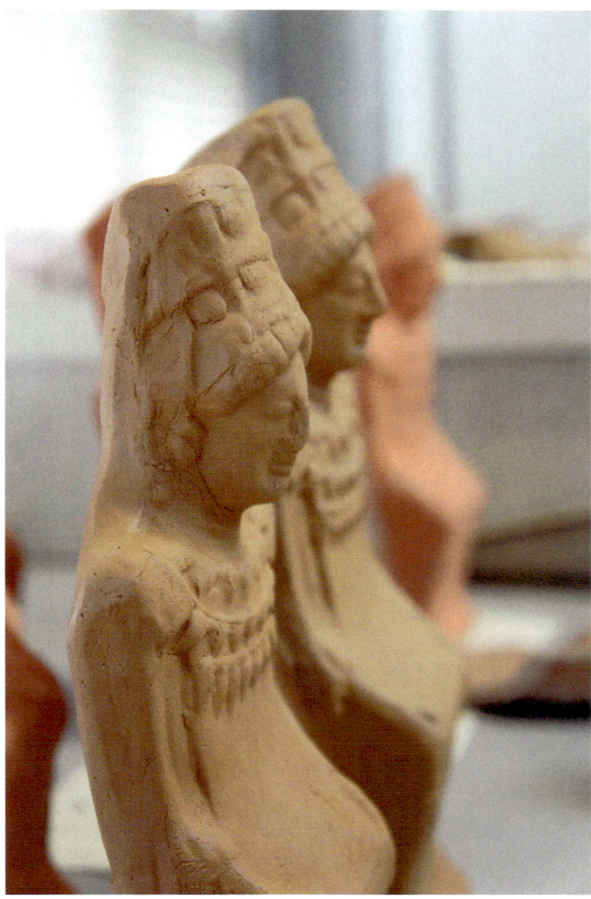

Figure 3.4: Second generation figurine replicas. The nose of the figurine at the front was damaged while being taken from the mould. The sides of the head and the neck were difficult to unload from the mould because it had become too narrow. The force required to take the figurine out caused cracks in the neck. Imitation of the reworking on the back of the head, removing the corners with a thin knife, resulted in forms very similar to the originals. While drying standing, the heavier head tends to bend to the front. On this replica, the line on the chest, just above the second row of pectoral pendants, can be clearly observed. This line indicates that the original or patrix of this replica was made in parts, possibly to combine a head and body. Photo after Van Rooijen et al. 2017.

is therefore more plastic, and in its levigated state appears rather sticky and dense. Combining the two materials with the addition of some silt as a tempering material resulted in a clay body with very good workability properties.[689] To generate more material as an alternative, Dutch commercial clay mixed with some temper was used. It was adapted to the properties mentioned above, and had shrinkage of 5%.

689 For an eventual slip layer, the white clay of Scala dei Turchi, provided that it would be finely ground, and dissolved in water, is suitable.

An overview of the consistencies and different properties of the clay can be found in table 3.1.

Both clays should be well kneaded to be properly mixed. Uneven mixing causes colour differences, as seen in **29**. The condition of the clay should be neither too wet nor too dry. The flexibility of a proper clay body is well visible in the imprint on the back of **146**. A too dry condition would cause cracks in the surface when pressing the lump into the mould, a defect that appeared during the experimental trials and is visible on **166**. The preparation took approximately half an hour extra because the secondary material from Scala dei Turchi had to be ground. Had this calcareous material not been finely ground, it could have caused lime-spalling on firing.[690] The effects of lime-spalling are also clearly visible on some figurines, for example, **139**. This destructive process can be caused by different forms of chalk, including marl, shell, micro-fossils, and crystalline-calcite.

The presence of small shell fragments in the ceramic structure of some figurines can be explained by the proximity of a beach.[691] Crushed shell could have been used as tempering material.[692] However, calcareous particles of 2-3mm in size increase the risk of lime spalling. To minimise this risk, it was necessary to thoroughly grind the shell in order to reduce particle size to mix the shell thoroughly with the clay in order to homogenise the clay body. In order to avoid lime-spalling, the firing temperature would also have to be kept below 750° C.

The processing of the raw materials – the collecting, grinding, sieving, purifying and mixing – were all labour intensive activities. Each step would only be undertaken by the coroplasts presumably, if they led to a noticeable improvement in the workability or final appearance of the clay bodies. The presence of crushed shell would indicate that it was necessary to improve upon the raw materials prior to processing.

Figurines **147** and **144** respectively show few and many inclusions, of which some are burned, resulting in cavities in their surfaces. In the experiment, tempering the two clays with some silt resulted in a workable clay body, which was not too sticky and turned pinkish beige after firing. By mixing the clay of Macalube di Aragona with the fine ground clay from Scala dei Turchi, shrinkage was also reduced by about 2.5%. The most important improvement, however, was the resulting openness of the clay structure, which improved the equal drying of the clay. As a result,

690 On firing, these particles change into calcium oxide. Later, as they absorb CO_2 from the atmosphere, they expand more quickly faster than the surrounding terracotta. a process that can be destructive.

691 Other examples, besides these two, with one or more chalk fragments are: **14**, **30**, **42**, **92** (many), **95**, **103**, **143**, **154**, **155**, **186**.

692 The shells would have been collected. Its availability might have led the coroplast of figurine **99** to use it as a tool in reworking the hair, impressing fine lines and a wavy structure.

no cracks appeared in the experimental figurines, whereas this was the case when pure Macalube clay was used.

The third sample of local clay from the modern beach of Giallonardo is a sticky clay in its pure form. Its shrinkage is not as high as the pure Macalube di Aragona clay due to the presence of small sand particles. In our experiment, only one figurine was made with this sample because the Macalube di Aragona clay was both a suitable clay and available much nearer to Akragas.[693]

It is by experiencing the outcomes of different levels of moistness and by kneading the material that we can learn the correct conditions for a workable clay body. The same is true for making a matrix. Here too the clay paste might easily crack if it is too dry or the relief too deep. This may have occurred with mould **32,** which displays some cracks on the sides. This is less problematic for a mould because the straight surface could be easily smoothed out when retouching the moulded figurine, although it means more work.

III.7.b Steps 2 and 3: Choice of patrix and creating the matrix

The patrices of our experimental figurine series were selected because they each represent a common mould series from Akragas, which was almost certainly developed locally.[694] While the physiognomy of the two series is each exemplary for the regional terracotta figurines, they also have Akragantine characteristics. The individual patrices were used because they were the sharpest examples in their mould-series. However, it is not clear to which generation they belong exactly. The larger **118** could have well belonged to one of the earlier generations, but for **42** this is less clear. The first one is 26.3cm tall and belongs to the group with decorated *polos*, described above. The statuette is rather detailed in the way she is adorned but lacks a chair. The second statuette, **42**, is an example of an earlier armless figurine, with a relatively low height of 13.9cm and a simple rendering of the body. She lacks decorative items on the chest except for one line. In this case, the chair was part of the mould and thus has not been added separately. On the original, **42**, used as patrix, the right corner of the chair, near the feet is broken off. This was reconstructed in the mould in our experiment.

Commonly, matrices are thick-walled and therefore rather heavy. The thickness can be locally more than 1cm and its model is based on C240, **90** in the catalogue. Surprisingly this mould of a standing figurine is able to stand by itself. The base is left open completely, which means that when a cast was formed the base needed to be cut off in order to have a straight and level surface for standing. The open base makes it possible to add a hand-modelled pedestal and elongate the figurine relatively easily. This mould, **90**, as well as mould S5 of a *kourotrophos*, are tilted, which is clearly visible at the feet as one is clearly positioned lower than the other.[695]

In the experiment, fine clay was used to create a sharp mould and, therefore, a sharp print-off. Derivative moulds may often become less precise, for example, S4, depicting a figure on a rooster. In this case, a sharp tool was used to cut away the edges between the rooster/figurine and their background, which is most clearly visible at the rooster's neck. This treatment might have been done to ease unloading (fig. 3.1).

When pressing clay onto the patrix, as well as when filling the mould, it is better to work with pieces of clay additively in order to not to over-stretch the clay and cause cracks. This is specifically a risk with parts that have deeper profiles, like the face. In our experiment, a better result was achieved when the clay for the nose and the head as a whole was pressed in separately. On **146** the face was clearly pressed in separately. The clay body would otherwise easily leave space unfilled. This way of working, in which different parts of the figurine are separately made, is visible on casts from derivate moulds (fig. 3.4).[696] The moulds found in Agrigento are frontal moulds, without 'fitting keys'.[697] Residues of clay or other material left behind in the mould cause marks on objects from new generations. This principle also works when there are cracks in the mould: **143** has a slightly protruding line, coming from the right side of the throne over the arm and the lap, caused by a fracture in the mould. It is exactly the same mark visible on **147**.

The figurines have a plain and unworked back which often shows tool marks or fingerprints of hand modelling, **34**. Sometimes the surface of the back is rather smooth and probably retouched. The back of other statuettes was scraped with a tool, for example, **135**. In particular, for larger figurines, the method of working with a slab of clay to form the back turns out to be faster and easier, compared to making use an extra mould. An example of a back formed with parts of clay

693 Van Rooijen et al. 2017, p.155.

694 See Section III.6 and n. 34.

695 Bold numbers refer to the catalogue. Other numbers mentioned, not bold and starting with 'S' or 'AG' are objects from the Arch. Mus. Agrigento, that are not included in the catalogue, because they belong to different categories or later date. They can be found in De Miro 2000, Albertocchi 2004.

696 Another example is the mould of a satyr AG8941.

697 Such 'fitting keys' are clearly visible on exceptional object **79**. This mould has three rather deep compartments. The lower, larger one is rectangular with rounded corners. There are six roughly circular shaped 'fitting keys' on the corners of the compartments, corresponding to another mould. The representation on this mould is not entirely clear.

is **135**. In the middle, diagonal folds are visible, where pieces of clay were added.

For the coroplast, the function of the back is a practical one: keeping the statuette upright. The three-dimensional shape gives the object more expression and a better spacial appearance, compared to flat plaques. It might have been technically possible to use a mould for the back, but this was not necessary for the design and would not have saved time. The back is plain at this time, the end of the sixth to the beginning of the fifth century BCE, and no figurative elements are visible on the reverse of the figurines.

III.7.c Step 4: Aspects of the shaping process and related items

III.7.c.i Making the front of the figurine

Moulded figurines, as opposed to hand-modelled objects, are recognisable by some features. First, they have smooth surfaces and soft edges, caused by moist clay paste taking the shape of the mould. Secondly, a seam marks the assemblage of the front and rear. This is a weaker part, see, for example, **53**, and was often smoothed away afterwards. An advantage of this mechanical method is the ease of producing finely detailed figurines. The method is comparatively quick and results in uniformity. An important factor is also that less skill is necessary compared to hand-modelling. The method of moulding creates figurines as a replica but still gives the coroplast some space to alter the model. The result of the imprint is first visible after unloading the object from the mould. In this phase of production, when the clay is in a soft-leather condition, certain changes and corrections can still be applied.

III.7.c.ii Making the back of the figurine

Instead of filling the hollow figurine with cloths and ropes, as done in the experiment, originally a less expensive material could have been used. It is possible that an animal bladder functioning as a balloon, supported the slab of clay in the back, temporarily. One reason to assume this sort of filling is the more or less regular convex shapes of the back of some figurines, and the almost perfectly oval opening formed by the front and rear base: **136**, **171**, **173**, **174**. The evenly roundish shape of an air-filled bladder would ensure more evenness and symmetry than propped up material. By inflating or deflating the bladder, different parts could be made more convex or concave. This technique is applied only for a small number of figurines. The thin body and flat back of **115**, for example, shows no indication of this technique, while **173** and **171** have comparable iconographic characteristics but a much more rounded back.

The Akragantine figurines are usually left open at the base in order to enable air circulation. There are a few instances of round openings in the middle of the back, which are too large to interpret as suspension holes. In the case of Akragas, these are believed to have facilitated assemblage.

III.7.c.iii Making an extra rim

When the clay is pressed into the mould, the clay that overlaps at the front could be handled in two different ways. It could be cut off to create the impression of a side or could be used to form an additional rim as if it were a plaque. When pressing the two parts together, some left-over clay could be cut off. This is the most common treatment. The removed piece of clay could have been applied on the inside to join the two parts and strengthen the seam between the two halves.

Several variants of these treatments within the same type are known from Selinous with different sorts of rims or without a rim.[698] On some Akragantine figurines, a group of objects from the same moulding genealogy has a rim worked out in different ways: **142-151**. The wide rim around the body might have strengthened the weak parts, such as the neck. Besides this functional perspective, the outline that was thus made around the head and upper part of the body connected with the bench creates a strong image, because it increases the figurine's size and places it in a sort of frame. The rim was retouched straight or with round edges. The inspiration to vary in this way might have come from Selinous.

III.7.c.iv Drying and deformation

Drying clay objects in the open air, exposed to direct sunlight and drafts, causes uneven evaporation and warps the clay. The drying of moulds is extra complicated in this respect because the wall is thicker in order to ensure its strength and to absorb moisture from the fill. Another reason that the drying takes longer lies in the character of the clay. The pure Macalube di Aragona clay was used in the experiment to create a sharp imprint. The clay is very fine in its pure form but lacks the openness of tempered clay. For the figurines, silt and/or ground Scala dei Turchi clay was added. As a result, the Macalube clay tends to warp when dried unevenly.

Uneven clay shrinkage caused by drying the mould turned out to be problematic. The sides tended to bend inwards, narrowing the space. This became clear when the mould was used to make a figurine. The narrow space was not wide enough to remove the head in a straight line, which caused damage to the sides of the head and the nose. At **143** a flattened nose and chin are visible

698 Dewailly 1992, p.86, Type B XV.

from the side, which similarly might have been caused by a narrow derivative mould (fig. 4). Some cracks in the neck also indicate difficulties unloading. The head became immovable in the mould. A possible solution is to bend the sides slightly outwards preventively and to dry the mould with its open side downwards.

Both the mould and the figurine should dry slowly and horizontally. If a tall figurine dries in a standing position, it tends to bend slightly. Because the head is rather heavy and the body is relatively thin and flexible, the figurine ends up looking downwards. Coroplasts certainly had to deal with comparable situations. The final drying may take a rather long time, up to a couple of days. A longer drying time also minimises the risk of cracks caused by a steam explosion.

III.7.c.v The derivative mould

As it dries, the clay turns from flexible to fragile. As a consequence, ceramic objects are hard but breakable. Breaking a mould would have been costly for the coroplast.[699] Extra time was necessary to make a new mould in order to continue production. If the coroplast had not kept the patrix, he could opt for a derivative mould made from one of the first generation figurines.[700] This solution, however, had some consequences. One of them is a considerable reduction in size compared to the broken mould, due to clay shrinkage of the figurine and the mould itself. In addition to shrinkage, malformation could also be caused by uneven drying. Because the thinner sides of the mould dry faster, there is an increased amount of vertical shrinkage relative to the horizontal. Specifically, the narrowness of the neck and face proved to be problematic when removing the figurine from the mould.

A rapid decline in quality could be observed through the course of the experiment. Figurines from a derivative mould were noticeably less sharp compared with previous generations. In particular, the detailed areas suffered the most. Facial expressions, for example, became less distinct. Pendants too lost parts of the relief but, nevertheless, remained recognizable. In order to remedy this deterioration, the best option was to replace the entire head or face, as the facial expression was essential and retouching the mould for the face would have been very difficult. **118** is an example of this solution (Van Rooijen 2014). In the new generation, the reduced size caused by clay shrinkage is often compensated with a raised pedestal, **144** for example, or elongated headgear.[701] Such a procedure, however, was not very common in Akragas.[702] There is an example, **136,** with her feet above the ground level. The *polos* is relatively low, compared with others from the iconographical typology 3a. Another way of compensating in order to enlarge the object as a whole was to make alterations to the seating. The benches, which are sometimes as wide as the length of the total figurine, balance the composition by adding a horizontal element. Figurines without benches appear heightened as the vertical element is emphasized. The sturdy, triangular shape is often created by adding extra 'ears' to the chair along with sizeable fibulae, **34**. This addition after moulding emphasizes the seated appearance. During the same period, at the end of the 6th century BCE, coroplasts at Paestum used deeper moulds from which a more bent and thus seated figure could be made.[703] One technical indicator that a figurine was printed from a derivative mould is a very thin upper body, as the depth of the mould inevitably decreased over the generations.

Impressions on the figurine of clay residues, straw, or wood pieces left in the mould are not necessarily an indicator of the use of a derivative mould, but rather of quick and careless handling. Figurine **111** has the impression of a piece of wood on her neck. If such a figurine were used as a patrix, the defect would be passed on to the new generations.

III.7.c.vi Time management and additions

During the experiment, the time required for each step was recorded. The modelling itself, making use of a mould, was quite rapid, and the most time-consuming element was the drying process. If the coroplast worked in a sequence and used all the available time for figurine production, three to four figurines could be worked on at the same time. Filling a mould with clay paste takes about 10 minutes. During the first drying phase, the rough-out remains in the mould. The initial desiccation takes about 40 minutes. For retouching after unloading, the time investment depends very much on additional parts and details. As a consequence, it is clear that differences in the major shapes of the figurine could have technological as well as iconographic causes.

The seated, standing or leaning posture of the figurines is not just a matter of aesthetic preference but linked closely to the technical skills of the coroplast. Because of its size, a broader chair or bench was not an integrated part of the mould but was added later. The making of a bench, which is symmetrically shaped on both sides, takes about 15 to 20 minutes. This estimation depends largely on the coroplast's skill. On **136**, for example, it can be clearly seen that the right half of the bench is positioned

699 See Jastrow 1938, p.5.

700 This was a common solution. For example, at Morgantina, Bell 1981, p.220.

701 Ammerman 1993, p.14.

702 In Paestum other means were found to compensate for shrinkage, such as relief or extra rims added in the derivative mould. See Ammerman 1993.

703 See Ammerman 1993, p.18.

relatively high to the arm. The hand modelling of this addition required creativity, skill, and extra time. It is probably because of this that the large bench from the mould series **118**, used in this experiment, was commonly left out by the coroplasts.[704] Though most of the benches are rather straightforward and unevenly shaped, there are also benches with soft curving on the edges and cushions, for example, **139**. This upper part of the bench could be made in a mould, to save time and create better symmetry. Large fibulae were probably mould-made and added separately.[705] The 5.8cm mould of an earring (**201**) could have been an individual object, as its size would otherwise only fit a near life-size figurine.

In summary, it can be assumed that specific additions that were not part of the frontal mould, such as larger chairs or benches, fibulae or other decorations, were moulded separately, for example, the pectoral pendants of **179**. Otherwise, the time taken to model these objects by hand would have been out of proportion for the achieved result.

III.7.c.vii Retouching and tools

An important element of retouching consists of fixing and smoothing the assemblage seam on the inside and outside. This is not only aesthetically important but also technically, as the joint needs to be firmly sealed to prevent splitting. Rolls of clay were pressed firmly onto the inside of the seam with a small stick. In this way, the two sections were slightly thickened. Next, the overlapping parts on the outside were cut away with a sharp, thin knife. Traces left by the coroplast are sometimes clearly visible. The 'hand of the coroplast' can often be distinguished from such marks. Despite this, however, the majority of the figurines are made with considerable care and eye for detail. For this reason, carefully retouching the figurines for aesthetic purposes was also part of the experiment. Interruptions of the surface were smoothed with water and a piece of leather or simply by hand. The use of a stick by the coroplast of **117** is clear from the traces of rolling in order to divide equally the clay for the back slab, and also because the stick, probably accidentally, touched her right cheek twice, leaving a clear impression.

The work surface of the coroplast's table would ideally have been made of smooth stone in order not to leave any impressions on the figurines. However, the thin straight lines visible on the backs of **34** and **139** might be impressions caused by the use of a wooden surface.[706] As long as the clay paste is in a leather-hard condition, it is susceptible to being imprinted by the working surface. For retouching the figurines, it is probable that wooden tools with differently shaped edges and tips were used. The tool traces mentioned above point to the use of a small knife with a sharp blade, which would have been useful for removing the rim that overlapped the mould. A thin rope or wire would have been used to divide large lumps of clay into smaller parts. Such tools can be identified by the different marks they leave, for example, scraping marks.[707]

III.8 The production of other types of objects

Most figurines from Akragas are thin-walled with a hollow inner space, with the exception of a few small solid figurines, such as a weathered statuette of a standing female figurine, **85-86**, and a small herm, **77**, with exceptional painting residues on the front and back, respectively about 7cm and 9cm high. The back of the herm is also pierced in the middle, while the base is widened to enable it to stand.

Other types of objects, such as plaques, are also solid, and usually pierced to be hanged. Many of the plaques and solid statuettes depict pygmies[708] or satyr-like figures with distinct faces. Though less common, the pygmy figurines could very well have been produced in Akragas itself in addition to the more common iconographic types.

Protomai also feature small holes, mainly in front, for attaching metal ornaments. Specific spots are pierced, like the forehead of a female head *protome* for the application of a diadem (S26). The ears were also sometimes pierced for earrings. Similar small holes on the top of some *protomai* were probably used to hang the objects on the wall, for example, S178.

In addition, some moulds have been discovered with a small hole in the middle of the back: **90**, S4, S5,

704 See Van Rooijen et al. 2017, and also AT 3392 (713) of the Pushkin Museum, Moscow, which has a wide bench. See Catalogue fig. 14, p.285.

705 The empty spots on the shoulders of a figurine indicate this. See AT 3392 (713) of the Pushkin Museum, Moscow. See Catalogue fig. 14, p.285.

706 Several thin straight lines of various length are imprinted diagonally on the upper part of figurine **34** and imply that the figurine picked and replaced a couple of times. This could well have been the result of additional retouching after the figurine was taken out of the moulds and turned face up in order to be retouched.
The impressed lines on **139** run vertically, but are less sharp and less straight as on **34**. The back of the head is scraped, probably because the figurine was moved over the wooden tabletop during retouching.

707 Neutsch describes scrapers with a loop intended for hollowing out clay objects. Marks made by such tools are not identified on the inside of Akragas' figurines. Neutsch described and photographed specific tools, but does not explain if this is based solely on modern potters' instruments. Neutsch 1952, p.3 and 9, Beilage I, 3.

708 C299 from Agrigento, a broken plaque depicting a pygmy with an axe and bell, is mentioned by Hariri 2017, p.185, pl.8.

S10, S11, C261.[709] They are not completely pierced, and were possibly intended to be hung in the coroplast's workshop. Hanging, they would be visible and well stored in an organised fashion. They could also have served as a kind of advertisement for the available figurines. The reason that seated figurines do not have suspension holes seems straightforward: they were intended to be used standing up.

There is a correlation between the subject depicted, the iconographic type and the technique by which the object is made. Plaques have a different function compared with figurines, which is explained by their application. Plaques are suitable as bearers of a scene, an action, or telling a story, with several figures in movement or displaying attributes, **198**. They often depict a ritual scene. In contrast to the figurines, the action is central rather than a single figure, so three-dimensional attributes are much less common on plaques, including in other materials like wood and metal. The common female figures, which serve as votives, have an iconographic focus on the head and specifically the face. To ensure sharp details for the facial expression, moulds were combined. This focus on the face made the female figurine also suitable to serve as a *protome*. The three-dimensional statuettes of seated or standing female figures were dedicated by individuals and represented individuals. Their three-dimensionality was an important part of the ritual, aiding the imagination of the observer. Functionality thus plays a role in the choice of object.

The upper part of the 'body' of the female figurine has a similar function to a plaque and could serve for displaying contextual scenes, such as the painted scenes on the dress or Greek korai. In the case of the Akragantine figurines, they display attributes in relief. These chest ornaments, of various shapes and number, and possibly the fibulae as well, convey symbols that provide an encrypted frame of reference in which the function of the dedication is often specified. These ornaments were sometimes rather irregularly shaped. The irregularity of roundish pendants and fibulae of early objects, probably modelled after real-life jewellery, could be an indication that they were hand-modelled and added separately to a patrix. Real jewellery was probably used to imprint the chest-chain in the mould of **172**. The choice of three-dimensional objects that could be adorned with jewellery items fits the anthropomorphism and intentional recognisability of the figurines. Such social aspects will be further discussed below.

709 C270 (broken), C272 and C262 are glued to their stand, which makes the tracing of a hanging hole impossible. AG8974, the mould of a bird with spread wings, does not have a hole. Its back is exceptionally coarse.

III.9 Interpretation and discussion

III.9.a Implications of the introduction of the moulding technique

Having described the techniques used above, it is worthwhile to analyse their implications. Jeffra states that only a few researchers engaging with experimental approaches to *chaîne opératoire* address the anthropological aspects of their research.[710] In this chapter, some of the questions addressing the 'who' and 'why' are discussed. The experiment was intended also to shed light on the social context of coroplastic activities, indicating how technical issues were solved and iconography altered to tailor the objects to their role as votives. Examining the 'who' and 'why' involves deduction and informed speculation, and therefore is naturally susceptible to a degree of uncertainty.

Using the moulding technique, the coroplast could work quickly and did not necessarily require much artistic skill. The mechanical method of production fitted into the tradition, common up to that time, of producing three-dimensional wooden figurines. Wooden statuettes were used as a patrix, **85-86**. The earliest terracotta figurines were produced using shallow moulds, but the appliance of terracotta developed from being a rather two-dimensional object to a more three-dimensional one, in order to create a figurine that could stay upright.[711] The rapid production of three-dimensional hollow ceramic figurines by moulding must have represented a major advance, leading to a significantly higher output and availability of the figurines. After its introduction, halfway through the sixth century BCE, moulding developed rapidly at Akragas, resulting in high-quality objects with very fine features, as well as a large number and variety of designs.

The early figurines were only partly hollow, and no attention was spent on their side profile. They often appear plank-like or with a blockish body. After altering their production, the coroplasts must have discovered new possibilities, indicated by the three-dimensional hollow construction of the figurines. The figurines could stand upright and be finely decorated with detailed designs. Another improvement was the increased size. The different angles, depths and larger proportions required a thin-walled construction in order to prevent the statuettes from cracking during drying and firing. The three-dimensional figurines constructed with a slab of clay for the back are technically similar to the *protomes*. It is therefore not surprising that these two sorts of objects were produced in high numbers. They have in common their unworked backs, and it was not before the second

710 See Jeffra 2014, introduction and p.141.

711 Both patrices and the techniques to produce them with a mould would have been imported from the metropoleis. Hinz 1998, p.88.

half of the fifth century BCE that moulds for creating the backs came into use.

Part of the work of the coroplast may be easy to learn, which means that with some experience one could produce moulded figurines.[712] In addition to the quality of the mould, the condition of the clay is essential for achieving a detailed result. Most of the coroplasts of Akragas were certainly skilled and experienced craftsmen, as they redefined certain techniques, combined moulds, and applied hand-modelled additions. Failures seem to occur rarely. Issues related to the production of new matrices using existing generations of figurines were solved in different ways. The reduced size of the statuettes, due to repeated reproduction, was not a problem, and relatively small figurines became as common as the full-sized objects. When the facial expression lost its sharpness, the most common solution was to replace the entire head. The replacement of the head meant that the neck had to be reworked to remove traces of the attachment. One of the earliest figurines on which this is visible is **64**. This was not always carefully executed, **148**, and could leave traces of the seam between the two parts. This rim sometimes looks like the upper hem of the dress but is more often turned into a necklace. The appearance of figurines produced with the moulding technique could, therefore, be called a 'technologically defined iconography'.

Reasons for applying this method may have been various. Both the material and the applied technique limit the choice for a random design but provide the freedom to vary a standard format. Altered details and additions, or retouching are signs of more conscious decisions about the appearance of the figurine. As discussed in the previous chapter, this often concerns the seated pose and the additional chair. Edits of the mould outline and design were changes that were intentionally made. Customers who desired a variation on the standard were served well by the coroplast. These edits were not technically necessary. The motivation could have been either iconographic or ritual.

The new technique opened up a scale enlargement for production, while at the same time variation was initially limited. Once coroplastic skills were fully mastered, around the beginning of the fifth century BCE, significantly more variation was introduced. Simple techniques like impressions of metal pendants, **172**, combinations of moulds for the head or body parts, **62**, **104**, and fine details in the execution of the dress or chair gave rise to a wide variety of figurines with differing details. The result would have been appealing in its uniformity from a distance and distinction through the details nearby. It is exactly this psychological concept of originality and conformism that could have made it so attractive for the inhabitants of the multicultural society of Akragas to obtain these objects. This mechanism is comparable to the process of emulation.[713] The advancement of coroplastic skills enabled the coroplasts to keep up with the fast-changing iconographic elements.

III.10 Identification of coroplastic workshops by different techniques

The workshops are assumed to have specialised in a specific category of ceramic objects, like statuettes, architectural elements or pottery. The daily production was for a great part dependant on the moulds available at the coroplastic workshops. For other parts of the process, like collecting clay or firing, it is very likely that coroplasts cooperated. Less purified clay was for example applied for larger objects. For small, hand-sized figurines, a fine clay was necessary. The clay of **3**-**7**, for example, is coarser, containing more and larger inclusions. The method of moulding figurines gives reasons to infer serial production. At least one generation with several objects from the same mould could have been produced by the same workshop. Since moulds were required for the instant production of numerous figurines, they would have been the most valuable possession of the workshop. The business model of generating several figurines depends on the availability of these matrices, or ultimately patrices. The lifespan of the moulds was, therefore, crucial for changes to the pattern.

During the experiment, there was no noticeable use-wear on the moulds even after producing up to twenty figurines with each. More intensive use may have caused wear and tear. Because ceramic is fragile, mechanical shock can easily cause the moulds to break. On moving, a small corner piece of one of the experimental moulds broke off. Reworking this minor damage required some additional time and effort, but no more than a couple of minutes.

Presumably different generations of figurines series were produced at the same workshop and probably within a limited timespan. Traces of reworking techniques reveal that new generations were made within a couple of years. A reason could be that a mould broke and a derivative mould had to be created after an object from the first generation. In different generations of a series, similar technical characteristics may identify specific workshops. Such details often match those of previous generations.

The manner of retouching at the back and sides of the statuettes was compared in order to identify specific coroplastic workshops. Examples of figurines that

712 "(...) motor skill learning takes between 2-3 years and 10 years and involves social learning." Gandon and Roux 2019. In this article it is suggested that adopting new ceramic styles can be challenging for motor skills and is not necessarily low-cost. Adapting to a completely different method, moulding, could have been challenging initially.

713 Nieuwenhuyse 2008, p.247-9.

display such characteristics are shortly described below. Certain workshops existed for many years and not all the figurines would have been made by the same individual. It is probable that coroplasts worked with apprentices and that specific techniques were passed on to their apprentices and successors.

III.10.a The Workshop of the White Clay

The most common colour among the Akragantine objects is a pinkish beige, and the Munsell colour code Pink 7.5 YR 7/3 or 7/4 appears throughout all iconographic groups. Mixtures to soften the red and darker tones remained the common solution to balance costs, workability and a light-toned result. One group of six early figurines stands out for its appealingly white or light pinkish fired clay. Whether they are from the same workshop is not entirely clear, because there are no objects from the same mould series. Most statuettes are early figurines without arms: **20**, **54**. Figurine **21** is remarkable because it combines a simple body with a clearly later head. Some of the statuettes are also exceptionally thin, **63**, or styled similarly to the Rhodian figurines, **71**. The latter shows on its back the typical marks of a wooden tool. One figurine, **80**, depicts a small-waisted girl with a flower and a particularly large head. This solid figurine was probably made from a wooden mould. The coarse forms indicate early fabrication, possibly due to the use of wooden patrices. The similarity of the head of **21** to other chubby faces and the large earring indicates local production.[714] Both **21** and **54** are from the same context. Because of the large amount of variation in iconographic types, an early workshop in Akragas is suggested. The clay mixture with light firing colours presumably contained a large percentage of white mudstone from nearby Scala dei Turchi. The light colours were possibly appreciated by Akragantine customers. The several types of figurines, their low total number and the absence of objects from the same mould series indicate that production from this workshop was limited.[715]

III.10.b The Workshop of the Convex Back

This group of rather simple figurines, iconographically, nevertheless introduced some technical novelties (table 3.3). The backs of the figurines were often sturdy and convex, while earlier objects were more block-shaped with a straight back. These differences in execution were often combined with a bench protruding on both sides, resulting in increased stability. The separately modelled chair was applied by hand and was often asymmetric in height or shape in relation to its counterpart. The smaller figurines, measuring not more than 15cm, **41-47**, were probably made by the same workshop, like the others of group 1c, some years later **(36-47)**. The latter group originates from the same mould series but is also similar in technical aspects. These figurines still surprise with their fine details, such as the carefully horizontally layered hair, impressed with a tiny stick tool on both sides of the head. However, an added hand-made chair with ears was in some cases executed with less attention to detail, **44**. The clays applied by this workshop were also of local origin and some were also mixed. This often resulted in very pale brown tones. Statuette **40** is exceptional in this respect because its clay was not so purified and probably not mixed in the same way as its firing colour is more red. The cavities are caused by burned or leached-out inclusions. Traces of reworking with a sharp tool are visible on some of the figurines.

By comparing details it became clear that the scratches on the back of figurine **37** match those on a figurine in a private collection (Catalogue figures 5 and 6), it is likely that both are from the same workshop.

III.10.c The Workshop of Straight Reworking

A figurine with the typical 'cut-away sides' can be recognised by these reworking techniques as originating from a specific workshop in Akragas (table 3.3).[716] In the case of figurines **49-53** of group 1d, the complete back has been reworked in this way. The back of **49** seems to have been made from an inferior sort of clay compared with the front. The back contains many inclusions and cavities caused by lime-spalling. The clays were badly kneaded and not entirely mixed, resulting in colour differences. Figurine **8** also has a rough back with sharp angles indicating that the coroplast used a knife or blade to cut away strokes of clay from the sides. When cutting away surplus parts, the sticky clay might heap up at some point. This appears to have happened with **9** on the right shoulder and with the hair at the neck. Its face seems to have been smoothed with a sponge, which resulted in the loss of its facial expression. Such details on early figurines, in group 1a, might point to rather common techniques, not necessarily all from the same workshop. If figurines executed in this way were from the same mould, it is likely that they were made by the same person. This might also explain the overlap with the following 'workshop' characteristics.

III.10.d The Workshop of the Chubby Faces and the One Pendant Necklace

This workshop was probably experimenting with combining moulds, and also introduced several new,

714 See the Workshop of the Chubby Faces.

715 See group 1a and 5d in Groups.

716 A figurine, sold at auction in Berlin in 2015, displayed such sharp sides very clearly. See http://www.the-saleroom.com/en-us/auction-catalogues/isa-auctionata-auktionen-ag/catalogue-id-srauctionat10008/lot-b2710dc4-71db-4ca5-ad28-a40100d3481a.

Characteristic or Workshop	Figurines
Workshop of the White Clay	**20; 21; 54; 63; 71; 80.**
Workshop of the Convex Back Side	**19; 23; 26; 27; 29; 30; 34; 35; 36; 37; 38-40; 41-47.**
Workshop of the Straight Reworking	**49-53; 56-57; 100; 115-117; 179-180; 176**
Workshop of the Chubby Faces	**105-106;**
Figurines with the Tight Necklace with One Pendant A Necklace, but without Pendant	**171, 173-175, 176-177, 178; 179-180; 189** **125; 133; 148; 152-153; 165; 188, 190**
Sharp Straight Lines on Back Side	**34; 37; 71; 100; 122; 147**
Convex Back Side	Group 1c and afterwards *e.g.* **136; 171; 173; 174;** etc.
Workshop of the 'Straight Reworking': Sharp Cut-Off on Seam and Back by Knife, Sometimes Causing Bulging of Clay	**49-53; 65; 100; 115; 117; 130; 136; 176; 179;** etc.
Back Slab Rolled with a Stick	**117; 148; 174**

Table 3.3: The characteristics of reworking, and other technically significant features that distinguish a workshop or an Akragantine technique.

and sometimes hand-modelled, additions. Interesting combinations of moulds for head and body parts differing in details, such as pendants, arms, chair and fibulae, can be found among a group of figurines with specific facial features. They have a particularly fleshy wide face and a clear smile between pronounced cheeks that characterise group 2d. The body of **179-180**, of which the arms are removed, is probably from an older mould in the series of **103-104**. The faces are similar in their chubbiness. Interestingly, the coroplast made different choices about what to alter. With figurine **179,** the head was replaced; while on **103,** the body was completely changed, including the exceptional removal of the pectorals. The head of **179** was borrowed from another mould series **171-177**. This mould series is surprisingly detailed and richly adorned. Including **178,** they often wear a thin hand-modelled veil over their *polos*. The latter series appears only in Akragas and also the mould previously used for **103-4** and **179** probably originates from Akragas. The Louvre object C5122 therefore probably also originates in Akragas (Catalogue fig. 9).

Several objects in this group possessed a tight necklace or choker with one pendant or bead on it. It is clearly distinct from the pectoral band by its placement high on the neck. The inspiration for such a necklace might have come from Selinous, but the first objects with an impressed version – directly on the freshly formed and unfired figurine, **179** – all possess a single pendant.[717] There are two reasons for identifying the use of this choker necklace as a trademark of a specific workshop. Many of these figurines bear similar iconographic traits, such as a chubby face, and method of manufacture. On most of them, the sides are sharply cut off, which could refer to the previously mentioned Workshop of Straight Reworking or even a specific coroplast from this workshop. By this, it becomes possible to date the tight necklace to the second decade of the fifth century BCE and onwards. The one pendant necklace is a common appearance on figurines from Mould I and II, appearing for the first time in group 2d and continuing in group 3. These series show similar signs of retouching on the sides and back.

Another characteristic of the Mould I and II figurines is their larger-than-average size and original, richly adorned appearance. The necklace might be a sort of 'signature' by the coroplast, or perhaps a sort of trademark for the workshop. Originally, the necklace had the practical function of concealing the place at the neck where head and body from different moulds were attached. These original, appealing designs with the tight one-pendant necklace thus became a kind of trademark. As a result, some figurines produced at the same workshop prior to the use of this characteristic design are datable, for example, **103-4**.

Based on certain shared characteristics, there is an overlap visible between the Workshop of Straight Reworking and the Workshop of the Chubby Face (table 3.3). The overlap concerns a number of figurines that were developed with the tight necklace at a time when the chubbier face had become the standard and when the straight reworking could have been used instead. Such common features marking transitions also occur between iconographic groups. Such overlaps confirm that coroplasts were not working alone. The workshop presumably comprised several coroplasts, who divided tasks between them. Their cooperation could have led to the exchange of moulds or parts of moulds. Chronological developments, both iconographical and technical, confirm intensive cooperation between coroplasts. One example of figurines with combined characteristics is **100**, which displays the chubby face, while also having a straight reworked back. Over any particular time period, iconographic and technical innovations would spread, while other features were discarded. One example of this is figurine **135**, a derivative of the Mould II series, with its sharp marks on the back. The one pendant necklace was omitted, but it possessed a novel, lighter toned slip layer. Together with **136,** the popularity of this design is revealed. On the one hand, the design was simplified, for

717 See Section II.6.h.iii.

example by the omission of the decorated *polos*, while on the other hand it was updated with the latest technical developments. **136** was painted white over the slip layer.

III.10.e The skills of the coroplast

Some of the examples above of very fine and elaborate work or, on the other hand, insufficient and unnecessary actions in the production process raise questions about the decision-making process of the coroplast. While some skilled coroplasts took considerable effort to execute the front of the figurines properly, they often neglected the back. The back is usually plain and convex. It would have been easy to smooth it with a bit of water, as, exceptionally, was done to **153**. In many instances, impressions or other unevenness was left untouched. Coroplasts worked with coarser materials on the back, and sometimes used less fine clay. They were certainly not aiming for the same detailed work as on the front. Coarse particles in the clay, clear cut-off tool marks, uneven shaping and coarser work are rarely seen on the fronts of figurines, but are all commonly visible on the backs. It is understandable that the coroplasts did not care for the backs, as these would not have been visible in the intended final resting places of the figurines.

The sides, though often thin, are usually executed with slightly more care than the backs. This makes it plausible that the figurines were placed in groups, standing side-by-side, with their backs turned away from the observer. The differences in size between the statuettes might have created the effect of a gathering or crowd of figures.

Their intended ultimate location was presumably outside sacred buildings, against the walls or on or next to altars, facing visitors and worshippers. Their size, importance, and instability make it less likely that they were placed directly on the uneven ground. The figurines were made to stand on a raised level, but their three-dimensionality is not fully exploited.

Caubet writes that the coroplast's work does not ask 'ni imagination ni savoir-faire particulier'. Yet the right conditions and uses of tools and materials led to well-constructed figurines for which the coroplast also created hand-modelled additions. The variation in figurines, their facial expressions, variety of adornments, and differing furniture show that coroplastic art was a well-developed profession by the end of the sixth century BCE in Akragas and other Sicilian towns. For such fine-tuned iconography, but also for maintaining the scale of production, both skilled and creative coroplasts were needed. Though modelling by hand might be more difficult and result in a unique object, the technical part of the coroplasts' work in itself seems to have been underestimated and their artistic skills undervalued. The significant variety among figurines in Akragas,[718] points to renewal or updating of the latest styles, using other techniques such as combining moulds and additional hand-modelling, instead of just blindly copying the models from earlier generations.

One example of creativity was the way in which coroplasts dealt with clay shrinkage by compensating with larger headgear or a lifted base. The choice of this solution points to the presence of a sufficient number of moulds or patrices of high quality. The coroplasts had options available for replacing certain body parts if necessary. It is also likely that their customers preferred an up-to-date iconography, rather than an older, derivate, lower quality figure. This could explain the rapid succession of iconographic types and variations, where different fashions can be identified. The coroplasts of Akragas were innovative, continuously chose new combinations of moulds, and altered the appearance of the figurines. Examples of this are the Ionian and chubby faces, and the addition of arms.[719] Although customers could have requested such changes, the rapid development in technical capabilities in parallel to iconographic advances points to the coroplasts having taken the initiative. In group 4, the details and fine quality reach the highest level, and the final technical innovation is a white clay slip or paint layer. However, while the fine details suggest depth on the front and sides, the figurines remain unworked on the back.

While there were variations in details and adornments, the figurines shared a common set of typical features: a seated position, unfolded dress, chest adornments, and *polos* (although no feature was omnipresent). The interaction between standard iconography and specific preferences is intriguing. The conservative effect of the mechanical method must have played a role in setting the standard, but the Akragantine coroplasts developed methods and tools to vary the figurines, and even to express individual motives.

III.11 The coroplastic exchange between Sicilian towns

There was an exchange of patrices and moulds not only between the coroplasts and workshops of Akragas, but also between different towns, containing culturally mixed communities, exchanging iconographical details and probably also technical innovations. The reason for this exchange was probably high demand for figurines. The continuous need for matrices can certainly be attributed

718 Another explanation for the limited number of derivative moulds at Akragas would be the existence of parallel moulds. This would mean that the coroplasts kept the patrix as reserve and made more matrices for quicker production or as a back-up. The differences between figurines from parallel moulds are hard to distinguish.

719 For the specific addition of the arms to the Mould II series, see Section I.4.a.i.

to the vulnerability of terracotta objects. Once figurines had been dedicated they could no longer be used as a patrix, as they were consecrated and placed permanently in a sanctuary.

There are in general more shared features between Akragantine and Selinuntine than between Akragantine and Geloan objects. This was different for the later figurines of the last group in the catalogue, which were iconographically similar to enthroned female figurines from Gela, as well as for other subjects such as the piglet-carrying figurines, which developed in the same period. Technical aspects, like a layer of slip and white paint, were features shared with figurines from Gela belonging to the same period and in the second half of the fifth century BCE. The connections and exchanges between Selinous and Akragas seem to have been established in an earlier phase. Some iconographic ideas, like the pendants, are a clear sign of influence in this period, at the end of the sixth to the beginning of the fifth century BCE. Iconographic and technological ideas were probably first developed in Selinous.[720] One would expect larger and simpler figurines as predecessors of the richly adorned ones, but this is not necessarily true for the exchanged objects.[721] A patrix or matrix was adapted to the locally preferred style, and pendants are often different. They could have been easily removed and replaced with separately moulded pendants. Pendants in the form of lion *protomes* appear only on Selinuntine figurines.[722]

The figurines from Selinous and Akragas described by Dewailly 1992 as B XV resemble each other. The extra rim, like a frame around the figurine, seems to have been a more common feature in Selinous.[723] Several figurines of the Akragantine mould series appear in different variations. In addition, one in Selinous and two in Akragas feature an opening at the back. This raises the question of whether a mould was transported to Akragas and used there. Or perhaps only one figurine was taken to Akragas which then inspired a local coroplast. Alternatively, these 'B XV' figurines could have been exchanged between Selinous and Akragas. An opening at the back was uncommon for Akragantine figurines. The small circular opening at the back of **150-151** is not large enough for

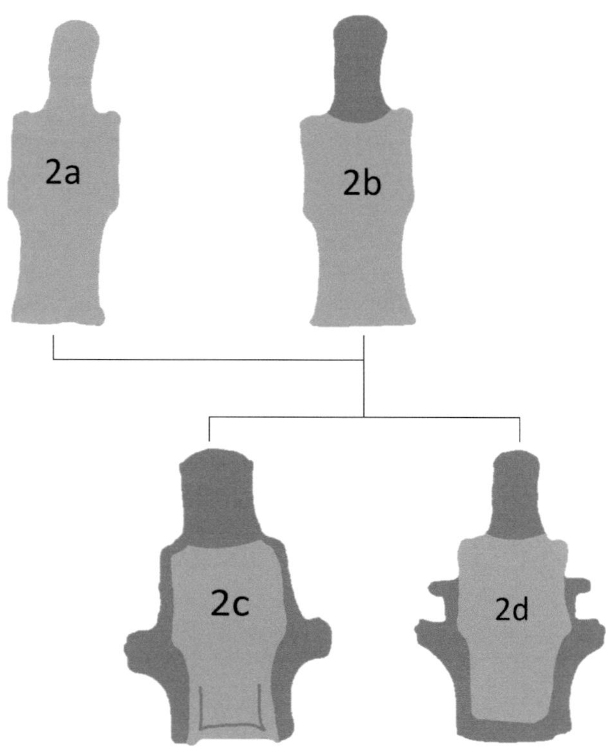

Figure 3.5: Entity relationship diagram of the casts of Mould II. A horizontal relation indicates direct reuse of the mould, while the vertical genealogy marks a continuation of the casts of 2b, as derivate. Light grey marks the older parts of the mould and darker grey alternations or additions. The casts of 2b, 2c and 2d all have a wider face. 2c and 2d are developed after 2b but with thrones, in two variations. Those two figurines are also characterised by intentional alterations: an outer rim and apron lines on 2c, lion paws and a high-backed throne on 2d. 2a= **115-117**; 2b=**118**; 2c= S 2218, Louvre Museum; 2d= AT 3392 (713) Pushkin Museum, Moscow.

working on the inside and could have functioned for air circulation, even though this is technically unnecessary. The last object, **151**, is also odd with respect to its size, smoothness and clay colour. The fact that such an opening for air circulation is unnecessary is confirmed by figurines **142-148** which lack such an opening.[724] Several figurines found at Selinous feature a similar opening in the back, which is similar in size and round-oval like the Akragantine figurines, **150-151**. The similarity in physiognomy between these figurines points to the use of shared moulds. Surprisingly, they also share production

720 It is striking that some figurines at Akragas, which appear otherwise quite similar to Selinuntine figurines, lack the pendants, but are usually smaller. Most of the Akragantine figurines of a certain mould series or iconographically similar figurines have only fibulae and a single or double band, empty, between them.

721 Albertocchi writes that a group of statuettes from Agrigento is derived from a type from Selinunte, without the chest pendants. Albertocchi 2004, p.58, p.101, n.78. In my opinion, certain elements of the pectoral pendants, as well as specific fibulae shapes were developed later at Akragas.

722 Dewailly 1992, p.114.

723 Dewailly 1992, p.84ff.

724 Figurine **23** has a similar hole in the middle of her back also, but somewhat lower and less regular. The very simple forms and similar reddish clay might indicate the same coroplast as **151**. Figurine **150** is made of the same clay, but with a slip of a lighter colour.

techniques. The coroplast might have been concerned about the air circulation or simply copied Selinuntine examples with a vent hole, without considering its precise function. With a mould for the front part only, the existence of a vent hole could not have been known. This phenomenon clearly confirms exchange between Akragas and Selinous.

Another example of patrix or mould exchange between the Sicilian towns is the Mould II series, of which S901, **118**, was used in the archaeological experiment. The large chair or bench is omitted in the Akragantine Mould II series. The figurine of itself has an obviously seated position (fig. 5).

Surprisingly, similar figurines from Gela and Selinous have different sorts of benches. Considering the way this series was produced, the Akragantine coroplast seems skilled enough. It might have been the time investment needed for such a hand-modelled addition that made the coroplast decide to omit the benches. The number of figurines made in this series, however, is high, and the many variations that appear in Selinous, Gelas and Akragas show that the design, in general, was popular. As the demand for figurines was high, the addition of a chair or other time-consuming extras that required hand modelling were simply omitted.

Another example of the continuous mould genealogy can be found with **135**. This figurine, found in tomb 834 at Necropolis Pezzino with a skyphos and a miniature lekythos, is similar to but smaller than the figurines of Mould II. Its head was exchanged for another and an extra line was added on the apron.[725] The third row of pendants was removed from the mould, but the shapes of the pendants are almost similar to a figurine from Selinous.[726] The pendants were not retouched to be triangular and pointy or with the chain itself bulging, as on **115**-**118** and **120**, but there are seven pendants on the first row and it is more rounded than on N.I. 7. It is possible that the body of **135** is made from a derivative mould, but by a different coroplast, like one of the Mould II series. The necklace with the round pendant is absent, but a bench with cushion, which was, in this case, part of the mould, is now present.

III.11.a Terracotta production at the kerameikos of Selinous and workshops in Akragas

The terracotta quarter or *kerameikos* of Selinous was set to the east of the town and separated from it by an uninhabited area, but still within its city walls. The location in the valley along the Cotone river, near the clay deposits in the east and a water drain, was not chosen at random.[727] A gate on the north side protected and connected the *kerameikos* to the inland, while the port on the south side directly outside the walls facilitated transportation of the goods over the sea. Both the seaside and the river formed possible resources of clay, sand, mineral and water applied in the production of terracotta. The long stretched area, the size of half a housing block, contained several workshops for different terracotta products that was industrial in scale. For the production of the hand-size figurines, the location across the so-called East Sanctuary[728] with three monumental temples created a direct market, positioned nearby.

The location close to the East Sanctuary implies that potential customers were directly approached by the coroplasts or their employees. The scale of the industry is surprising but could be explained by the local market for the products and the trendsetting innovations that spread from here over the eastern part of Sicily. An architectural structure on the highest terrace is thought to have been the warehouse or shop, where the figurines were sold to the passing devotees. Intermediaries might have transported the votives to, for example, the Malophoros Sanctuary, where indeed a large number of figurines was found. Another possibility is that the dedicants would have acquired their votives on their way, carrying the objects that are usually not over thirty centimetres tall and of relatively low weight. In itself, this could have been regarded as cultic handling or part of the act of dedication. The organised industries were a result of intensified production serving the increased demand and had definite implications for the local economy.

The nearby port facilitated transportation of larger architectural terracottas produced at the terracotta quarter.[729] A kiln measuring 5.3m in diameter functioned probably for firing roof terracottas. The workshop with this large oven was preserved so well that its interior can be reconstructed. The water resource in a corner of the workshop facilitated the softening and kneading of the clay, which was done in large bowls. On the other side, a tumbled over wooden shelf held containers of probably the clay tempers, such as sand or ground marlstone. A plate on a foot may have eased the coroplasts' work on three-dimensional objects. Apart from that, the remains of objects connected to food preparation were found. This may be an indication for long working hours, which necessitated facilities in the workshop for preparing

725 Not inventorised figurine: N. I. 7.

726 Dewailly 1992, p. 101-2.

727 The present name used by archaeologists for this part is Insula S16/17-E, of which the southern half forms the terracotta production quarter. S16-E is a street connected with a large open space. Over time, when the industries grew larger the quarter was extended along the wall.

728 There are three monumental temples here: E, F and G dating from the sixth and fifth century BCE.

729 Rheeder 2019.

and eating food. A small altar with several figurines[730] also demonstrates that religious needs were met at the workshop. Two of the statuettes represent an enthroned goddess from the second half of the fifth century BCE.[731] The portable objects were originally set up in a niche in the wall, together with miniature vessels and a treasury with some coins that confirm the period.

This industrial area dates from the mid of the sixth century BCE and activities continued after a renovation in the fifth century BCE until the Carthaginians destroyed the city in 409 BCE. The terracotta hand labour was well structured over four sections (terraces A-D) of a terrain measuring over 1200m². A total of seventy kilns, both rectangular and circular, most of them measuring more than two meters, were localised by geomagnetic detection. A part of the terrain has been excavated and a workshop brought to light. There are several working spaces and the complex holds large open spaces that might have facilitated the drying process and storage. The terracotta workshops were up to now thought to be small businesses run by extended family, even though it concerns serial production. This large space and production centre proves different for the case of Selinous.[732] Due to the scale of production, we may speak of mass production, though the main production method was manual production employing a large number of people, who directly or indirectly lived from the terracotta industries.

The oldest phase of the terrain in the eastern end of the insula, from the sixth century BCE, was separated by a wall that was demolished when space was required for two rectangular kilns. One of them was later levelled to build a larger kiln, in which three phases of use have been detected. In the lowest level, figurine fragments from the same mould have been found, dating from the third quarter of the sixth century BCE. The fired fragments are of at least twenty-two figurines of a Daedalic kore[733] and were discarded. This could indicate that the figurines were collected to be fired together with possibly larger objects, in order to fill the space left in the kiln. The fact that all figurines are from the same mould shows the scale of production for a similarly scaled market.[734] Figurative objects were produced in this workshop from an early stage and in large quantities. They were found here together with several other fragments of figurines and tools for their production: a matrix, clay residues, the raw, unprepared clay, and small objects to keep the distance between the stacked objects in the kiln.[735]

The terracotta quarter must have played a large role in the economy of Selinous and its direct environment. The area contained about twenty large companies and some small ones and might have provided a living for at least a tenth of the inhabitants, including the families, as calculated.[736] Not only did the monumental temple building start in the second half of the sixth century BCE, but also houses were provided with roof tiles and households with pottery for daily use. The votives were certainly part of this wide variety of terracotta products on the market.[737] The demand for terracotta figurines, the innovation of the moulding technique, the absence of high-quality stone material, and the presence of clay form the foundation of the expansion of terracotta production in the second half of the sixth century BCE.

The production location in the vicinity of the final destination of the terracotta figurines and near a gate for the delivery of the necessary material is comparable to the situation in Akragas, where two workshops have been found, both near the City Sanctuary. The first location, close to gate V, contained two kilns and yielded several moulds for figurines. This was probably a large-scale production workplace for terracotta figurines, as the two kilns might indicate. In continuous production, the firing process included, two kilns, fired alternately are involved. Although at first, the architectural structures were interpreted as a sanctuary, De Miro concludes that a workplace for terracotta figurine production is more likely.[738] The uncertainty of the attribution was caused because several figurines (**58**, **107**, **108**, **111**, **139**) were found on the spot next to moulds.[739] It might seem less probably to connect the presence of moulds to a sanctuary, but at a bothros in Himera several moulds were also dedicated.[740] However, the number of moulds found,

730 The figurines are identified by Bentz as Athena, Demeter, Artemis, and a smaller male figure.

731 The folds of her dress indicate this date, but otherwise one of the figurines is quite comparable to the Akragantine figurines. She sits in a similar pose, rather rigidly, on an elaborate throne with cushion or lion paws and a footstool. Bentz et al. 2016, fig. 17 and 18.

732 Bentz 2015, p.63.

733 For an extensive description and figure of this solid figurine that wears earrings and a necklace, see Bentz et al. 2014, p.69, n.4, fig.4.

734 Bentz et al. 2014, p.68-9.

735 There are several sorts, of which the wedge-shaped and perforated cylinders were the most common. They often have marks, which refer to the workshop or coroplast.

736 The numbers mentioned in this excavation report are as follows. Approximately 20,000 people lived in an area, Selinous, of 100 ha, in about 2,500 houses. This means that the average household would have been about 8 people. If about 2-3 people of each household were providing for it, the direct employees or workers were about 500-750 for 250 households. These numbers fit with the large-scale quarter that has been found and the labour intensive production of some of their products.

737 Bentz 2016, p.79.

738 De Miro 2000, p.42-3.

739 One example of a near-by deposit contained a mould as well, **90**. See description of the other objects in this context. Griffo 1955, p.109-10.

740 Himera, Piano del Tamburino, at the votive deposit (ST 13-15) and bothros (ST11). Mango and Edel 2015, p.118, 120, Abb.2.

together with the presence of kilns at Akragas, points rather to a workshop than a sanctuary.[741] Also, the other workshop dates from the Archaic and Classical period and both are thus contemporary with the first phase of the Selinuntine terracotta quarter, which matches with the products in both towns. The second workshop would be an unpublished find from 1971 on the west side of the same hill.[742] The workshop near Gate V might have been small, but its production quite intense. It seems that the terracotta production at Selinous started earlier and reached a larger scale, and probably more industrialised organisation than Akragas. However, considering the number of figurines and their generations, the terracotta figurine business was also flourishing at Akragas. Another workshop near gate II was specialised in pottery.[743] The collective use of kilns to fire different sized clay products is not directly evidenced at Akragas. Unlike Selinous, the workshops were scattered. Specialisation could have been a reason for this situation. In the case of Akragas, distinctive techniques, like wheel- or mould-made models, were probably separated. Akragantine terracotta products do not show the application of combined techniques.[744]

In both cities, the production of figurines reached a peak in this period. It is probable that kilns were shared, particularly as the small objects could be used to fill the kiln. It seems likely that the coroplast was a specialist in figurines and would not have produced pottery or large architectural terracottas on the side. Other similar and mould-made categories like the *protomes* or plaques could well have been produced by the same coroplasts, as they were also produced using a mould. The customs and outcomes of the production of these small objects are clearly local. Though moulds were probably exchanged, the coroplasts were not itinerant, as other craftsmen may have been.[745] This is supported by the technical differences between objects of the same mould series from Akragas and Selinous.

III.12 Conclusions

This chapter investigated the material aspects of the Akragantine terracotta figurines. It reconstructs the *chaîne opératoire* of these objects by making use of an archaeological experiment. Two methods were applied in this research to reveal the techniques applied in the late sixth and early fifth century BCE coroplastics. A method of deductive inquiry was combined with experimental imitation. By carefully investigating specific features and traces on the figurines, the handling of both coroplasts and consumer was reconstructed, from clay to its application as a votive. Other hypotheses were also tested by experiment. Some of the trials in the experiment had surprising outcomes. Such features were noted first with the experimental figurines and could then be understood as consequences of specific approaches.

The first reason that the coroplastic art in Akragas could flourish is because of the availability of large quantities of high quality, local clays and, as a result of the first, the fine-tuned techniques and methods of the coroplasts. The availability of good materials and well-developed technology enabled the coroplasts to produce large amounts of fine and aesthetic figurines. The clay sourced at Macalube di Aragona was easily accessible and of excellent quality, as shown by the experimental results. Its fine-grained and compact structure makes it very suitable for the production of moulds and statuettes. The combination with the white marl of Scala dei Turchi creates, on the other hand, a very workable clay for the production of statuettes. Though it is time and labour intensive to grind, the resulting soft firing-colour might have been preferred over the more reddish colour as it seems more natural, closer to the colour of female skin. A disadvantage of this particular is the shrinkage rate of the material, while the addition of a grind temper increases the risk of lime-spalling. These determined recipes are thus good candidates for the production of the statuettes and can form a further guideline to determine the origins of raw material procurement for these statuettes and the relation with other ceramic materials, such as architectural ceramics and pottery.

A second reason for the flourishing coroplastic activity at Akragas and the high number of figurines is certainly the mechanical method of moulding, which was applied extensively. Moulding intensifies the production and in itself does not require much of the coroplasts' artistic skills. Yet the coroplasts of Akragas can certainly not be blamed for a lack of artistic skill and originality. Their eye for detail and general experience in terracotta manufacture is proven by the detailed figurines. They exploited the artistic freedom available within the boundaries of the prescribed iconographic standards. Though dependent on moulds, the coroplasts developed technical and iconographic variation in design towards the end of the sixth and early fifth century BCE. Under these two conditions, Akragas could develop a thriving coroplastic industry.

From an economic perspective, the coroplastic activity offered a great cost-effective improvement compared to the production of their wooden predecessors. Inspired by the iconography of those and the technical aspects of a plaque, the several steps in the *chaîne opératoire*, from patrix via matrix to the final figurine, were well developed.

741 The excavations were carried out in the fifties by Pietro Griffo, but are not extensively published.

742 It is mentioned by Cuomo di Capri 1992, p.71.

743 Orsola 1991.

744 Except for a horse with a wheel-made body and handmade legs and head that forms a combination of the three methods, because it carries a mould-made couple on its back. Mus. Agrigento R220. See Section II.7.b.iii.

745 Rheeder 2019.

It is the moulding method in combination with the use of a clay slab for the back of the figurine that kept the statuettes rather two-dimensional in character for such a long time. The convex or column-shaped back does not reflect the anatomy of a human body but helped keep the figurine upright. In relation to this, is the question about form and function: were some details made as an intentional choice or were they simply a result of the moulding method? The answer differs depending on the detail and shows that improvements on the technical level went hand-in-hand with those on an iconographic level. The rendering of a more clearly seated posture and a more natural depiction of the human body appeared when the moulds became deeper and more three-dimensional. The moulding thus limited the iconographic possibilities while extending the scale of production. The balance between quantity and quality created the prerequisites for an affordable, but still fine figurine. It was probably not the customers who were requesting personalisation, but rather that moulds, in particular, the jewellery, were constantly being adapted to the latest styles. Such emulation and variation ensured the continuation and prospering of the business.

Differences in local techniques are distinctive: objects of similar iconography from Selinous have a vent hole in the back, while at Akragas an opening at the base is preferred. In both towns, the scale of production was large, but at Selinous the work was probably better organised and concentrated in one specific area, the *kerameikos*. Selinuntine coroplasts reached a comparatively high technical and organisational level, which served as an example for Akragantine coroplasts, resulting in the exchange of moulds and techniques. Within Akragas itself, several workshops can be distinguished such as the Workshop of the White Clay, the Workshop of the Convex Back Side, the Workshop of the Straight Reworking, and the Workshop of the Chubby Faces and the One Pendant Necklace. The characteristics of their output are distinguishable by clay composition, rendering of the back, details of reworking, and the specific execution of the head. One of those details, for example, is a tight necklace, which was presumably added to cover the attachment of a separately moulded head. In addition, a specific necklace with a pendant could have functioned as a trademark of the workshop.

The high number of objects and workshops account for the presence of industrialised production, directly related to the market requesting the objects. Religiosity and the custom of dedication provided such an impulse. On form and function, the morphology of the figurines was largely dictated by the technological methods used and the religiously prescribed iconographic standards for such votives.

Migration might have resulted in the introduction of the method of moulding and the use of terracotta as a material for votives. Exchange of products could have influenced the specific techniques applied in the production. Remaining questions, such as on the origin of certain features could be answered by research on the exact clay composition of individual moulds and figurines. The different consistency of the clay is the result of the mixing of clays, probably taken from sites near to Akragas. A study of the chemical composition of the figurines might provide insight into the origin of clays and differences between terracotta objects from Selinous and Akragas or even from workshops within the towns. The precise chemical composition could be determined by various geo-chemical techniques, such as X-ray fluorescence. The origin of both the raw materials as well as certain morphologies could in that way be distinguished more precisely.

Chapter IV

Technically and iconographically defined typology

The defined typologies are presented as the result of the findings in the previous two chapters. In this overview, the chronological development and relation of the figurines to each other is described. There are four groups, 1-4, which describe the locally produced figurines, followed by group 5 with several imported objects, which were found at Agrigento, and the last group, group 6, which concerns other figurine categories that were produced locally. For a number of notable iconographic features (the presence or form of arms, chair, polos, pectorals, and fibulae), the percentages of incidence are calculated in order to give an overview of the development within the group and over a longer period of time. In the chapter on iconography, the details and possible external influences on these features are described. Technical aspects of moulding and other methods that could indicate a chronological development or even a specific workshop in Akragas are connected to the iconographic characteristics. This aims to provide insight into the coroplastic development and the numbers of figurines produced at Akragas from about the second half of the sixth to the first half of the fifth century BCE.

Each group table presents several subgroups, mainly based on iconographic features. Sometimes these subgroups are contemporary, sometimes ordered chronologically. The table presents the individual catalogue numbers of the figurines, the total number of objects and of unique mould series. Figurines' numbers in the tables are separated by a comma if they are from the same series. When they are from the same mould generation, a hyphen is used for continuing numbers. A semi-colon indicates that figurines are not related by mould series. The division into groups is presented in chronological order. The combined results follow up on the production, the cultural influences or intensification of such contacts. An explanation for the choices of the coroplasts might be found in cultural identity, economic relations, and social exchanges.

Group 1

The first group of the locally produced figurines is a large group of in total 55 figurines, of which 38 are from unique mould series, divided into four subgroups (table 4.1). These figurines form the earliest completely mould-made figurines in a particular local style. This

Group name	Concerning numbers	Total number of objects	Number of unique mould series	Time-range
1a	8; 9; 10; 11; 12; 13; 14; 15-17; 19; 20; 18; 64; 63	15	13	Last quarter or decade of the 6th century BCE
1b	22; 23; 24; 25; 26; 27; 28; 29; 30; 31-32; 33; 34-35	14	12	Last decade of the 6th century BCE
1c	37; 36; 38-39, 40; 41-47	12	4	Last decade of the 6th century BCE
1d	48; 49-53; 54, 55; 56-57, 58, 59, 60; 61	14	8	Last decade of the 6th century BCE

Table 4.1: Overview of object in group 1.

style is characterised in the first place by the shape of the body, which is particularly block-like and has a characteristic leaning pose. The subdivisions mark the gradual changes and additions. Some of these characteristics continue in later-dated figurines but found their origin in this group from the last quarter of the sixth century BCE.

The first subgroups, 1a and 1b, are of plain-bodied figurines. Some of them have no visible garment nor chair, feet, pendants, fibulae, or polos. However, it is the shape of the body, which is characteristic: a rectangular, but not very deep, block forms the lower part of the body and serves also to keep the figurine upright. The sloping upper part, as if bending at the knees, suggests a seated or leaning back position. All the figurines in group 1a are without a visible seat, while those in 1b and 1c, are seated on a variety of benches and chairs. The figurines of 1d share the same pose but are adorned with pectoral pendants. The addition of a chair or pectoral band and pendants in group 1c and 1d did not change the basic shape and pose. They share not just their appearance but mark the swift development towards a deeper, more three-dimensional mould, more purified clay, finer details applied in the mould, and subtle handmade additions.

Group 1a

This group together with 1b forms the oldest dated figurines in the local tradition, characterised by the block-like body, a shape derived directly from its wooden predecessors.[746] Within these groups, the figurines are ordered chronologically. Of 1a, some figurines are very, 15 in total from 13 different mould series. The first figurine, **8**, has an irregularly shaped body, while numbers, **9, 10, 11, 12** have straighter lines and smoother surfaces. The coroplasts might have gained experience over time. The bodies are plain, usually just dressed in the rectangular apron or ependytes. The outline of this garment on the front on each side, close to the edge, except for **8** and **64**, marks the geometrical shapes and straight lines. Only at the shoulder and the knees, the edges are softened and a more rounded shape points to a natural body and seated pose. The impression is of a seated figure. It is as if the ependytes, which must have been a thick and heavy garment is draped over a frame, hanging down from the shoulders and only pushed forward at the height of the knees. Only **18, 63** and **64** reveal how such a garment could have been attached to the body: with large objects, that could be called fibulae, because they keep the dress in place. The round fibulae on **63** are clearer than the irregularly shape **64**, which also lacks the ependytes. **64**, however, has a line at the neck, that could be seen as the upper hem of the ependytes. Another indication of the human body that is covered by the ependytes is the feet, visible from under the garment. On **11,** there is just the suggestion of these feet, while on **12** and **19** they are placed clearly on a small base that could be seen as a footstool. The ependytes is arching over it, leaving just the front of the feet visible. On the sides of the footstool, the garment continues and reaches the ground.

The head of **8** is relatively large compared to the others. The face common in this group is quite fleshy and has pronounced cheeks and a big chin. Deep dimples next to a small mouth and high cheekbones strengthen the impression of a smile. The nose is also sizeable and often has a particularly large bridge. Large eyes make the forehead small, especially with the high arching eyebrows, which make the eyes look even bigger. A particularly round face is common in this group (**12, 14, 15-17**). The hairstyle is divided into two parts, the fringe, which runs on the forehead as a band from ear to ear, and hair on the sides of the neck and face. Both fringe and hair seem to be pushed forward by the headgear. The bulging hair that seems to reach the shoulder or fall over it to the back is typical of this group. The fringe is smooth or divided into bulbs (**9**, **12**, **14**, and **20**). On **15-17** it seems to be parted in the middle. This fringe is often substantial and stays visible, while a veil or polos is worn on top. Together with the rim of the polos, they mark and draw attention to the face . The veil, often thick, creates an extra rim as well. These shapes are reminiscent of an aureole or halo for a saint. The fringe is usually detailed, while the parts of the hair next to the sides of the head and neck are rather simple, often slightly bulging, but usually smooth. Both parts of the hair frame the face. To be more specific on the date: the increasing details and neat working might indicate a chronological order. The first part of group 1a, up to figurine **12** might be dated around the last quarter of the sixth century BCE. From **19** onwards, the appearance of the polos indicates a next step, for which they might be dated around five years later, as they appear otherwise similar, with a very simple body.

Group 1b

This group is mostly contemporary with group 1a. The figurines presented are also simple-bodied, but have a visible seat. Concerning the body and its adornment, the same developments take place as in group 1a, but with some new alterations in the iconography. The first figurines, **22**, **23**, **24** and **25**, have no clear indication of dress. Yet the shape of their bodies is geometrical and in straight lines like the figurines described above in group 1a. **28** wears a garment that is just visible from the feet sticking out from under it. On **29**, **30**, **31**, **32**, **34** and **35**, the ependytes is clearly depicted as an upper garment, reaching the ankles and laid on top of a longer undergarment. **28**, **30** and **34** wear fibulae.

746 For that reason, purely technically speaking, **85** and **86** would have belonged to this group, except that their dress and the shape of the body is significantly different from those of group 1a.

The faces, except for **33**, are more oval than the rounded faces of group 1a. The hairstyle is similar, however, a smooth or bulb fringe. The hairstyle on the sides of the neck is bulges slightly only on **34**. On **33**, this part of the hair has bulbs or horizontal lines.

There is a large variation in seats, such a benches, narrow (**22, 26**) or wide (**25**), straight (**23, 25, 29**) or curving upwards (**27, 28, 34**), with a diagonal (**23**), straight (**28, 33**) or a roundly curved front (**25, 27, 29, 34, 35**). The wide benches sometimes have a wide back (**33, 34, 35**). Some combine features such as having a straight front on the left and the curved one on the right (**30**). This variation is explained by the manufacturing technique; the seats, if wide, were handmade. Smaller ones, like the chair with the round 'armrests', could be moulded (**31, 32**). The order here is that of increasing detail and additional aesthetic refinement, such as the shape of the sides of the throne (**34, 35**). The last objects in this group, **34** and **35** are similar in their iconography, but the second is much more finely detailed. Again, the details of adornment might indicate where they should be placed chrono-logically.

Many heads are missing, but the surviving ones all still wear a polos (**23, 24, 33** and **34**). It seems that the majority of the figurines, which are dated slightly later, wear a polos. **8-18** do not, but after them, where it is possible to observe, all figurines except **58** have a polos. The polos itself is usually quite low and has a rim. **34** has a particularly tall and flaring polos. This part of the group can be dated to the last decade of the sixth century The polos had become standardised, while the seat, which was developed in the same period, did not become a standard feature.

Group 1c

This part of group 1 consists of twelve figurines, from only four mould series. They have much in common iconographically and technically, but their size indicates that a large part dates from some years later in the sixth century BCE. Disregarding the shrinkage in later generations, they share their appearance: they are seated on a wide bench and have a particularly short body and a relatively small head. This group continues through just one iconographic development shared with the previous groups: the dress, which is indicated on **37**, but not marked on **36**. These two objects are very similar: their shoulders are wide and their heavy short body gives a heavy impression. The disc fibulae are large while the polos is low and wide. Both figurines are seated on a wide bench. This iconographic scheme continues through the other figurines of group 1c.

The clearly protruding line between the fibulae on **36** might be the earliest appearance of the pectoral band on Akragantine figurines. **38** is the first to have a double band on the chest. The bands are clearly held by the fibulae. In this part of the group, all figurines have fibulae. They form together with the polos the first steps in the adornment of the figurines. However, in the next part of the group, 1d, there are some exceptions. In general, however, the fibulae seem to precede the pendants, together with the pectoral band. They are usually disc-shaped fibulae or marked as rounded or oval shapes. Only in part 1d is there variation from the standard.

In part 1c all figurines also all wear the polos. It is clear that this is a development towards a more detailed rendering. The polos has become a standard feature. While **36** and **37** had a simple wide bench, the bench in **38-40** has the 'ears' and with figurines from the same mould series (**41-47**), these 'ears' are sometimes decorated with a disc, particularly clearly on **42**. The hairstyle seems to develop from a smooth fringe towards one with bulbs and the hair on the sides of the neck of **41-47** is indicated with horizontal lines. In the facial expression, with their chubby cheeks, sizeable nose, small – often scarcely visible – mouth and protruding chin, they reveal a very strong similarity to **36** and **37**. The last indication that **38-47** were developed from these or similar figurines is their small size. The nearly complete **37** measures more than 20cm while **38-48** range between 12.6 and 14.2cm high. As a result, these fourth-fifth generation figurines could be dated later with certainty. It is, however, impossible to know whether the old moulds were used and precisely how much later they are. Considering the intensive use of moulds and the vulnerability of the material, they would not have lasted over a decade if in use. A significant novelty in this group is the appearance of a column-shaped lower body, particularly visible on the back. This convex-shaped rear enables the figurine to stay upright and is more natural than the earlier block-based body. Based on those specifications they are therefore dated towards the end of the century and made by the same workshop, the 'Workshop of the Convex Back Side.'[747]

Group 1d

The final part of group 1, comprises 14 figurines, among which are 9 unique mould series. This group shows the first pectoral pendants. They occur in triple form, except **60** and **61**, and often in a strict symmetry: if different shapes are shown, the pendant in the middle is the different one. There are four variants of the triple pectoral pendants:

1. All discs, often similar in shape and just slightly smaller than the fibulae, as on **58**, but also appearing without the disc-shaped fibulae, **54**, **55** and **56-57**.
2. A pointed pendant, flanked by discs, only **48**.
3. A disc flanked by crescents, **49-51**.
4. A crescent flanked by discs, **59.**

747 For a more detailed description of this workshop, see section III.10.b.

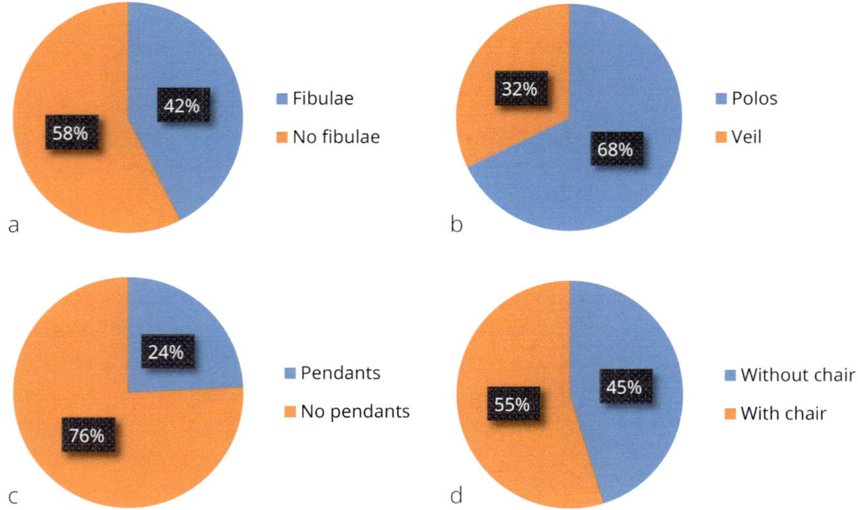

Figure 4.1:
(a) Division of figurines with and without fibulae in group 1;
(b) Division of figurines with a polos or a veil in group 1;
(c) Division of figurines with and without pendants in group 1d;
(d) Division of figurines with and without a chair in group 1.

On this last sort, the double discs flanking the crescent are a variation (**60**). The intention of keeping the adornments symmetrical and giving the middle object a different shape kept the total number of pendants odd. The next step in the development partly broke with this rule, in the first place with the addition of a higher number of smaller pendants. The last figurine in this group (**61**), shows, on the one hand, the five pendants, similar to **60**, but on the other hand, the disc is replaced with an ovoid shape and several rows of pectoral pendants lessen the strong symmetry of earlier figurines.

The correlation between fibulae and pectoral bands was noted above. The band is usually clearly visible in this group, but on **54, 55, 56-57, 59** and **61** the fibulae are absent. This makes clear that the pectoral pendants hang from a band. Whether this band, which was an aesthetic part of the iconography in itself in group 1c, was always attached or needed to be fixed to the dress by fibulae remains unclear. Real fibulae, found in high numbers on Sicily as well[748] have a very different shape. The discs might have had rather an aesthetic than a practical function. On **49-51,** they are shaped like rosettes and the pectoral band curves down slightly in the middle as if the disc is heavier. On **60,** the fibula is small and seem to repeat the shape of the discs.

With just one exception (**58**), the figurines wear a polos. There is also only one figurine with a bench (**48**). The body is still shaped in the same way, but the feet are always there, sticking out from under the long garment. This omnipresence shows that it has become fixed in the iconographic scheme and a standard for all newly produced figurines.

Some of the figurines in this group (**49-53**), as well as some individual objects in group 1a, share a particular detail. The sides on the back of the figurine are cut away to give it a less angled, more column-shaped appearance. This fits in the development in which the rear of the figurine was made convex.[749]

The rounded faces with the small mouth and chubby cheeks that were noted in 1c and earlier on **19**, for example, continue here on **49-53**. Though the larger polos and divided hair change the impression slightly, the facial features are the same on **56-57**. The eyes can be particularly large, as on **54** and **58**. The figurines in this group can also be dated to the end of the sixth century BCE. The last object of this group, **61**, marks the transition to the fifth century BCE with its extension of the pectoral bands.

Calculations for group 1

Below, the main developments of the changes in iconography are calculated as percentages for the group as a whole. The percentages for the absence or presence of certain characteristics are visualised in the pie charts below. In the order discussed, these are: the presence/absence of a chair, a polos, fibulae, and pectoral pendants. The statistics are not calculated for individual figurines but their mould series. There are figurines from the same mould series in 1a **15-17**, 1b **31-32, 34-35,** 1c **38-40** and a series with seven objects, **41-47**, and in 1d **49-53, 56-57.** Because some figurines are incomplete, the total number on which the discussed characteristic was absent or present differs. To make this clear, the numbers and total for the presence/absence of a chair are written out.

Out of the 37 individual mould series in group 1, just 14 lack a chair (**8, 9, 10, 11, 12, 19, 63, 64, 49-53, 54-55, 56-57, 58, 59, 60**) and of 6 figurine heads or upper parts it is unknown (**13, 14, 15-17, 18, 20, 61**). When the figurines on which the presence or absence of a chair can be seen are

748 See section II.6.f.

749 For a more detailed description of this characteristic, see section III.7.c 'Making the back of the figurine'.

Group name	Concerning numbers	Total number of objects	Number of unique mould series	Time-range
2a	154; 170; 163, 164; 165; 155; 159, 156-158; 160	11	7	End of the 6th cent to beginning of the 5th century BCE
2b	98; 99; 107, 108, 109; 62; 87; 101-102	9	6	First decades of the 5th century BCE
2c	65, 70, 66-68; 69; 88; 89; 90, 92, 91; 93	12	6	First quarter of the 5th century BCE
2d	105-106; 100; 103, 104; 21; 179, 180; 171- 173-174, 172-175 and 178; 177, 176; 182, 183	18	8	The first three decades of the 5th century BCE

Table 4.2: Overview of object in group 2.

counted, the seated group's total number is 17 from a total of 31 in group 1 (fig. 4.1). This brings the percentage to 45% without and 55% with a chair. The majority of figurines in group 1 is seated.

In group 1, the total number of polos-wearing figurines is 19 out of 28. This means that a large majority, 68% wears a polos. Out of the 33 mould series in group 1 – those of which the chest is visible – 14 have fibulae, which is 42% (fig. 4.1). Group 1d forms the group with the pectoral pendants. The chest is visible in this group on all eight mould series. They form the 24% within group 1 that wears pectoral pendants (fig. 4.1).

To conclude the description and calculation of the group as a whole, it can be observed that the seated pose and the absence or presence of the seat is not a development through time, but occurs right from the start. The other characteristics noted in the development of the figurines seem to win more terrain over time. Figurines without marked ependytes are rare, as is the presence of feet or a footstool. Other developments started slightly later. The polos, for example, was in the first half of this group, 1a and b, only depicted about half the time, while for the group as a whole it is depicted on more than two thirds. In the last half of the group, 1c and d, there is just one figurine with a veil. For the pendants, the case is even clearer. They gain quickly in popularity from one point and the variation in numbers and sorts increased from there onwards. For the fibulae, though they are connected through pectoral bands to the presence of pendants, the absence on some figurines with pendants is striking. Yet they appeared at a stage when pendants were not yet applied and precede them. In general, it can be concluded that in particular, the disc-shaped fibulae became a standard part of the iconographical scheme of the figurines, connecting the fibulae. In the following groups, the developments described above continue: the dress, body and limbs, headgear, fibulae and pectoral pendants will all evolve in shape, size or detail. An iconographic scheme, including the rendering of the body and the different parts and aspects, became an established framework within the space of roughly two decades, upon with successive coroplastic versions were all based.

Group 2

The second group comprises four subgroups with a total of 50 figurines from 27 unique mould series. In group 2d, some figurines are very similar and originate probably partly from the same mould with both a seated and a standing version. These are counted as two mould series. The group continues at the point where group 1 stopped, at the end of the sixth and beginning of the fifth century BCE. Group 1 ended with the triple pendant, while this group, except for the last subgroup, contains the figurines with a double row of pendants. The development evolved quickly, probably because production intensified and possibly because the exchange of ideas and items of coroplastic traditions from elsewhere intensified. The use of combined and exchanged moulds resulted in diverging appearances.

From this group onwards, two styles of pectoral pendants are distinguishable, as well as some figurines on which the two are combined (fig. 4.2 and 4.3). They develop in this group, apparently parallel to each other. The first is the one used for nearly all figurines with pendants in group 1, a smaller number of usually relatively large pendants in each row. An additional feature of the same objects as pendants occurs in group 2, an alternating pattern (**98**[750] and especially group 2d). This pattern originates in the triple and quintuple-form pendants, which had a different pendant in the middle (**48**, **60**). A transitional form can be seen in those figurines with a second or third row consisting of identical or different objects, but never exceeding a total of five pendants on one band (**61** in group 1; **62**, **100**, **70**, **88** in group 2). The second style of the pectoral pendants is that of higher numbers of equally sized, ovoid pendants on several, at least two, rows. The pendants give a rounder, three-dimensional impression (**99**, **107-109**). Characteristic of the first style is the variation in shapes of the pectoral pendants, often alternating, while the second style is known for its identical, usually ovoid, pendants. In the description below these styles will be referred to.

In the first part, 2a, some large heads are discussed that show a variation in hairstyles and facial features (fig. 4.2).

750 The pointed ovoid pendants on the second row could count as a reason to see these as transitional objects. They are similarly shaped on the first row, where they alternate with the discs.

The partly chronologically parallel group 2b focuses first on the development of the pectoral pendants of the second style. A second development is a change in the appearance of the body. With that development, a major change takes place, because from here onwards the poses become more varied. Figurines with a slightly curving body appear to be standing. These developments continue in group 2c. Details of the dress, such as folds and fibulae distinguish the group from the previous one. Group 2d continues where 2c left off, with additional details such as the larger sized earrings. It continues, however, with a major change in the facial features towards a chubbier and eventually a round face. The standing and seated poses were also common, and the early style of pectoral pendants saw a final comeback as an archaism. This intentional return is also visible from the block-shaped body. The details and face, however, reveal that they should be dated much later than group 1. As we saw in group 1, alterations are not introduced one-by-one and continue in a majority of later dated figurines, but not without exceptions. The polos is the clearest example, as the majority wears this headgear with a larger number (but not all) of group 2 than group 1.

Group 2a

Group 2a comprises 11 heads from 7 mould series. The details of the head are remarkable and it is in contrast to the body, much more three-dimensional. Coroplasts paid attention to the sides of the head as well, while for the body the sides are often just smoothed. This attention to the head and expression was noticeable from the start. It gives an idealised, but still naturalistic impression. Greek influences, such as the archaic smile and the forehead-nose line are very clear in this subgroup. It might that the attention to the head was a Greek inspiration.

This subgroup comprises heads, ordered chronologically, from the same time-range and slightly before the more complete figurines of group 2b. Heads from the same mould series are also ordered by size, as the larger heads are earlier due to shrinkage during drying and firing causing newer generations to be considerably smaller. The first generation of heads measure 10-11cm or even more with a high polos. Their size compared to the smaller heads in group 1 is distinctive. To order them chronologically, the specific details of the face, hairstyle, and polos will be discussed. Besides the size, the heads in this group differ from the mostly rounded heads of the majority of figurines in group 1. The form of the face is more elongated. The eyes are very large and not detailed with eyelids on, for example, **154**, as would later be more common. The same large eyes and sharply marked mouth, placed almost directly under the nose, is characteristic of **163** as well. Though her oval face, in particular, the jaw, is much wider than **154**, it shares the same characteristics.

Another indication of the choronology is the ears and their development. The tiny ears on **154** and **163** are hardly noticeable and rendered as a cut-out on the hair. Their relative size is very small. There is a clear development towards larger and more detailed ears, for example, **156-157**.

Many figurines, with or without polos, have a particular kind of fringe, a thick rim of hair arching across the forehead, which is sometimes slightly triangular. The fringe is divided into ‘bulbs’, vertically placed strands of long hair. **154**, **155** and **170** are examples of this hairstyle. They are exemplary for the development towards more rounded and separate bulbs. It would remain the most common hairstyle. It is likely that the head of **20**, of which the body type fits in group 1, is from a later mould series. This replacement of the head was a very common method and proves again the importance of that part of the figurine. A similar development, not concerning the bulbs, but the general roundness of the fringe, is evident on **163-164**, which have a rectangularly shaped fringe compared to the fully rounded fringe of **165**. The vertical lining on the fringe of **163** is similar to that of **154** and confirms their synchrony stated above, based on the facial features.

The hair on the sides of the heads varies, from plain as on **154** or lined horizontally as on **155** and **165**. The hairstyle and its changes are an indication of the rapidly changing trends in appearance and indicate a certain chronology. The ‘dogtooth’ hairstyle of the fringe, much less common, is a double row with waves. Probably from the same mould series are heads **156**, **157** and **158**, in three generations, possibly also of the same series as **159**, which would form the earliest generation and brings the total to four. On **160**, the fringe seems to have more than two rows, though the shape is similar. Because of that and the large size of this head, it is also placed in this subgroup. The hairstyle also appears in group 2b, but those figurines do not wear a polos (**112**, **113**, **114**). The continuation in group 2c on **91** and **92** (vague), marks the popularity of it during this period.

All heads wear a polos in this group. It is in most instances a quite large one with a clearly distinct rim. A very large polos is worn by **160** and **165**. The general shape is straight to slightly flaring to the top. Again **160** is increasingly flaring. The rim angles clearly and runs in the same way as the fringe around the forehead. The increased size compared to the figurines in group 1 is clear from the larger heads. While in group 1 most poloi were quite low, a development towards taller ones is clear in this group.

Chronological development can also be distinguished by the hairstyle. While the earlier bulging division, together with the presence of the polos, is an indication of a date from the last decade of the sixth century BCE. Some large heads, such as **154**, could even be dated to the last quarter of the century. The dog-tooth hairstyle of **159** is dated on a similar head from Gela or Akragas by Higgins between 490-470 BCE.[751]

751 Higgins 1954, p.303, no.1105 and 1106.

Considering the size of the head, a slightly earlier date is justified: the first quarter of the fifth century BCE.[752]

Group 2b

The second subgroup consists of 9 figurines from 6 unique mould series. This group runs nearly parallel in time to group 2a and introduces some novelties as well. The focus in this subgroup is the changes of the body and pendants.

The first object, **98**, is a remarkable piece. It is part of the chest of what must have been a relatively large figurine. Without arms, but with a variation of pendants in two rows, the object might be dated around the turn of the century. The ependytes is noteable, raised in relief with a straight line running parallel to the edge of the body. The same is visible on **99** and **107**. Any indication of a naturally shaped body or an arm is absent from these figurines. The upper part is an inverted triangle. However, **109**, a later generation of **107**, reveals more rounded shapes for the shoulders. The arms appear very vague and flat on **87**. As in group 3, the upper arm is formed from the edge of the body, next to the raised ependytes. Only the lower arms are three-dimensional. The next step to more rounded, natural arms, placed along the body next to the ependytes and with a sleeve, is **100**. The arms and hands from these figurines onwards are always placed in the same way. The arms are palced along the body with outstretched hands and the thumb separate from the other fingers. When the figure is seated, the arms reach the knees.

In the introduction to this group, the two styles of pectoral pendants were described. The distinction in other groups is clear, but here, where the second style finds its origin, there are some hybrid examples. The first style is represented by **98**. The alternation between different larger pendants is clear. The second line shows the ovoid pendants. **62** would belong to this group as it has only disc-shaped pendants with just four in each row, although the even number of pendants on a row is exceptional and it might also be seen as a hybrid. The second style, which has a larger number of equally designed pendants, is represented in this group by **99**, **107-109**, **87**. A combination of these two styles marks perhaps the start of the second style, particularly the use of ovoid and three-dimensional pendants. On the figurines with a combination of those pendants, we see that the first row consists of disc-shaped pendants and the second of more elongated ovoid ones (**100**). On **101-102** the same combination is found. They are probably of a later date and the ovoid pendant has become thinner. This is the next step in the development of the second style.

In group 2b, the ears of **99** are rendered with just the concha in outline, while those of **107** are very clear, detailed, and relatively large. The lobe of the ear seems, in particular, large or carries a disc-shaped ear stud. This could have been seen as aesthetically pleasing. The large earrings appeared more often in subgroup 2d. This figurine is remarkable because it seems exceptional in different regards. It would be the first to introduce more naturalistic, round arms, a sleeve with a seam in the middle. Also, for the first time, the large, shaped earrings also appear. The chair is unusually shaped. It is very narrow and visible only from a small rim next to the body. The high placement of the 'ears' of the wide-backed throne is also unusual. The face is quite chubby, with a large nose. The figurine might be interpreted as a 'forerunner,' considering the sleeves and the large earring. For these reasons, it could also have been placed in group 2d. The production date would be rather towards the end of the period. Its direct imitations, **101** and **102**, are much smaller and slightly different. The sleeves have diagonal folds and the pendants on the second row are just four in number, instead of the five on **100**.

Up until this time, only round fibulae, disc-shaped and similar to the disc-shape pendants, were produced. Figurines **99**, **107-109** and **100** all have round fibulae. In this group, there is a longer model introduced, though there seems to be no correlation with improving its functionality in fastening the pectoral bands. Most of the time the second band somehow just stretches from one side to the other. The new shape of the fibulae is on some figurines vaguely oval (**87**), and on others more clearly the outline of a double palmette (**62**). The disc-shaped fibulae became relatively smaller. While those of **98** and **99** are quite large, the ones of **100** and **70** (in group 2c) are much smaller, considering the ratio to the size of the rest of the body, the pendants, and the head.

Group 2c

This subgroup consists of 12 figurines from 7 unique mould series. The tall standing figurines are characteristic of this group. The faces of **65** to **70** are narrow and the tall polos strengthens this effect. The body of these figurines is not bent at the knees. Some figurines still lean a bit backwards and have a rounded, bulging lower body (**88** and **87**, group 2b).

In this group, the first style of pendants is not represented, only the second one (**90**, **92** and **93**). These figurines have an increased number of pendants and the next step in the development is the adidition of a third row (**93**). Some figurines mark the stage of change, such as **70**, and also **88**. The pendants are disc-shaped but much smaller than on **62** of group 2b and other earlier figurines. The exceptional disc-shaped fibulae of **65-70** is peculiar to this group, shaped similarly to the pectoral pendants on the first row of **70**. While the figurines that appear to stand usually have mainly shaped fibulae, this figurine still has round ones. They are, however, relatively smaller than those in group 1 and 2b. The pectoral pendants themselves

752 The facial features of the head are more similar to the fleshy faces, like those of the decorated polos.

develop into smaller and more numerous items. Relatively smaller and thinner ovoid pectoral pendants are the result. There are seven pendants on each of the pectoral bands of **90-92**. Sometimes the ovoid pendants became more pointed too. The pendants on the second row of **70** are an example of this. These figurines are grouped together because they share their standing pose and pendants in the second style.

Group 2d

This subgroup consists of 18 figurines and heads from 8 mould series (table 4.2). The larger scale production and exchange of moulds resulted in a large variety. The specific mould series **171-178** and **176-177** are almost similar, except for the pose and some details. They are counted as two mould series because each series has different objects and the differences concern both head and body. The head of **176-177**, for example, has no veil. Other small details can be found on the body. The first figurines in this group, **105-106**, link up directly with **100**, because of the specific head, though the body is earlier. These heads are from the same mould series. The smaller head on **100** indicates that the whole figurine is younger. The earrings are a clear indication as well. It is in group 2d that these large earrings become common, and they are visible on all the figurines. The face becomes chubbier and the Ionian influence results in very fleshy faces, with chubby cheeks and a large nose. From **21** onwards, the figurines in this subgroup have the same fatter face. From **179** onwards, the eyes have eyelids.

The variation in hairstyles in this group is remarkable ranging from previously common hairstyles such as a smooth fringe on **103-104**, an edged or rounder fringe with thin bulbs, **105-106** and **179-180**, to divided but naturally looking hair on **21,** and a fine tongue-shape with a thin outline on **171-177**. The last heads in this subgroup have a sort of small tube-shaped hairstyle. Both the tongue and the tube shape are ordered vertically to form a rounded fringe. The hairstyle on the sides of the neck is sometimes bulging, and has on **179** a double incised line. On this figurine, as well as on **180** from the same mould, there is an incised tight necklace with one pendant. This necklace also appears on many of the successive figurines – now in the mould – in this group and continues to be used on the figurines in the group after. Another detail that appears on all figurines in this group and continued into the next group is the large earring. The use of the specific head, jewellery and the addition of the tight necklace might indicate that it was the same workshop producing the figurines.[753]

The variety in pose and body type in this group is also very large. Again, it seems we are returning to characteristics of group 1 with a figurine like **21** that has a very simple block-shaped body with flaring shoulders. It is the head and large sizes of earrings that characterises the figurine as belonging to this period. Figurines **179-180** have a similarly shaped body, but the sticking out shoulders seem to suggest that the arms have been taken off on purpose. This might have been done to create the triangular body shape, common in groups 1 and 2b. Most figurines in this subgroup have roundish arms. Especially the upper arms of **103-104** look very naturalistic. The pose of some figurines is clearly standing, **176**, but a slight leaning backwards is still clear. On others, the bent knees are reminiscent (**21**, **180**). This might be seen as a clear development because **105-106** and some previous objects in subgroup 2b still have bent knees. The pose of the seated figurines also changed. While **105-106** still has a sloping upper body, the angle of the lap to the upper body in the following figurines becomes close to ninety degrees and looks more naturalistic. This is visible on **103**, **171**, **173** and **174**. The chest remains flat, except for figurine **103**, on which the possibly removed pectoral pendants resulted in a smoothed but slightly protruding chest. The seats, in connection with the pose, also provide a variety of different types, from a block-seat like **21** to a wing-backed throne of **103** and **171**, **173**, **174**. The latter mould series also has a finely detailed footstool.

The different aspects of dress also appear in various forms. The polos in this group seems, except for **103-104**, rather low. The veil over the polos is also exceptional (**171** and **178**). The fibulae in this subgroup range along a scale from being absent on **21** to the rosettes that also appeared in group 1 -which can also be seen as a conservative element- to the double palmette outline on **103** and the palmette on **171**, **173**, **174**, **175** and **176**. A surprising new and unique fibula portrays wheat sheaves bound in the middle, on **105-106**.

The pectoral pendants reflect the same intentional return to the first, style one pendants. They add, however, a third band and some new pendants, such as the shell-shapes and the satyr and calf protomes. The alternating pattern that we saw earlier in this group is also used. **179-180** have a pattern that is closest to the second style. The pendants are a bit more pointed and hang from a sort of knob. The seven pendants on the second band show that it clearly belongs to the second style.

Calculations for group 2

The polos is more commonly worn in this group than in the previous one. Of the 19 mould series of which the head is clear, 15, or 75%, wear a polos, but one mould series, **171-175** and **178** wears both. Figurine **21** seems exceptional with a veil with a band. Those four figurines, missing a polos, also lack arms, which were introduced much later and did not appear at all on figurines in group 1. This was possibly was an intentionally conservative style feature. In group 2, however, there are 11 figurines with arms out

753 For a description of The Workshop of the Chubby Faces and the One-Pendant-Necklace, see section III.10.d.

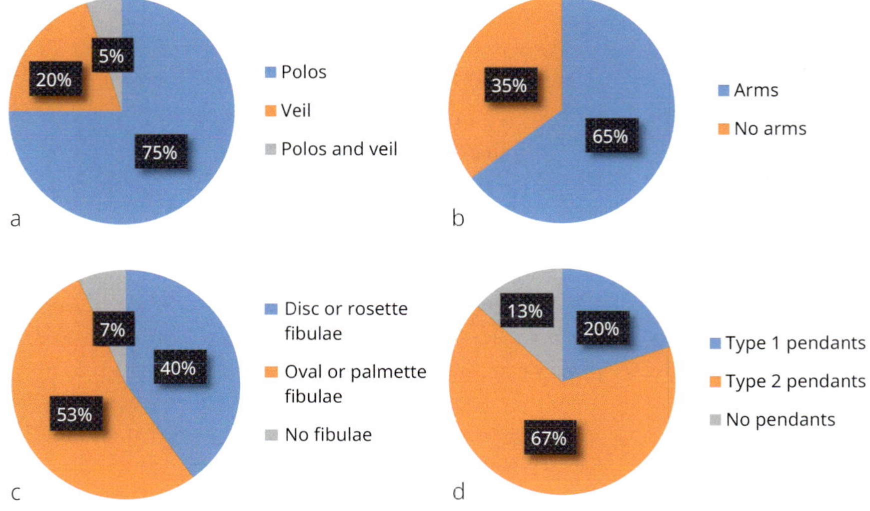

Figure 4.2:
(a) Division of figurines with a polos or a veil in group 2;
(b) Division of figurines with and without arms in group 2;
(c) Division of figurines with disc and oval/palmette shaped fibulae in group 2;
(d) Division of figurines with first and second style pendants in group 2.

of the 17 mould series to which the question of absence or presence of arms is applicable. This means that a majority of this group, 65%, has arms.

As far as it is noticeable, all figurines seem to wear fibulae in group 2. Some wear the traditional disc or rosette-shaped ones and some the newly introduced oval or palmette-shaped fibulae. One figurine, **93**, is not included in these calculations, because the figurine was too small and indistinct to see whether it originally had fibulae. If it had, it would likely have also had the palmette-shaped fibulae. The total number of mould series with fibulae is 15, of which just over half, 8, wear the palmette or oval fibulae. There is one figurine without fibulae.

The sort and number of pendants change in this period. While in group 1 we saw mostly figurines with three pendants, the figurines in this group are mostly adorned with a larger number, in each row and in total. The pendants are also more often similarly shaped. As explained above, the latter are called style two pendants, while those with a smaller number of pendants, up to five in each row and in a variety of shapes belong to the first style. A majority of 67% of the 15 mould series has pendants in the second style, 20% in the first style. The figurines that could be seen as transitional have been added to the second style, for they have already the ovoid pendants. There are two figurines without pendants.

The figurines, heads and bodies in this group are in general larger and taller than in group 1. Within the group, there are quite large differences between figurines. The coroplasts were searching for new ideas and tried different possibilities. The result is that in a short period of time there are many changes affecting almost all aspects of the figurine. Hairstyles and even facial features are changed. A clear example is the ears that become both larger, more detailed, and more naturalistic. The fringe becomes more round and the bulbs more clear. A variation in the hairstyle appears with the waving fringe. This remains a popular hairstyle through this time-period, though the round 'bulbs' also continue. In the last part, some exceptionally fine and detailed hairstyles appear on figurines.

The calculations make clear that some traditions are quite strong and continue to be applied, such as the polos. The size, however, varies from large and flaring at the beginning of the group towards, in 2d, lower headdresses with rounded corners, and even a veil draped over it in one instance. This shortening would have been applied after the moulding. On **179**, the polos is even removed.

New features, such as arms were added and became the standard, although group 2d, possibly because of Archaism, has two exceptions. The other arms became rounder and more naturalistic following the flat-edged arms in subgroup 2b. The pose as a whole is altered to create standing figurines. The body itself becomes more naturalistic with the addition of arms aa nd gradually developed towards a more rounded shape. The broadened shoulders were changed into a straighter body shape.

For the adornment of the chest with fibulae and pectoral pendants, the variation is larger. The majority of figurines display the disc-shape fibulae. The introduction of other shapes for the fibulae comes later than the variation in pendants and is a separate development. It seems that most of the standing figurines also had more oval or double palmette fibulae.

Group 2 has a majority of pectoral pendants in the second style (with more and ovoid pendants) which began here. Though it does not replace the first style, there are in subgroup 2b several objects, which seem to mark a transition from a smaller number of larger pendants towards larger numbers of smaller pendants. Group 2c has figurines with an increased number of relatively smaller and sometimes pointier pendants. Subgroup 2d, however, uses the first style of pectoral pendants, with even new sorts of pendants, and a division in three rows. The transitional figurines could be seen in two ways. They could represent a transitional phase from one style to the other or an intentional combination of features from both, perhaps even sometimes literally a combination of different moulds.

The large variety, particularly in the last decades of this period, is what characterises the group. A development in body and pose is clear and the attention to detailed additions, such as the differently shaped fibulae. Some of these returning details mark the final period, which is contemporary with the next group: the tight necklace with one pendant and the large earring. At the same time, the last part of this group is striking in the absence of certain features: polos, arms, fibulae, pendants, ependytes, and even feet. This might be explained by the wish to return to the simpler, more geometrical shapes of the earlier figurines and is an intentional conservative element. Such constants or returning elements of form and dress for the figurine have been dictated by the requirements for their function as votives. The rounder face is seen as an Ionian influence but might fit in the same trend as well.

Group 3

Group 3 is a large group because it contains the two most successful mould series among other similar figurines and some objects with intentional conservative elements. Like all objects presented here, they were found at Agrigento, but in this particular group, they were probably also produced there. The first subgroup contains a mould series, which produced the most figurines found at Akragas, together with its generations, parallels, altered objects, and other similar figurines. The discussion will therefore often draw comparisons with that mould series. The figurines are characterised by a specifically decorated polos, which was found in this quantity only at Akragas and is therefore likely to have originated there. The many imitations and parallel series, which are counted as individual moulds, bring the total of this subgroup to 29, with 12 figurines from unique moulds. If these minor and detailed differences are left aside and the partial moulds are counted as belonging to the same series, it would be just half the number. Even though those numbers are much higher than in other subgroups, they belong together in their iconography and give a clear impression of the development of the figurines (table 4.3).

Subgroup 3b comprises 25 figurines from 9 unique mould series, of which one was among the most popular in Sicily. Mainly because of production in high numbers at Selinous and the increasing exchange between the towns, the series was also produced in high numbers at Akragas. Most figurines are similar in their general iconographic scheme to group 3a, as far as the body is concerned. Besides the head, however, there were several other modifications made. One reason for this may have been because the body type originated in Selinous, not Akragas. This clearly did not prevent local coroplasts from producing them in high quantities, adding different heads and details according to their own taste and customs. The development within the group is thus quite clear. By looking at the details, they can be placed within the larger framework and chronology.

The absence of original moulds and the probable use of figurines to create new moulds resulted in smaller, less distinct figurines, particularly when compared with the mould series discussed in 2d, that are probably contemporary to 3a. New features, particularly related to technical aspects, were introduced in this group. Together with the usual alterations in the details, they form an example of the extensive coroplastic industry and the increasing exchange of artisanship and objects. The use and combinations of old mould parts, including imported ones from Selinous, together with new features, results in a mixture that characterises, in particular, the last three mould series of subgroup 3b.

Group 3a

The group consists of 29 individual objects of which 11 figurines belong to the main mould series in different generations (1st generation: **115-117**; later: **119**, **120**, **126-127**, **122**, **128**, **129**) and including a parallel series (**118**, **126**, **127**) (table 4.3). From here on, these objects will be referred to as the main mould series to which many other figurines will be compared. Four large heads in two mould series are thought to be predecessors of the heads of the main mould series. The first heads, **124** and **123**, from the same mould, have faces almost a centimetre larger than that of the main mould series. One generation later is **121**, which lacks a slip-layer and is, therefore, darker in colour. The hairstyle of these heads is similar to that of the

Group name	Concerning numbers	Total number of objects	Number of unique mould series	Time-range
3a	124-123, 121; 125; 115-117, 119-120, 118, 126-127, 122, 128-129; 130; 131-132; 133-134, 161-162; 135; 136; 137; 166; 167; 168-169	29	12	The first and second decade of the 5th century BCE
3b	138; 140; 142-151; 139; 152-153; 141; 112, 114, 111, 110; 113, 95, 96, 94, 97	25	9	The second and third decade of the 5th century BCE

Table 4.3: Overview of object in group 3.

main mould series, but the fringe is smaller and the hair on the sides of the head is horizontally lined. They have no earrings like the main mould series. On **124,** the large ear is visible as an outline. The polos has an intriguing pattern that is characteristic for almost all figurines in this group: space is divided into two rows of squares filled with discs. Compared to the main series, the discs in the squares, on the polos of these three heads, **124-121**, are much larger. They also lack the pearl-rim of the later heads. The facial features are similar, though the mouth is slightly wider. The larger size, horizontally lined hair and less complexity point to an earlier date for these figurine heads than that of the main mould series, 495-485 BCE. It is likely a parallel series as well, because the details would have been difficult to add in a new generation. The fringe of hair of **125** is very large and thick, while that on **123-124** and **121** is very thin in the middle. The main mould series seems to be in between those hairstyles. The same figurine head, **125**, wears a necklace, tight around her neck, but without a pendant. Her polos is similar to that of the main mould series with smaller discs inside the squares. Another difference with the larger heads **123-124** is that **125** has earrings, like the main-mould series. Her hair on the sides of her neck has horizontally incised lines. This part is almost cut away and seems quite flat on the main mould series. It is probably used to attach the body and the head and therefore lacks the more common bulging hair on the sides like on **124** and **125**. The body of this main-series is striking with its seated pose, although a bench is missing. Though the upper arms are flat, a new detail like the bracelets on the much more naturalistic lower arms shows that they should be dated to the second decade of the 5th century BCE. It is clear that they are composed of different parts of moulds. The third band with pendants is quite different from the upper two. The fibulae are not really clear; they are roughly rectangular but not carefully worked and not added straight but slightly turned. Whether they were originally painted or something was placed over them is not clear. Due to the change of mould, the heavy working to cover the seams between different parts from the mould resulted in a smooth lower body. There is no indication of the apron. The feet also were probably formed from another mould and therefore stick out oddly, without the usual dress draped over them and without a footstool.

A later and much smaller variation on these mould series, **135**, as well as **136**, has many different details, such as a different head, the outline of the apron and a wide bench. There must have been many variations of this series, like a different head and thicker sleeves. The reworking and combination of moulds often result in the loss of details. The feet of **135** are a clear example. Figurine **137** looks like an imitation or is also heavily reworked. What counts for the body, applies also for the heads. Variation in hairstyle or polos decoration, like the head of the main mould series, can be seen on **130** and **131-132**. This decorated polos head is known from a figurine body, similar to **90.** It is very possible that these sorts of figurines were the original ones introducing the decorated polos. It would fit with the above-noted extension of the pectoral pendants in the second style. A new hairstyle appears with the zigzag-like hairstyle (**133**, **134**, **161**, **162**). Another hairstyle that did not occur earlier is the wavy layer (**168-169**).

Group 3b

This subgroup discusses first a number of figurines that are similar in general iconography to group 3a (fig. 5). This means that there is a continuation, such as in the pose, the rather tall polos and the second style of pendants. On the other hand, there are some details that are quite divergent. There are fibulae in rectangular form, **138**; **140**; **139**, oval, **143-152**; **152-153** and even small disc shapes appear, **141**. Other details disappear, like the pendant on the tight necklace. What characterises this part of the subgroup is one extensive mould series again, **143-152**, which has considerable variation. The first variation concerns the head, distinguishable by the hairstyle in a parted smooth fringe or a fringe with bulbs. The second variation concerns the production of the figurines. On some, the outer rim that overlaps the mould is used to create a rim along the upper part of the figurine. In the table below the variations are summed up. Of this mould series, **142** is the oldest, indicated by the larger size. This is surprising because the fringe with bulbs is much more common in Akragas. The rim, around the figurine, as a leftover from the mould, becomes popular but is not seen on any other mould series in Akragas. Another technical feature that shows influence on the production of figurines is the small opening in the back of figurines **150** and **151**. The absence of these two features might indicate that these figurines are actually imports from or exchange with Selinous, rather than locally made objects (table 4.4).

The benches in this group all have a pillow and one of them, **141**, has a particular curly shape. The latter figurine also shows for the first time very fine folds and is draped over the feet very naturally, though those on the arms, horizontally, would be rather aesthetic and less realistic. The folds on the arms of **139**, **152-153** with the seam in the middle are very fine as well. A similar fineness is visible in the hair of **152-153**, which gives a very natural look. Her

	Without rim	**With rim**
Smooth parted fringe	**142**, **143**	**144** (partial) **145**, **146**, **147**, **148**
Fringe with bulbs	no figurines	**149**, **150**, **151**

Table 4.4: Fringe types in group 3.

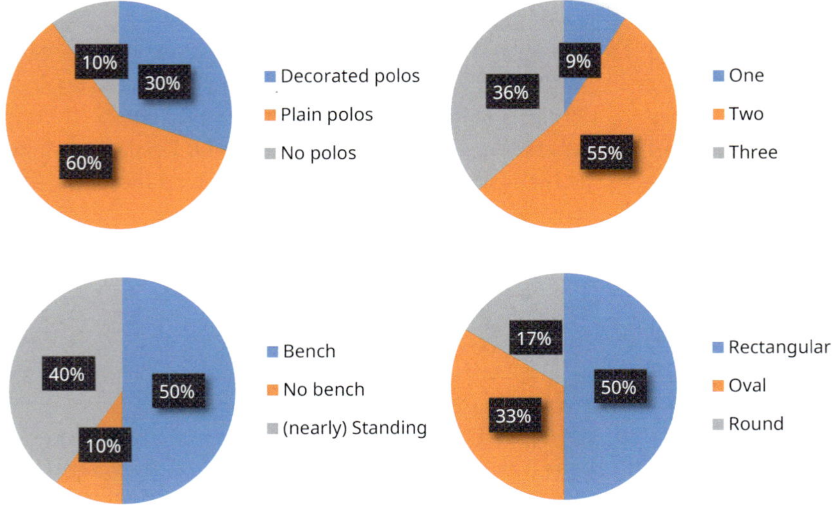

Figure 4.3:
(a) Division of figurines with a decorated, plain or no polos in group 3;
(b) Division of figurines with two and three pectoral bands in group 3;
(c) Division of figurines on the pose and seat in group 3;
(d) Division of figurines with rectangular, oval or round fibulae in group 3.

earrings are relatively small and therefore more realistic as well. They still have the same shape as the ring with a pendant. Figurine **141** is exceptional in the fact that the pectoral pendants are unordered and though in a straight line, look chaotic in comparison with, for example, **139**. A reverse development towards previously used shapes of the pendants such as the crescent is visible on **152**. This could be seen as an Archaising trend, even though it is combined here with the ovoid pendants on the first band. The following figurines, **114** and **110** from the same mould series and **94**, shows the same characteristic, and even nearly identical pendants, though other details of these figurines are very different from each other. The coroplasts intentionally combined other, older figurine bodies, such as here for the series of **114**: a figurine body of **60** from group 1, with another head, **107**, and contemporary details: in this case the fine folds of the undergarment in the neck and on the arms. This implies again an increase of detail over time. The range **95**, **96**, **94**, **97** run also from larger to smaller objects and, also the result of the moulding technique, from sharply defined to less distinct. The series as a whole might have been started in the second decade of the fifth century BCE, based on several details and the increased number of pendants.

Calculations for group 3

Calculations for this group could be done based on small details. Because the figurines' general iconography is very similar, most figurines have a polos and all of them have arms. The tendency to use old moulds, or maybe intentional Archaism, resulted in two figurines without a polos. Of all figurines, 60% wear a plain polos, and 30% a decorated one, though the latter comes in slightly different sorts. There are two mould series, and 10% wear no polos. These two have a sort of rim above their fringe, but no clear indication of a veil. One figurine head, **112**, seems to wear a polos while it is removed from **114** from the same mould series.

The majority of the fibulae are rectangular, 50%, while about one third is oval shaped and just two, (17%) are round. Most of the mould series, 55%, have two bands with pectoral pendants and 36% has three, while just one series has one pectoral band. Of these pectoral bands, in one or two rows, three have a crescent in the middle. There seems to be a correspondence between the sort of polos and the number of pectoral bands: a figurine with a decorated polos is more likely to have three pectoral bands. This is accords with the trend of an ever-increasing number of adornments and details. It is possible that the workshop where figurines with the decorated polos were made also had a preference for richer adornment of the pendants. This explains the combinations of moulds of which the figurines from a first generation, **115-117**, are formed. This workshop might have specialised in richer decoration and the figurines might have been costlier as a result.

Most figurines, 90%, are seated, most of them on a wide bench. In the main mould series in group 3a, this bench is often omitted, while in a later variation on that series and most objects in 3b the bench is depicted. In subgroup 3b, the latter part, some figurines, forming 10% of all mould series, are standing or have just very slightly bent knees.

To conclude this group, it should be noticed in the first place that the production methods intensified the application of partial moulds and combine a large number of details. The main mould series in both groups are clearly combined from different parts of moulds. The reworking and combination of even small parts of moulds becomes clear from the numerous versions and parallel series in these groups. Small details such as the tight necklace and the indication of bare feet in sandals point to synchrony of the main mould series in subgroup 3a with the mould series from 2d (**171-175**, **178**). The main mould series in

Group name	Concerning numbers	Total number of objects	Number of unique mould series	Time-range
4	185, 186, 187; 188; 190; 191; 192; 193; 194, 195, 196, 189; 197	13	8	The third and fourth decade of the 5th century BCE

Table 4.5: Overview of object in group 4.

subgroup 3b shows different technical novelties, probably as a result of influences from Selinous.

Previously noticed developments like the addition of details are noted in the jewellery and the dress. The fine folds in the sleeves of the garment are prominent in 3b. Bracelets are a new feature in group 3a, though not as popular as the earrings and not appearing in other mould series. The third row with pendants is applied here, as in group 2d, but continues on the second style, taking up the sort of pendants of **90** and **92** in 2c. It contains eight pendants on the third line of the main mould series in both subgroups. New as well is that the symmetry is no longer kept for all parts. Besides the pendants on **139** and **141**, the fibulae are striking in their odd rectangular form and diagonal placement.

Other characteristics do not change much. Though some new hairstyles are introduced, the most common one remains the fringe with bulbs. This hairstyle comes in a variation of thickness and is sometimes parted in the middle. A wide bench is the usual seat, though it has a fine mattress-like pillow on it in this group. The bench is sometimes curved for aesthetic reasons. The cushion, the fine folded garments, and the increasing number and fineness of jewellery items, are a sign of luxury, and would have been costly goods in real life. Possibly figurines with extensive features, such as a chair and details that needed reworking of the mould or the moulded object, were also more costly. Some figurines at the end of the group, from **112** onwards, are intentionally Archaising and use a double row of pectoral pendants with a crescent in the middle of the lower band. The removal of the polos, **114** and **113**, is another feature that could be interpreted as an Archaism. The characteristic, slightly bent body of **94** is surely also an Archaism.

Group 4

This group has no subgroups and is much smaller than previous groups, consisting of just thirteen objects from eight mould series (fig. 6). The reason this group is much smaller is not that fewer figurines were produced in this period, but rather that new subjects were found, such as the worshipper carrying a votive object in her hand. These other categories are not discussed here, just the objects that are a continuation of the previous groups, that is polos-wearing female figures, standing or seated, adorned with pectoral pendants. This continuation also includes some details, the folds in the undergarment, and a tight necklace, both with and without a pendant. At the same time, heads may have been interchanged between these categories and the newer categories of figures, for example, the worshippers carrying a piglet – which were very common at Akragas. The broadness of the fringe and polos, as well as the often elaborate hairsyle, give the heads a very different impression. This change went together with a more conservative style for the body of the standing figurines. The roundness of the arms, however, reveals the later date. The body seems relatively small for the large heads. Another part of the group, again slightly later in time, is seated on very elaborate thrones. There is a clear distinction between sitting and standing figures. The difference creates a new type of figurine: the worshipper.[754] These objects could have been placed together as a set. It would have recreated the dedication in miniature:worshipper in front of the seated deity. This interpretation would explain the rather simple forms of the standing figures, in contrast to the very elaborate seated figures. The furniture received the attention of the coroplasts and is shaped in detail, probably after the latest developments in real furniture. A last technical characteristic of the group is that most of the figurines had a lighter, whitish coloured slip-layer, covering the red clay.

Figurines **185-187** and **188**, the standing figurines, have a thin and flat body. Their pose is comparable to that of the standing figurines in subgroup 2c. The figures hold their arms alongside their body with hands outstretched, as if they are grabbing their dress, lifting it to step forward or preparing to take a seat. The dress and decoration on **185-186** are rather simple. There are small round fibulae, just two cords with pendants, and a chiton with relatively coarse folds. The number of pectoral pendants indicates that the rigid symmetry has made place for a more flexible and natural way of dress. Five small discs are combined with five or six (only **185**) pointed pendants. The combination of round and pointed pendants are reminiscent of some figurines in group 2b, like **100** and **70**. However, the pectoral bands seem to hang lower on the chest. A part of the undergarment is visible behind and above it. Figurine **188** has a similar widened polos and large fringe with curly hair. Her face looks small and so

754 The worshipper itself was the dedicated object. Its pose and facial features are not very different from the next step in the development, that of the worshipper carrying a piglet to be sacrificed to the goddess.

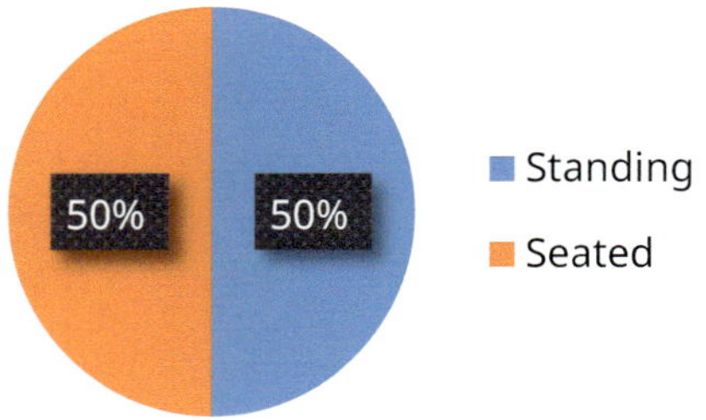

Figure 4.4: Division of figurines on the pose: sitting or standing in group 4.

does her body, contrasted with the large volume carried on her head. The same goes for **189**, which seems to have a small face, because the hair and polos are relatively very large. The hair on the sides of the neck is often detailed as well, as on **190-193**. Figurine **189** is seated and from **194** onward elaborate thrones are listed.

The sort of polos changes slightly in this period. **190-191** have a polos that flares much more than the previous ones, compared with **185-186**. One figurine, **192**, wears a Corinthian helmet, of which the lophos, the middle and highest part, has been broken off, as well as the curl on the other side. The furniture, in particular, the references to horse legs are a striking characteristic of the chairs in this period. It might be a way to show a certain status. A horse is a costly possession. References to lions symbolize rather power and strength. A lion with a ring is part of the decorative construction of a chair on **197**. Figurines **187**, **188** and **189** have/had a white slip-layer.

Calculations group 4

There are not many calculations to be done for this group, because the differences between the objects are very minor when it comes to the head and general iconography. Striking however is the dichotomy between standing and sitting. In total, there are four mould series on which this pose is clear; half are standing, the other two seated.

In conclusion, the large polos was new and unique for this group. In shape, it comes close to a kalathos, a wide basket, carried on the head. The face, and the body, appear relatively small compared to this large polos and hairstyle that increased in size in this group. Besides that, the hairstyle became very elaborate and finely detailed, sometimes in structured geometrical shapes, otherwise with more movement, more curly and naturally arranged. There is continuation mainly with the standing figurines in this group that are reminiscent in their pose, fibulae and pectoral pendants of some objects from group 2. The specific adornments on the latter, particularly the round disc refer to earlier common shapes for pendants. This might be again interpreted as an intentional conservative element, but the simple-bodied standing figurines form such a contrast with the seated figurines that there might be another explanation. The very elaborate thrones with specific decoration are a novelty. While in the previous groups, there was just some variation in the furniture, here there are completely new constructions depicted. The figure on it follows the previously set standards of the rich adornment, such as the numerous pendants in three bands and the folded dress. The head and hairstyle seem not distinctively different between the standing and the seated objects. From the small details, it is not possible to place them in one or the other pose. The body, however, of the two poses is very different in its adornment. The standing one is of striking simplicity. This gives reason to speculate about a possible new distinction between the depicted persons. The objects might have been placed in a group in which the seated, larger figure represents the goddess and the standing the worshipper. Because other indications of such an interpretation are lacking, it remains speculative. The several new features, combined with older ones point to a chronological development and a date in the third and fourth decade of the fifth century BCE. The white slip-layer is also a technical innovation that can be dated to this period.

Group 5

In this group, the objects are mostly and probably imported objects, though all are found in Agrigento, as well as figurines inspired by those or made from imported moulds (fig. 7). They are distinctively different sorts of objects of which most are unlikely locally produced because they do not fit in the local coroplastic developments described above. Some date also from very early onwards in the sixth and other from the first half of the fifth century BCE. This group has several subgroups for these different iconographic schemes. The order of the subgroups is chronological. These objects serve to identify possible influences on locally produced figurines and their source. Calculations are absent because of the different nature of the objects.

The first subgroup, 5a, has a striking feature: the pectoral bands. The second subgroup is similar to the Akragantine in iconography but very different in size and technique. The third subgroup, 5c, concerns East Greek imports and influences, in particular on the pose. The last group might give an insight into the transition from wooden statuary to mould-made terracotta and shows some figurines with dress that is rare for Akragas.

Group 5a

The first group consist of just two objects: handmade and thought to be from Akragas, **1** and **2**, now in Mus. Munich. They are striking because of their seated position: a support behind their bent body gives the impression of sitting and keeps the figurine up. This idea, to keep the figurine up and increase its stability might have had quite

Group name	Concerning numbers	Total number of objects	Number of unique mould series	Time-range
5a	1; 2	2	Not applicable, handmade	The first half of the 6th century BCE
5b	3; 4; 5; 6; 7	5	1, face only	The third quarter of the 6th century BCE
5c	71; 72; 73; 74; 75; 76	6	6	End of the 6th century BCE
5d	85, 86; 77; 78; 80; 81; 82; 83; 84	9	8	6th and first half of the 5th century BCE

Table 4.6: Overview of object in group 5.

an impact on the development of Akragantine coroplastics. Another aspect, that of the double band between disc-shaped fibulae on the shoulders, could have been an inspiration as well. Other characteristics seem to be very different from other Akragantine figurines: the pinched face, the crown with a specific raised part on **2** and the wide-stretched arms. Technically, there is, of course, the fact that these figurines are handmade. Outstretched limbs were not easy to make in clay and this might be one of the reasons that arms were omitted in so many early figurines from Akragas. The roundish shapes and narrow waist are in contrast to the mould-made figurines as well. The eyes and strands of hair, on **1**, as well as the fibulae, are made of separately created clay pellets. The figurines are very similar to Argive objects from the sixth century BCE, which are found in Catania and Syracuse as well.

Group 5b

The relatively large objects in this group seem similar in iconography to the Akragantine figurines: they share the rigid pose and a polos. For that reason, and because the objects were probably brought to Akragas, they are covered here. The objects are presently in the Archaeological Museum of Agrigento and one in Mus. Munich.

This group shares a mould-made face, a particular hairstyle with a hollow, widening polos, placed on top of the head and a broad chest. However, the body part is not the same for all: three were standing, and two seated. The seated figures have their arms stretched along the body, in line with the sloping body; the standing ones probably had separate wooden arms, which were sticking out, placed over the terracotta stumps. The clay is similar to each other with glimmering sand and quite a lot of insertions, less fine than most other Akragantine figurines, but of the same colour. The similarities with the figurine in Mus. Munich, **5**, make it very likely that it is indeed from the same origin as the others, whether Akragas or another place. Paint has been used to highlight details, such as the hair and lips. The way of reworking is comparable, though it varies slightly. While **4** has a large opening on the side for firing, **6** has two small holes on the same spot and others have no fire-holes at all.

Except for figurine **3**, the faces have a characteristic cleft chin the pointed chin, a deep vertical groove is made on the pointed chin. On figurine **7**, the part between nose and mouth has a groove as well. Though not straight, it clearly marks a continuation of the chin groove. The narrow mouth with its thick lips is striking, but may not have appealed to everyone, as seen by the reworked mouth of **7**. The mouth has become much wider, with thinner lips, slightly open and curling up. A reason for doing so could also have been the indistinctness caused by a worn mould. This is clear on **6**. This gradual change in sharpness indicates a chronological order. This order coincides with the changed pose, from standing with the lower arms stretched out to seated with arms along the body. The seated pose, in particular, the leaning back to the backrest of **6** and **7**, and the upraised head give her a distinguished look.

Because the sizes of the face are very similar, it is plausible that the same mould was applied for all five. The small mouth, very narrow but with thick lips, and its placement just below the nose, as well as the deep dimples creating a smiling face by lifting the cheek-bones slightly, are a common characteristic on Akragantine statuary, though less pronounced. The placement and relative size of the polos, though hollow because of the size, leaving hair visible at the front, as well as the plain body and round ear studs are common features as well. It is very possible that these are characteristics common in a wider area, in this case, Southern Italy. The small lips are typical for the South of Italy. Both the upper bodies on the standing and seated figurines are very similar to figurines from Locri.[755] At the same time, it is clear that the figurines influenced the local coroplastics in some aspects.

Group 5c

The iconography of the figurines discussed in this subgroup differs greatly at first sight from that of the block-like figurines thought to be from around the same period. Most of them were imported, but some might be locally made from moulds of the imported objects. The

755 Ferri 1929, p.37-8, tav.XXVIII.

seated figurine on a visible chair might well be inspired by East Greek and Attic figurines. One example is an Attic figurine on a wide-backed throne, **76**. The block-shaped lower part of the body of **75** is similar in its pose. A figurine like **21** could be inspired as well by this sort of pose. **71** is clearly inspired by the round shapes of so-called Rhodian figurines, of which **72** is an example. The latter was clearly a popular model on Sicily.[756] The round shapes and continuing smooth outlines, particularly that from polos to shoulders are typical for these figurines. They might have inspired the imitation of the high polos and continuing outline onto the hair on **73** and **74**. The dress is different also from the apron, commonly seen on Akragantine figurines. An undergarment reaches halfway down the lower legs with a draped cloak, open to the front, over it. A similar garment is worn by **83** and **84**.

In addition to the iconography, techniques and materials used, the characteristics like colour and inclusions often reveal where an object was made. Figurine **71** was made locally, because the clay is similar to **63**, a white clay, and found in the same context, though it has a thin block-shaped body. Thus, a distinction can be made between iconographically close figurines. Numbers **72** and **76** are imported, numbers **71**, **73**, **74** and **75** were locally made.

Group 5d

This group consist of some outliers and objects with special iconographic features, nine in total from 8 different mould series. Some can be compared to others within the group, but they are collected together here as exceptional items. Their difference often concerns the dress and therefore the outline of the body.

One flattened model usually wears a peplos, accentuating the narrow waist (**80**, **81**, **85** and **86**). They are thin figurines with a roughly-shaped back. Their posture and thinness suggest that they are derived from wooden origins, from which a mould in terracotta was made. For the last two, **85** and **86**, which are both from the same mould, this is certain. Their mould was made after one of the three wooden figurines found in Palma di Montechiaro.

No. 77 is a herm-shaped figurine with shoulders and head on top of a rectangular column. Its pose is not comparable to the block-like figurines. The horizontally lined hair is an element that appears more often on early figurines. It is an exceptional object and probably imported. **78** is a mould for a female figurine with a polos, but the shape of the body and its cloak-like garment have no similarities with other Akragantine figurines, except some figurines in this group, and 5c, with a similar dress. **80-83** are female figurines, holding an object in their right hand on their chest. **83** has a second object in her left hand, a wreath, while she holds a bird in her right on her chest. **84** holds her long garment the same way. This long garment, open to the front, is worn by several standing figurines (**82-84**).

Although these figurines would not fit directly into the iconographic scheme of the figurines described in the groups above, they might have formed an inspiration for several aspects of the local coroplastics. Their size, production technique and certain specific features distinguish them from the other groups and they are likely to have been imported into Akragas, some probably already in the second half of the 6th century BCE, where they might have influenced the local style from the start and throughout both the 6th and 5th century BCE. Precisely the features of the polos, as in 5b, pectoral bands and seated pose, as in 5a, could have been derived from objects like these. Influences from different traditions and directions were adopted by the Akragantine coroplasts to create a wider variation. This is particularly clear from subgroup 5c. The elongated polos, for example, seems directly inspired by East Greek figurines.

Group 5b raises the question of inspiration from reality because of a dimple, roughly in the middle, that marks the protruding chin. This peculiarity draws the attention and is not seen in other Akragantine figurines. The small mouth with thick lips, however, is a characteristic common on Akragantine figurines. There are some facial features that are reminiscent of the Cretan faces, also found in Akragas, such as the nose-eyebrow line that runs continuously, the straight mouth and split chin.[757] In addition, the ear studs are made in the same way.

The absence of direct and iconographically comparable predecessors makes it difficult to draw conclusions. The introduction of the mould resulted on the one hand in the production of terracotta figurines, similar to the previously wooden objects. These are however distinctively different, particularly concerning the body, from the objects that would be produced shortly afterwards. One of the explanations might be that the locally most popular pose was developed after the introduction of the mould and has no direct link to that technical invention. The change from flat to more three-dimensional is merely a matter of the wish to keep the figurines upright. Another striking difference between the figurines is the dress. The local dress, the stiff ependytes might have created the difference in outline and does not look like the belted peplos.

Group 6

Though this is called a group, it actually contains just five objects of different nature that do not fit into the

756 See references to other figurines at **72** in the Catalogue.

757 See section II.5.c.i.

Group name	Concerning numbers	Total number of objects	Number of unique mould series	Time-range
6a	198; 199; 200	3	3	The first half of the 5th century BCE
6b	201; 202	2	2	End of the 6th century BCE to the first half of the 5th century BCE.

Table 4.7: Overview of object in group 6.

other categories described above. These objects serve as comparative objects and are added because they have not been discussed in relation to the Akragantine coroplastic production. They are therefore not arranged chronologically but based on their category. The first category is that of a figure-group: a satyr is running away with a 'statue' on his shoulder and two objects are kourotrophoi, figurines carrying a smaller figure on their left shoulder. A second subgroup contains two objects from different categories, a mould and part of what must have been a near life-size statue, both concerning an earring. For the different nature of these objects, there will be no further calculations or discussion, just a description.

The first, **198**, is a curious object, which with a similar object from the Louvre could be reconstructed as a satyr carrying a female figure on his left shoulder (Catalogue fig. 28). The figure he carries could be interpreted as a statuette because its appearance and pose are close to figurines of group 1. She wears a polos and pectoral pendants on her chest. The satyr's legs are bent, implying that he is running. The pun made in this object seems to contrast the gender and virginity of the deity with the sexual behaviour of the satyrs. The excited satyr runs off, stealing the figurine. He seems to steal the deity or at least her image as in an abduction marriage.

The pose is interesting, because it does not seem random, but rather reflects a way of carrying that is common among kourotrophoi. Two of them, **199** and **200** from Akragas show continuity in this category through time. The first, **199**, is, with the polos as headgear and the block-like body of the smaller figurine, clearly from the second half of the sixth century BCE, while the second, **200**, is with its folded garment and naturalistic body, with arms, rather from the first half of the 5th century BCE.

The following two objects are included in order to be compared with the earrings of the figurines because they are larger and therefore better visible. The first, **201**, is a mould of an earring, consisting of the three parts we saw on the earrings of figurines, knob, ring and pendants. The details seem slightly different from the ones depicted on the figurines (**21**, **96**, **100**, **103-106**, **115-8**, **133**, **161**, **176**, **177**, **178** and **179**). These also have a knob, though a decoration on it might have been painted, the ring in this mould is elongated and has a lyre-like shape with small curled tips. Similar to the earrings on the figurines is that the ring is 'boat-shaped' with a thicker lower part. The ring on **202** is very thick and hangs from a much smaller knob. **202** omits the pendant, while **201** has four. As we saw above, the figurines wear earrings with usually one larger pendant. This is particularly clear on **133**, which has a dotted decoration. In general, earrings were an important part of the jewellery, appearing third in frequency after the pectoral and fibulae.

The categories of the figurines are different from the seated and standing figurines discussed above. In this group, some parts are discussed because of similar details appearing on figurines, such as the earrings from larger statuary. It is very likely that larger statuary functioned as an example for the iconography of smaller figurines. The figurine groups refer probably as well to other material, large or small, or even to real life events in which an object or person was carried on the left shoulder.

Chronological overview of the groups

The defined typologies are depicted here with figurine examples and some notes on their appearance. A visual overview of the iconographic development is presented.

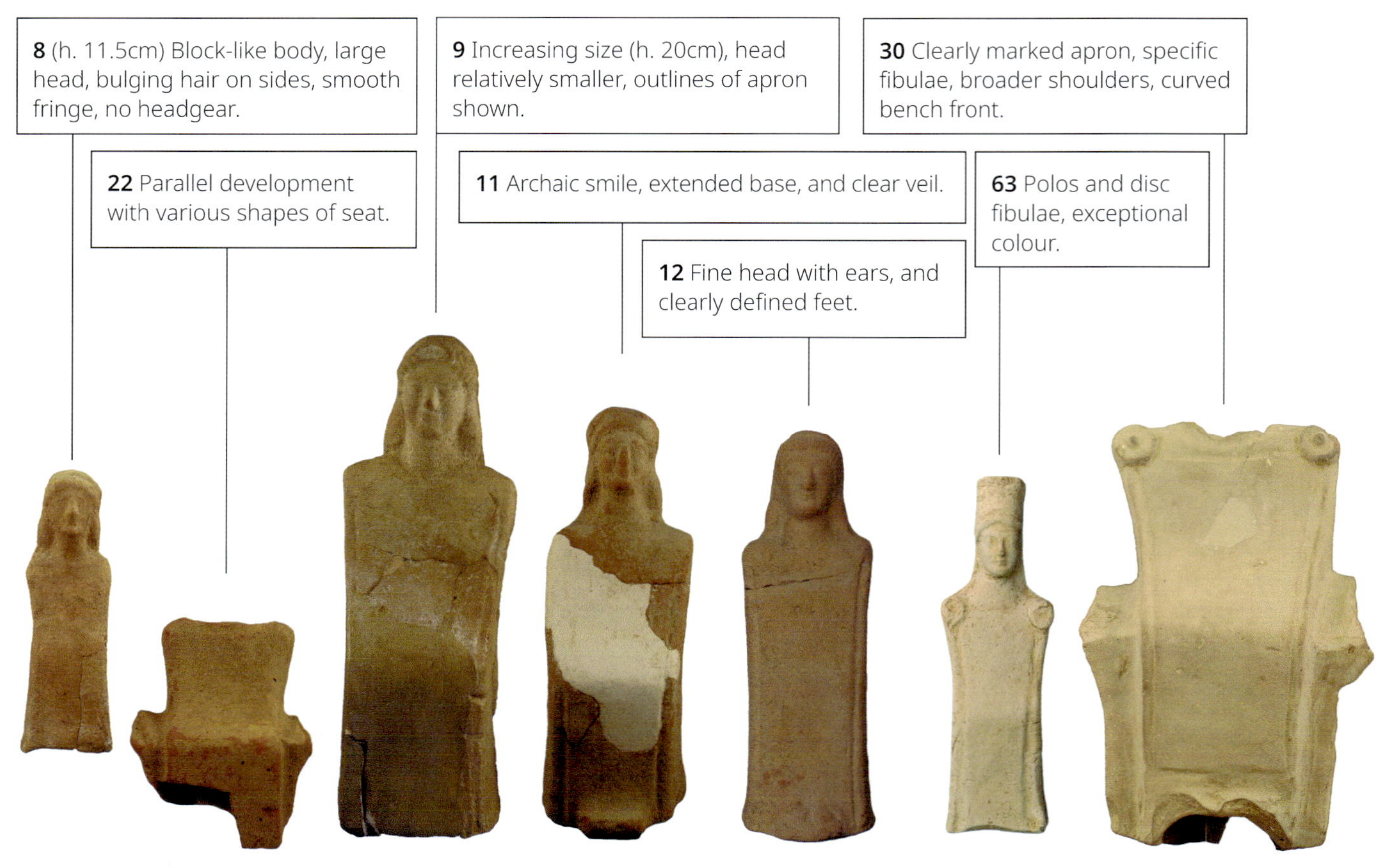

Figure 4.5: Chronological overview of the Group 1 characteristics: block-shaped bodies, round faces and a development marked by additions to dress, apron, fibulae, polos, and pectoral. All objects are scaled 1:3.

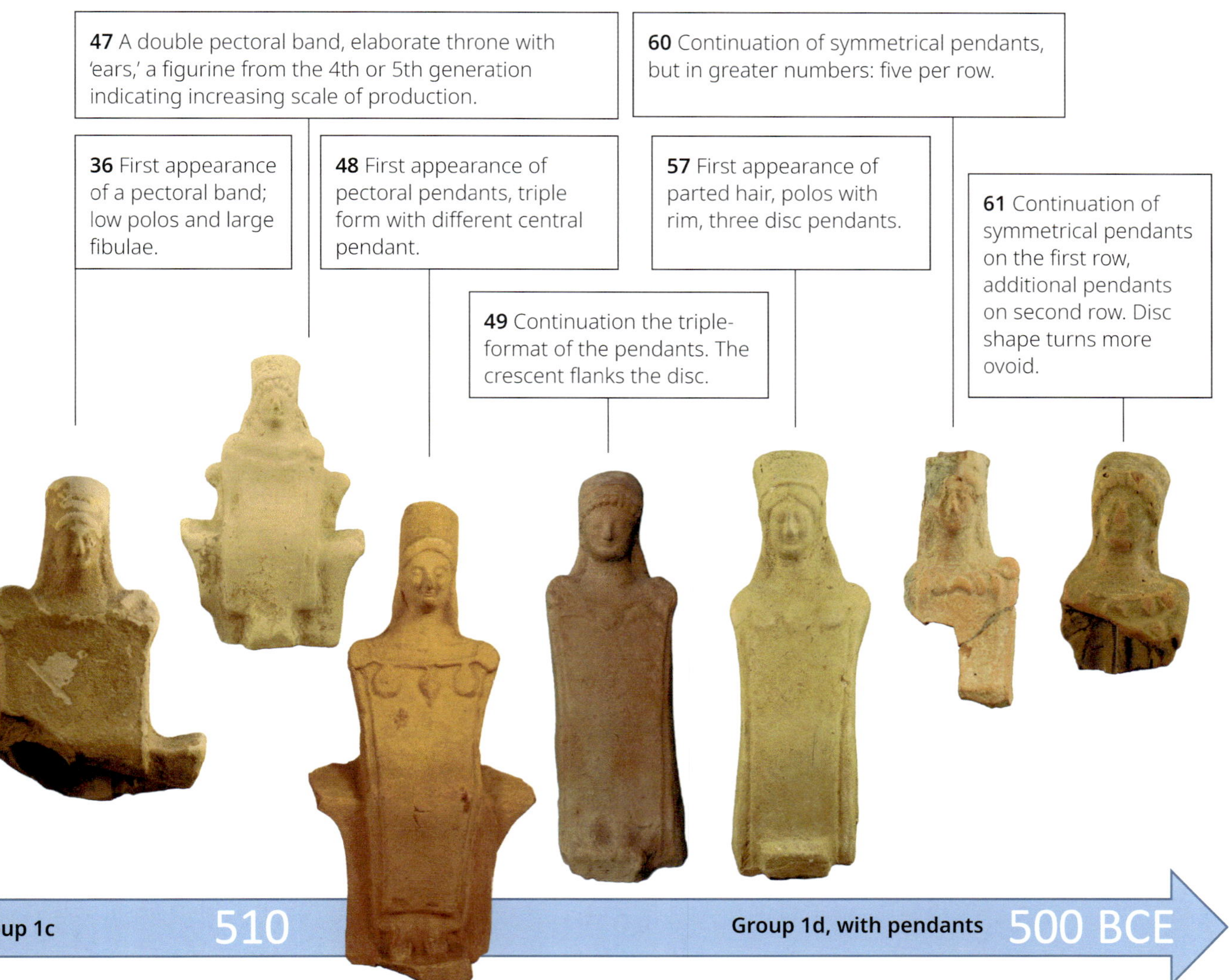

47 A double pectoral band, elaborate throne with 'ears,' a figurine from the 4th or 5th generation indicating increasing scale of production.
60 Continuation of symmetrical pendants, but in greater numbers: five per row.
36 First appearance of a pectoral band; low polos and large fibulae.
48 First appearance of pectoral pendants, triple form with different central pendant.
57 First appearance of parted hair, polos with rim, three disc pendants.
61 Continuation of symmetrical pendants on the first row, additional pendants on second row. Disc shape turns more ovoid.
49 Continuation the triple-format of the pendants. The crescent flanks the disc.
Group 1c
510
Group 1d, with pendants
500 BCE

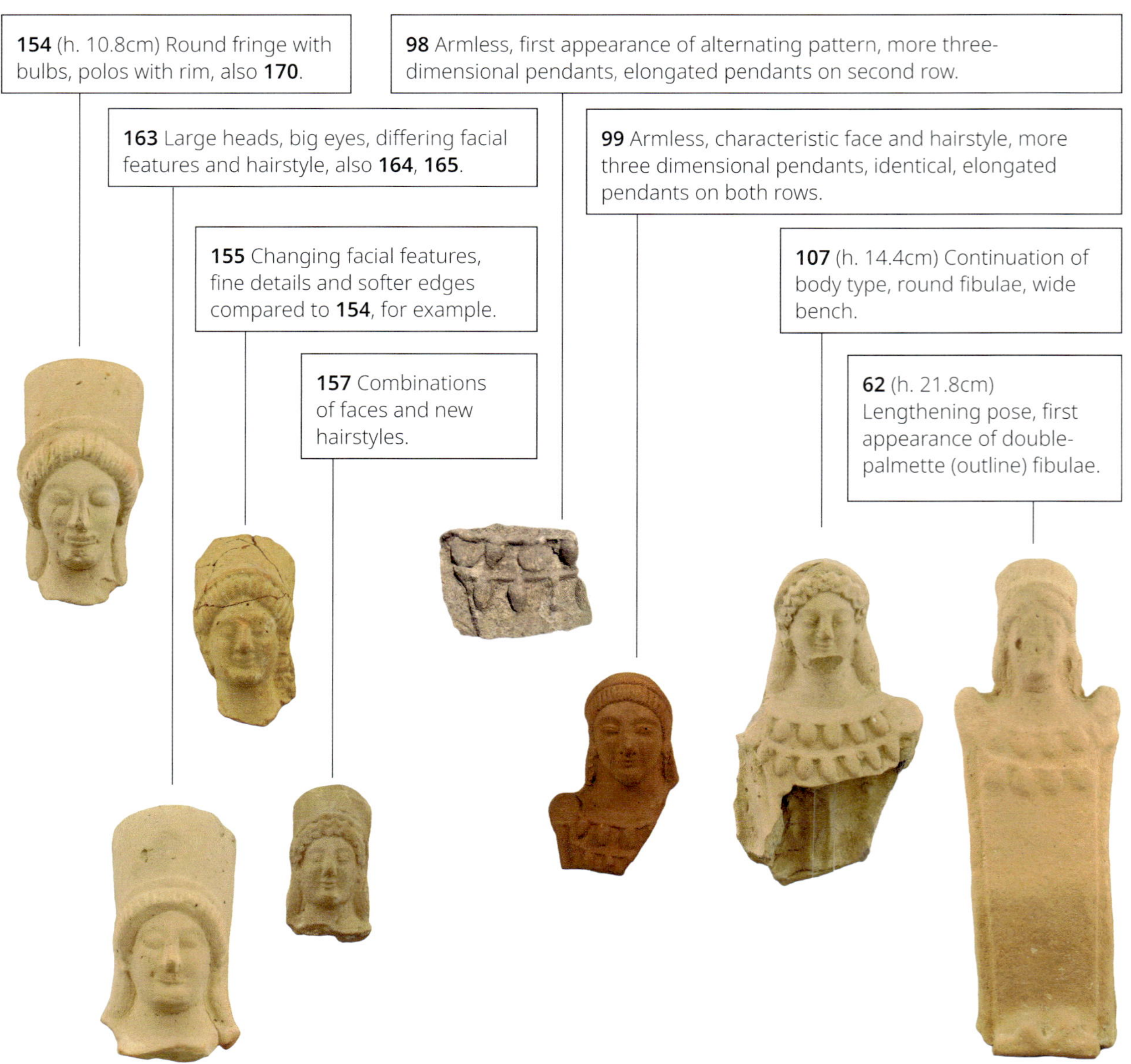

Figure 4.6: Chronological overview of the Group 2 a-c characteristics: changes in hairstyle, face, body and pose, standardisation of pendants in two rows, introduction of arms and double-palmette fibulae. All objects are scaled 1:3.

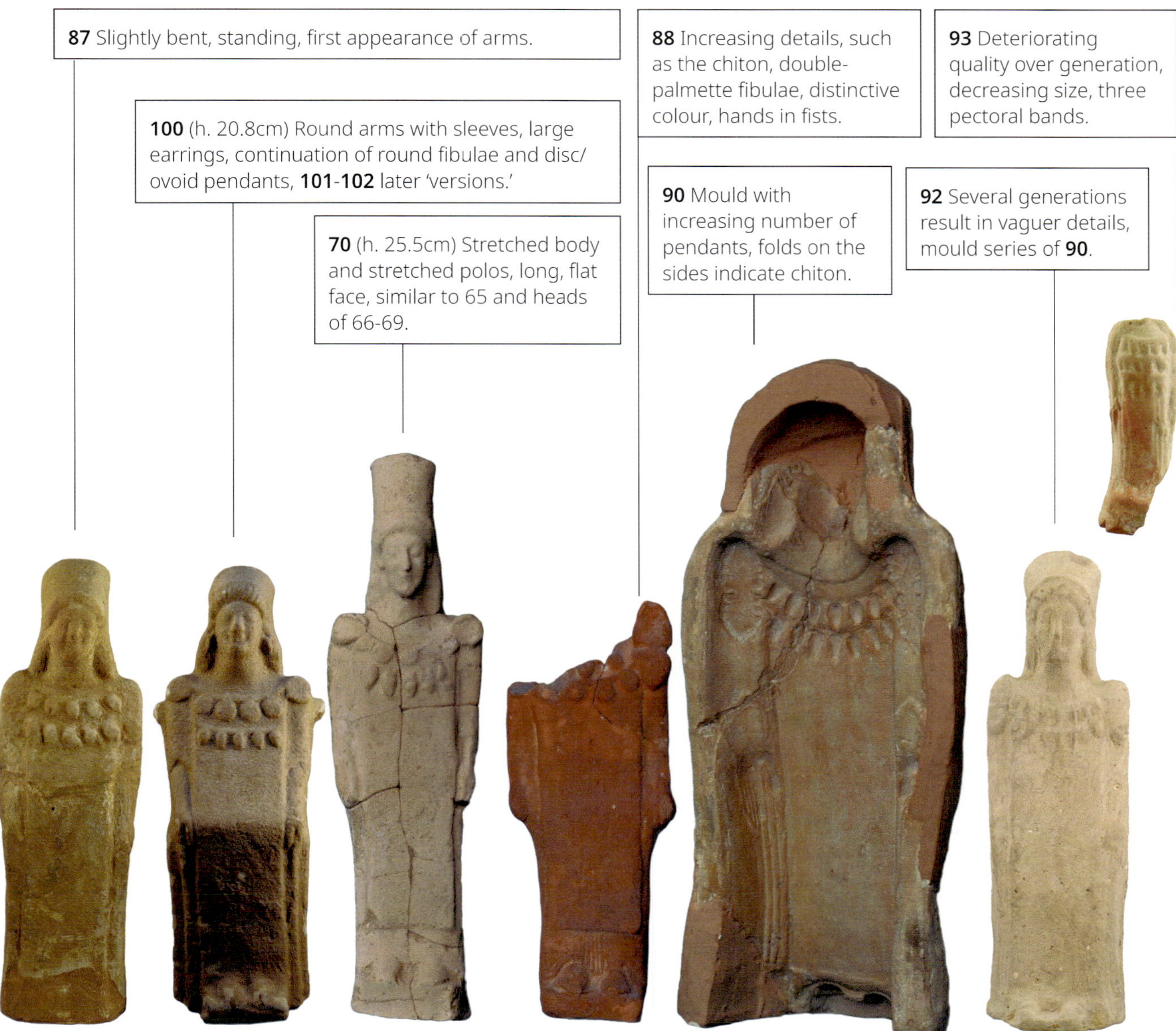

87 Slightly bent, standing, first appearance of arms.
100 (h. 20.8cm) Round arms with sleeves, large earrings, continuation of round fibulae and disc/ ovoid pendants, **101**-**102** later 'versions.'
70 (h. 25.5cm) Stretched body and stretched polos, long, flat face, similar to 65 and heads of 66-69.
88 Increasing details, such as the chiton, double-palmette fibulae, distinctive colour, hands in fists.
90 Mould with increasing number of pendants, folds on the sides indicate chiton.
93 Deteriorating quality over generation, decreasing size, three pectoral bands.
92 Several generations result in vaguer details, mould series of **90**.
480
2c: faces and hairstyle
470 BCE

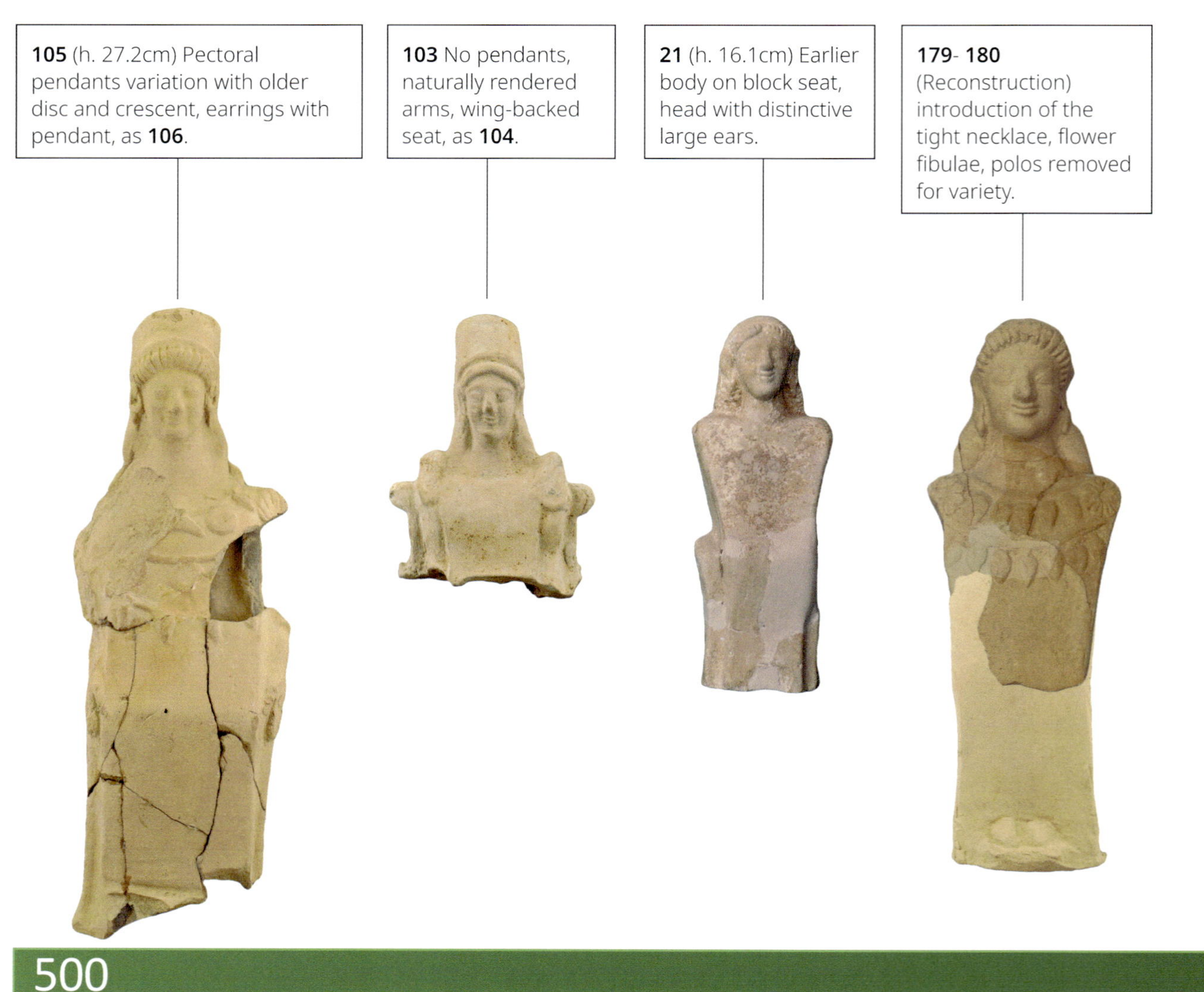

Figure 4.7: Group 2d characteristics: large, chubby face, fibulae and earrings, varying pectoral pendants, standing and seated versions, low polos. These figurines express wealth. All objects on this page are scaled 1:3.

171-175, **178** (h. 30.5cm, **171**) New sorts of pectoral pendants, polos with veil for variety, detailed throne.

176 (h. 29.5cm) Mould **177** additional details, variation of pose, standing, painted details, large earrings, and fibulae.

182 (h. 7cm) Fleshy face, clear smile, eyelids, and fine hair rendering.

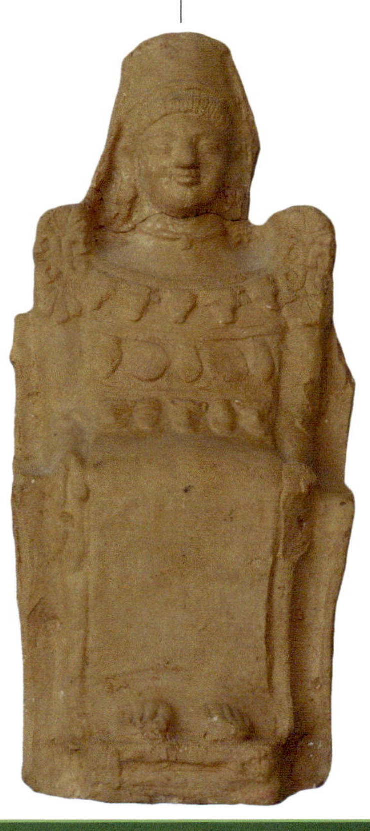

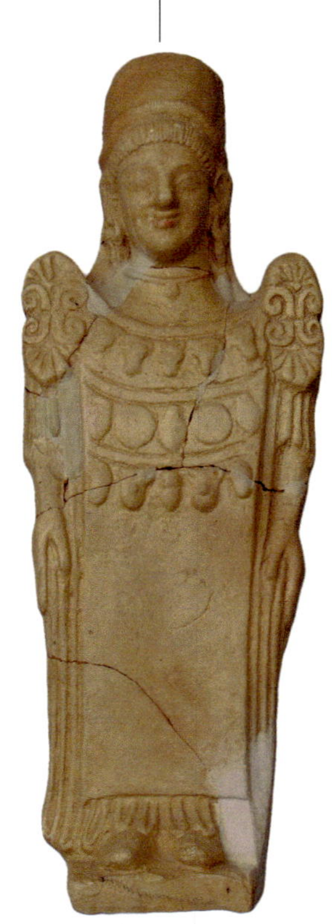

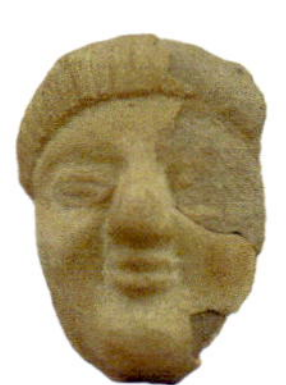

470 BCE

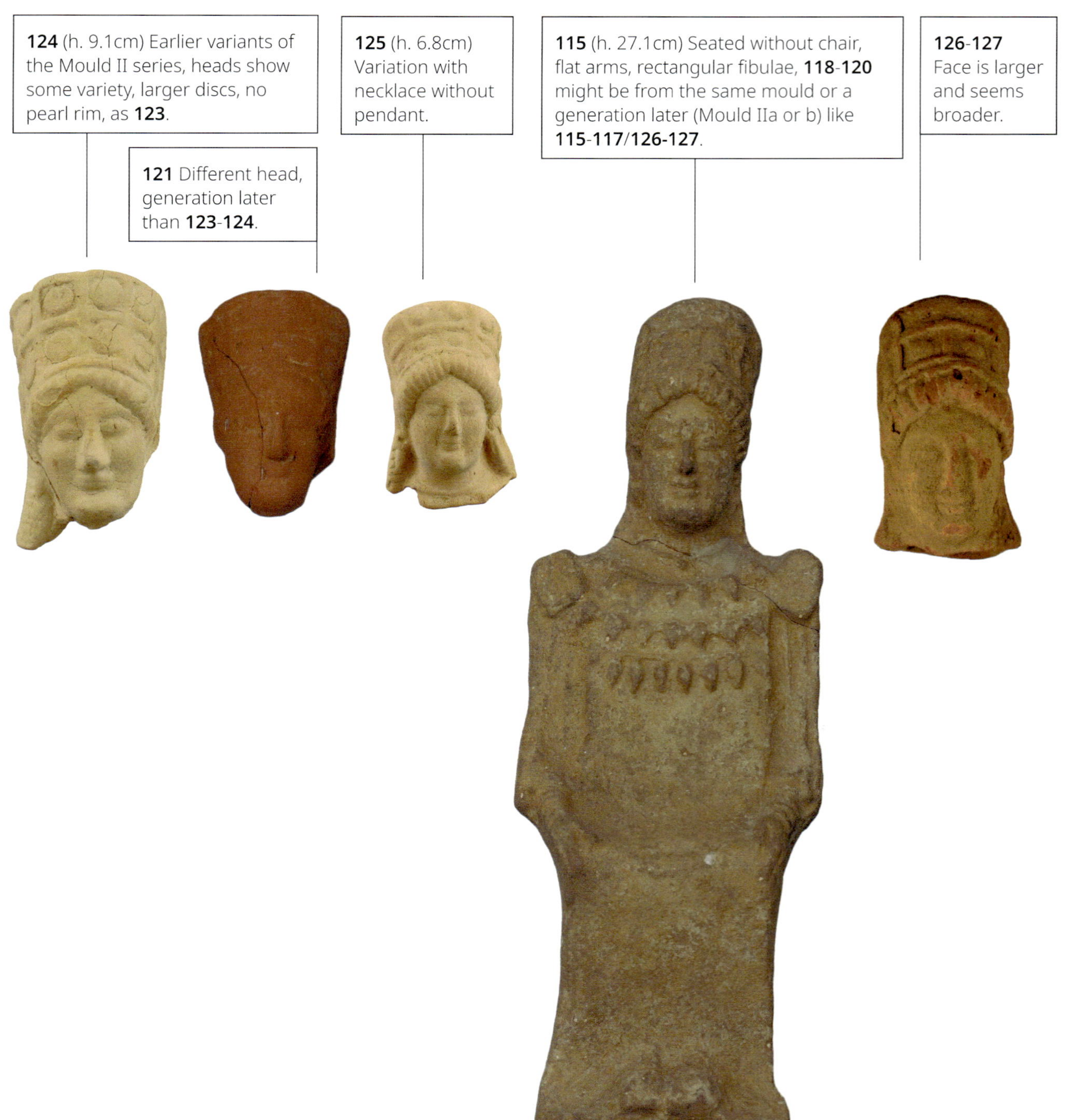

Figure 4.8: Chronological overview of the Group 3a characteristics: newly introduced decorated polos, different variations on the Mould II series, imitation and emulation. All objects are scaled 1:2.

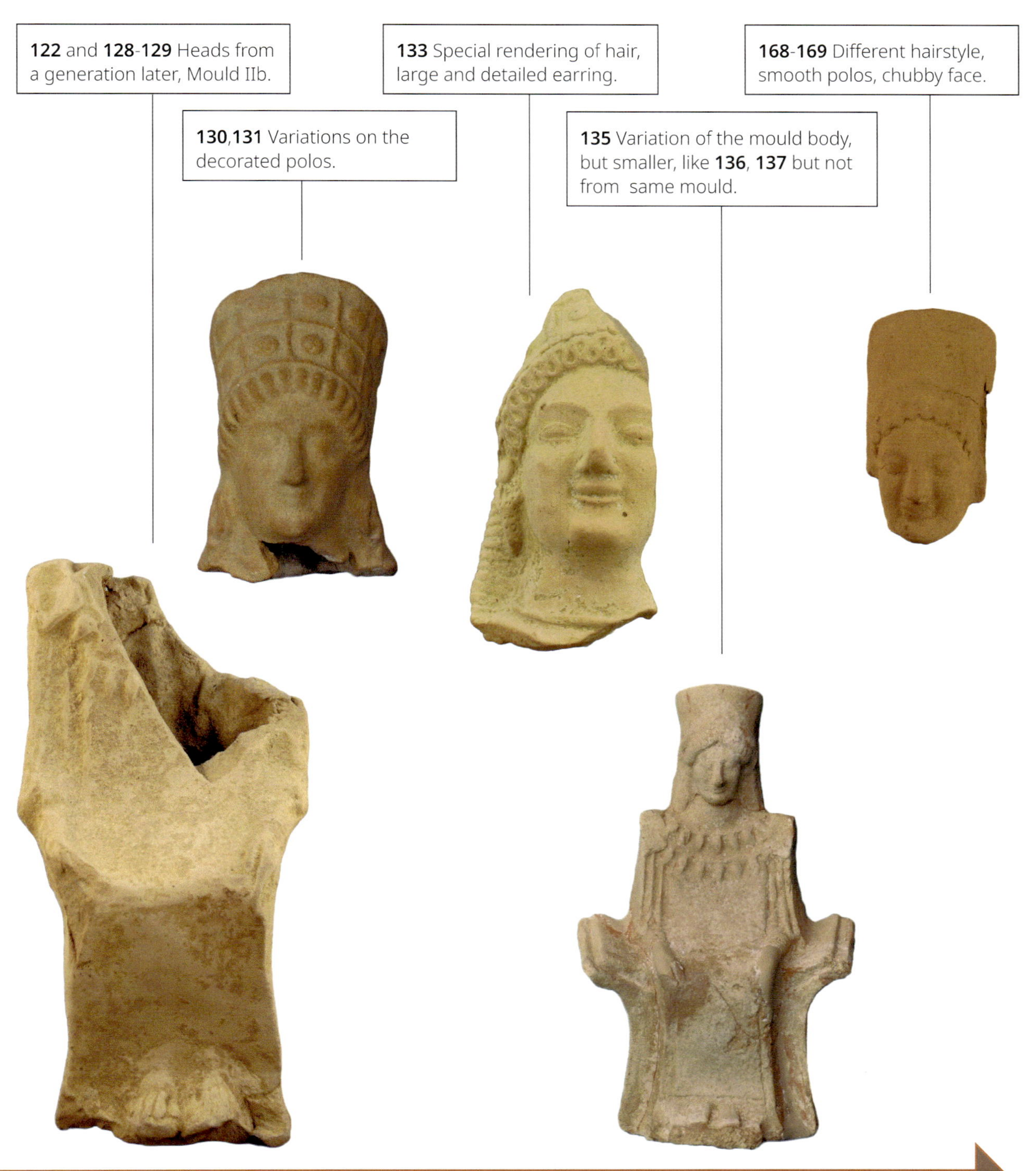
122 and **128**-**129** Heads from a generation later, Mould IIb.
130,**131** Variations on the decorated polos.
133 Special rendering of hair, large and detailed earring.
135 Variation of the mould body, but smaller, like **136**, **137** but not from same mould.
168-**169** Different hairstyle, smooth polos, chubby face.
480 BCE

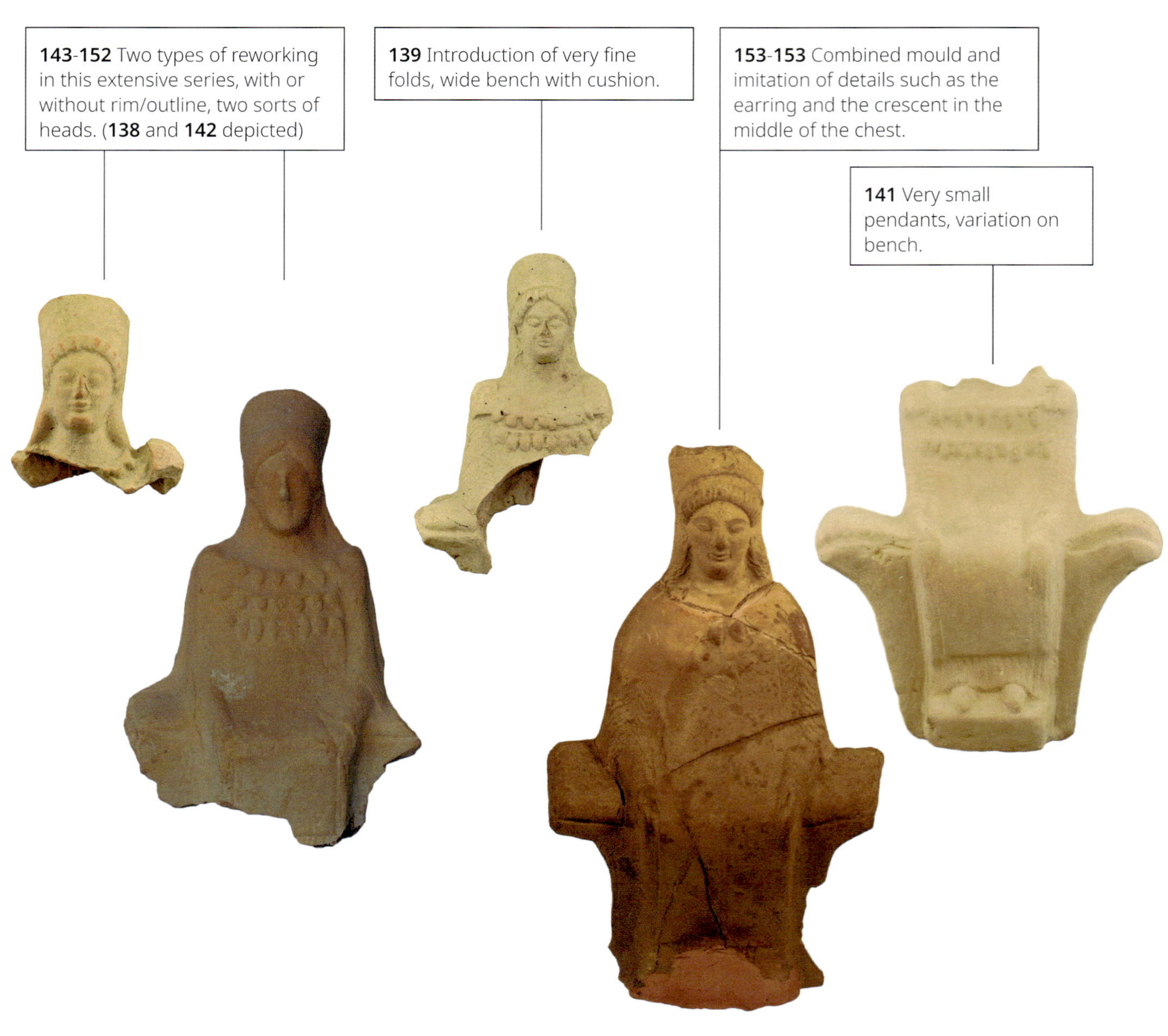

Figure 4.9: Chronological overview of the Group 3b characteristics: continuation of the general iconographic scheme, exchange with other production centres brings new forms and inspiration. All objects are scaled 1:3.

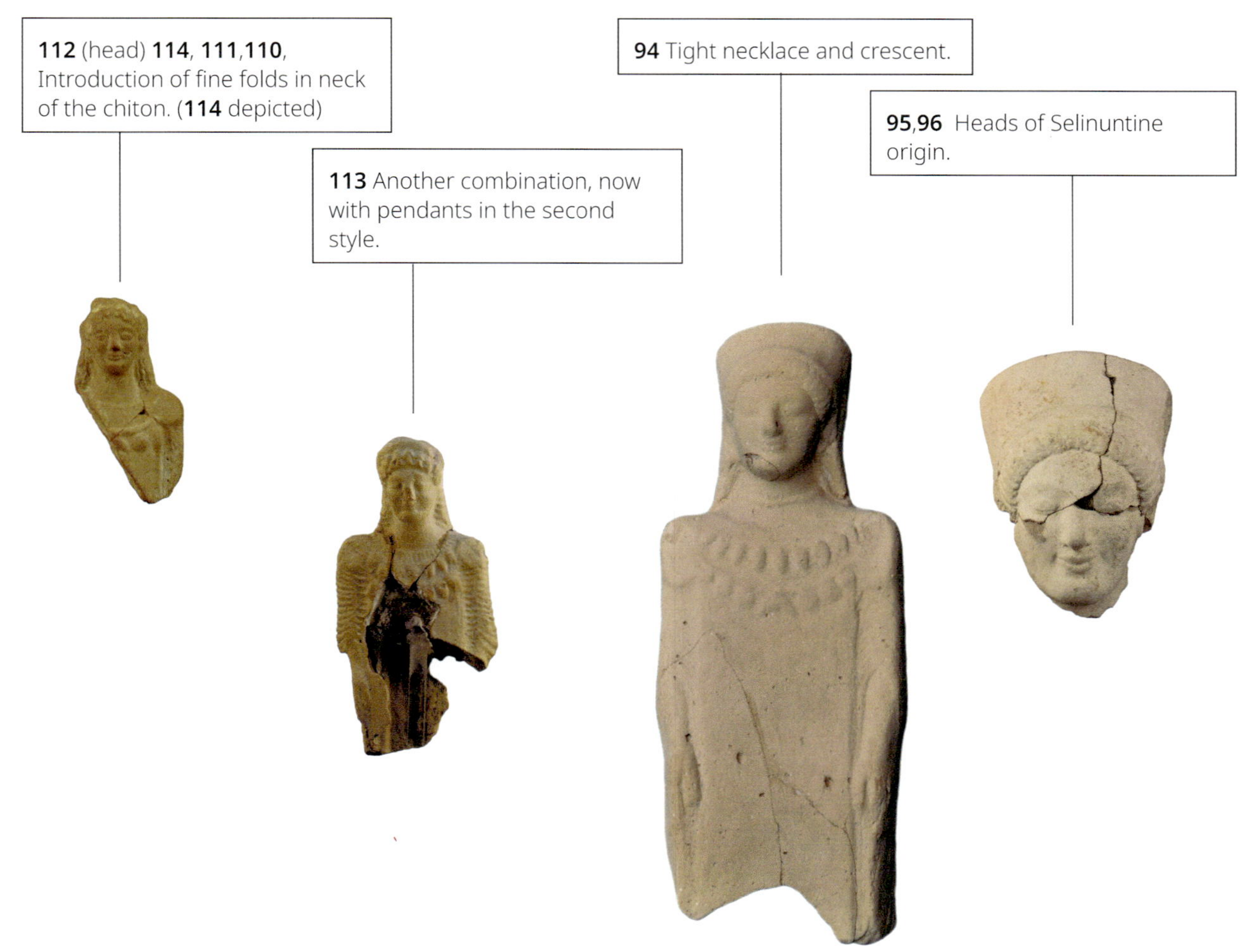
112 (head) **114**, **111**,**110**,
Introduction of fine folds in neck
of the chiton. (**114** depicted)
113 Another combination, now
with pendants in the second
style.
94 Tight necklace and crescent.
95,**96** Heads of Selinuntine
origin.
470 BCE

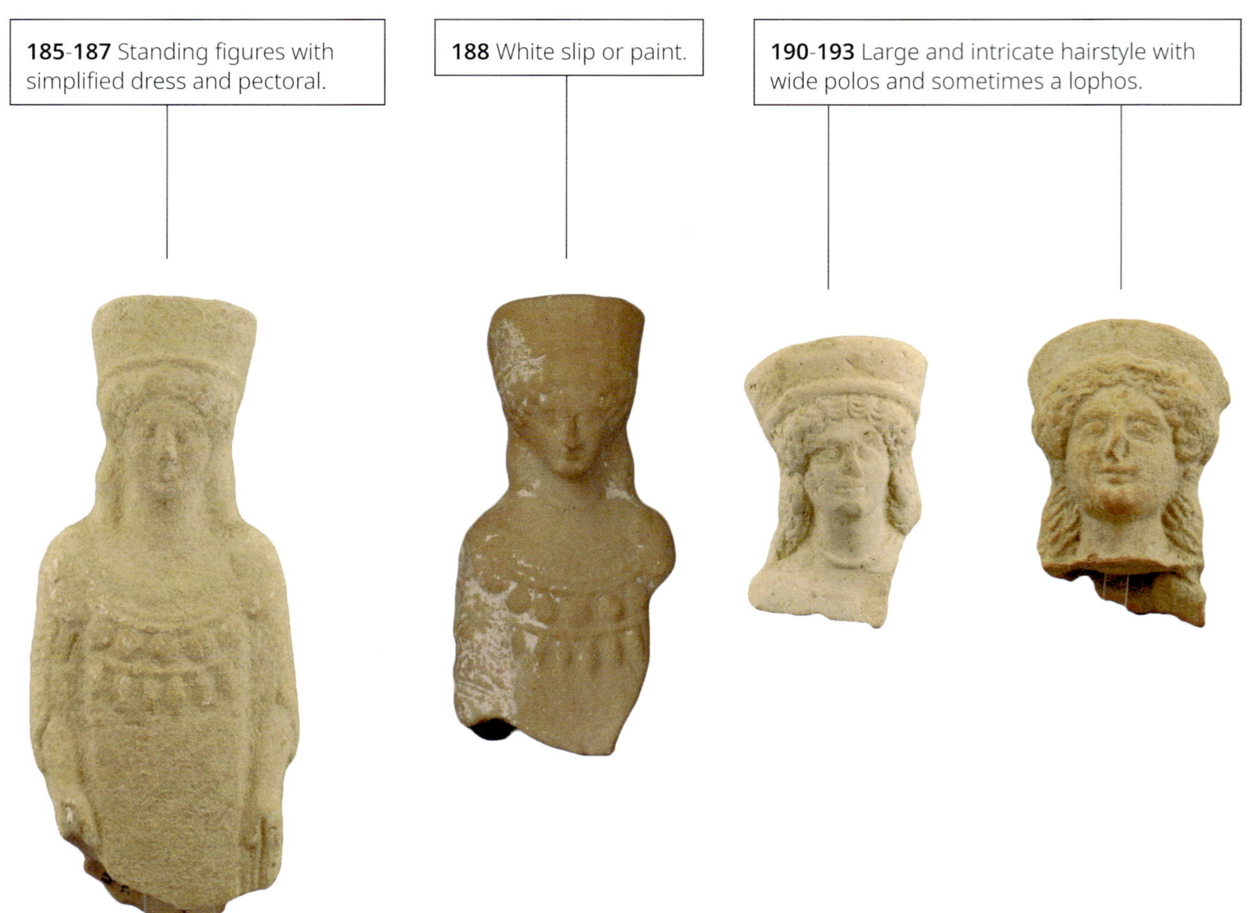

Figure 4.10: Chronological overview of the Group 4 characteristics: standing and seated female figures, new model hairstyle and polos, smaller bodies and faces, larger polos and hair. All objects are scaled 1:2.

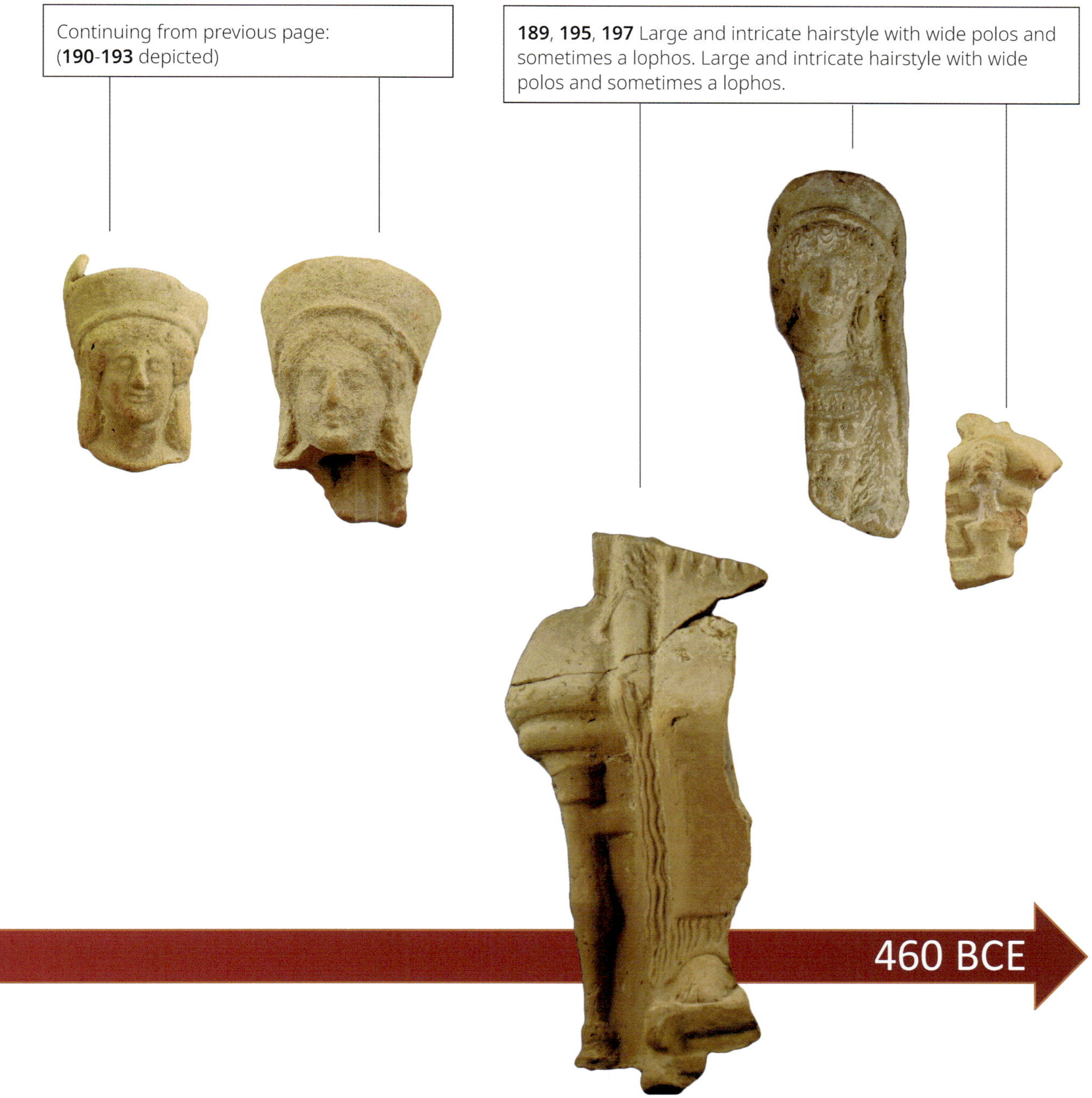
Continuing from previous page:
(**190**-**193** depicted)
189, **195**, **197** Large and intricate hairstyle with wide polos and sometimes a lophos. Large and intricate hairstyle with wide polos and sometimes a lophos.
460 BCE

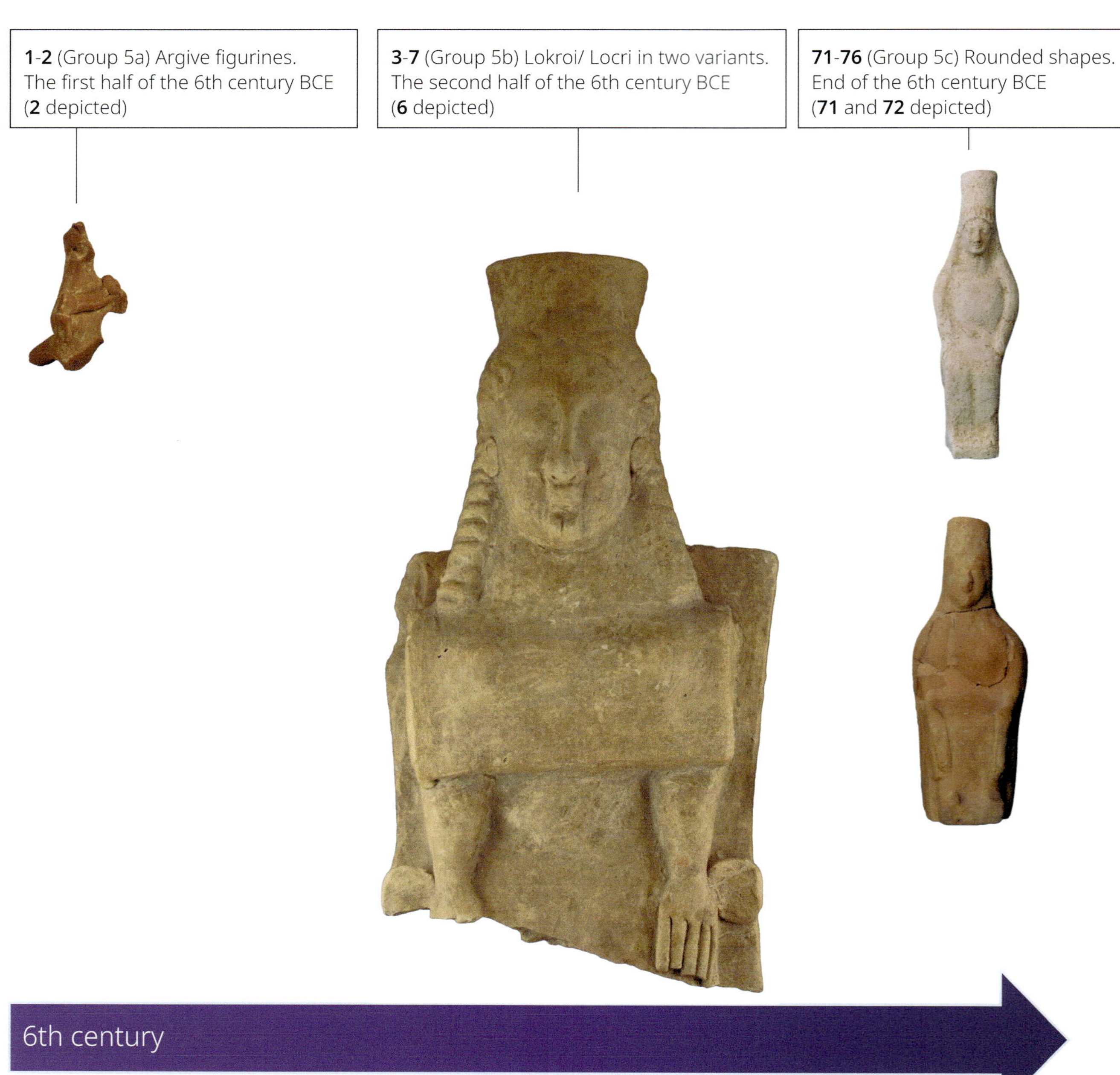

Figure 4.11: Chronological overview of the Group 5: imported and imitated objects. All objects are scaled 1:2.

77-**78**, **78**, **80**-**86** (Group 5d) Wooden thin figurines and other exceptional objects from various origins.
6th century BCE
(**78**, **83**, **86** depicted)

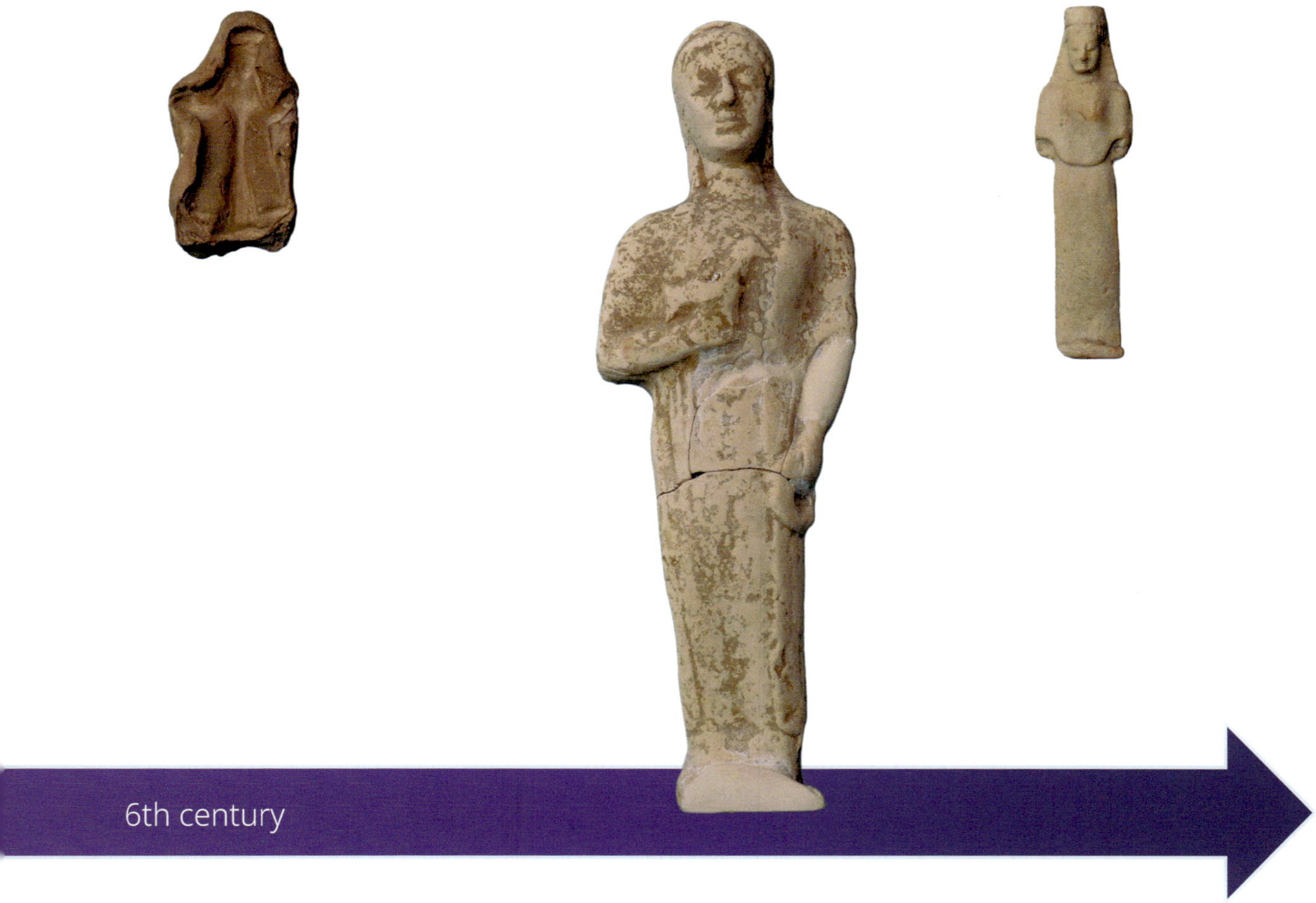

6th century

Chapter V

Conclusion

This study provides a description and analysis of the iconographic and material development of approximately 200 female terracotta figurines produced in Akragas during a period of about one hundred years, from the second half of the sixth century BCE onwards. It also addresses the social implications of the developments, particularly on cultural diversity and ritual, using the iconography of the figurines to read their implicit expression of norms and values. The terracotta figurines are unique in that they are locally designed and produced, non-utilitarian objects, and, as such, are artistic expressions of thoughts and acts that usually leave no direct trace in the archaeological record. Shifts in appearance may indicate changes in cultic life or mark a specific development in the wider context of society. The overarching question of this research is how terracotta votives were shaped, both literally, in their production, as well as iconographically. To what extent were religious structures and cultic rituals defined by these figurines? Which aspects of society contributed to the form and formation of these representations?

The town of Akragas provides a perfect case study in which the local nature of its iconography, and its production techniques and organisation can be studied. When comparing the Akragas figurines with regional coroplastics or specifically with figurines from Gela, Akragas' metropolis, and Selinous, another *apoikia* with large-scale figurine production, the typically Akragantine features become clear. Within the relatively short period of one hundred years, both the iconography and production method of the Akragas figurines underwent major changes: from hand-modelling to moulding, from individual objects to serial production, from small, simple-bodied figurines to larger and extensively adorned examples, and from block-shaped to naturalistic representations.

This research not only serves as a case study for terracotta production more generally on the rest of the island of Sicily, but also provides a detailed account of local developments in coroplastics. In addition to providing an analysis of the available literary sources in the light of the archaeological finds, this study also provides an in-depth investigation of the appearance of the figure represented, in particular, her dress and adornment. Material aspects were investigated using an archaeological experiment in order to scrutinise the applied moulding method and the development of the production techniques. By combining the technical and iconographical analyses, the study provides a conclusion on how the figurines came into being, and on their shape, function and meaning.

V.1 Concerning literary sources

Literature or mythology can lend additional support to what can be inferred from the archaeological material. For example, Diodorus states that Akragas was known for being wealthy, and the Phoenicians were known for trading in metals. These statements appear to be supported by the expensive adornments and the metal jewellery visible on the figurines.

Thucydides mentions large numbers of Phoenicians living in the same places as the later Greek colonists before the Greeks forced them into three cities. This would fit with the early, Phoenician-influenced form of the figurines and several references to Phoenician iconography, such as the crescent.

V.2 Concerning iconography

From the beginning of this category of female figurines, the fineness of their facial expression and the level of detail is surprising. On earlier figurines, the head is relatively large in order to convey expression better, which is important not only for their anthropomorphism, but also for the personal setting of the dedication. In the final stage of development, the head of the figurine is rather small, but nevertheless finely detailed. The facial features are clearly reminiscent of Greek korai, but with several local characteristics: the roundness of the face, the pronounced nose, large eyes, overall plumpness, combined sometimes with a less feminine jaw and protruding chin. All share the same 'Archaic smile'. On the 'Locrian' faces, a change in the shape of the mouth marks the moment of introduction of the Archaic smile, superseding the earlier Phoenician styled narrow mouth. Under the influence of the 'Ionian face', the cheeks and lips become more pronounced and the smile is a broader one, giving the face a healthy and well-fed appearance, which indirectly expresses abundance and welfare. In general, the facial features develop towards more naturalism: a thinner nose, detailed ears, and eyelids. The unpainted eyes keep a certain distance from the viewer. The bulging fringe of stylized hair parts or waves typically frames the face. In the first half of the fifth century, the Greek styled *krobylos* becomes the favoured hairstyle, as it is depicted on coins, though it remains a frontal view and the back of the head is rarely reworked. The last group of figurines is marked by large and elaborate coiffures.

The block-shaped body of early statuettes, which lack a clear pose and defined limbs, probably derives from aniconic objects, possibly a geometric cult statue, comparable to a cippus. The block-like body is very different from its wooden and terracotta predecessors with their belted dresses and flaring skirts. The rigidity and stillness of the early figurines are stressed by their stiff pose. The sloping upper body bends slightly halfway before continuing straight down. The angle creates the impression of bended knees and therefore a seated pose. However, several other standing figurines with a slight bend mean it is difficult to draw a clear distinction. The difference with imported objects and wooden predecessors is particularly apparent in the shape of the body: statuettes not made in Akragas are standing and wear a belted dress. The Akragantine figurines in a standing pose would not have been able to stay upright unsupported. The block-shaped body in a seated pose could be formed after earlier figurines with a stand or even chair legs, which were covered or connected. It is in this respect, as well as in the pectorals, that they are reminiscent of Argive/Boeotian figurines, which could very well have inspired them, as several have been found on Sicily in addition to similarly influenced figurines from Selinous. It is therefore not entirely clear if originally the representation was intended to be seated from the start or if they were provided with seating as a practical necessity. One does not exclude the other, and the numerous chairs added after moulding indicate the importance of an enthroned representation. The pose of the figure accompanied often by a large bench upon which to sit, later with additional cushions or decorations, indicate the status of the seated. The lion pawns or protomes could well refer back to Phoenician representations of a female deity on a throne flanked by lions or sphinxes, while the horse-leg-shaped chair leg is reminiscent of Greek furniture. Over time, the seats become more and more extensive and elaborate, even including a footstool. There are some series, the 'Locrian', and the Mould I group that present a similar figurine in both a standing and a seated pose. As this is the only difference, there is no reason to believe that two different persons are intended to be represented.

One disadvantage of a seated pose is size, as standing figures were naturally taller. Height seems to have been appreciated in figurines, and there is a clear tendency to an increasing size over time, up to about 30cm in height per figurine. Another development over time was the more naturalistic representation of the human body: feet, arms and rounded forms. Surprisingly, however, there was little indication of the female nature of the figurine, as breasts are not clearly modelled (in contrast to both earlier wooden objects and imported figurines). While the block-shaped body gradually became more anthropomorphic, the focus remained on the adornments of the body, as if the body itself were an abstraction or merely a carrier. The apron sometimes referred to as 'ependytes', a rectangular frontal garment attached with a knob on each shoulder emphasizes this view. Unlike the dress of Greek korai, the apron only follows the contours of the knees but otherwise hides the shape of the body underneath. This element of dress remained the same, although with the addition of finely detailed undergarments at the beginning of the fifth century.

The figurines also almost all bear one specific form of headgear, the polos. While in earlier figurines, group 1, nearly 70% wear the polos (with most others wearing a veil instead), the polos continued to gain in popularity over time, passing through five, distinct styles. One of those is originally Akragantine: a tall slightly diverging polos with a disc-filled square pattern. The pearl rim, between hair and polos, appears in this style. By the time the hairdo became extended into large hair creations, the polos was shaped similarly to a kalathos. The polos was already worn in Sicily and would have been a common sight. Both polos and veil were probably a typical part of female dress and, as such, were also applied to the goddess. It is possible that the veil and polos could have expressed marital status, and may thus have been applied to states of transition to another world. Although this idea would fit with the Greek narrative of Persephone (who was seized by Hades in Sicily), it is nevertheless not very likely that the figurine is depicted as a bride, both because of her pose and also because she is represented as a mature woman. The polos therefore is more likely to mark her status as a goddess.

The pectoral or *hormos* is a form of jewellery hanging between clasps on a cord or chain. Additional fastening to the dress appears on one figurine. The pendants, often with geometrical shapes, are most characteristic for Sicilian figurines. The wearing of a pectoral was a common cultural practice for both migrants and locals: several Corinthian objects appear with one or more pectorals with pendants, the Argive/ Boeotian objects wear large pectoral bands, and a local custom of wearing several metal chain pectorals and necklaces with amber pendants could all have inspired the dress of the figurine and its application in a cultic context.

The pendants appear in several forms, which can be divided into four categories, with some chronological overlap. The first and earliest category, A, is that of discs and downward-facing crescents, which usually appear in triplicate with alternating discs and crescents, usually in a single row. In the second and third category, B and C, more rows, to a maximum of three are added. In the following category, D, the pendants multiply with up to nine per row, and up to three rows in total. The pendants themselves no longer have a strictly defined shape but are generally oval or 'fruit-shaped'. With the exception of one specific pendant collection, they are not identifiable as representations of anything specific but clearly have an aesthetic function. In Category C, which is partly contemporary to Categories B and D, the form of the pendants were meaningful and refer to a specific concept. This was also the case to a slightly lesser extent for Category A, in which the pendants clearly refers to the sun and moon. The exceptional collection part c in Category C refers to masculinity and male fertility with its depictions of acorns, bucrania and satyrs.

The symbols depicted are derived from specific original contexts; the disc, for example, is common in Etruscan iconography and was developed later into the bulla; the crescent is Phoenician in origin; and the satyrs, bucrania, and acorns are Greek. Their symbolic application might have fit in earlier traditions of pendant dedication and adornment, and could have specified the wish of the dedicant. Some objects appear to be small containers that are reminiscent of miniature grave good vessels. Category B appears to express wealth and abundance in general. Pendants shaped like satyr protomes and female heads found at S. Anna, Akragas, probably dedicated at the sanctuary, demonstrate the link between real jewellery and that depicted on the figurines. The disc and oval shapes are known from pendants found at the Malophoros Sanctuary in Selinous and on the Acropolis of Gelas, while other images were found at the Demeter Sanctuary in Cyrenaica. The pendants could be attached individually by their tube-shaped suspension, held in place by additional beads on the cord.

Jewellery might also have been dedicated and applied to the larger terracotta objects in ritual adornment. Several life-size busts and the libation tubes with pierced ears point to metal ornamentation of terracotta objects. Necklaces or pectorals could have been around busts and figurines in an act of dedication. The increasing number of pectoral chains reflects the accumulation of several such dedications. In addition to the pectorals, large earrings, bracelets and a necklace were also added to the extensive jewellery representation. The dedications of jewellery would have not only sent a message to the immortals but also to fellow citizens: the prosperity of the inhabitants of Akragas was reflected in the abundance of precious jewellery. The fine metalworking and jewellery forms seem to have Phoenician origins, and influenced also Etruscan, Cyprian, Iberian and Argive representation of jewellery. Gold bowls, such as the one from a tomb at Sant'Angelo Muxaro, appear with symbols similar to those on the figurines. The figurines with specific pectorals are thus to be identified as votives. The later, similarly shaped multiple pendants may serve either as a sign of wealth or represent a prayer for such a luxury. Matching jewellery, in particular when earrings are styled in a similar way to the pectorals, indicate the loss of the symbolic functioning of the pectorals.

The 'head'-side of Siracusan silver tetradrachms, from the fifth century also shows a very similar style and development to the jewellery (and the earrings in particular) depicted on the figurines. The pendants may also have had a musical function in real-life as the pendants clashed together. However, this is unlikely to have been a primary function. In addition, bracelets, which can also be used for musical effect, are only depicted in a few instances.

Sicilian terracotta iconography probably influenced terracotta dedications elsewhere, such as the typical Iberian terracottas, which include metal rings, and possibly the amulets of toddlers and 'temple-boys', originally from Cyprus, but spread over a larger area, including Sicily. Two Greek korai also wear strikingly similar sets of jewellery: Phrasikleia and the Berlin Goddess. Both also wear a polos. On these korai, the jewellery and polos might be wedding attire.

The fasteners of the pectorals, the apron, or both, are in the earliest stages shaped into discs that seem directly derived from the local custom of wearing bone or metal fibula decorations with this shape. Later the figurines also use other forms such as the rosette, the mirrored palmette and a shape resembling a wheat sheaf, inspired by architectural ornamentation. Their function is similar to that of Argive/Boeotian figurines, while their role as a marker of status is similar to that of the large Etruscan fibulae. The fasteners also had a clear, practical function, in that they held a ring in place onto which the pectoral chains were attached.

The extensive dress and attention for fine jewellery indicate the importance of the attire, which is clearly out of the ordinary. The special clothing could have been for a marriage, with the figurine representing the bride. This would possibly explain the polos, the large seats and other specific indications of her appearance. However, it does not explain why the figure is solitary, as if she were to be wedded off and sent away to the family of the husband. If the figurine were to depict a bride, the boundary between deity and mortal would perhaps purposely be left vague to leave space for identification with the goddess. The goddess as a bride would fit the Greek narrative of Persephone, whose abduction took place on Sicily. In the context of intermarriage, where male migrants married local women, such a setting and the specific attention to marriage would not be surprising.

The exchange of symbols and shapes between neighbouring cities went both ways. The direct exchange of iconographic novelties with Selinous is clear, but both maintained their distinctive characters. Lions are a recurring motif in Selinous, whereas lion protome pendants do not appear at Akragas. It is possible that craftsmen of neighbouring towns were inspired by the works of their colleagues, in addition to the direct exchange of moulds or figurines. Compared with Gela, the distance, both literally and politically, between Akragas and Selinous was much larger. It is therefore surprising that exchange with Gela took a different form. Protomes or masks were more common than the figurines at Gela. In one case, the pendants on a mask from Gela are similar to those on Akragantine figurines: bucrania and vaselets. Akragas' figurine production is more extensive and iconographically it is following its own path. The exchange of figurine forms with Gelas starts later, in the fifth century BCE. Some Akragantine figurines are comparable to Geloan objects representing Athena with a helmet. Another category of figurines is clearly inspired by Geloan examples: the kourotrophos, in particular, the sort in which the child is seated on the left shoulder.

There are several indicators that the figurines were produced and dedicated for a specifically female cultic practice. In the first place, the figurines themselves are female and over the years they became more feminine in appearance and dress. The lead pendants at the sanctuary of S. Anna could also indicate that women dedicated their jewellery. The lead pendants are similar to the pendants depicted on some figurines, i.e., the satyr-protomes. In addition, two different lead pendants from S. Anna depict female heads. The opposition with masculine pendants and objects, such as acorns returns in the depictions of satyrs, and a figurine in which a typical Sicilian statuette, a female figure, is abducted by an aroused satyr (Catalogue fig. 28). Similar figurines are carrying a child, representing the figurine as female. Female cultic practice nor female deities do necessarily mean an exclusively female cult. The gender distinction could have been less strong originally and changed during the time of intermarriage and under the influence of the Greek migrations, as the majority of migrants were male.

V.3 Concerning production techniques

The moulding technique was probably introduced by migrants. Migrants to Sicily would have brought with them objects of other materials, such as wood, metal or ivory, as well as terracotta figurines, along with their methods of production. Wooden figurines were used as the patrix: a wooden figure, found at Palma di Montechiaro, was the direct patrix for two moulded terracotta figurines. Similarly shaped terracotta figurines were now produced not only faster but also at lower cost. Their size and three-dimensionality were initially limited due to their solidity and small base. When a single mould was applied, its depth created new possibilities, while air circulation was guaranteed by the open base.

The form of the figurine depends in the first place on the method of moulding. A general similarity of form should therefore be expected. However, new forms, sizes and details were rapidly developed for the moulded figurines. They are discussed here in the same order as their iconographic categories. The face was the first part to be moulded, as facial details are vital for proper expression and a face is difficult to shape precisely. For the same reason, the deterioration and increasing lack of detail in newer generations of figurines were often solved by replacing the head with a sharper imprint. In the archaeological experiment, it became clear that moulding the face is the most difficult part, because of the varying depths. The nose, in particular, is easily damaged when removed from the mould. The earlier appearance of the feet, as the first part of a naturally shaped body, probably has a simple explanation in that feet could easily be added to the mould because of their small size. Arms were much more complicated because they initially protruded and were therefore made of wood in earlier models. These wooden armed examples are rare in Akragas. The solution was to stretch the arms all the way along the sloping upper body, down to the knees. On some figurines, the process is clearly visible: part of the apron is removed to create space for the arms. This deeper part must have been originally created on a moulded object, which later became the patrix of a new series. Most significant is the increasing three-dimensionality of the figurine. This overall depth had functioned in the first place to keep the figurine upright but was later developed to create more realistic images of a seated figure with the help of a chair or bench. The specifically bent body created a stable base for the figurine, even though it was a bit more difficult to unload from the mould. The chair is sometimes hand-made, which meant an additional investment of time. Surprisingly, the chair is excluded from the so-called Mould II series, which is otherwise characterised by a detailed appearance, and originally had a throne, as one figurine (Catalogue fig. 14) is from the same mould series. The extended series, with several generations of figurines, may explain this lack: the demand for figurines may have been at such a level that no time was spent on extra details.

Larger objects, such as busts, were made so that metal ornaments could be attached, with pierced ears, or so that objects could be hung around their necks or on their shoulders. For the smaller figurines, this was not the case. Jewellery was added in terracotta, with some being made separately, such as the fibulae. Real pendants on a cord with beads were used in one case to imprint pectoral pendants into the mould, **172**. Another mould for an earring has such fine details that it is very possible that a real earring was used to make it, **201**. Most figurines, therefore, demonstrate the skills of the coroplasts both as craftspeople but also as artists. Figurines were adapted to the latest designs of female fashion and were kept up-to-date with innovative techniques, such as painting, mould exchange and the application of imprints. Their fineness increased over time and it comes therefore as something of a degradation when, in the following category of figurines, the piglet-carrying figurines, the rendering is rather coarse. The large number of figurines may explain this drop in quality, together with the apparent increase in standardisation. For the piglet-carrying figurines it was perhaps sufficient to be able to recognise the subject of the representation. How different from the case of depicting a deity.

The tight necklace or choker is a detail that appears on several figurines and is at first carved in after the object was moulded, possibly to hide the connection between a body and head from different moulds. Later, the choker was included in the mould and thus was no longer a technical solution, but rather a characteristic of the coroplast or workshop, whose statuettes might have been recognised by this necklace. In addition, there are several other indicators of specific workshops. The generations and development of a series could often be reconstructed, providing insight into the preferred appearance of that time. The workshop of the necklace used heads, probably also hand-formed, with a particular chubby face, distinctive large earrings, and sometimes with both a polos and a veil, Mould I. These newly designed figurines were also larger than previous models. The same workshop applied symbolic references in large-sized pendants, representing bucrania, satyrs and acorns. This workshop also introduced the decorated polos. Looking at the details of the iconography, it is very possible that Mould I and Mould II were made by the same coroplast or workshop. This workshop could well have been the largest, as several series were produced here, and a variety of types could be supplied by one workshop. There might have been another, smaller and probably earlier workshop, in which a particular white clay was used. It seems a rather experimental one, as there is no clear connection between the iconography of these figurines. The details of reworking and cutting angles on the rear of the head could point to a general technique used in Akragas. The same applies for figurines with a specific convex-shaped back. Their presence on several similarly shaped figurines and a large number of objects from one mould series could well point to the large workshop mentioned above. The technical indications are in this case more difficult to interpret, as they could differ by object and, unlike iconographic features, are not a characteristic of a complete series.

The main reason such a large number of figurines could be produced is the availability of its primary material: clay. Within a relatively short distance of Akragas, a high quality clay is available on the surface: Macalube di Aragona clay. This fine clay is very suitable for moulds but has a high rate of shrinkage. Its red colour after firing was probably not appreciated that much. For these reasons, probably, it was combined with sand, silt, and a specific marlstone, which could all also be found within 15 km of Akragas. The more open structure of the clay facilitates the drying process and the outcome after firing is softer in tone, closer to natural skin colour. On the other hand, the grinding of the marl is labour intensive, and larger particles increase the risk of damage during the firing process. The majority of figurines from Akragas are probably made from a combination of these locally sourced materials. The nearly infinite availability of clay and marl made the production of figurines economically viable. Red figurines were also made, and there is a single exceptional group of white figurines. Only in the final phase, in the second quarter of the fifth century BCE, a layer of slip or white paint was more commonly applied.

Using a coroplastic experiment in which similar statuettes were made using the same techniques, believed to have been used in antiquity, provided new insights into the details of the production of the figurines. For example, the use of a filling to support the slab of clay on the back was examined, as the column shape suggests the application of an object. Using a figurine from the previous generation in order to produce a new mould results not only in a decrease in size but also a considerable loss of quality. The clay tends to warp and distort, particularly around the face, with a consequent reduction in detail. The experiment also revealed insights into the fragility of fired objects. The seam between the two halves needed to be strengthened. If this is done from the inside, an opening at the rear of larger objects is helpful. Also, the heavy head tends to bend if the object is left to dry standing. When dried lying down, the object is inevitably imprinted by the surface underneath. The experiment also provided insight into the tools used, such as a sharp knife. Fine motor skills, carefulness, and patience must have been qualities of the coroplast.

As well as an exchange of iconographic ideas between cities, it is possible that there was also an exchange of techniques and tools, such as moulds. Gela already had an extensive production of hand-made figurines in the first half of the sixth century, which were different from the block-like statuettes from Akragas. From the perspective of coroplastics, Akragas is not a derivative of Geloan production. Akragas' terracotta figurine production was fully independent, although iconographic influences seem to have been exchanged between cities along with moulds. The striking number of Rhodian, Argive, Cretan and other imported objects at Akragas does not prove foundation myths right, but may rather explain the spread of large numbers of migrants over the island from an early date, which resulted eventually in the most successful groups of migrants growing into larger political entities. These groups subsequently required cultic objects, which were produced locally.

The large workshops at Selinous produced even more figurines than have been found in Akragas. The archaeological remains of workshops have not yet been identified at Akragas. The figurines from Selinous can be distinguished from those made in Akragas by some technical differences. An opening in the back is common on figurines from Selinous, even though it is technically superfluous. Whether Akragantine coroplasts were inspired by objects or the figurines were brought in from Selinous is not entirely clear. The exchange, however, was mutual. Another aspect which was inspired by Selinun-tine coroplastics that could be considered both iconographic and technical is the rim along the outline of the figurine. This strengthens the upper part of the body, the neck in particular, and, at the same time, forms a frame.

V.4 Concerning meaning and use

Iconographic research and the archaeological experiment together give us insight into the production process and development, into the decisions made by the coroplasts based on a number of variables, which are divided into iconographic and technical aspects, while indirectly several other considerations of cultic, social and economic nature are in play. The unique appearance of the Akragantine figurines is a direct result of these aspects and its development could be used to trace them retrospectively. Indications of economic well-being are plenty: adornments, large and multiple, represent costly jewellery; fleshy faces are an indication of the food surplus and agricultural prosperity. The choice of terracotta is much more than a cheap alternative. The flexibility of the material, in shape, colour, and serial production, extends the possibilities of the coroplasts. It is probably that different variations of figurines were available at different costs. Alternatives or even personalisation, such as the addition of lion paws, would perhaps have been possible on request. The seated or standing variants could be seen in this light. Within certain boundaries, both cultic and technical, there were options. The availability of decorated and cushioned furniture in itself is another indication of luxury.

The moulding technique and therefore the iconography follow a linear development, in which a mould, shaped after an object forms another copy, though smaller. This would seem to limit the coroplasts and hinder innovative designs. However, the variation of figurines reveals a different picture. The Akragantine coroplasts were creative and versatile, not only in combining moulds but also by adding hand-shaped parts or even forming completely new patrices with original design variations. The artistic and technical skills of the craftsmen makes the absence of aesthetic appreciation of their work in Greek literary sources unfair. Given the scale and the quality of the production of coroplastics at Akragas and its neighbours, the situation is not comparable to the Athenian case, where terracotta figurines as dedications might have been no more than a cheaper alternative for statuettes made of more valuable materials. The popular appreciation of the figurines at Akragas itself must have been high, given the number of figurines, their size, and, above all, their fineness and level of detail. The Akragantine production is much less linear, served by several skilled coroplasts and different genealogies. Their creativity resulted in contemporary objects of varied designs. The precise dating is relative, based on the chaîne d'opératoire. The sometimes abrupt changes in iconography or technique provide us with additional and valuable information on preferences of that moment.

The value of the figurine is thus extrinsic: neither the material nor the manner of production were probably highly valued in themselves. The details, however, which could express local and personal expressions would have been appreciated by the customers of the coroplasts. The value of the figurines is determined mainly by their application as a votive. Such appreciation speaks from the handlings of objects after the dedication: when their numbers became too high, they were stacked and ritually buried in the sanctuary. The figurine's lower intrinsic or 'production' value made it, however, an affordable dedication, that would be similar to that of others and therefore had possibly a social function as an acceptable votive gift. Larger, more detailed (such as the Mould I and II series), or even personalised figurines, might have been more expensive than the average. The artistic approach led to complete new figurines, for which a patrix needed to have been made first by hand. The combination of low intrinsic and high extrinsic value led to the massive use of these figurines.

The Akragantine figurines were produced to be dedicated, in most cases at sanctuaries or as a grave gift. It is likely that they were carried by the dedicant, after being acquired, individually or in a group. The size of the average figurine is therefore between about 5-35cm, which is not too large nor too heavy to be carried for a certain distance. This distance would be from the shop, which was probably located – as at Selinous – at the workshop, to the place of dedication. In the case of Akragas, one of the possible workshops is very near to the City Sanctuary, where a majority of the objects was unearthed.

The dedication would have commemorated a votive act of giving in a miniature scene, replacing the dedication of adornment with a more affordable figurine. This representation shifts halfway through the fifth century BCE from the receiver, the goddess, to the dedicant. The dedicant carries her dedication, in the case of Akragas usually a piglet to be sacrificed, while the deity wears it after having received the dedication. In addition, the standing or seated pose came to mark the difference between dedicant and deity. A dedication of dress is also reminiscent of the peplos dedication to Athena at the yearly Panathenaia in Athens.

The establishment of certain rituals, of which the votive figurines are the material record, could be ascribed to the integration of newcomers in society, as well as the adaption of the original inhabitants of the region. A middle ground was created on which a new local identity was set out with the help of a locally developed iconography, applied on votive figurines. The cultic context and the iconographic borrowings allowed multiple cultures to form a socially cohesive town. The figurines bear literally the traces of this standardisation of a cultic image. Taking part in rituals together and dedicating similarly shaped objects unified a large group. The local identity was established with the help of specific Akragantine outfits for the goddess. This social construct of an Akragantine common identity overruled other differences. The common basis was formed by adapting and transforming an existing female deity and a communal act, celebrating the local identity. The later narratives of Greek literature confirm such constructions with foundation myths and a goddess, Demeter, who represents the agricultural prosperity of the island as a whole.

The female figurines seem to have been initially a generic goddess. Additional attributes, painting or simply its context could have altered the interpretation of her identity. Locally and only in the fifth century, the goddess would have been identified as Athena. A headgear with *lophos* indicates the helmet of Athena. This model, mostly applied in Gela, representing her in her role as Athena Polias, was chosen for political reasons. Such identifications with specific Greek goddesses seem to appear only towards the mid-fifth century, and have been only clear for Athena. While Greek iconographic influences are clear at a much earlier stage, such an identification takes place only after the standardisation of the votive statuette in a context in which popular cult and polis-cult are merged. Neither the Akragantine nor the Geloan figurines appear to have anything to do with Athena Lindia, other than that a similar process took place in a Rhodian context.

The figurines must have been artistically and aesthetically appealing from an early stage. Uniformly shaped from a distance and recognisable by certain features, the process of emulation allowed details to be altered, which would have pleased plural identities in the multicultural society of Akragas.

Bibliography

Ackermann, HC and Gisler, J-R (eds) 1981-2009, *Lexicon iconographicum mythologiae classicae (LIMC)*, Artemis, Zürich.

Adamesteanu, D and Orlandini, P 1956, 'Gela – ritrovamenti vari,' *Notizie degli scavi di antichità*, vol 10, Accademia Nazionale dei Lincei, Rome, pp.203-401.

Adornato, G 2012a, 'Phalaris: Literary Myth or Historical Reality? Reassessing Archaic Akragas,' *American Journal of Archaeology*, vol. 116, no. 3, pp.483-506.

Adornato, G 2012b, 'Supplemental images,' for Adornato, G, 'Phalaris: Literary Myth or Historical Reality? Reassessing Archaic Akragas, *American Journal of Archaeology*, vol 116.3, published online at www.ajaonline.org/imagegallery/1154, DOI: 10.3764/ajaonline1163.Adornato.suppl.

Agostiniani, L, de Cesare, M, Landenius Enegren, H 2014, 'Garments for a goddess? Apropos of an inscribed loom weight from Segesta,' *Rivista di Archeologia*, vol. 38, L'Erma di Bretschneider, Rome, pp.57-67.

Akimova, L 2013, 75. *БОГИНЯ В ПЕКТОРАЛИ НА ТРОНЕ*, published online at www.antic-art.ru/data/italy_sicily/75_gpddess_on_throne/index.php.

Albertocchi, M 1999, 'Note di coroplastica punica: le figure femminili con collane di semi', *Koinà, Miscellanea di studi archeologici in onore di P. Orlandini, a cura di M. Castoldi*, Milan, pp.355-368.

Albertocchi, M 2000, 'Le terrecotte di "Athena Lindia": il problema dell'influsso ionico nella creazione di un tipo coroplastico,' in F Krinzinger, *Die Ägäis und das westliche Mittelmeer*, pp.349-356.

Albertocchi, M 2004, *Athana Lindia, Le statuette siceliote con pettorali di età arcaica e classica*, L'Erma di Bretschneider, Rome.

Albertocchi, M 2009, 'Daedalica Selinuntia II. Osservazioni sulla coroplastica selinuntina d'età tardo-orientalizzante,' in C Antonetti and S Vido (eds), *Temi Selinuntini*, Edizioni ETS, Pisa, pp.9-27.

Allegro, N 1972, 'Tipi della coroplastica imerese,' *Quaderno Imerese*, vol 1, University of Palermo, Rome, pp.7-51.

Ammerman, RM 1991, 'The Naked Standing Goddess: A Group of Archaic Terracotta Figurines from Paestum,' *American Journal of Archaeology*, vol.95, pp.203-230.

Ammerman, RM 1993, *The Sanctuary of Santa Venera at Paestum II: The Votive Terracottas*, University of Michigan Press, Ann Arbor.

Ammerman, RM 2007, 'Children at Risk: Votive Terracottas and the Welfare of Infants at Paestum,' *Hesperia Supplements 41, Constructions of Childhood in Ancient Greece and Italy*, pp.131-151.

Antonaccio, C 2003, 'Hybridity and the cultures within Greek culture,' in C Dougherty and L Kurke (eds), *The Cultures within Ancient Greek Culture: Contact, Conflict, Collaboration*, Cambridge University Press, Cambridge, pp.57-74.

Antonaccio, C 2007, 'Colonization Greece on the Move, 900-480,' in H Shapiro (ed), *The Cambridge Companion to Archaic Greece*, Cambridge University Press, Cambridge, pp.201-224.

Anzalone, RM 2015, 'Kretikon keimelion. Nota su una testa fittile da Arigento,' *Archeologia Classica*, vol. 66, L'Erma di Bretschneider, Rome, pp.417-427.

Arias, PE 1940, 'La fonte sacra di Locri dedicata a Pan ed alle Ninfe,' *Le Arti*, vol 3, la Libreria dello Stato, Rome, pp.177-180.

Attema, P, Burgers, GLM, van Leusen, M 2010, *Regional pathways to complexity: settlement and land-use dynamics in early Italy from the Bronze Age to the Republican period*, Amsterdam University Press, Amsterdam.

Aubet, ME 1993, *The Phoenicians and the West: Politics, Colonies and Trade*, trans. M Turton, Cambridge University Press, Cambridge.

Baitinger, H 2017, 'The Metal Votive Objects from the Sanctuary of S. Anna in their Sicilian Context,' in N Sojc (ed), *Akragas. Current Issues in the Archaeology of a Sicilian Polis*, Leiden University Press, Leiden, pp.109-127.

Bakhuizen, SC 1988, 'Italy and Sicily in the Perception of the Early Greeks,' *Mededelingen van het Nederlands Instituut te Rome*, vol.48, pp.9-23.

Bald Romano, I 1995, *Gordion Special Studies II: The Terracotta Figurines and Related Vessels*, University of Pennsylvania Press, Philadelphia.

Barfoed, S 2013, 'The Mystery of the Seated Goddess, Vessels and Variety. New Aspects of Ancient Pottery,' *Acta Hyperborea*, vol 13, Museum Tusculanum, Copenhagen, pp.85-105.

Barfoed, S 2017, 'The Cults of Kalydon. Reassessing the Miniaturised Votive Objects,' *Proceedings of the Danish Institute at Athens*, vol 8, Aarhus University Press, Aarhus, pp.131-148.

Bell, M 1981, *Morgantina Studies I: The Terracottas*, Princeton University Press, Princeton.

Bellia, A 2014, 'Uno sguardo sulla musica nei culti e nei riti della Magna Grecia e della Sicilia,' in A Bellia (ed), *Musica, culti e riti nell'Occidente greco*, Istituti Editoriali e Poligrafici Internazionali, Pisa-Rome, pp.13-46.

Bellia, A 2012, 'Iconografia e culti: statuette di suonatrici di tympanon,' in M Albertocchi, A Pautasso, and U Spigo (eds), *Philotechnia*, Istituto per i Beni archeologici e Monumentali (CNR-IBAM), Catania, pp.253-263.

Bencze, A 2008, 'Une tête de terre-cuite tarentine du musée barracco au point de rencontre de traditions multiples,' *Numismatica e Antichità Classiche, Quaderni Ticinesi*, vol 37, Lugano, pp.15-37.

Bencze, A 2010, 'Symposia Tarentina The Artistic Sources of the First Tarentine Banqueter Terracottas,' *Babesch*, vol 85, Peeters, Leuven, pp.25-41.

Bennett, MJ and Paul, AJ (eds) 2002, *Magna Graecia: Greek Art from South Italy and Sicily*, Cleveland Museum of Art, Cleveland.

Bentz et. al. 2014= Bentz, M, Adorno, L, Albers, J, Garaffa, V, Miß, A, and Müller, JM 2014, 'Das Handwerkerviertel von Selinunt – Die Werkstatt der Insula S16/17-E Vorbericht zu den Kampagnen 2013-2014,' *Kölner und Bonner Archaeologica: Zeitschrift der Archäologischen Institute der Universitäten zu Köln und Bonn*, vol 4, LIT, Berlin, pp.67-74.

Bentz, M 2015, 'Töpferhandwerk in der griechischen Stadt Selinunt,' *Akademie Aktuell*, vol 02, Bayerische Akademie der Wissenschaften, Munich, pp.62-66.

Bentz et. al. 2016= Adorno, L, Albers, J, Bentz, M, Broisch, M, Dally, O, Franceschini, M, Miß, A, Müller, JM, Schlehofer, J, and von Hesberg, H 2016, 'Selinunt, Italien, die Arbeiten der Jahre 2014 und 2015,' *e-Forschungsberichte des DAI 2016 Faszikel 1*,deutsches Archäologisches Institut, Berlin, pp.67-84.

Bertesago, SM 2009, 'Figurine fittili da Bitalemi (Gela) e dalla Malophoros (Selinunte): appunti per uno studio comparato di alcune classi della coroplastica votiva,' in C Antonetti & S De Vido (eds), Temi Selinuntini, Edizioni ETS, Pisa, pp.53-7.

Bintliff, JL 2006, 'Multi-ethnicity and population movement in Ancient Greece: Alternatives to a world of 'Red-Figure' people,' in E Olshausen and H Sonnabend (eds), *"Troianer sind wir gewesen" – Migrationen in der antiken Welt*, Franz Steiner Verlag, Stuttgart, pp.108-114.

Bintliff, JL 2007, 'Emergent complexity in settlement systems and urban transformations,' in U Fellmeth, P Guyot and H Sonnabend, (eds), *Historische Geographie der alten Welt. Grundlagen, Erträge, Perspektiven. Festgabe für Eckart Olshausen*, Georg Olms, Hildesheim, pp.43-82.

Bintliff, JL 2010, 'Classical Greek Urbanism: A Social Darwinian View,' in R Rosen and I Sluiter, (eds), *Valuing Others in Classical Antiquity*, Brill, Leiden, pp.15-41.

Blinkenberg, Chr 1912, 'La Chronique du temple Lindien', *Bulletin de de l'Académie royale des sciences et des lettres de Danemark*, pp.317-467.

Blinkenberg, Chr 1917, *L'image d'Athena Lindia*, AF Høst, Copenhagen.

Blondé, F and Muller, A 2000, *L'artisanat en Grèce ancienne, les productions, les diffussions. Actes du colloque de Lyon 1998*, L'université Charles de Gaulle, Lille.

Boardman, J and Hammond, NGL (eds) 1982, *The Cambridge Ancient History Vol 3, part 3: The Expansion of the Greek World, Eighth to Sixth Centuries BC*, Cambridge University Press, Cambridge.

Boardman, J 2002, *The Archaeology of Nostalgia. How the Greeks recreated their Mythical Past*, Thames & Hudson, London.

Boehringer, E 1929, *Die Münzen von Syrakus*, de Gruyter, Berlin.

Böhm, S 2007, *Dädalische Kunst Siziliens*, Ergon Verlag, Würzburg.

Bolmarcich, S 2010, 'Communal Values in Ancient Diplomacy,' in R Rosen and I Sluiter, (eds), *Valuing Others in Classical Antiquity*, Brill, Leiden, pp.113-136.

Brandherm, D 2006, 'Zur Datierung der ältesten griechischen und phönizischen Importkeramik auf der Iberischen Halbinsel. Bemerkungen zum Beginn der Eisenzeit in Südwesteuropa,' *Madrider Mitteilungen*, vol. 47, Reichert, Wiesbaden, pp.1-23.

Breitenstein, N 1945, 'Analecta Acragantina,' *Acta Archaeologica*, vol 16, Copenhagen, pp.133-53.

Brijder, H (ed) 2014, *Nemrud Dağı: Recent Archaeological Research and Preservation and Restoration Activities in the Tomb Sanctuary on Mount Nemrud*, De Gruyter, Berlin.

Burn, L 2012, 'Terracottas,' in Smith, TJ and Plantzos, D (eds), *A Companion to Greek Art I*, Blackwell, Oxford, pp.221-234.

Byvanck-Quarles van Ufford, L 1940, *Les terres-cuites siciliennes: une étude sur l'art sicilien entre 550 et 450*, Van Gorcum, Assen.

Canciani, F 1984, *Bildkunst*. Archaeologia Homerica N, Teil 2, Göttingen.

Caputo, G 1938, 'Tre xoana e il culto di una sorgente sulfurea in territorio Geloo-Agrigentino,' *Accademia Nazionale dei Lincei: Monumenti antichi*, vol 37, pp.585-684.

Caubet, A 2009, 'Les figurines antiques de terre cuite,' *Perspective* 1, placed online 8 June 2013, consulted 7 August 2014, URL: http://perspectiverevuesorg/1690; DOI: 104000/perspective1690.

Cerchiai, L, Jannelli, L and Longo, F 2004, *The Greek Cities of Magna Graecia and Sicily*, Getty Publications, Los Angeles.

Christiansen, J, Fischer-Hansen, T & Johansen, F 1974, *Antik kunst i dansk privateje: et udvalg af oldtidskunst fra Middelhavsområdet og de tilgrænsende Lande; udstilling i Ny Carlsberg Glyptotek, 16 maj-31 august 1974*, Ny Carlsberg Glyptotek, Copenhagen.

Clack, T 2011, 'Syncretism and religious fusion,' in T Insoll (ed), *The Oxford Handbook of the Archaeology of Ritual and* Religion, Oxford University Press, Oxford.

Costamagna, L and Sabbione, C 1990, *Una città in Magna Grecia. Locri Epizefiri*, Laruffa Editore, Calabria.

Culican, W 1973, 'Phoenician Jewelry in New York and Copenhagen,' *Berytus*, vol 37, pp.31-52.

Cuomo di Caprio, N 2014, *Morgantina Studies, Volume III: Fornaci e Officine da Vasaio Tardo- ellenistiche*, Princeton University Press, Princeton.

D'Andrea, B 2014, 'Nuove stele dal tofet di Mozia,' *Vicino Oriente*, vol XVIII, Sapienza University, Rome, pp.123-144.

De Angelis, F 2003a, 'Equations of Culture: the meeting of Natives and Greeks in Sicily (ca. 750-450 BC),' in Tsetskhladze G R (ed), *Ancient West and East*, vol. 2.1, Brill, Leiden, pp.19-50.

De Angelis, F 2003b, *Megara Hyblaia and Selinous. The Development of Two Greek City-States in Archaic Sicily*, Oxbow, Oxford.

De Angelis, F 2016, *Archaic and Classical Greek Sicily: A Social and Economic History*, Oxford University Press, Oxford.

De Miro, E 1962, 'La fondazione di Agrigento e l'ellenizzazione del territorio fra il Salso e il Platani,' *Kokalos*, vol 8, Fabrizio Serra, Rome, pp.122-152.

De Miro, E and Fiorentini G 1976-7, Relazione sull' attivita della Soprintendenza alle antichita di Agrigento *Kokalos*, vols 22-23, Fabrizio Serra, Rome, pp.423-52.

De Miro, E 1980-1, 'Agrigento Necropoli greca di Contrada Mosè,' *Kokalos*, vol 26-27, Fabrizio Serra, Rome, pp.566-571.

De Miro, E 1988, 'Akragas, città e necropoli nei recenti scavi,' in L Franchi dell' Orto, *Veder Greco: Le necropoli di Agrigento*, L'Erma di Bretschneider, Rome, pp.235-52.

De Miro, E 2000, *Agrigento I santuari urbani: l'area sacra tra il tempio di Zeus e porta V*, L'Erma di Bretschneider, Rome.

De Orsola, D 1991, 'Il quartiere di Porta II ad Agrigento,' in *Quaderni di archeologia*, vol. 6, Università di Messina, Messina, pp.71-105.

De Waele, JA 1971, *Acragas Graeca. Die historische Topographie des griechischen Akragas zu Sizilien I. Historischer Teil*, Staatsdrukkerij, The Hague.

Demargne, P 1984, 'Athena', *LIMC* II, 1984, pp. 955-1044.

Deppert-Lippitz, B 1985, *Griechischer Goldschmuck*, Philip von Zabern, Mainz am Rhein.

Dewailly, M 1992, *Les statuettes aux parures du sanctuaire de la Malophoros à Sélinonte*, Cahiers du Centre Jean Bérard XVII, Naples.

Dewailly, M 2010, 'La polyvalence sacree, sociale et ethnique du port de parures: quelques exemples,' in *La Dama De Baza Un Viaje Femenino Al Mas Alla Actas Del Encuentro Internacional Museo Arqueologico Nacional 27 Y 28 Noviembre 2007*, Ministerio de Educación, Madrid, pp.211-222.

Die Etrusker: Weltkultur im antiken Italien 2017, Theiss in Wissenschaftliche Buchgesellschaft, Darmstadt.

Diodorus Siculus, *Library of History*, vol V, books 12.41-13, trans CH Oldfather, 1950, Loeb, Cambridge, Massachusetts.

Doak, B 2015, 'Phoenician Aniconism in its Mediterranean and Ancient Near Eastern Contexts,' *Archaeology & Biblical Studies*, vol 21, SBL Press, Atlanta.

Donahue AA 1988, Xoana and the Origin of Greek Sculpture, Scholars Press, Atlanta.

Domínquez, AJ 2006, 'Greeks in Sicily,' in GR Tsetskhladze (ed), *Greek Colonisation. An Account of Greek Colonies and other Settlements Overseas Vol I*, Brill, Leiden, pp.253-357.

Dougherty, C 1993, *The Poetics of Colonization. From City to Text in Archaic Greece*, Oxford University Press, Oxford.

Dougherty, C and Kurke, L (eds) 2003, *The Cultures within Ancient Greek Culture: Contact, Conflict, Collaboration*, Cambridge University Press, Cambridge.

Dover KJ 1965 (ed), Thucydides, *History*, Book VI, Clarendon Press, Oxford.

Dunbabin, TJ 1948/1968, *The Western Greeks: the history of Sicily and South Italy from the foundation of the Greek colonies to 480 BC*, Clarendon Press, Oxford.

Eaverly, MA 2013,*Tan Men/Pale Women. Color and Gender in Archaic Greece and Egypt. A Comparative Approach*, University of Michigan, Ann Arbor.

Ferguson, JR 2010, *Designing Experimental Research in Archaeology: Examining Technology through Production and Use*, University of Colorado, Colorado.

Ferri, S 1929, *Divinità ignote; nuovi documenti di arte e di culto funerario nelle colonie greche*, Valecchi, Florence.

Fiertler, G 2001, 'La produzione agrigentina di "statuette con pettorali",' *Quaderni dell'Istituto di Archeologia della Facoltà di Lettere e Filosofia dell'Università di Messina*, vol 2, Messina, pp.53-76.

Fiorentini, G 1969, 'Il santuario extraurbano di S Anna presso Agrigento,' *Cronache di Archeologia e di storia dell' arte* 8, Catania University, Catania, pp.63-80.

Fiorentini, G, Calì, V, and Trombi, C 2010, *Agrigento. Le fortificazioni: catalogo dei materiali* , Gangemi Editore, Rome.

Forsdyke, S 2002, 'Herodotus on Greek History, 525-480,' in E Bakker, I de Jong and H van Wees, (eds), *Brill's Companion to Herodotus,* Brill, Leiden, pp.521-549.

Frisone, F 2012, 'Rivers, land organization, and identity in Greek Western Apoikíai,' *Mediterranean Historical Review*, vol. 27:1, Taylor & Francis, Abingdon pp.87-115.

Gabrici, E 1927, 'Il santuario della Malophoros a Selinunte,' *Monumenti Antichi dei Lincei*, vol 32, Rome, pp.1-419.

Gandon, E and Roux, V 2019, 'Cost of motor skill adaptation to new craft trait. Experiments with expert potters facing unfamiliar vessel shapes and wheels,' *Journal of Anthropological Archaeology 53*, Elsevier, Amsterdam, pp.29-239.

Gehrke, HJ 1986, *Jenseits von Athen und Sparta, Das dritte Griechenland und seine Staatenwelt*, Beck, München.

Gehrke, HJ 2005, 'Identität in der Alterität: Heroen als Grenzgänger zwischen Hellenen und Barbaren,' in E S Gruen (ed), *Cultural Borrowings and Ethnic Appropriations in Antiquity Oriens et Occidens 8*, Steiner, Stuttgart, pp.50-67.

Gleba, M 2008, 'Textile tools in ancient Italian votive contexts: Evidence of dedication or production?,' in Places and Rituals in Etruscan Religion: Studies in Honour of Jean MacIntosh Turfa. Brill, Leiden, pp.69-84.

Gombrich, EH 1979, *The Sense of Order. A Study in the Psychology of Decorative Art*, Phaidon, Oxford.

Graham, AJ 2001, 'Religion, women and Greek colonization,' in AJ Graham (ed), *Collected papers on Greek colonization,* Brill, Leiden, pp.293-314.

Gras, M, Treziny, H and Broise, H 2005, *Mégara Hyblaea. 5, La ville archaïque: l'espace urbain d'une cité grecque de Sicile orientale*, l'École française de Rome, Rome.

Greenwood, E 2006, *Thucydides and the Shaping of History*, Duckworth, London.

Greco, E (ed) 2002, Gli Achei e l'identita' etnica degli Achei d'Occidente, Atti del Convegno Internazionale, Pandemos, Paestum

Grethlein, J 2006, 'The Manifold Uses of the Epic Past: The Embassy Scene in Herodotus 7.153-63,' *American Journal of Philology*, vol.127.4, John Hopkins University, Baltimore, pp.485-509.

Griffo, P 1958, *Sulle orme della civiltà gelese : scavi e scoperte nell'antica Gela e nei territori della sua espansione*, Agrigento.

Grotta, C 2010, *Zeus Meilichios a Selinunte*, L'Erma di Bretschneider, Rome.

Hadzisteliou Price, T 1978, *Kourotrophos: Cults and Representations of the Greek Nursing Deities*, Brill, Leiden.

Hall, J 2003, 'How 'Greek' were the Early Western Greeks?' in K Lomas (ed), *Greek Identity in the Western Mediterranean*, Brill, Leiden, pp.35-54.

Hall, JM 2008, 'Foundation stories,' in GR Tsetskhladze and AJ Graham, (eds), *Greek Colonisation: an Account of Greek Colonies and other Settlements Overseas,* vol 2, Brill, Leiden, pp.383-426.

Hamdorf, FW 1996, *Hauch des Prometheus. Meisterwerke in Ton*, Staatliche Antikensammlungen und Glyptothek, Munich.

Harden, DB 1963, *The Phoenicians*, Thames & Hudson, London.

Hariri, M 2017, 'A Short History of Pygmies in Greece and Italy,' in K Lomas, *Greek Identity in the Western Mediterranean, Papers in Honour of Brian Shefton, Mnemosyne Supplements* 246, Brill, Leiden, pp.163-190.

Hawkes, C 1954 'Archaeological Theory and Method: Some Suggestions from the Old World,' *American Anthropologist*, vol. 56, no. 2, pp. 155-168.

Haynes, S 2000, *Etruscan Civilization: A Cultural History*, British Museum Press, London.

Higbie, C 2003 *The Lindian chronicle and the Greek creation of their past*, Oxford University Press, Oxford.

Higgins, R 1961, *Greek and Roman Jewellery,* Methuen, London.

Higgins, RA 1954, *Catalogue of the terracottas in the Department of Greek and Roman Antiquities*, British Museum, London.

Hinz, V 1998, *Der Kult von Demeter und Kore auf Sizilien und in der Magna Graecia*, Dr Ludwig Reichert Verlag, Wiesbaden.

Hodos, T 2006, *Local Responses to Colonization in the Iron Age Mediterranean*, Routledge, London.

Hodos, T 2009, 'Colonial Engagements in the Global Mediterranean Iron Age,' *Cambridge Archaeological Journal*, vol.19, Cambridge University Press, Cambridge, pp.221-241.

Hodos, T 2010, 'Globalisation and colonisation: a view from Iron Age Sicily'. *Journal of Mediterranean Archaeology*, vol 23, pp. 81-106

Hornblower, S 1996, *A Commentary on Thucydides: Books IV-V.24*, Oxford University Press, Oxford.

Hornblower, S 2002, 'Herodotus and his Sources of Information,' in E Bakker, I de Jong and H van Wees (eds), *Brill's Companion to Herodotus*,Brill, Leiden, pp.373-386.

Hornblower, S 2008, *A Commentary on Thucydides: Books V.25-VIII.109*, Oxford University Press, Oxford.

Huysecom-Haxhi, S 2016, 'Création et transformation des images dans la coroplathie ionienne archaïque,' in *BCH Supplement*, vol 54., Peeters, Leuven, pp. 65-78.

Hurschmann, R, 'Polos,' in H Cancik and H Schneider (eds), *Brill's New Pauly*, vol 4, consulted online on 17 October 2016 http://dx.doi.org/10.1163/1574-9347_bnp_e1000840.

Insoll, J 2017, The Oxford handbook of prehistoric figurines, Oxford University Press, Oxford.

Jastrow, E 1938, 'Abformung und Typenwandel in der antiken Tonplastik,' *Opusula Archaeologica*, vol 2 fas 1, CWK Gleerup, Lund.

Jeffra, CD 2014, 'Experimental approaches to archaeological ceramics: unifying disparate methodologies with the chaîne opératoire,' *Journal of Archaeological and Anthropological Sciences*, vol 7, pp.141-9.

Jenkins, I and Sloan, K 1996, *Vases & Volcanoes: Sir William Hamilton and his Collection*, British Museum Press, London.

Jung, H 1982, *Thronende und sitzende Götter: zum griechischen Götterbild und Menschenideal in geometrischer und früharchaischer Zeit*, Habelt, Bonn.

Kallet, L 2001, *Money and the Corrosion of Power in Thucydides: the Sicilian Expedition and its Aftermath*, University of California Press, Berkeley.

Karoglou, K 2016, 'The Collection of Greek Terracotta Figurines at The Metropolitan Museum of Art,' *Les Carnets de l'AcoSt*, vol 14, Association for Coroplastic Studies, pp.1-4.

Kekulé von Stradonitz, R 1884, *Die antiken Terrakotten (Band II): Die Terracotten von Sicilien*, Spemann, Berlin.

Kekulé von Stradonitz, R and Winter, F (eds) 1903, *Die antiken Terrakotten,* Band III, Spemann, Berlin.

Kistler, E 2012, 'Glocal responses from Archaic Sicily,' in *Ancient West & East,* vol. 11, Brill, Leiden, pp.219-232.

Kistler, E 2014, 'Die Phönizier sind Händler, die Griechen aber Kolonisatoren – Zwei alte Klischees Ulfs Kulturkontaktmodell und das archaische Westsizilien,' in R Rollinger and K Schnegg, (eds), *Kulturkontakte in antiken Welten: von Denkmodell zum Fallbeispiel, Proceedings des internationalen Kolloquiums aus Anlass des 60. Geburtstages von Christoph Ulf, Innsbruck, 26. bis 30. Januar 2009 (Colloqiua Antiqua 10)*, Peeters, Leuven, pp.67-108.

Ladurner, M 2010, 'Terrakotten im Schutt Katalog und Auswertung der Terrakottafunde aus den österreichischen Grabungen in Elea-Velia 1973-2003,' published online.

Langlotz, E and Hirmer, M 1963, *Die Kunst der Westgriechen in Sizilien und Unteritalien*, Hirmer, Munich.

Lanza, MT 1975, 'Tre nuovi cippi dalla necropolis di Camarina,' *Sicilia Archeologica*, vol 8, Palermo, pp.39-46.

Lee, MM 2015, *Body, Dress, and Identity in Ancient Greece*, Cambridge University Press, Cambridge.

Leighton, R 1999, *Sicily before History. An Archaeological Survey from the Palaeolithic to the Iron Age.* Duckworth, London.

Leighton, R 2000, 'Indigenous society between the Ninth and Sixth centuries BC: Territorial, Urban and Social Evolution,' in C Smith and J Serrati (eds), *Sicily from Aeneas to Augustus: New Approaches in Archaeology and History*, Edinburgh University Press, Edinburgh, pp.15-40.

Leschhorn, W 1984, *'Gründer der Stadt': Studien zu einem politisch-religiösen Phänomen der griechischen Geschichte*, Steiner, Stuttgart.

Levi, A 1926, *Le Terrecotte figurate del Museo Nazionale di Napoli*, Vallecchi, Florence.

Lippolis, E 1996, *Arte e artigianato in Magna Grecia,* Electa, Naples.

Lippolis, E 2009, 'Oreficeria e società nel mondo greco' in I Baldini Lippolis and MT Guaitoli (eds), *Oreficeria antica e medievale. Tecniche, produzione, società*, Ante Quem, Bologna.

Lomas, K (ed) 2004, *Greek Identity in the Western Mediterranean: Papers in Honour of Brian Shefton*, Brill, Leiden.

Lunsingh Scheurleer, TH 1986, *Grieken in het klein*, Allard Pierson Museum, Amsterdam.

MacLachlan, B 2009, 'Women and Nymphs at the Grotta Caruso,' in G Casadio and PA Johnston (eds), *Mystic Cults in Magna Grecia*, University of Texas, Austin.

Malkin, I 1987, *Religion and Colonization in Ancient Greece*, Brill, Leiden.

Malkin, I 2004, 'Postcolonial Concepts and Ancient Greek Colonization,' *Modern Language Quarterly*, vol 65.3, Duke University Press, Durham, pp.341-364.

Malkin, I 2011, *A Small Greek World: Networks in the Ancient Mediterranean*, Oxford University Press, Oxford.

Mango, E, and Edel, M 2015, 'Vierter Vorbericht zu den Forschungen in Himera,' *Antike Kunst*, vol. 59, Vereinigung der Freunde Antiker Kunst, Basel, pp.112-122.

Marconi, P 1929, *Agrigento: topografia ed arte*, Vallecchi, Florence.

Marconi, P 1933, *Agrigento arcaica: il santuario delle divinità Chtonie e il tempio detto di Vulcano*, Collezione meridionale, Ser. 3, Rome.

Marconi, C 2007, *Temple Decoration and Cultural Identity in the Archaic Greek World: the Metopes of Selinus*, Cambridge University Press, Cambridge.

Marconi Bovio, J 1930, Agrigento. Scoperta *di* matrici fittili *e di terrecotte figurate negli anni 1926-1927*, in *Notizie degli scavi di antichità*, Accademia nazionale dei Lincei, Rome, pp.73-105.

Marincola, J 2007, *A Companion to Greek and Roman Historiography*, Blackwell, Oxford.

Mattusch, C 1989, *Greek Bronze Statuary: From the Beginnings Through the Fifth Century BC*, Cornell University Press, Ithaca.

Mendel, G 1908, *Musées Impériaux Ottomans. Catalogue des figurines grecques de terre cuite*, Hachette, Paris.

Merker, GS 2000, *The Sanctuary of Demeter and Kore: Terracotta Figurines of the Classical, Hellenistic, and Roman periods*, The American School of Classical Studies at Athens, Princeton.

Meijden, H van der, 1993 *Terrakotta-arulae aus Sizilien und Unteritalien*, Hakkert, Amsterdam.

Mertens, D 2006, *Städte und Bauten der Westgriechen: von der Kolonisationszeit bis zur Krise um 400 vor Christus*, Hirmer, Munich.

Mertens-Horn, M 2005, 'I pinakes di Locri: Immagini di feste e culti misterici dionisiaci nel santuario di Persefone,' in Bottini A (ed), *Il rito segreto: misteri in Grecia e a Roma*, Electa, Milan, pp.49-57.

Meurer, M 1914, 'Die mammae de Artemisia Ephesia,' *Mitteilungen des Deutschen Archäologischen Instituts, Römische Abteilung*, vol 19, pp.200-219.

Mikalson, JD 2005, *Ancient Greek Religion*, Blackwell, Oxford.

Miller, M 1970, *The Sicilian Colony Dates (Studies in Chronography 1)*, State University of New York Press, Albany.

Miller Ammerman, R 2007, 'Children at Risk: Votive Terracottas and the Welfare of Infants at Paestum,' in A Cohen and JB Rutter (eds), *Constructions of Childhood in Ancient Greece and Italy, Hesperia Supplement* 41, American School of Classical Studies at Athens, Princeton, pp.131-151.

Miro, de E 1988, 'Akragas, città e necropoli nei recenti scavi,' in L Franchi dell' Orto, *Veder Greco: Le necropoli di Agrigento*, L'Erma di Bretschneider, Rome, pp.235-52.

Mollard-Besques, S 1963, *Les terres cuites grecques*, Presses Universitaires de France, Paris.

Mollard Besques, S 1954, *Catalogue raisonné des figurines et reliefs en terre-cuite grecs, étrusques et romains. I: Époque préhellénique, géométrique, archaique et classique*, Éditions des Musées Nationaux, Paris.

Morakis, A 2011, 'Thucydides and the Character of Greek Colonisation in Sicily,' *The Classical Quarterly*, vol. 61, Cambridge University Press, Cambridge, pp.460-492.

Morgan, KA 2015, 'Pindar and the Construction of Syracusan Monarchy in the Fifth Century BC,' Oxford Scholarship Online.

Müller, V 1915, *Der Polos, die griechische Götterkrone*, (diss.), Universitäts-Buchdruckerei von Gustav Schade, Berlin.

Müller, A (ed) 1997, *Le moulage en terre cuite dans l'Antiquité. Création et Production dérivée, Fabrication et Diffusion*, Presses universitaires du Septentrion, Lille.

Muller, A 1997, 'Description et analyse des productions moulees: Proposition de lexique multilingue, suggestions de méthode,' in A Muller (ed), *Le moulage en terre cuite dans l'Antiquité Création et production dérivée, fabrication et diffusion*, Presses universitaires du Septentrion, Lille, pp.437-463.

Muller, A 2000, 'Artisans, techniques de production et diffusion le cas de la coroplathie,' in F Blondé and A Muller (eds), *L'artisanat en Grèce ancienne, les productions, les diffussions Actes du colloque de Lyon 1998*, L'université Charles de Gaulle, Lille, pp.91-106.

Muller, A 2010, 'The technique of Tanagra coroplasts. From local craft to "global industry" in Tanagras, figurines for life and eternity,' in V Jeammet (ed), *Tanagras: Figurines for Life and Eternity. The Musée du Louvre's collection of Greek figurines*, Paris, pp. 100-103.

Mussini, E 2002, 'La diffusione dell'iconografia di Acheloo in Magna Grecia e in Sicilia Tracce per l'individuazione di un culto,' *Studi Etruschi*, vol. 65-68, L'Erma di Bretschneider, Rome, pp.91-120.

Neutsch, B 1952, 'Studien zur vortanagräisch-attischen Koroplastik,' *Jahrbuch des Deutschen Archäologischen Instituts*, vol 17, de Gruyter, Berlin.

Nicholls, RV 1952, 'Type, group and series: a reconsideration of some coroplastic fundamentals,' *Annual of the British School at Athens*, vol 47, British School at Athens, London, pp.217-226.

Nieuwenhuyse, O 2006, *Plain and Painted Pottery. The Rise of Neolithic Ceramic Styles on the Syrian and Northern Mesopotamian Plains*, Brepols, Turnhout.

Nijboer, AJ 1998, *From household production to workshops: Archaeological evidence for economic transformations, pre-monetary exchange and urbanisation in central Italy from 800 to 400 BC*, PhD thesis, University of Groningen.

Nijboer, AJ 2006, 'The Iron Age in the Mediterranean: A Chronological Mess or "Trade before the Flag", Part II,' *Ancient West & East*, vol. 2, Brill, Leiden, pp.255-277.

Nunn, A 2000, *Der figürliche Motivschatz Phöniziens, Syriens und Transjordaniens vom 6 bis zum 4. Jahrhun-*

dert v. Chr., Vandenhoeck & Ruprecht Verlage, Göttingen.

Orlandini, P 1968, 'Gela Topografia dei culti e documentazione archeologica dei culti,' *Rivista del R Istituto d'Archeologia e Storia dell'Arte (RIA)*, vol. 15, L'Erma di Bretschneider, Rome, pp.20-66.

Orsi, P 1900, 'L'Heroon di Antifemo,' *Notizie degli scavi di antichità*, Accademia nazionale dei Lincei, Rome, pp.272-77.

Orsi, P 1909, 'Locri Epizefiri, Resoconto Sulla Terza Campagna Di Scavi Locresi,' in *Bollettino d'Arte*, vol 3, Ministero della Publica Istruzione, Rome, pp.406-35.

Orton, C and Hughes, M 2013, *Pottery in Archaeology*, Cambridge University Press, Cambridge.

Osborne, R and Cunliffe, B (eds) 2005, *Mediterranean Urbanization 800-600 BC*, Oxford University Press, Oxford.

Panvini, R 1998, *Gela, Il museo archeologico: Catalogo*, Soprintendenza per i beni culturali e ambientali di Caltanissetta, Caltanissetta.

Panvini, R and Sole, L 2005, *L'Acropoli di Gela. Stipi, depositi o scarichi*, L'Erma di Bretschneider, Rome.

Panvini, R and Sole, L (eds) 2009, *La Sicilia in età arcaica. Dalle apoikiai al 480 a.C.*, Assessorato dei Beni Culturali, Ambientali e della Pubblica Istruzione, Palermo.

Parisi, V 2017, *I depositi votivi negli spazi del rito : analisi dei contesti per un'archeologia della pratica cultuale nel mondo siceliota e magnogreco*, L'Erma di Bretschneider, Rome.

Paul, E 1959, *Antike Welt in Ton. Griechische und römische Terrakotten des archäologischen Institutes in Leipzig*, VEB Seemann, Leipzig.

Pautasso, A 2015, 'Spazi, contesti, funzioni. Osservazioni sulla coroplastica dal versante meridionale della Patela di Priniàs,' in A Pautasso and O Pilz (eds), ΠΗΛΙΝΑ ΕΙΔΩΛΙΑ. *New Perspectives in Cretan Coroplastic Studies, Creta Antica*, vol 16, pp.59-84.

Pautasso, A 1996, *Terrecotte arcaiche e classiche del Museo Civico del Castello Ursino a Catania, Studi e materiali archeologia greca* 6, Catania University, Catania.

Perna, K 2015, 'La coroplastica di Priniàs nel contesto culturale cretese della tarda età del bronzo,' in A Pautasso and O Pilz (eds), ΠΗΛΙΝΑ ΕΙΔΩΛΙΑ. *New Perspectives in Cretan Coroplastic Studies, Creta Antica*, vol 16, pp.29-44.

Perlès, C 2007, *The Early Neolithic in Greece. The First Farming Communities in Europe*, Cambridge University Press, Cambridge.

Picard, C 1984, 'Demeter et Kore à Carthage – Problèmes d'iconographie,' *Kokalos*, vols 28-9, Fabrizio Serra, Rome, pp.187-94.

De Polignac, F 1999, 'L'installation des dieux et la genèse des cités en Grèce d'Occident, une question résolue? (Retour à Mégara Hyblaea),' in *La colonisation grecque en Méditerranée occidentale. Actes de la rencontre scientifique en hommage à Georges Vallet*, Collection de l'Ecole française de Rome, Rome, pp. 209-229.

Poma, L 2009, 'Le terrecotte figurate arcaiche e classiche,' in ML Famà (ed), Il Museo Regionale 'A. Pepoli' di Trapani, Le collezioni archeologiche, Bari, pp.223- 248.

Prückner, H 1968, *Die Lokrischen Tonreliefs*, Philipp von Zabern, Mainz.

Pülz, AM and Bühler, B 2009, *Goldfunde aus dem Artemision von Ephesos*, Verlag der Österreichischen Akademie der Wissenschaften, Vienna.

Raffiotta, S 2007a, *Terrecotte figurate dal santuario di San Francesco Bisconti a Morgantina*, Editopera, Assoro.

Raffiotta, S 2007b, 'Il santuario di Demetra in contrada San Francesco Bisconti a Morgantina. Terrecotte figurate di età arcaica,' in R Panvini and L Sole (eds), *La Sicilia in età arcaica. Dalle apoikiai al 480 a.C.*, Assessorato dei Beni Culturali, Ambientali e della Pubblica Istruzione, Palermo, pp.417-24.

Rapp, GR 2002, *Archeomineralogy*, Springer, Berlin.

Rheeder, A 2019, *Architectural terracottas from Akragas: investigating monumental roofs from the Archaic and Classical period*, Leiden University PhD thesis, Leiden.

Richter, GMA 1966, *The Furniture of the Greeks, Etruscans and Romans*, Phaidon, London.

Richter, GMA and Frantz, A 1968, Korai: archaic Greek maidens: a study of the development of the Kore type in Greek sculpture, Phaidon, London.

Rives, JB 2007, *Religion in the Roman world*, Blackwell, Oxford.

Robb, JE 1998, 'The Archaeology of symbols,' *Annual Review of Anthropology*, vol 27, Palo Alto, California: Annual Reviews Inc. pp.329-346.

Ross Holloway, R 1969, 'Architect and Engineer in Archaic Greece,' *Harvard Studies in Classical Philology*, vol 73, Harvard University Press, Cambridge, Massachusetts, pp.281-290.

Russenberger, C 2015, 'Bildproduktion und gesellschaftliche Entwicklung der indigenen Kulturen West- und Zentralsiziliens in archaischer Zeit,' in E Kistler, B Öhlinger, M Mohr and M Hoernes (eds), *Sanctuaries and the Power of Consumption Networking and the Formation of Elites in the Archaic Western Mediterranean World*, Harrassowitz Verlag, Wiesbaden, pp.99-136.

Rutishauser, W 2017, *Etrusker: Antike Hochkultur im Schatten Roms*, Philipp von Zabern, Mainz.

Salapata, G 2015, 'Terracotta Votive Offerings in Sets or Groups,' in S Huysecom-Haxhi and A Muller (eds), *Figurines grecques en contexte: présence muette dans le sanctuaire, la tombe et la maison*, Presses universitaires du Septentrion, Lille, pp.179-197.

Sapouna-Sakellarakē, E, Kilian-Dirlmeier, I and Betzler, P 1978, *Die Fibeln der griechischen Inseln, Prähistorische Bronzefunde*, Abteilung 14, Fibeln, vol 4, Beck, Munich.

Schneider-Herrmann, G 1968, 'Silen mit Göttin und mit Nymphe,' *Antike Kunst*, vol 11, Vereinigung der Freunde Antiker Kunst, Basel, pp.110-13.

Schürmann, W 1989, *Katalog der antiken Terrakotten im Badischen Landesmuseum Karlsruhe*, Paul Aström, Göteborg.

Shapiro, HA 2002, 'Demeter and Persephone in Western Greece: Migrations of Myth and Cult,' in Bennet, M (ed), *Magna Graecia: Greek art from south Italy and Sicily*, Cleveland Museum of Art, Cleveland., 82-97

Shepherd, G 1995, 'The Pride of Most Colonials: Burial and Religion in the Sicilian Colonies,' *Acta Hyperborea*, vol. 6, Museum Tusculanum Press, Copenhagen, pp.51-82.

Shepherd, G 1999, 'Fibulae and Females: Intermarriage in the Western Greek Colonies and the Evidence from the Cemeteries,' in Tsetskhladze, GR (ed), *Ancient Greeks West and East*, Brill, Leiden, pp.267-300.

Shepherd, G 2000, 'Greeks bearing gifts: religious relationships between Sicily and Greece in the Archaic period,' in Smith, CJ and J Serrati, *Sicily from Aeneas to Augustus: new approaches in archaeology and history*, Edinburgh University Press, Edinburgh, pp.55-70.

Shepherd, G 2005, 'Dead men tell no tales: ethnic diversity in Sicilian colonies and the evidence of the cemeteries,' *Oxford Journal of Archaeology 24* (2), Blackwell, Oxford, pp.115-136.

Simpson, E 2011, *The Gordion Wooden Objects: The Furniture from Tumulus MM*, vol 1, Brill, Leiden.

Sinn, U 1977, *Antike Terrakotten, Staatlichen Kunstsammlungen Kassel*, Thiele & Schwarz, Kassel.

Snodgrass, A 1994, 'The Nature and Standing of the Early Western Colonies,' in GR Tsetskhladze and F de Angelis (eds), *The Archaeology of Greek Colonisation: Essays Dedicated to Sir John Boardman*, Oxbow, Oxford, pp.1-10.

Sojc, N 2010, 'The formation of visual culture in Akragas: Investigating the social significance of non-figurative symbols within a Polis in Ancient Sicily,' (unpublished project outline) Faculty of Archaeology, Leiden University.

Sojc, N 2016, 'Excavation at the Suburban Sanctuary at S. Anna in Agrigento. Preliminary Insights of the 2015 Campaign', in MC Parello and MS Rizzo (eds), *Paesaggi urbani tardoantichi. Casi a confronto, Atti delle Giornate Gregoriane VIII edizione* (29-30 novembre 2014), Bibliotheca Archaeologica 39, Edipuglia, Bari, pp.269-274.

Sojc, N (ed) 2017, *Akragas. Current Issues in the Archaeology of a Sicilian Polis*, Leiden University Press, Leiden.

Spanò Giammellaro, A 1995, 'Necropoli punica di Palermo. Aspetti inediti di cultura materiale dalla necropoli punica di Palermo,' *Cuadernos de Arqueología Mediterránea*, vol. 1, Universitat Pompeu Fabra, Barcelona, pp.33-56.

Stibbe, CM and Stibbe-Heldring, B 2006, *Agalmata: Studien Zur Griechisch-archaischen Bronzekunst, Babesch Supplement* 11, Peeters, Leuven.

Straten, van FT 1981, 'Gifts for the Gods,' in HS Versnel (ed), *Faith, Hope and Worship: Aspects of Religious Mentality in the Ancient World, Studies in Greek and Roman Religion*, Brill, Leiden, pp.65-151.

Surgeon, MC 2017, 'Hellenistic Sculpture at Corinth. The state of the question,' in O Palagia (ed), *Regional Schools in Hellenistic Sculpture*, pp.1-13.

Swett, K 1993, *A Study of the Syracusan Coins from the Ottilia Buerger Collection*, Lawrence University Honors Projects, no 68, https://lux.lawrence.edu/luhp/68

Taylor, R 2014, 'The Cult of Sirens and Greek Colonial Identity in Southern Italy 183-90,' in B Alroth and C Scheffer (eds), *Attitudes towards the Past in Antiquity: Creating Identities*, Stockholm University, Stockholm, pp.183-190.

Thucydides, *History of the Peloponnesian War*, vol III, books 5-6, trans CF Smith, 1921, Loeb, Cambridge, Massachusetts. Tribulato, O 2012, *Language and Linguistic Contact in Ancient Sicily*, Cambridge University Press, Cambridge.

Trombi, C 2003, 'Il materiale indigeno presente nelle colonie greche di Sicilia. La Sicilia occidentale. Parte I', in *Quaderni dell'Università di Messina*, vol 3, pp.91-118.

Trombi, C 2016, 'Il material votivo e di uso rituale nel Sanctuario di S. Anna (Agrigento): note sugli aspetti cultuali e socio-politici,' in N Sojc (ed), *Akragas, Current issues in the Archaeology of a Sicilian Polis*, Leiden University Press, Leiden, pp.95-108.

Uhlenbrock, JP 1988, *The Terracotta Protomai from Gela: A Discussion of Local Style in Archaic Sicily, Studia Archeologica 50*, L'Erma di Bretschneider, Rome.

Uhlenbrock, JP 1992, 'History, Trade, and the Terracottas,' in D White (ed), Gifts to the Goddesses: Cyrene's Sanctuary of Demeter and Persephone, Expedition *34 (1-2)*, University of Pennsylvania Press, Philadelphia, pp.16-23.

Uhlenbrock, JP 2010, 'Terracotta Types of Enthroned Females from the Extramural Sanctuary of Demeter and Persephone at Cyrene,' in M Luni, (ed), *Cirene e la Cirenaica nell'Antichita'*, L'Erma di Bretschneider, Rome, pp.85-100.

Urquhart, LM 2010, *Colonial Religion and Indigenous Society in the Archaic Western Mediterranean: Religious Integration in Sicily and Sardinia between 750 and 400 BCE*, Stanford University dissertation, Stanford.

Van Rooijen, GK, Jacobs, L, Braekmans, D and Sojc, N 2017, 'Figuring out: coroplastic art and technè in Agrigento, Sicily: the results of a coroplastic exper-

iment,' *Analecta Praehistorica Leidensia*, vol 47, Sidestone, Leiden, pp.151-161.
Veder Greco: Le necropoli di Agrigento 1988, l'Erma di Bretschneider, Rome.
Verger, S 2011, 'Dévotions féminines et bronzes de l'extrême Nord dans le thesmophorion de Géla,' in F Quantin (ed), *Archéologie des religions antiques : contributions à l'étude des sanctuaires et de la piété en Méditerranée (Grèce, Italie, Sicile, Espagne)*, University of Pau and Pays de l'Adour, Pau, pp.15-76.
Veronese, F 2006, *Lo* spazio *e la* dimensione *del* sacro *Sanctuari greci e territorio nella Sicilia arcaica*, Esedra, Padua.
Versluys, MJ 2016, 'The global Mediterranean: a material-cultural perspective,' in T Hodos (ed), *The Routledge Handbook of Globalisation and Archaeology*, Routledge, London, pp.597-601.
Virgilio, P 1969, *Randazzo e il museo Vagliasindi*, Scuola salesiana del libro, Catania.
Wallenstein, K 1971, *Korinthische Plastik des 7. und 6. jahrhunderts vor Christus*, Bouvier Verlag Herbert Grundmann, Bonn.
Warden, PG 1992, 'Gift, Offering, and Reciprocity: Personalized Remembrance and the "small finds",' in D White (ed), *Excavations at the Extramural Sanctuary of Demeter and Persephone at Cyrene, 1969-1981. Gifts to the goddesses: Cyrene's Sanctuary of Demeter and Persephone*, Expedition, vol 34, no. 1-2, University of Pennsylvania Press, Philadelphia, pp.50-58.
Wegner, M 1982, 'Terrakotten einer Frau mit einem Ferkel,' in M L Gualandi, L Massei, and S Settis (eds), *ΑΠΑΡΧΑΙ: Nuove ricerche e studi sulla Magna Greciae la Sicilia antica in onore di Paolo Enrico Arias*, Pisa, pp.201-219.
Wentker, H 1956, 'Die Ktisis von Gela bei Thukydides,' *Mitteilungen des Deutschen Archäologischen Instituts, Römische Abteilung*, vol 63, Schnell & Steiner, Regensburg, pp.129-139.
White, D 1975, 'Archaic Cyrene and the cult of Demeter and Persephone', Expedition, vol 17.4, pp.2-17.
White, D and Reynolds, J 2012, *The Extramural Sanctuary of Demeter and Persephone at Cyrene, Libya, Final Reports, vol 8, The Sanctuary's Imperial Architectural Development, Conflict with Christianity, and Final Days*, University of Pennsylvania Press, Philadelphia.
Williams, D and Ogden, J 1994, *Greek Gold: Jewelry of the Classical World*, Harry N Abrams, New York.
Winter, F 1903, *Die Typen der figürlichen Terrakotten III*, Spemann, Berlin.Wünsche, R and Steinhart M (eds) 2010, *Schmuck der Antike: ausgewählte Werke der Staatlichen Antikensammlungen München*, Kunstverlag Fink, Lindenberg im Allgäu.
Whitley, J 2001, *The Archaeology of Ancient Greece*, Cambridge University Press, Cambridge.
Wiederkehr Schuler, E 2004, *Les protomés féminines au sanctuaire de la Malophoros*, Cahiers du Centre Jean Bérard 22, Publications du Centre Jean Bérard, Naples.
Xydopoulos, I 2007, 'The concept and Representation of Northern Communities in Ancient Greek Historiography: The Case of Thucydides,' in J Pan-Montojo and F Pedersen (eds), *Communities in European History: Representations, Jurisdictions, Conflicts*, Pisa University Press, Pisa, pp.1-21.
Zancani Montuoro, P 1954, 'Note sui soggetti e sulla tecnica delle tabelle di Locri,' *Atti e memorie della Società Magna Grecia*, NS1, Associazione Nazionale per gli Interessi del Mezzogiorno d'Italia, Rome, pp.71-106.
Zuntz, G 1971, *Persephone: three essays on religion and thought in Magna Graecia*, Oxford University Press, Oxford.

Websites

The Coroplastic Studies Interest Group: www.coroplasticstudies.org
Comparative finds excavated in Cyrenaica: www.cyrenaica-terracottas.org

Catalogue

How to use the catalogue

The catalogue is organised according to the iconographic development of the figurines over time, The figurines are categorised according to their mould series, which have been labelled as Types A to P. Those figurines that could not be categorised according to mould series have been grouped thematically and then chronologically, such as the Type L heads. The mould series are discussed in order of completeness, followed by the sharpness of detail. The catalogue provides a full list and description of the figurines, as well as a detailed comparison with other objects from Akragas, the rest of Sicily or beyond. References are provided directly after the description. The external colour of the object is described with reference to the Munsell Color System.

Overview of the locations and contexts of findspots for figurines

City Sanctuary: At the southwestern corner of the city, directly next to Gate V. The complex comprised several buildings, including monumental temples such as temple L, built in the first half of the fifth century BCE with a large altar. There were various other buildings and altars in use until at least the fourth century BCE. The cult has been interpreted as chthonic because of its numerous altars, some specifically connecting to the underworld, and finds of lamps and votives similar to those from the sanctuary of Bitalemi, Gela. For this reason, it is also known as the Chthonic Sanctuary. Most of the figurines of which the findspot is known stored at the Mus. Agrigento are from the City Sanctuary. The figurines of the Mould I and II series, including several variations on the series, are from here. In addition, several other figurines ranging in date from early to late periods were also found at the City Sanctuary. Several moulds were also discovered here. This makes it more likely that they were produced nearby. Mertens 2006, p.397; Hinz 1998, p.79-90.
Objects (86): **12**, **15-17**, **18**, **22**, **23**, **30**, **32-33**, **38-39**, **41-47**, **50**, **52- 53**, **56**, **59**, **62**, **64**, **66-68**, **82**, **87**, **89**, **92**, **94**, **100**, **103-104**, **118**, **120**, **122**, **123-124**, **126-127**, **128-129**, **130**, **131-132**, **133-134**, **136**, **137**, **141-151**, **155**, **157-159**, **161-162**, **163**, **164**, **166**, **168-169**, **174-175**, **177**, **182-183**, **186**, **188**, **189**, **195-196**, **202**

City Sanctuary. At the base of the southwest wall of the sanctuary: In the area west of the City Sanctuary and near the workshop, on the west side, a votive deposit was found at the base of the fortification wall, excavated in the fifties by Pietro Griffo. In addition to figurines, the deposit contained different sorts of miniature and normal pottery, eighteen simple lamps and three female masks. Sporadic finds in the area yielded the pinakes of Herakles with the Cercopes and a figurine representing three female figures. Griffo 1955, p.109-10, n. 1453
Some of the figurines are very similar in iconography or reworking and were probably produced at the workshop. The moulds, **90** and **201**, differ both in nature and time period, **201**, from the other objects in the deposit.
Objects (13): **8**, **49**, **55**, **57**, **90**, **115-117**, **121**; **171**, **176**, **179**, **201**

S. Anna Sanctuary: This sanctuary consisted also of several buildings, but of smaller proportions and located outside the city walls on a hill, presently known as S. Anna, overlooking the southwestern part of the valley. In the seventies, a building with stone foundations was excavated. A large terracotta jar, decorated with triangles and concentric circles, containing a bronze hoard of about 150kg was found inside the building. Other finds from this first building are as yet unpublished. Fiorentini 1969. Recent and ongoing excavations undertaken by Natascha Sojc (Leiden University, Augsburg University) have revealed other architectural structures and a high number of vessels, figurine parts, bronze phialai and knifes, as well as lead pendants and glass paste beads that confirm the active cult in this sanctuary up to the first half of the fourth century BCE. Sojc 2017.
Objects (6): **16**, **31**?, **72**?, **88**?, **98**, **115**, and comparable objects. Objects from the earlier excavations have an inventory number starting with 20XXX

West Archaic sanctuary underlying the bouleuterion: In a previous building phase, where presently there is the bouleuterion from the 4th-3rd century BCE, the museum, and the S. Nicola church, at the higher part of the agora and next to the Temple of Zeus and the Temple of Hercules, there might have been a sanctuary from the Archaic Period. Fiorentini, Calì, Trombi 2016, p.26; De Miro 2000, p.90; Hinz 1998, p.90-1.
Objects (4): **29**, **95**, **153**, **160**. Numbers starting with 15.XXXX

Dioscuri Temple: This temple is dated to around 430 BCE and has a corner still standing today. The figurine would predate the building. De Angelis 2018, p.115; Mertens 2006, p.396-7.
Object (1): **34**

One of the sanctuaries, S. Biagio: Some figurines are from 'one of the sanctuaries.' This means that they are from a drawer of the Mus. Agrigento archives in which a note stated 'santuari vari.' More specific information is unfortunately not known. It is possible that they were part of the dedications found at S. Biagio, excavated by P.Marconi. Hinz 1998, p. 74-9, n. 443.
Objects (3): **10**, **26**, **75**. They are mainly early and have an inventory number of five digits starting with 20XXX:

Temple of Hercules: Alternatively named Temple A, it was for a long time named the Temple of Hercules, as it was mentioned by Cicero (Verr. 2.4.43). This building, dated to the end of the 6th century BCE, is ascribed by Adornato to Apollo. The excavations were undertaken together with the Temple of Zeus in 1958-9 and 1962. The rear of the figurine probably gives details on the findspot. The temple would have been built by Phalaris. Adornato 2012, p.483-4
Object (1): **192**

Temple of Zeus: This temple was built on the Acropolis around the mid-sixth century BCE under the reign of Phalaris and possibly dedicated to Zeus Polieus or Atabyrios. The excavations were undertaken together with the Temple of Hercules in 1958-9 and 1962. The rear of the figurines sometimes provides details on the findspot. The later female figurines, such as group 4, appear at this temple, but otherwise, it concerns exceptional objects for their form or date. Mertens 2006, p.195-7; De Miro 2000, p.86
Objects (6): **93**, **181**, **185**, **191**, **193**, **197**

Sanctuary near Villa Aurea: Traces of a small architectural structure have been found under the Villa Aurea, a modern building. Hinz 1988, p.91, n. 546
Objects (2): **97**, **125**
Southern city wall Construction of the city wall was thought to have begun after the city was officially founded, under the reign of Phalaris during the first half of the sixth

century BCE, but the remains suggest a starting date of about 500 BCE. Most parts of the wall were actually built in the fourth century BCE. Mertens 2006, p.195.
Objects (4): **76**, **102**, **110**, **180**

Workshop/sanctuary near Gate V: Gate V forms the entrance to the Chthonic temple complex. East of the gate, a temple was built in the mid sixth century BCE. A small workshop with two kilns was located here. The structure has been interpreted as a sanctuary also. De Miro 2000, p.42-3. Mertens 2006, p.198
Objects (5): **58**, **107**, **108**, **111**, **139**. Inv. numbers 89xx-90xx

Necropolis di Contrada Mosè: On the east, along the road to Gelas lies the necropolis on a flat-topped hill. The graves date from the 6th and 5th century BCE from different building phases. There are also several deposits. Figurines are from the lower layer, dated towards the end of the 6th century BCE. Veder Greco: le necrópolis di Agrigento 1988, p.244-8
Objects (4): **21**, **54**, **83**, **173**

Necropolis di Contrada Pezzino: Not far from the city, on the northwest side, along the street to Megara, this necropolis had three phases between 580-430 BCE. The graves are in particular rich in pottery, but also figurines. Poorer graves are in one area of the necropolis. Veder Greco: le necrópolis di Agrigento 1988, p.248-252.
Objects (7): **25**, **35**, **63**, **70**, **71**, **80**, **135**

Akragas, Museo Civico: Numbers starting with C37X or C38X are figurines from the Mus. Agrigento, which was previously part of the Museo Civico. Except for C380 and C383, of which Albertocchi mentions the City Sanctuary, they are all without findspot information. Their findspot is here referred to by 'Akragas.' These figurines are often without pendants. Earlier excavated figurines from Selinous were also stored in the Museo Civico in Agrigento, but have been moved to Mus. Palermo. Extra numbers written, usually on the back of the figurine, in addition to the inventory number are noted between brackets as the 'Museum and Inventory number.' This number probably gives more specific information on the findspot.

Abbreviations/references for museum collections with figurines from Akragas:

Mus. Agrigento	Museo Archeologico Regionale "Pietro Griffo", Agrigento, Italy The largest collection of terracotta figurines from Akragas.
Mus. Aidone	Museo Archeologico Regionale di Aidone, Italy
Mus. Catania	Museo di Adrano, Castello Normanno, Catania, Italy
Mus. Eraclea Minoa	Antiquarium di Eraclea Minoa, Italy
Mus. Naples	Museo Archeologico Nazionale di Napoli, Naples, Italy
Mus. Palermo	Museo Archeologico Regionale "Antonino Salinas", Palermo, Italy A small collection of figurines from Akragas, a large collection from Selinous.
Mus. Randazzo	The Archaeological Civic Museum "Paolo Vagliasindi", Randazzo, Italy
Mus. Reggio Calabria	Museo Archeologico Nazionale di Reggio di Calabria, Reggio Calabria, Italy

Mus. Syracuse	Museo Archeologico Regionale "Paolo Orsi", Syracuse, Italy A small collection of figurines from Akragas.
Mus. Tarent	Museo Archeologico Nazionale di Taranto, Tarent, Italy
Mus. Trapani	Museo Regionale "A. Pepoli" di Trapani, Italy
Mus. Munich	Staatlichen Antikensammlungen München, Munich, Germany Several figurines, included in this catalogue, probably from Akragas.
Mus. Bonn	Akademische Kunstmuseum der Universität Bonn, Germany Several figurines from Selinous, some possibly from Akragas.
Mus. Karlsruhe	Antikensammlung des Badischen Landesmuseums
Mus. Berlin	Antikensammlung der Staatlichen Museen zu Berlin, Germany
Mus. Amsterdam	Allard Pierson Museum, University of Amsterdam, the Netherlands Some figurines from Akragas, some from Selinous. Most objects are from the private collection in the Hague of C.W. Lunsingh- Scheurleer.
Mus. Copenhagen	National Museum of Denmark, Copenhagen, Denmark. Some figurines from Sicily.
Louvre	Musée du Louvre, Paris, France Some figurines from Sicily.
British Mus.	British Museum, London, United Kingdom Several objects, previously part of the private collection of Douglas Sladen, are similar to figurines and possibly originally from Akragas. See Museum website.
Mus. Athens	National Archaeological Museum of Athens, Greece
Mus. Moscow	The Pushkin State Museum of Fine Arts, Moscow, Russia
Mus. Bardo	The National Bardo Museum, Tunis, Tunisia
Mus. Istanbul	İstanbul Archaeology Museums, Istanbul, Turkey

Catalogue

Type A: Argive Type (no.1-2)

These two handmade objects are from Akragas but might be imported. The support on the back for keeping them upright and the large pectoral bands are noteworthy.

No.1:

‣ *Museum and Inventory number:* Mus. Munich 9580
‣ *Findspot and context:* Akragas
‣ *Publications:* Hamdorf 2014, p.96, no.C 208
‣ *Dimensions in cm:* h.4.4
‣ *Material:* Terracotta.
‣ *Techniques:* Handmade. Several separately attached parts such as eyes, hair, earring, fibula and bands.
‣ *Colour:* Pink 7.5 YR 8/4
‣ *Date:* First half of the sixth century BCE
‣ *Workshop:* Unknown
‣ *Typology:* Argive: group 5a
‣ *Short description:* Left arm broken off. Upper part of a figurine with pinched face and big eyes. On the right, she wears a round earring. Long hair in three parts at the back and draped in two circular shapes on the head. She stretches her right arm holding the double lined band up. She has a round fibula on the left.
‣ *Comparable objects:* Similar to **2**, except for the hair. Posture and shape of body comparable with a figurine from Akragas, though the face is very different. Marconi 1933, pl. VI.2.

Other Argive figurines would have been found at the City Sanctuary and are dated to around mid-sixth century BCE. Hinz 1998, p.85.

No.2

‣ *Museum and Inventory number:* Mus. Munich 8929
‣ *Findspot and context:* Akragas
‣ *Publications:* Hamdorf 2014, p.96, no.C 207
‣ *Dimensions in cm:* h.6.9
‣ *Material:* Terracotta.
‣ *Techniques:* Handmade. Several separately attached parts such as polos/crown, fibulae and bands. Painted white (?)
‣ *Colour:* Pink 7.5 YR 7/4
‣ *Date:* First half of the sixth century BCE
‣ *Workshop:* Unknown
‣ *Typology:* Argive: group 5a
‣ *Short description:* Upper part of a figurine with pinched face and big eyes. On the right, she wears a round ear stud. Long hair in three parts at the back and draped in two circular shapes on the head. She stretches her right arm holding the double lined band up. She has a round fibula on the left. The body curves just below the waist: a sitting pose, supported by a leg on the back.
‣ *Comparable objects:* Similar to **1**, though it has no headgear.

The stand on the back of the figurine, also as the hand-modelled body and the fibulae with double band are reminiscent of a figurine from Syracuse, which has however a head with a fringe of bulbs and a polos. Winter 1903, p.121, no.1

Similar headgear and face, though with a different pectoral band and a necklace are seen on a figure from Tegea. Nat. Mus. Copenhagen Inv. no.8044 h.10cm, See museum website.

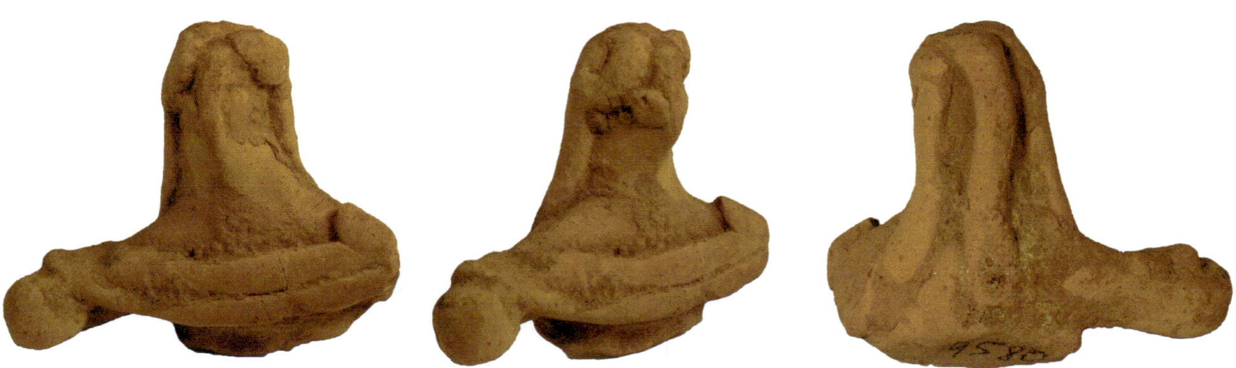

No. 1; Scale 1:1 (Staatlichen Antikensammlungen München).

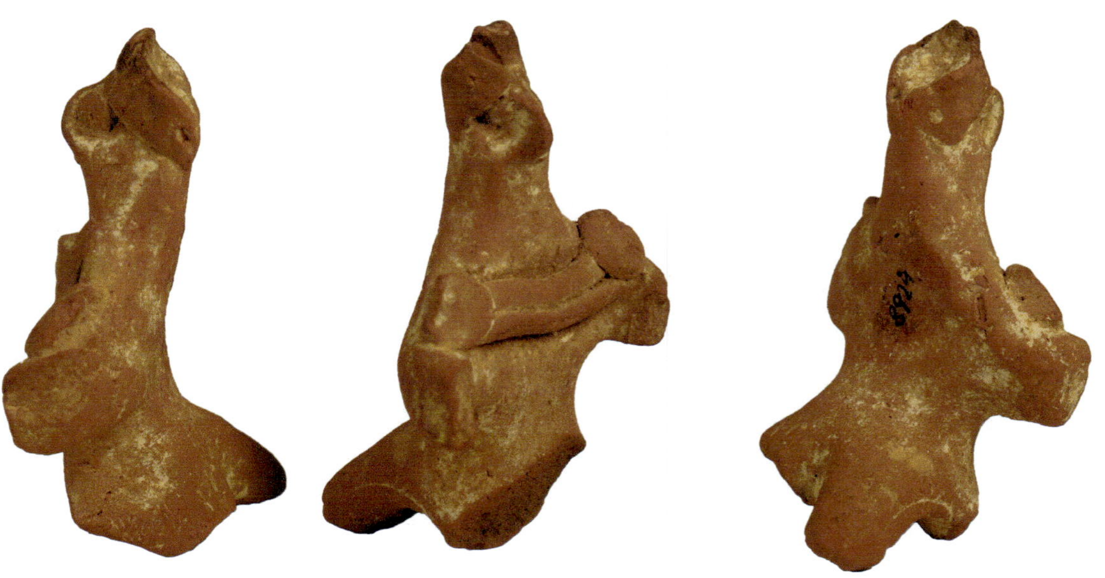

No. 2; Scale 1:1 (Staatlichen Antikensammlungen München).

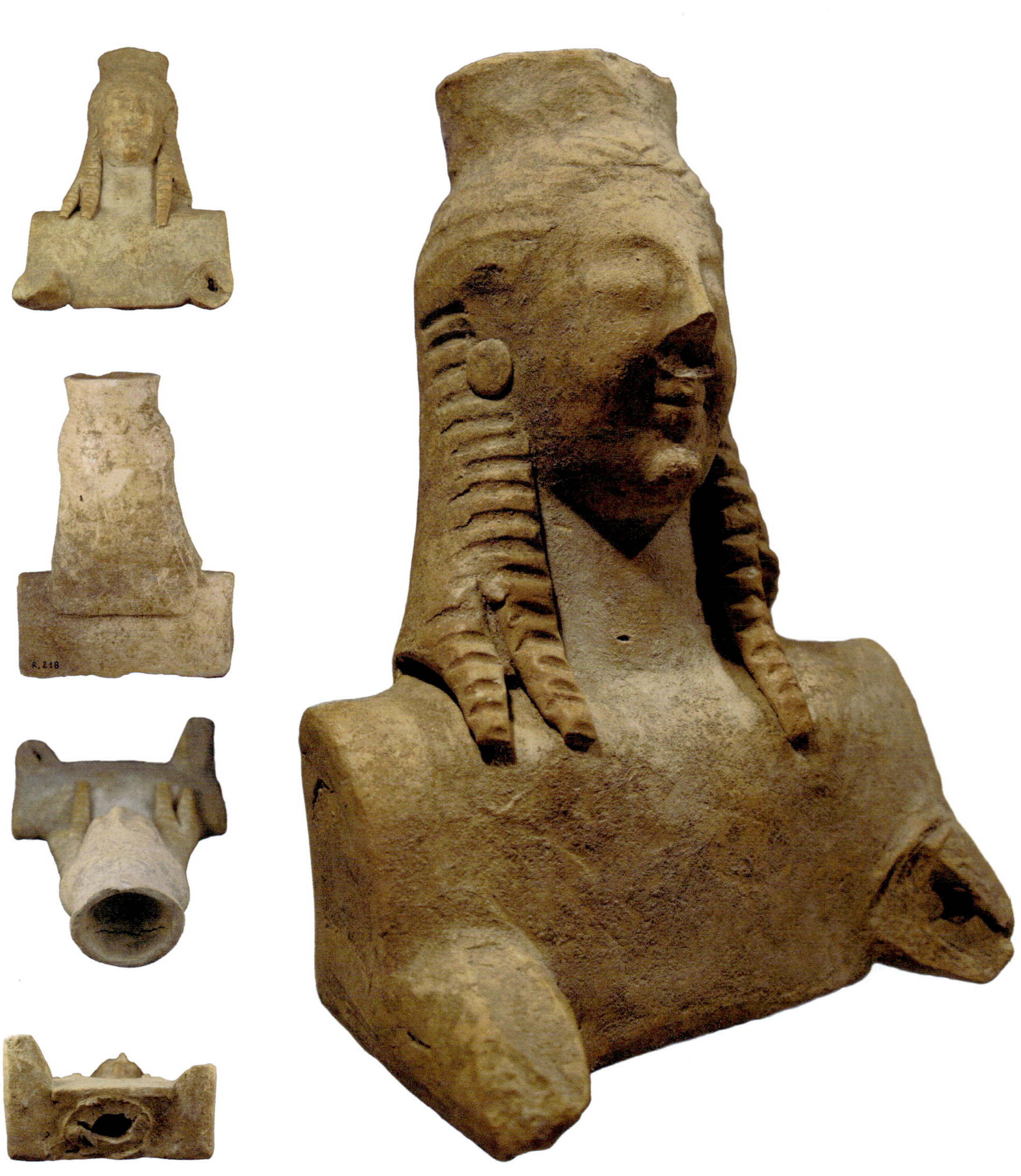

No. 3; Side view. Scale 1:1½; Left: Different angles of no. 3; Scale 1:5 (Museo Archeologico Regionale "Pietro Griffo", Agrigento).

Type B: Face-moulded figurines (no.3-7)

These figurines have been made with a mould for the face only. They appear in two variations: seated or standing. In the latter case only the upper part, the bust, remains. They could have been imported to Akragas from Locri.

No.3

- *Museum and Inventory number:* Mus. Agrigento R218
- *Findspot and context:* Akragas (?)
- *Publications:* -
- *Dimensions in cm:* h.21.2
- *Material:* Terracotta, with glittering sand insertions. The lips and cheek have little residues of red paint. The hair seems a bit darker, possibly because it was once painted black.
- *Techniques:* Mostly handmade. Mould-made face. An impression of a finger and a sharp tool inside the polos. On the left arms, the clay displays waves as if the arm was pushed. Hair reworked with round stick. Strands of hair made of separate clay coils, attached later, like the earrings. Body made out of a bent thick slab of clay. The sides of the statue are not worked, just smoothed. The sticks in the place of the lower arms were probably meant to remain unseen, as wooden arms might have been placed over them. The lower part of the original figurine fit a hole in the upper part. The flattened 'base' of the upper part shows that it was made separately.
- *Colour:* Pink 7.5 YR 7/4
- *Date:* The third quarter of the 6th century BCE
- *Workshop:* Face-moulded figurines
- *Typology:* Hollow polos: group 5b
- *Short description:* Terracotta bust, upper part of a female. Nose, parts of hair and arms, a piece of the polos and small parts next to a vertical break – from the polos downwards – on the left side at the back are broken off. The lower part of the original figurine with short body and feet probably on a base are missing. Her oval face on a flat long neck has a high forehead, big round eyes, protruding cheekbones, a narrow mouth with thick slightly smiling lips and a pronounced protruding chin in two parts. Her hair at the front is parted, incised with diagonal lines turning horizontal on the upper back and on the double strand of hair in front, hanging over her shoulders and thinning towards the ends. At the back, her hair with more roughly incised lines on the upper part, ends straight below the shoulder. Her ears are marked by an oval impression in the hair and placed rather high, in particular the left one. She wears round ear studs. Her body both front and back is very straight. Below the strands of hair, two elevations indicate collarbones or breasts. Her right breast is placed higher, and her shoulders are very wide. On the bottom of the bust, an oval shaped stand was created around a hole.
- *Comparable objects:* Very similar to **4** and **5**. Face from the same mould for the face, also as of **6** and 7.

These sort of figurines, called 'a leggio', appear in different sorts, standing and seated, also as a siren-shaped vase. They are found at sanctuaries in Locri and its subcolonies Hipponion and Medma. A. Anselmi 2012. 498ff.; Müller 1995, p.211; Costamagna and Sabbione 1990, p.100; Zuntz 1971, p.161. A similar but complete statue is found in Lokroi Epizephyrioi, sanctuary of Persephone, Manella. It includes the tall cylindrical dress. Forming the lower part of the body. Mostly handmade, 61.1cm tall. Feet and footstool are restored. Arms have been broken off but are restored. Otherwise, complete. Mus. Reggio Calabria Inv. 5804. Langlotz and Hirmer 1963, p.56, no.6.

Another figurine from Locri with a slightly different pose, holding something up on her chest with her left hand, the right hand outstretched along the body. The facial features, polos and hairstyle are very similar. Levi 1926, p.6, fig.4.

There are several figurines, both standing and seated, also as a variant of the seated one with a very long neck, in the Mus. Tarent. Ferri 1929, p.37-8, fig.25 and tav.XXVIII; Winter, Typen I, 121,6.

‣ *Other notes:* It is possible that the whole group was once bought and came into the collection of the museum through the donation of a private collection. The museum numbering with the letter R, like many vases, but no other terracotta figurines, would point in this direction. There are in total five rather similar objects, of which one, **5**, came into the collection in Munich in the year 1960 from the private collection of Eduard Schmidt, who acquired the object in Agrigento.

No.4

‣ *Museum and Inventory number:* Mus. Agrigento R217
‣ *Findspot and context:* Akragas (?)
‣ *Publications:* -
‣ *Dimensions in cm:* h.18.2
‣ *Material:* Terracotta, with glittering sand insertions.
‣ *Techniques:* Mostly handmade. Face, possibly made from a mould after the mostly handmade 3, but with some additions by hand. The clay was spread and smoothed with a sharp tool. On the right, there are some sharp lines, as if made with a knife. On the bottom, an oval stand was created around the hole. It is broken off, but was probably the upper component of the lower part of the figurine.
‣ *Colour:* Pink 7.5 YR 7/4. The surface is finished with a special layer: 7.5 YR 6.3, light-brown), visible on the face and chest. Other parts might have been painted.
‣ *Date:* The third quarter of the 6th century BCE
‣ *Workshop:* Face-moulded figurines
‣ *Typology:* Hollow polos: group 5b
‣ *Short description:* Terracotta bust, upper part of a standing female figure. Arms are partly broken off. Lower part of figurine missing. Her oval face on a flat long neck has a high forehead, big round eyes, protruding cheekbones, an Archaic smile and a pronounced protruding chin in two parts. Her hair is in the front parted, indicated by diagonal lines, turning horizontal on the upper back and on the double strand in front, hanging over her shoulders and thinning towards the ends. At the back, her hair with more roughly incised lines on the upper part, ends straight below the shoulder. The straight back and sides strengthen the impression of a sitting image. She wears on her very high ears, an oval impression in the hair, round studs as earrings, placed separately after moulding the head. The left ear is placed very high (a clear sign of similarity with **3**). She wears a low hollow polos on top of her head, leaving her hair visible around it. The arms, though partly broken off, become thinner towards the front as if a wooden longer arm could be placed over it. The left arm is smaller and thinner than her right arm. Her body both front and back

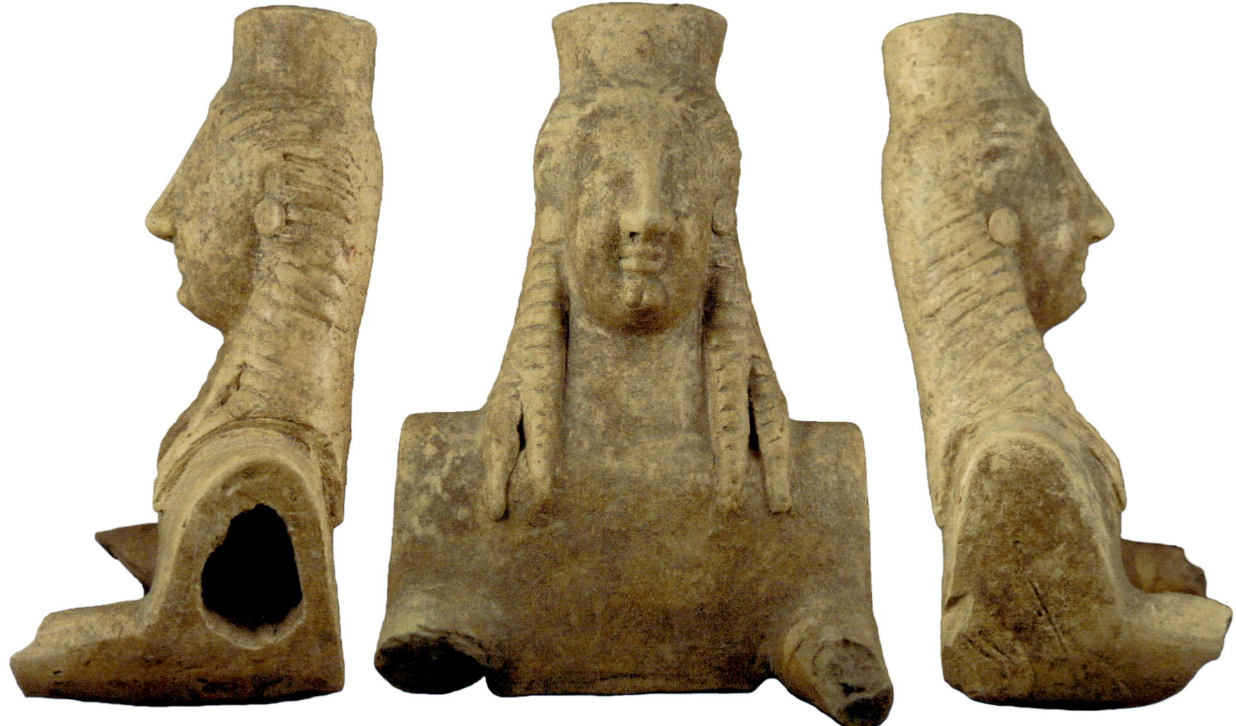

No. 4; Scale 1:2 (Museo Archeologico Regionale "Pietro Griffo", Agrigento).

is very straight. Below the hair strands, two elevations indicate breasts or collarbones. Her right breast is higher.
‣ *Comparable objects:* Almost identical to **3** and **5**, but a bit smaller in most regards, for example, the polos, also the face is narrower. Face from the same mould, also as that of **6** and 7. The mould for the face might have been made after **3**, which is mainly handmade. This one has a smoother surface and less sharp edges and could be therefore dated later: the mould was a bit worn. In some parts, it differs from **3**. There are more lines down the back to indicate the hair. These were made after moulding by hand. The statue was put down, because the clay is pressed a bit into the lines. For this statue, more clay is used on the back than on **3**. No.**4** is thicker in most places. On her left side, there is a large hole, while a similar hole on **5** is closed with clay. The lines on the hair strand are thinner than on **3**.

No.5

‣ *Museum and Inventory number:* Mus. Munich NI 8923
‣ *Findspot and context:* Akragas
‣ *Publications:* Hamdorf 2014, p.110, no.C 263
‣ *Dimensions in cm:* h.21.5
‣ *Material:* Terracotta. Inclusion of many glittering sand particles. Dark red-brown paint on the ends of the hair strands on the left, as well as a bit of the same colour on the cheek. Munsell colour 2.5 YR 4/6: red.

Some small holes in the clay burned away inclusions, and some dark-red inclusions: neck and back.
‣ *Techniques:* Mostly handmade, but mould-made face. The lower part of strands of hair was made of flattened rolls of clay and attached separately. The ear studs were also added later. The lower part inside consists of the front of two layers of clay. An extra layer is separate from the rest of the inside and partly broken off. This was probably part of the lower part of the figurine, which was attached here. Lines indicate where the arms were; around the arms, a quarter of a circle was incised, more clearly on the right. It is clear that a layer of clay was folded to form the shoulder and that this dried differently than the part that closed the shoulder off on the side. Cracks show on the left shoulder how the hole was filled. Parts of the body, at the front between the arms, and on the right side, were smoothed with a piece of fabric (?), which resulted in thin lines. With a sharp tool, the hair was marked to be distinguished from the body, on the left shoulder, while on the right shoulder a small piece of clay was added. With a similar stick, the lines were incised to mark the hair, but they are a bit flattened in the middle.

There is a diagonal groove on the hair of the back. On the inside on the right, there are pieces of branches included in the clay.
‣ *Colour:* Pink 5 YR 7/4 on broken part of the arms outer side, inside: grey 7.5 YR 6/1, slip layer: pink 7.5 YR 7/3
‣ *Date:* The third quarter of the 6th century BCE
‣ *Workshop:* Face-moulded figurines
‣ *Typology:* Hollow polos: group 5b
‣ *Short description:* Upper part, bust, of a female figurine. Both arms broken off. Right shoulder restored. Piece of the chin broken off. Piece of the polos broken off at the back and a small piece of the rim of the front left side. Large part of the back broken off connected with the inside. The hole on the bottom was probably meant to attach the lower body. Part of this might be the clearly separate piece.

Terracotta bust of a female figure, wearing a low hollow polos. Her face is oval above a flat broad and long neck. She has a high forehead, big round eyes, which are rather indistinct. She has protruding cheekbones, next to the nostrils. The mouth has two very thick lips, which are not wider than the nose, creating a very characteristic mouth. The nose is finely shaped and proportioned. Her hair is parted at the front, indicated by diagonal incised lines, turning horizontal on the upper back and on the double strands of hair in front, hanging over her shoulders and ending in two thin parts. The oval impressions on her hair are her ears. She wears round knobs as ear studs, placed separately. Her body both front and back is very straight. Below the hair strands, two elevations indicate collarbones or breasts. The left one is slightly higher. At the back, her hair with more roughly incised lines, 13 in total, on the upper part, ends straight below the shoulder. The sides of the statue are not worked, just smoothed.
‣ *Comparable objects:* Very similar to **3** and **5**. Face from the same mould for the face, also as that of **6** and **7**. The face of this figurine is slightly more elongated than the others of this type, but at max. 6mm longer. The coroplast of this figurine is very likely to be the same person as for **4**, because even the hand-worked hair on the back is similar.

No.6

‣ *Museum and Inventory number:* Mus. Agrigento R219 (68)
‣ *Findspot and context:* Akragas (?)
‣ *Publications:* -
‣ *Dimensions in cm:* h.26
‣ *Material:* Terracotta, with glittering sand insertions.
‣ *Techniques:* Mostly handmade, but mould-made face. With a tool, the distinction between the throne and the body was made sharper; the lines are visible on sides. The horizontal lines on the hair were created with a stick. The ear studs, consisting of a 2-3mm round knob, are pressed onto the ears and hair. On the right side of the upper body, there are two small vent holes. The size suggests that a stick was used. Possibly the same as for the hair.
‣ *Colour:* Pink 7.5 YR 7/4
‣ *Date:* The third quarter of the 6th century BCE
‣ *Workshop:* Face-moulded figurines
‣ *Typology:* Hollow polos: group 5b
‣ *Short description:* Upper part of an enthroned female figure. Her face is a bit out of proportion: very long and

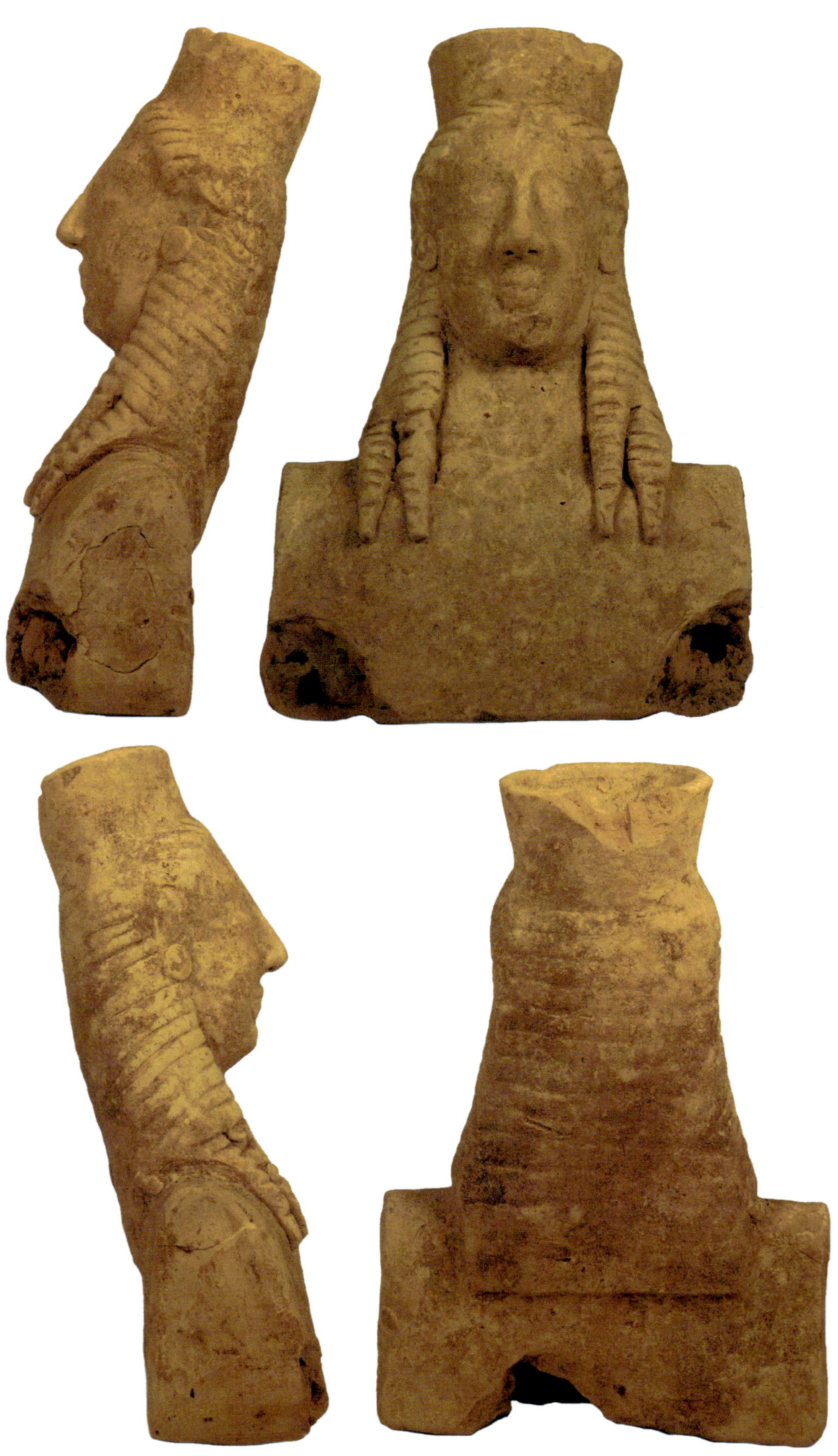

No. 5; Scale 1:2 (Staatlichen Antikensammlungen München).

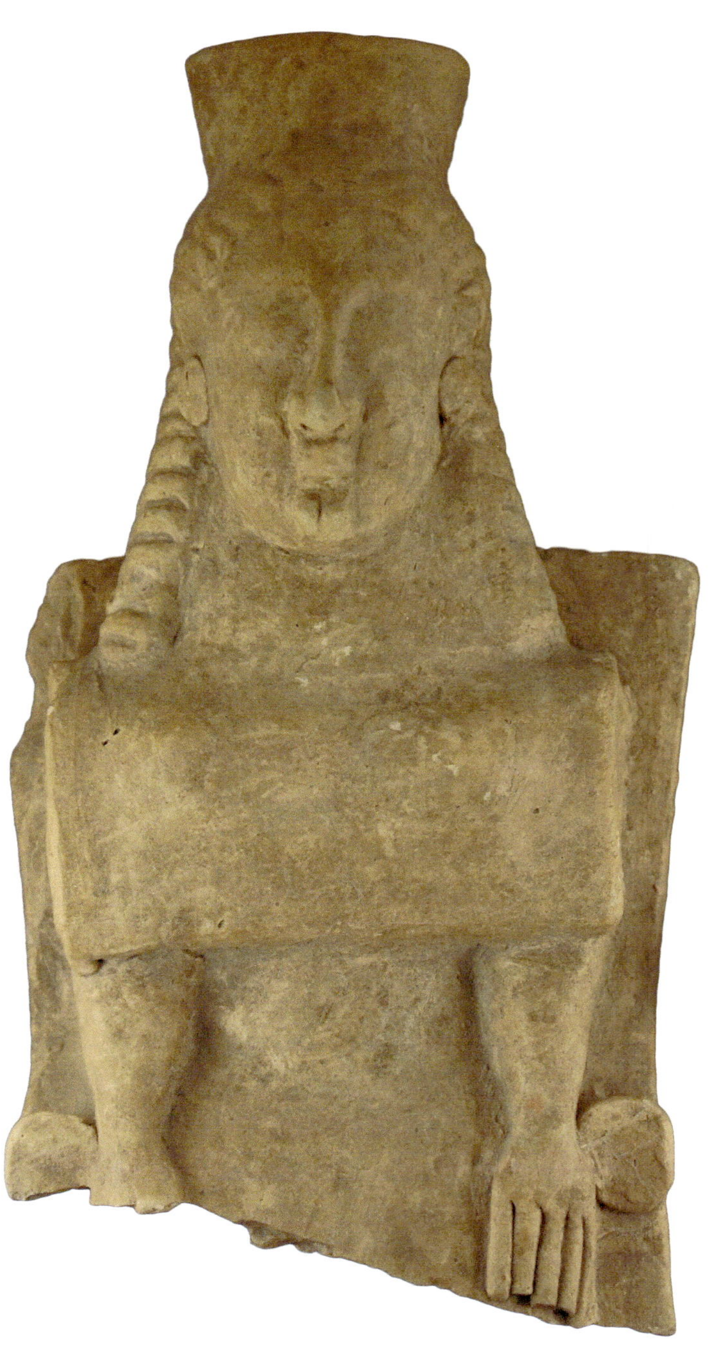

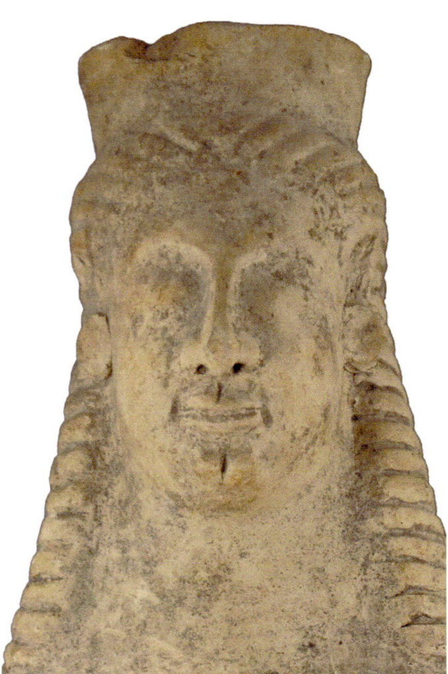

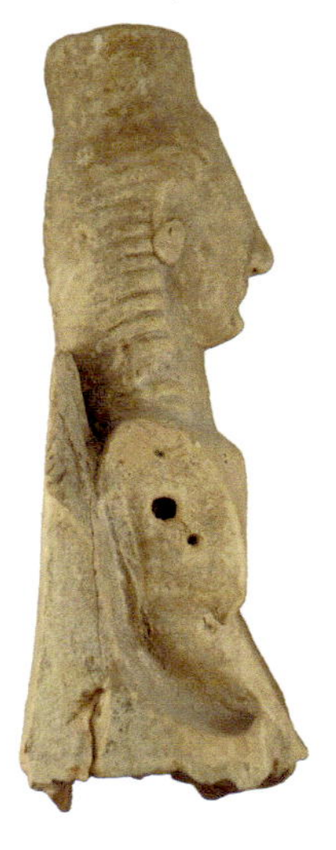

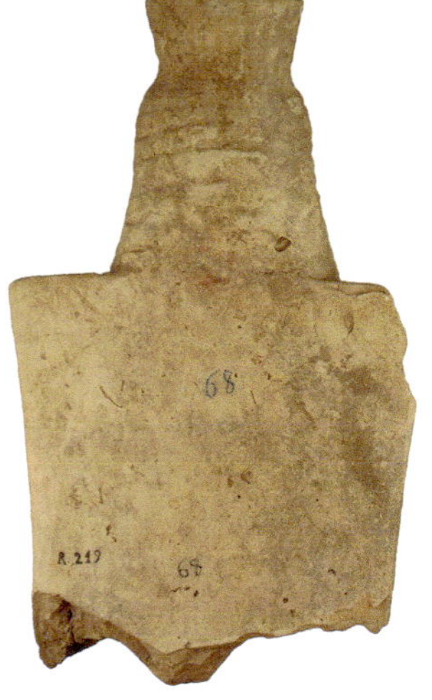

No. 6 (above); Front; Scale 1:1.5
No. 7 (top right); The face; Scale 1:1.5
Right: Details of no. 6; Scale 1:4
(Museo Archeologico Regionale "Pietro Griffo", Agrigento).

with a small jaw and pointed chin. The cheeks and the nostrils are low, and not very pronounced. She has a high forehead. The eyebrows arch in a sharp line from the nose over the large but indistinct eyes. Her dorsum is long but thin, with rounded nostrils and deep nares. A deep split line marks the chin. The mouth has the width of the nose and is very indistinct. Its placement is directly under the nose. At the corner of the mouth, there are small but deep dimples. A vertical line runs along both sides of the nose, mouth and chin. The polos is rather narrow and placed high up, leaving her hair to all sides visible. Diagonal course lines, starting from the middle, where it is parted, mark her hair. The strands of hair run diagonally parallel to each other towards the side of the head where they turn horizontal, bending to the front and back. On the top and right side, these lines are rather indistinct. Her neck is broad and rather flat and creates together with the head and hair strands a triangular shape. The strict geometrical shapes continue into her shoulders and upper part of the body, covered with a rectangular peplos-like garment, with just slight elevations to indicate her breasts or clavicles. These are placed unnaturally high and to the sides. The sides of her upper body are just smoothed Her pose is stiff and she sits straight. Her lower arms appear from under the chest and are rounded, tapering towards the wrist, and slightly bent. Her hands have five similar shaped long straight fingers. The suggestion of a seated pose is strengthened by the backrest, which rises behind her shoulders and neck. The rectangular shape repeats the chest. This backrest runs down to end in a knob. Though she is leaning against the backrest, she only touches the armrests with her wrists. Her belly is rounded and she has a clear waist, though there is no belt. The lap is small and rounded also.
‣ ***Comparable objects:*** Very similar to **7**, except for the facial reworking of the latter. Her neck is longer than that of **7**, just like the body and face, which are more elongated. No. **7** does not have vent holes. This figurine is more complete than **7**. The throne of this figurine continues up to the shoulders, and because the figurine is broken off lower than **7**, the knobs on the throne are visible, as are the lap and hands. Face from the same mould for the face, also as that of **4**, **5**, and **6**. Nos. **6** and **7** bear strong likeness to a nearly complete, 53cm tall figurine, seated in the same pose, from Locri, based on a drawing from two incomplete objects at Mus. Reggio Calabria. Winter 1903, p.121, no.6. They are very similar also to the upper part of a figurine from Locri (38.2cm), which has a very long neck, a more clear indication of the breasts, a flaring and slightly bent body leaning against a bench-like seat. Its head is very different also and does not originally belong to the figurine. Langlotz and Hirmer 1963, p.59-60, no.18.

No.7

‣ ***Museum and Inventory number:*** Mus. Agrigento R220
‣ ***Findspot and context:*** Akragas (?)
‣ ***Publications:*** -
‣ ***Dimensions in cm:*** h.25.6
‣ ***Material:*** Terracotta, with glittering sand insertions. Some small holes show that there were insertions, which burned during firing.
‣ ***Techniques:*** Mostly handmade. Mould-made face, but heavily reworked nose and mouth. With a tool the distinction between the upper part of the dress and the arms/belly was made sharper (lines visible). Mouth, chin and nose lines were worked on after moulding to sharpen the expression. Probably the lines in the hair, which were faded in the mould (as on the top), were sharpened by hand after moulding. This is visible because the clay bends in and is flattened in the lines. This reworking took place before the knob was added. Ear studs were applied separately. The ear studs, 2-3mm round discs, are pressed onto the ears and hair.
‣ ***Colour:*** Pink 7.5 YR 7/4
‣ ***Date:*** The third quarter of the 6th century BCE
‣ ***Workshop:*** Face-moulded figurines
‣ ***Typology:*** Hollow polos: group 5b

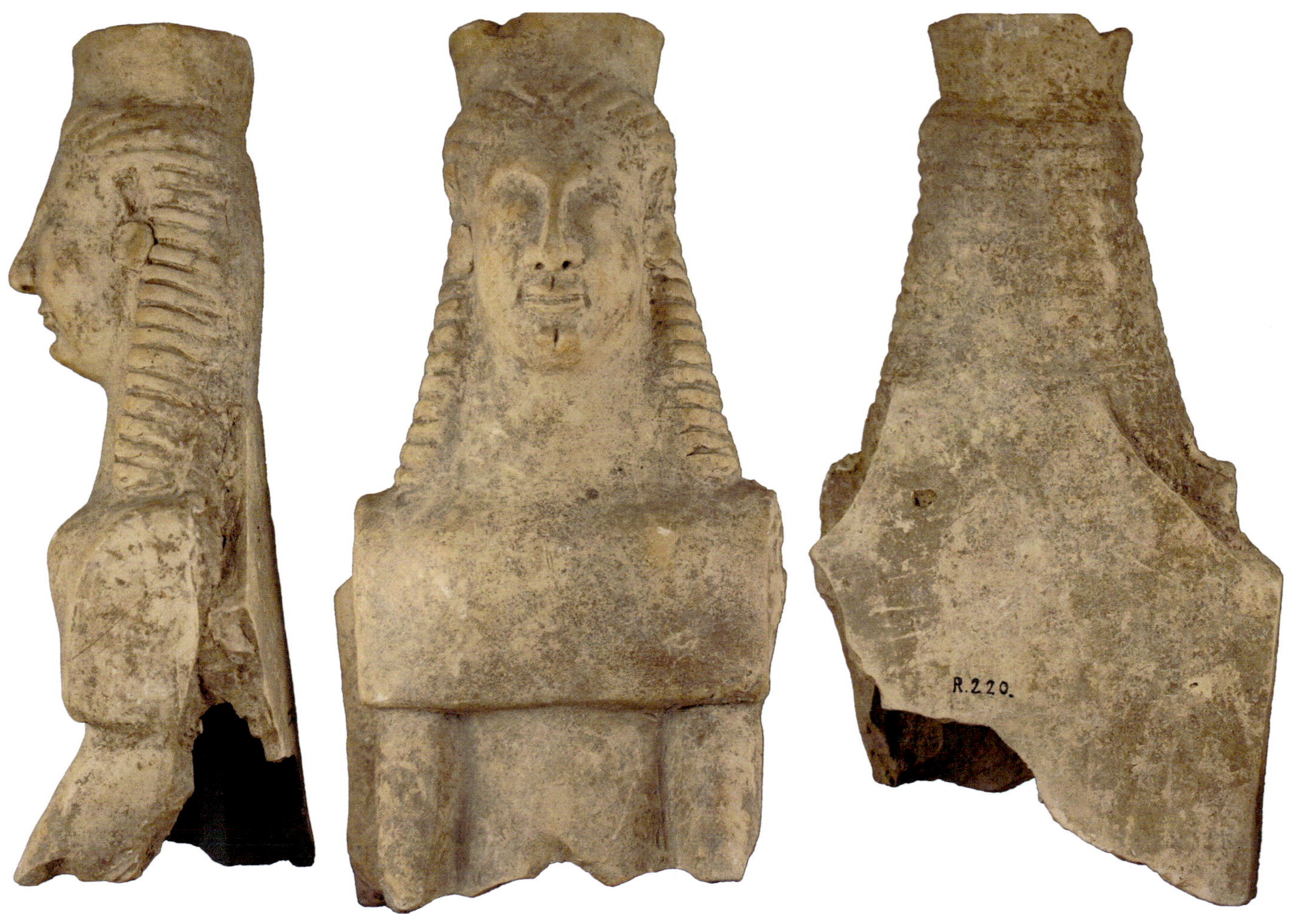

No. 7; Scale 1:2 (Museo Archeologico Regionale "Pietro Griffo", Agrigento).

‣ *Short description:* Upper part of an enthroned female figure. Lower part and corners of the throne broken off. Polos damaged.

Her face is a bit out of proportion: very long and with a thin jaw and pointed chin. The cheeks are low, next to the nostrils and not very pronounced. She has a high forehead. The eyebrows arch in a sharp line from the nose over the large but indistinct eyes. She has a very large nose. The dorsum is long but thin, with rounded nostrils and deep nares. A deep split line, both not completely straight, marks the philtrum and the chin. The mouth has the width of the nose and is slightly opened. They form a straight line, as if talking rather than smiling. At the corner of the mouth, there are small but deep dimples. The polos is smaller than the head and placed high up, leaving her hair to all sides visible. Diagonal course lines, starting from the middle, where the hair is parted, run diagonally parallel to each other towards the side of her head where they turn horizontal on the front hair strands and back. Her neck is broad and rather flat and creates together with the head and hair a triangular shape, placed on the straight shoulders. The strict geometrical shapes continue into her shoulders and upper part of the body, covered with a rectangular peplos-like garment, with just slight elevations to indicate her breasts. These are placed unnaturally high and to the sides. They could be seen as clavicles also, because of the small size and odd position. Her pose is stiff and she sits straight. Her lower arms appear from under the chest and are rounded, tapering towards the lower arm, and slightly bent. The suggestion of a seated pose is strengthened by the backrest, of which the corners are broken off. This backrest is also visible on the right side, next to her arms and upper body.

‣ *Comparable objects:* Very similar to **6**, except for the facial reworking. Face from the same mould for the face, though here it is heavily reworked, as that of **4**, **5** and **6**.

Type C: block-like figurines (no.8-64)

This large group of earliest local production is characterised by its body shape. The head might be defined, but the body is very much abstracted, lacking arms and rectangular rendered.

No.8

- *Museum and Inventory number:* Mus. Agrigento 1162
- *Findspot and context:* City Sanctuary. At the base of the southwest wall of the sanctuary
- *Publications:* De Miro 2000, p.128, no.9
- *Dimensions in cm:* h.11.5
- *Material:* Terracotta, many inclusions
- *Techniques:* Front moulded. From very worn mould and coarsely reworked. Just the lower part of the body is hollow.
- *Colour:* Light Pale Brown 7.5YR 6/4
- *Date:* Last quarter of the 6th century BCE
- *Workshop:* Unknown
- *Typology:* Block-like body: group 1a
- *Short description:* Complete, restored. Relatively large head on a thick neck. The face is indistinct, but with big eyes, a large nose and small mouth. She wears a flat veil on top of the head. Bulging hair on each side of the head. Simple body, coarsely shaped, with bent knees and flaring at the shoulders.
- *Comparable objects:* Though more coarse, both head and simple body are reminiscent of **13**. Head is similar but much indistinct than **19**.

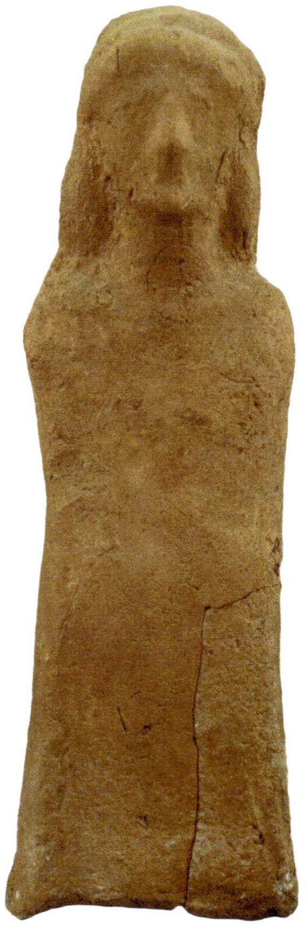

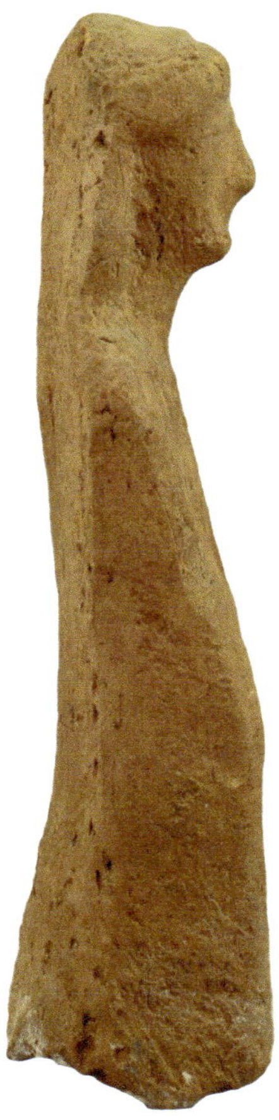

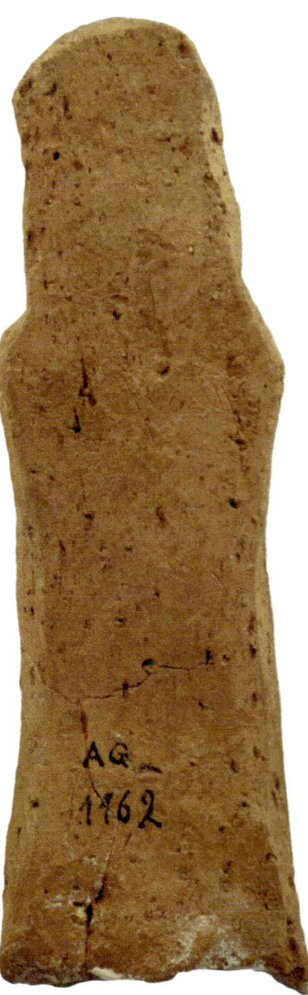

No. 8; Scale 1:1 (Museo Archeologico Regionale "Pietro Griffo", Agrigento).

No.9

‣ *Museum and Inventory number:* Mus. Agrigento C379
‣ *Findspot and context:* Akragas
‣ *Publications:* -
‣ *Dimensions in cm:* h.20
‣ *Material:* Terracotta. Lighter coloured thick slip layer. Back worked with fingers, bulging clay at edge of head and right shoulder.
‣ *Techniques:* Front moulded
‣ *Colour:* Light reddish brown 2.5 YR 7/4
‣ *Date:* Last quarter of the 6th century BCE
‣ *Workshop:* Workshop of 'straight reworking'
‣ *Typology:* Block-like body: group 1a
‣ *Short description:* Nearly complete figurine, infill at lower part and feet, 5 fragments, broken nose.

Round face with small mouth and deep dimples running along the mouth. It marks the fleshy cheeks. Together with the high cheekbones, the smile seems clear. Her hair bulges along the sides of the neck. On the forehead, the fringe is divided into thick bulbs. On top of her hair, she wears a veil. She has slightly flaring shoulders; the right shoulder is higher than the left. Simple block-like body, bending at the knees. She wears an apron, which covers almost the complete front. The sides are straight; the back is slightly rounded, but straight.
‣ *Comparable objects:* The body is similar to **10**. Although the face is quite different, the statuette is similar to **11**. The facial features are reminiscent of **18**.

No.10 (not illustrated)

‣ *Museum and Inventory number:* Mus. Agrigento 20.184
‣ *Findspot and context:* Akragas: one of the sanctuaries
‣ *Publications:* -
‣ *Dimensions in cm:* h.10.3
‣ *Material:* Terracotta, coarse
‣ *Techniques:* Front moulded, back rather coarsely reworked.
‣ *Colour:* Reddish-yellow 5 YR 6/6
‣ *Date:* Last quarter of the 6th century BCE
‣ *Workshop:* Workshop of 'straight reworking'
‣ *Typology:* Block-like body: group 1a
‣ *Short description:* Headless figurine in six fragments. Simple model of the body, leaning backwards dressed in an apron, defined in neck with a rounded hem and along the sides, on a sloping body with a slight bend at the knees. At the shoulders and the base, the body flares slightly. The back is straight on the lower part, but curves parallel with the upper part.
‣ *Comparable objects:* The body is similar to **9**, but not from the same mould series.

No.11

‣ *Museum and Inventory number:* Mus. Agrigento C381
‣ *Findspot and context:* Akragas
‣ *Publications:* -
‣ *Dimensions in cm:* h.17.2
‣ *Material:* Terracotta. Lighter coloured slip layer.
‣ *Techniques:* Front moulded. From worn mould: damaged nose.
‣ *Colour:* Light red 2.5 YR 6/6
‣ *Date:* Last quarter of the 6th century BCE
‣ *Workshop:* Unknown
‣ *Typology:* Block-like body: group 1a
‣ *Short description:* Nearly complete figurine, infill at front and knees, in three fragments. Chubby face with large flattened nose, big chin and jaw. She has large but undetailed eyes with high arching eyebrows. Her hair is smooth on the fringe, but might have had structure in the original mould. On the sides, next to the neck the hair is bulging. She wears a veil, which is thick and rounds her hair. Simple block-like body. Knees bending straight down, sloping upper body. She wears an apron. Feet not visible but footstool sticking out. Flat back, on the upper part parallel to the body, again straight at the back of the head.
‣ *Comparable objects:* The body of the figurine, though not the face and the feet, is similar to **9** and **10**. No. **12** has a similar body also, but feet that are more detailed.

No.12

‣ *Museum and Inventory number:* Mus. Agrigento S91
‣ *Findspot and context:* City Sanctuary
‣ *Publications:* Fiertler 2001, p.70, tav.X BII
‣ *Dimensions in cm:* h.16.3
‣ *Material:* terracotta
‣ *Techniques:* front moulded
‣ *Colour:* Very Pale Brown 10 YR 7/4
‣ *Date:* Last quarter of the 6th century BCE
‣ *Workshop:* Unknown
‣ *Typology:* Block-like body: group 1a
‣ *Short description:* Complete figurine, restored. Relatively large head. The face is round with large eyes and nose and a small mouth. An ear is indicated, by a bulging part on the side, but rather unclear. Fringe of hair with vertical lines. Hair hanging down on the sides of the neck. She wears a veil on top of her head, leaving her hair visible. It runs just along the upper part and seems to hang down behind her hair, if seen from the side. Very simple block-like body, with knees bending. Feet on irregular-shaped footstool(?). She wears an apron, which covers her front body from shoulders to the floor, leaving just a small part on the sides uncovered. It is draped over her feet. Flat back.
‣ *Comparable objects:* Possibly from the same mould series as head **13** and **14**. The hairstyle is slightly different but sharper than the face, and was probably renewed with a mould or reworked by hand on the moulded object. Both head and body are reminiscent of **8**. There are four examples from Agrigento, of which one was found at the temple of Zeus and Gate V, the other two are from the excavations by Marconi and found at the City sanctuary. Fiertler 2001, p.66, n. 67, with reference to a figurine from the City Sanctuary, AG 9207, headless, 13.5cm, De Miro 2000, p.240, no.1407; Allegro 1972, tav.LXXV, fig.14; Marconi 1933, pl. VIII.3, head, and pl. XV.9, a complete figurine. The facial features are reminiscent of **99**.

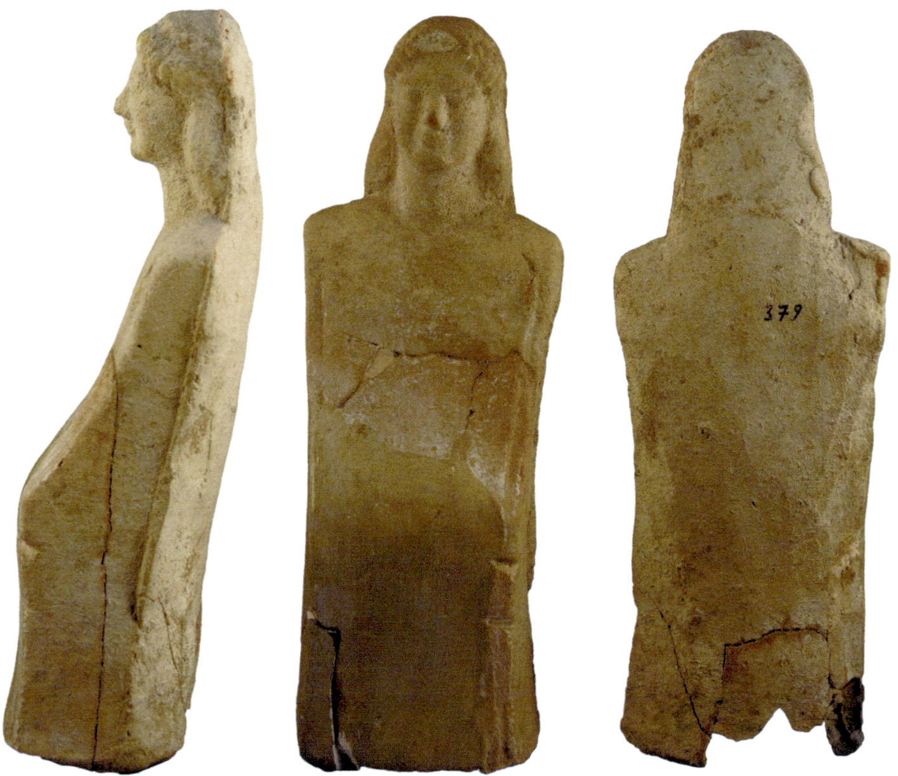

No. 9; Scale 1:2 (Museo Archeologico Regionale "Pietro Griffo", Agrigento).

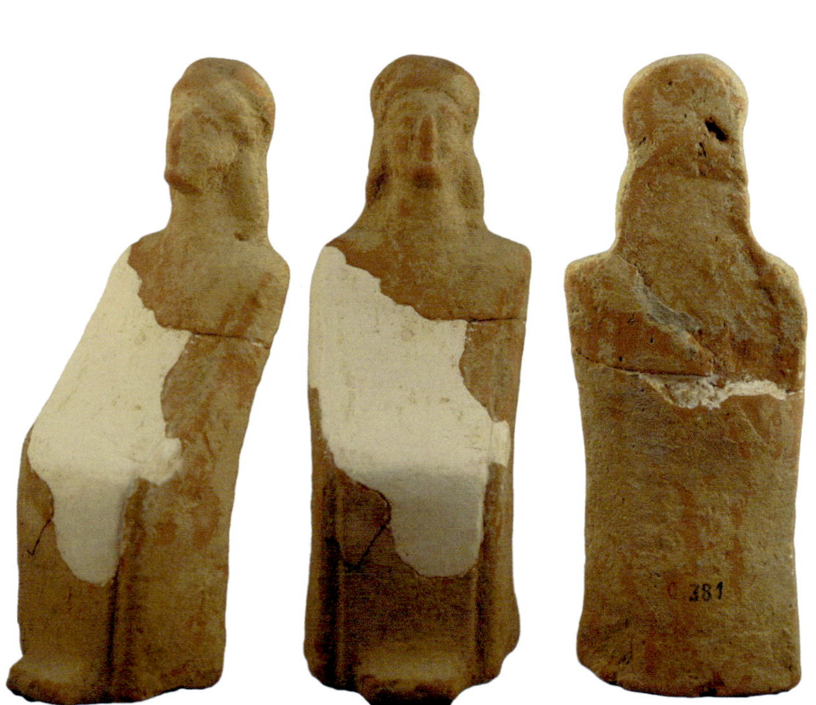

No. 11; Scale 1:2 (Museo Archeologico Regionale "Pietro Griffo", Agrigento).

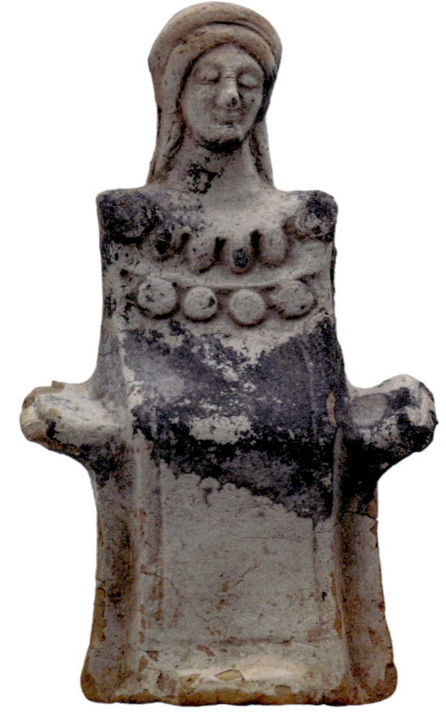

Figure 1a: The head of this figurine is similar to the head of no. 11 but larger and sharper, probably from the same mould series, AT 2709 Mus. Moscow, h.18.5cm. (Photo Mus. Moscow, Scale 1:2)

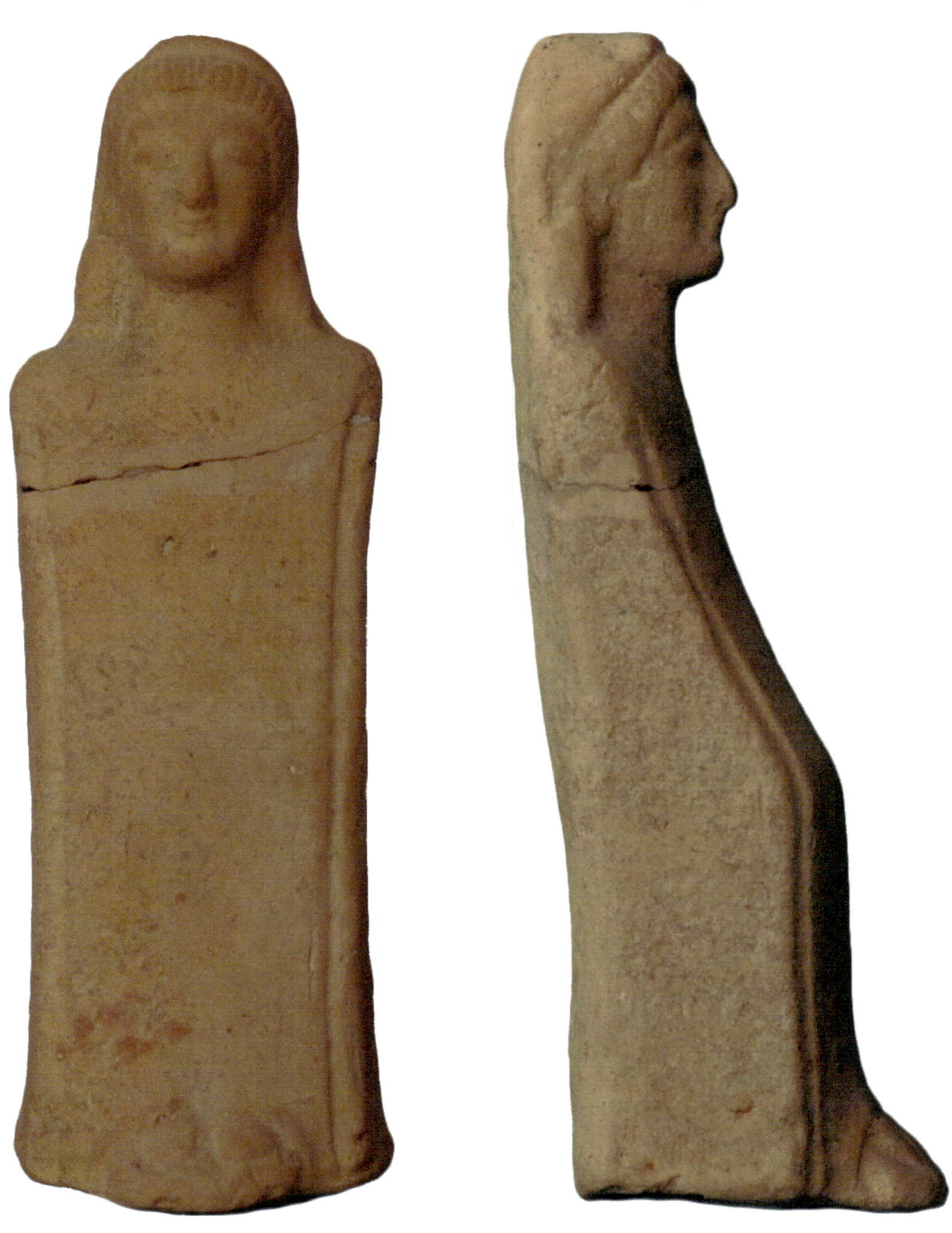

No. 12; Scale 1:1 (Museo Archeologico Regionale "Pietro Griffo", Agrigento)

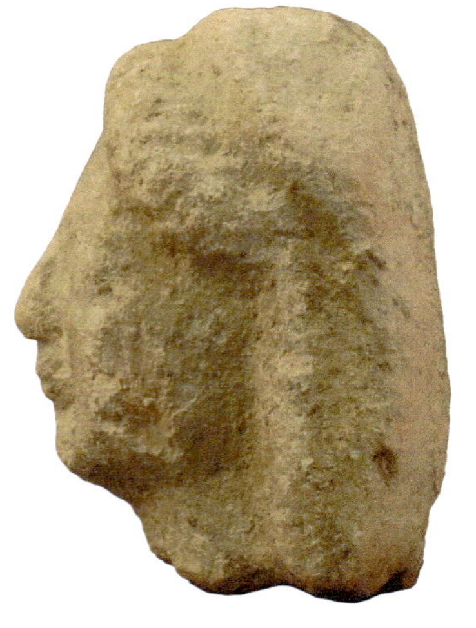
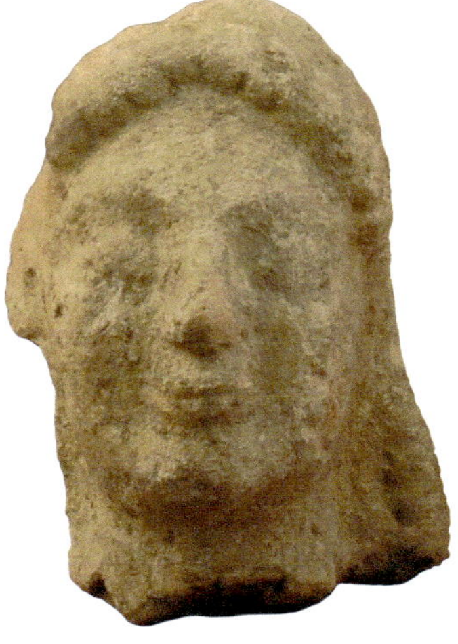

No. 13; Scale 1:1 (Museo Archeologico Regionale "Pietro Griffo", Agrigento).

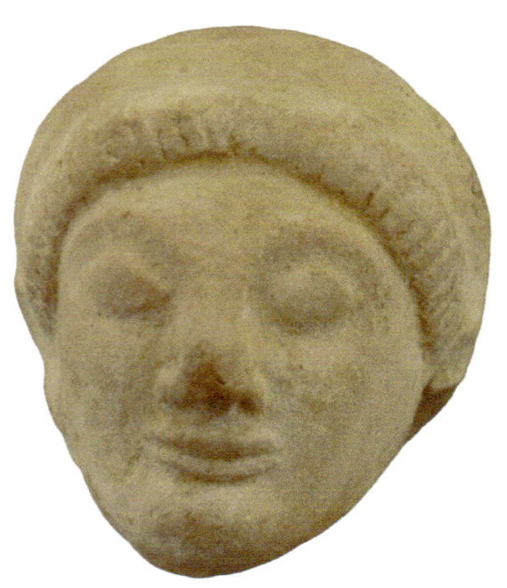
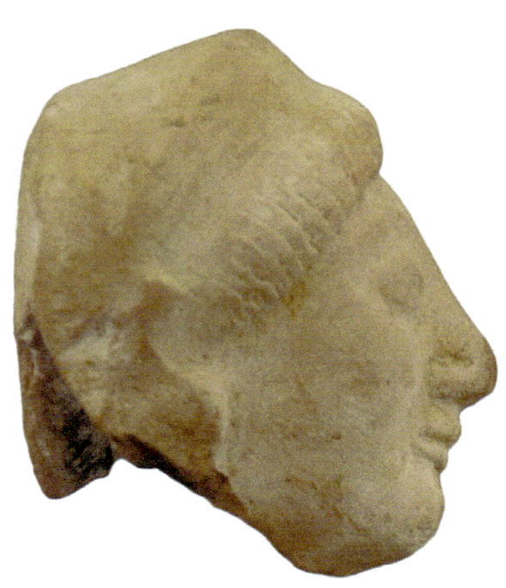

No. 14; Scale 1:1 (Museo Archeologico Regionale "Pietro Griffo", Agrigento).

No.13

- *Museum and Inventory number:* Mus. Agrigento SA/C1
- *Findspot and context:* S. Anna, Coordinates: 298, 582 Left of C40 (excavated in 2013)
- *Publications:* -
- *Dimensions in cm:* h.6.1
- *Material:* terracotta
- *Techniques:* front moulded
- *Colour:* Very Pale Brown 10 YR 7/4
- *Date:* Last quarter of the 6th century BCE
- *Workshop:* Unknown
- *Typology:* Block-like body: group 1a
- *Short description:* Head and neck of a figurine, from a worn mould. Left side partly broken off. The face is rounded with large eyes and nose and a small mouth with thin lips in a soft smile. Fringe in coarse bulbs and hair hanging down on each side of the neck. She wears a veil on top of the head. Flat back.
- *Comparable objects:* Possibly from the same mould series as head **12** and **14**. The hairstyle is slightly different. Based on size, this would be the second in a row. The figurine must have been reworked in different stages. In addition, the indication of ears might have been added later. There are four examples from Agrigento, of which one was found at the temple of Zeus and Gate V, the others are from the excavations by Marconi and found at the City Sanctuary. Fiertler 2001, p.66, n. 67; Marconi 1933, pl. 15.9. Therefore, it was probably produced in Akragas.

No.14

- *Museum and Inventory number:* Mus. Agrigento S86
- *Findspot and context:* Akragas
- *Publications:* Marconi 1933, tav.VII.8
- *Dimensions in cm:* h.5.5
- *Material:* Terracotta. Shell fragment.
- *Techniques:* Front moulded.
- *Colour:* Very pale brown 10 YR 7/3
- *Date:* Last quarter of the 6th century BCE
- *Workshop:* Unknown
- *Typology:* Block-like body: group 1a(?)
- *Short description:* Head in fragments. Rounded triangular face with large eyes. The nose runs in one line from the

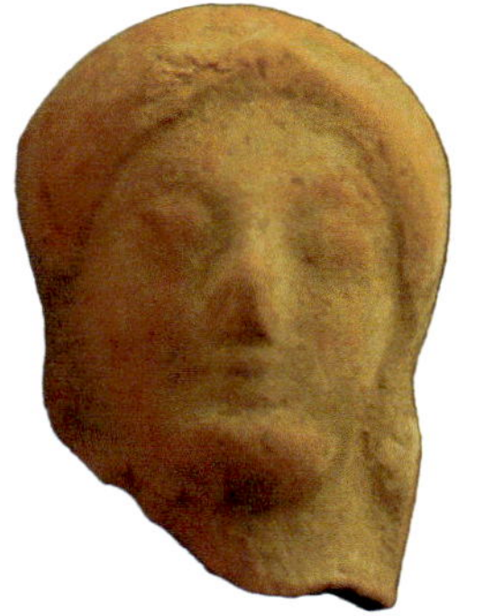
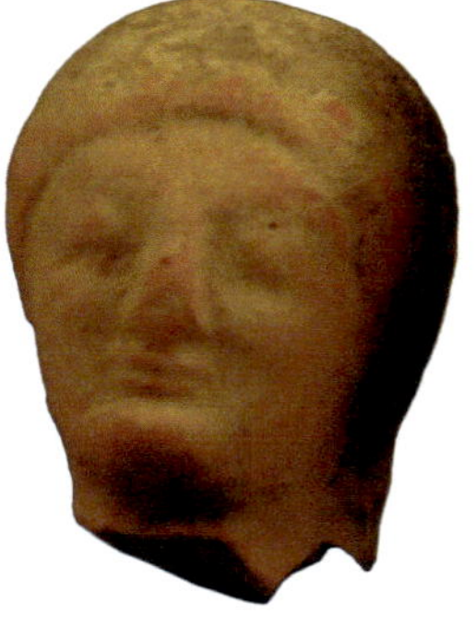
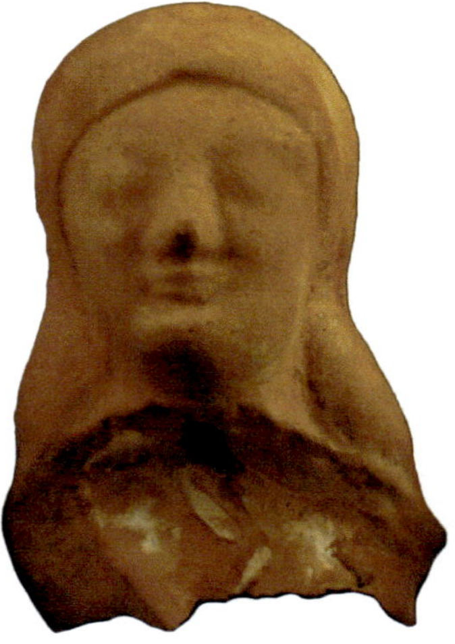
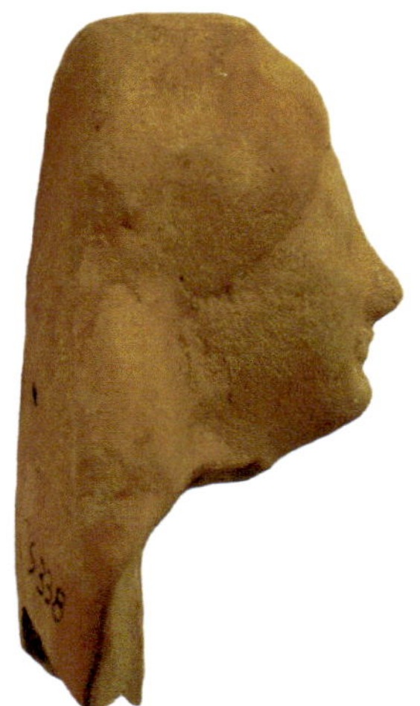

No. 15, 16, 17 in front and en-face view.; Scale 1:1 (Museo Archeologico Regionale "Pietro Griffo", Agrigento). Head S352 (below).

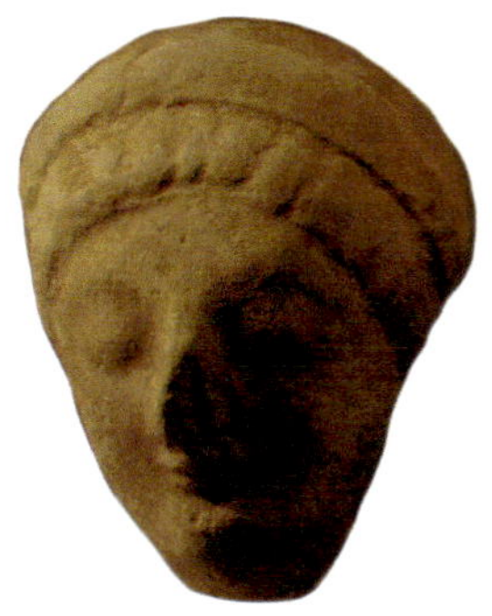

Figure 1b: Head similar to 15-17. Inv. no. S352 (Museo Archeologico Regionale "Pietro Griffo", Agrigento).

forehead and has a rounded tip, but small nostrils. The lips of the slightly curved up mouth are thin. The fringe of hair on the short forehead in a thick band consists of small vertical bulbs. Above this, a rim might indicate a veil. The indistinct shape on the side of the fringe might indicate an ear. This would be impressed after moulding.

‣ *Comparable objects:* Possibly from the same mould series as heads **12** and **13**. Marconi places this head among the Ionian faces, but I think the face is not as fat.

No.15, 16, 17

‣ *Museum and Inventory number:* Mus. Agrigento S452; S339; S338

‣ *Findspot and context:* City Sanctuary

‣ *Publications:* -

‣ *Dimensions in cm:* h.4.5; 4.3; 6.2

‣ *Material:* Terracotta. Many insertions. Dried clay caused cracks. Fingerprints on back.

‣ *Techniques:* Front moulded.

‣ *Colour:* Reddish-yellow 5 YR 7/6 (all)

‣ *Date:* Last quarter of the 6th century BCE

‣ *Workshop:* Unknown

‣ *Typology:* Block-like body: group 1a(?)

‣ *Short description:* Heads of figurines. The last, **17**, including the hair next to the sides of the neck. Very specific shape: rounded head with parted, smooth hair. Her chin is sturdy, and she has pointed cheeks. She has large eyes and a small mouth with pronounced lips. Though the mouth itself is not particularly curling, the deep dimples and lifted cheeks give the impression of a smile. Straight back.

‣ *Comparable objects:* These three are from the same mould. The round face and the absence of a polos indicate that it was probably the head of a simple or block-like figurine. Another head from Akragas is probably from the same mould series. Breitenstein 1945, p.125 fig.18, Nat. Mus. Copenhagen. Another two heads from the same mould, also from Akragas, and even broken at the same heights: British Mus. Inv. no.1931,0513.6 and 1931,0513.5 respectively h.7.7 and 6cm. Higgins 1954 301, no.1097-1098, pl.150-151. See museum website. Except for the hair divided into 'tongues,' the heads are very similar to S352 (fig.1) and S354 from Akragas, Mus. Agrigento.

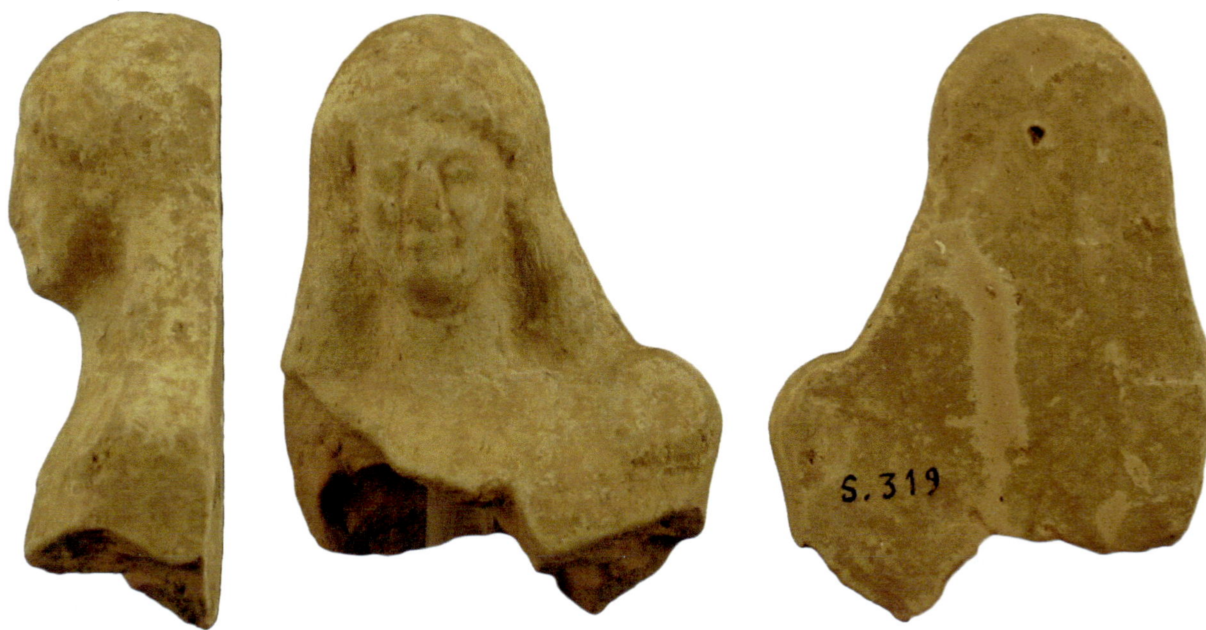

No. 18; Scale 1:1 (Museo Archeologico Regionale "Pietro Griffo", Agrigento).

No.18

- *Museum and Inventory number:* Mus. Agrigento S319
- *Findspot and context:* City Sanctuary
- *Publications:* -
- *Dimensions in cm:* h.8.0
- *Material:* Terracotta. From worn mould. Lighter coloured slip layer. Lime-spalling on back of the head. Head and neck are solid.
- *Techniques:* Front moulded, flattened nose
- *Colour:* Very pale brown 10 YR 7/4; Inside: Pink 7.5 YR 7/4
- *Date:* Last quarter of the 6th century BCE
- *Workshop:* Unknown
- *Typology:* Block-like body: group 1a(?)
- *Short description:* Upper part of a figurine with left shoulder. Chubby oval face with large flattened nose, chin and jaw. Her fringe originally had bulbs, but is now smoothed. Hair along the side of the neck is plain and slightly flaring. She wears a veil and a large round fibula on her shoulder. She wears small knob earrings. The back is very straight.
- *Comparable objects:* The facial features are reminiscent of **9**.

No.19

- *Museum and Inventory number:* Mus. Agrigento C378
- *Findspot and context:* Akragas
- *Publications:* -
- *Dimensions in cm:* h.13.4
- *Material:* Terracotta
- *Techniques:* Front moulded. Clay on left side of the face folded. Made in a mould by layering. Layer broken off at many places. Face seems preserved relatively well, compared to the body but from a worn mould.
- *Colour:* Pink 7.5 YR 8/3
- *Date:* Last decade of the 6th century BCE

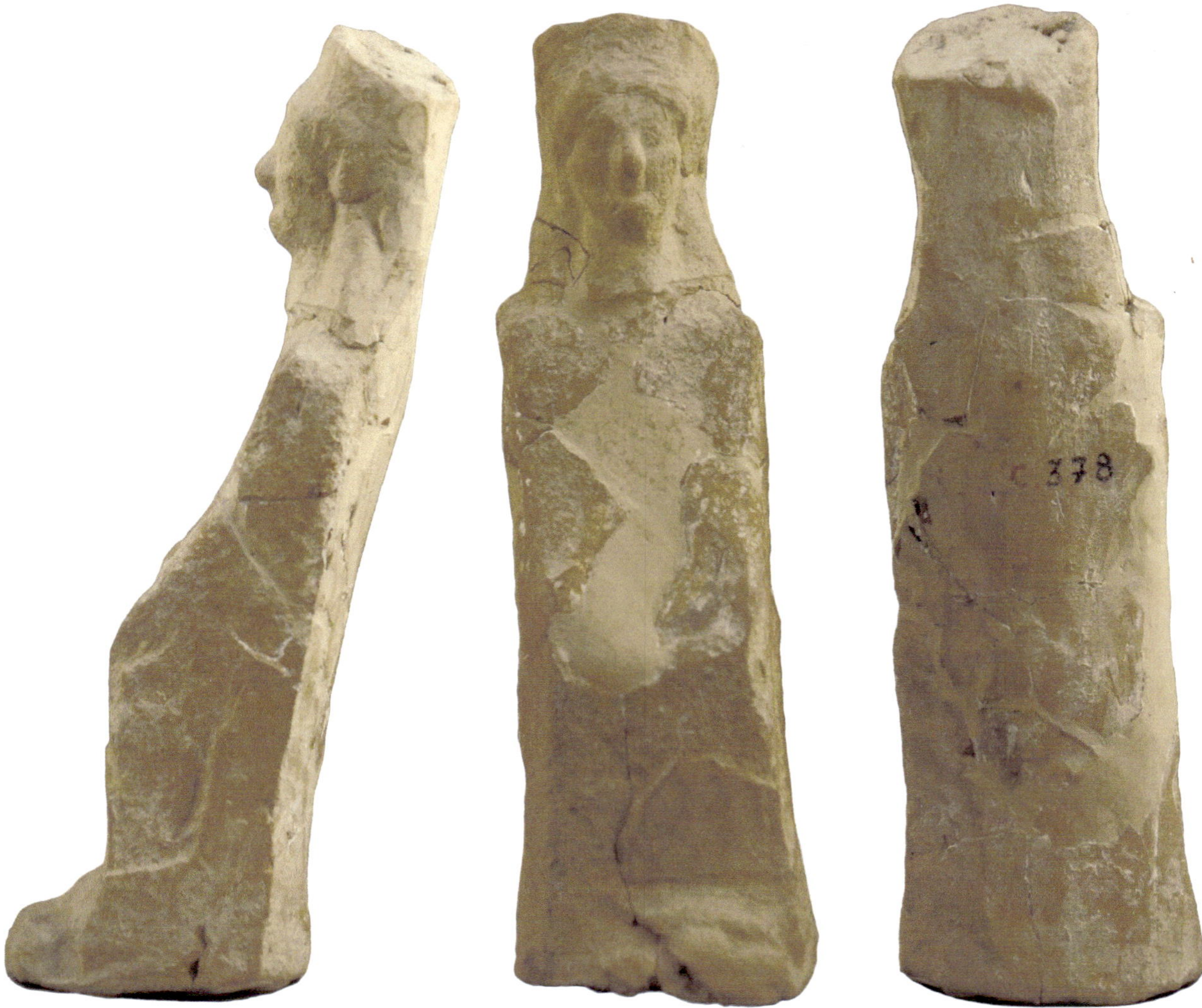

No. 19; Scale 1:1 (Museo Archeologico Regionale "Pietro Griffo", Agrigento).

- ***Workshop:*** Workshop of the convex back (?)
- ***Typology:*** Block-like body: group 1a
- ***Short description:*** Nearly complete figurine, infill at front and knees, several fragments. Chubby face with pronounced chin and fleshy cheeks. She has a large nose with a round tip. Her mouth is small, and her smile creates deep dimples next to it. She has large round eyes. Her fringe on her forehead is wavy, but quite indistinct. Her hair bulges out slightly next to the sides of her neck. She wears a wide, low polos with a small rim, just above the fringe. Simple block-like body. Knees bending straight down, sloping upper part of body. She wears an apron, of which only a small part is left. It reaches her ankles and covers the front. An undergarment is draped over her feet, which are placed on a footstool. Flat back.
- ***Comparable objects:*** The simple body and chubby face are reminiscent of **11**, but it is not from the same mould. The head with its pronounced cheeks and sizeable nose, is probably from the same mould as the head of a figurine dated to around 490-470 BCE from Akragas, now in Mus. Karlsruhe inv. no.B 418. Schürmann 1989, p.90, no.307, tav.52. Because of the small size of the figurine's body, several generations and variations later in the series, the head from such a small figurine fitted. See **137** in comparison. Both head with low polos and block-shaped body are comparable with a figurine from S. Anna. This figurine wears five small oval pendants on her chest Trombi 2016, p.101-2, fig.9.

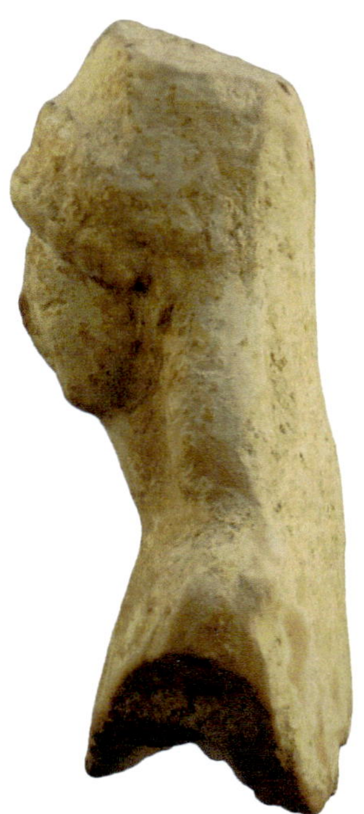
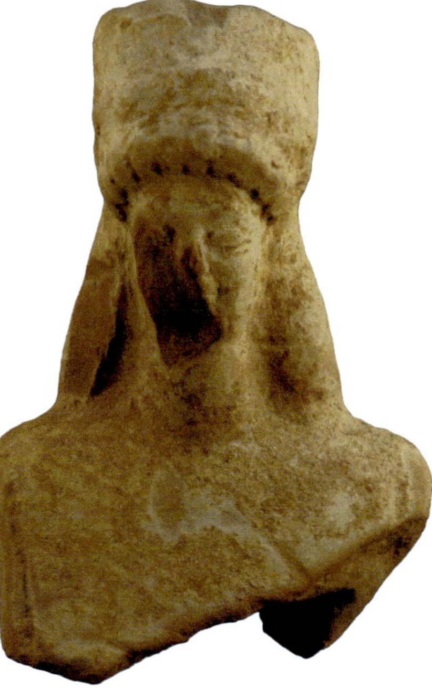

No. 20; Scale 1:1 (Museo Archeologico Regionale "Pietro Griffo", Agrigento).

No.20

- *Museum and Inventory number:* Mus. Agrigento C387
- *Findspot and context:* Akragas
- *Publications:* -
- *Dimensions in cm:* h.8.5
- *Material:* Terracotta
- *Techniques:* Front moulded.
- *Colour:* Pinkish white 5 YR 8/2
- *Date:* Last quarter of the 6th century BCE
- *Workshop:* Workshop of the white clay
- *Typology:* Block-like body: group 1a
- *Short description:* Upper part of a figurine: chest and head of a simple bodied female figurine. Face and hair heavily damaged. Fine face with sharp eyes with eyelids. The mouth, directly below the nose, has thick lips. A large and thick fringe of hair in large bulbs is placed around her forehead. On top of it in the same size, she wears a low polos with a wide rim. Next to the sides of her neck, but placed rather towards the back, her hair is bulging. The space between neck and hair is deeper. On her straight, almost rectangular upper body, the apron leaves just a small part visible on both right and left side. The back is straight.
- *Comparable objects:* The body is similar to **10** and **12**. Of course, nothing indicates that this figurine was not seated on a chair. It could therefore also belong to iconographic type 1b and compared with figurine **24**.

No.21

- *Museum and Inventory number:* Mus. Agrigento 23120
- *Findspot and context:* Necropolis di Contrada Mosè. Besides several terracotta figurines of different sorts, there is miniature pottery, oil lamps and no.**54**, **83** and **173** from a deposit pit (fig.4 and 22).
- *Publications:* Veder Greco: le necrópolis di Agrigento 1988, p.271
- *Dimensions in cm:* h.16.1
- *Material:* terracotta
- *Techniques:* Front moulded. Handmade chair.
- *Colour:* Pink 7.5 YR 7/3
- *Date:* 490-470 BCE
- *Workshop:* Workshop of the white clay
- *Typology:* Block-like body type, but also chubby-face: group 2d
- *Short description:* Partly restored figurine with significant infill on the lower body. Simple body, flaring at the shoulders, seated on block-shaped chair that follows the outline of the body and slightly runs up. Large triangular head with big eyes and large nose. Her lips are thin and curve up in a smile. Big ears with triangular earrings, rings with triangular pendant. She has a short forehead, above which a fringe is parted in the middle and divided into small vertical bulbs. Her hair on the sides of her neck has some structure and falls down to her shoulders behind the ears and earrings. She wears a hairband or veil with a rim. Rounded back, straighter at the shoulders.
- *Comparable objects:* Face and earrings comparable to **179**. The body type with flaring shoulders and the sitting position on a small block is similar to fig.G IV, a from Veio, complete 15cm, Vagnetti 1971, p.67, tav.XXX. She describes that the object derives from the 'Athena Lindia' -type.

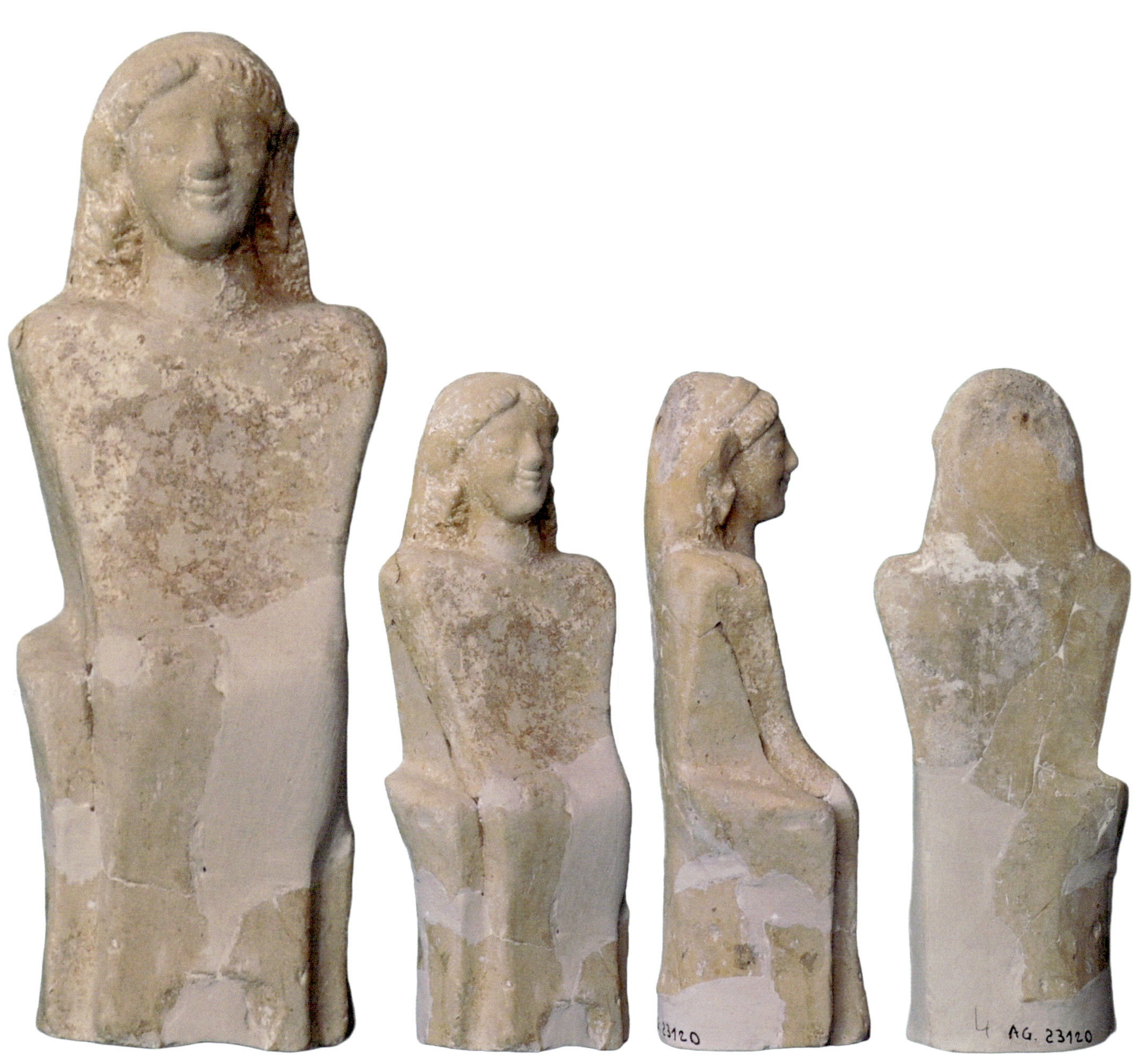

No. 21 front; Scale 1:1; Different angles; Scale 1:1½; (Museo Archeologico Regionale "Pietro Griffo", Agrigento).

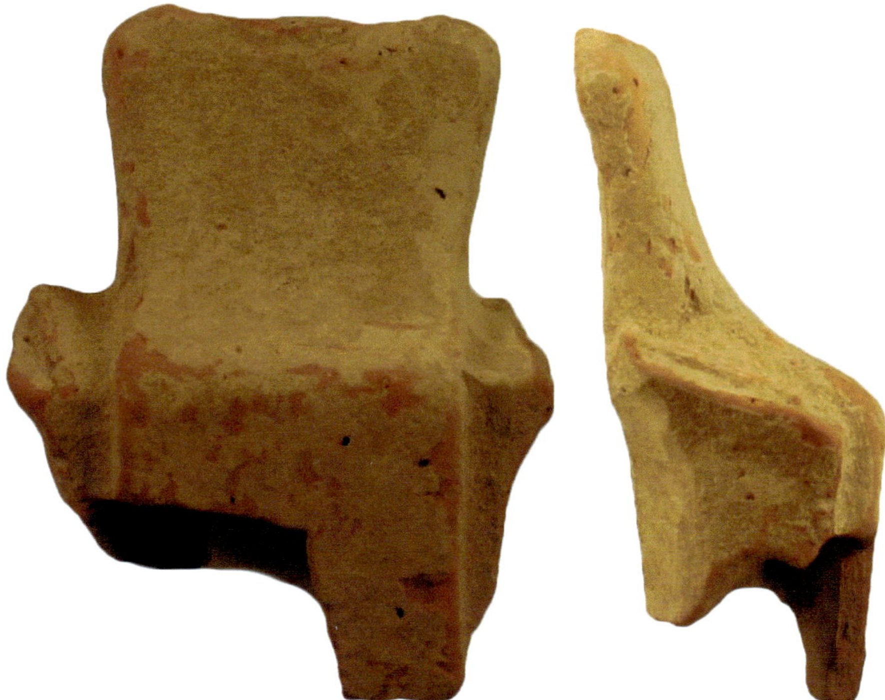

No. 22; Scale 1:1 (Museo Archeologico Regionale "Pietro Griffo", Agrigento).

No.22

- ***Museum and Inventory number:*** Mus. Agrigento 'without number'
- ***Findspot and context:*** City Sanctuary
- ***Publications:*** -
- ***Dimensions in cm:*** h.9.2
- ***Material:*** Terracotta. Many insertions, fingerprints.
- ***Techniques:*** Front moulded. Probably a lighter coloured slip layer: inside dark red. Bench partly widened out of the mould.
- ***Colour:*** Very pale brown 10 YR 7/3
- ***Date:*** Last decade of the 6th century BCE
- ***Workshop:*** Unknown
- ***Typology:*** Block-like body: group 1b
- ***Short description:*** Headless figurine, feet and bench on both sides broken off. Simple body, with rounded shoulders; slightly flaring upper body. Her knees are bent at a sharp angle. The part below her knees is straight. She wears an apron of which the upper hem is visible on the chest. The bench has a short sloping seat and just a bit wider than the body. The edge of it is visible by a line, but the coroplast decided to make it a little wider, out of the mould. The front of the chair curves inwards, down the sides of the lower body. Back straight at upper part, rounded for lower part.
- ***Comparable objects:*** The figurine is not typical of its sort, because the angle of the body is greater: the upper body is straighter than **27**, for example. The body is relatively broad.

Very similar, even in size, is a figurine from Sicily in the British Mus. Inv. no.1956,0216.34, headless h.9cm, See museum website.

No.23

- ***Museum and Inventory number:*** Mus. Agrigento S892
- ***Findspot and context:*** City Sanctuary
- ***Publications:*** Fiertler 2001, p.70, tav.X BIIIa
- ***Dimensions in cm:*** h.15.2
- ***Material:*** Terracotta.
- ***Techniques:*** Front moulded. Small vent at the back, max. 2cm wide. Finger impressions visible on the inside of the back. Lighter coloured slip layer.
- ***Colour:*** Light brown 7.5 YR 6/4
- ***Date:*** Last decade of the 6th century BCE
- ***Workshop:*** Workshop of the convex back(?)
- ***Typology:*** Block-like body: group 1b
- ***Short description:*** Nearly complete figurine. Oval face, very indistinct, with large nose and narrow mouth. Fringe of smooth hair and straight falling down on the sides of the neck. She wears a medium-sized, slightly flaring polos. The polos is narrower than the head. Simple body with a short neck. Block-like body slightly bent at the knees and wider at the rounded shoulders. Feet sticking out under garment, placed on a small footstool of the same width as the body. She sits on a wide bench, which bends out from the height of the feet to the seat. The back is rounded, and smoothed by hand. Small vent hole at the back.
- ***Comparable objects:*** Similar features, but not from the same mould as **28**.

The figurine is reminiscent of the characteristics of **33** and onwards, but is simpler.

- ***Other notes:*** The hole in the back was not very common at Akragas. The figurine might be imported from Selinous where such a vent hole was commonly applied.

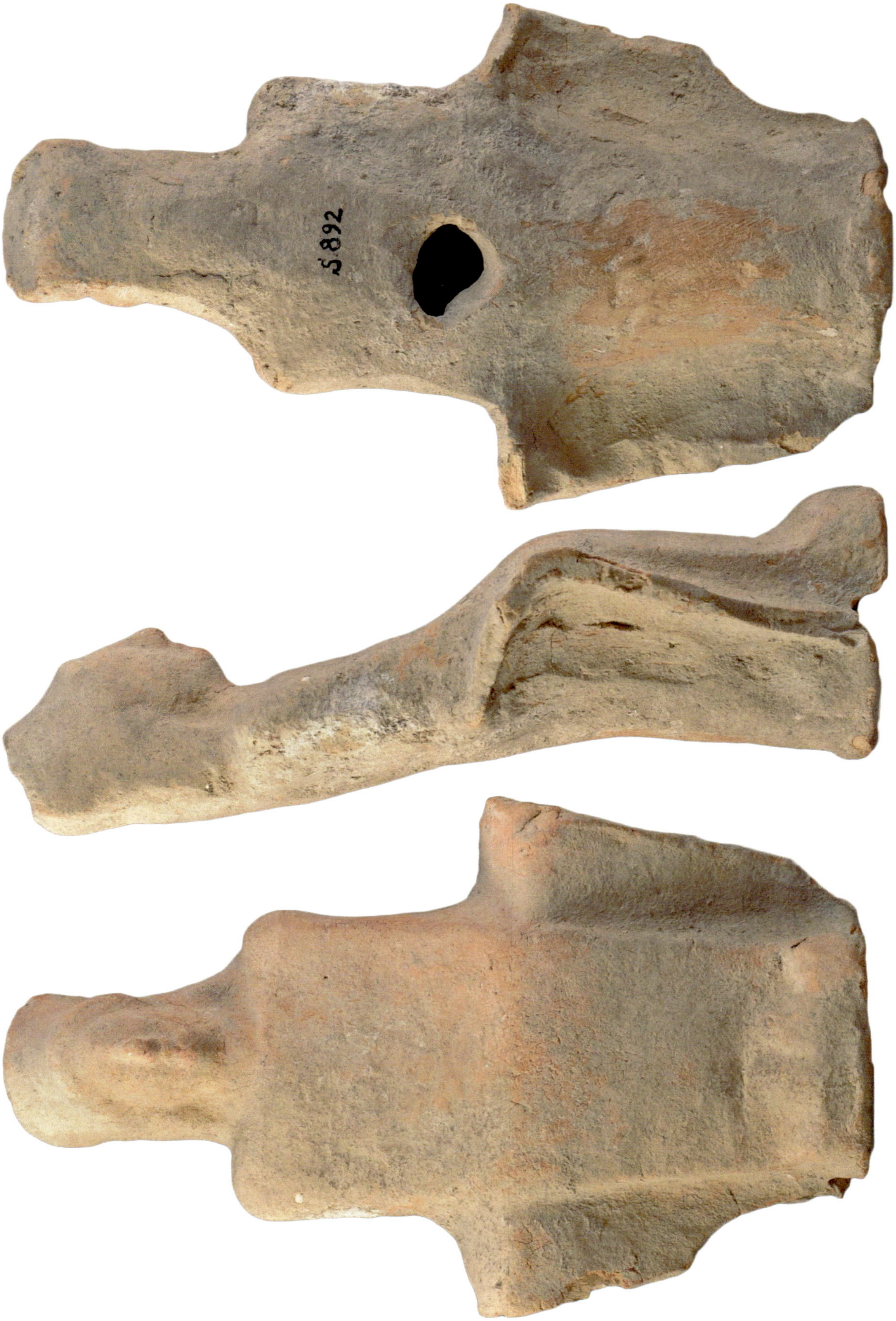

No. 23; Scale 1:1 (Museo Archeologico Regionale "Pietro Griffo", Agrigento).

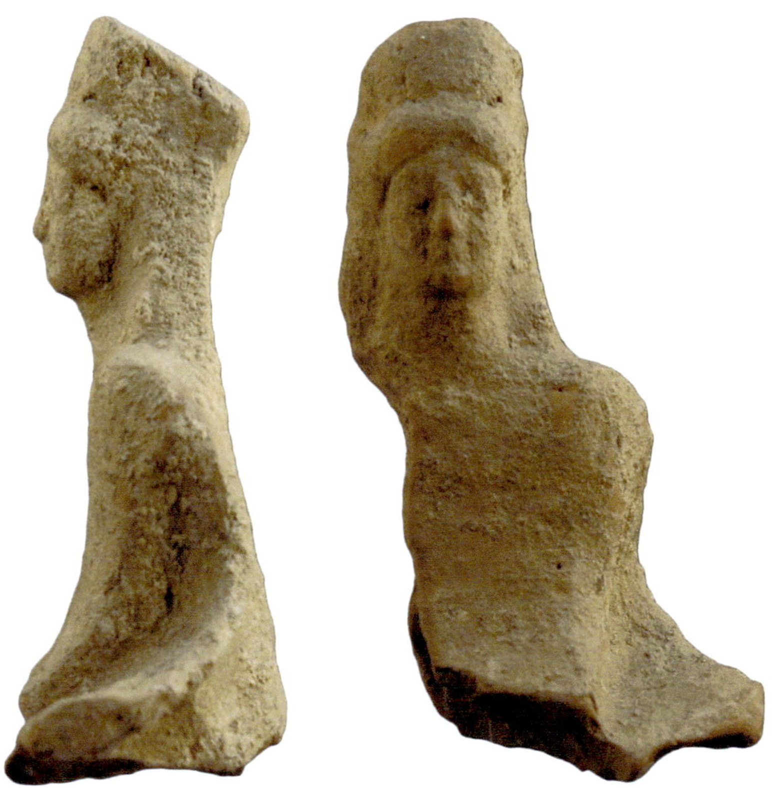

No. 24; Scale 1:1 (Museo Archeologico Regionale "Pietro Griffo", Agrigento).

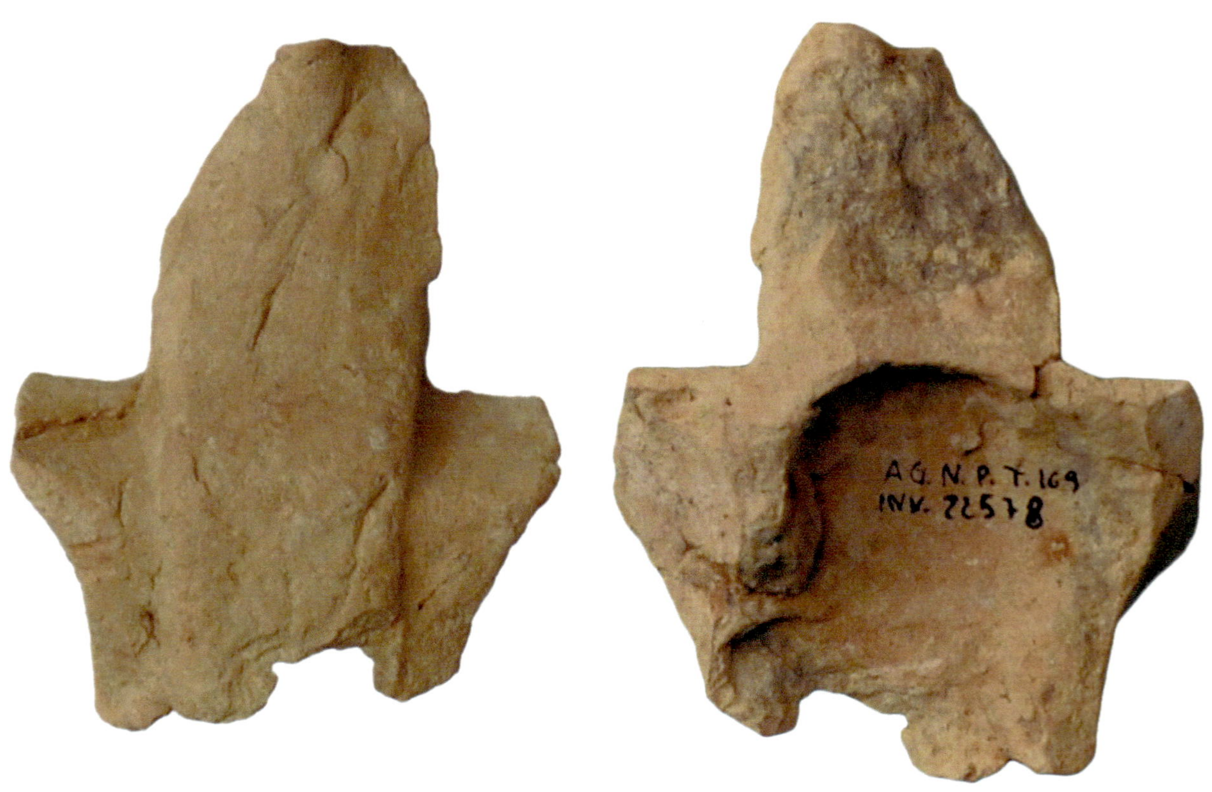

No. 25; Scale 1:2 (Museo Archeologico Regionale "Pietro Griffo", Agrigento).

No.24

‣ *Museum and Inventory number:* Mus. Agrigento C377
‣ *Findspot and context:* Akragas
‣ *Publications:* -
‣ *Dimensions in cm:* h.10.1
‣ *Material:* Terracotta
‣ *Techniques:* Front moulded. The body is solid from the chest onwards. Handmade chair.
‣ *Colour:* Pink 5 YR 7/3
‣ *Date:* Last decade of the 6th century BCE
‣ *Workshop:* Unknown
‣ *Typology:* Block-like body: group 1b
‣ *Short description:* Upper and left part of a figurine, broken from the knees downwards and the right part.

Oval face with large bulging eyes, sizeable nose and narrow mouth with thick lips. A smooth thick fringe of hair on her forehead seems parted in the middle. Smooth and straight hair falls down on both sides of the neck. She wears a medium-sized polos without rim, which leans slightly to the back. She is seated on a bench. Her body widens slightly towards the rounded shoulders. There is no further adornment nor arms.

‣ *Comparable objects:* The face is very similar to **63** and is reminiscent also of **66-68**, though it has no rim on the polos. It is similar to a figurine from Grammichele, Mus. Syracuse Inv. no.14319.

No.25

‣ *Museum and Inventory number:* Mus. Agrigento 22578
‣ *Findspot and context:* Necropolis di Contrada Pezzino, tomb 169, together with two other figurines, 63 and 71.
‣ *Publications:* Veder Greco: le necrópolis di Agrigento 1988, p.307

De Miro 1989, p.36, tav.XXVI

‣ *Dimensions in cm:* h.8.6
‣ *Material:* Terracotta. Inferior quality of clay.
‣ *Techniques:* Moulded. Clay folded in the mould. It seems moulded without care.
‣ *Colour:* Pink 7.5 YR 7/4
‣ *Date:* Last decade of the 6th century BCE
‣ *Workshop:* Unknown
‣ *Typology:* Block-like body: group 1b
‣ *Short description:* Body and bench of a figurine. Damaged surface and edges. Block-like body with bent knees, rounded on the edges, seated on a wide bench, curving inwards along the body in front on each side. Large vent hole in the back (?).
‣ *Comparable objects:* Its simply shaped body on a wide bench is reminiscent of **22** and **23**. Again, a vent hole was not a common feature in Akragantine coroplastics. It might be an imported object, but of Sicilian origin.

No.26 (not illustrated)

‣ *Museum and Inventory number:* Mus. Agrigento 20.195
‣ *Findspot and context:* One of the sanctuaries
‣ *Publications:* -
‣ *Dimensions in cm:* h.12.7
‣ *Material:* Terracotta
‣ *Techniques:* Front moulded Probably a lighter coloured slip layer: inside dark red.
‣ *Colour:* Pink 7.5 YR 7/4
‣ *Date:* Last decade of the 6th century BCE
‣ *Workshop:* Workshop of the convex back(?)
‣ *Typology:* Block-like body: group 1b
‣ *Short description:* Middle part of a figurine, head and feet broken off.

A simple body with backwards bending rounded shoulders. She wears an apron, which covers the sloping front of the body almost to the sides. The hems are marked clearly. She is seated on a chair with a sloping seat. The front curves inwards, along the shape of the lower body. Back straight at upper part, rounded lower part.

‣ *Comparable objects:* The figurine is similar to **29**, but larger. Because of missing parts and re-working after moulding it is not possible to say whether it is from the same mould series. It is similar to **27**.

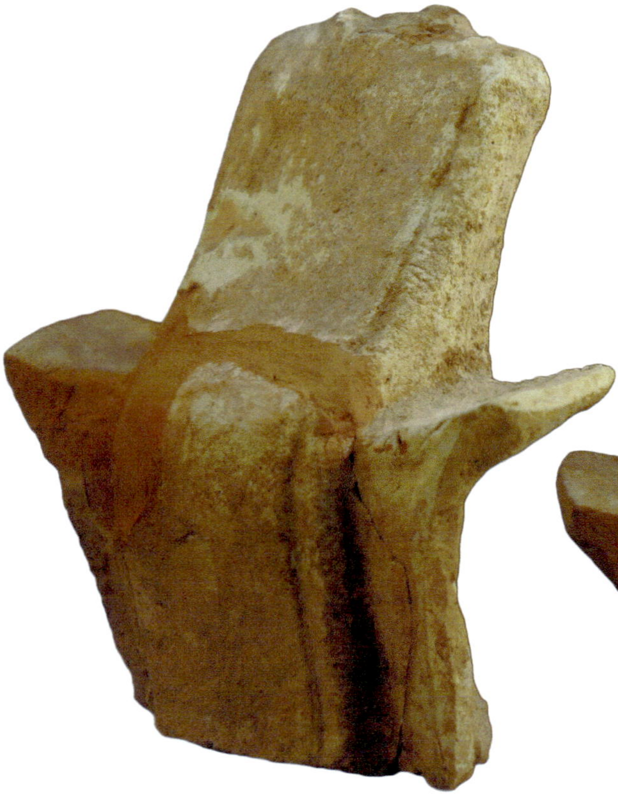

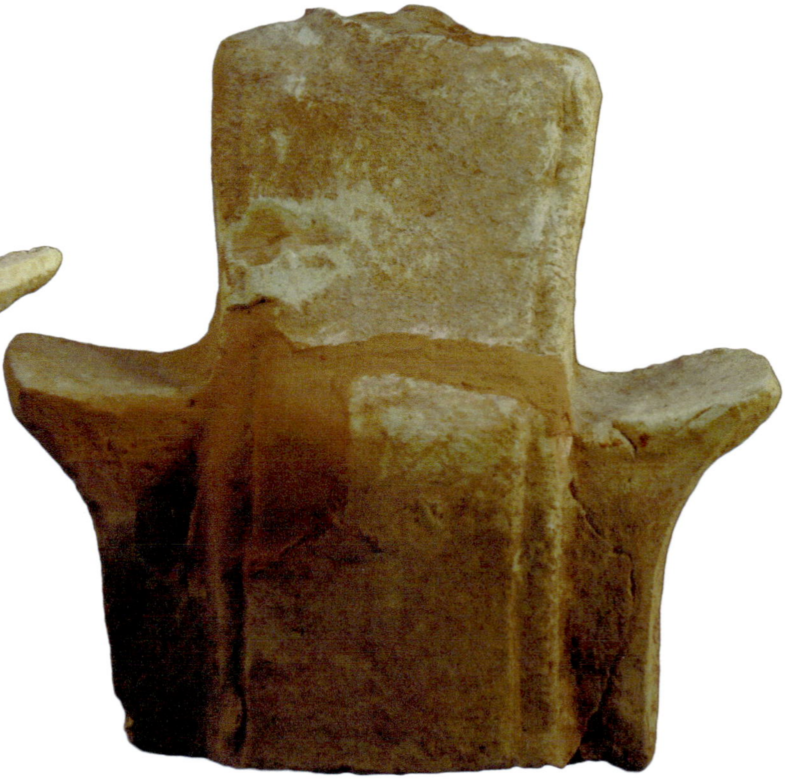

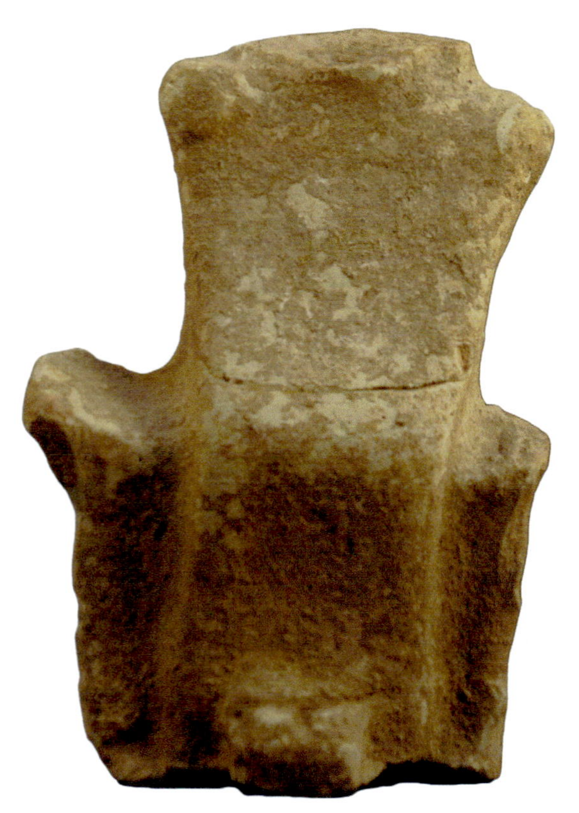

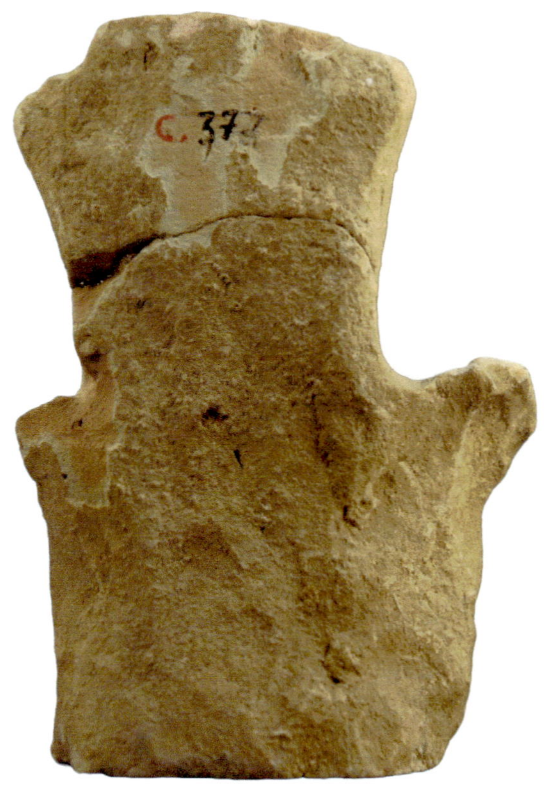

No. 27 (left page); Scale 1:1 (Museo Archeologico Regionale "Pietro Griffo", Agrigento).

No.27

- *Museum and Inventory number:* Mus. Agrigento C374
- *Findspot and context:* Akragas
- *Publications:* -
- *Dimensions in cm:* h.10.2
- *Material:* Terracotta
- *Techniques:* Front moulded. Bench handmade. Fingerprints on bench.
- *Colour:* Very Pale Brown 10 YR 8/2
- *Date:* Last decade of the 6th century BCE
- *Workshop:* Workshop of the convex back(?)
- *Typology:* Block-like body: group 1b
- *Short description:* Headless figurine in several fragments, restored with considerable infill on lap and knee. Very simple block-like body, seated on an upwards-curving bench. Its pose is characterised by a sloping upper body and an angle at the height of the knees. No feet or arms. An apron covers the front of the figurine, leaving just an edge visible at the side.
- *Comparable objects:* Similar to **29**, though without feet. The upwards-curving bench and the simple body are reminiscent of **28**.

No. 28 (left page); Scale 1:1 (Museo Archeologico Regionale "Pietro Griffo", Agrigento).

No.28

- *Museum and Inventory number:* Mus. Agrigento C373
- *Findspot and context:* Akragas
- *Publications:* -
- *Dimensions in cm:* h.10.1
- *Material:* Terracotta
- *Techniques:* Front moulded. Bench handmade. Coarsely shaped rear. Solid upper part. Drying while standing might have caused the bending to the left. Possibly lighter coloured slip layer.
- *Colour:* Very Pale Brown 10 YR 8/2
- *Date:* Last decade of the 6th century BCE
- *Workshop:* Unknown
- *Typology:* Block-like body: group 1b
- *Short description:* Headless figurine in two fragments, restored. The figurine bends over to the left. Seated on an upwards-curving bench. Round fibulae with a point in the middle, on each shoulder. Simple block-like body, though with rounder shapes and more flaring shoulders. Feet on a small footstool. Dress draped over upper part of the feet, but no indication of another garment.
- *Comparable objects:* Similar features, but not from the same mould as **23**. Possibly from the same mould as a complete figurine. Mus. Catania Inv. no.MC 5406. Pautasso 1996 67, no.59, tav.VII h.12.7cm dated to the sixth to beginning of the fifth century BCE.
- *Other notes:* Glue on the neck might indicate that there was a head attached.

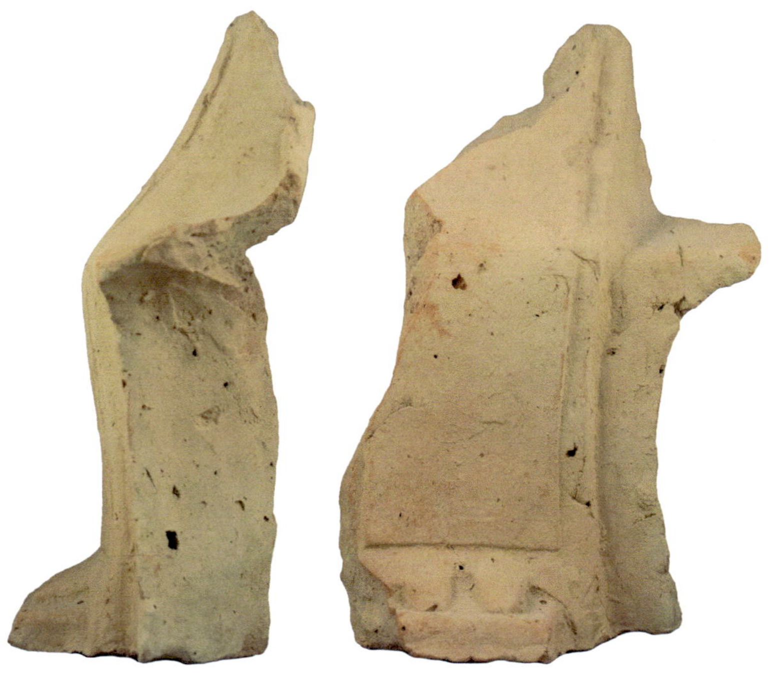

No. 29; Scale 1:2 (Museo Archeologico Regionale "Pietro Griffo", Agrigento).

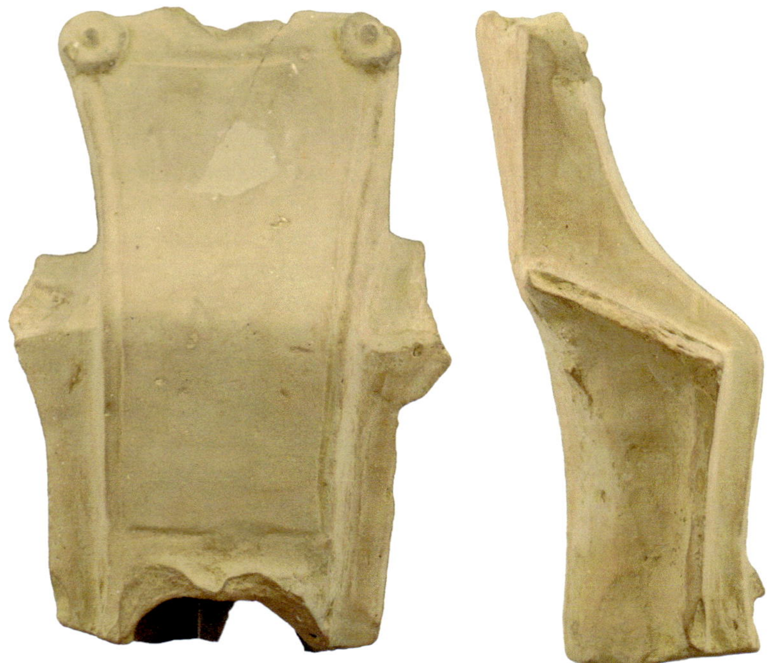

No. 30; Scale 1:2 (Museo Archeologico Regionale "Pietro Griffo", Agrigento).

No.29

- *Museum and Inventory number:* Mus. Agrigento 15.1355 (2307)
- *Findspot and context:* West Archaic sanctuary underlying the bouleuterion
- *Publications:* -
- *Dimensions in cm:* h.16.9
- *Material:* Terracotta. Several instances of lime-spalling.

The difference in colour on one figurine might be caused by clay mixtures that are not well kneaded, like on 29, or the coincidental closeness to another object in the kiln when the figurines where fired.

- *Techniques:* Front moulded. Handmade bench. From a relatively new mould.
- *Colour:* Pink 7.5 YR 7/3
- *Date:* Last decade of the 6th century BCE
- *Workshop:* Workshop of the convex back(?)
- *Typology:* Block-like body: group 1b
- *Short description:* Lower left front part of a figurine. Back, head and right side broken off. Figurine with a

simple body, sloping upper part and bent at the knees, seated on a small bench, with a front curving inwards down next to the lower body. She wears an apron over an undergarment, which is draped over the feet and the footstool. Feet in shoes are placed a bit apart from each other on a small, low block-like footstool. Back straight at upper part, rounded at the lower part.

‣ *Comparable objects:* Iconographically similar to **30**. It shares with **30** its size and sharpness. The figurine is similar to **26**, but larger. It is reminiscent of **27** also, though it has feet.

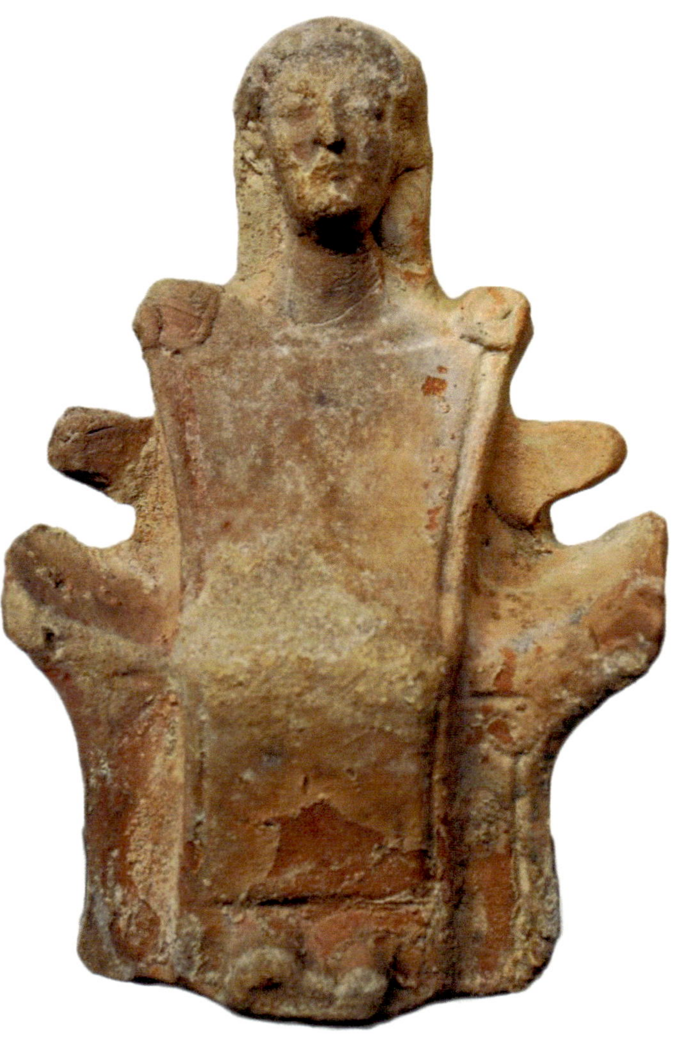

Figure 2: A figurine probably from Akragas from the same mould series as no.30 but two or three generations later and complete. Scale 1:1 © Trustees of the British Museum.

No.30

‣ *Museum and Inventory number:* Mus. Agrigento S93
‣ *Findspot and context:* City Sanctuary
‣ *Publications:* Fiertler 2001, p.61, tav.XII, type BXVI
Marconi 1929, p.58, fig.35a
‣ *Dimensions in cm:* h.17
‣ *Material:* Terracotta. Several shell inclusions.
‣ *Techniques:* Front moulded. Handmade chair.
‣ *Colour:* Very pale brown 10 YR 7/3
‣ *Date:* Last decade of the 6th century BCE
‣ *Workshop:* Workshop of the convex back
‣ *Typology:* Block-like body: group 1b
‣ *Short description:* Headless figurine. Chair on both sides and feet broken off. Shoulder broken, restored with infill. Figurine from a fresh mould. She wears an apron, which hangs in front of her body, between the fibulae, just slightly smaller than the block-like shaped body. It has a hem on the chest also. Round fibulae with a knob in the middle on the shoulders. A line above the dress suggests a pectoral band. Very smooth surface. Feet were placed on a footstool probably. The chair has a sloping seat and curves slightly down at the front, along the sides of the body. On the left, the front of the chair has an angle. Back straight at upper part, rounded lower part.

‣ *Comparable objects:* The figurine is comparable to **26**, which lacks the fibulae. It shares many features with **29**, also its size and sharpness. It is very likely that figurine from Akragas or Selinous is from the same mould series, headless h.18cm in the British Mus. Inv. no.1956,0216.20. See museum website. Also another exemplar from Akragas or Gelas could well be from the same mould series, two or three generations later. It is complete but just h.13.4cm. The latter has a chair with ‘ears’ and a characteristic head (see fig.2). British Mus. Inv. no.1953,0825.6. See museum website. Another figurine with the same head as the figurine above but a slightly less detailed body and different hand-modelled chair is again, however, larger: 15.7cm. Christiansen et al. 1974, p.37 nr. 214. According to Fiertler there were two from the City Sanctuary, excavated by Marconi. Fiertler 2001, p.61, n.73. A figurine, complete 15cm, with similar body, seat and fibulae is depicted on a drawing in Winter 1903, p.125, no.5. A figurine with similar body and fibulae with a knob in the middle, but turned into flowers: Louvre Inv. no.MNB 1716, complete, 15.5cm. Mollard Besques 1954, p.79, tav.LII, B 554.

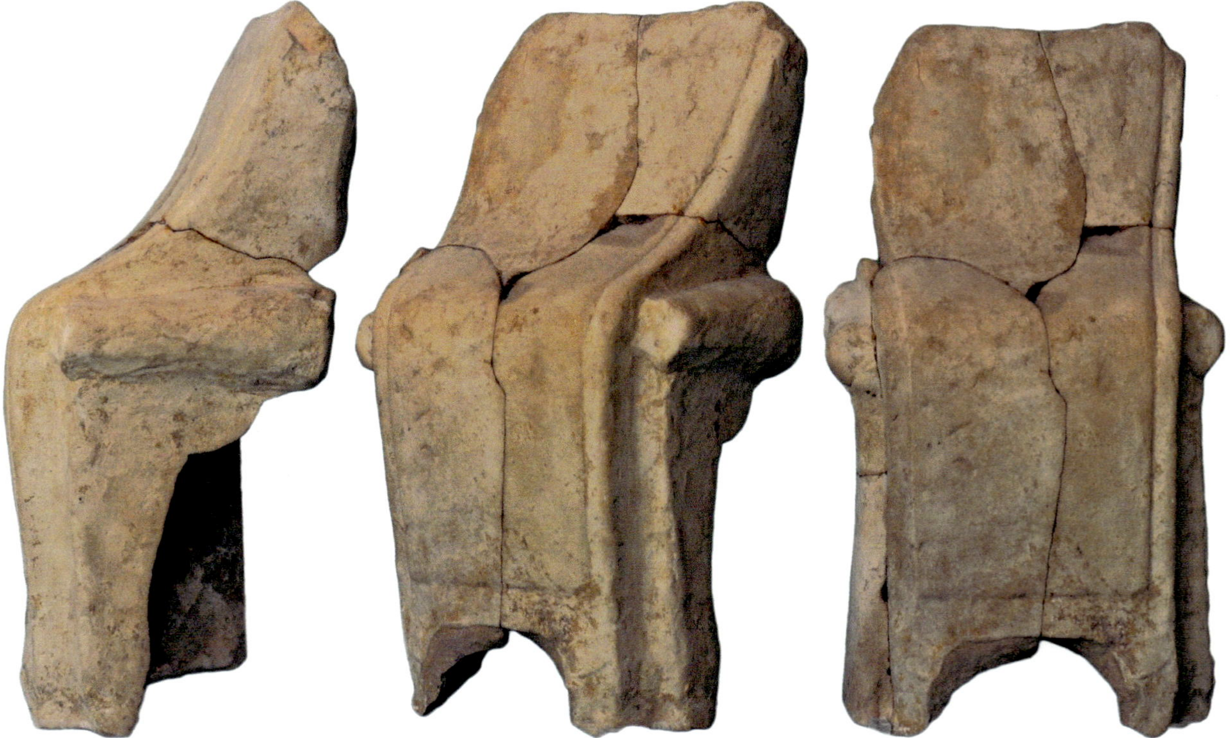

No. 31; Scale 1:2 (Museo Archeologico Regionale "Pietro Griffo", Agrigento).

No.31

- *Museum and Inventory number:* Mus. Agrigento 20417
- *Findspot and context:* S. Anna (?)
- *Publications:* -
- *Dimensions in cm:* h.18.8 w. 10.3 d. 9.1
- *Material:* Terracotta.
- *Techniques:* Front moulded.
- *Colour:* Light grey 2.5 YR 7.2
- *Date:* Last decade of the 6th century BCE
- *Workshop:* Unknown
- *Typology:* Block-like body: group 1b
- *Short description:* Front part of a figurine, head and feet broken off.

Simple block-like body bent at the knees, seated on a high block-shaped chair, with round armrests. She wears an apron, leaving the edges uncovered. It did not reach the feet.

- *Comparable objects:* Mould **32** is very likely from the same series, but a later generation.

Possibly from the same mould series is a complete figurine of 28.3cm tall. Her smoothed shoulders show that handmade clasps were originally applied. Paint residue of dark-red was found on the throne and polos, and blue on the dress. Her face and tall polos are reminiscent of the head 66-68. The large size confirms the early date for the body, but shows evidence also for the early origin of this facial form. Mus. Karlsruhe Inv. no.B411. Schürmann 1989, p.89, no.304, tav.52; Winter 1903, p.125, no.4. A figurine from Selinous has round armrests also: Mus. Palermo Inv. no.SM Pal T292. Dewailly 1992, p.127, fig.92.

No.32

- *Museum and Inventory number:* Mus. Agrigento 8965
- *Findspot and context:* City Sanctuary
- *Publications:* De Miro 2000, p.251, no.1529
- *Dimensions in cm:* h.12
- *Material:* Terracotta.
- *Techniques:* Imprint from an object, the patrix.
- *Colour:* Very pale brown 10 YR 7/4

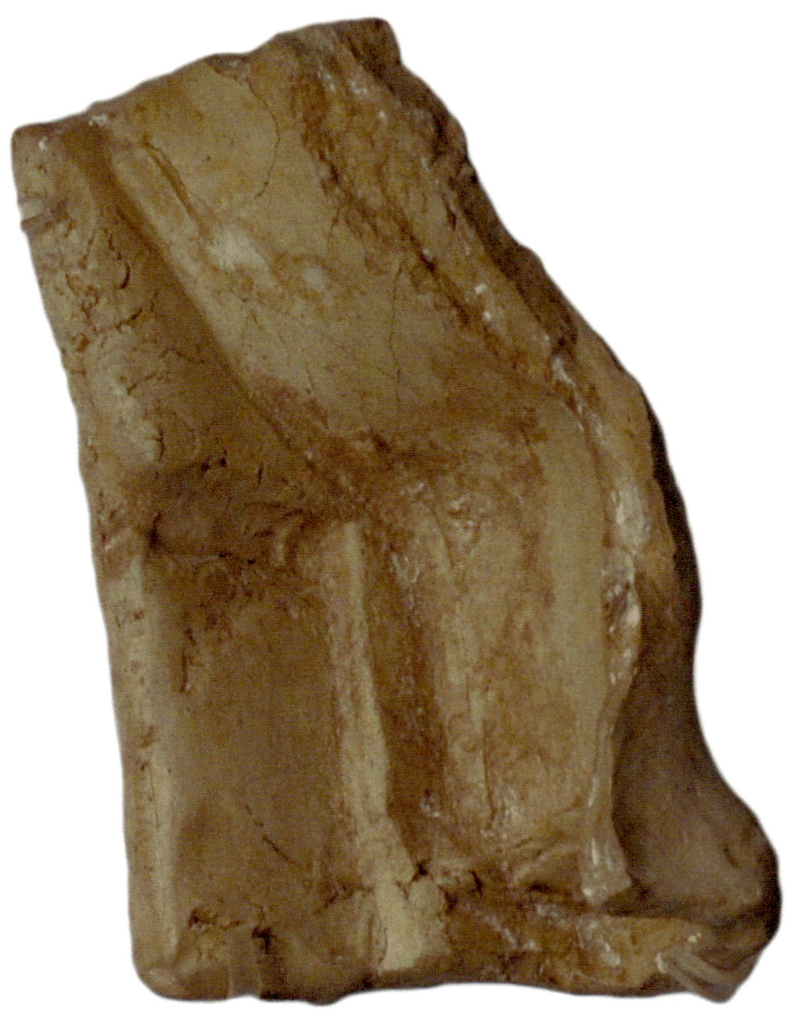

No. 32 front; Scale 1:1;
Below: cast and different angles; Scale 1:1½; (Museo Archeologico Regionale "Pietro Griffo", Agrigento).

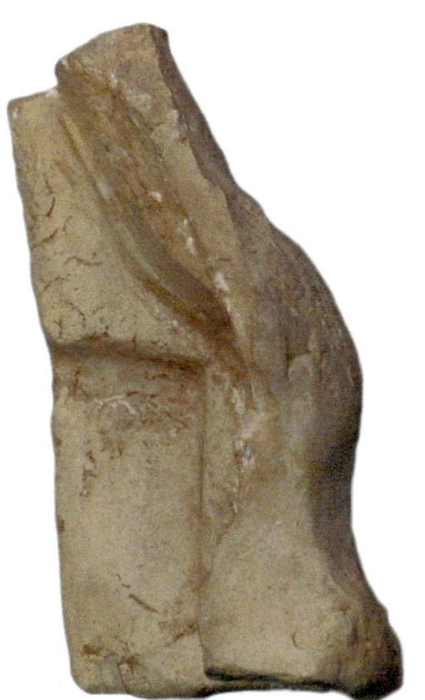

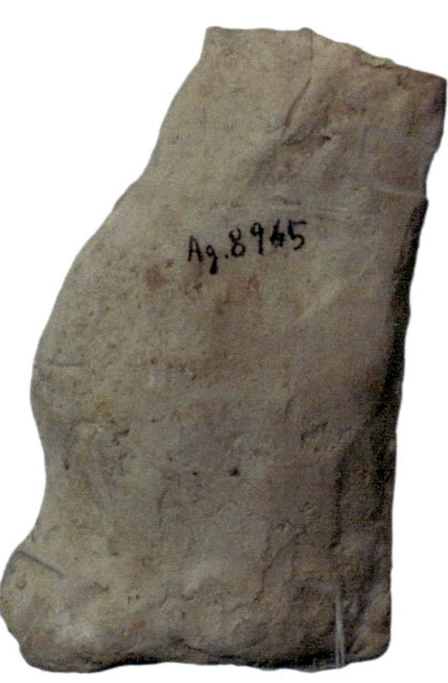

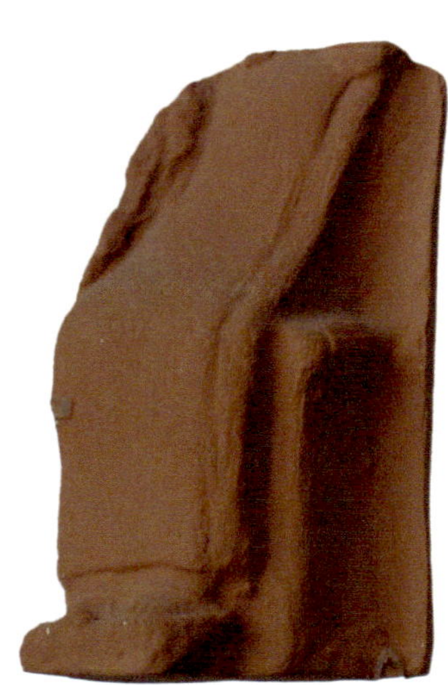

‣ *Date:* Last decade of the 6th century BCE
‣ *Workshop:* Unknown
‣ *Typology:* Block-like body: group 1b
‣ *Short description:* Part of a mould of a seated figurine. Upper part broken off. Block-like body with a sloping upper part and bent at the knees, without arms, but with feet and fingers indicated. She wears an apron that covers the body almost completely; just an edge is left on the sides. The apron reaches above the ankles. Below that, an undergarment is visible, which is longer, reaching the feet and draped over it. She is seated on a block-like chair with rounded edges on the seat. These could be seen as armrests. On the shoulder, which widens slightly, part of a round fibula is visible. The back of the mould is roughly rounded.
‣ *Comparable objects:* Very similar to **30**, probably from the same series, but a younger generation, considering the size.
‣ *Other notes:* Photograph with modern cast on the left.

No.33

‣ *Museum and Inventory number:* Mus. Agrigento S267
‣ *Findspot and context:* City Sanctuary
‣ *Publications:* Marconi 1929 57 fig.33d
‣ *Dimensions in cm:* h.21.5
‣ *Material:* Terracotta.
‣ *Techniques:* Front moulded.
‣ *Colour:* Pink 5 YR 7/4
‣ *Date:* Last decade of the 6th century BCE
‣ *Workshop:* Unknown
‣ *Typology:* Block-like body: group 1b
‣ *Short description:* Nearly complete figurine, lower back part broken off. Small face with large eyes and high arching eyebrows. Her small mouth is smiling. Her fringe of hair

No. 33; Scale 1:2 (Museo Archeologico Regionale "Pietro Griffo", Agrigento).

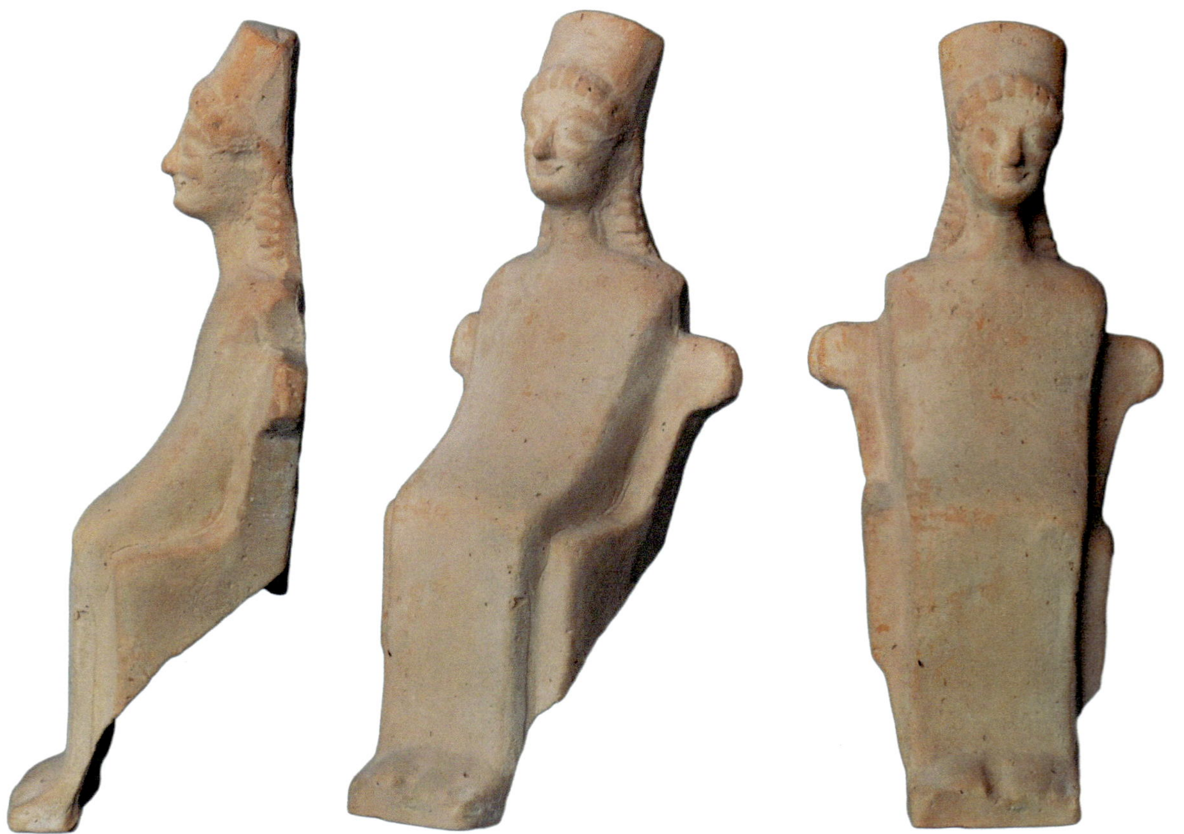

in vertical bulbs continues horizontally along the sides of the neck. She wears a slightly flaring polos. Block-like body, slightly wider at the shoulders and narrower at the feet with a very thin neck. She is seated on a chair, just a bit wider than her body, with a winged back just below the height of the shoulders. The angle of the seat is quite sharp and in contrast with the sloping body. Her feet stick out and are placed on a low footstool with the width of her body. Her dress seems to reach her ankles but is not otherwise indicated.

‣ *Comparable objects:* -

No.34

‣ *Museum and Inventory number:* Mus. Agrigento 1156

‣ *Findspot and context:* In or on the bothros of the Dioscuri Temple

‣ *Publications:* Langlotz and Hirmer 1963, p.263, no.19; Marconi 1929, S. 57

De Miro 2000, p.130, no.30.

‣ *Dimensions in cm:* h.21.3

‣ *Material:* terracotta

‣ *Techniques:* Front moulded, back and possibly upper part of throne made out of slab of clay, sides sharply cut away. Impressions of sharp straight lines on the back, possibly by a blade used for reworking.

‣ *Colour:* Light Yellowish Brown 10 YR 6/4

‣ *Date:* Last decade of the 6th century BCE

‣ *Workshop:* Workshop of the convex back

‣ *Typology:* Block-like body: group 1b

‣ *Short description:* Nearly complete figurine. Piece of the head has been broken off. Crack on the head and right part of the throne, restored. Figurine with narrow, almost triangular face, widening to the upper part. She has large slightly bulging eyes, a long nose with a round tip and large ears. She wears a very tall lean polos and large disc-shaped fibulae. A chiton under her apron is indicated by a fold between feet. Her feet are placed on a footstool and she sits on a wide throne: an upwards-curving bench with curved ending. The winged back seat is much higher on the right side than on the left.

‣ *Comparable objects:* Possibly from the same mould series as **34**. It looks similar, except for the pendants, to **48** and also to **103**, except for the fibulae and arms.

Face and polos look very alike **70**, though the body of that figurine is different, as is the clay colour. The polos of this figurine is more flaring than the one of **70**, narrower and straight, but the reworking of the sides is similar. It is very likely that they come from the same workshop and the coroplast used the same mould for the heads. The chair with winged back and the pose of the figurine are comparable with **33**, though the style of the figurine is very different. The fibulae are similar to **36** and **37**.

No.35

‣ *Museum and Inventory number:* Mus. Agrigento 22583

‣ *Findspot and context:* Necropolis di Contrada Pezzino Tomb 918 together with **70**, two reliefs of which one with a sphinx(?), and a phallus(?)

‣ *Publications:* De Miro 1989, p.37, tav.XXVII

Veder Greco: le necrópolis di Agrigento 1988, p.309.

‣ *Dimensions in cm:* h.14.7

‣ *Material:* terracotta

‣ *Techniques:* Front moulded.

‣ *Colour:* Very pale Brown 10 YR 6/7

‣ *Date:* Last decade of the 6th century BCE

‣ *Workshop:* Workshop of the convex back

‣ *Typology:* Block-like body: group 1b

‣ *Short description:* Lower part of a seated figurine. The body is bent at the knees. She wears an apron of which the outline is clearly marked, reaching almost to the edges of her straight body. Shoes are visible from under the straight dress and placed on a podium. The throne consists of a wide bench, curving down on the front. The backrest, which is visible next to the body, has a winged back.

‣ *Comparable objects:* Possibly from the same mould series as **34**.

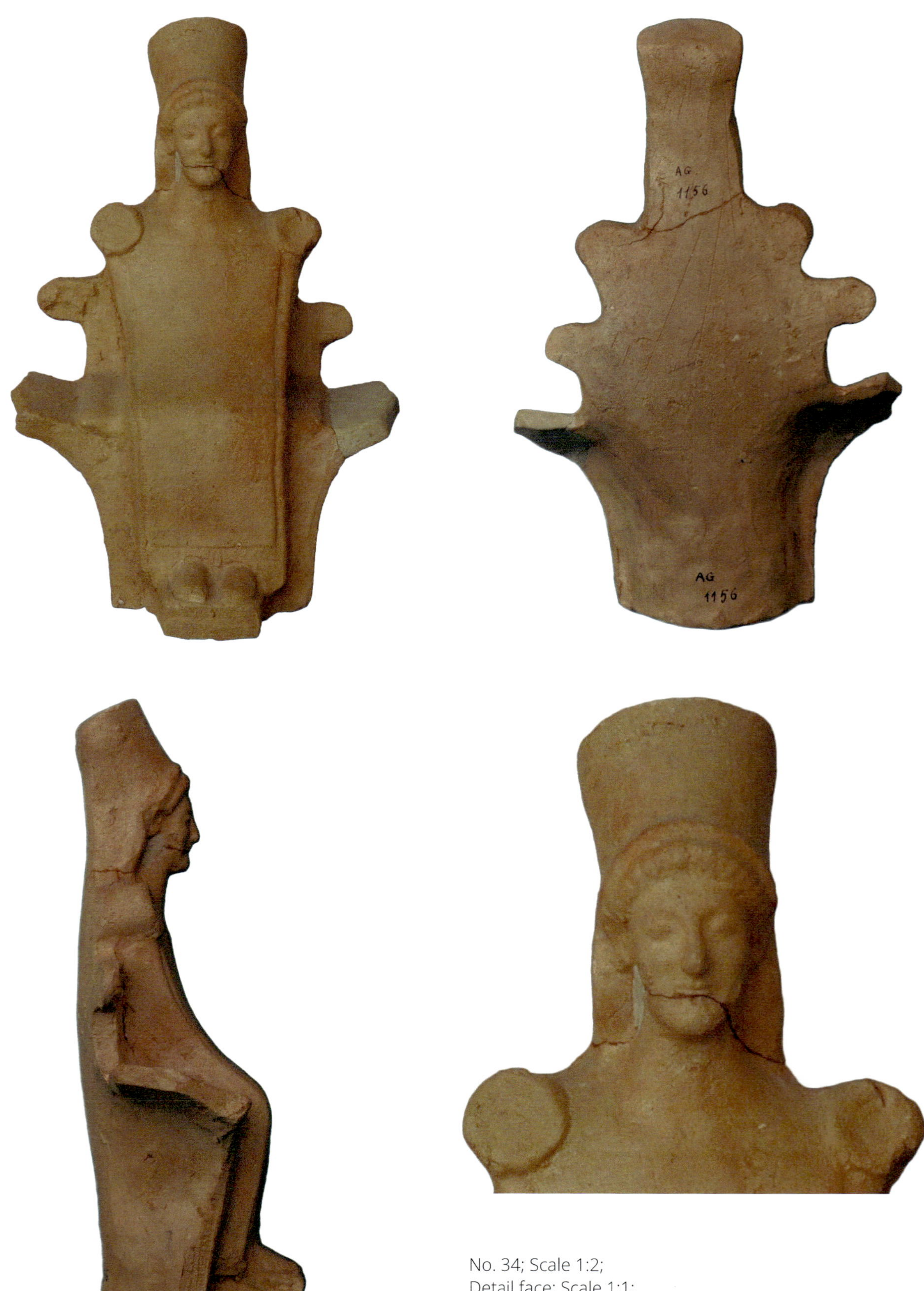

No. 34; Scale 1:2;
Detail face; Scale 1:1;
(Museo Archeologico Regionale "Pietro Griffo", Agrigento).

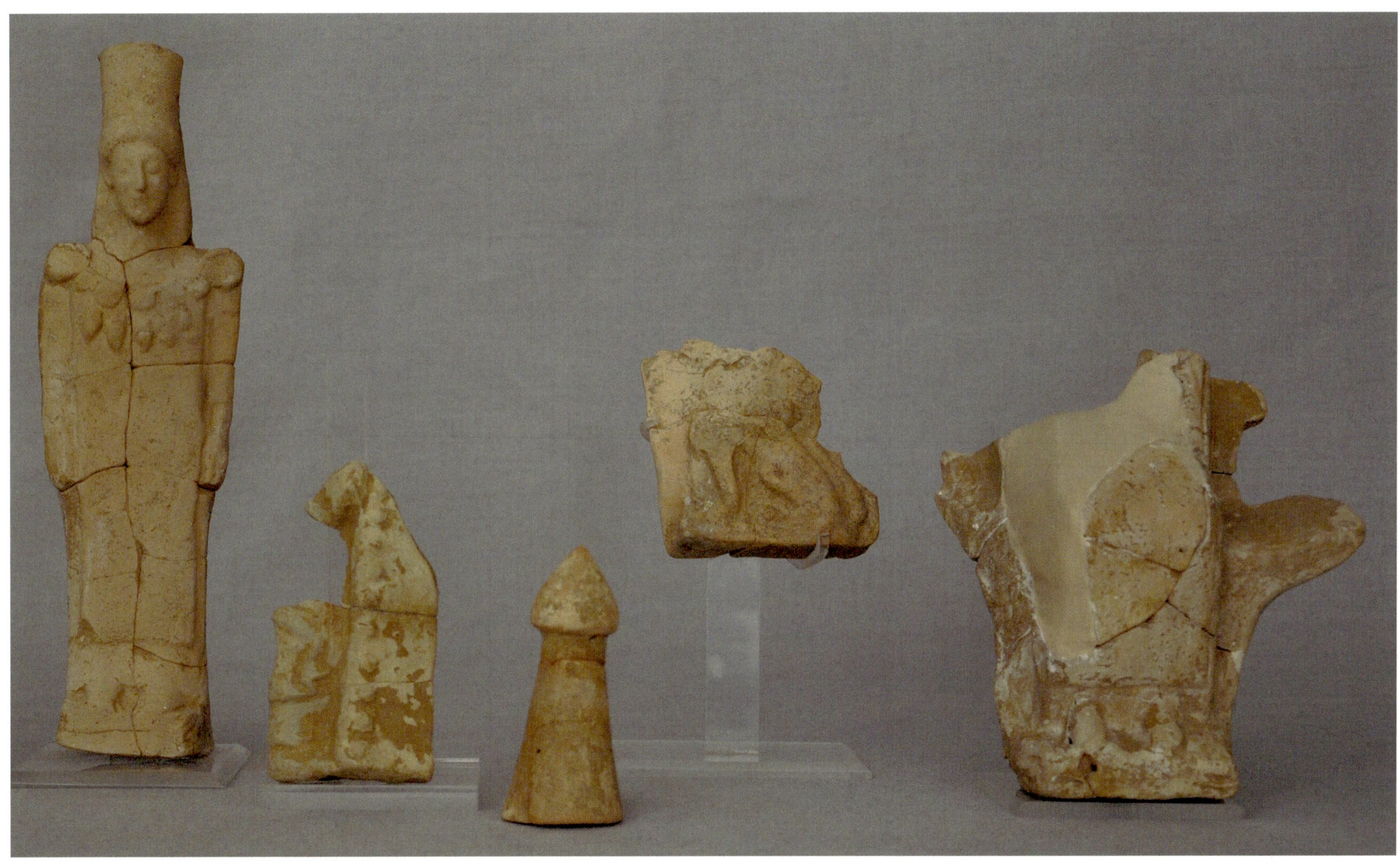

No. 35 on the right, with objects from the same context; Scale 1:2 (Museo Archeologico Regionale "Pietro Griffo", Agrigento).

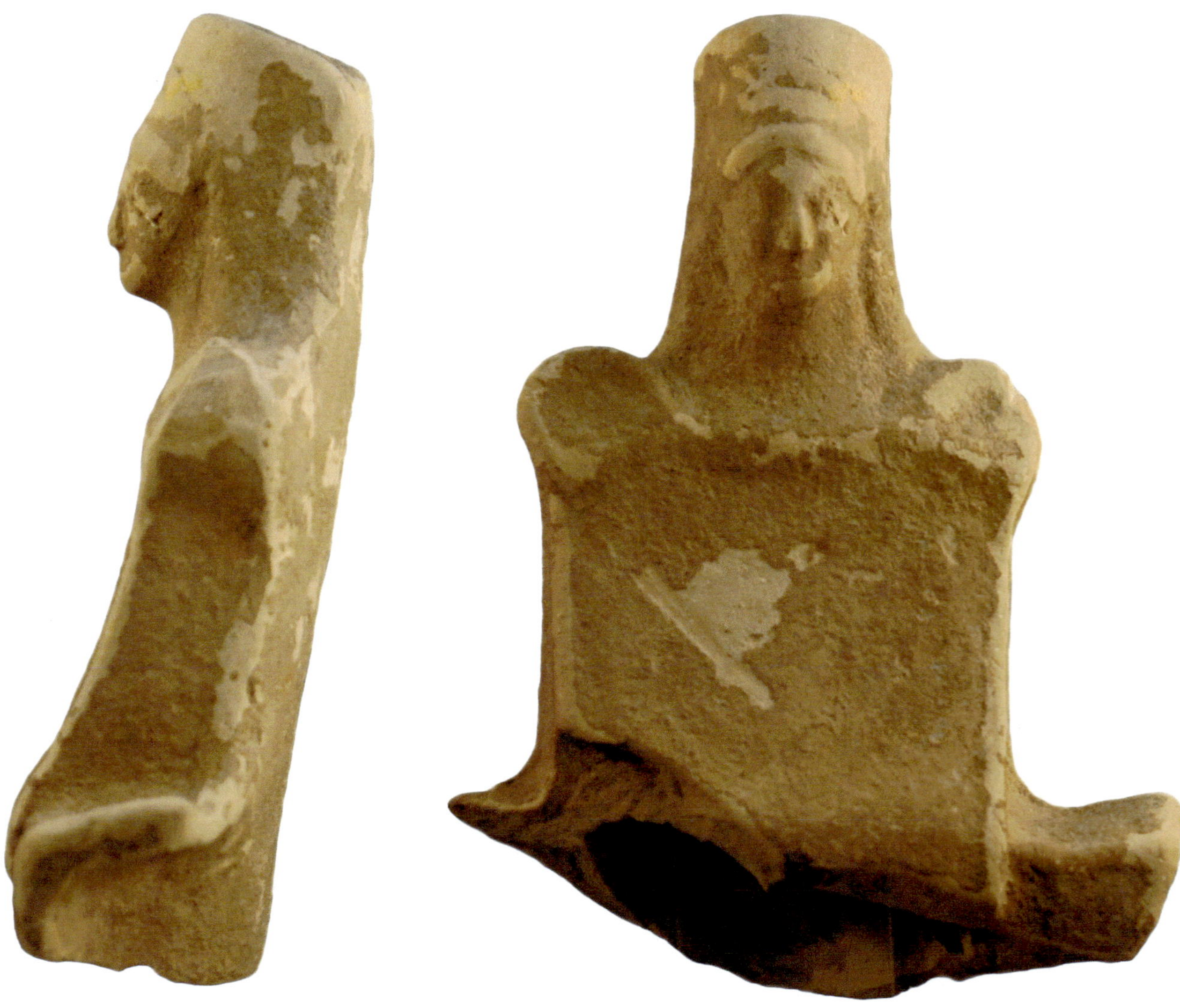

No. 36; Scale 1:1 (Museo Archeologico Regionale "Pietro Griffo", Agrigento).

No.36

- *Museum and Inventory number:* Mus. Agrigento C372
- *Findspot and context:* Akragas
- *Publications:* -
- *Dimensions in cm:* h.13.8
- *Material:* terracotta
- *Techniques:* Front moulded
- *Colour:* Pink 7.5 YR 8/3
- *Date:* Last decade of the 6th century BCE
- *Workshop:* Workshop of the convex back
- *Typology:* Block-like body: group 1c
- *Short description:* Upper part of a figurine. Right knee and part of the bench broken off. Film of dirt. Female figurine with a small face, on a large body with large round fibulae on the shoulders. The face is quite indistinct, but the nose is sizeable. Eyes are slightly bulging and the mouth is small. She has a smooth fringe of hair, with straight, medium-high sized polos with a rim on top. Her body is very flat and there is no indication of any garment, unless the protruding line between the fibulae is interpreted as the upper hem of a dress. The upper part of the body is sloping, and bent at the knees. She sits on a slightly upwards-curving bench, of which the right side is higher than the left. Between the large fibulae, there is an empty cord or pectoral chain.
- *Comparable objects:* Similar in colour, techniques and iconography to **37**. The head is reminiscent of the small face and low polos of figurines **41**-**47**. Fibulae look similar to **34**. It could well be from the same mould series as a figurine from Akragas or Selinous: Mus. Bonn Inv. no.: D 189.33, headless, h.15.6cm Hübinger-Menninger 2007, no.204. The hem of the apron on the edges at the front is not visible on **36**.

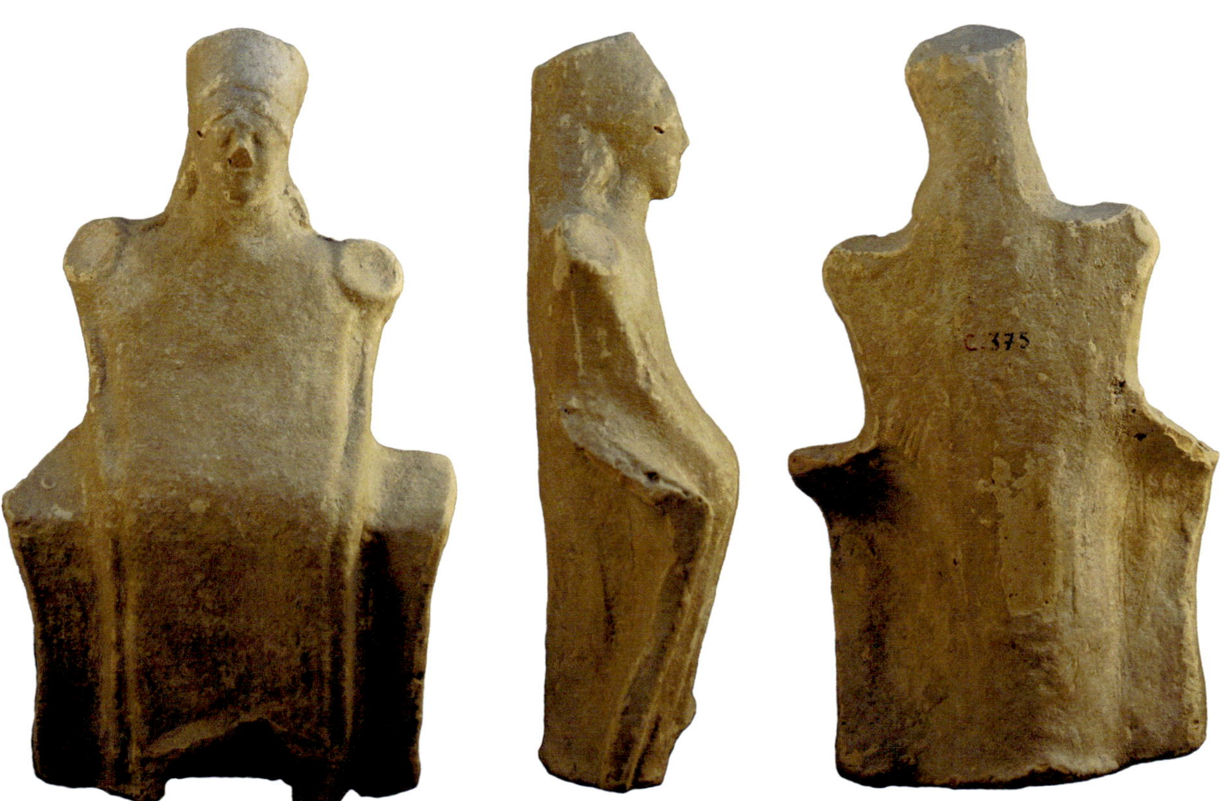

No. 37; Scale 1:2 (Museo Archeologico Regionale "Pietro Griffo", Agrigento).

No.37

‣ *Museum and Inventory number:* Mus. Agrigento C375
‣ *Findspot and context:* Akragas
‣ *Publications:* -
‣ *Dimensions in cm:* h.20.5
‣ *Material:* Terracotta
‣ *Techniques:* Front moulded. Lime-spalling: right side of head and on the back. Bench probably handmade. Reworking with a tool visible on the back.
‣ *Colour:* Pink 7.5 YR 8/3
‣ *Date:* Last decade of the 6th century BCE
‣ *Workshop:* Workshop of the convex back
‣ *Typology:* Block-like body: group 1c
‣ *Short description:* Nearly complete figurine, feet and nose broken off, part of bench broken off. Female figurine with a small rounded face, a small chin, but wide jaws. She has bulging eyes, and a wide-bridged nose with a small mouth directly under it. Her hair on her forehead is thin and parted in two, falling along her temples. She wears a medium-high polos with rim. Simple body with bent knees. Flaring, very wide shoulders with large round fibulae. She sits on a wide bench, of which the right side is higher. The front on the right curves lightly inwards, while on the left this part is straight.
‣ *Comparable objects:* Probably from the same mould as Inv. 5865 Selinous, complete 19.5cm Mus. Palermo. Strikingly the figurine is damaged at exactly the same spots: nose damaged, feet and right back corner of bench broken off. See Poma 2009, p.236, no.30. The figurine is not made from a double mould.

Similar to **41**-**46**. The general shape of body and chair, also as facial features are reminiscent of type B XVII from Selinous, though pendants, fibulae and backrest of the chair are different. Dewailly 1992, p.104-106, fig.64.

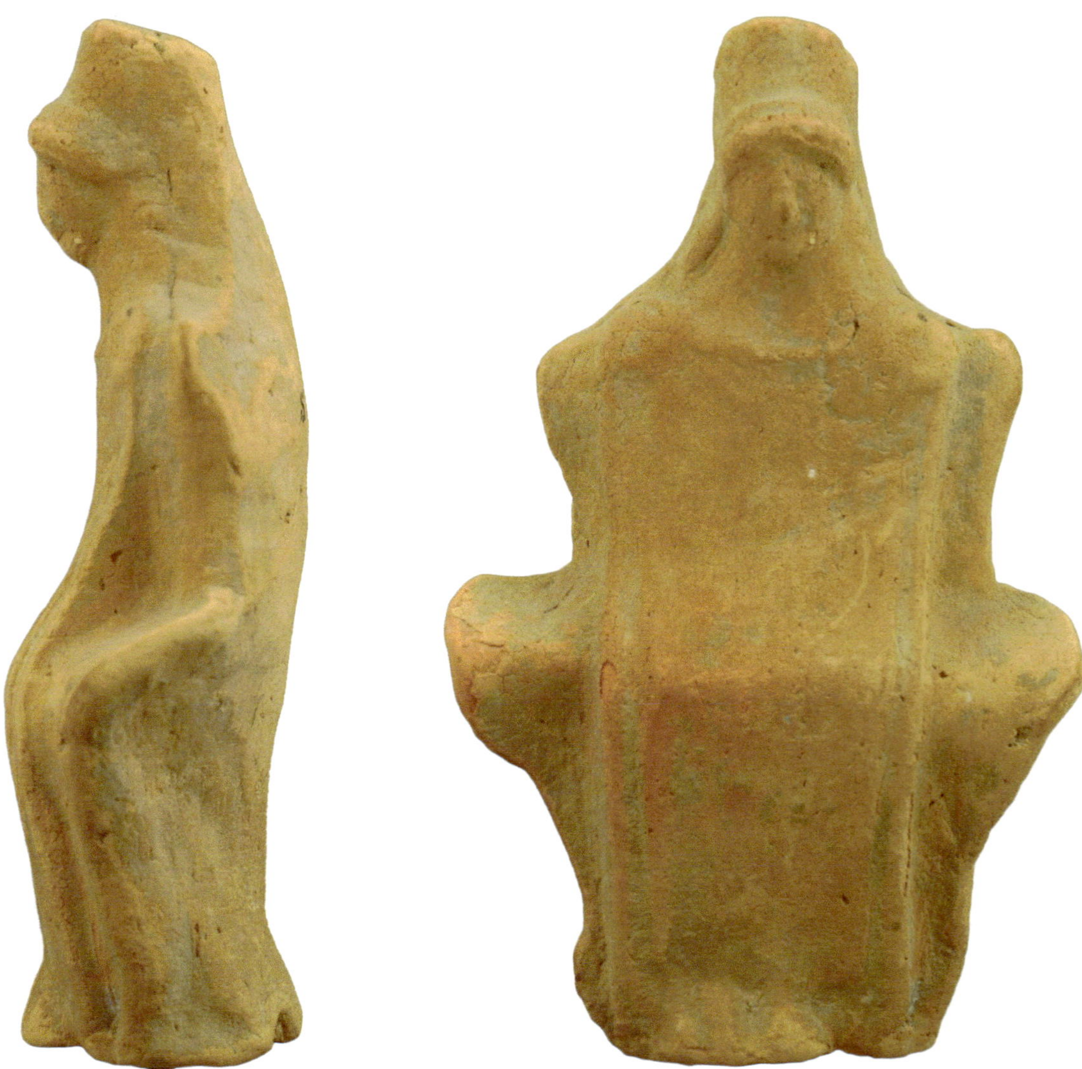

No. 38; Scale 1:1 (Museo Archeologico Regionale "Pietro Griffo", Agrigento).

No.38

‣ *Museum and Inventory number:* Mus. Agrigento S891
‣ *Findspot and context:* City Sanctuary
‣ *Publications:* -
‣ *Dimensions in cm:* h.13.9
‣ *Material:* Terracotta.
‣ *Techniques:* Front moulded. From worn mould. The narrowed head is the result of several generations in the same mould series. See Section III.7.c.iv. The compressed, but wide body, might also be the result of the same. Lighter-coloured slip layer.
‣ *Colour:* Reddish-yellow 7.5 YR 6/6
‣ *Date:* Last decade of the 6th century BCE
‣ *Workshop:* Workshop of the convex back
‣ *Typology:* Block-like body: group 1c
‣ *Short description:* Nearly complete figurine. Small face, very indistinct. Smooth rim of hair, medium-sized polos with thin rim. Hair bulging in the neck. Straight dress on top of slightly bent block-like body, slightly wider at the shoulders. Round fibulae and a double band on the chest. Feet sticking out. She is seated on a wide bench with small rounded ears at the height of the shoulder. Round decorations at the ears of the chair also, but very indistinct. The back, made out of a slab of clay, is bulging in the middle and rounded.
‣ *Comparable objects:* Probably from the same mould series as **39**, though it omits the double band on the breast and is much sharper. The figurine is, except for the pendant, similar to type B XXVII and of similar size. The Selinuntine figurine N.I. 70 features an amphoriskos/vaselet-shaped pendant on a lower-placed but similarly thin pectoral band. It is much sharper. Dewailly 1992, p.128-9 fig.94.

No.39

‣ *Museum and Inventory number:* Mus. Agrigento S890
‣ *Findspot and context:* City Sanctuary

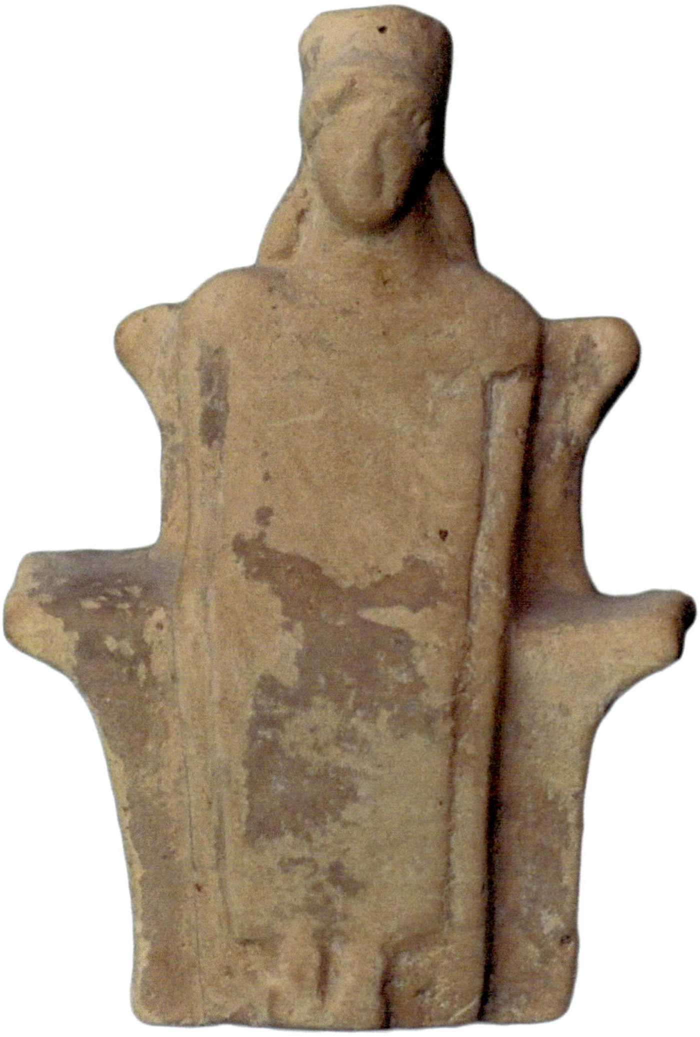

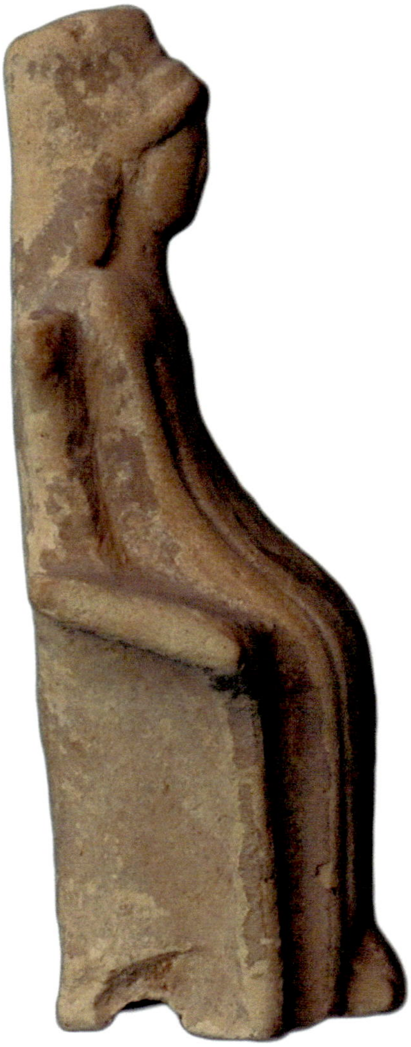

No. 39; Scale 1:1 (Museo Archeologico Regionale "Pietro Griffo", Agrigento).

- ***Publications:*** -
- ***Dimensions in cm:*** h.13.6
- ***Material:*** Terracotta.
- ***Techniques:*** Front moulded. From worn mould.
- ***Colour:*** Very pale brown 10 YR 7/4
- ***Date:*** Last decade of the 6th century BCE
- ***Workshop:*** Workshop of the convex back
- ***Typology:*** Block-like body: group 1c
- ***Short description:*** Nearly complete figurine. Small face, very worn and indistinct. The mouth seems small and the eyes slightly bulging. The nose has become flattened. Fringe of hair in bulbs, creating a triangular forehead. Hair falling down bulging along the sides of the sturdy short neck. Medium-sized polos. A straight apron, following the contours of the block-like body and bent knees. Round fibulae, faded, overlapping the edge of the apron. Feet without much detail, sticking out under apron. She is seated on a wide bench, which is unequal in height. The lower left

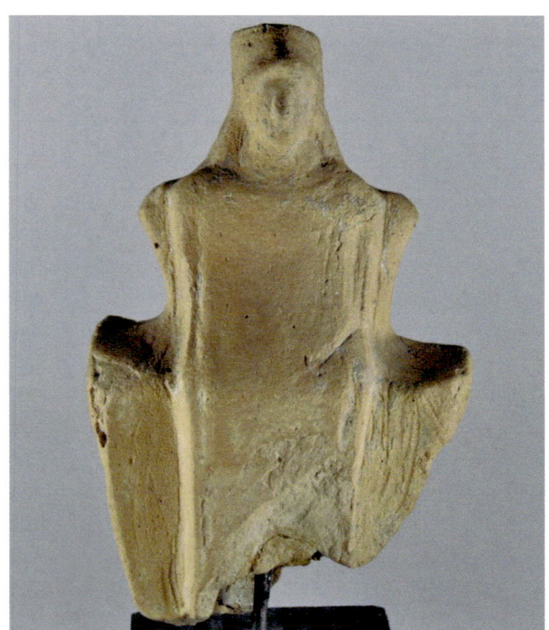

Figure 3: Similar figurine from a private collection. Unknown size

side is also placed slightly diagonally. The backrest along the sides of the body runs rounded on the left and straighter at the right, ending in round ears just below the height of the shoulders. At the frontal side of the seat, the bench curves inwards and runs along the sides of the body. The back, except for the sides of the throne, is convex and column-shaped to enable the figurine to stay upright.

‣ *Comparable objects:* Probably from the same mould series as **38**.

Figurine comparable and possibly from the same mould series as a figurine of 18cm in height from a private collection (see fig.3).

No.40

‣ *Museum and Inventory number:* Mus. Munich 8553
‣ *Findspot and context:* Akragas
‣ *Publications:* Hamdorf 2014, p.98, no.C 213; Knauss 2012 455
‣ *Dimensions in cm:* h.12.3
‣ *Material:* Terracotta. Several small holes and inclusions.
‣ *Techniques:* Front moulded. Placed on a podium, not belonging to the mould. From a worn mould. Bench partly added by hand.
‣ *Colour:* Reddish-yellow 7.5 YR 7/6
‣ *Date:* Last decade of the 6th century BCE
‣ *Workshop:* Workshop of the convex back
‣ *Typology:* Block-like body: group 1c
‣ *Short description:* Complete figurine placed on a thin irregular shaped podium. Unclear details, particularly at the face. Wide, large polos, placed on her thick fringe of hair. Her hair is bulging at the sides also. The body is typically block-like, with bent knees at height of the bench. However, it seems an extra layer was added on the right side of her body. She is seated on a wide bench with backrest. She has two round fibulae, in between which there seem to be two elevated lines, which are not clear. The apron appears to be doubled. One runs all the way down, the other ends above the feet. The back is convex in the middle. The extra rim on the underside or 'podium' increases the figurine's stability.
‣ *Comparable objects:* Very similar to **38** and **39**, except for the 'podium.' Considering the smaller size and the podium, it might be from the same mould series, but a later generation, of which the mould was reworked.

No.41 (not illustrated)

‣ *Museum and Inventory number:* Mus. Agrigento S888
‣ *Findspot and context:* City Sanctuary
‣ *Publications:* -
‣ *Dimensions in cm:* h.14.2
‣ *Material:* Terracotta.
‣ *Techniques:* Front moulded. From a worn mould, flattened nose.
‣ *Colour:* Very pale brown 10 YR 7/4
‣ *Date:* Last decade of the 6th century BCE
‣ *Workshop:* Workshop of the convex back
‣ *Typology:* Block-like body: group 1c
‣ *Short description:* Nearly complete figurine. Small round face with a pronounced chin and a large, but flattened nose. The eyes have become indistinct and a small mouth is just visible by the dimples next to it. Her fringe of hair consists of bulbs in a neat round-shaped row; her hair along the sides of her short neck is marked by horizontal waves on the side. She wears a medium-sized, flaring polos with rim. She wears a straight apron on top of her slightly bent block-like body, widening at the shoulders. She wears round fibulae and a thick double band on the chest. Both her undergarment and the apron reach to her ankles, where her feet stick out. This part is coarsely-shaped and lacks details: the feet might be placed on a small footstool. She is seated on a wide bench with rounded ears on the backrest, just below the height of the shoulder. The front of the bench bends inwards on her left but is straight to her right. The back is column-shaped.
‣ *Comparable objects:* From the same mould as **42**-**47**, but slightly larger than **42** and **43**.

No.42

‣ *Museum and Inventory number:* Mus. Agrigento S273
‣ *Findspot and context:* City Sanctuary
‣ *Publications:* Fiertler 2001, tav.IX, type BXV
‣ *Dimensions in cm:* h.13.9
‣ *Material:* Terracotta.
‣ *Techniques:* Front moulded. From worn mould. Black discolouring on back. Shell fragment on the right back of the seat.
‣ *Colour:* Very pale brown 10 YR 7/3
‣ *Date:* Last decade of the 6th century BCE
‣ *Workshop:* Workshop of the convex back
‣ *Typology:* Block-like body: group 1c
‣ *Short description:* Nearly complete figurine. Lower part of the bench on the left broken off. Small round face with a pronounced chin and a large, but flattened nose. The eyes have become indistinct and a small mouth is just visible by the dimples next to it. Her fringe of hair consists of bulbs in a neat round shaped row; her hair along the sides of her short neck is marked on the side by horizontal waves. She wears a medium-sized, flaring polos with rim. She wears a straight apron on top of her slightly bent block-like body, widening at the shoulders. She wears round fibulae and a thick double band on the chest. Both her undergarment and the apron reach to her ankles, where her feet stick out. This part is coarsely shaped and lacks details: the feet might be placed on a small footstool. She is seated on a wide bench with rounded ears on the backrest, just below the height of the shoulder. The front of the bench bends inwards on both sides. The back is column-shaped.
‣ *Comparable objects:* From the same mould as **41** and **43**-**47**, but sharper than **43**.

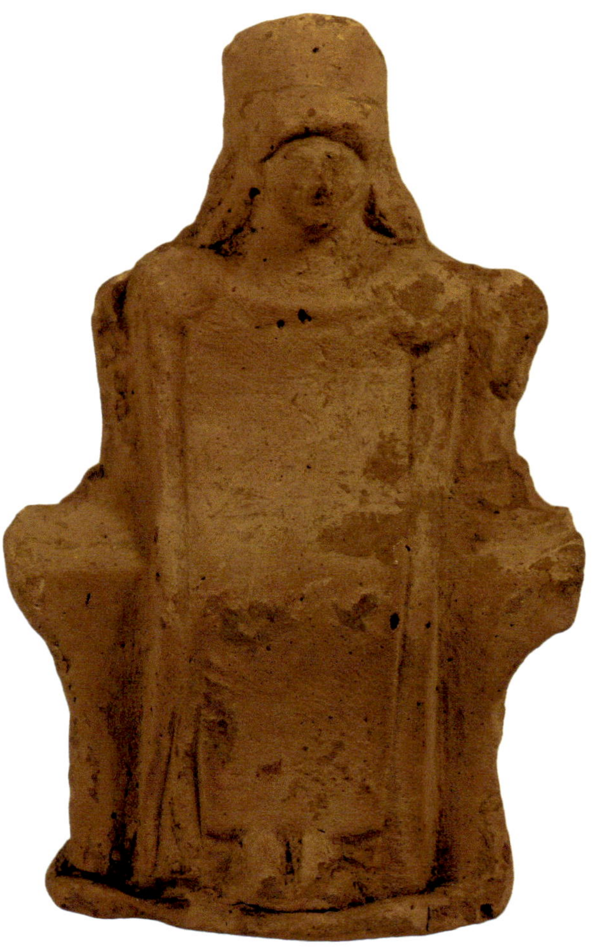

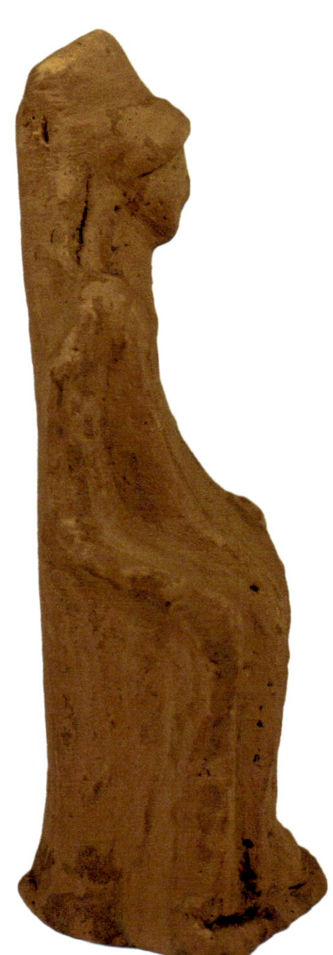

No. 40; Scale 1:1 (Staatlichen Antikensammlungen München).

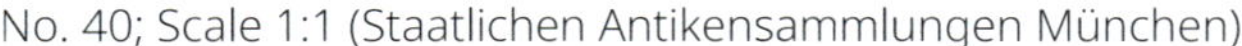

‣ *Other notes:* This figurine is used in the coroplastic experiment as patrix of the series.

No.43 (not illustrated)

‣ *Museum and Inventory number:* Mus. Agrigento S886
‣ *Findspot and context:* City Sanctuary
‣ *Publications:* -
‣ *Dimensions in cm:* h.13.6
‣ *Material:* Terracotta.
‣ *Techniques:* Front moulded. Weathered mould.
‣ *Colour:* Very pale brown 10 YR 7/4
‣ *Date:* Last decade of the 6th century BCE
‣ *Workshop:* Workshop of the convex back
‣ *Typology:* Block-like body: group 1c
‣ *Short description:* Nearly complete figurine. Right 'ear' of the backrest broken off. Small round face with a pronounced chin and a large, but flattened nose. The eyes have become indistinct and a small mouth is just visible by the dimples next to it. Her fringe of hair consists of bulbs in a neat round shaped row; her hair along the sides of her short neck is marked on the side by horizontal waves. She wears a medium-sized, flaring polos with rim. She wears a straight apron on top of her slightly bent block-like body, widening at the shoulders. She wears round fibulae and a thick double band on the chest. Both her undergarment and the apron reach to her ankles, where her feet stick out. This part is coarsely shaped and lacks details: the feet might be placed on a small footstool. She is seated on a wide bench with rounded ears on the backrest, just below the height of the shoulder. The front of the bench bends slightly inwards. The back is column-shaped.
‣ *Comparable objects:* From the same mould as **41-42**, **44-47**. Less sharp than **42**.

No.44 (not illustrated)

‣ *Museum and Inventory number:* Mus. Agrigento S887
‣ *Findspot and context:* City Sanctuary
‣ *Publications:* -
‣ *Dimensions in cm:* h.13.2
‣ *Material:* Terracotta.
‣ *Techniques:* Front moulded. Very weathered. Handmade throne

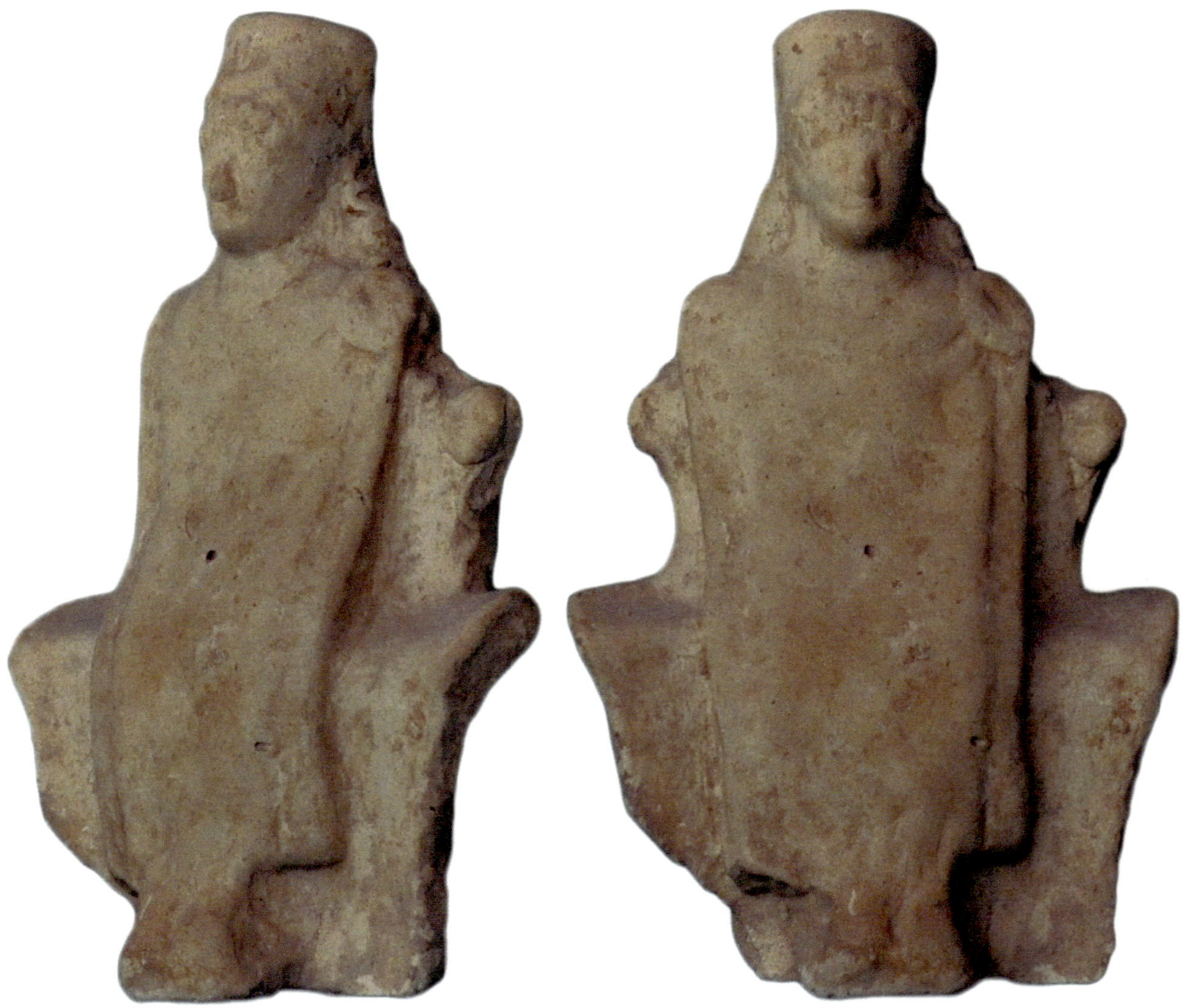

No. 42; Scale 1:1 (Museo Archeologico Regionale "Pietro Griffo", Agrigento).

- *Colour:* Very pale brown 10 YR 7/4
- *Date:* Last decade of the 6th century BCE
- *Workshop:* Workshop of the convex back
- *Typology:* Block-like body: group 1c
- *Short description:* Complete figurine. Small round face with a pronounced chin and a large, but flattened nose. The eyes have become indistinct and a small mouth is just visible by the dimples next to it. Her fringe of hair consists of bulbs in a neat round shaped row; her hair along the sides of her short neck is marked on the side by horizontal waves. She wears a medium-sized, flaring polos with rim. She wears a straight apron on top of her slightly bent block-like body, widening at the shoulders. She wears round fibulae and a thick double band on the chest. Both her undergarment and the apron reach to her ankles, where her feet stick out. This part is coarsely shaped and lacks details: the feet might be placed on a small footstool. She is seated on a wide bench with rounded ears on the backrest, just below the height of the shoulder. The one on the right is slightly higher placed the one on the left. The seat of the throne runs in a slope. The fronts of the seat are more or less straight. The back is column-shaped.
- *Comparable objects:* From the same mould as **41-43**, **45-47**.

No.45 (not illustrated)

- *Museum and Inventory number:* Mus. Agrigento S885
- *Findspot and context:* City Sanctuary
- *Publications:* -
- *Dimensions in cm:* h.13.2
- *Material:* Terracotta.
- *Techniques:* Front moulded. Weathered mould.
- *Colour:* Very pale brown 10 YR 7/4
- *Date:* Last decade of the 6th century BCE
- *Workshop:* Workshop of the convex back
- *Typology:* Block-like body: group 1c

‣ *Short description:* Complete figurine. Small round face with a pronounced chin and a large, but flattened nose. The eyes have become indistinct and a small mouth is just visible by the dimples next to it. Her fringe of hair consists of bulbs in a neat round shaped row; her hair along the sides of her short neck is marked on the side by horizontal waves. She wears a medium-sized, flaring polos with rim. She wears a straight apron on top of her slightly bent block-like body, widening at the shoulders. She wears round fibulae and a thick double band on the chest. Both her undergarment and the apron reach to her ankles, where her feet stick out. This part is coarsely shaped and lacks details: the feet might be placed on a small footstool. She is seated on a wide bench with rounded ears on the backrest, just below the height of the shoulder. The one on the right is smaller and not sticking out like the one on the left. The front of the seat bends inwards slightly. The back is column-shaped.
‣ *Comparable objects:* From the same mould as **41-44**, **46-47**.

No.46 (not illustrated)

‣ *Museum and Inventory number:* Mus. Agrigento S889
‣ *Findspot and context:* City Sanctuary
‣ *Publications:* -
‣ *Dimensions in cm:* h.12.8
‣ *Material:* Terracotta.
‣ *Techniques:* Front moulded.
‣ *Colour:* Very pale brown 10 YR 7/4
‣ *Date:* Last decade of the 6th century BCE
‣ *Workshop:* Workshop of the convex back
‣ *Typology:* Block-like body: group 1c
‣ *Short description:* Nearly complete figurine. 'Ears' of backrest are broken off. Small round face with a pronounced chin and a large, but flattened nose. The eyes have become indistinct and a small mouth is just visible by the dimples next to it. Her fringe of hair consists of bulbs in a neat round shaped row; her hair along the sides of her short neck is marked on the side by horizontal waves. She wears a medium-sized, flaring polos with rim. She wears a straight apron on top of her slightly bent block-like body, widening at the shoulders. She wears round fibulae and a thick double band on the chest. Both her undergarment and the apron reach to her ankles, where her feet stick out. This part is coarsely shaped and lacks details: the feet might be placed on a small footstool. She is seated on a wide bench, which had rounded ears on the backrest, just below the height of the shoulder. The front of the seat is bends inwards slightly, but is straight, not curved. The back is column-shaped.
‣ *Comparable objects:* From the same mould as **41-45** and **47**.

No.47

‣ *Museum and Inventory number:* Mus. Agrigento S274
‣ *Findspot and context:* City Sanctuary
‣ *Publications:* -
‣ *Dimensions in cm:* h.12.6
‣ *Material:* Terracotta.
‣ *Techniques:* Front moulded. Weathered mould, flattened nose.
‣ *Colour:* Very pale brown 10 YR 7/3
‣ *Date:* Last decade of the 6th century BCE
‣ *Workshop:* Workshop of the convex back
‣ *Typology:* Block-like body: group 1c
‣ *Short description:* Nearly complete figurine. Sherd on the back broken off. Small round face with a pronounced chin and a large, flattened nose. The eyes have become indistinct and a small mouth is just visible by the dimples next to it. Her fringe of hair consists of bulbs in a neat round shaped row; her hair along the sides of her short neck is marked on the side by horizontal waves. She wears a medium-sized, flaring polos with rim. She wears a straight apron on top of her slightly bent block-like body, widening at the shoulders. She wears round fibulae and a thick double band on the chest. Both her undergarment and the apron reach to her ankles, where her feet stick out. This part is coarsely shaped and lacks details: the feet might be placed on a small footstool. She is seated on a wide bench, which had rounded ears on the backrest, just below the height of the shoulder. The left one sticks out further. The front of the seat curves inwards. The back is column-shaped.
‣ *Comparable objects:* From the same mould as **41-46**, but the smallest in this group.

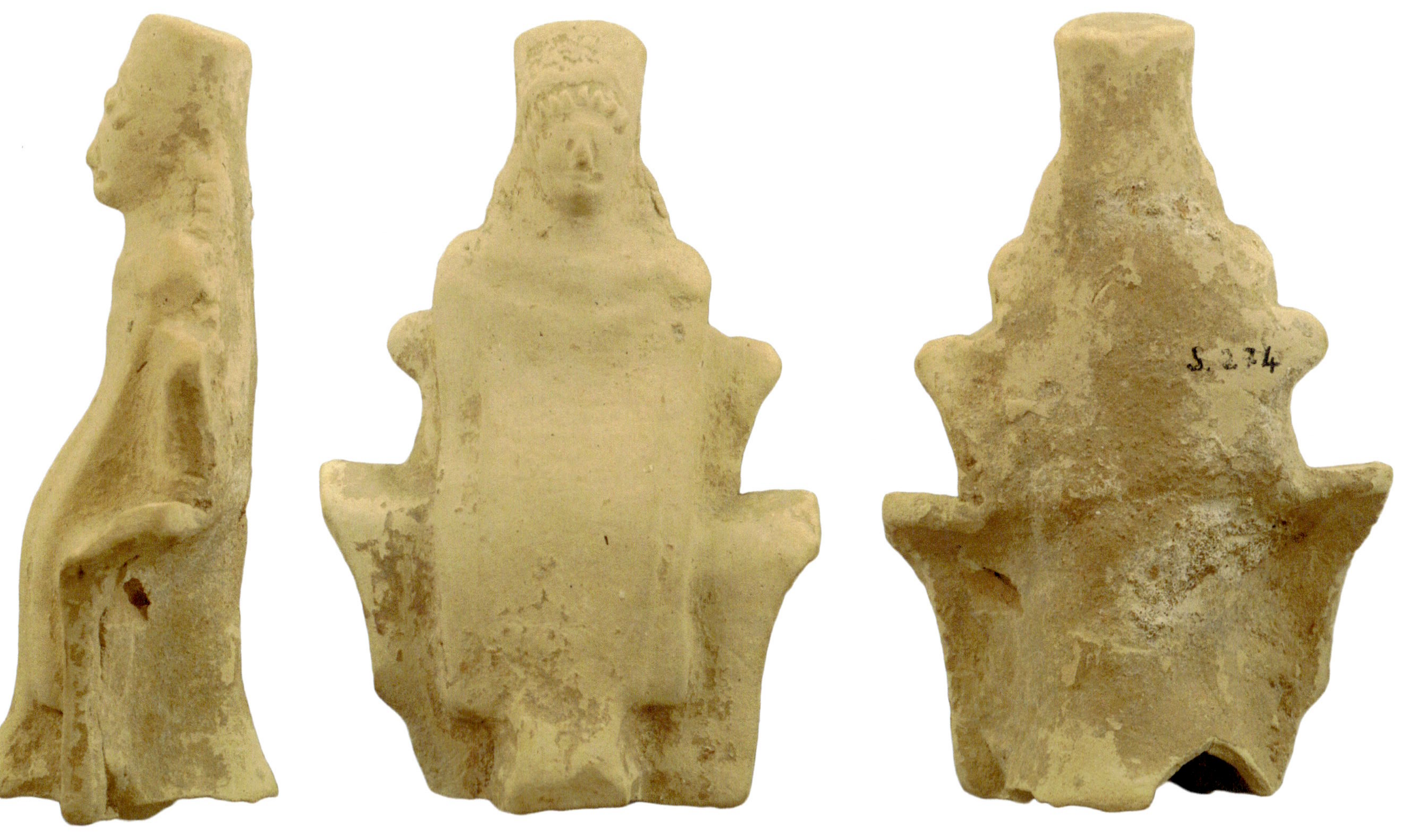

No. 47; Scale 1:1 (Museo Archeologico Regionale "Pietro Griffo", Agrigento).

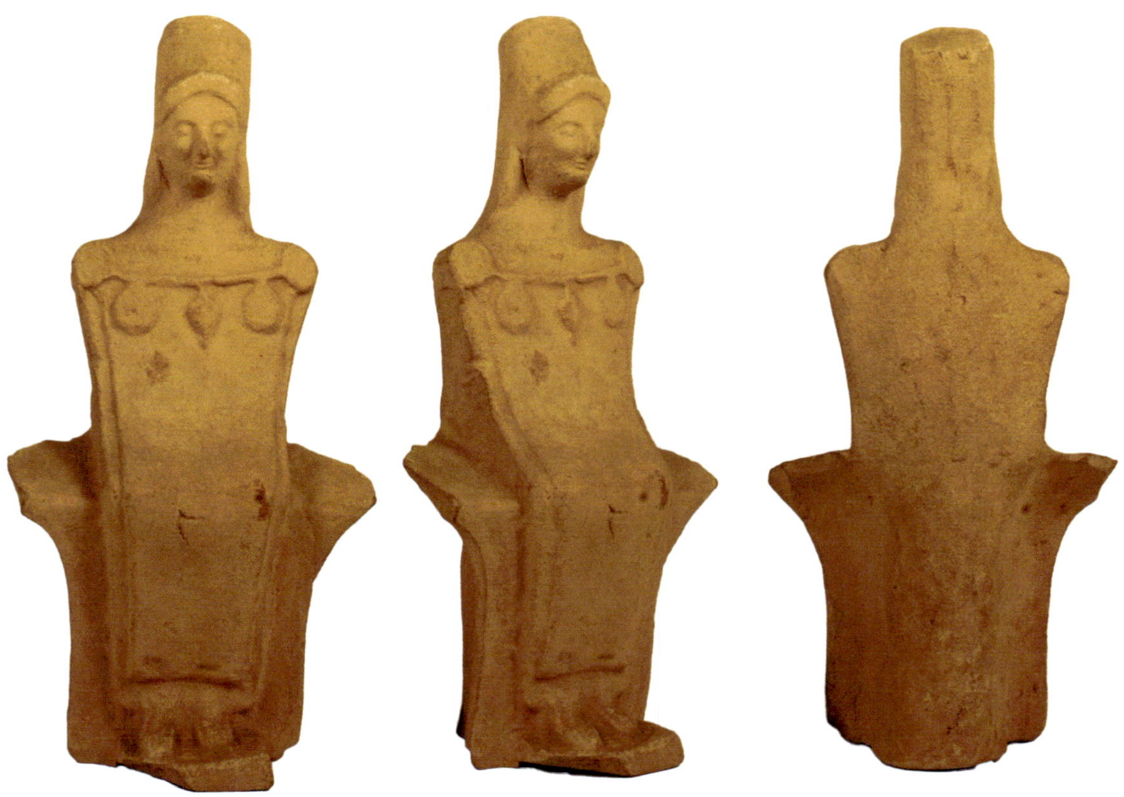

No. 48; Scale 1:2 (Staatlichen Antikensammlungen München).

No.48

- *Museum and Inventory number:* Mus. Munich 5272
- *Findspot and context:* Akragas
- *Publications:* Hamdorf 2014, p.97, no.C 212
- *Dimensions in cm:* h.20.5
- *Material:* Terracotta. Two black lines on the apron above her feet, paint (?)
- *Techniques:* Front moulded.
- *Colour:* Light Grey 10 YR 7/2
- *Date:* End of the sixth century BCE
- *Workshop:* -
- *Typology:* Block-like body: group 1d
- *Short description:* Nearly complete female figurine. In the neck, chin and knee there are cracks. Parts of seat broken off. Smiling face with protruding chin and cheeks. Narrow mouth with deep dimples. She has simple bulging eyes under arching eyebrows. She wears a tall straight polos on top of smooth and flat fringe of hair. She is seated on a wide bench. Her body is block-like; her undetailed feet placed on a small footstool, the right foot placed a bit further forwards. She wears an apron, just a bit shorter than her undergarment, which falls over her shoes/feet. On her shoulders, there are round fibulae with a band between them: attached to this clear line are three pendants: a pointed pendant in the middle, pear-shaped, and a disc on each side. All of them have visible attachments to the line.
- *Comparable objects:* The figurine belongs to Type A XXXIII, which are mostly from Gelas. Albertocchi 2004, p.53-4. Probably from the first generation in the same mould series is this figurine: Mus. Berlin Inv. no.6618. It measures 24.3cm and is described on the back as being from Akragas. Albertocchi 2004, p.50, no.680; Kekulé von Stradonitz 1884, p.17, fig.22; Müller 1929, p.350, pl. 32; Winter 1903, p.125, no.2. Also from the same mould is probably a figurine from Selinous: Mus. Palermo N.I. 9, complete, h.24.5. Dewailly writes that type BXXVI is likely originally from Gelas or Akragas. Dewailly 1992, p.126-8. The face is reminiscent of that of **34** and **70**, but this one is more rounded, chubby and cheeky. Very similar to a figurine from Grammichele: Mus. Syracuse Inv. no.14319, which has a thicker fringe of hair. Similar and partly from the same mould series is a figurine from the Mus. Catania Inv. no.MC 5414. Pautasso 1996, p.66, no.55, tav.VII h.12.7cm dated to the last quarter of the sixth century BCE.

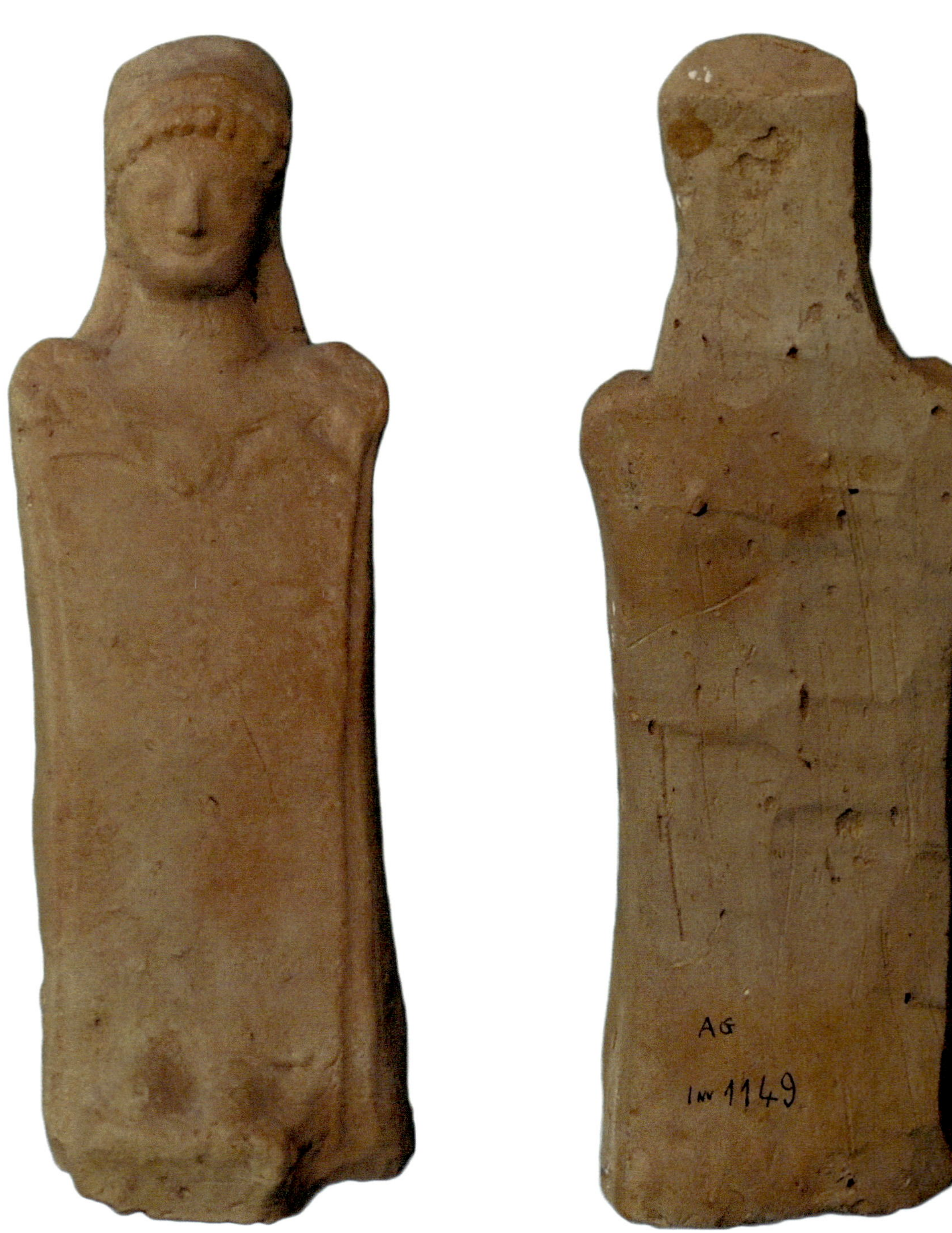

No. 49; Scale 1:1 (Museo Archeologico Regionale "Pietro Griffo", Agrigento).

No.49

‣ *Museum and Inventory number:* Mus. Agrigento 1149

‣ *Findspot and context:* City Sanctuary. At the base of the southwest wall of the sanctuary

‣ *Publications:* Albertocchi 2004, p.94, no.1701; De Miro 2000, p.128, no.17

‣ *Dimensions in cm:* h.17.6

‣ *Material:* Terracotta. Colour differences, many inclusions.

‣ *Techniques:* Front moulded. Sides and back straightened with sharp tool. Lighter coloured slip layer

‣ *Colour:* Very pale brown 10 YR 7/4

‣ *Date:* End of the sixth century BCE

‣ *Workshop:* Workshop of 'straight reworking'

‣ *Typology:* Block-like body: group 1d

‣ *Short description:* Complete figurine. Figurine as a whole bends over to the right and the footstool is placed more to the right side. Female figure. She has a round face with bulging eyes, a pronounced chin and a small mouth, placed directly under the nose. She wears a low polos with rim, on top of a fringe of hair in bulbs. Her slightly bulging hair falls down next to the sides of her sturdy neck. She has a simple block-like body, which is slightly bent halfway, as if her knees are bent below her apron. The apron reaches almost to the corners of the body and runs down to the base. She wears rosette-shaped fibulae on her shoulders with a curving band in between, lower in the middle. Three pendants with two crescents, pointing down, and a disc in the middle. Feet, undefined, on a relatively high footstool. The back is roughly straightened with a sharp tool.

‣ *Comparable objects:* From the same mould as **50-53**, also as AG 1159, Museo "Griffo", De Miro 2000, p.129, no.18 pl. LX.

No.50 (not illustrated)

‣ *Museum and Inventory number:* Mus. Agrigento S266

‣ *Findspot and context:* City Sanctuary

‣ *Publications:* Albertocchi 2004, p.94, no.1703

‣ *Dimensions in cm:* h.17.2

‣ *Material:* terracotta

‣ *Techniques:* Front moulded. Sides and back straightened with sharp tool. Lighter coloured slip layer. Weathered mould. Some lime-spalling

‣ *Colour:* Light pink 10 YR 8/4

‣ *Date:* End of the sixth century BCE

‣ *Workshop:* Workshop of 'straight reworking'

‣ *Typology:* Block-like body: group 1d

‣ *Short description:* Complete figurine in two parts, restored: the head and neck have been attached to the body. Figurine as a whole bends over to the right and the footstool is placed more to the right. For a further description, see **49**.

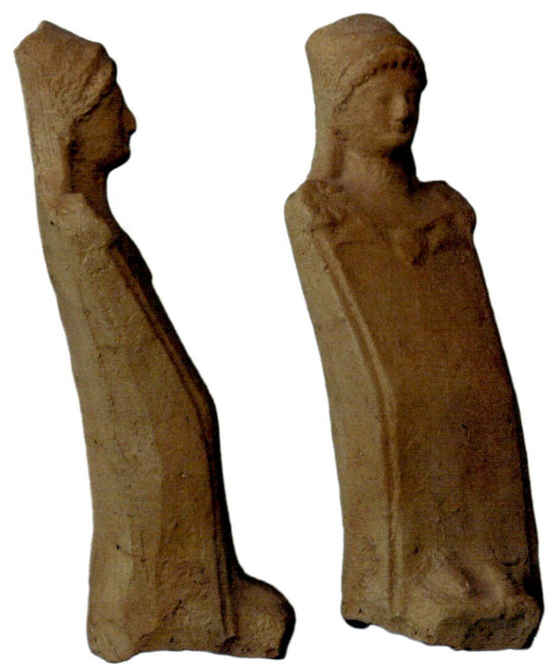

No. 49; Scale 1:2 (Museo Archeologico Regionale "Pietro Griffo", Agrigento).

‣ *Comparable objects:* From the same mould as **49**, **51-53**, also as AG 1159, Museo "Griffo", De Miro 2000, p.129, no.18 pl. LX. Like **51**, damaged on lower part of body. It is likely that they were made by the same workshop.

No.51 (not illustrated)

‣ *Museum and Inventory number:* Mus. Agrigento C382

‣ *Findspot and context:* Akragas

‣ *Publications:* Albertocchi 2004, p.94, no.1704

‣ *Dimensions in cm:* h.17.2

‣ *Material:* Terracotta

‣ *Techniques:* Front moulded. Sides and back straightened with sharp tool.

‣ *Colour:* Pink 5 YR 7/4

‣ *Date:* End of the sixth century BCE

‣ *Workshop:* Workshop of 'straight reworking'

‣ *Typology:* Block-like body: group 1d

‣ *Short description:* Complete figurine in two parts, restored: the head has been attached to the body. A film of dirt covers the entire object. Figurine as a whole bends over to the right and the footstool is placed more to the right. For a further description, see **49**.

‣ *Comparable objects:* From the same mould as **49-50**, **52-53**, also as probably AG 1159, Museo "Griffo", De Miro 2000, p.129, no.18 pl. LX. Though this object is more weathered, the imprint is sharper. Like **50** there are scratches between the knees and the feet. It is likely that they were made by the same workshop.

No.52 (not illustrated)

- *Museum and Inventory number:* Mus. Agrigento S411
- *Findspot and context:* City Sanctuary
- *Publications:* -
- *Dimensions in cm:* h.5.2
- *Material:* Terracotta.
- *Techniques:* Front moulded. Lighter coloured slip layer
- *Colour:* Reddish-yellow 5 YR 7/6
- *Date:* End of the sixth century BCE
- *Workshop:* Workshop of 'straight reworking'
- *Typology:* Block-like body: group 1d
- *Short description:* Head and neck of a figurine. Solid. The face is round, but slightly widening to the forehead. Otherwise weathered and difficult to see. Pronounced chin and nose. Fringe of hair in short bulbs. Ear (?). She wears a low polos with rim. The polos runs a bit sideways, lower at her right side. Slightly bulging hair falls down next to her neck.
- *Comparable objects:* From the same mould series as **49-51**, **53**, also as AG 1159, Museo "Griffo", De Miro 2000, p.129, no.18 pl. LX.

No.53

- *Museum and Inventory number:* Mus. Agrigento S350
- *Findspot and context:* City Sanctuary
- *Publications:* -
- *Dimensions in cm:* h.6.0
- *Material:* Terracotta
- *Techniques:* Front moulded.
- *Colour:* Reddish-yellow 5 YR 6/6
- *Date:* End of the sixth century BCE

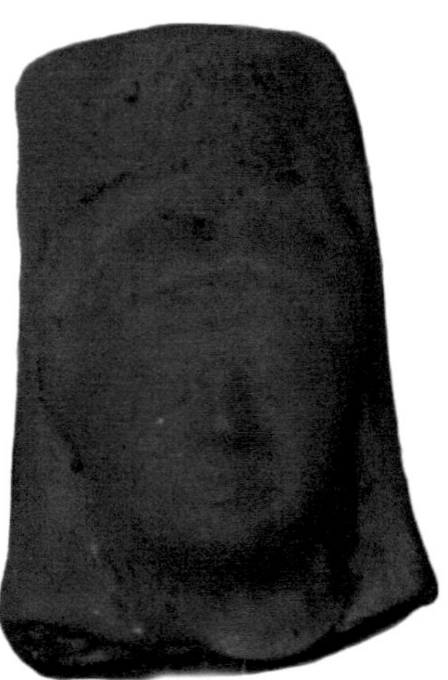
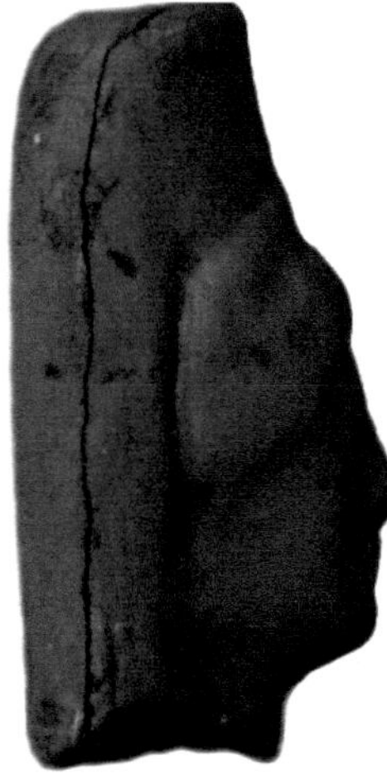

No. 53; Scale 1:1 (Museo Archeologico Regionale "Pietro Griffo", Agrigento).

- *Workshop:* Workshop of 'straight reworking'
- *Typology:* Block-like body: group 1d
- *Short description:* Head and neck of a figurine. Solid, cracked at the seam where front and back were attached. The face is a rounded triangular shape, widening towards the forehead. Otherwise weathered and difficult to see. Pronounced chin and nose. Fringe of hair in short bulbs. She wears a low polos with rim. The polos runs a bit sideways, lower at her right side. Straight hair falls down next to her neck.
- *Comparable objects:* Probably from the same mould series as **49-52**, also as AG 1159, Museo "Griffo", De Miro 2000, p.129, no.18 pl. LX.

No.54

- *Museum and Inventory number:* Mus. Agrigento 23114
- *Findspot and context:* Necropolis di Contrada Mosè. Besides several terracotta figurines of different sorts, there is miniature pottery, oil lamps and no. **21**, **83** and **173** from a deposit pit (fig.4 and 22).
- *Publications:* Veder Greco: le necrópolis di Agrigento 1988, p.271, no.14; Albertocchi 2004, p.90, no.1681; De Miro 1980-81, tav.XLIII fig.4
- *Dimensions in cm:* h.18.7
- *Material:* terracotta
- *Techniques:* Front moulded. Lighter coloured slip layer.
- *Colour:* White 5 Y 8/1
- *Date:* End of the sixth century BCE
- *Workshop:* Workshop of the white clay
- *Typology:* Block-like body: group 1d
- *Short description:* Nearly complete figurine. Restored from several fragments and with considerable infill on the back and the left shoulder.

Oval face with large bulging eyes, a large nose with very flat bridge and tip. Upwards curving lips in an archaic smile. The rim of hair on her forehead is formed by a curving double line. She wears a low polos with a rim, right on top of the fringe. Hair along the sides of her face and neck is bulging. Flat and block-like body, with rounded shoulders. Across her shoulders, she wears a band on her chest with originally probably three discs. The middle one is slightly larger and hangs lower on the chest. There is some distance between the pendants. She leans slightly and has a bit of bending at the 'knees'. On top of her straight body, she wears an apron, of which just the edge is indicated on the sides.

- *Comparable objects:* From the same mould series as figurine **55**, but differently reworked and an earlier generation.

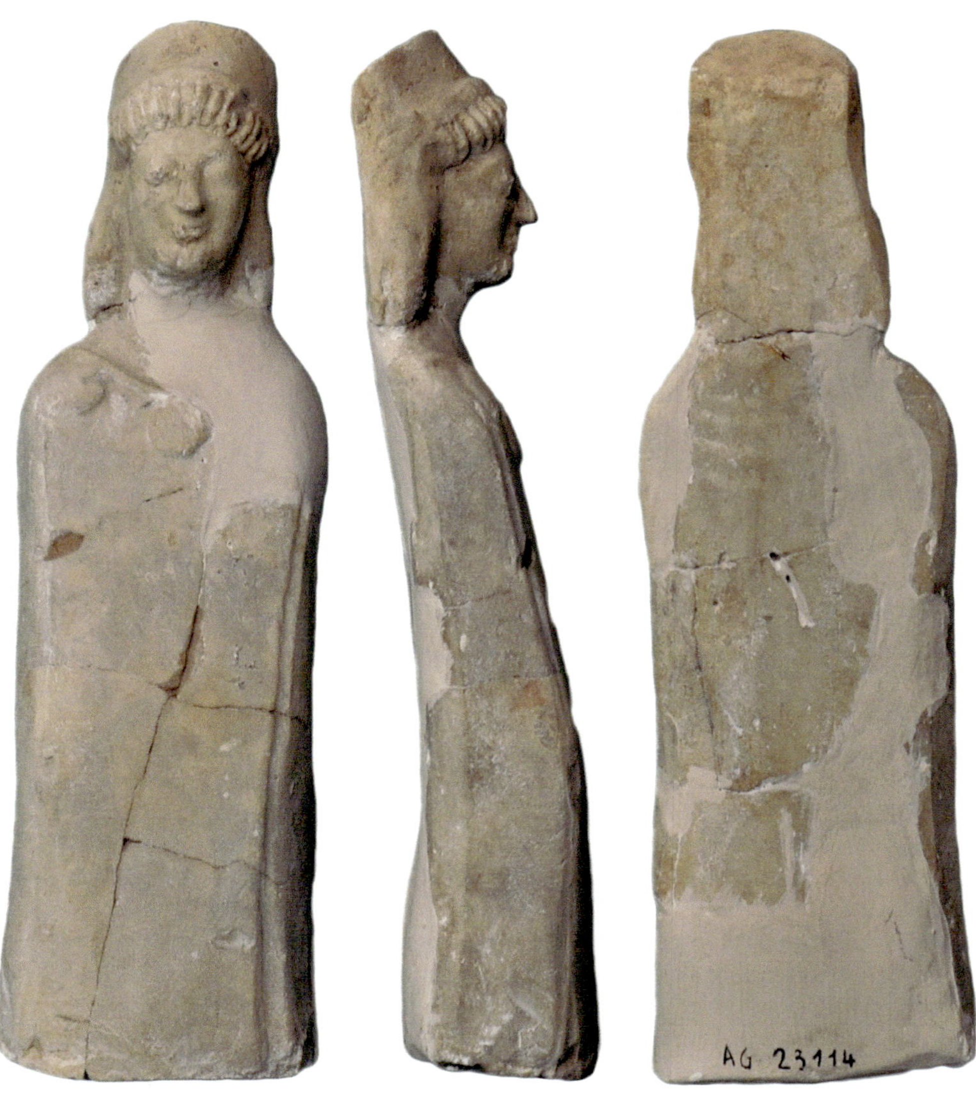

No. 54; Scale 1:1½ (Museo Archeologico Regionale "Pietro Griffo", Agrigento).

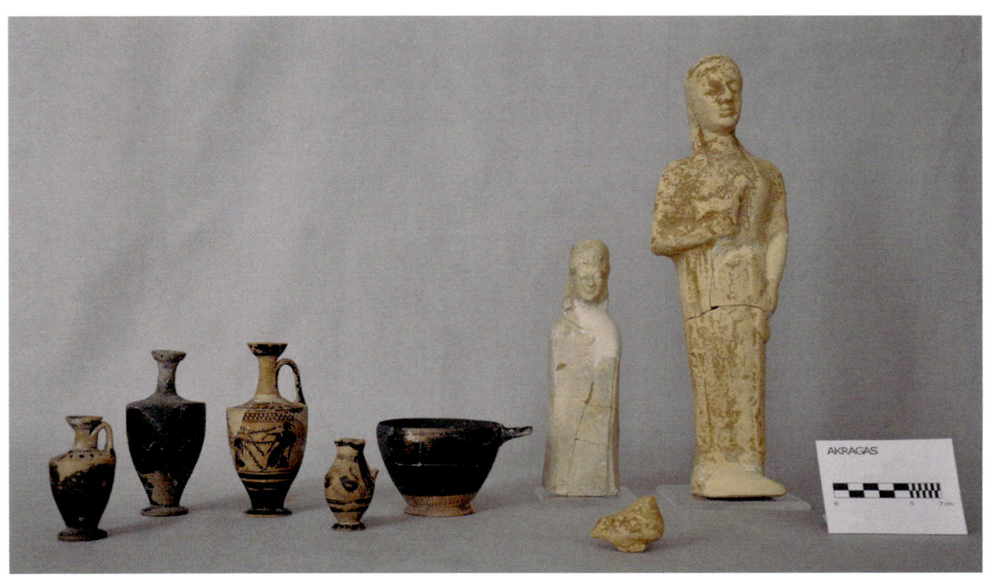

Figure 4; Some of the contents of a deposit pit at the Necropolis di Contrada Mosè. Context of no.21, 54, 83 and 173. See for other items figure 22 (Museo Archeologico Regionale "Pietro Griffo", Agrigento).

No.55

‣ *Museum and Inventory number:* Mus. Agrigento 1165

‣ *Findspot and context:* City Sanctuary. At the base of the southwest wall of the sanctuary

‣ *Publications:* Albertocchi 2004, p.92, no.1693; De Miro 2000, p.128, no.12; Dewailly 1992, p.73, n. 69

‣ *Dimensions in cm:* h.14.5

‣ *Material:* terracotta

‣ *Techniques:* Front moulded. Reworked: Line carved in at the hem of the dress.

‣ *Colour:* Pink 7.5YR 7/3

‣ *Date:* End of the sixth century BCE

‣ *Workshop:* Unknown

‣ *Typology:* Block-like body: group 1d

‣ *Short description:* Headless figurine in three fragments, restored. Block-like body, wider near the feet and upper part of body. Bending at the knees hardly visible, but the figurine as a whole leans back. Three round pendants hang on a band at some distance from each other on the chest, just below the neck. The middle pendant is slightly larger, as if the outer two were cut off by the dress. She wears the typical apron, which ends slightly above the feet. Feet on footstool undefined, merely a protruding footstool.

‣ *Comparable objects:* From the same mould series as figurine **54**, but probably a generation later and differently reworked. The outcome from using different clays is clear from the irregularities in this body. The lower hem of the apron and the feet are additions in this generation. From the same mould as AG 1150, a complete figurine, 19.5cm including hem and feet and a different head, without polos, Museo "Griffo". Albertocchi 2004, p.92, no.1690, De Miro 2000, p.128, no.11. Though comparable in iconographic scheme, this is not from the same mould as AG 1153, Museo "Griffo". See comparable objects of **58**. The shape of, and distance between, the discs, the fibulae, the different shape of the body, the different sizes, the hairstyle and the veil are not comparable.

No.56

‣ *Museum and Inventory number:* Mus. Agrigento C380

‣ *Findspot and context:* City Sanctuary

‣ *Publications:* Albertocchi 2004, p.90, no.1677; Dewailly 1992, p.71, n. 64

‣ *Dimensions in cm:* h.18.1

‣ *Material:* Terracotta

‣ *Techniques:* Front moulded. Worn mould

‣ *Colour:* Pinkish grey 7.5 YR 7/2

‣ *Date:* End of the sixth century BCE

‣ *Workshop:* Workshop of 'straight reworking' probably

‣ *Typology:* Block-like body: group 1d

‣ *Short description:* Complete figurine. Chubby face with rounded jaw and large chin. Indistinct bulging eyes, big nose, small smiling mouth with the same width as the nose. She has pronounced cheeks and dimples next to her mouth. Hair parted in the middle of the forehead, otherwise smooth. Hair falling down along the sides of the neck, slightly bulging. Medium-sized polos with rim. Block-like body with outward bending rounded shoulders and slight bending at the knees. The shoulder is rounded as if it had a round fibula. Three disc-shaped pendants hang in a straight row on the upper hem of the apron. The apron reaches almost to the sides of the body and continues to the base. A footstool without feet sticks out, on top of garment. Straightened back.

‣ *Comparable objects:* From the same mould as **57**. The figurine is probably from the same mould series as S192, nearly complete, 13.4cm from necropolis Pezzino, the debris of Cave B, above tomb 1927 and 1930, stratum 3. De Miro 1989, p.16, 18 and fig.15.4. He dates it in the second half of the 6th century BCE. Probably also from the same mould series is a head from Akragas. Breitenstein 1945, p.125, fig.17, Nat. Mus. Copenhagen.

In Eraclea Minoa a figurine from the same mould was found in tomb 61. This figurine had a white slip layer: Mus. Eraclea Minoa Inv. no.4907. Albertocchi 2004, p.91, no.1685. From the same mould series as AG 1164, Museo "Griffo". Albertocchi 2004, p.90, no.1680; De Miro 2000, p.128, no.16, complete 19.1cm, which was found at the same location. From the same mould series are also two other figurines, both from the living quarter West of the Temple of Zeus: AG 9205, no head or feet, 13.4cm and AG 9206, headless 12.6cm. Albertocchi 2004, p.90, no. 1682-3; De Miro 2000, p.221, no.1177 and 1176. With its double row of four pendants and large fibulae, but the same block-like body and pose, **62** seems a further elaboration on the same type. It is probably not a figurine from the same mould series. Dewailly describes it as the second generation of type A VII from Selinous.

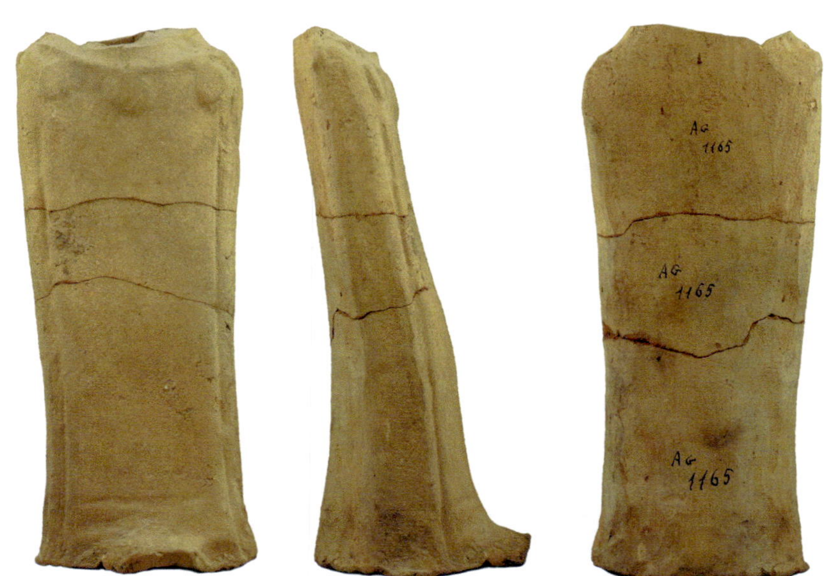

No. 55; Scale 1:2 (Museo Archeologico Regionale "Pietro Griffo", Agrigento).

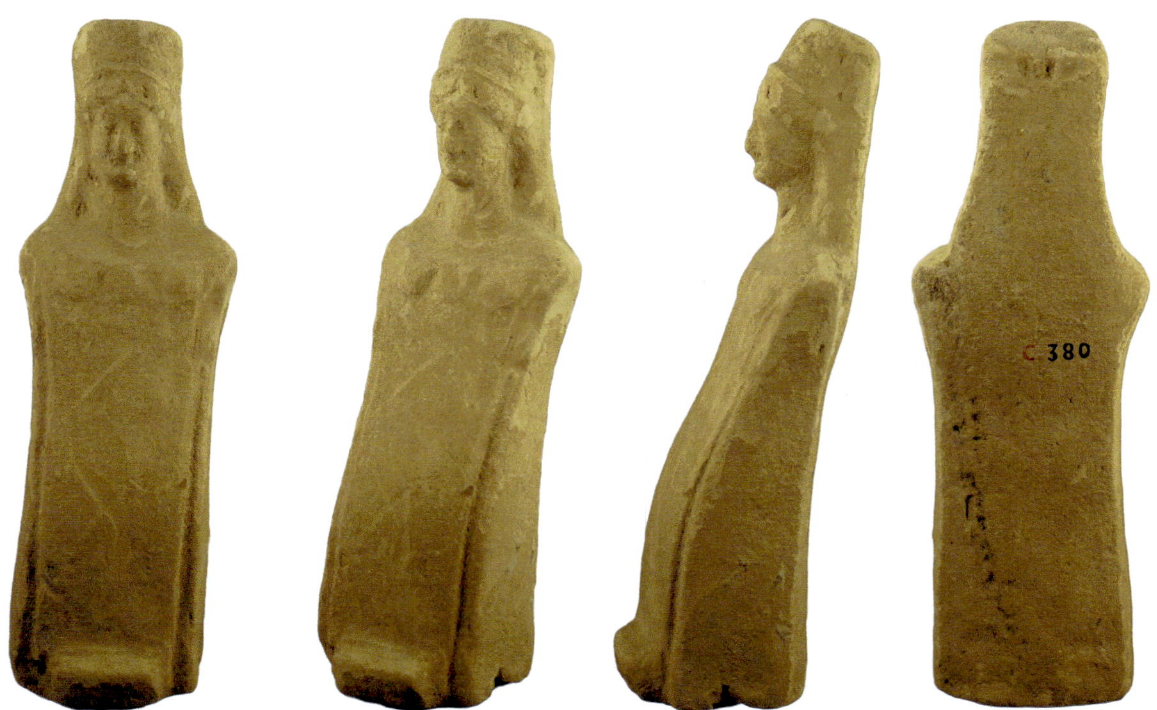

No. 56; Scale 1:2 (Museo Archeologico Regionale "Pietro Griffo", Agrigento).

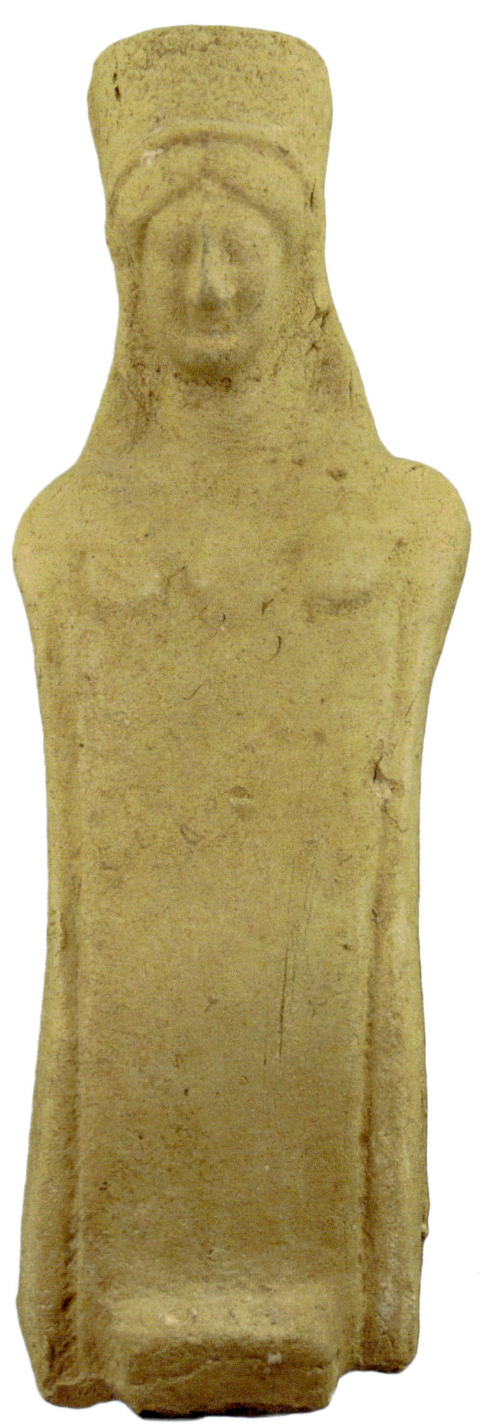

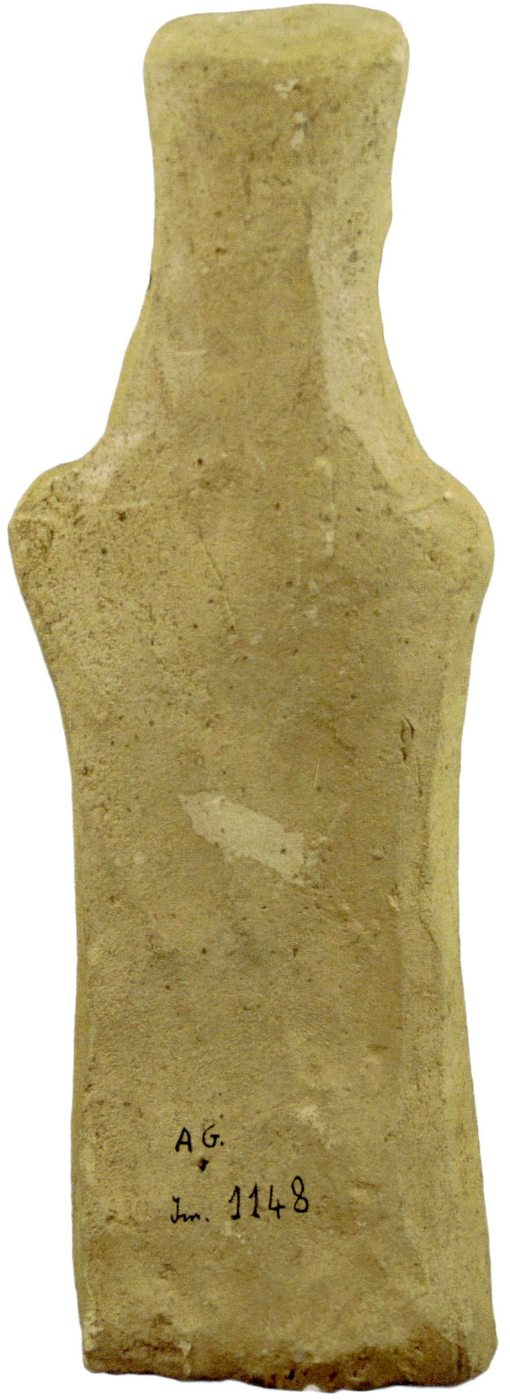

No. 57; Scale 1:1 (Museo Archeologico Regionale "Pietro Griffo", Agrigento).

No.57

- *Museum and Inventory number:* Mus. Agrigento 1148
- *Findspot and context:* City Sanctuary. At the base of the southwest wall of the sanctuary
- *Publications:* Albertocchi 2004, p.90, no.1679; De Miro 2000, p.128, no.15, tav.LX; Dewailly 1992, p.71, n. 64
- *Dimensions in cm:* h.18.5
- *Material:* Terracotta
- *Techniques:* Front moulded
- *Colour:* Very pale brown 10 YR 7/4
- *Date:* End of the sixth century BCE
- *Workshop:* Workshop of 'straight reworking'
- *Typology:* Block-like body: group 1d
- *Short description:* Complete figurine. Fleshy face with rounded jaw and big chin. Indistinct bulging eyes, big nose, small smiling mouth with the same width as the

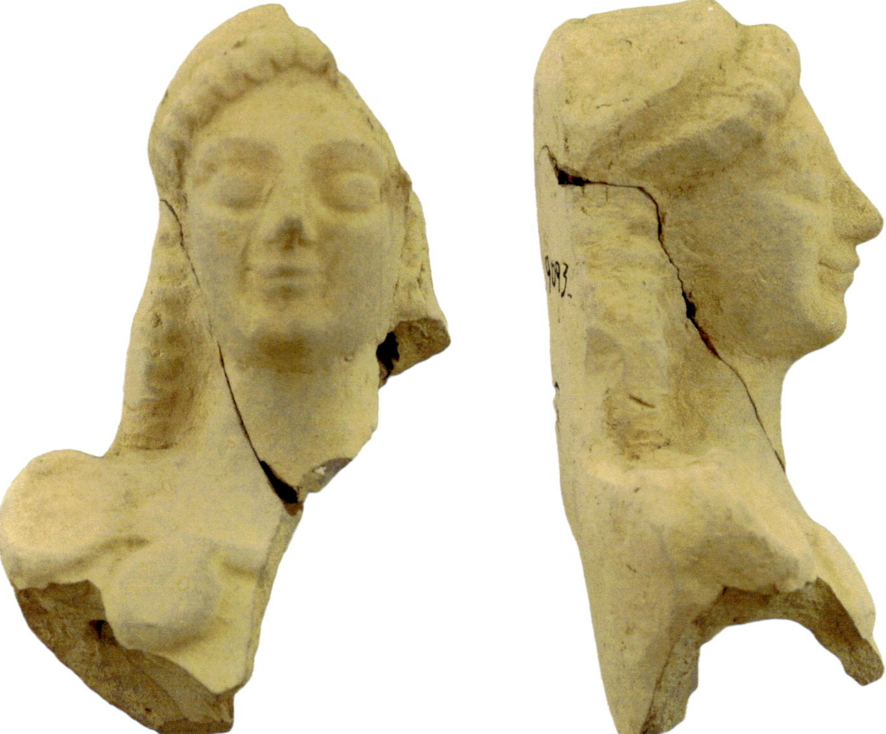

No. 58; Scale 1:1 (Museo Archeologico Regionale "Pietro Griffo", Agrigento).

nose. She has pronounced cheeks and dimples next to her mouth. Hair parted in the middle of the forehead, otherwise smooth. Hair falling down along the sides of the neck, slightly bulging. Medium-sized polos with rim. Block-like body with outward bending rounded shoulders and a slight bending at the knees. Three pendants, disc-shaped hang in a straight row on the upper hem of the apron. The apron reaches almost to the sides of the body and continues to the base. A footstool without feet sticks out, on top of garment. Straightened back and sides.

‣ *Comparable objects:* From the same mould as **56**. Other comparable objects, see **56**.

No.58

‣ *Museum and Inventory number:* Mus. Agrigento 9093 (169)

‣ *Findspot and context:* Workshop/ sanctuary near Gate V

‣ *Publications:* Albertocchi 2004, p.92, no.1695; De Miro 2000, p.241, no.1412; Dewailly 1992, p.71, n. 64

‣ *Dimensions in cm:* h.9.8

‣ *Material:* Terracotta

‣ *Techniques:* Front moulded. Slip layer in lighter colour, on grey clay. Pure and fine clay.

‣ *Colour:* Very pale brown 10 YR 8/4

‣ *Date:* End of the sixth century BCE

‣ *Workshop:* Unknown

‣ *Typology:* Block-like body: group 1d

‣ *Short description:* Head and right shoulder of a figurine in two fragments. Oval face, large eyes with eyebrows and a very pointed nose, smiling mouth with thin lips. Dimples next to the mouth. Hair in big bulbs vertically placed on the forehead and along the sides of the neck, horizontally

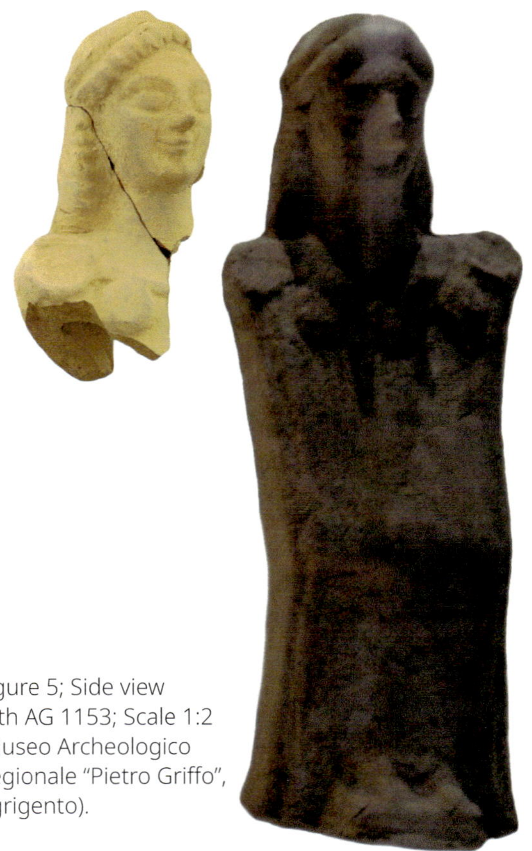

Figure 5; Side view with AG 1153; Scale 1:2 (Museo Archeologico Regionale "Pietro Griffo", Agrigento).

placed. A rather thick veil covers the top of the head, but is not visible behind the hair on the sides. Another possibility is that this is an ampyx, a headband. Albertocchi 2004, p.93. Large round fibula, quite similar in shape to the pendant, but larger, attached to a cord on the chest with originally three discs. Straight back.
‣ *Comparable objects:* Probably from the same mould is AG 1153, complete, h.21.3cm, has a block-like body, three discs as chest pendants and feet on a footstool, Museo "Griffo" (fig.5). Albertocchi 2004, p.92, no.1691; De Miro 2000, p.128, no.13, tav.LIX. Face and hair, but not the headgear, are reminiscent of **138**.

No.59

‣ *Museum and Inventory number:* Mus. Agrigento S 92
‣ *Findspot and context:* City Sanctuary
‣ *Publications:* Albertocchi 2004, p.95, no.1705
‣ *Dimensions in cm:* h.19.2
‣ *Material:* terracotta
‣ *Techniques:* Front moulded
‣ *Colour:* Very Pale Brown 10 YR 8/3
‣ *Date:* End of the sixth century BCE
‣ *Workshop:* Unknown
‣ *Typology:* Block-like body: group 1d
‣ *Short description:* Complete figurine. Small face, indistinct, sizeable nose. Hair in bulbs. Low polos with rim. Block-like body, bending at the knees. She wears a long straight apron that continues over the footstool. Three pendants on the chest, attached to a band: a crescent, pointing down, in the middle and on each side a disc, each reaching the hem of the apron. Straightened back.
‣ *Comparable objects:* Fiertler considers this type to originate from Akragas. Fiertler 2001, p.57, 59-60, tav.BXXI, type BXXI), but inspired by a 'secondary prototype' from Selinous. According to Albertocchi a head, AG 1175, Museo "Griffo", is from the same mould series. See De Miro 2000, p.131, no.42, tav.LXVII. From the same mould as Marconi 1930 37 fig.34.2. A figurine from Akragas is probably of the same mould series: Mus. Bonn Inv. no.D 171a, head on chest, h.9cm. Hübinger-Menninger 2007, no.204. A similar figurine, also in size, upper part h.6.2cm, but without pendants, is thought to be from Akragas or Selinous: British Mus. Inv. no.1956,0216.61.See museum website. **60** and **61** are variations on this figurine: the number of pendants is extended, also as fibulae on **60**.

No. 59 (right); Scale 12 (Museo Archeologico Regionale "Pietro Griffo", Agrigento).

No.60

‣ *Museum and Inventory number:* Mus. Agrigento 2598
‣ *Findspot and context:* Akragas
‣ *Publications:* -
‣ *Dimensions in cm:* h.11.2
‣ *Material:* Terracotta.
‣ *Techniques:* Front moulded. The back might have had a large firing hole, which is suggested by the rounded break.
‣ *Colour:* Reddish-yellow 5 YR 6.6
‣ *Date:* End of the sixth century BCE
‣ *Workshop:* Unknown
‣ *Typology:* Block-like body: group 1d
‣ *Short description:* Upper part of a figurine. Head and right side heavily damaged. In two pieces, restored. Female figurine with an oval face, pointed nose and upwards-curving mouth. She has a smooth fringe of hair on the forehead and hair falling down straight along the sides of the neck. She wears a very low polos. Her body is simple, slightly flaring to the shoulders, diagonally shaped at the front, with a sharp bend at the knees. She wears an apron on top of which at the chest five pendants are hanging in a row. In the middle, there is a crescent with the points down, flanked by a disc on her right side and two

No. 60 (right); Scale 1:1 (Museo Archeologico Regionale "Pietro Griffo", Agrigento).

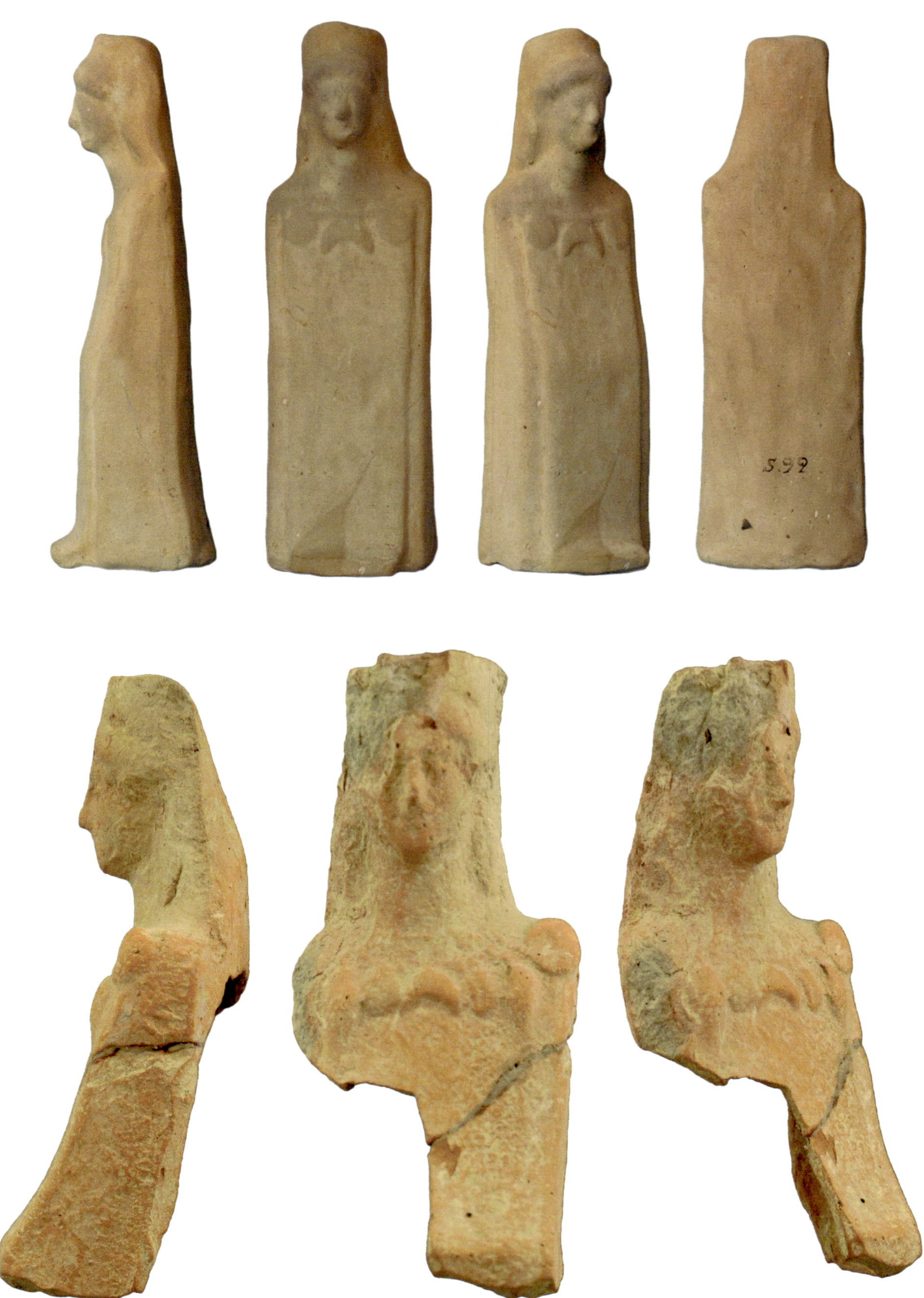
5.99

shell or seed-shaped pendants on the left. It is unclear and could very well have been a disc. Considering the strong symmetry of the figurine overall, this seems more likely. Something might have prevented a proper print in the clay. On her left shoulder, a small round fibula seems in line with the pendants. The sides are cut off straight. The back might have had a firing hole.

‣ *Comparable objects:* Almost same pendants as **59**, without the seed-shaped pendants. Very similar body, except for the arms as **114**. **61** has a similar head and pose, but the pendants have been extended with another row, and two ovoid pendants next to the crescent in the middle. If the ovoid pendants are not seen as a misprint when moulded, the figurine might be an example of the transformation of pendant types: from discs to seeds and ovoids, and also an increase in the number of pendants and rows. A figurine part from Selinous, chest and head 14cm tall, from an earlier generation, has exactly the same upper pectoral band, but a different head, necklace and fibulae: Mus. Palermo SM Pal T19560. Dewailly 1992, p.75, fig.40.

No.61

‣ *Museum and Inventory number:* Mus. Agrigento S497
‣ *Findspot and context:* City Sanctuary
‣ *Publications:* -
‣ *Dimensions in cm:* h.9.6
‣ *Material:* Terracotta
‣ *Techniques:* Front moulded. Numerous small holes: lime-spalling or other inclusions. The clay is rather red. Lighter coloured slip layer
‣ *Colour:* Light red 2.5 YR 7.6
‣ *Date:* End of the sixth to beginning of the fifth century BCE
‣ *Workshop:* Unknown
‣ *Typology:* Block-like body: group 1d
‣ *Short description:* Upper part of a figurine. Very worn and damaged, particularly on the protruding parts and edges. Right shoulder broken off. Though very indistinct, the rounded face shows a large nose, big eyes and a smiling mouth. A fringe in bulbs rounds her forehead in a thick band. She wears a low polos with a rim on top of the fringe of hair. She wears knob earrings. It is unclear whether she has arms. Two visible rows with pendants hanging from a clear cord on her chest, without shoulder clasps: five pendants in total are still visible: a crescent pointing down in the middle and two ovoid pendants on the sides. The second row has two left of probably originally five ovoid shapes. Flat back, side cut off.
‣ *Comparable objects:* No. **60** has a similar head with low polos, but the pectoral pendants with shoulder clasps are different.

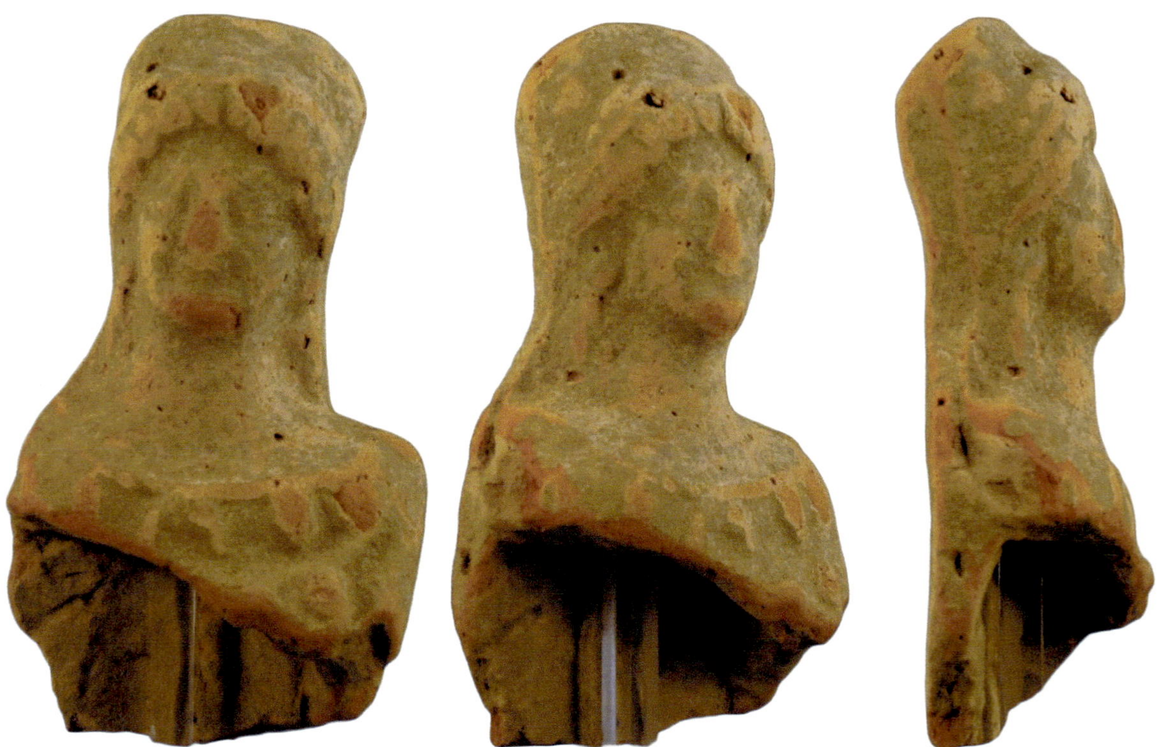

No. 61; Scale 1:1 (Museo Archeologico Regionale "Pietro Griffo", Agrigento).

No. 62; Scale 1:1½ (Museo Archeologico Regionale "Pietro Griffo", Agrigento).

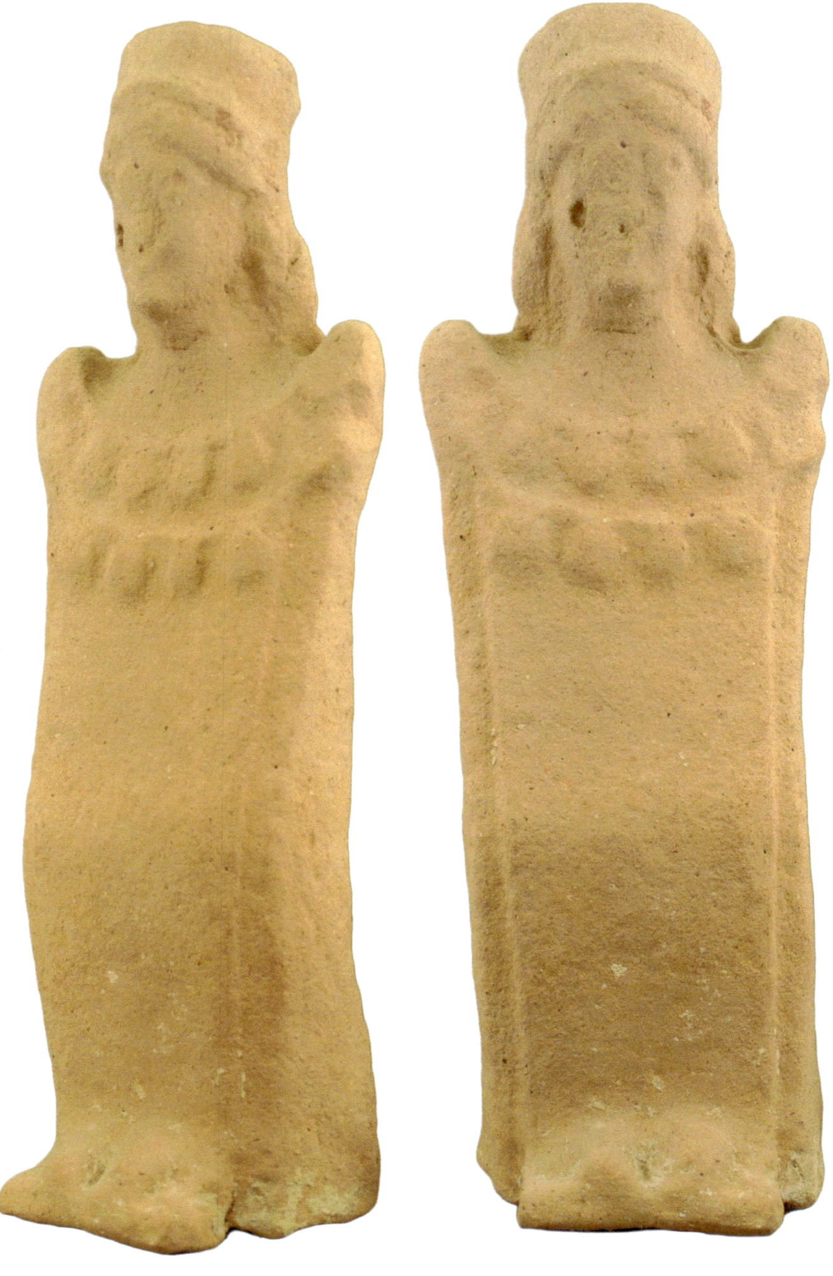

No.62

‣ *Museum and Inventory number:* Mus. Agrigento S884

‣ *Findspot and context:* City Sanctuary

‣ *Publications:* Albertocchi 2004, p.96, no.1710; Dewailly 1992, p.76, n. 73

‣ *Dimensions in cm:* h.21.8

‣ *Material:* Terracotta.

‣ *Techniques:* Front moulded. Worn mould

‣ *Colour:* Pink 7.5 YR 7/4

‣ *Date:* 500-480 BCE

‣ *Workshop:* Unknown

‣ *Typology:* Block-like body: group 2b

‣ *Short description:* Nearly complete figurine. Heavily damaged face. Oval face with protruding chin. Smooth fringe of hair, parted in the middle, bulging along the sides of the neck. Low polos with small rim. Thin block-like body with apron. Fibulae shaped as a double palmette, but without details. Two bands, the upper reaching the fibulae, the second the edge of the apron. Each cord contains four disc-shaped pendants. Low footstool on which undefined feet. Flat back, slightly flaring at the lower part.

‣ *Comparable objects:* Upper body is from the same mould as **88**, except for the arms and the reworked dress. The head and body type are reminiscent of **56** and **57**, but the pendants and fibulae have been altered in this figurine. Figurine AG 1152, Museo "Griffo", could be a type that is in between, because of the four disc-shaped pendants, complete 20.37cm Mus. Agrigento. Albertocchi 2004, p.90 no.1678; De Miro 2000, p.128, no.14, tav.LIX. The head, however, with the fringe band in bulbs, does not give reason to think so. It is very well possible that these heads and body-moulds were combined during the same period. From the same mould as AG 1146, Museo "Griffo". Albertocchi 2004, p.96, no.1711; De Miro 2000, p.129, no.19.

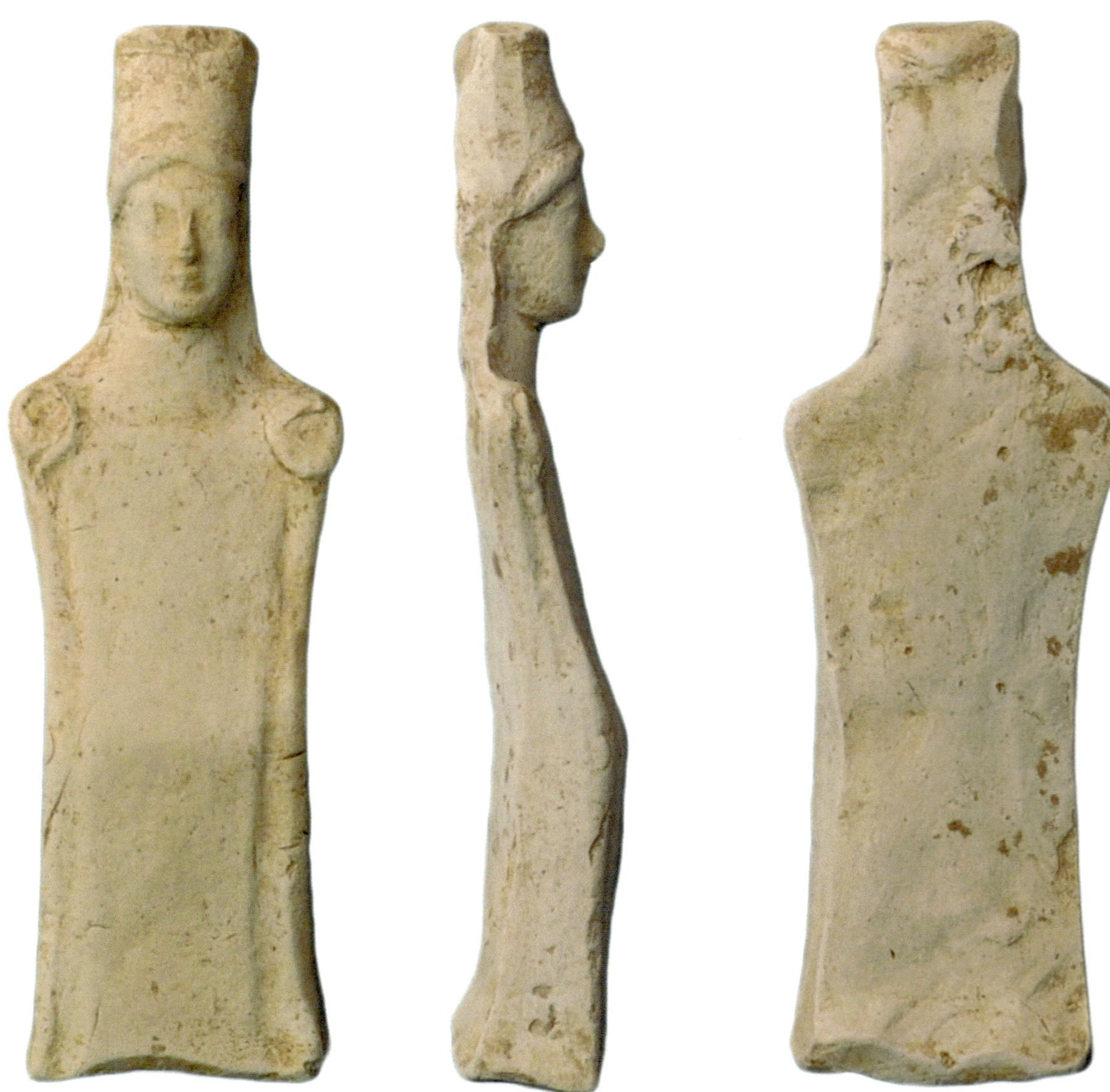

No. 63; Scale 1:1 (Museo Archeologico Regionale "Pietro Griffo", Agrigento).

No.63

- *Museum and Inventory number:* Mus. Agrigento 22577
- *Findspot and context:* Necropolis di Contrada Pezzino Tomb 169, together with two other figurines, **25** and **69**.
- *Publications:* Veder Greco: le necrópolis di Agrigento 1988, p.307; De Miro 1989, p.36, tav.XXVI
- *Dimensions in cm:* h.13.4
- *Material:* terracotta
- *Techniques:* front moulded
- *Colour:* White 2.5 Y 8/1
- *Date:* Last decade of the 6th century BCE
- *Workshop:* Workshop of the white clay
- *Typology:* Block-like body: group 1a
- *Short description:* Complete figurine with a very thin block-like body, bending slightly at the knees. The face is oval but quite flat with round eyes and a small mouth. Straight high polos. She wears an apron attached with fibulae on the flaring shoulders. The garment has a hem in the neck and on both sides of the front of the slim body.
- *Comparable objects:* The face is reminiscent of **48** and **70** but is more round and flat than those are. **71** is from the same findspot and likely from the same workshop, because of the style of the head and the colour of the clay. It appears to be a variation on this figurine and the Rhodian figurines with their round shoulders, seated on a block-shaped seat.

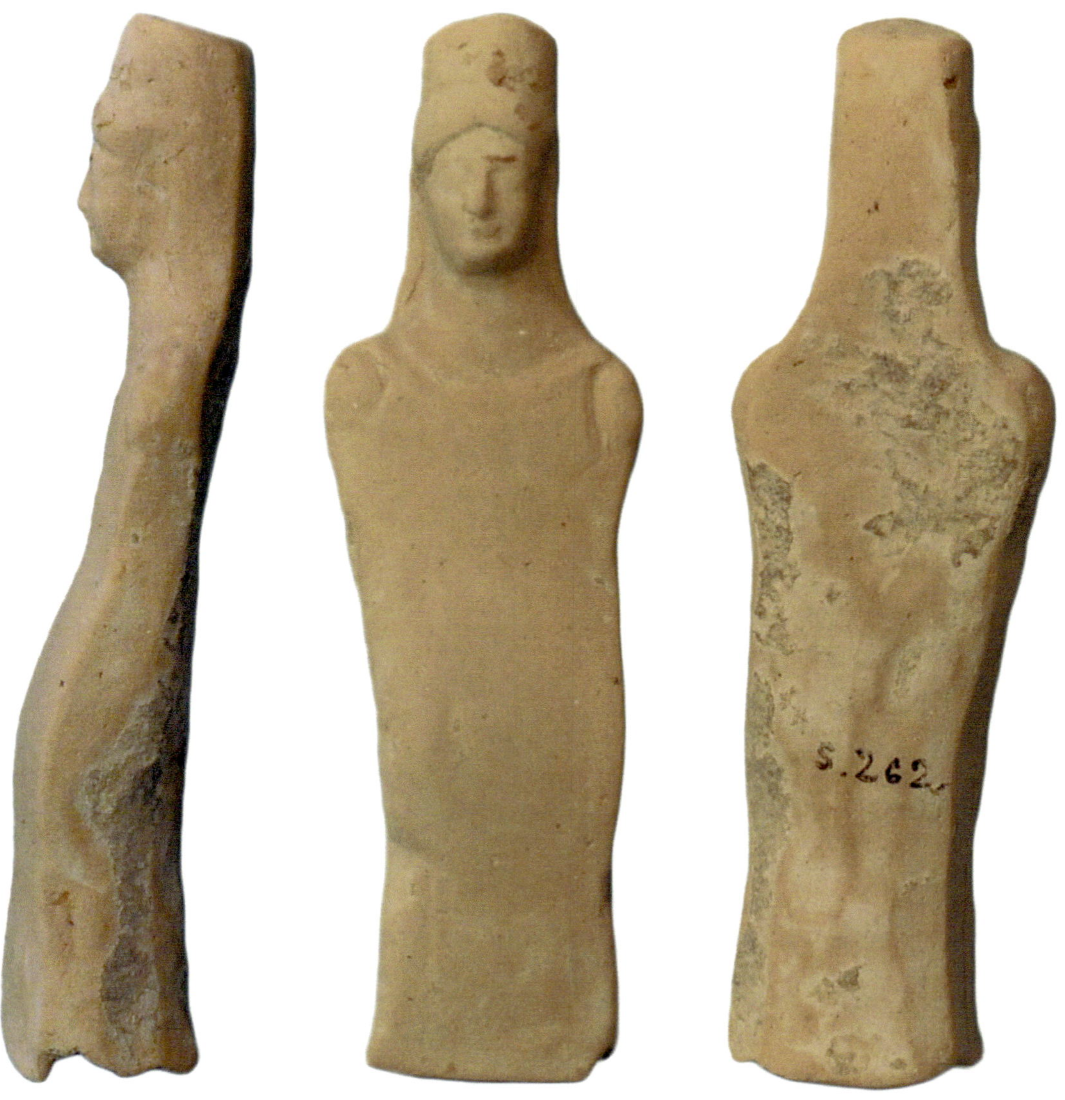

No. 64; Scale 1:1 (Museo Archeologico Regionale "Pietro Griffo", Agrigento).

No.64

- *Museum and Inventory number:* Mus. Agrigento S262
- *Findspot and context:* City Sanctuary
- *Publications:* Fiertler 2001, p.61, n. 66
- *Dimensions in cm:* h.14.2
- *Material:* Terracotta
- *Techniques:* Front moulded. Incised with tool to mark possible pectoral chain and fibulae.
- *Colour:* Pink 7.5 YR 7/3
- *Date:* Last decade of the 6th century BCE
- *Workshop:* Unknown
- *Typology:* Block-like body: group 1a
- *Short description:* Nearly complete thin figurine. Some chips broken off at the base. Oval face with indistinct eyes and small mouth. Straight, medium-high polos, placed high up on her head, leaving a rim of hair visible. Hair parted in two, hanging down along the sides of the neck. Two incised lines in the neck create a band. It might concern reworking because of a body-head combination from different moulds. Fibulae, oval-round in shape, are formed by incised lines. The thin body bends at the knees on the front and is slightly flared at the shoulders.
- *Comparable objects:* The face is very similar to **24** and reminds also of **63**, though it is less round. It also looks like the faces of **65** and **66**-**68**. Fiertler refers to the similarities on the sides of the body. Fiertler 2001, p.61, n. 66. Similar but not from the same mould series as head **69**, in particular the small polos, which is placed more to the back of the head.

Type D: Some characteristic faces and standing figurines (65-70)

This small group contains some tall figures with a narrow face and a tall polos.

No.65

‣ *Museum and Inventory number:* Mus. Agrigento C385
‣ *Findspot and context:* Akragas
‣ *Publications:* -
‣ *Dimensions in cm:* h.12.3
‣ *Material:* Terracotta. The flakes broken off, show that the quality of the clay was not high.
‣ *Techniques:* Front moulded. Polos on the back smoothed on the sides with a sharp tool.
‣ *Colour:* Pink 5 YR 7/4
‣ *Date:* First quarter of the 5th century BCE
‣ *Workshop:* Angled back of polos group
‣ *Typology:* Narrow-face: group 2c
‣ *Short description:* Upper part of a figurine: chest and head of a female figurine. Chest heavily damaged. Narrow oval face with a pointed chin, large bulging eyes, indistinct, a sizeable nose and a very small mouth. A rounded thin and smooth fringe of hair runs around her forehead. On top of it, she wears very tall, slightly flaring polos with a rim that repeats the fringe. Next to the sides of her narrow neck, but placed rather towards the back, her hair falls down straight. On her right shoulder, she wears a small round fibula, while her left shoulder is empty. The hem of a thick apron is visible on the chest, running horizontally straight. The back is straight, while the 'corners' of the polos on the back are cut away sharply.
‣ *Comparable objects:* Possibly from the same mould series as **70**. The sizes are comparable, but **65** has a pectoral on the chest and forms a variation in the series. The face and polos are similar to **66-68** and might be also from the same mould series. The face and the reworking on the sides of the head are reminiscent of **34**.

No.66, 67, 68

‣ *Museum and Inventory number:* Mus. Agrigento S421, S424, S422
‣ *Findspot and context:* City Sanctuary
‣ *Publications:* -
‣ *Dimensions in cm:* h.5.4, 6.5, 6.3
‣ *Material:* Terracotta
‣ *Techniques:* Front moulded
‣ *Colour:* Pink 7.5 YR 7/4, Pink 7.5 YR 8/4, Pink 7.5 YR 7/4
‣ *Date:* First quarter of the 5th century BCE
‣ *Workshop:* Unknown
‣ *Typology:* Narrow-face: group 2c
‣ *Short description:* Head and neck of three figurines. Lower part of face with mouth and chin broken off from two of them. Oval face. Large eyes, a pronounced nose. An earring is visible on her left. The fringe is smooth. Bulging hair next to the neck. She wears a very high outward-bending polos with a rim. The rim is as big as the hair.
‣ *Comparable objects:* The three heads are from the same mould. They might be from the same mould series as **65** and **70**. The face and polos are similar to **24** (without rim) and **34** also.

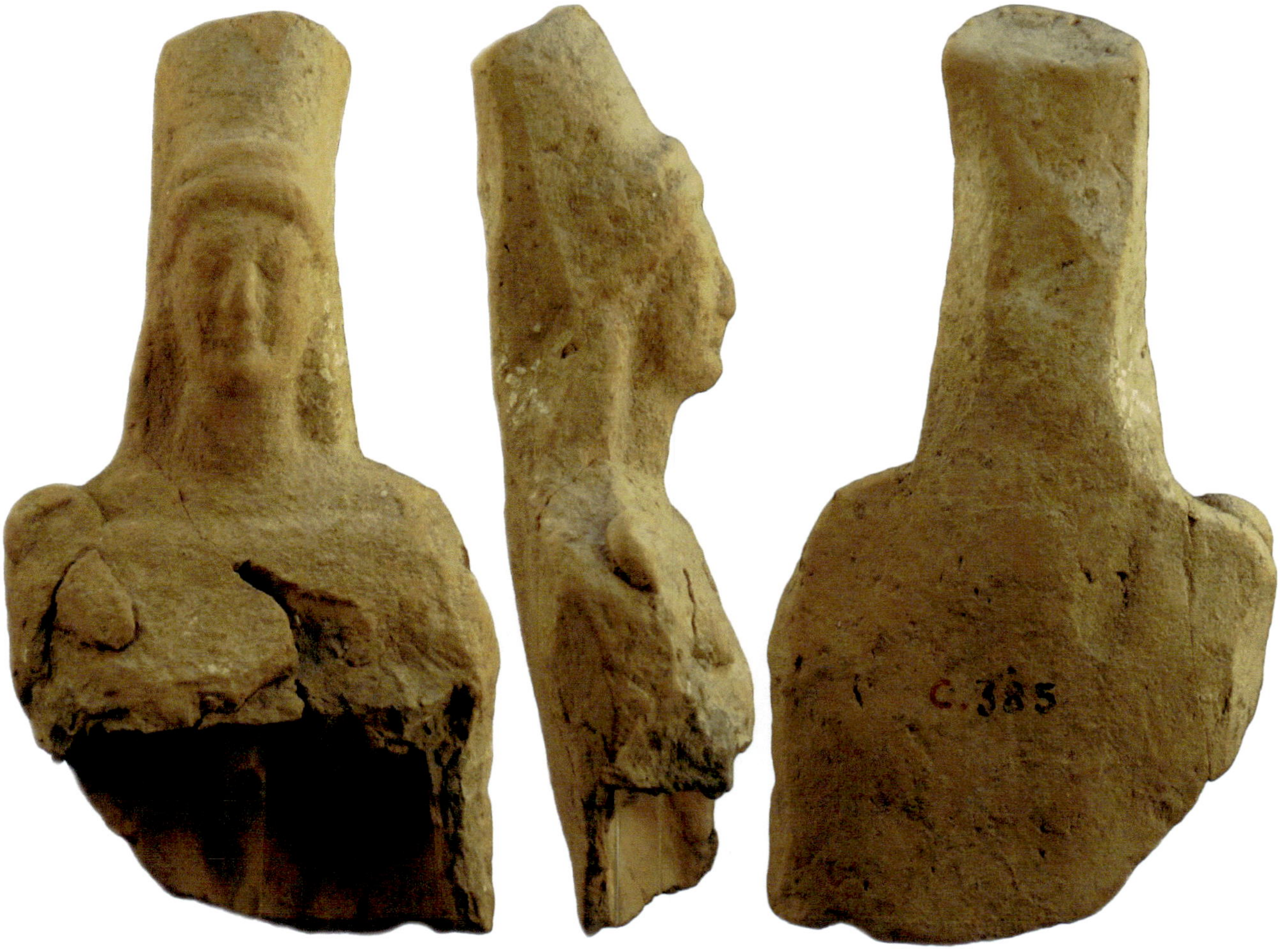

No. 65; Scale 1:1 (Museo Archeologico Regionale "Pietro Griffo", Agrigento).

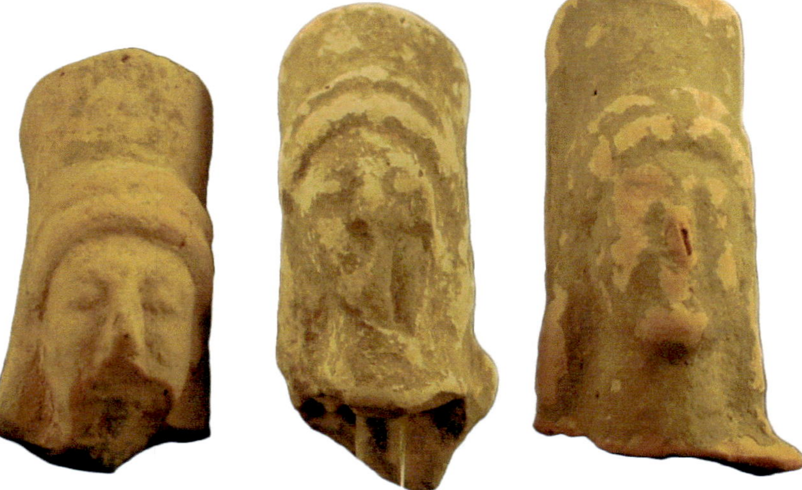

No. 66, 67, 68; Scale 1:1 (Museo Archeologico Regionale "Pietro Griffo", Agrigento).

No.69

‣ *Museum and Inventory number:* Mus. Agrigento S399
‣ *Findspot and context:* Akragas
‣ *Publications:* -
‣ *Dimensions in cm:* h.6.3
‣ *Material:* terracotta
‣ *Techniques:* Front moulded.
‣ *Colour:* Light yellowish brown 10 YR 6/4
‣ *Date:* First quarter of the 5th century BCE
‣ *Workshop:* Unknown
‣ *Typology:* Narrow-face: group 2c
‣ *Short description:* Head of a figurine. Her face is narrow and her eyes round and bulging. The chin is pronounced. Her fringe has a vertical structure and the hair on the sides of her face is thick. She wears a small cylindrical polos high-up on her head with a thick round rim.
‣ *Comparable objects:* Similar but not from the same mould series as figurine **64**. The polos and its placement are comparable to **28**.

No.70

‣ *Museum and Inventory number:* Mus. Agrigento 22582
‣ *Findspot and context:* Necropolis di Contrada Pezzino Tomb 918 together with **35**, two reliefs of which one with a sphinx (?), and a phallus (?)
‣ *Publications:* Albertocchi 2004, p.65, no.1061; Veder Greco: le necrópolis di Agrigento 1988, p.309; De Miro 1989, p.37, tav.XXVII
‣ *Dimensions in cm:* h.25.5
‣ *Material:* Terracotta
‣ *Techniques:* Front moulded
‣ *Colour:* Very Pale Brown 10 YR 7/3
‣ *Date:* First quarter of the 5th century BCE
‣ *Workshop:* Angled back of polos group
‣ *Typology:* Narrow-face: group 2c
‣ *Short description:* Nearly complete figurine. Restored from several fragments. Narrow face, triangular face with large bulging eyes and a smiling mouth. Her ears are visible in front of her fringe with bulbs, which is smoothed and similar to the rim of the polos she wears. The polos is very tall and straight. She also has a veil. Standing with arms outstretched along flat body. She seems to look downwards. She wears an apron on top of an undergarment, draped over feet on a footstool. The apron itself is narrower than her body and does not reach her ankles. She wears two rows of pendants, the first with five discs, in line with her disc like fibulae. The second row comprises five oval but pointed shaped pendants, varying in size, some shaped like small containers. The rim might also represent the suspension tube.
‣ *Comparable objects:* Possibly from the same mould as **65**. Facial features are comparable with **66-68**, but might be from the same mould as the head of **34**, even though the polos is slightly different. Again, the reworking might show that they are from the same workshop. The larger face of **73** is similar also, but quite indistinct. The figurine is also comparable to Marconi 1933, p.57, fig.34.1, which has no arms, but also the combination of disc and ovoid pendants (see fig.). The small circular fibulae seem a continuation of the pendants on the first band. The latter is probably from the same mould series as AGS6807 (14cm headless): De Miro 2000, p.281, no.1898.

It is the same combination of discs and pointed pendants, also as the long face that is reminiscent of a complete, 20cm tall figurine from Gelas. Adamesteanu D. and P. Orlandini 1956, p.369, fig.13. Its pose is not standing and is reminiscent of **100**. The arms of the figurine here are one of the following steps in the iconographic development. The rim of the 'undergarment' is often applied to create the arms. As a result, the fibulae changes often at that moment. This is visible in figurine **88**, which is very comparable in pose and iconographic scheme, but the fibulae have been altered.

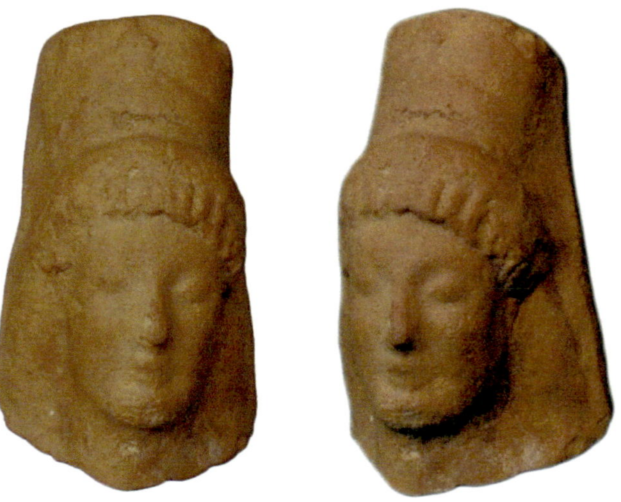

No. 69; Scale 1:1 (Museo Archeologico Regionale "Pietro Griffo", Agrigento).

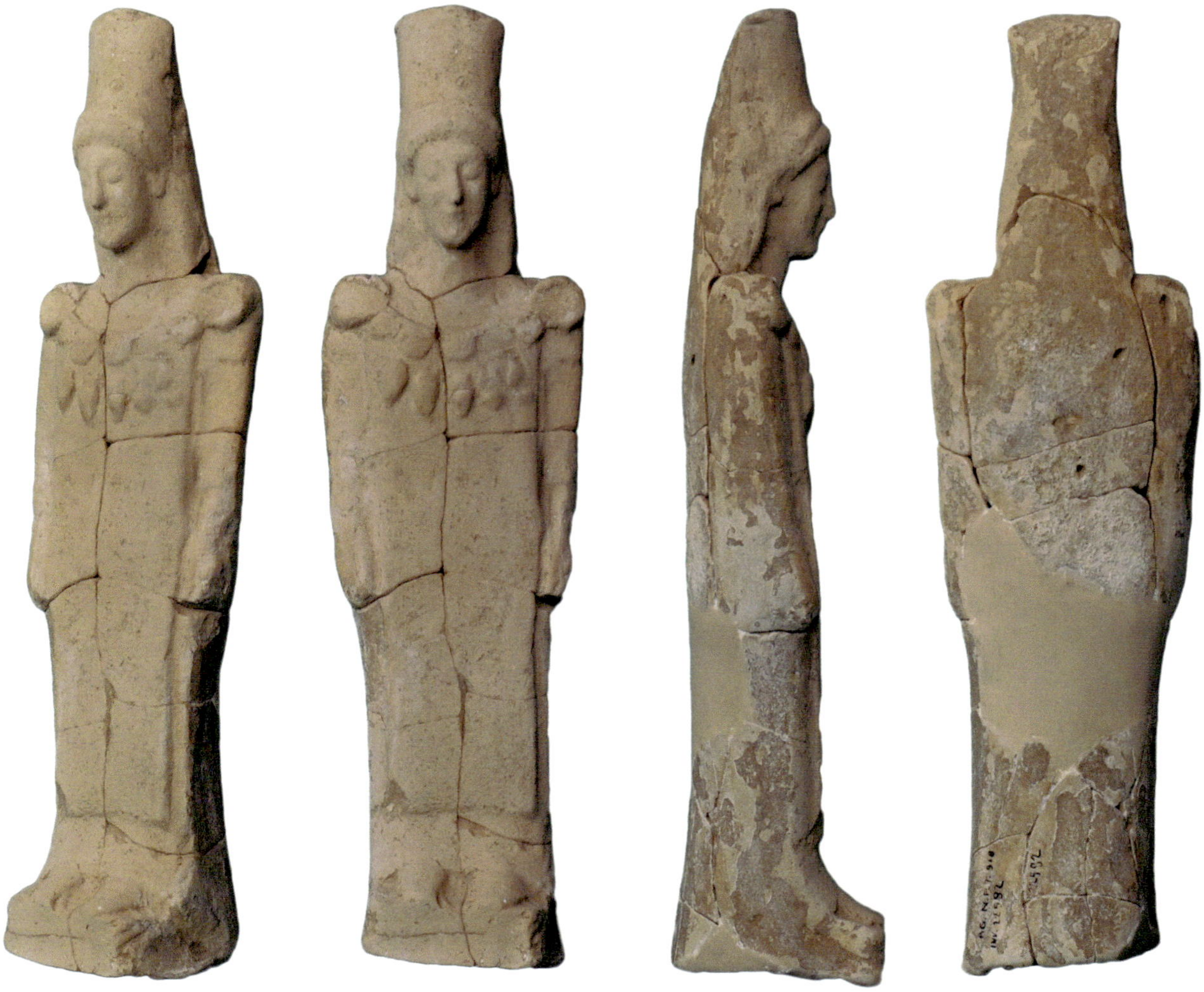

No. 70; Scale 1:2 (Museo Archeologico Regionale "Pietro Griffo", Agrigento).

Type E: Imported figurines with rounded shapes, and objects inspired by them (71-76)

Imported objects with a seated figure with rounded arms, and their local imitations.

No.71

- *Museum and Inventory number:* Mus. Agrigento 22576
- *Findspot and context:* Necropolis di Contrada Pezzino Tomb 169, together with two other figurines, **25** and **63**.
- *Publications:* Veder Greco: le necrópolis di Agrigento 1988, p.307; De Miro 1989, p.36, tav.XXVI
- *Dimensions in cm:* h.13.4
- *Material:* terracotta
- *Techniques:* Moulded. Solid. Incised lines on the back.
- *Colour:* White 2.5 Y 8/1
- *Date:* End of the 6th century BCE
- *Workshop:* Workshop of the white clay
- *Typology:* Inspired by East Greek figurines: 5c
- *Short description:* Complete figurine. Oval face with large eyes. Big fringe with wavy hair and a very high polos flaring at the top. The outline of the figurine is rounded and curves from the polos to the arms. The rounded arms are attached to the upper part of the body and end at the lap, smoothly without hands. The lower part of the body is square, and smaller than the upper part. On the legs, a line indicates the two attached legs. A base under the whole statue includes a footstool. The surface of the figurine is smooth and not interrupted by detailed parts. Sides and back are smooth and straight also.
- *Comparable objects:* Its rounded body is reminiscent of Rhodian figurines, such as **72**: the outline of the polos and arms has the same shape. Common in Akragas and Gelas, De Miro 1989, p.36, n. 7. There are several more in the Museum of Second Choice, the exhibited part of the archive of the Archaeological Museum in Agrigento. They vary in size between about 10 to about 20cm tall and are clearly inspired by East Greek or Attic figurines in their pose, and their rounded contours are very similar. Marconi 1933, tav.XV.3; De Miro 2000, p.162, no.395, p.257, no.1593-4, p.281, no.1895-6, tav.LVII).

No.72

- *Museum and Inventory number:* Mus. Agrigento 20180 (20421)
- *Findspot and context:* S. Anna(?)
- *Publications:* Fiertler 2001, p.61, n. 66
- *Dimensions in cm:* h.14.3
- *Material:* Terracotta
- *Techniques:* Front moulded
- *Colour:* Reddish-yellow 7.5 YR 6/6
- *Date:* End of the 6th century BCE
- *Workshop:* Unknown
- *Typology:* East Greek: 5c
- *Short description:* Nearly complete figurine. Restored with minor infill. Seated female figurine with a rounded body and high polos. Her face is unclear, but the nose protrudes. Her polos runs without interruption into her head and hair, giving her a smooth outline. The body is more naturally depicted. Rounded shoulders, and her breasts are indicated. She sits straight up, body at almost 90 degrees to her lap. Her hands rest on her knees. The elevation below her hands is created by drapery of the dress, continuing under her hands to her lower legs. Her undergarment reached her ankles. She sits on a square chair with backrest and a small footstool. The surface on the sides and back is smooth and is rounded at the corners.
- *Comparable objects:* Similar to **52**, though with a rounder face. Comparable to the head AG 9024. De Miro 2000, p.194, no.848, tav.LVIII. Four statuettes from Selinous are very similar. SM T 2805, SM T 2903, SM T 2852, SM T 2977. Dewailly 1983, p.5-12. Similar to some statuettes with a very high polos and similar large nose from the Athenaion of Gelas. Panvini and Sole 2005, p.38-9 type I. D1 II tav IIIc and d, IV and V a; Panvini 1998 171 V. 7

Also similar to a figurine from Palma di Montechiaro De Miro 1962, tav.XLIII fig.1 Mus. Syracuse. The typical parts of the mantle with the hands on top are clearly distinguished on a figurine from Rhodes. Nat. Mus. Copenhagen: photo 6298, See museum website. Comparable to a figurine from Kos, h.15cm in Mus. Istanbul Inv. No.1822. Mendel 1908, p.132, no.1657. See museum website. The following figurines share a likeness with the iconography of the body and face, but wear a veil instead of a polos: From Akragas: De Miro 2000, p.257, no.1593-1594, tav.LVII. From Selinous: Poma 2009, p.231, no.14; Gabrici 1928, tav.XXXIX.Similar to a figurine from Taormina, with the drapery/folds, with long hands (h.13.1cm, Inst. Leipizg T2354. Paul 1959, p.71, no.74, pl. 22. And a figurine from the necropolis of Eraclea Minoa. De Miro 1962, p.145-6, tav.LXIII, fig.1 on the right. Similar to figurine TW80 (h.19.8cm, Göttingen, Germany), which is from Sicily. Hubo 1887, p.455.2. This Rhodian type is also known from a small vase, for example, from Naucratis. British Mus. Inv. no.1886,0401.1398 nearly complete h.14.2cm Higgins 1954, p.49, no.63 pl. 14. See museum website. A figurine from Medma Rosarno, complete h.21.4cm is clearly inspired by this type also, but has been given a different head. Langlotz and Hirmer 1963, p.61, no.22. The body of this type could be even combined with a local head. Poma 2009, p.230, no.12. Several without veil from Rhodes. Nat. Mus. Copenhagen: photo 5895, See museum website. Several figurines from Paestum, particularly Ammerman 1993, p.94, no.195 and 196, pl. XXII-XXIII. There are many more similar figurines. See for more references, ordered by location, Ammerman 1993, p.989, n.16.

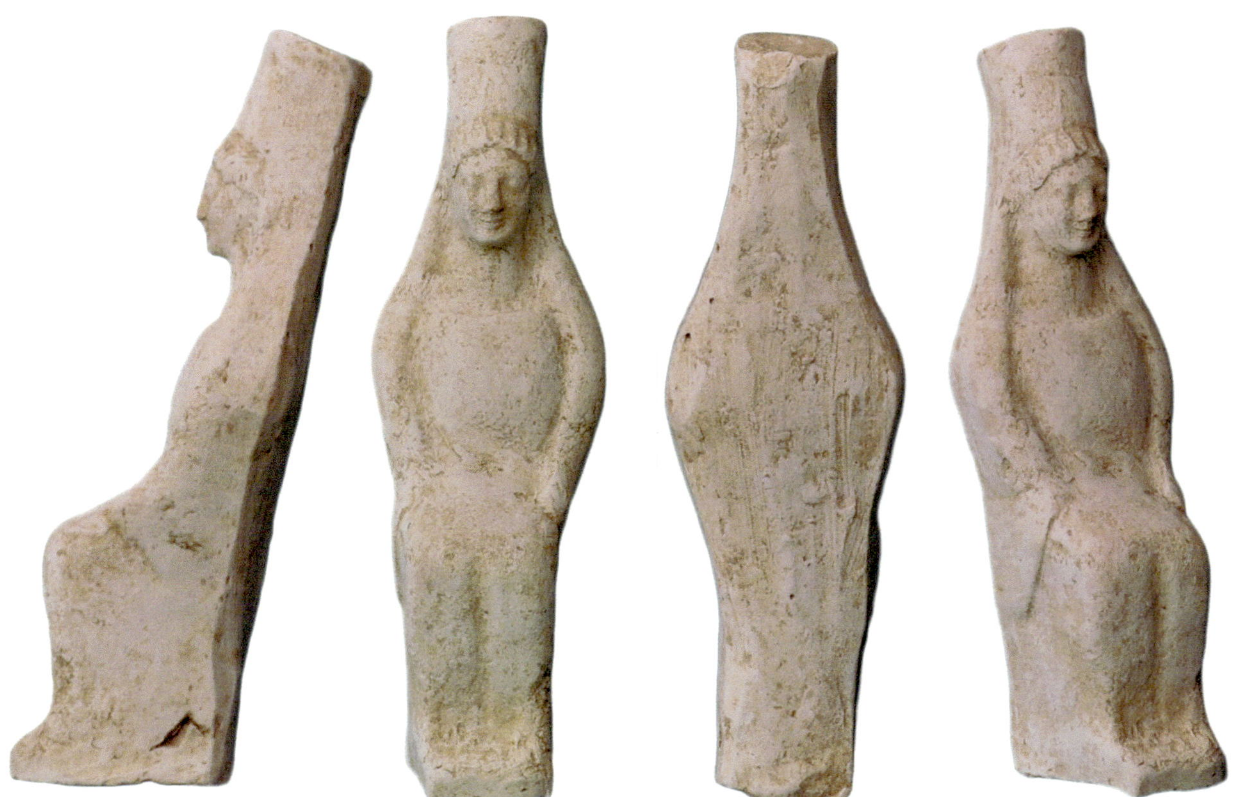

No. 71; Scale 1:1½ (Museo Archeologico Regionale "Pietro Griffo", Agrigento).

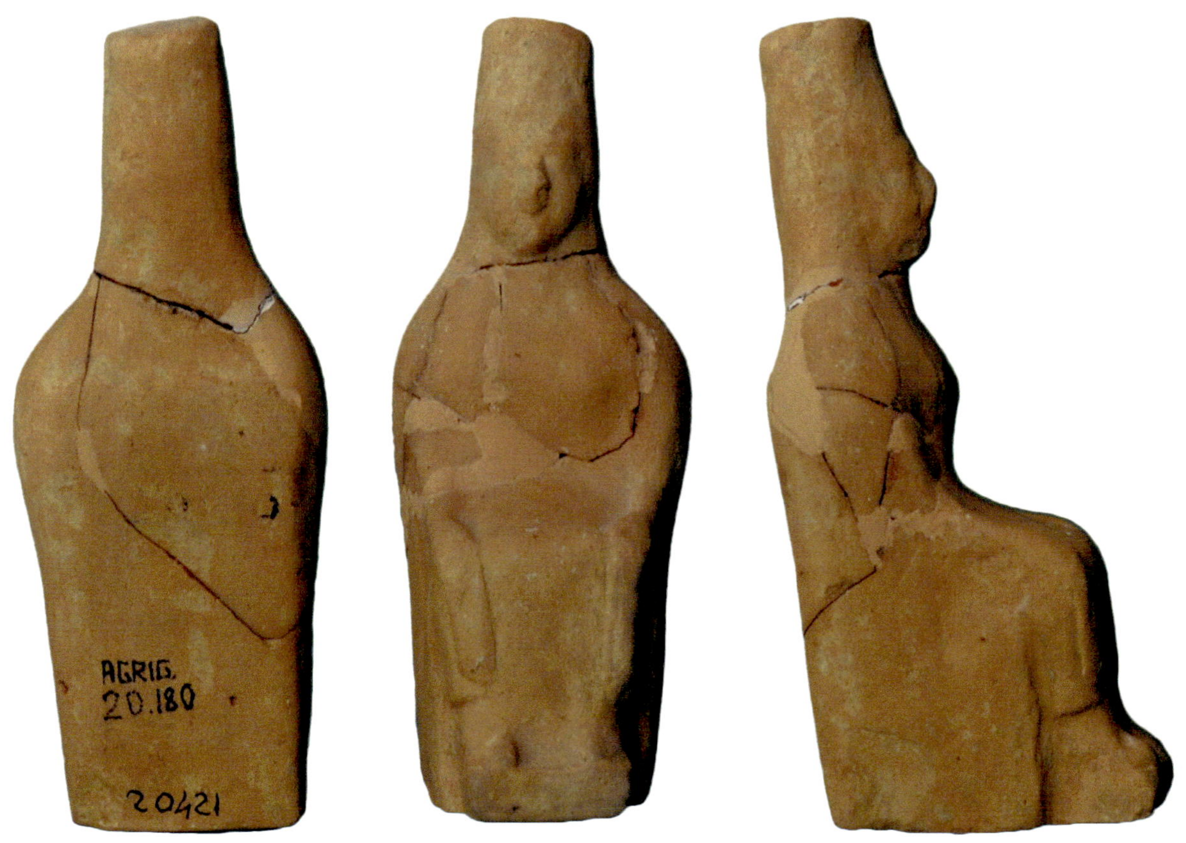

No. 72; Scale 1:1½ (Museo Archeologico Regionale "Pietro Griffo", Agrigento).

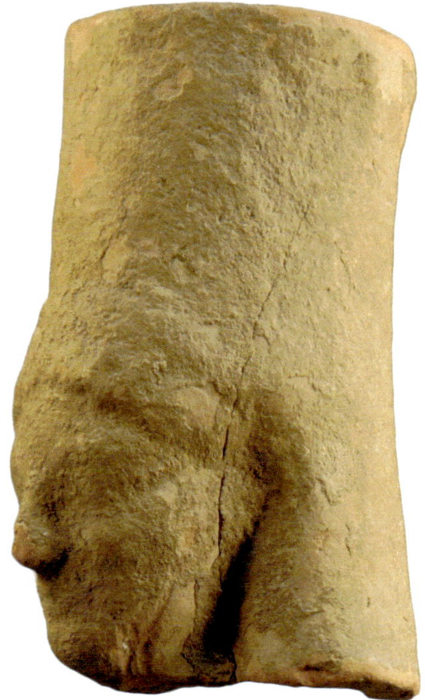
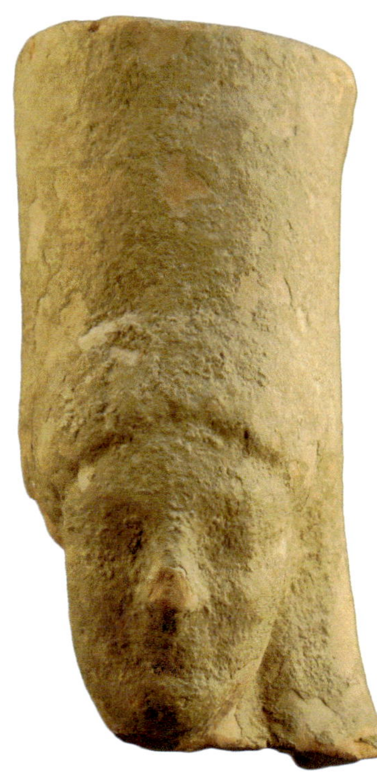

No. 73; Scale 1:1 (Museo Archeologico Regionale "Pietro Griffo", Agrigento).

No.73

‣ *Museum and Inventory number:* Mus. Agrigento C402
‣ *Findspot and context:* Akragas
‣ *Publications:* -
‣ *Dimensions in cm:* h.9.4
‣ *Material:* Terracotta
‣ *Techniques:* Front moulded.
‣ *Colour:* Pink 7.5 YR 8/3
‣ *Date:* End of the 6th century BCE
‣ *Workshop:* Unknown
‣ *Typology:* Inspired by East Greek figurines: 5c
‣ *Short description:* Head of a figurine. Right side and neck broken off. Crack in the left side of the head. Narrow face, quite indistinct with sizeable nose, indistinct round eyes and small mouth. She wears a very tall, slightly flaring polos with a rim on top of her fringe. On the sides the polos continues into her thick hair next to the sides of the face and neck, suggesting a veil over the polos.
‣ *Comparable objects:* While the facial features are reminiscent of **34** and **70**, the polos and the outline created are typically 'Rhodian inspired.'

No.74

‣ *Museum and Inventory number:* Mus. Agrigento S366
‣ *Findspot and context:* Akragas
‣ *Publications:* -
‣ *Dimensions in cm:* h.9.0
‣ *Material:* terracotta
‣ *Techniques:* Front moulded. Numerous small holes because of lime-spalling. Clay mixture has turned out redder on face and polos. Weathered mould. White slip layer (?)
‣ *Colour:* Reddish-yellow 5 YR 6/8
‣ *Date:* End of the 6th century BCE
‣ *Workshop:* -
‣ *Typology:* Inspired by East Greek figurines: 5c
‣ *Short description:* Upper part of a figurine. From the waist down broken off. Nose damaged. Small face with large eyes. Smooth fringe of hair. High polos, slightly flaring with rim. Long hair or veil falling over the shoulders in a continuing outline from the headdress to the shoulders. Rounded body and arms. Arms held tight to body.
‣ *Comparable objects:* Very similar to **71**.

No.75

‣ *Museum and Inventory number:* Mus. Agrigento 20194
‣ *Findspot and context:* One of the sanctuaries
‣ *Publications:* -
‣ *Dimensions in cm:* h.8.0
‣ *Material:* Terracotta
‣ *Techniques:* Front moulded. Probably a lighter coloured slip layer: inside dark red. Clay bulging at feet. Upper part of the figurine must have been solid. Very thick walls, on right: 1cm thick. Incisions with sharp tool on right side of the figurine.
‣ *Colour:* Pink 7.5 YR 7/4
‣ *Date:* End of the 6th century BCE
‣ *Workshop:* Unknown
‣ *Typology:* Inspired by East Greek or Attic figurines: 5c
‣ *Short description:* Lower part of the body of a figurine. This part is block-shaped and stable due to its depth, but it tilts to the right. Feet sticking out, placed on footstool

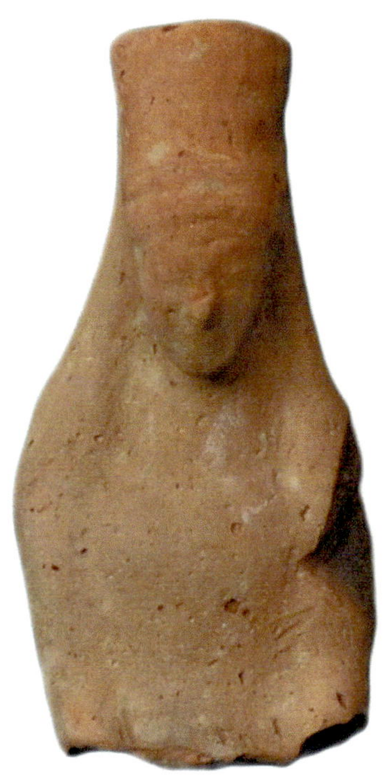
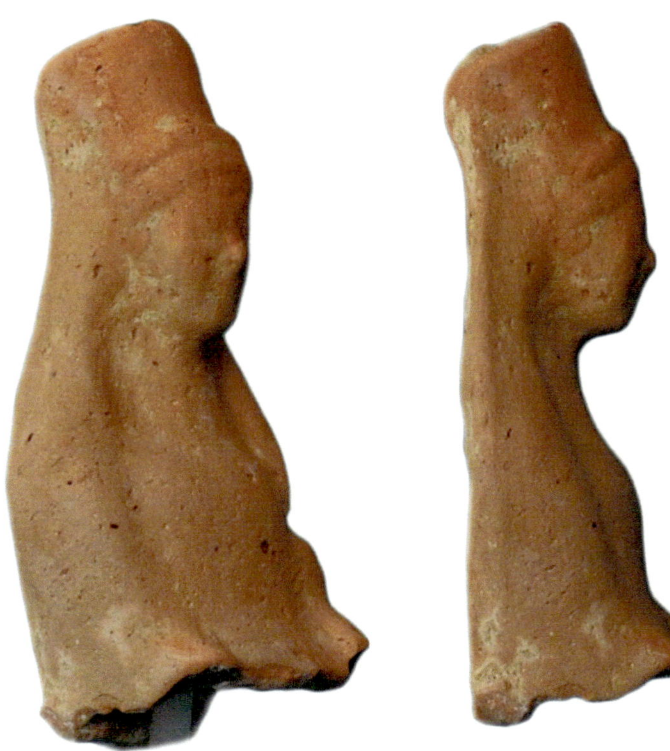

No. 74; Scale 1:1 (Museo Archeologico Regionale "Pietro Griffo", Agrigento).

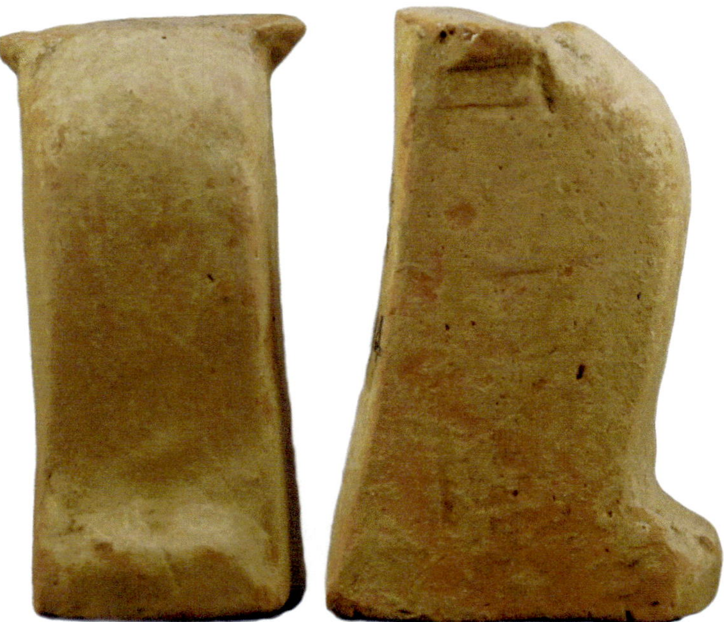

No. 75; Scale 1:1 (Museo Archeologico Regionale "Pietro Griffo", Agrigento).

with the same width as the body. Very rounded knees and straight sides. On both upper sides a small part sticks out.
‣ *Comparable objects:* The figurine is not typical at all, because its depth is larger than average and the shape of the very rounded knees and flat lap is totally different from the sloping or semi-sloping bodies of most other figurines. However, the feet and their placement look similar to other figurines and it might be locally made, after a non-Sicilian example, such as **72** and **76** with the strongly angled lap.

No.76

‣ *Museum and Inventory number:* Mus. Agrigento 9034 (285)
‣ *Findspot and context:* Southern city wall
‣ *Publications:* De Miro 2000, p.168, no.463, tav.LXXXVIII
‣ *Dimensions in cm:* h.9.5
‣ *Material:* Terracotta
‣ *Techniques:* Front moulded. Front and sides painted: completely white base layer with dark red on the front of the throne. Several holes caused by lime-spalling.
‣ *Colour:* Light brown 7.5 YR 6/4
‣ *Date:* Early 5th century BCE
‣ *Workshop:* Unknown
‣ *Typology:* Attic or East Greek imported object: 5c
‣ *Short description:* Nearly complete figurine. Right ear of the throne and feet broken off.

Female figurine on throne. Round face with large eyes. Expression indistinct. Veil with rim rounding her head. Band with wavy hair in three rows on her forehead. Veil runs in a continuous curve on to her arms, which are attached to body. Pointed breasts, of which the right one is placed higher on the chest. She is seated on a block-based throne. Chair with backrest and ears, rounded endings. Straight back.
‣ *Comparable objects:* Very similar, except for the paint, to a figurine from Santa Venera. Ammerman describes an example from Paestum that is originally Attic or East Greek, complete h.9.9cm. Ammerman 1993, p.98, no.215 pl. XXV. Similar to some other figurines from Magna Graecia, now in Louvre Inv. no: N 4524, C 4950, N 4397, S 2215 Mollard Besques 1954, p.75-6 pl. XLVIII.B528-B531. Similar to a figurine from Cuma Mus. Naples Inv. no.84909 complete, h.10.8cm. The type originates probably from Attica. Scatozza Höricht 1987, p.54-6, tav.VIII. The iconographic elements of a figurine are comparable: British Mus. Inv. no.1966,0328.20, which is much taller h.22.8cm. See museum website. Also as others from the British Mus. Inv. no.1856,1226.257 Higgins 1954, p.175-6, no.655-9, tav.85. See museum website. A figurine from Selinous. Poma 2009, p.230, no.11.

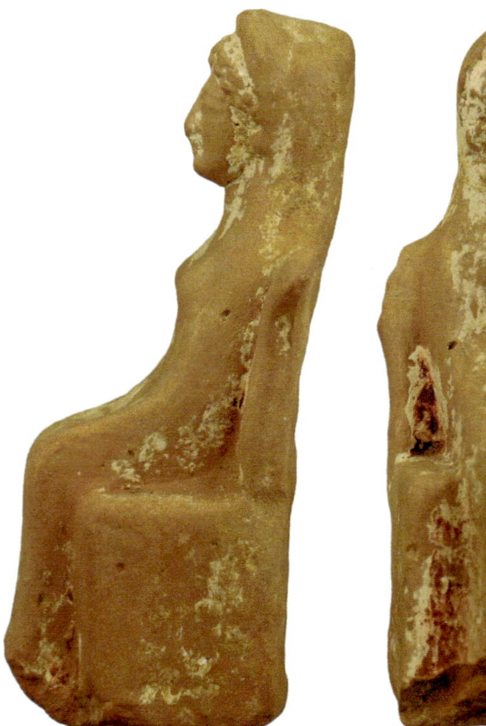
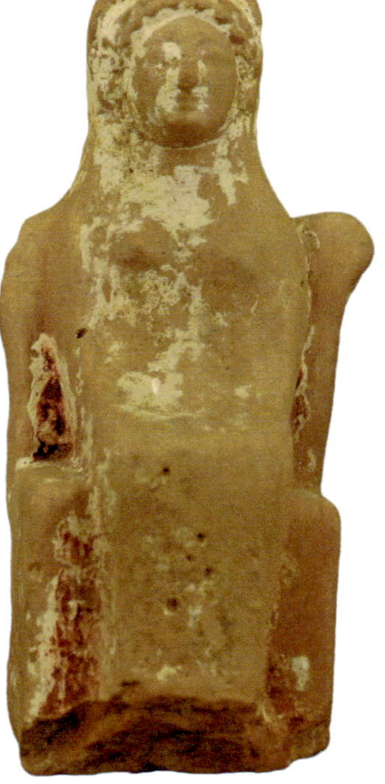
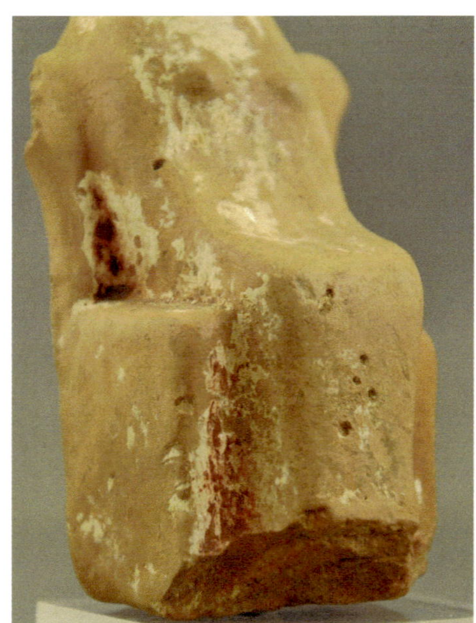

No. 76; Scale 1:1 (Museo Archeologico Regionale "Pietro Griffo", Agrigento).

Type F: Exceptional objects (77-86)

Some exceptionally shaped moulds and figurines. This group contains the early plank-like figurines, and those wearing a wreath or holding another object in their hands.

No.77

- *Museum and Inventory number:* Mus. Agrigento S172
- *Findspot and context:* Akragas
- *Publications:* -
- *Dimensions in cm:* h.9.3
- *Material:* Terracotta
- *Techniques:* Handmade. Painted with dark red, grey and black colours.
- *Colour:* Reddish-Yellow 5 YR 7.6
- *Date:* Mid of the 6th century BCE
- *Workshop:* Unknown
- *Typology:* Imported: 5d
- *Short description:* Complete. Pillar-shaped figurine with a relatively small head with large eyes and a wide jaw. The hair next to the face and neck has horizontal lines and is long and wide. The face could be male. The hair on the head is bulging on the forehead but plain. The wide chest and large shoulders, with just a small part of the upper arm, are painted dark red, like the hair. On the pillar-like body, which flares at the base to increase stability, concentric rectangular blocks are depicted in dark red paint. At the base, there is another dark red horizontal line. Sides and back are painted completely dark-red and black. There is a suspension (?) hole in the back.
- *Comparable objects:* Comparable or even from the same mould series as an upper body fragment from the acropolis of Gelas. Mus. Inv. no.8322. Panvini 2005 56 FR2 2, tav.XIXa.

No. 77; Scale 1:1 (Museo Archeologico Regionale "Pietro Griffo", Agrigento).

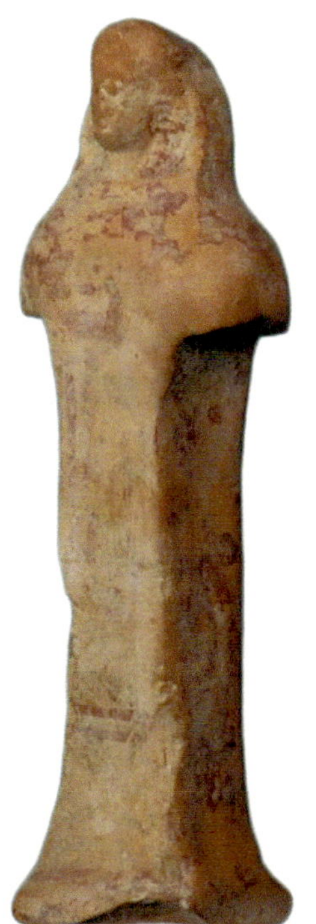

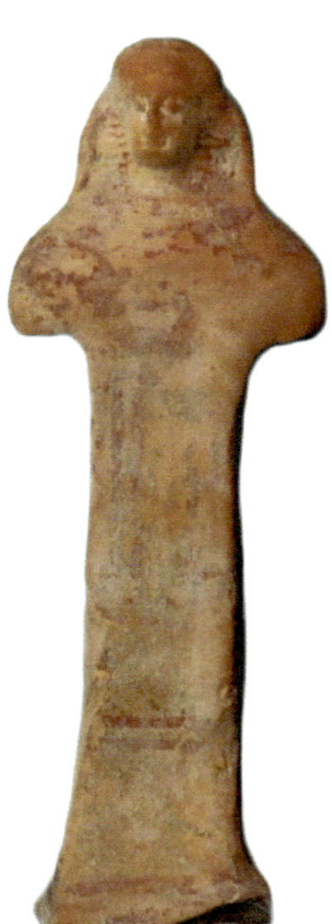

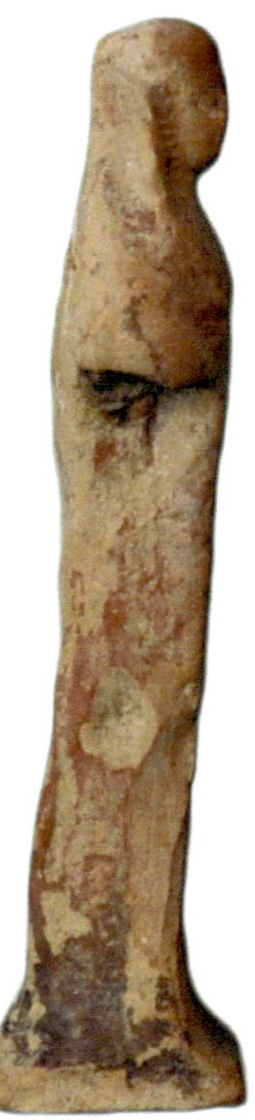

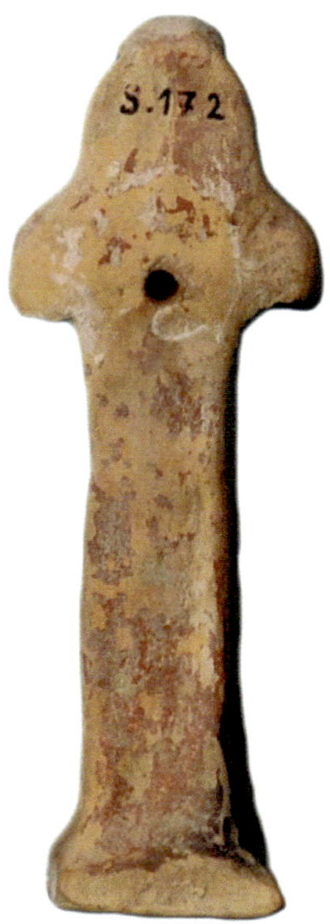

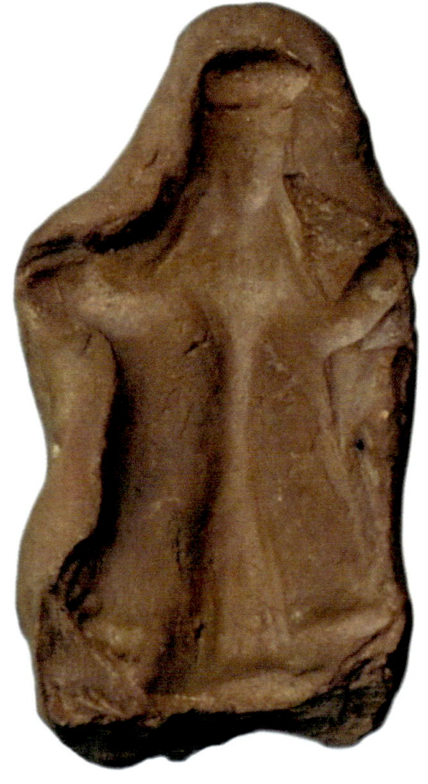

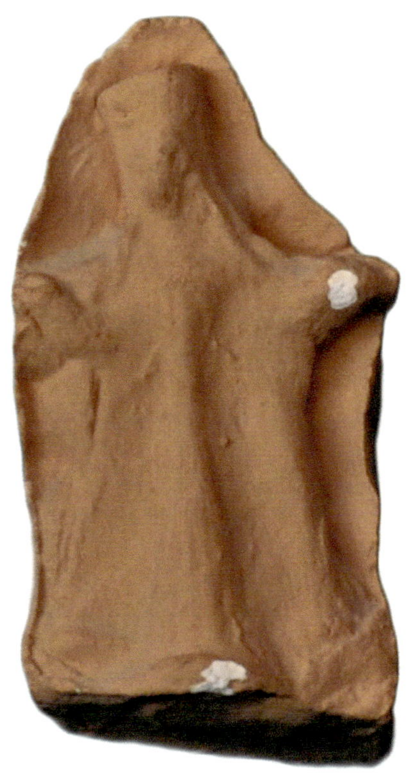

No. 78; Scale 1:1 (Museo Archeologico Regionale "Pietro Griffo", Agrigento).

No.78

- *Museum and Inventory number:* Mus. Agrigento C262
- *Findspot and context:* Akragas
- *Publications:* -
- *Dimensions in cm:* h.10.1
- *Material:* terracotta
- *Techniques:* Imprint from an object, the patrix.
- *Colour:* Light brownish grey 2.5 Y 6/2
- *Date:* End of the 6th century BCE
- *Workshop:* Unknown
- *Typology:* Probably imported: 5d
- *Short description:* Complete mould of a standing and probably female figurine. The thick mould is glued to its stand. Her head is turned slightly to the right and looks down, but the face is very indistinct. She stands on a small base and stretches out the rounded arm stumps. Her hair is long and on each shoulder, there are two separate parts hanging down. She wears a long coat or dress with a protruding rim at the bottom hem. Hair on top of her head and the low polos, with a rim at the top, together form an impressive headgear. It is not clear whether the part in the middle, starting from the chest that protrudes and widens towards the base, is supposed to be the body proper. Back rounded on the edges, flat in the middle.
- *Comparable objects:* A similar thin figurine with a protruding middle part and arm stumps originates from Rhodes. Nat. Mus. Copenhagen Inv. no.2969, photo 6211, link to databse. A similar coat, but then the inverse (the body is deeper than the coat), seems to be worn by the satyr in mould AG8941 .
- *Notes:* Photograph with modern gypsum cast on the right.

No.79

- *Museum and Inventory number:* Mus. Agrigento 20398
- *Findspot and context:* Akragas
- *Publications:* -
- *Dimensions in cm:* h.13.7
- *Material:* Terracotta.
- *Techniques:* Front moulded.
- *Colour:* Light reddish brown 5 YR 6/4
- *Date:* 5th century BCE
- *Workshop:* Unknown
- *Typology:* Mould of the back (?)
- *Short description:* Mould of a general shape for a figurine or the back (?). It has three rather deep compartments,

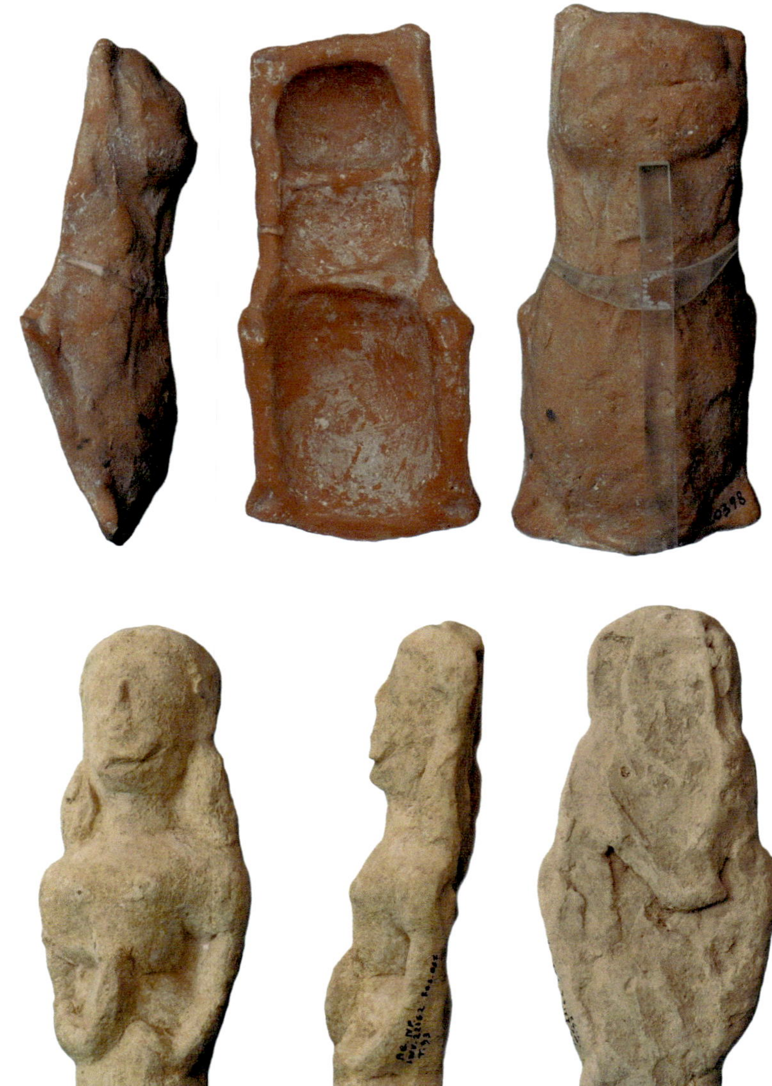

No. 79; Scale 1:2 (Museo Archeologico Regionale "Pietro Griffo", Agrigento).

No. 80; Scale 1:2 (Museo Archeologico Regionale "Pietro Griffo", Agrigento).

rounded and rectangular shaped. The lower, larger one is rectangular with rounded corners and the two upper ones are smaller and divided horizontally by a lower division edge. There are six keys to fit another mould on the corner of the compartments, shaped roughly circular.

No.80

- *Museum and Inventory number:* Mus. Agrigento 22162
- *Findspot and context:* Necropolis di Contrada Pezzino Tomb 93, external pit, together with a figurine of a big-bellied male, a miniature pomegranate-shaped object and a miniature kylix.
- *Publications:* Veder Greco: le necrópolis di Agrigento 1988, p.308; De Miro 1987 459-60
- *Dimensions in cm:* h.13.8
- *Material:* terracotta
- *Techniques:* Moulded. Solid. Weathered mould. Very coarse back.
- *Colour:* Pale Brown 2.5 Y 8/2
- *Date:* Second half of 6th century BCE
- *Workshop:* Workshop of the white clay
- *Typology:* Figurine holding object: 5d
- *Short description:* Upper part of a standing figurine. Relatively large head. Long hair bulging at the sides with diadem (?), along the sides of the neck. Female holding pointed oval-shaped flower bud in her right hand. Her left arm is placed along her body, but it seems she holds her hand on her belly. Dress with short 'sleeves' and sizable upper part covering breasts. Tight waist but wide shoulders.
- *Comparable objects:* The same pose is seen on the three figurines of the triad: AG 1278, Museo "Griffo". De Miro 2000, p.245-6, no.1474, tav.XLIX.

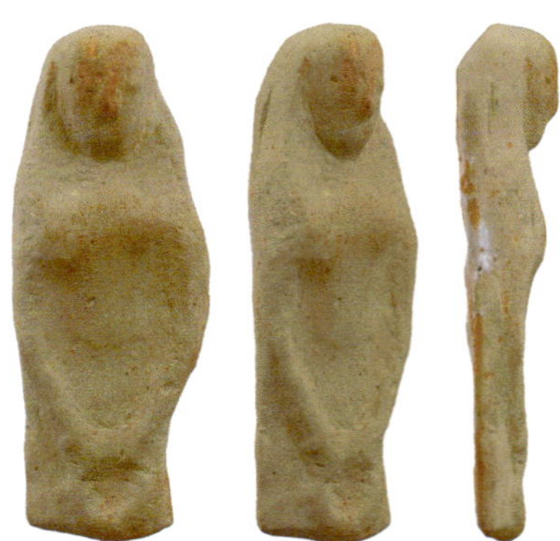

No. 81; Scale 1:2 (Museo Archeologico Regionale "Pietro Griffo", Agrigento).

No.81

- *Museum and Inventory number:* Mus. Agrigento S85
- *Findspot and context:* Akragas
- *Publications:* Marconi 1933, tav.VI, 4
- *Dimensions in cm:* h.9.5
- *Material:* Terracotta.
- *Techniques:* Front moulded. Solid. Worn mould
- *Colour:* Very pale brown 10 YR 7/3
- *Date:* Mid of the 6th century BCE
- *Workshop:* Unknown
- *Typology:* Figurine holding object: 5d
- *Short description:* Nearly complete standing figurine, lower part of body broken off. Glued to its stand. Female figurine in rigid standing pose with a smooth wreath held in front of lower body with both hands. Rounded head with big eyes and large nose, too indistinct for other details. Hair, in block-shaped strands, is visible only at the sides and continues on the chest. Thin figurine, but rounded shapes of body indicated, such as breasts. Arms close to the body, but rounded and naturalistically rendered.
- *Comparable objects:* The figurine is reminiscent of **82**, which also holds a wreath in the same pose. Hair arrangement similar to **77**. The triangular shape of the hair is reminiscent of the face on the marble lamps from Selinous. Parisi 2017, p.55, fig.13.

No.82

- *Museum and Inventory number:* Mus. Agrigento S96
- *Findspot and context:* City Sanctuary
- *Publications:* -
- *Dimensions in cm:* h.16.8
- *Material:* terracotta
- *Techniques:* Front moulded
- *Colour:* Pink 7.5 YR 8/3
- *Date:* Beginning of the 5th century BCE
- *Workshop:* Unknown

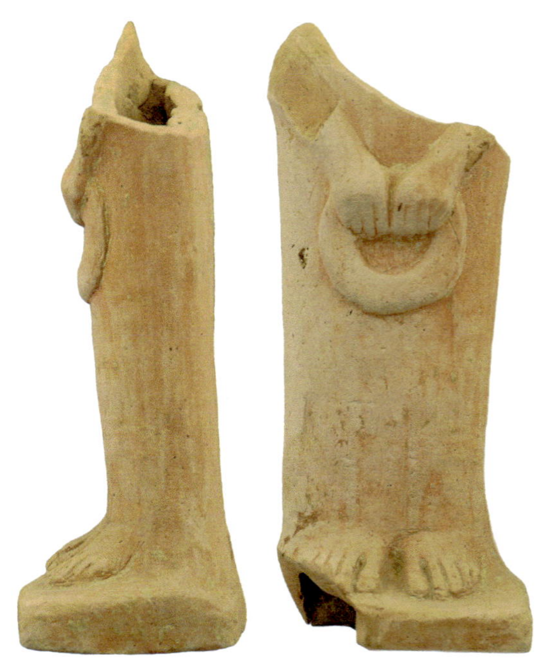

No. 82; Scale 1:2 (Museo Archeologico Regionale "Pietro Griffo", Agrigento).

- *Typology:* Figurine holding object: 5d
- *Short description:* Lower part of a standing figurine. Piece broken off at the base. Standing female figurine holding a wreath in front of her lower body with both hands. The part of the lower arms are brought together with the fists to the front, next to each other, holding the large smooth wreath. She wears a long garment, open a bit to the front, that runs smoothly from her body onto the rectangular low base she is standing on without any seam or rim. Her bare feet with long fingers are placed close together and are partly visible from under the garment. The back and sides are smooth and rounded like the front.
- *Comparable objects:* Could be from the same mould series as a figurine from the Sanctuary of Malophoros,

Selinous, which is complete and 27cm tall. Gabrici 1927, p.254, tav.L.3. It is reminiscent of figurine **81** with a similar wreath. The long dress, open to the front is similar to that of **83** and **84**. It can be compared also to other figurines holding a wreath in the same way. Two stone ones, from Gelas, are both dated to the end of the 6th century BCE and comparable, also like a terracotta figurine, found at Piazza S. Francesco, Catania. Mus. Catania. The wreath and pose is comparable also with two figurines from Gelas, of which one is from Bitalemi. Byvanck-Quarles van Ufford 1940, p.78, fig.30.

No.83

- *Museum and Inventory number:* Mus. Agrigento 23119
- *Findspot and context:* Necropolis di Contrada Mosè. Besides several terracotta figurines of different sorts, there is miniature pottery, oil lamps and no.21, 54 and 173 from a deposit pit (fig.4 and 22).
- *Publications:* Veder Greco: le necrópolis di Agrigento 1988, p.271, no.12
- *Dimensions in cm:* h.32.4
- *Material:* terracotta
- *Techniques:* Front moulded
- *Colour:* Very pale brown 10 YR 7/3
- *Date:* The first half of the 5th century BCE
- *Workshop:* Unknown
- *Typology:* Figurine holding objects: 5d
- *Short description:* Nearly complete figurine. Small infill on the left arm at the base. Standing female figurine holding a wreath and a bird. She has an oval- shaped flat face with large eyes. She has thick lips and a straight mouth. On her forehead, she has a rim of hair with bulbs, topped by a veil. Next to her narrow neck, her hair falls down. She is standing, with her legs tightly next to each other. Her chest indicates breasts and she has large rounded shoulders. With her right hand, she holds a bird, a dove maybe, in front of her chest. In her left hand, stretched out along her body she holds a small but thick and smooth wreath. She wears a long garment, open to the front. Whether the sleeves are long or reach only to the elbow is not clear. She stands on a small base and keeps balance by leaning a bit to the back.
- *Comparable objects:* Is reminiscent of figurine **81** and **82** with a similar wreath and **82** and **83** with a similar long garment, open to the front.

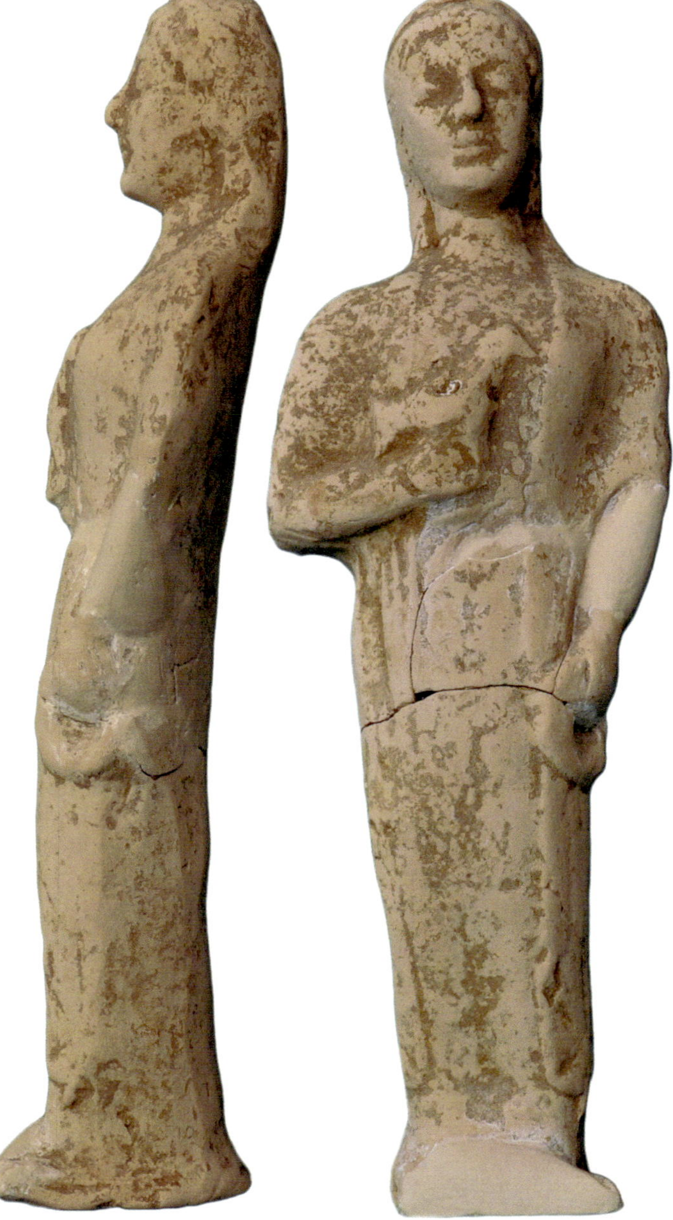

No. 83; Scale 1:2 (Museo Archeologico Regionale "Pietro Griffo", Agrigento).

No.84

‣ *Museum and Inventory number:* Mus. Munich 5409
‣ *Findspot and context:* Akragas (?)
‣ *Publications:* Hamdorf 2014, p.100, no.C 221
‣ *Dimensions in cm:* h.17.6
‣ *Material:* Terracotta
‣ *Techniques:* Front moulded. Reworked with a stick. Clay cracks from drying (?) Disc ear studs separately attached by hand. Only the base is hollow.
‣ *Colour:* Reddish-yellow 7.5 YR 7/6
‣ *Date:* The first half of the 5th century BCE
‣ *Workshop:* Unknown
‣ *Typology:* Figurine holding object: 5d
‣ *Short description:* Complete figurine. Left eye damaged (infill?) Some pieces from headgear broken off. Rigidly straight, standing female figure on a rectangular block base, leaning slightly to the right. Oval face with high forehead, slanted eyes and thick eyelids. They are placed diagonally. The nose is a bit bent. Mouth with thick straight lips. Flat cheeks and a small chin. She has long hair strands, three at each side. The small rim of hair high on her forehead is divided into vertical parts. She wears large disc ear studs. She wears a high polos, which curves first inwards and then out at the top at the front. She wears a long garment, a kind of cloak, covering her shoulders and arms and from there hanging down, open in the middle, with, on each side, three folds reaching the ground. Her bare feet, placed slightly outwards and with toes are visible from under the garment. With her right hand, she holds her dress up and in her left hand, placed higher up, close to the chest, she holds something round. This might be her dress also. Very flat back, straight sides.
‣ *Comparable objects:* Facial features, the style of the polos, dress with folds and clay colour are different from figurines from Agrigento. It is probably an imported statuette. The long mantle and pose is reminiscent of figurines from Corcyra. Higgins 1954, p.295-6, no.1081-6. Comparable in pose and dress is a figurine from Selinous, then in the Mus. Agrigento (Civico). Byvanck-Quarles van Ufford 1941, p.50-1, p.77 fig.26. This sort of mantle marks Corinthian figurines according to Ufford.

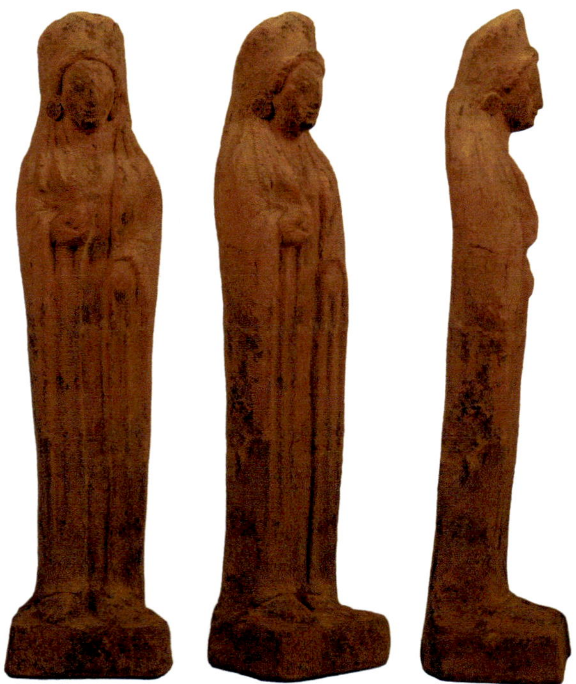

No. 84; Scale 1:2 (Staatlichen Antikensammlungen München).

No.85

‣ *Museum and Inventory number:* Mus. Agrigento S84
‣ *Findspot and context:* Akragas
‣ *Publications:* Marconi 1933, tav.VI, 6
‣ *Dimensions in cm:* h.7.1 w. 4.1 d. 2.3
‣ *Material:* Terracotta
‣ *Techniques:* Front moulded. Solid. Holes for wooden arm-inset. Lighter coloured slip layer. Worn mould.
‣ *Colour:* Very pale brown 10 YR 7/3
‣ *Date:* Mid of the 6th century BCE
‣ *Workshop:* Unknown
‣ *Typology:* Figurine from wooden original: 5d
‣ *Short description:* Upper part of a figurine with a very thin body. The face has big eyes and a small mouth, but is quite indistinct. Hair with horizontal lines. Small polos, placed high on the hair and head. She has rounded shoulders and breasts. Peplos bulging over the waist (apotygma). Holes for the placement of under-arms. In the left there is a hole, while the right has a pin in the middle.
‣ *Comparable objects:* From the same mould as **86**, with the same dimensions, though slightly thicker. Figurine made after a wooden patrix, Inv. no.47136 from Mus. Syracuse (fig.6 on the right).

No.86

‣ *Museum and Inventory number:* Mus. Agrigento S30
‣ *Findspot and context:* Unknown
‣ *Publications:* Marconi Bovio 1930, p.79-80, fig.10
‣ *Dimensions in cm:* h.14.5 w. 4.1 d. 2.1
‣ *Material:* terracotta
‣ *Techniques:* front moulded; red paint residue on left arm; solid; holes for wooden arm-inset
‣ *Colour:* Pink 7.5 YR 7/3
‣ *Date:* Mid of the 6th century BCE
‣ *Workshop:* Unknown
‣ *Typology:* Figurine from wooden original: 5d
‣ *Short description:* Complete figurine with very thin body. Standing female figurine. Oval face with wide jaws and big eyes, a large nose and a narrow mouth. Hair on forehead scalloped and next to face and neck with horizontal lines. Low polos, placed high on the hair and head, leaving a rim

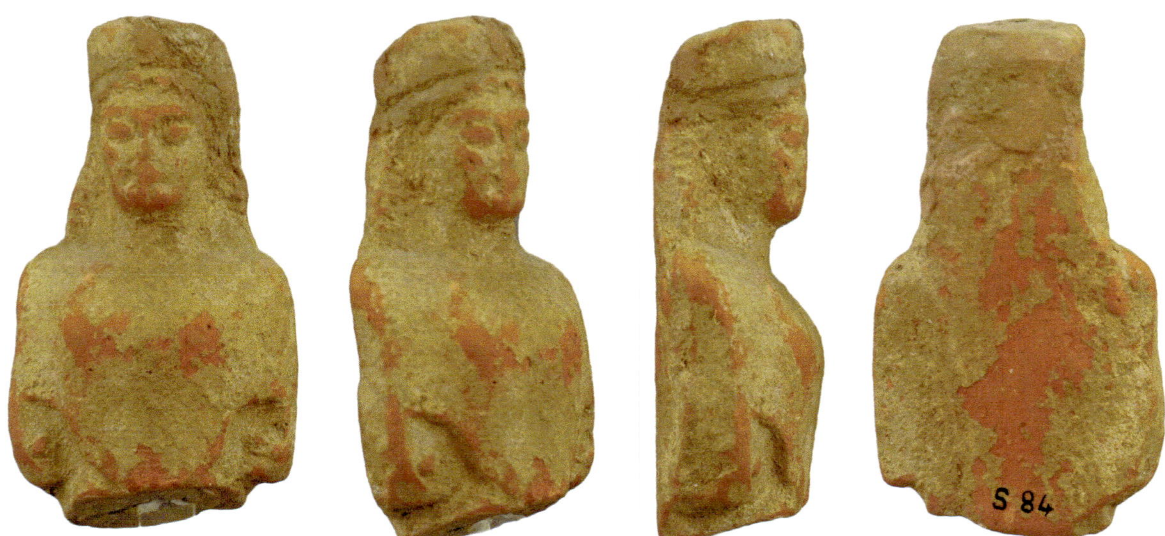

No. 85; Scale 1:1 (Museo Archeologico Regionale “Pietro Griffo”, Agrigento).

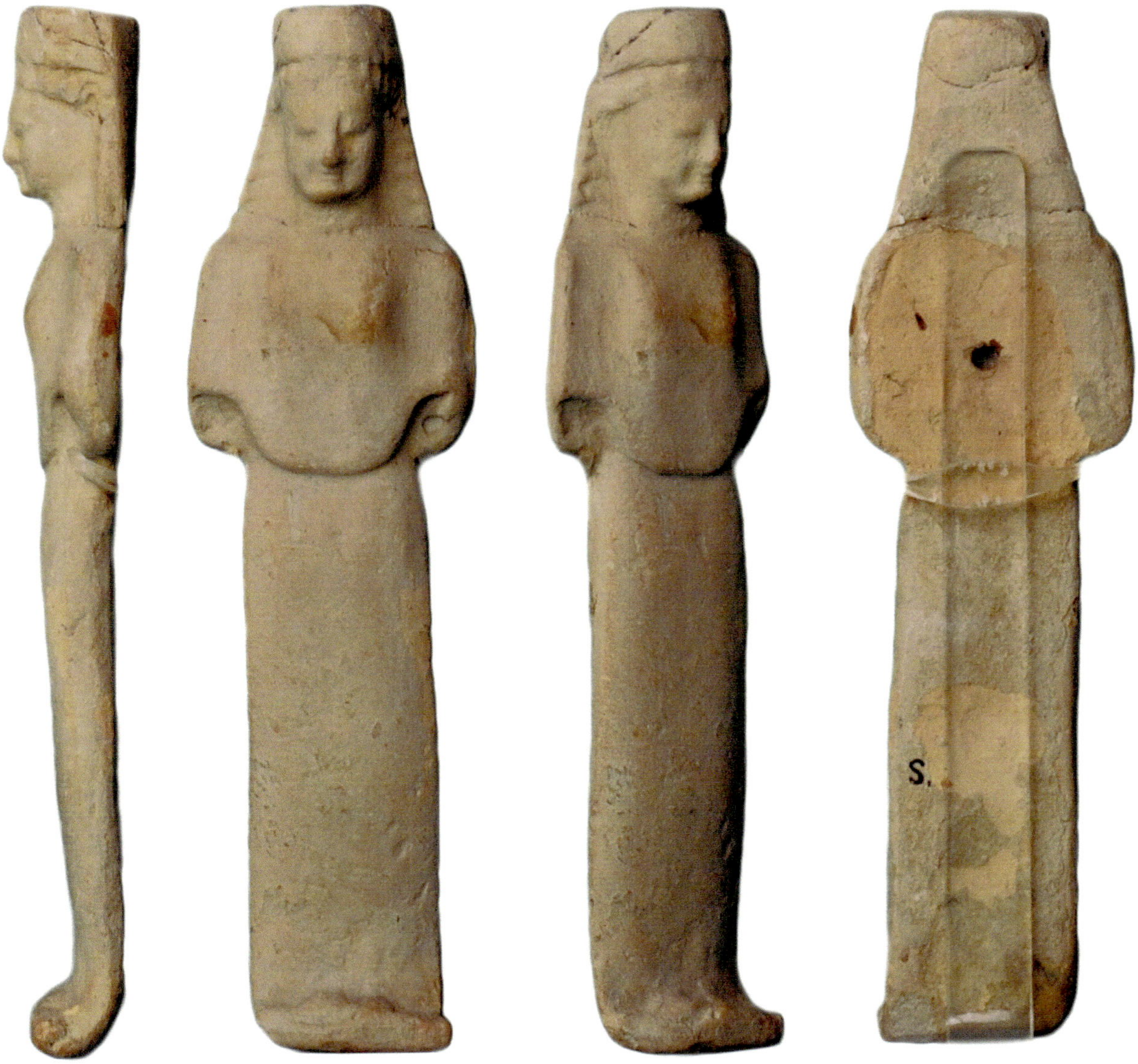

No. 86; Scale 1:1 (Museo Archeologico Regionale “Pietro Griffo”, Agrigento).

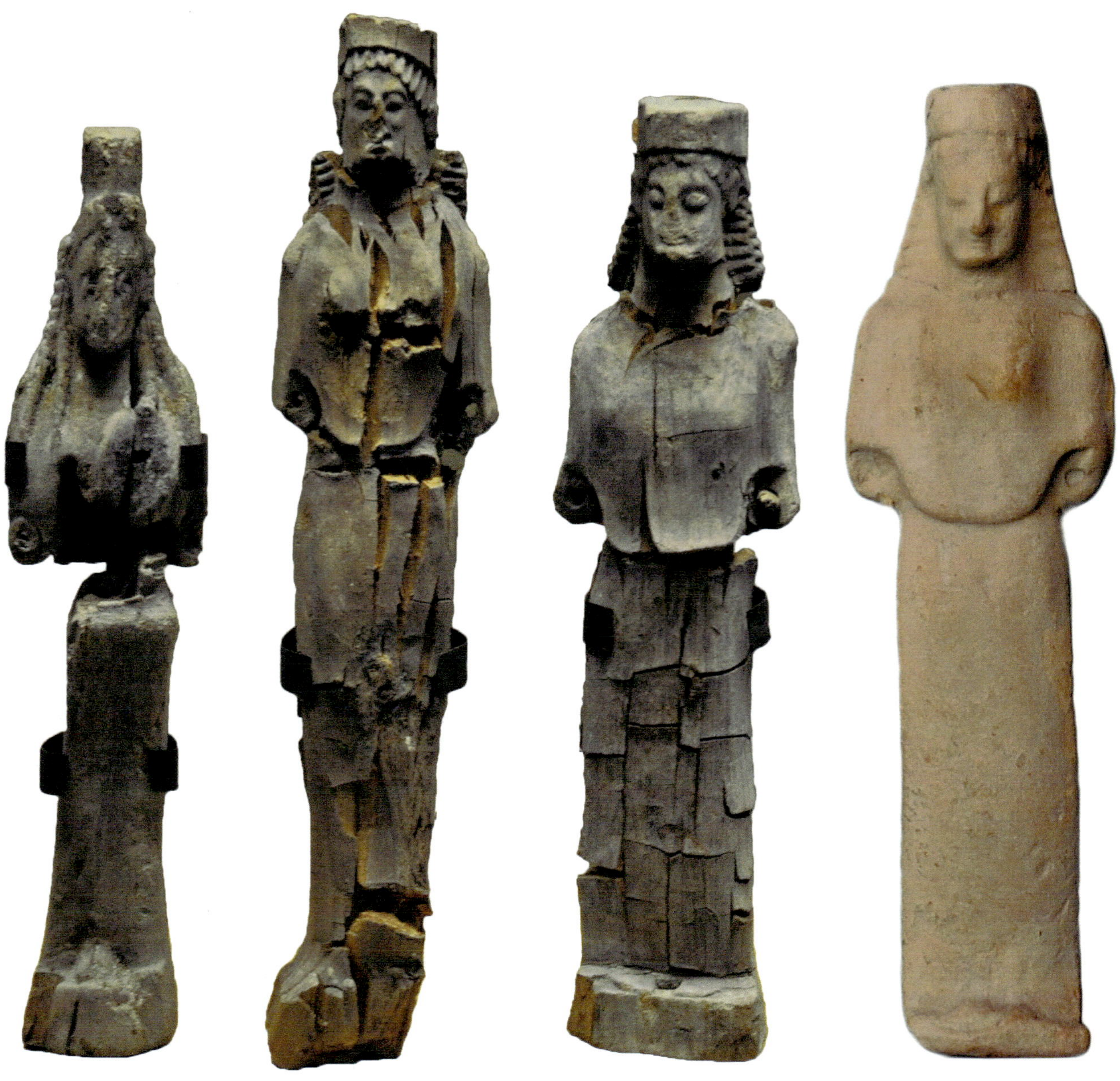

Figure 6; Scale 1:1; Wooden figurines, Inv. no.47134, 47135 and 47136 (Museo Archeologico Regionale "Paolo Orsi", Syracuse), combined with no. 86, see previous page.

of hair. Feminine shapes, such as breasts and hips. Feet on footstool. Peplos bulging over the waist (apotygma). Holes for the placement of under-arms. In the left, there is a hole, while the right is smoothed.

‣ *Comparable objects:* From the same mould series as **85**.

Figurine made after a wooden patrix, Inv. no.47136 from Mus. Syracuse (fig.6, on the right). Comparable are figurines from Selinous. Their pose, the arm-inset, girded dress and low polos are similar. These Corinthian-inspired figurines are dated to the end of the 7th-beginning of the 6th century BCE. Albertocchi 2012, p.93-4, fig.12. Marconi Bovio 1930, p.79-80, fig.9 is similar in the pose and sort of dress, but has a different head. Several characteristics like facial features, horizontal lines in the hair, the low polos, the dress with an upper and lower part are comparable to a figurine found at the Asklepion. A difference is the veil, visible behind the hair. The upper part of the dress that seems to continue on the side is merely the result of the shallow mould and not intentionally another type of dress. De Miro 2003, p.183, pl. 89.1.

Type G: Standing group (87-97)

Figurines with a standing pose.

No.87

- *Museum and Inventory number:* Mus. Agrigento C384
- *Findspot and context:* City Sanctuary
- *Publications:* Albertocchi 2004, p.71, no.1234
- *Dimensions in cm:* h.20.2
- *Material:* Terracotta
- *Techniques:* Front moulded.
- *Colour:* Pink 7.5 YR 8/3
- *Date:* 500-480 BCE
- *Workshop:* Unknown
- *Typology:* Block-like body group: 2b
- *Short description:* Nearly complete figurine, infill on the base, broken in two, restored. Female figurine. Chubby face with pronounced chin and fleshy cheeks. She has a large nose with a round tip. Her mouth is small, and her smile creates deep dimples next to it.

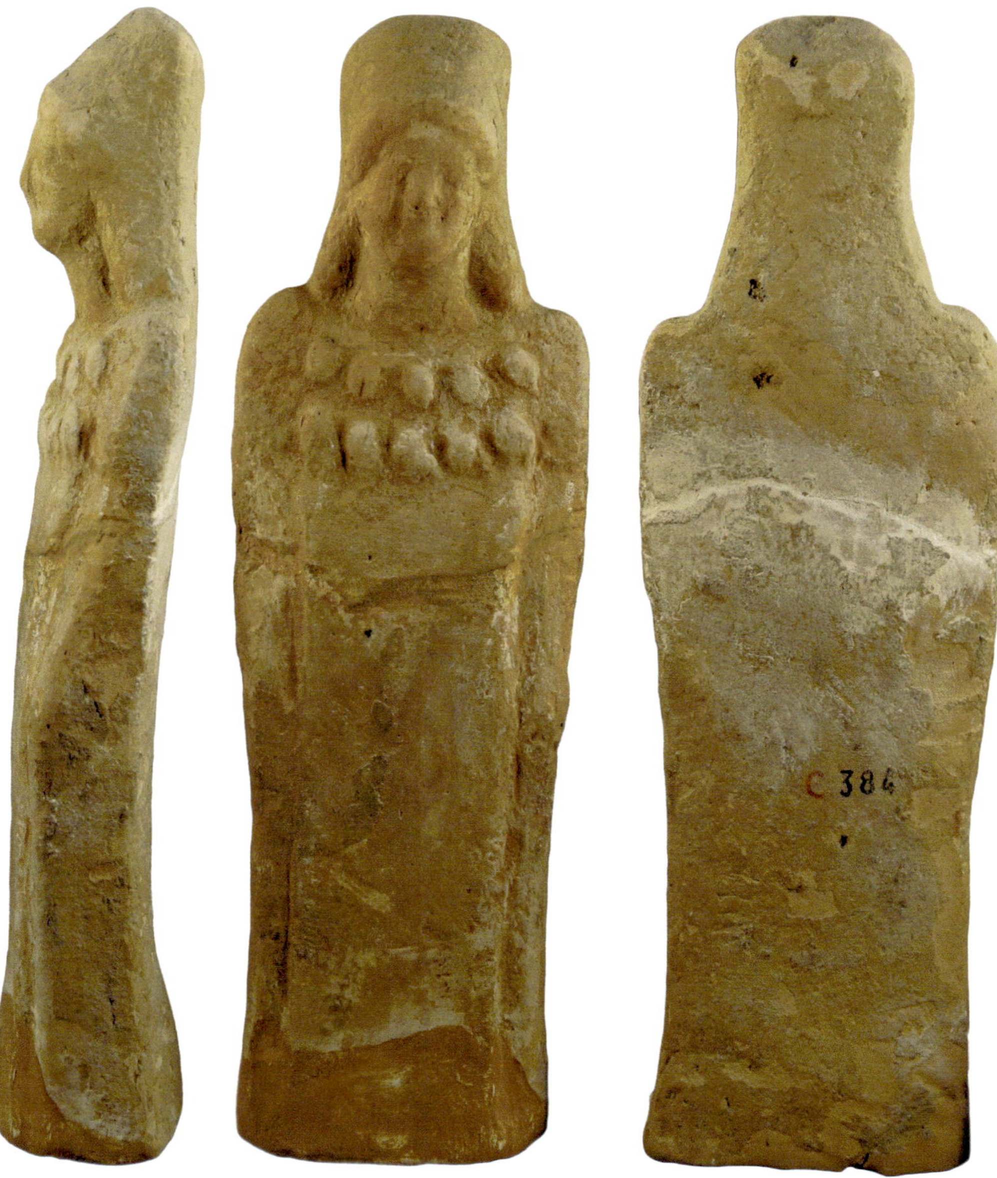

No. 87; Scale 1:1½ (Museo Archeologico Regionale "Pietro Griffo", Agrigento).

This part is very indistinct. She has large round eyes. The fringe on her forehead is smooth. Thick bulging hair next to the sides of her neck. She wears a straight, tall polos, just above the fringe. She has a simple straight rectangular body in standing pose, while holding her arms on the side. It seems she holds her hands outstretched with the thumb separated, as if she is grasping her dress. Her body has rounded shoulders and just a very slightly bending at the knees. The body becomes thinner at the top. This is visible from aside. She wears an apron, which leaves the side parts of her undergarment visible. On her chest, she wears two rows – the cords themselves are not visible – with five irregular ovoid pendants each. The egg-shaped pendants are close to each other, in particular on the second row, and irregularly shaped. The ones on the upper row are slightly smaller. The ones on the second row have been smoothed at the bottom. The outlines of the oval fibulae appear on the shoulder. Flat back, slightly flaring at the base to increase stability.

‣ *Comparable objects:* The chubby face is reminiscent of **19**, but more indistinct and wearing a straight and tall polos. The facial features are also reminiscent of the stubby face of **36**, and figurines **62** and **88**.

No.88

‣ *Museum and Inventory number:* Mus. Agrigento 20189 (20420)
‣ *Findspot and context:* S. Anna (?)
‣ *Publications:* Albertocchi 2004, p.66, no.1065; Dewailly 1992, p.76, n.75
‣ *Dimensions in cm:* h.18.9
‣ *Material:* Terracotta.
‣ *Techniques:* Front moulded.
‣ *Colour:* Yellowish red 5 YR 5/6
‣ *Date:* First quarter of the 5th century BCE
‣ *Workshop:* Unknown
‣ *Typology:* Standing group: 2c
‣ *Short description:* Headless figurine. Right shoulder and part of chest broken off. Thin block-like body with arms along the sides and hands in fists. The body runs slightly at a slope, but without a clear angle. The upper part is thinner. She wears an apron on top of an undergarment of which the thin straight folds are visible at the feet. It has an incised line, as a hem, curving along with the feet, over which the dress is draped. Fibula shaped like a double palmette, but without details. Two bands on the chest, the lower attached to the fibula, the second at the edge of the apron. This cord contains four relatively small disc-shaped pendants. Above it, two pendants of the first row look irregularly round or ovoid-shaped. Low footstool with pointed, naturalistically shaped feet on it. Flat back, curving slightly at the upper part of the body.
‣ *Comparable objects:* Similar upper part of the body as **62**. Pose and pendants are comparable to **70**. Dewailly writes that the similar type A XI from Selinous might have originally been based on an Akragantine example. Comparable to Kekulé von Stradonitz 1884, p.18, fig.25 (fig.7). That figurine is different, because it has five thin ovoid pendants on the first band and an equal number of disc-shaped ones on the second. De Miro refers to it, mentioning a figurine fragment from the southern city wall that had similar pectoral pendants, but oval fibulae: Mus. Agrigento without inv. no. De Miro 2000, p.164, no.412.

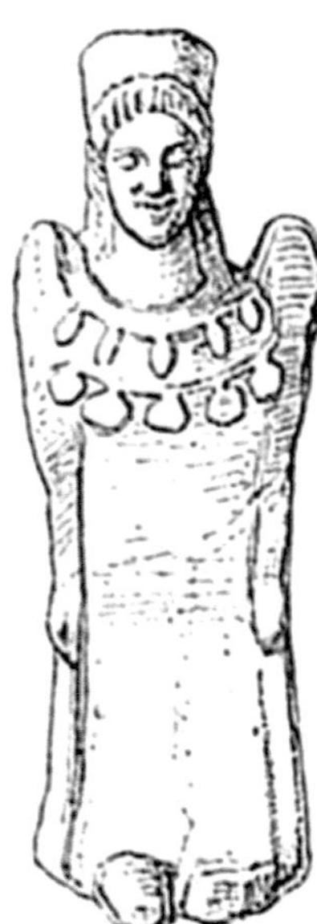

Figure 7; Drawing of a figurine similar to no.88. Drawing after Kekulé 1884 p.18 fig.25

No.89

‣ *Museum and Inventory number:* Mus. Agrigento S318
‣ *Findspot and context:* City Sanctuary
‣ *Publications:* -
‣ *Dimensions in cm:* h.9.3 The sherd is rather thin for its size.
‣ *Material:* Terracotta.
‣ *Techniques:* Moulded
‣ *Colour:* Reddish-yellow 7.5 YR 7/6
‣ *Date:* First quarter of the 5th century BCE
‣ *Workshop:* Unknown
‣ *Typology:* Standing group(?): 2c
‣ *Short description:* Lower front part of a what was once a large figurine. Bare feet on a low podium stick out from under a garment. The feet are placed somewhat away from each other and are finely modelled: the five fingers can be distinguished. The undergarment has fine straight vertical lines, folds, draped over the feet. The upper garment, reaching to just above the ankles, is plain.
‣ *Comparable objects:* **88** has a similarly folded undergarment, which is draped over the feet. The fabric is long and flexible enough to drop between the feet.

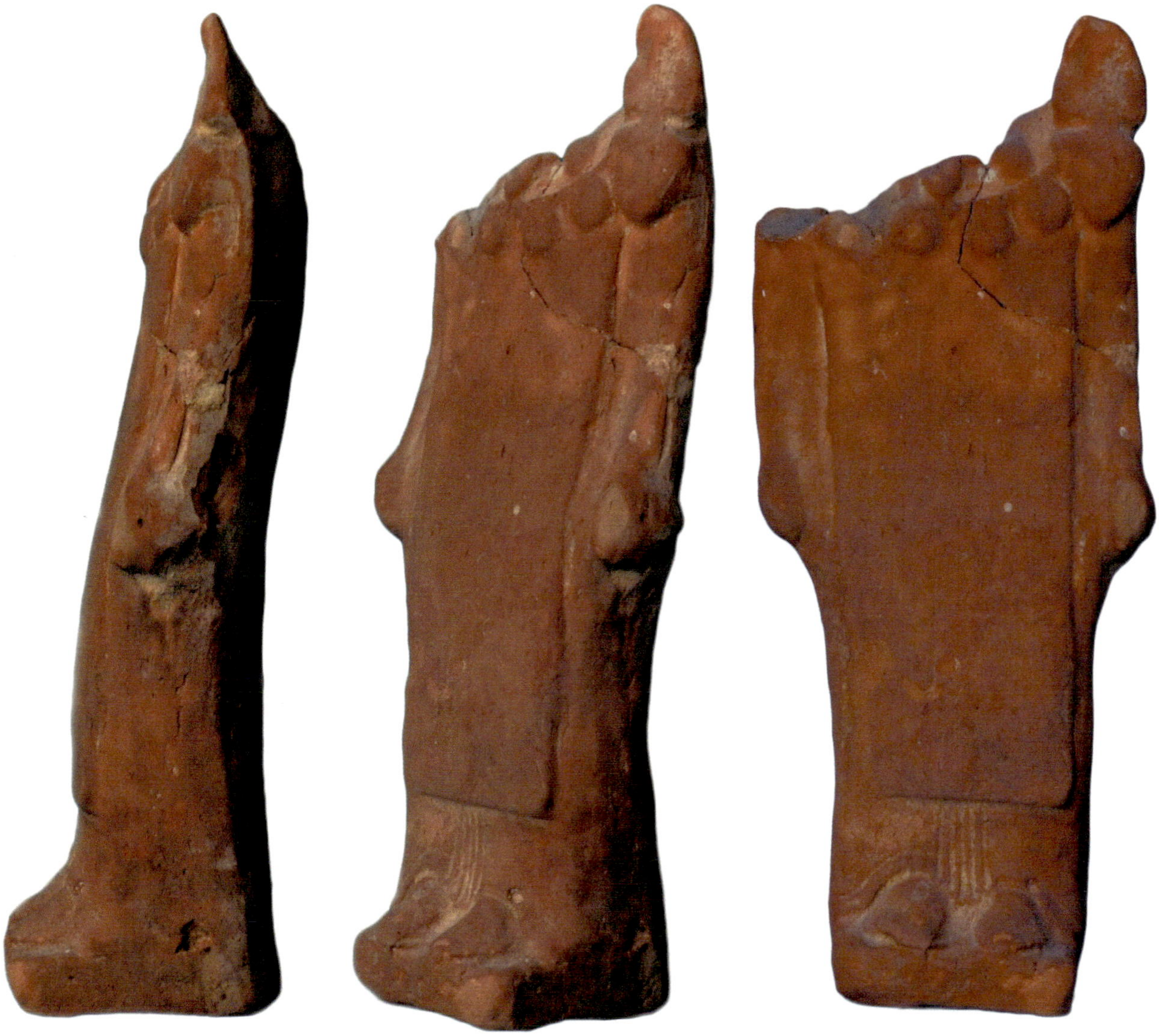

No. 88; Scale 1:1½ (Museo Archeologico Regionale "Pietro Griffo", Agrigento).

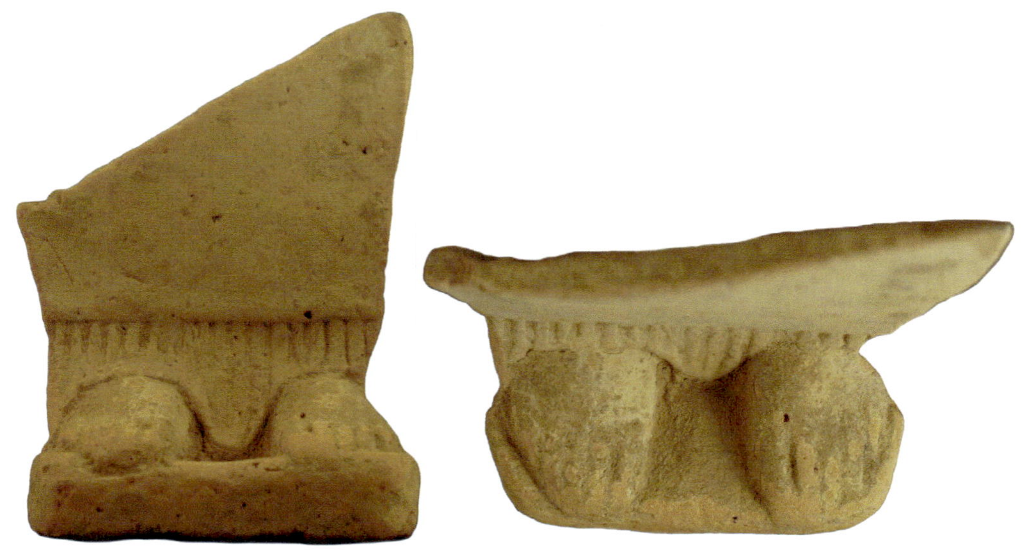

No. 89; Scale 1:1½ (Museo Archeologico Regionale "Pietro Griffo", Agrigento).

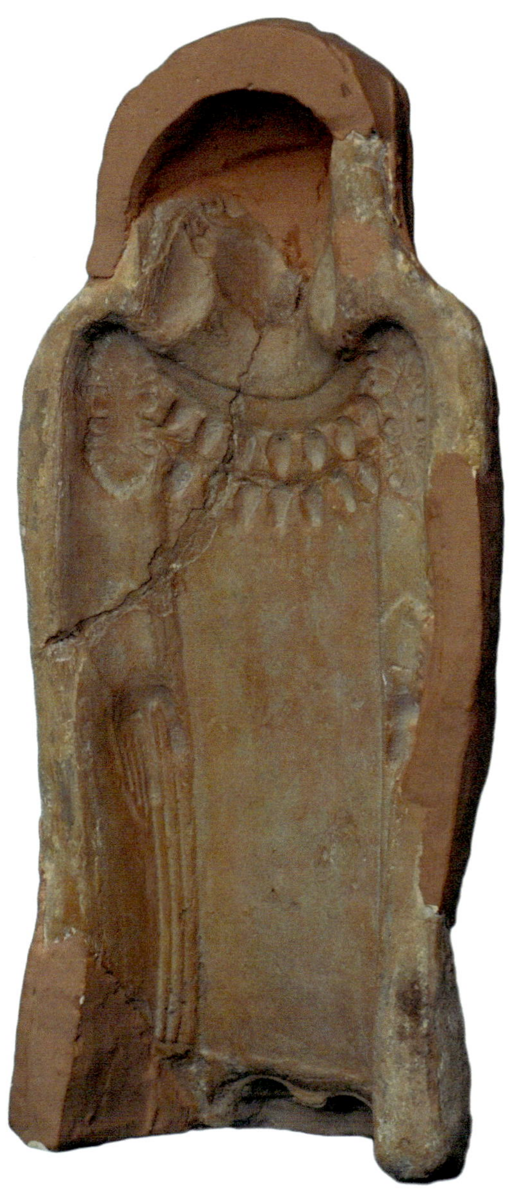
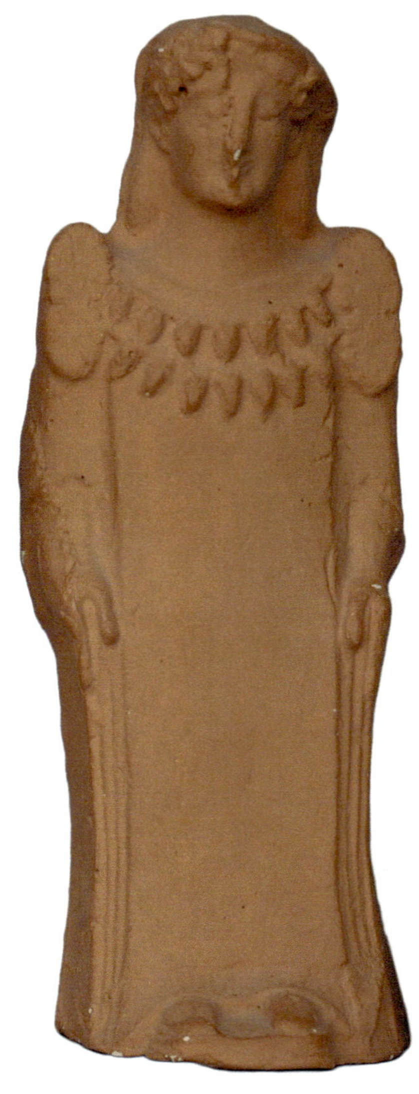

No. 90; Scale 1:2 (Museo Archeologico Regionale "Pietro Griffo", Agrigento); continued on next page.

No.90

‣ *Museum and Inventory number:* Mus. Agrigento C240 (20A -3 638)

‣ *Findspot and context:* City Sanctuary. At the base of the southwest wall of the sanctuary

‣ *Publications:* Albertocchi 2004, p.70, no.1231; Rizzo 1897, p.306

‣ *Dimensions in cm:* h.29.8

‣ *Material:* terracotta

‣ *Techniques:* Imprint from an object, the patrix.

‣ *Colour:* Light grey 10 YR 7/2

‣ *Date:* First quarter of the 5th century BCE

‣ *Workshop:* Unknown

‣ *Typology:* Standing group: 2c

‣ *Short description:* Mould of figurine, matrix. Part of head, one side and a corner near the feet broken off. In two fragments, restored with infill. Standing, leaning backwards, pose of a female holding her hands tight to her body. Wide oval head with a long nose and a very small mouth with thick lips, smiling. Her eyes are rounded and placed close to the nose. Scalloped fringe on the forehead and next to the side of the neck bulging, undefined hair. Her ears are placed in front of the hair. She wears large double palmette shaped fibulae, sticking out from her shoulders and marking the finials of the two cords on her dress on each of which hang seven small ovoid pendants. Below the rectangular apron, which runs to the base, draped over her feet, she wears an undergarment, a chiton with a hem at the

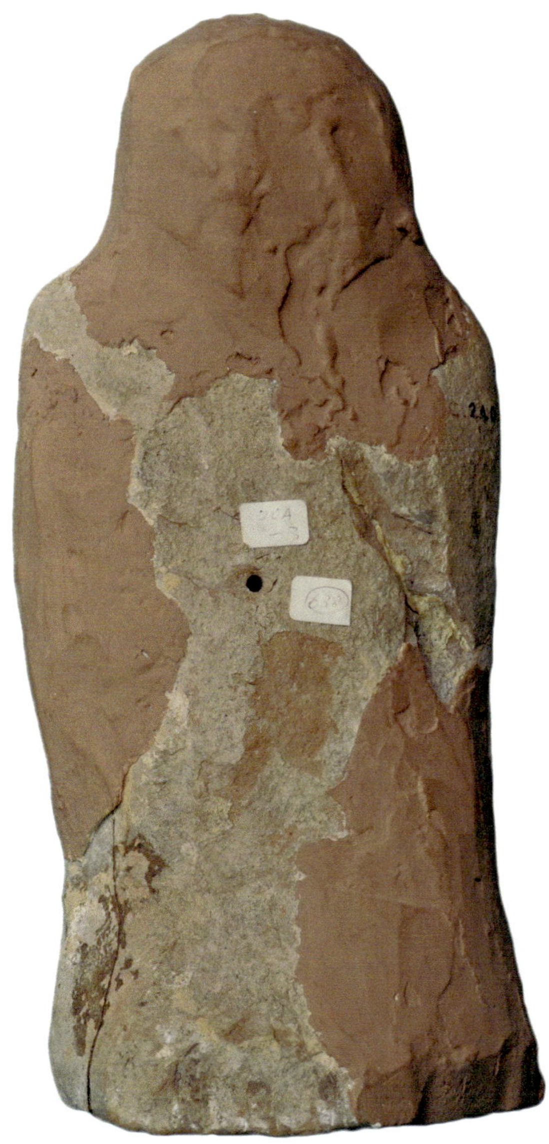

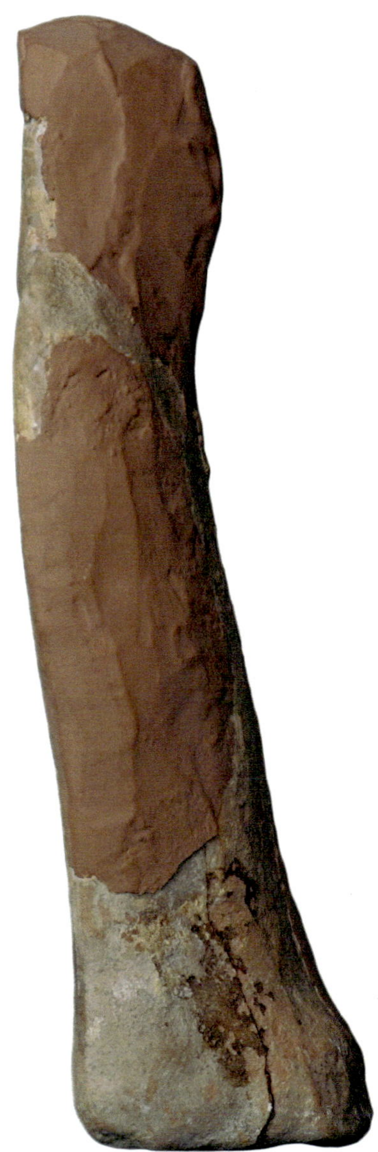

neck and folds on the sides of the apron. On her arms, the sleeves end in a delta-shape just below her elbow. She holds her hands halfway down her body, with the long fingers outstretched and thumbs to the front.

The mould is thick and roughly reworked on the outside. It has a small hole on the outer side in the middle. The mould can stay upright by itself.

‣ *Comparable objects:* Similar to figurine **91** and **92**, though those are much smaller and more indistinct. There are not directly from this mould, but possibly from the same mould series, some generations later. The pectoral chains, each with seven ovoid pendants are very similar to the ones of Mould II, usually on three cords, but on **135** just two. Two figurines from tomb 4 at Tharros, Sardinia, were clearly inspired by, and possibly made locally, with Sicilian moulds. British Mus. Inv. no.1856,1223.466 and 1856,1223.467, complete h.20cm and h.16.9cm Higgins 1987, p.138-9 pl. 32. See museum website.

In addition, a standing figurine from Montelusa is similar in pose and fibulae, but has a third row with pendants: complete, h.34,9cm. Langlotz and Hirmer 1963, p.60, no.20 left. The number of pendants on the first two rows is eight and not seven. The head that has been combined with that figurine is very different and resembles **131**. A similar figurine from the southern city wall, Akragas: AG 20487, complete, h.21.5cm. Albertocchi 2004, p.67, no.1068; De Miro 2000, p.130, no.32, tav.LXIII. It has three rows of pendants with seven pendants on each.

‣ *Other notes:* Photograph with modern cast.

No.91

‣ *Museum and Inventory number:* Mus. Munich 1090
‣ *Findspot and context:* Akragas
‣ *Publications:* Hamdorf 2014, p.97, no.C 210
‣ *Dimensions in cm:* h.15.9
‣ *Material:* Terracotta with a lighter-coloured slip layer, inside light red.
‣ *Techniques:* Front moulded. Sides cut off, resulting in clay heaping on the edges of the back. The line on the upper part of the body might indicate that different moulds were used to form the figurine.
‣ *Colour:* Very pale brown 10 YR 8/2
‣ *Date:* First quarter of the 5th century BCE
‣ *Workshop:* Unknown
‣ *Typology:* Standing group: 2c
‣ *Short description:* Near complete standing female figurine. Part at the base broken off. Crack in the neck and chest. Details have become very indistinct.

Standing female figurine. She has an oval face, with round protruding eyes, a long nose and a very small mouth with thick lips. Her fringe of hair is formed from relatively long, scalloped waves. She wears a low polos on top of her fringe. Her hair hangs down to the sides but is very indistinct. Arms, with three folds, indicate an undergarment. With both hands, she reaches next to her knees, which are indicated by a slight curve as if she is holding her dress up a little. Two rows of pendants, with seven ovoid pendants on each line. Under the second cord, though itself not visible, there seems to be a sort of protruding line. The shape of the fibulae is hardly visible, but seems more oval or double palmette-shaped. Back worked roughly.

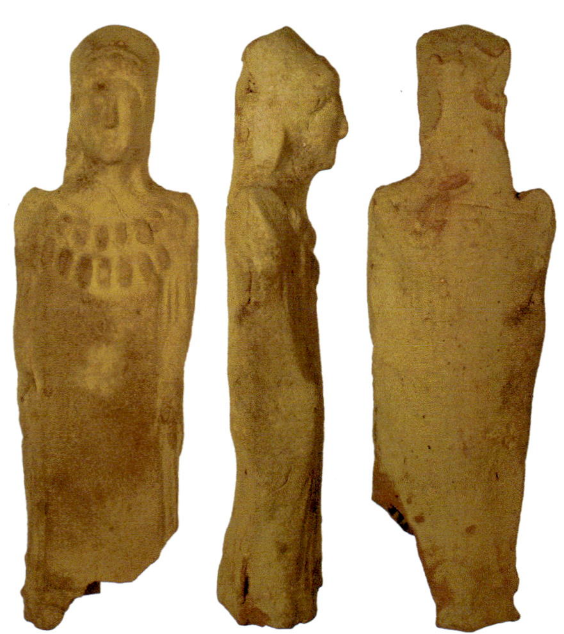

No. 91; Scale 1:2 (Staatlichen Antikensammlungen München).

‣ *Comparable objects:* Similar to figurine **90** and **92**, though much smaller and more indistinct. Possibly from the same mould series but some generations later.

Very similar and possibly an earlier generation of the same mould is a figurine from Birgi: Mus. Trapani Inv. no.5292 complete h.26.3cm. Poma 2009, p.235, no.25. Such a figurine would be typical of Akragantine coroplastics.

No.92

‣ *Museum and Inventory number:* Mus. Agrigento S883
‣ *Findspot and context:* City Sanctuary
‣ *Publications:* Albertocchi 2004, p.70, no.1229
‣ *Dimensions in cm:* h.21.6
‣ *Material:* Terracotta. Numerous shell inclusions.
‣ *Techniques:* Front moulded. Worn mould
‣ *Colour:* Very pale brown 10 YR 8/3
‣ *Date:* First quarter of the 5th century BCE
‣ *Workshop:* Unknown
‣ *Typology:* Standing group: 2c
‣ *Short description:* Complete figurine. Small piece of polos off. Standing, leaning backwards, female holding her arms tight to her body. The slight sloping of the upper part of the thin body, with the arms along the sides is clear from the side view. She reaches with her hands halfway down her body, the long fingers outstretched, and thumbs to the front. Oval elongated head with a long nose and a very small mouth with thick lips, smiling. Her eyes are round and very indistinct. The face is smoothed from the arching eyebrows down to the cheek. There is a fringe of hair with a double row of waves, and hair at the sides of the neck falling down straight and undefined. She wears a slightly flaring tall polos with a thin rim. She wears large double palmette-shaped fibulae, sticking out from her shoulders and marking the finials of the two cords on her dress, each of which carry seven thin ovoid pendants. Below the rectangular apron, which runs to the base, draped over her feet, she wears an undergarment, a chiton with vertical folds. The back is slightly bulging, but straight. The angles at the sides are sharp, the edge at the front a little less.
‣ *Comparable objects:* Pose and pendants are similar to the mould **90** and possibly it is the same mould series. Similar and somewhat larger than **91**. See **91** for other comparable objects. Probably from the same mould series, also from the City Sanctuary. Mus. Agrigento Inv. no.AG20487. Dewailly 1992, p.65, n.49; Albertocchi 2004, p.67, no.1068; De Miro 2000, p.130, no.32, tav.LXIII.

Similar to Type A IV 3 a 3 from Selinous. Dewailly 1992, p.65 fig.29

No.93

‣ *Museum and Inventory number:* Mus. Agrigento 2150
‣ *Findspot and context:* South of the Temple of Zeus
‣ *Publications:* Fiertler 2001, p.58, n.37; Albertocchi 2004, p.83, no.1317; De Miro 1963, p.162 fig.76c

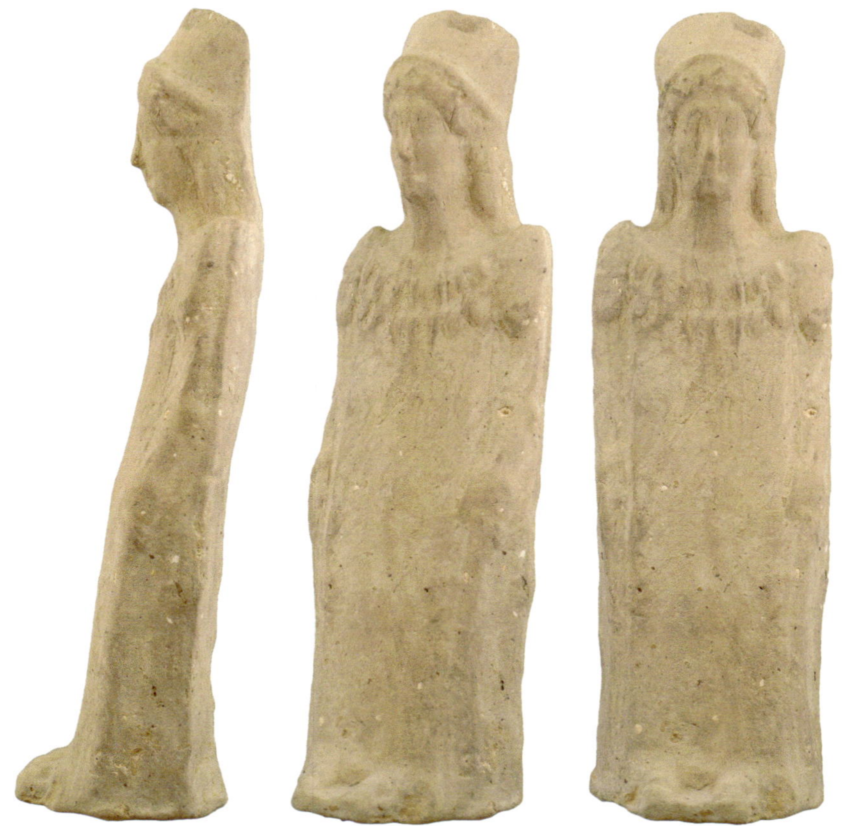

No. 92; Scale 1:2 (Museo Archeologico Regionale "Pietro Griffo", Agrigento).

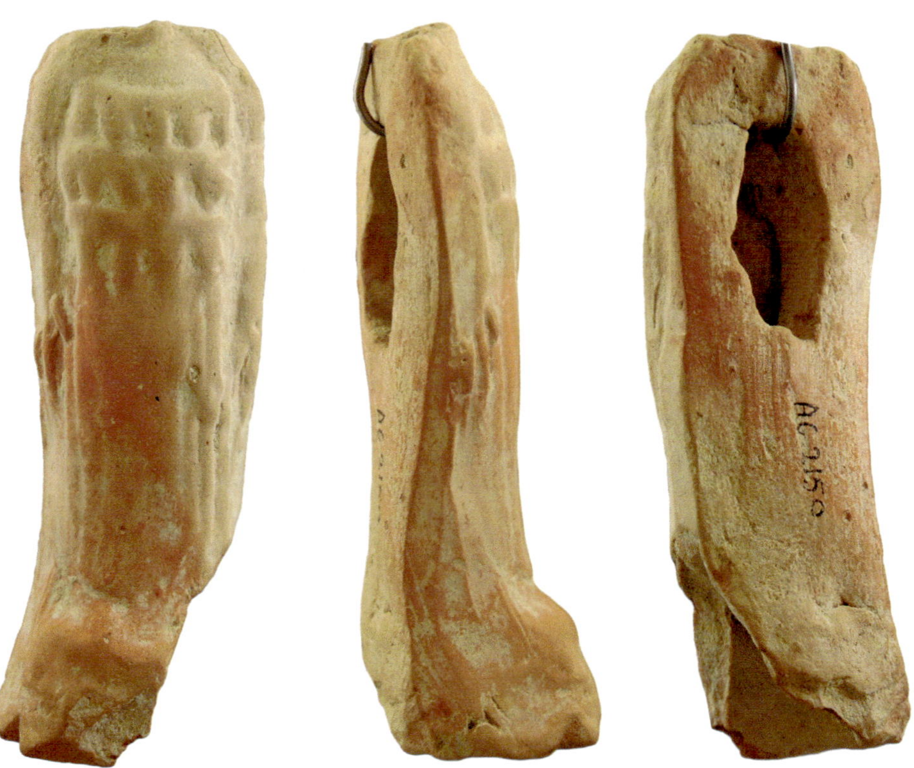

No. 93; Scale 1:1 (Museo Archeologico Regionale "Pietro Griffo", Agrigento).

‣ *Dimensions in cm:* h.9.8
‣ *Material:* Terracotta
‣ *Techniques:* Front moulded. Its relatively small size, the podium and the indistinct details make it likely this is quite some generations after the original patrix and matrix. The opening in the back could have served for assemblage from the inside.
‣ *Colour:* Reddish-yellow 5 YR 7/8 Lighter coloured slip layer over red original.
‣ *Date:* 490-470 BCE
‣ *Workshop:* Unknown
‣ *Typology:* Standing group: 2c
‣ *Short description:* Headless, relatively small figurine from a worn mould. Left corner broken at base. Fully standing pose on a high, widening base. There is no leaning or bending at the knees. She holds her arms close to her somewhat rounded body, reminiscent of a column. Her outstretched hands reach halfway. She wears an undergarment with vertical folds on the sides of the apron, below the hands. There are no fibulae on her rounded shoulders, but there are three cords with pectoral pendants. Five large ovoid pendants are attached to the first two cords. The third carries four. The back has an oval hole on the upper part and is otherwise reworked straight.
‣ *Comparable objects:* Iconographic scheme similar to **91** and **92**, though fibulae and pectoral pendants differ.

No.94

‣ *Museum and Inventory number:* Mus. Agrigento S293
‣ *Findspot and context:* City Sanctuary
‣ *Publications:* Albertocchi 2004, 87, no.1416
‣ *Dimensions in cm:* h.26
‣ *Material:* Terracotta. Lime-spalling
‣ *Techniques:* Front moulded. Reworking with a knife on the back caused some clay bulging.
‣ *Colour:* Very pale brown 10 YR 7/4
‣ *Date:* The second decade of the 5th century BCE
‣ *Workshop:* Angled back of polos group (?)

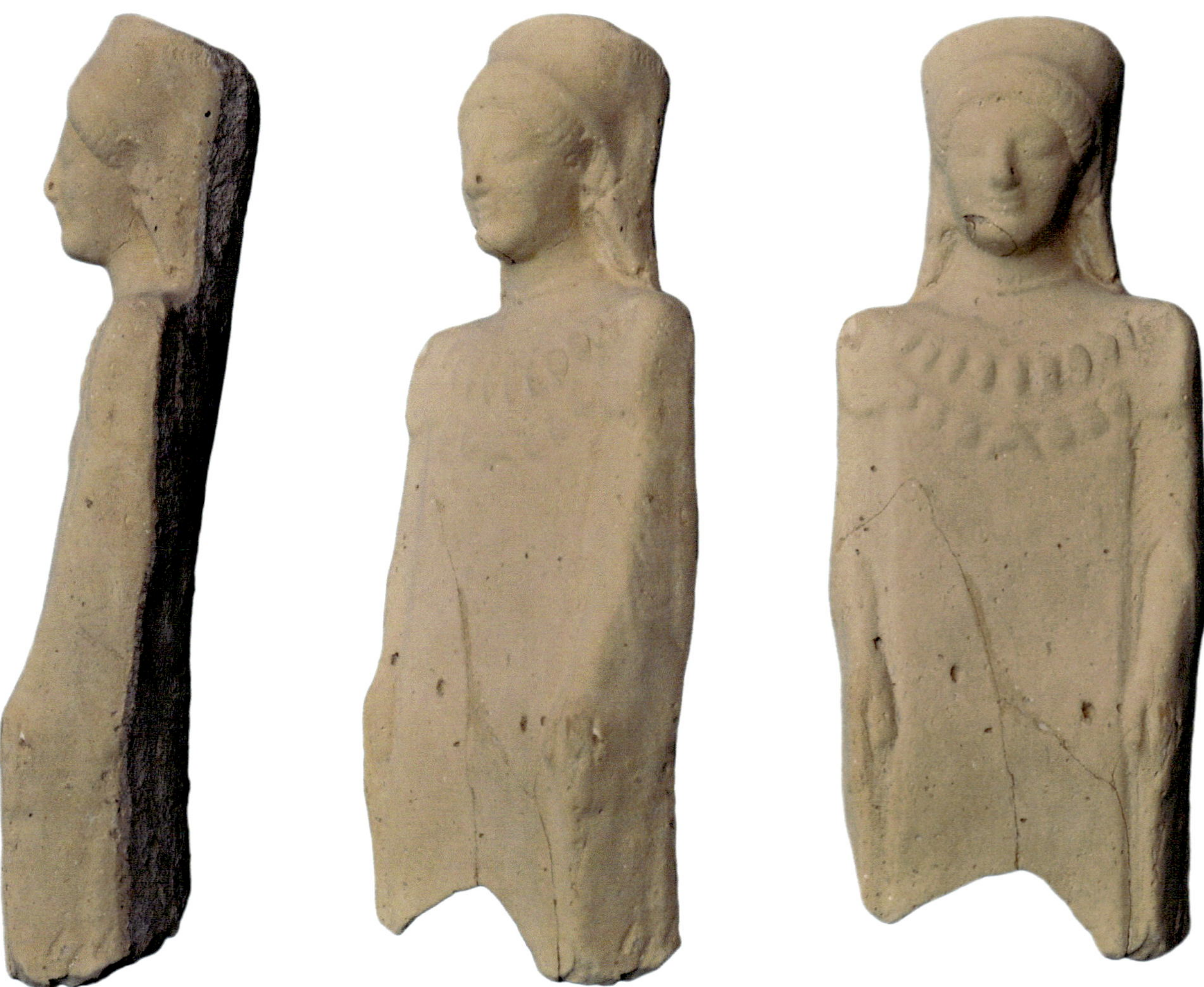

No. 94; Scale 1:2 (Museo Archeologico Regionale "Pietro Griffo", Agrigento).

‣ *Typology:* Fine folds chiton-group, the head: wide polos group: 3b

‣ *Short description:* Nearly complete figurine, base and feet broken off. In three parts, restored. Standing female figurine. The face is wide, with a big nose and large eyes. She has relatively thick lips. Her hair in a fringe with bulbs on her forehead is thinner in the middle. The outline of ears is placed on top of it at the finials. She wears large earrings with a knob, ring and pendant. She wears a low, wide polos, flat on the front, with a rim, just above the hair. Next to the sides of her neck, her hair is flaring, falling behind her shoulders. She wears a thick necklace tight around her short neck. She is standing upright with bent knees and her arms tight to her body, her knees reaching with outstretched hands, the thumb separate. From there the lower part of the body is straight. The upper part of her body is a very steep slope. Her fibulae are oval but details are indistinct. She wears a chiton, the upper hem is elevated at the neck, with sleeves to just below her elbows that show fine folds in a regular manner. The seam in the middle creates a triangular shape on the arm. Below her hands, the outer rim of the undergarment is visible. She wears two cords with ovoid or round seed-shaped pendants, nine on the first row, a crescent with the points down, flanked by three small discs on the second. Straight back.

‣ *Comparable objects:* The heads of **95** and **96** might be from the same mould series.

The arrangement of the pectoral pendants is reminiscent of **152**, though on that figurine the crescent is flanked by two discs instead of three. Posture is reminiscent of mould **67** and figurine **135**. There are six more heads from this mould series. Albertocchi 2004, p.87, no.1417-22. She writes that the type originates in Selinous. Albertocchi 1999, p.361, fig.13. The oldest figurines from Akragas of this type are therefore seen as the second generation. Dewailly 1992, p.49-55. A very similar figurine from Selinous: Mus. Palermo Inv. no.5754, upper part, 20cm. It has a rounder running fringe and polos. Poma 2009, p.234, no.23. A similar figurine from the necropolis of Kerkouane is exceptional for its size. It has three cords with pectoral pendants instead of two and a longer neck. Mus. Bardo, Inv. no.2914, complete, h.40.5cm. Albertocchi 1999, p.361, fig.13. Cf. Type AI, Dewailly 1992, p.47-9.

No.95

‣ *Museum and Inventory number:* Mus. Agrigento 15.1345 (2266)

‣ *Findspot and context:* West Archaic sanctuary underlying the bouleuterion

‣ *Publications:* -

‣ *Dimensions in cm:* h.10.8

‣ *Material:* Terracotta. Shell fragment on nose and hair.

‣ *Techniques:* Front moulded.

‣ *Colour:* Pinkish grey 7.5 YR 7/2

‣ *Date:* The second decade of the 5th century BCE

‣ *Workshop:* Unknown

‣ *Typology:* Wide polos group: 3b

‣ *Short description:* Head of a figurine, back and sides broken off; in three fragments, restored. Rounded oval face with pronounced chin. Almond shaped eyes with eyelids under arching eyebrows. Nose with rounded tip.Smiling mouth with thick lips and dimples on the finals. Thick flattened round fringe of hair in vertical bulbs, larger towards the sides. These 'bulbs' are hollow at the front and indicate waves. On the finals of the fringe, there are ears, of which the auricle is distinct. The size is relatively small and it is placed diagonally. Low slightly flaring polos with rim, just above the fringe. Straight back.

‣ *Comparable objects:* Probably from the same mould series as **96**, but a generation earlier. The head of **94** is very similar also. Comparable to facial features and the specific hairstyle of **99**, in particular the eyes.

No.96

‣ *Museum and Inventory number:* Mus. Munich 7144

‣ *Findspot and context:* Akragas

‣ *Publications:* Hamdorf 2014, p.99, no.C 220

‣ *Dimensions in cm:* h.10.8

‣ *Material:* Terracotta. Several holes, probably caused by lime-spalling.

‣ *Techniques:* Front moulded.

‣ *Colour:* Pink 7.5 YR 7/4

‣ *Date:* The second decade of the 5th century BCE

‣ *Workshop:* unnown

‣ *Typology:* Wide polos group: 3b

‣ *Short description:* Head. Female figurine with a rounded face. She has big slightly bulging eyes with thin eyelids. Her thin nose has a rounded tip. Her mouth is narrow, curved into a smile. Her hair is placed in a thick fringe with rounded vertical bulbs. These 'bulbs' are hollow at the front and indicate waves. She wears a low flaring polos with a rim. Along the sides of her neck, her hair hangs down straight. She wears large earrings with a knob, ring and pendant.

‣ *Comparable objects:* Probably from the same mould series as **95**, one generation later. Whether the earlier generation also had earrings is not clear. The head of **94** is very similar also.

‣ *Other notes:* The shiny yellowish layer might be the result of restoration processes.

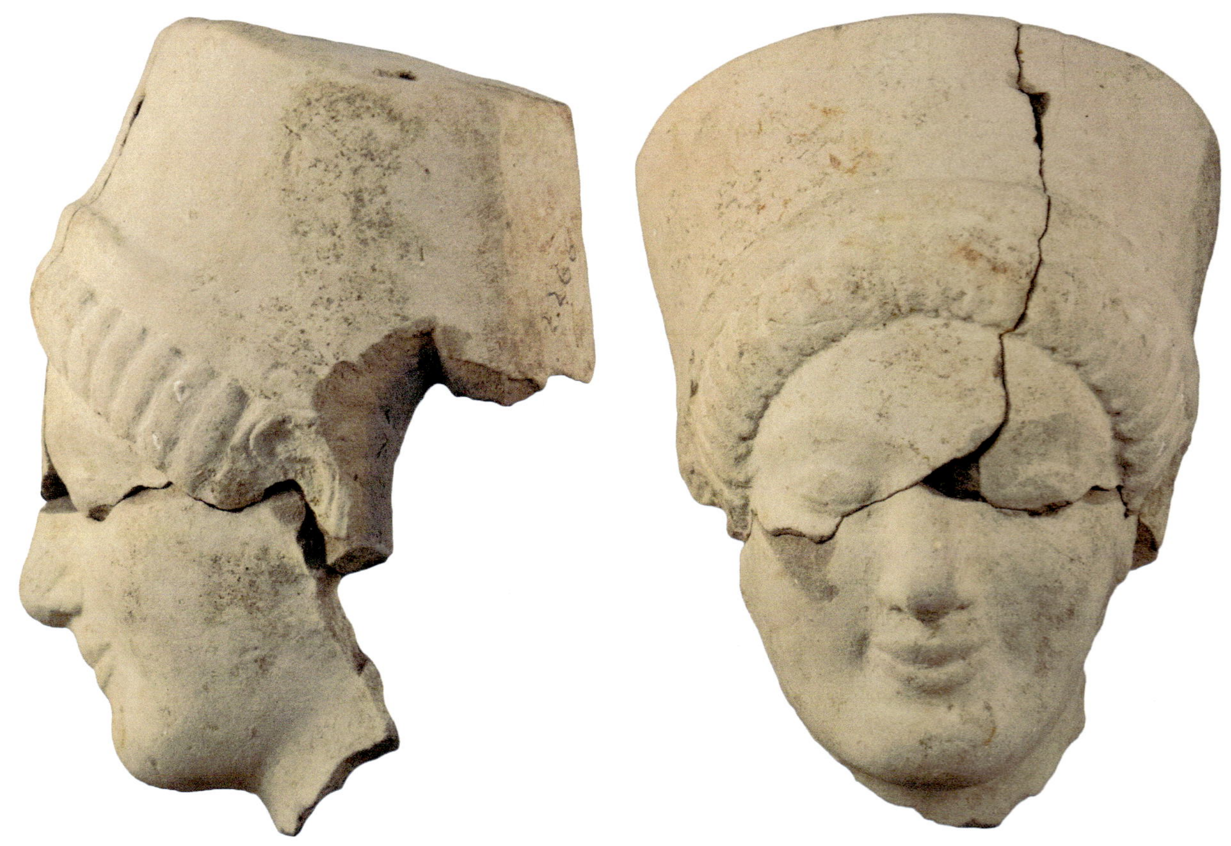

No. 95; Scale 1:1 (Museo Archeologico Regionale "Pietro Griffo", Agrigento).

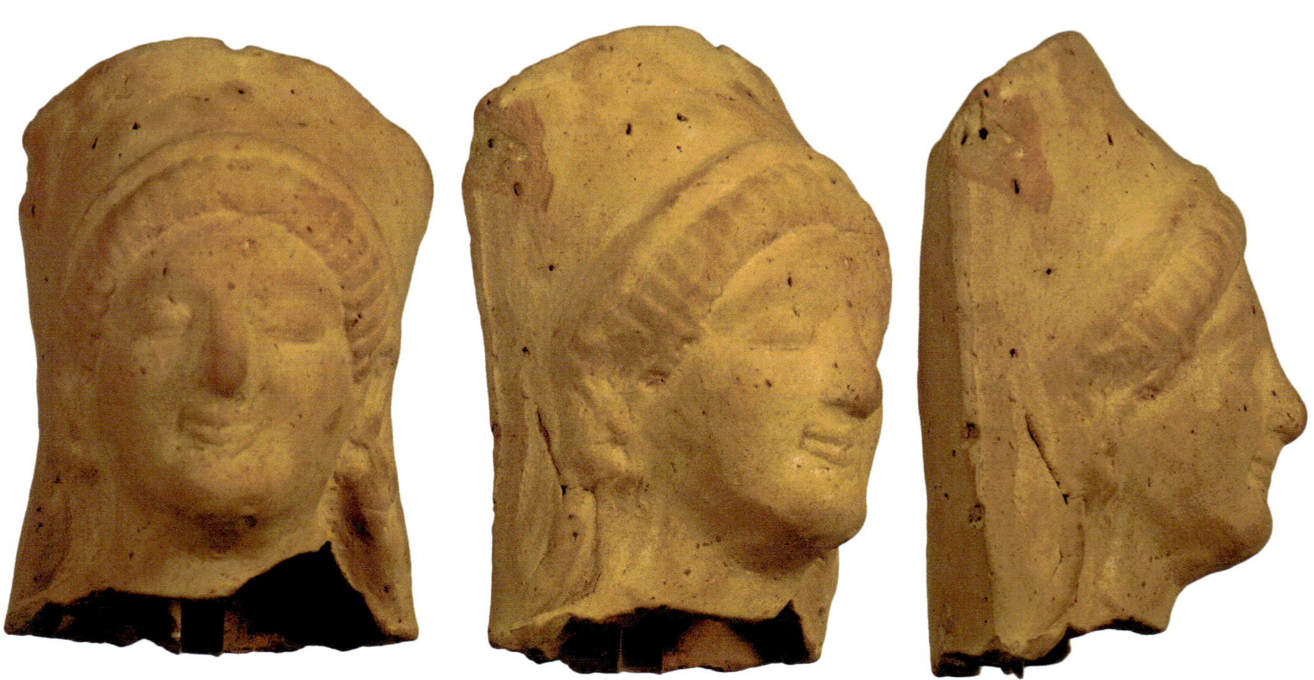

No. 96; Scale 1:1½ (Staatlichen Antikensammlungen München).

No.97

‣ *Museum and Inventory number:* Mus. Agrigento S21

‣ *Findspot and context:* Sanctuary near Villa Aurea

‣ *Publications:* Albertocchi 2004, p.69, no.1225; Marconi Bovio 1930, p.80-1, fig.13

‣ *Dimensions in cm:* h.12.4 w. 9.9

‣ *Material:* Terracotta.

‣ *Techniques:* Front moulded.

‣ *Colour:* Light Yellowish Brown 2.5 Y 6/3

‣ *Date:* The third decade of the 5th century BCE

‣ *Workshop:* Unknown

‣ *Typology:* Fine folds chiton-group: 3b

‣ *Short description:* Upper part of the body of a figurine. Head part below the knee and back part are broken off. Very sharply moulded standing figurine. A small part of the hair besides the neck is left: it has horizontal lines. She is standing upright with bent knees and her arms tight to her body, reaching her knees with outstretched hands, the thumbs separate. From there, the lower part of the body is straight. The upper part of her body has a very steep slope. Her fibulae are oval, but details are indistinct. She wears a chiton; the upper hem is elevated on the chest and shows fine vertical folds above the pectoral cords. The undergarment has sleeves till just below her elbows with fine folds in a regular manner and a seam in the middle. She wears on top of her apron, three cords with ovoid seed-shaped pendants, hanging close together. There are nine on the first row, flattened at the end, as if smoothed. Also on the other two cords, there are nine similarly shaped pendants. The sides have been cut with a sharp tool.

‣ *Comparable objects:* It is reminiscent of mould **90**, but this one has three rows of pectoral pendants, folded sleeves and plain fibulae. The posture, however, is very similar. It could well be a variant in the same series. In the same way, it is similar to figurine **94**. With this figurine just the pendants and necklace are different. Both mould and figurine are less sharp than this example. It is also reminiscent of another tall standing figurine from

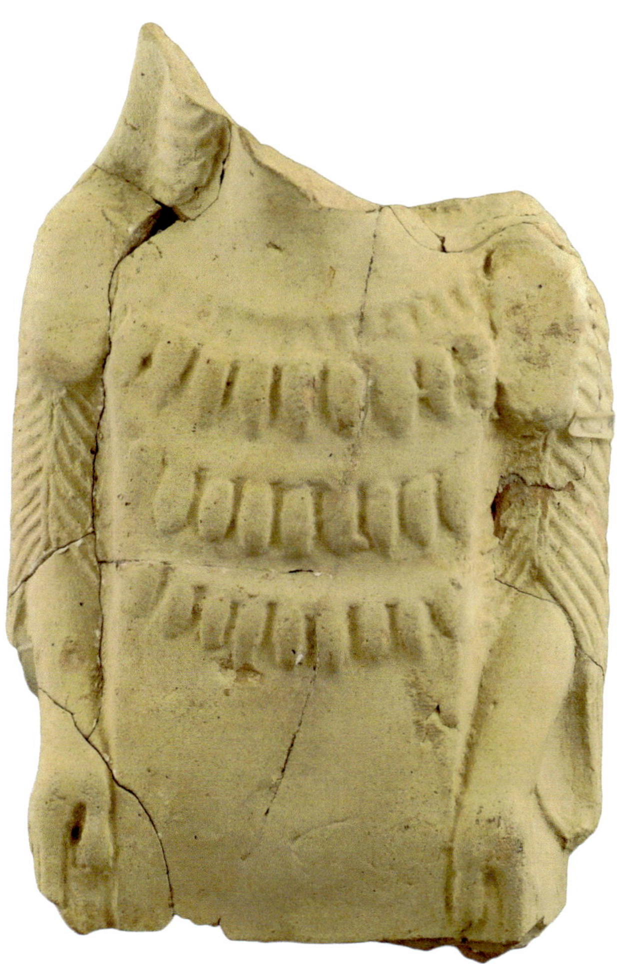

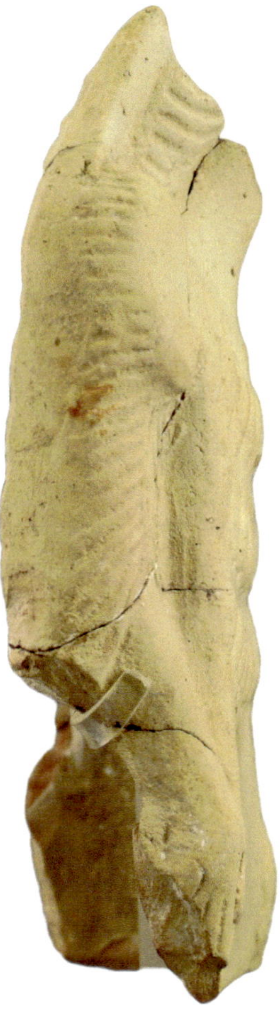

No. 97; Scale 1:1 (Museo Archeologico Regionale "Pietro Griffo", Agrigento).

Akragas: AG2313, h.35.1cm. Albertocchi 2004, p.67, no.1069; Langlotz and Hirmer 1963, p.263-4, fig.20. A similar headless figurine from the extra-urban Sanctuary of Contrada San Francesco Bisconti Morgantina, Mus. Aidone Inv. no.EN 10656H. h.17cm. Raffiotta 2007, p.70, no.1. Its pose with the finely dressed arms, the multiple pendants and the oval fibulae is similar to a figurine from Selinous. The fourth row with disc pendants and the bracelets are different, however. Mus. Louvre Inv. no.Cp 5137, complete h.32.7cm.

Type H: A variety of pendants (98-106)

This group comprises figurines with various types of pendants, marking the development towards an increased number of identical pendants.

No.98

- *Museum and Inventory number:* Archive of the Soprintendenza Archeologica di Agrigento (without number)
- *Findspot and context:* Sporadic find at S. Anna Sanctuary survey 2011
- *Publications:* -
- *Dimensions in cm:* h.5.1
- *Material:* Terracotta
- *Techniques:* Moulded
- *Colour:* Pinkish
- *Date:* 500-480 BCE
- *Workshop:* Unknown
- *Typology:* Block-like body group: 2b
- *Short description:* Right part of the chest, just front. Weathered, but sharply moulded. The relief is relatively deep, up to 5mm. Simple bodied figurine with two rows of pectoral bands and alternating disc and ovoid shaped pendants on the first cord, only ovoid or seed shapes on the second. The latter are pointier than oval, but not very thin and thick or three-dimensional. Each of the pendants hangs on a thicker piece, like the rim of vases. Yet the disc is not an aryballos, because it is flat. The part on the upper side of the pendant shows the construction of how the attachment to the band is constructed. It seems to be a small bead.
- *Comparable objects:* The large discs and alternation are reminiscent of **171-174**. The combination of disc and ovoid or seed-shaped pendants is more common, but not on armless, probably block-like bodied, figurines.

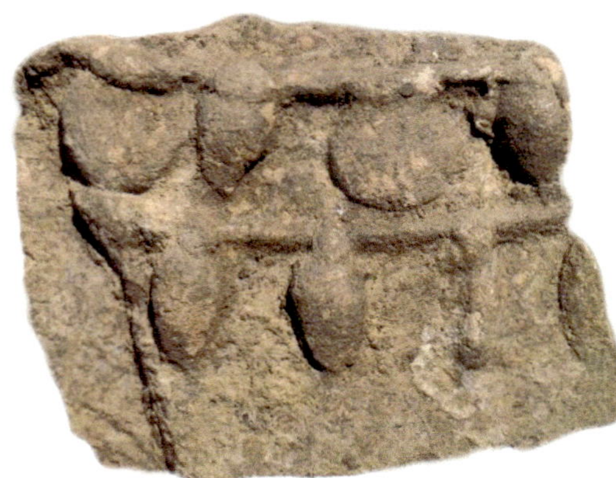

No. 98; Scale 1:1 (Museo Archeologico Regionale "Pietro Griffo", Agrigento).

No.99

- *Museum and Inventory number:* Mus. Munich 6867
- *Findspot and context:* Akragas
- *Publications:* Hamdorf 2014, p.99, no.C 217
- *Dimensions in cm:* h.8.9
- *Material:* Terracotta. The imprint of a shell is visible behind the right ear.
- *Techniques:* Front moulded from a fresh mould. Eyes probably sharpened afterwards with a tool. Hair along sides of the neck reworked with a round stick.
- *Colour:* Pink 7.5 YR 7/4
- *Date:* 500-480 BCE
- *Workshop:* Unknown
- *Typology:* Block-like body group: 2b
- *Short description:* Head and right part of the chest of a figurine. Female figurine with a round face and a short forehead. She has slanting, bulging eyes and sharply marked eyelids with high arching eyebrows. A pointed nose with precisely indicated nostrils, flat cheeks and a pronounced chin. Her mouth is thin and narrow, no wider than the nose width, curving upwards into a smile. Her very finely wavy hair is placed in a thick band with small waves on her forehead. She wears a veil, visible on top of her hair and cut straight off on the back of the head. Along the sides of her neck, the hair is reworked with a stick, resulting in unequal small impressions, horizontally arranged in scallops. Her ears with large lobes or ear studs are placed where the two parts of the hair meet. The thin lines of the part with the shell impression on the back at

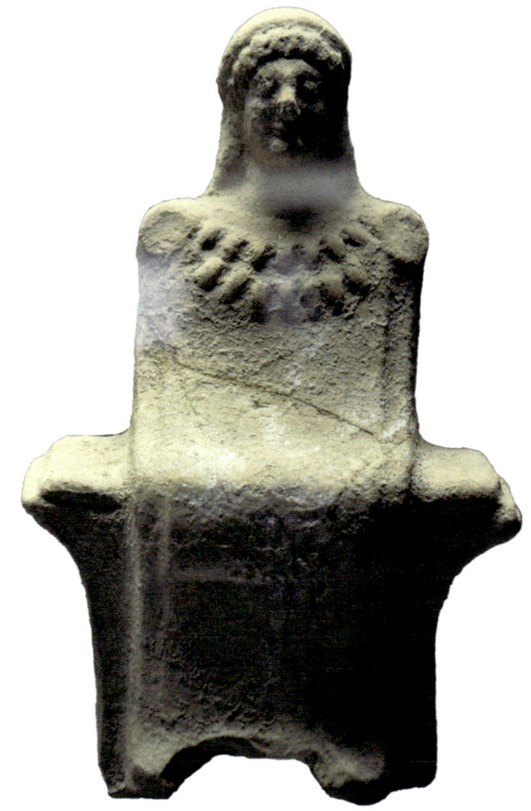

Figure 8; Figurine from Akragas. Inv. no.2017 (Museo Archeologico Regionale "Paolo Orsi", Syracuse).

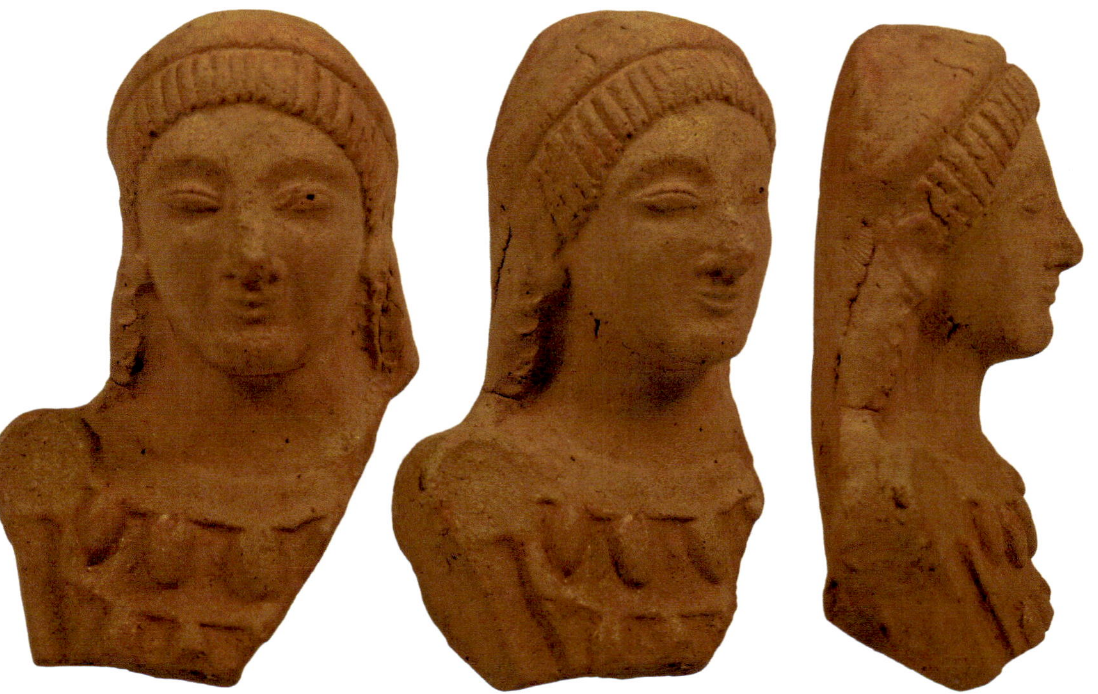

No. 99; Scale 1:1 (Staatlichen Antikensammlungen München).

the right side are also scalloped. The impression seems intended rather than coincidental. She has a broad and sturdy neck. A round, slightly hollow fibula is placed on the wide shoulders. There are two bands on the chest, and the upper band is attached to the fibula. On the first band, five ovoid pendants, and, on the second band, three are still visible. The pendants near the fibula are more pointed. An apron covers the flat body reaching close to the edge and following the same triangular shape. The hem of the apron or an undergarment is visible at the neck. The neckline runs from the fibula to low in the neck. The back is straight.

‣ *Comparable objects:* A head, probably from the same mould series is mentioned by Marconi Marconi 1933, tav.VIII. 3. A complete figurine of 14.7cm is from the same mould series but several generations later. Mus. Karlsruhe Inv. no.B 1824. Schürmann 1989, p.90, no.305, tav.52. Comparable, but probably not from the same mould as **107**-**109**. See group I below. The facial features are reminiscent of **12** and **95**. The figurine has a different hairstyle than **107**, but is comparable in iconography of face, body and pendants. It is larger in size also. Though the hairstyle is different, it is reminiscent of type B XXI from Selinous. Dewailly 1992, p.117-20. It is likely that the figurine was seated on a wide bench, comparable to the Selinuntine figurines and the other Akragantine figurines (no.**107**- **109**). A figurine from Akragas has a similar body, though it is straighter. The hairstyle is different also. See Albertocchi 2004, p.59, no.785; Meurer 1914, p.211, fig.8,1. Mus. Syracuse, AG 20176 looks, nearly complete 21cm (fig.8 and 10). Probably from the same mould series as inv. no.6087, from Selinous, complete, h.19.7cm, Mus. Palermo. According to Dewailly the type originates in Agrigento, but Albertocchi brings up the few larger figurines and finds it more likely the type originates from Selinous. Albertocchi 2004, p.60; Dewailly 1992, p.120. Similar to a head from Selinous, but with a necklace. Poma 2009, p.235, no.24. These facial features, in particular the almond-shaped narrow eyes, but also the mouth, nose and eyebrows, are seen as Akragatine production. A protome found in Selinous is probably from Akragas, based on its style: Wiederkehr Schuler 2004, p.209-10.

No.100

‣ *Museum and Inventory number:* Mus. Agrigento C383

‣ *Findspot and context:* City Sanctuary

‣ *Publications:* Albertocchi 2004, p.28, no.525

‣ *Dimensions in cm:* h.20.8

‣ *Material:* terracotta

‣ *Techniques:* Front moulded. Impression of straws on the left side. On the back and corners, leftover clay was roughly cut away. A scratch from a sharp tool is visible also.

‣ *Colour:* Very pale brown 10 YR 8/2

‣ *Date:* 500-480 BCE

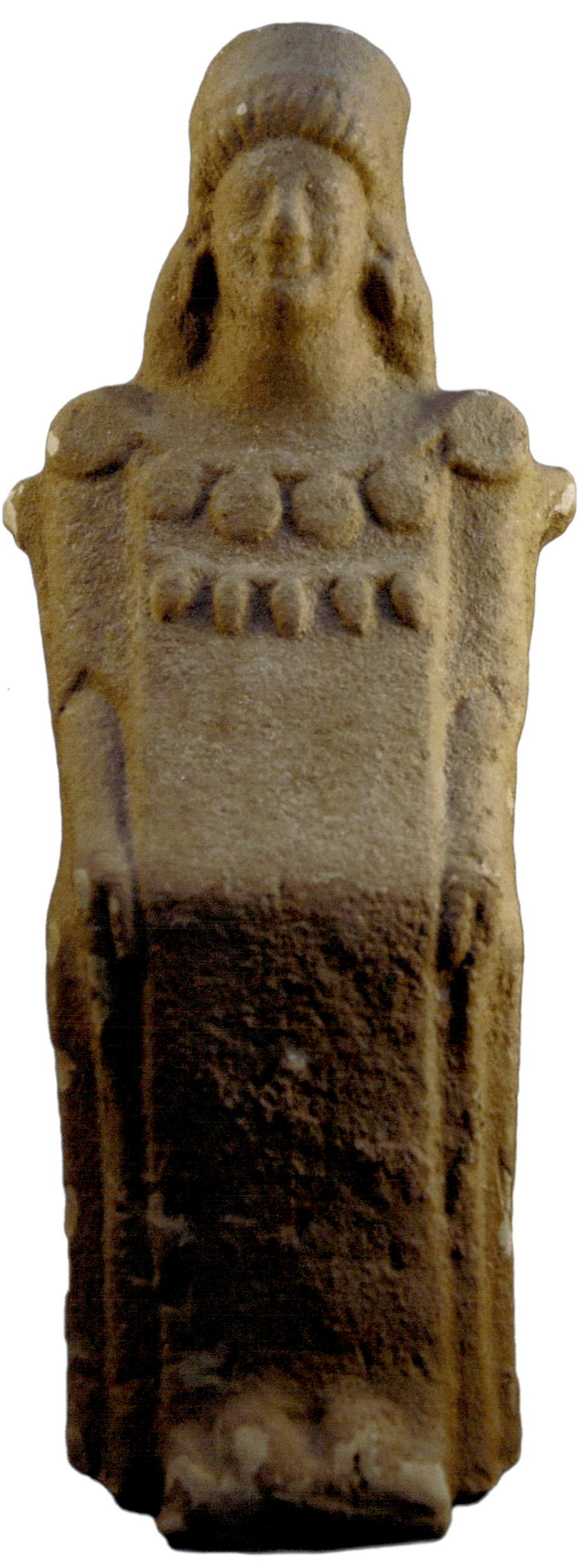

No. 100; Scale 1:1 (Museo Archeologico Regionale "Pietro Griffo", Agrigento); continued on next page at scale 1:2.

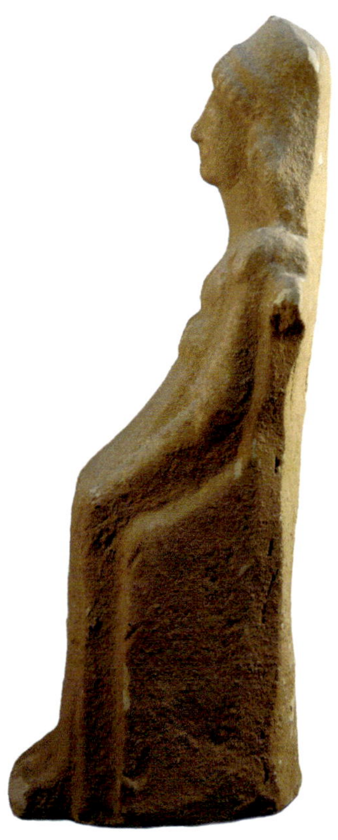

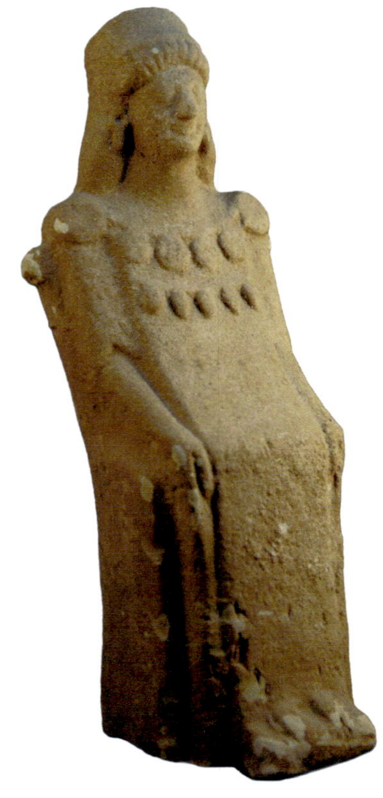

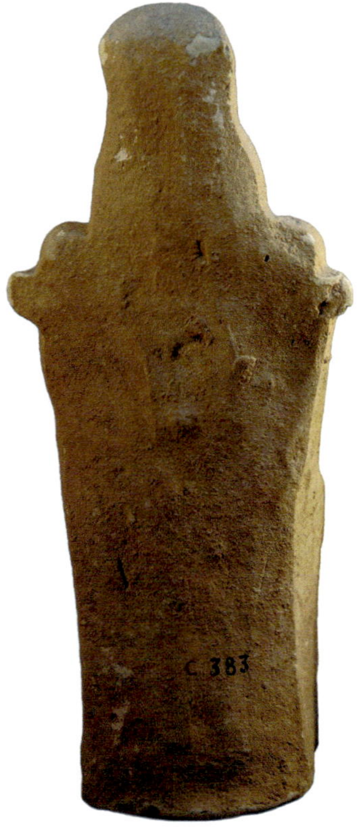

‣ *Workshop:* Chubby face group, though with earlier body: 2d
‣ *Typology:* Workshop of 'straight reworking'
‣ *Short description:* Nearly complete figurine. Film of dirt. On the inside, a metal placeholder has been attached by the museum. Seated female figurine. Round chubby face with large eyes, big nose and small mouth with thick lips. A fringe of hair in vertical round bulbs over her forehead and along the sides of the sturdy neck bulging hair with a large earring with a knob, a thick ring, and a pendant between the two strands of hair. She wears a low polos with a rim. Her simply shaped body runs diagonally towards the knees and bends from there straight down. Her arms are closely attached to the upper part of the body, but are rounded, her hands resting on her knees with the thumbs to the front. She wears an apron over an undergarment with sleeves. They reach the elbow with a v-shape to the front. On top of her dress, she wears pectoral pendants in two rows. On the first band, attached between the disc-shaped fibulae, there are four discs, on the second, five ovoid pendants, some pointed others more rounded. The cords themselves are clearly visible. She is seated on a throne, block-like, but with indications of the armrest on each side. The wide-backed backrest runs up high almost to the height of her shoulder and ends in small 'ears.' Her feet rest on a part of the base functioning as footstool. She wears shoes. The back is rounded, but straight.
‣ *Comparable objects:* A generation later from S. Biagio, Agrigento is AG 9388 (left side and chest 10.9cm slightly different chair. Albertocchi 2004, p.28, no.526. Also like some other figurines from the same mould series from Akragas, Himera and Sabucina, see Albertocchi 2004, p.28. From a later generation is a figurine from Himera, upper part, 12cm. Albertocchi 2004, p.28, no.530; Allegro 1972, p.46, fig.XX.7. A head from the same mould series: Mus. Agrigento Inv. no.AG9088. Albertocchi 2004, p.97, no.1716; De Miro 2000, p.131, no.41. The head of **105-106** is from the same mould series, one or two generations older and therefore larger. The body of a later figurine from Akragas is very similar. It is once more a proof that the bodies were applied for a long period while the head would be changed for a more contemporary one. Nat. Mus. Copenhagen Inv. no.8023, h.14.9cm, See museum website. Breitenstein 1941, p.24, no.234, tav.24. The body might be from the same mould series as that of a figurine from Gelas, though the pectorals are sharper and on straight cords, complete h.20cm. Adamesteanu and Orlandini 1956, p.369, fig.13. Its head is more similar to **70**.

No.101

‣ *Museum and Inventory number:* Mus. Agrigento S522
‣ *Findspot and context:* Akragas
‣ *Publications:* -
‣ *Dimensions in cm:* h.9.5
‣ *Material:* Terracotta
‣ *Techniques:* Front moulded.
‣ *Colour:* Light red 2.5 YR 7/6
‣ *Date:* 490-470 BCE
‣ *Workshop:* Unknown
‣ *Typology:* Combined pendants: 2b
‣ *Short description:* Headless figurine. Seated female figurine. Her pose is stiff and she holds her arms stretched along her sloping upper body. The arm reaches in the direction of the knees, but there are no hands. Her body is rectangular shaped, but the shoulders are rounded, also as the arms. On her left side, some bulging hair next to her neck is left. She wears an undergarment with folds on the sleeves. On her arms, these curving lines of the folds run diagonal, parallel to each other. The upper hem is visible in the neck. On top and just on the front part she wears an apron. This apron covers the front completely. On her chest and with the same width as the apron there are two pectoral chains: On the upper one, four discs and on the lower one four pointed seed-shaped pendants are attached to thick cords. The back is slightly rounded.
‣ *Comparable objects:* From the same mould as **102**, probably a generation earlier, because it is slightly larger. The types and combination of pendants are reminiscent of figurines **100** and **185-186**, with discs on the first row and pointed seed-shaped pendants on the second. The number of pendants on the comparable figurines, however, is greater.

No.102

‣ *Museum and Inventory number:* Mus. Agrigento 8999 (115)
‣ *Findspot and context:* Southern city wall
‣ *Publications:* Albertocchi 2004, p.90, no.1676, tav.XXX, b; De Miro 2000, p.163, no.406, tav.LXVI
‣ *Dimensions in cm:* h.9.2
‣ *Material:* Terracotta
‣ *Techniques:* Front moulded.
‣ *Colour:* Light grey 10 YR 7/2
‣ *Date:* 490-470 BCE
‣ *Workshop:* Unknown
‣ *Typology:* Combined pendants: 2b
‣ *Short description:* Headless figurine. Upper part of the chest broken off. Seated female figurine. Her pose is stiff and she holds her arms stretched along her sloping upper body, reaching her knees. The arms end in stumps. Her body is rectangular, but the shoulders and arms are rounded. She wears an undergarment with vertical wavy folds on the lower body reaching the footstool and draped over her feet. On her arms, there are some diagonal folds also. On top and only on the front, she wears a small apron, reaching her ankles. On her chest and with the same width as the apron, there are two pectoral chains. On the upper one, four discs and on the lower one four pointed seed-shaped pendants are attached to thick cords. Her feet in shoes are placed a bit away from each other on a footstool. The back is straight.
‣ *Comparable objects:* From the same mould as **101**, probably a generation later, because it is slightly smaller.

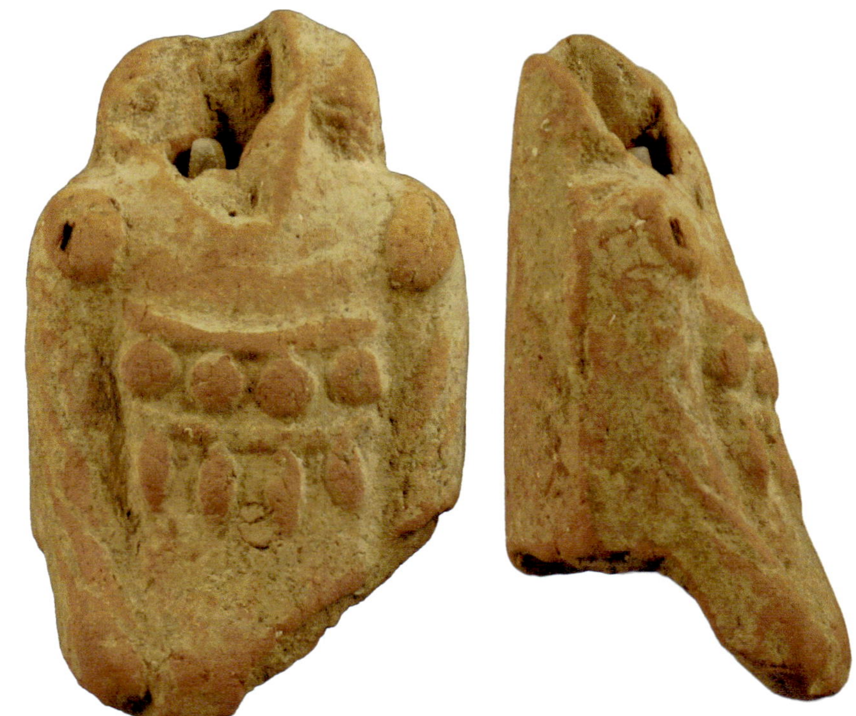

No. 101; Scale 1:1 (Museo Archeologico Regionale "Pietro Griffo", Agrigento).

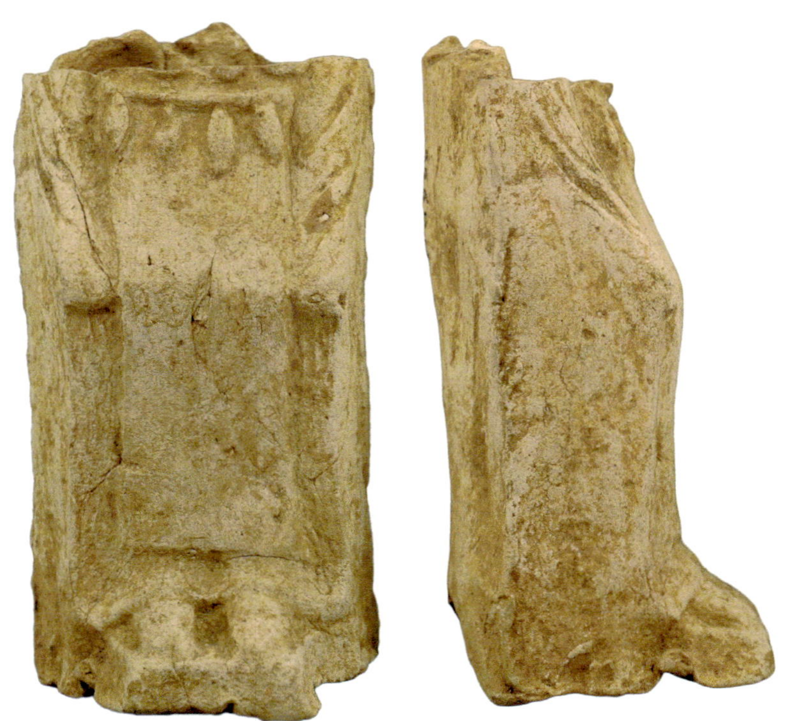

No. 102; Scale 1:1 (Museo Archeologico Regionale "Pietro Griffo", Agrigento).

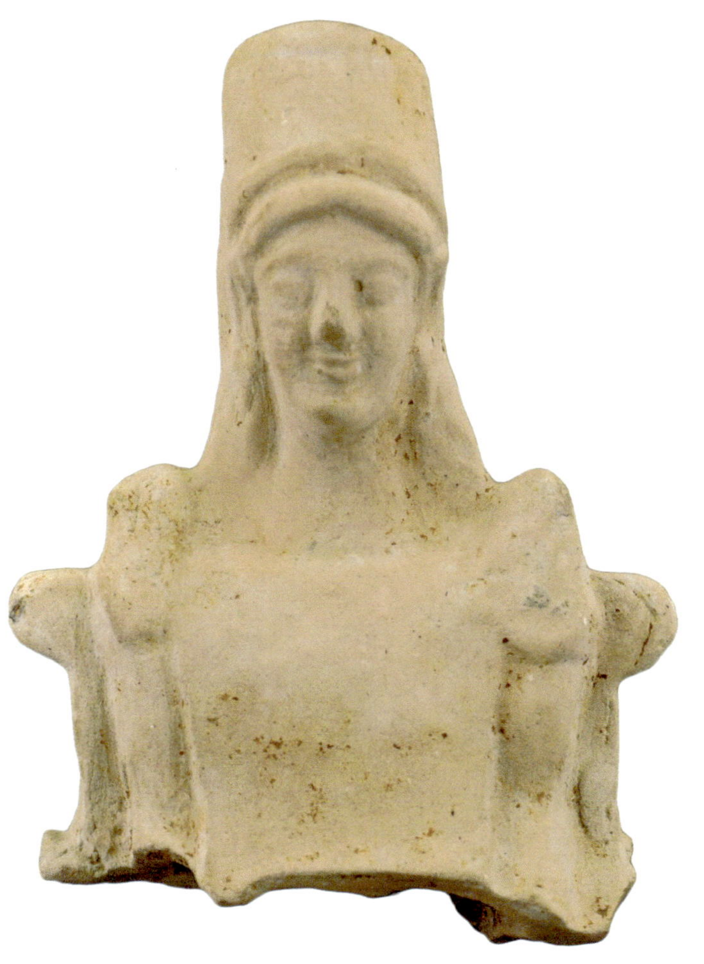

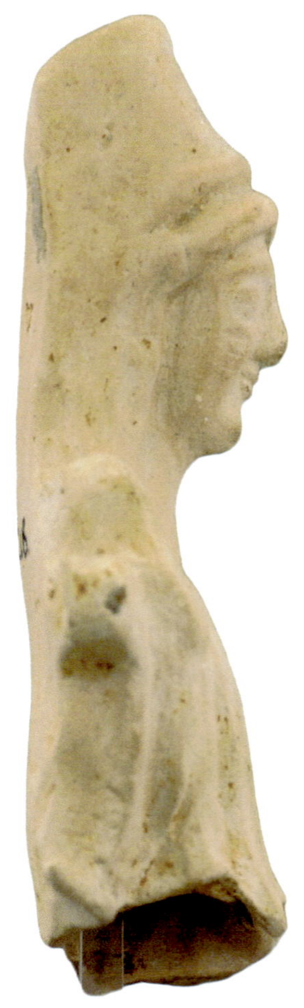

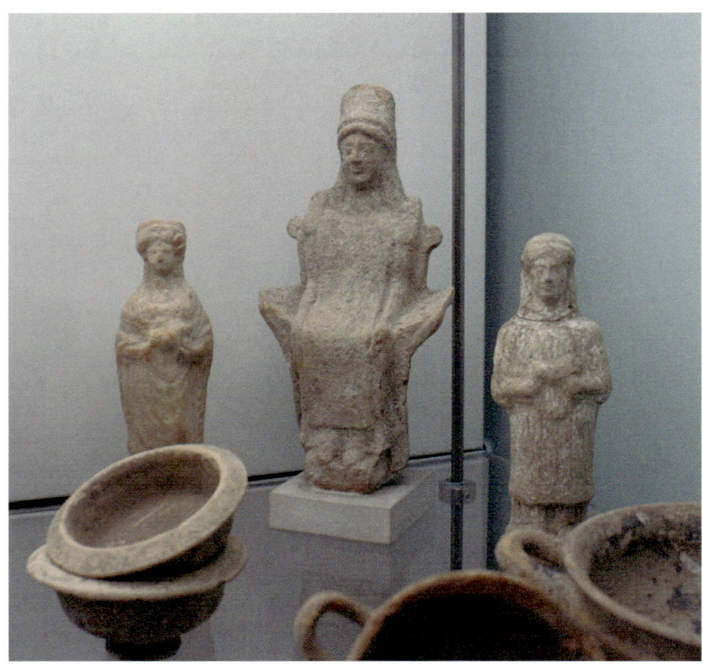

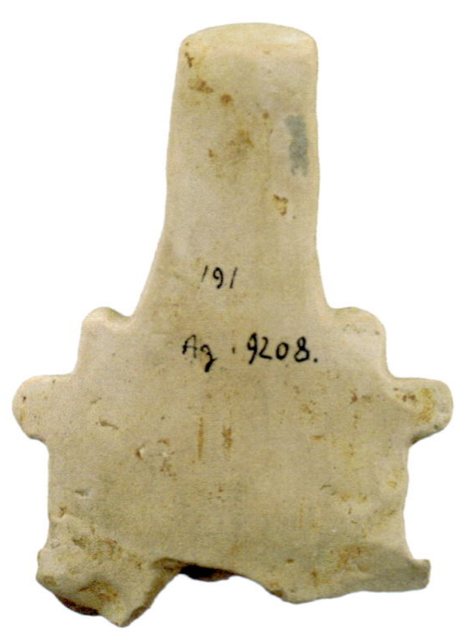

No. 103; Scale 1:1 (Museo Archeologico Regionale "Pietro Griffo", Agrigento). Other angles; Scale 1:2; A similar, but complete figurine is exhibited in the Palermo museum, and probably from S. Biagio, Agrigento.

No. 104; Scale 1:1 (Museo Archeologico Regionale "Pietro Griffo", Agrigento). Upper part of a figurine, Louvre C 5122 (photo: Mollard Besques 1954).

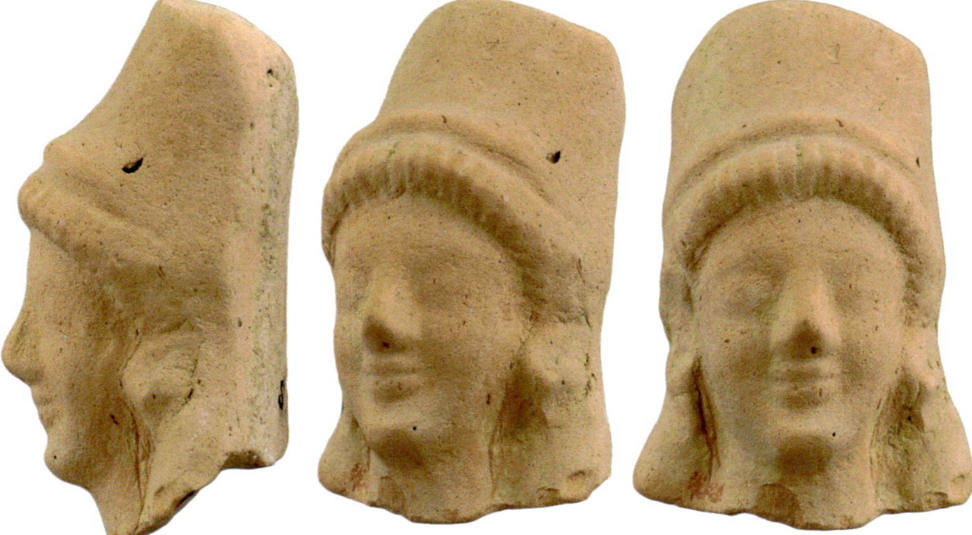

No.103

‣ *Museum and Inventory number:* Mus. Agrigento 9208 (191)
‣ *Findspot and context:* City Sanctuary
‣ *Publications:* De Miro 2000, p.240, no.1410
‣ *Dimensions in cm:* h.12.3
‣ *Material:* Terracotta
‣ *Techniques:* Front moulded. Painted reddish-yellow and white(?). shell fragment on the back. Incised line on the left ear of throne.
‣ *Colour:* Very pale brown 10 YR 8/2
‣ *Date:* 490-470 BCE
‣ *Workshop:* Unknown
‣ *Typology:* Chubby face group: 2d
‣ *Short description:* Upper half of a figurine. Narrow face, big chin. Large eyes with eyelids, big nose, smiling narrow mouth but thick lower lip.Pronounced cheeks. Hair parted in the middle. Very large ears with earrings with pendant. Its outline is placed in front of smooth fringe of hair and high polos with rim. Thin neck, separated from hair that falls over her shoulders. She holds her arms next to her body. Arms depicted naturally with thicker upper part and bending at elbow. She has a slightly elevated chest and narrowed waist, but wears the standard apron of which the hem is visible in the neck. She is seated on a wide-backed throne with 'ears' just below the shoulders. The right 'ear' of the throne is placed higher and slightly smaller than the left. She wears large, fibulae shaped like the outline of a double palmette and large earrings: a ring with a large pendant. Straight back, sides with sharp edges.
‣ *Comparable objects:* From the same mould is the upper half of the figurine: Mus. Agrigento Inv. no.AG20486, h.12cm. Part of the lap, lower arms and the bench on the left remained also. De Miro 2000, p.129, no.27, tav.LXIV.

The figurine looks very similar to a figurine from Selinous Louvre Inv. no.CA 421, complete, h.21cm. It could be from the same mould. Mollard Besques 1963, p.56-7, pl. IX,4; See museum website. The figurine has a similar smoothed chest and is seated on an upwards-curving bench. It is likely from the same mould and generation.

Face, polos and earring are similar to Marconi 1930, tav. VII.7, but has a necklace. This necklace links the figurines to the objects of the Mould I group, with which they share their large eyes, broad nose and fleshy lips, *e.g.* **171**.

The head **104** is from the same mould series probably one generation earlier. The fringe of hair on **104** is not smoothed.

No.104

‣ *Museum and Inventory number:* Mus. Agrigento S403
‣ *Findspot and context:* City Sanctuary
‣ *Publications:* -
‣ *Dimensions in cm:* h.7.3
‣ *Material:* Terracotta.
‣ *Techniques:* Front moulded.
‣ *Colour:* Pink 7.5 YR 7/4
‣ *Date:* 490-470 BCE
‣ *Workshop:* Unknown
‣ *Typology:* Chubby face group: 2d
‣ *Short description:* Head. Female figurine. Oval fleshy face, pronounced chin. Large eyes, sizeable nose, smiling narrow mouth but thick lips. Chubby cheeks and dimples next to her mouth. Fringe on the forehead in vertical bulbs. Very large ears: outline in front of fringe of hair. Earrings with pendant (? indistinct). She wears an at the top outward bending polos with rim. Thin neck, separated from hair that falls down next to it.
‣ *Comparable objects:* Figurine **103** is from the same mould series probably one generation later, because the face is slightly smaller. The fringe of hair on **103** is smoothed. For others see **103**.

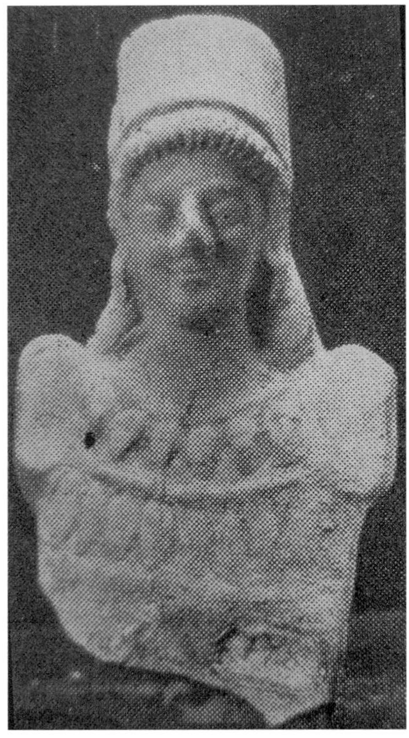

Figure 9; Upper part of a figurine, h.15cm; Inv. no. C 5122, coll. Campana 178, Louvre. Photo after Mollard Besques 1954, tav.LI, B 555.

This head is the same mould series as a figurine from Akragas, chest and head, h.15cm, Louvre Inv. no.C 5122, coll. Campana 178, (fig. 9). That head is probably older, because it is sharper, though not much different in size. Mollard Besques 1954, p.79, tav.LI, B 555.

In the later generations, like **103**, arms and a chair have been added, the chest is smoothed and fibulae have been altered to the double palmette-outline. See also **179** for the original body.

No.105

‣ *Museum and Inventory number:* Mus. Agrigento 9086 (306)

‣ *Findspot and context: City Sanctuary :*

‣ *Publications:* Albertocchi 2004, p.97, no.1715; De Miro 2000, p.130, no.28; Dewailly 1992, p.77, n.71.

‣ *Dimensions in cm:* h.27.2

‣ *Material:* Terracotta. Clay turned black inside in places.

‣ *Techniques:* Front moulded in a new mould. On several chest pendants, the earrings also, there is a double line visible, as if the object was removed and then pressed intoto the mould again. This creates a more three-dimensional effect, particularly with the discs. It's not clear, however, whether this was intended. The mould is filled first by a thin layer of clay to ensure a sharp impression. Back and sides are smoothed with a sharp tool.

‣ *Colour:* Pink 7.5 YR 7/4

‣ *Date:* 500-480 BCE

‣ *Workshop:* The double impression at the chest pendants are reminiscent of figurine 179.

‣ *Typology:* Chubby face group: 2d

‣ *Short description:* Figurine in several parts, restored with small infill on chest. Shoulders and sides of upper part, left part of the base broken. For description, see **106**. Her hands, not visible on **106** are outstretched, reaching the height of the knees and with the thumb forward. Other fingers are not separately indicated. On this figurine, the other shoulder has been preserved better. The pointed pendant has a vertical attachment to the band. This would strengthen the interpretation of a flower bud. Other objects, like the disc in the middle of the second line have a tubular attachment. This attachment indicates that an element of metal decoration is represented.

‣ *Comparable objects:* From the same mould as **106**, which is sharper than **105**. The face is slightly narrower than **106** and the polos a bit higher. The head of **20** is very similar, but lacks the earrings. A head from the same mould series AG9088. Albertocchi 2004, p.97, no.1716; De Miro 2000, p.131, no.41. The head of **100** is from the same mould series, one or two generations younger and therefore slightly smaller. Some Selinuntine figurines have two rows with pendants with the combination of crescent and disc. They lack, however, the third cord and seem earlier than **105** and **106**. Dewailly 1992, p.104, fig.64, 65. There would be another similar figurine from Agrigento in Syracuse, mentioned by Dewailly 1992, p.107, n.127. This figurine has a disc flanked by crescents on the first cord. Inv. no.20175. The combination with rosette-shaped fibulae and a patterned polos head is odd. The head is also out of proportion. See Meurer 1914, p.211, pl. 8,2 (fig.10). The pendants and earrings are reminiscent of **179**. The

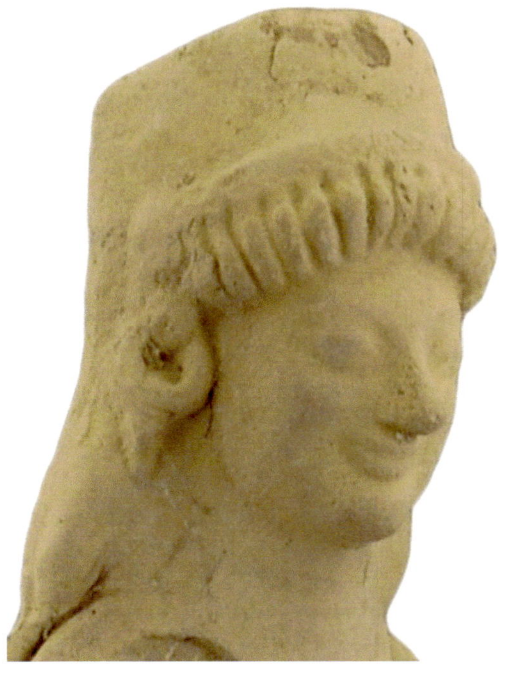

No. 105; Detail of the head (Museo Archeologico Regionale "Pietro Griffo", Agrigento).

fibulae outline and the lower seed-shaped pendants, though different in number, are similar to a figurine from Akragas, mentioned in old descriptions, which is now lost. The figurine would have been exceptional because it has on the first band a pendant, not known from any other Archaic figurine: a gorgoneion. Kekulé von Stradonitz 1884, p.17, fig.22; Winter 1903, p.127, no.1.

No.106

- *Museum and Inventory number:* Mus. Agrigento 9087 (307)
- *Findspot and context:* City Sanctuary
- *Publications:* Albertocchi 2004, p.97, no.1714, tav.XXXIV, a; De Miro 2000, p.130, no.29, tav.LXIV; Dewailly 1992, p.77, n. 71
- *Dimensions in cm:* h.27.2
- *Material:* Terracotta. Clay turned black inside in places.
- *Techniques:* Front moulded in a new mould. Head is left open at the back to ease drying and firing. On several chest pendants, there are double lines visible, as if the coroplast took the figurine out of the mould and pressed it in again. The face is made by application of a thin layer of clay to ensure a sharp impression, before adding more clay. Back and sides are smoothed with a sharp tool.
- *Colour:* Pink 7.5 YR 7/4
- *Date:* 500-480 BCE
- *Workshop:* Unknown
- *Typology:* Chubby face group: 2d
- *Short description:* Upper part and left front part of a tall figurine. Chin, back, left fibula, right side of body and feet broken off. Restored with infill. Oval face with large eyes and thick lips in upwards-curving smile. She looks downwards slightly, her head bent to the front. Her hair is divided into bulbs on an edged fringe on the forehead with bulging undefined hair along the sides of the sturdy neck. She wears a low polos with rim. Her ear itself is not visible, just a knob as an ear stud on the sides of the fringe, higher than where an ear would be expected. On the knob, a ring with a triangular pendant is attached. A simple body outline with a rectangular sloping front and a slight bending at the knees, but a more rounded outline as a whole, as rounded arms were attached to the sides. Fibulae in the shape of tied wheat sheaves on rounded shoulders. She wears an apron, to just above the feet. On top of the apron, on her chest, she has three bands, of which the middle one ends with a knob. On the upper band, a disc and a long pointed pendant flank a crescent pointing down. The crescent has a clear attachment part, like a tube. On the second band, there are three discs in the same style, but slightly larger than on the first band. On the furthest right one, the attachment tube is also visible. On the third band, there are four pointed shaped pendants, of which the two ones furthest to the right look like shells, with a curved line on it. The double moulding here gives a misleading impression because the other two, and the same pendant on figurine **105**, are not marked with a line. The two on the left are more elongated, with a clearer knob attachment to the band and a similar but smaller tip. The feet were probably sticking out from under the dress and placed on a small footstool.
- *Comparable objects:* From the same mould as **105**, which is less sharp. The face is slightly wider than **105** and the polos lower. For other comparable figurines see **105**.

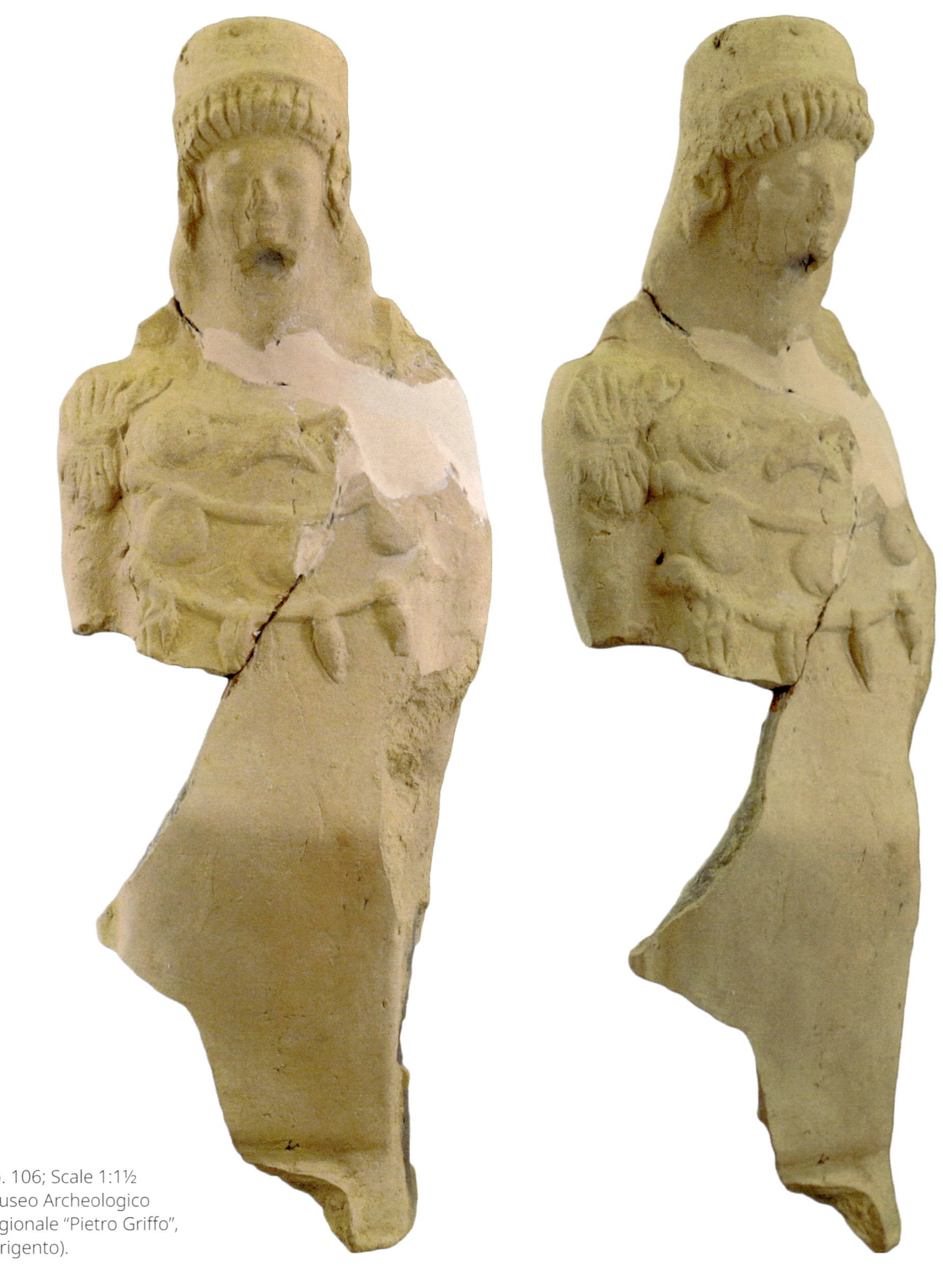

No. 106; Scale 1:1½ (Museo Archeologico Regionale "Pietro Griffo", Agrigento).

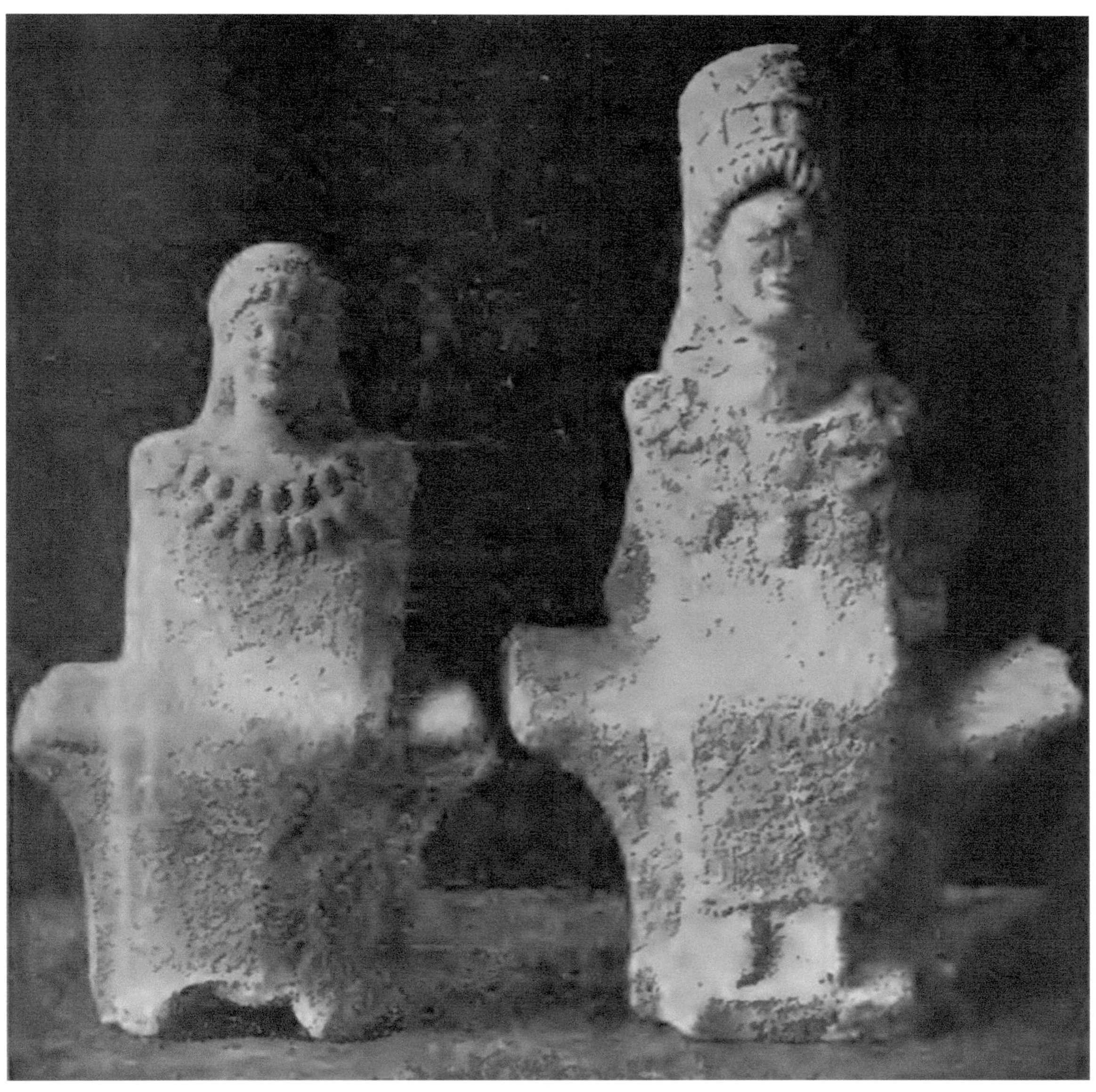

Figure 10; Two figurines from Akragas no.20176 and 20175 in Mus. Syracuse. Photo after Meurer 1914, p.211, pl.8,2.

Type I: The same head, a different body (107-114)

Figurines with a particular hairstyle in common, but with variations in their facial features and bodies.

No.107

- *Museum and Inventory number:* Mus. Agrigento 9090 (246)
- *Findspot and context:* Workshop/ sanctuary near Gate V
- *Publications:* De Miro 2000, p.165, no.429
- *Dimensions in cm:* h.14.4
- *Material:* Terracotta
- *Techniques:* Front moulded. Pressed in twice, visible from the double print of the pendants.
- *Colour:* Pink 7.5 YR 7/3
- *Date:* 500-480 BCE
- *Workshop:* Unknown
- *Typology:* Block-like body group: 2b
- *Short description:* Upper half of a figurine, chin and ears of throne broken off. Round face with slanted eyes, sharply marked by a line. Broad nose radix, large nose. Smiling mouth with thin lips, no wider than the nose. Ears in front of hair with a knob-shaped ear stud. Fringe with two rows of wavy scallop hair on the forehead, bulging hair along the sides of the neck. A thick veil covers the top of the head. Sturdy and long neck. Round fibulae with two bands in between with respectively, five and seven ovoid pendants, worn on top of an apron. The garment runs along the edge of the body, leaving just a small part uncovered. The body is very flat on the front and widening towards the shoulders. A small part on the back and a broken extension might indicate the wide-backed backrest of a chair. The 'ears', which were just below the height of the fibulae are broken off.
- *Comparable objects:* Probably from the same mould series as **108** and **109**. The body and head, but not the chair-ears are similar to a figurine from Akragas, necropolis Pezzino, the debris of Cave B, above tomb 1927 and 1930, stratum 3: Mus. Agrigento Inv. no.S191, h.14cm. De Miro 1989, p.16 and fig.15. He dates it to the second half of the 6th century BCE. The figurine is very similar to type B XXI from Selinous. Dewailly 1992, p.117-20.

No.108

- *Museum and Inventory number:* Mus. Agrigento 9076 (247)
- *Findspot and context:* Workshop/ sanctuary near Gate V
- *Publications:* De Miro 2000, p.240, no.1411, tav.LXV
- *Dimensions in cm:* h.14.9
- *Material:* Terracotta
- *Techniques:* Front moulded, smoothed front and back, handmade bench.
- *Colour:* Very pale brown 10 YR 8.3
- *Date:* 500-480 BCE
- *Workshop:* Unknown
- *Typology:* Block-like body group: 2b

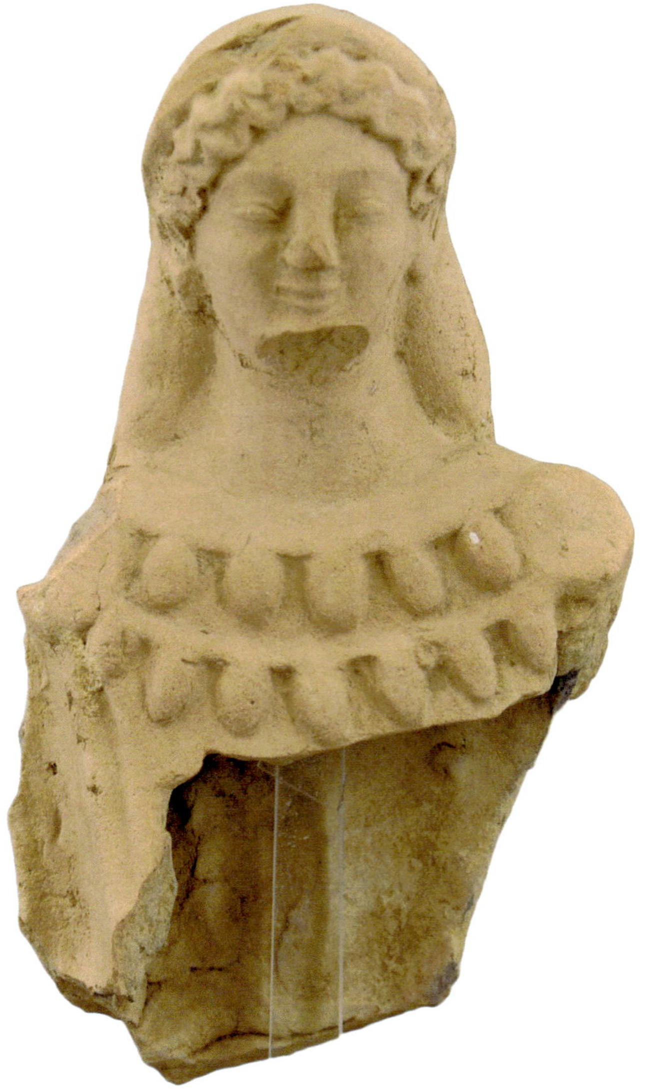

No. 107; Scale 1:1 (Museo Archeologico Regionale "Pietro Griffo", Agrigento); continued on next page.

- *Short description:* Body with lower part of the head of a figurine. Right shoulder, parts of bench and right part at base broken off. The chin is sizeable and fleshy. The mouth is very narrow with thick lips. Along the sides of the neck, the hair is bulging. Block-like body with outward bending rounded shoulders, a sloping upper body and a clear bending at the knees. The body, which is dressed in an apron reaching the floor, curves slightly inwards on both the upper and lower part. It flares at the base. The shoulder is a rounded shape as if it had a round fibula. Next to it is a band with five ovoid pendants. On a second cord, the number of pendants is unclear, because it has been smoothed. The pendants are closer together and may have been six of seven in number. She sits on a wide bench, curving up slightly and topped with a cushion. The back is rounded.
- *Comparable objects:* Probably from the same mould series as **107** and **109**.

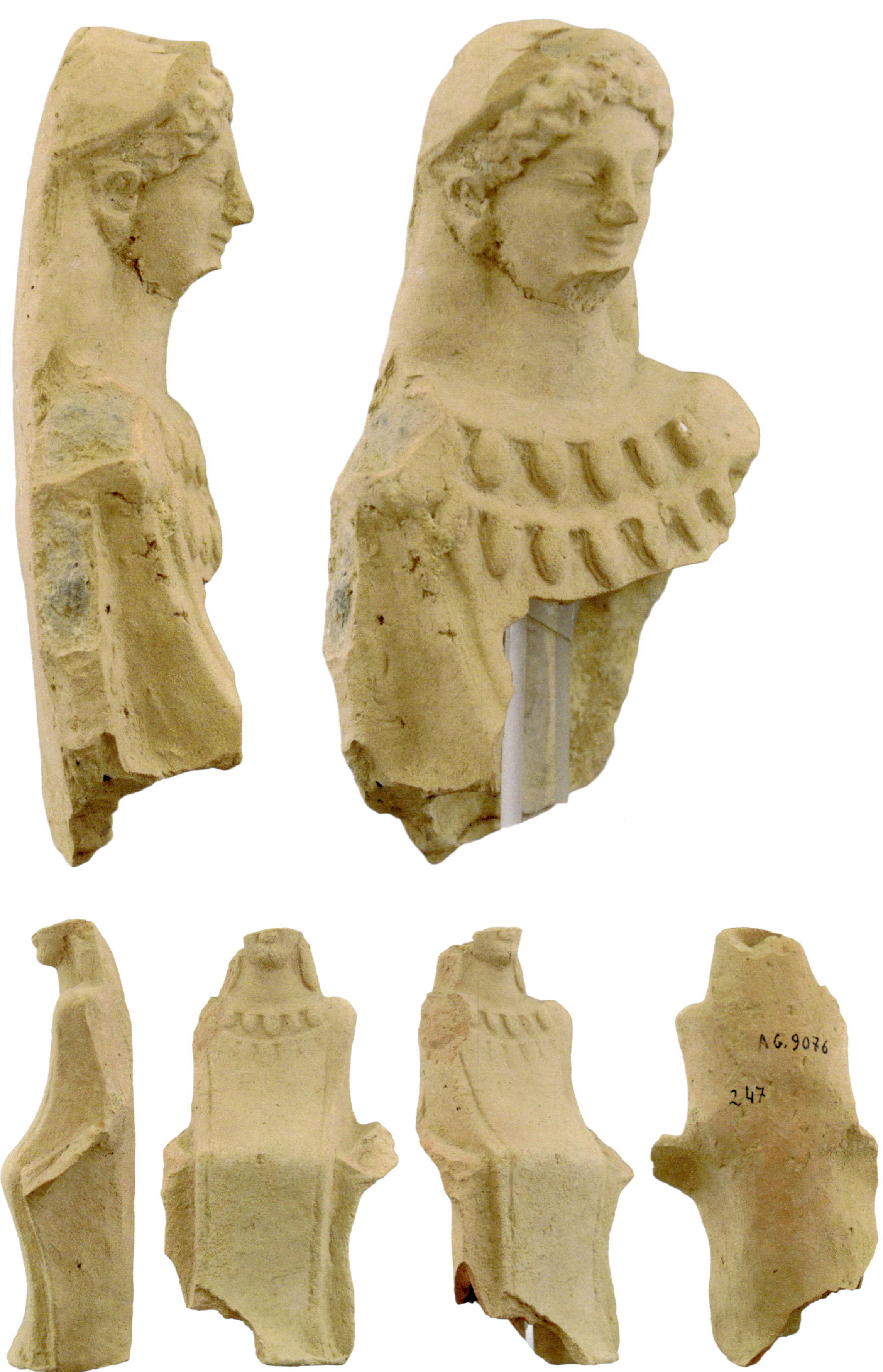

No. 108; Scale 1:2 (Museo Archeologico Regionale "Pietro Griffo", Agrigento).

Similar to S195 from necropolis Pezzino, the debris of Cave B, above tomb 1927 and 1930, stratum 3. See De Miro 1989, p.16, 18 and fig.15.2. It has the same indistinctness on the second row of pectoral pendants. Probably from the same mould.

No.109

- *Museum and Inventory number:* Mus. Agrigento S95
- *Findspot and context:* City Sanctuary
- *Publications:* Albertocchi 2004, p.59, no.786; Marconi 1933, p.58 fig.35.3
- *Dimensions in cm:* h.16.2
- *Material:* Terracotta, many inclusions
- *Techniques:* Front moulded. Very worn mould. White slip layer. Pressed-in fibulae. Handmade bench.
- *Colour:* Light grey 10 YR 7/2
- *Date:* 500-480 BCE
- *Workshop:* Unknown
- *Typology:* Block-like body group: 2b
- *Short description:* Nearly complete figurine, in many fragments, part of back missing. Round face, damaged nose, indistinct large eyes, pronounced chin. Hair in thick rhizomes, veil(?) A sturdy neck with hair on each side. Round fibulae at the flaring shoulders. On the upper part of the apron, two rows with five and seven ovoid pendants. Seated on an upwards-curving wide bench with a cushion. Slightly protruding part at the base.

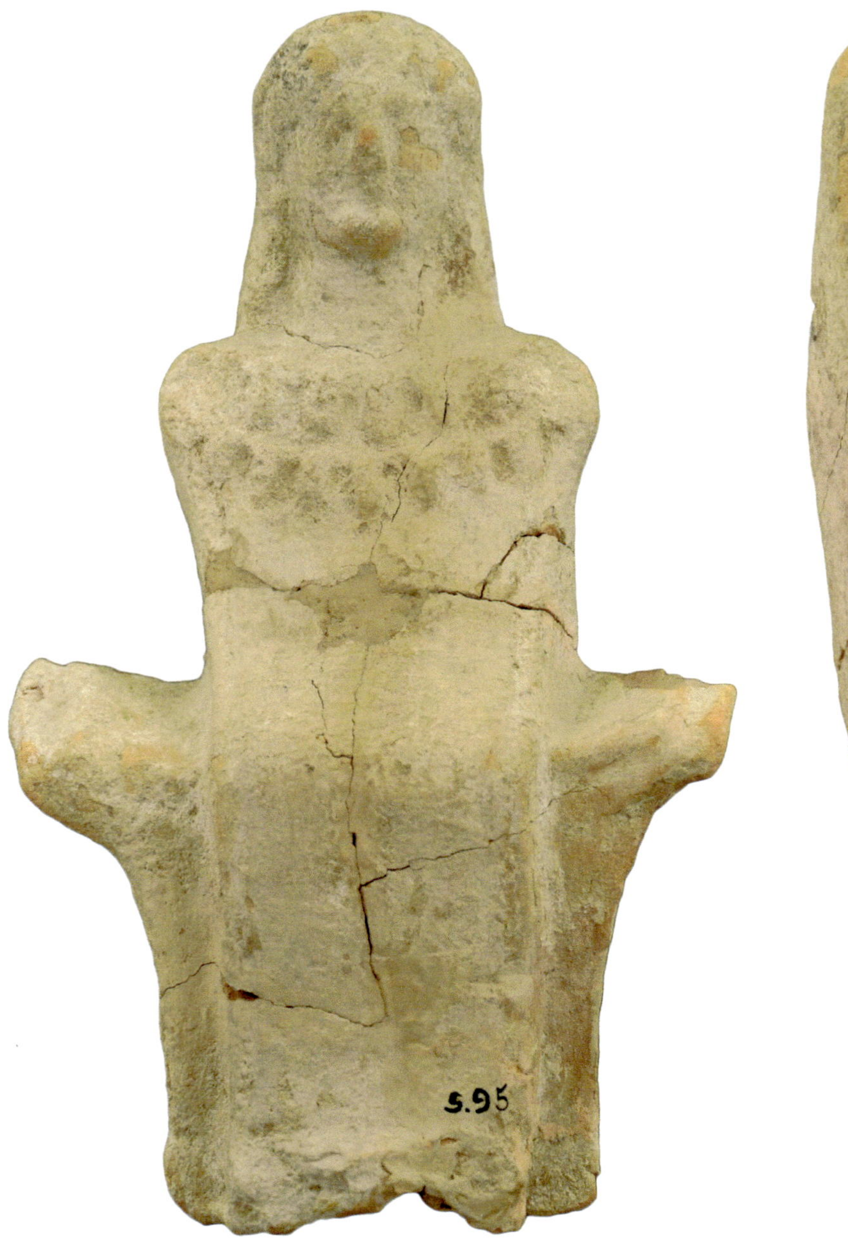

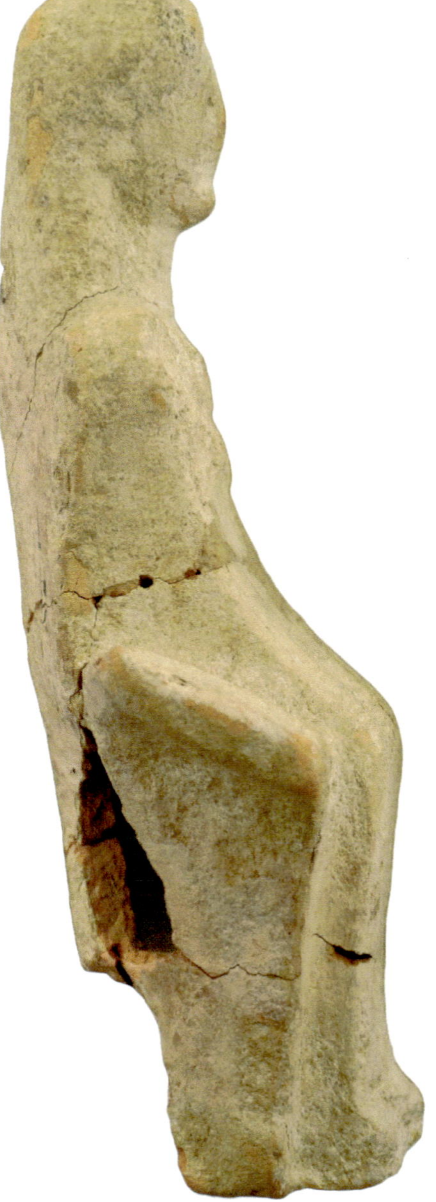

No. 109; Scale 1:1 (Museo Archeologico Regionale "Pietro Griffo", Agrigento).

‣ *Comparable objects:* Probably from the same mould series as **107** and **108**.

AG 20176 (fig. 8 and 10) is from the same mould, though the shape of the body is rectangular, according to Albertocchi 2004, p.59, no.785; Meurer 1914, p.211, fig.8, nearly complete, h.21cm. Probably from the same mould series as Inv. no.6087 from Selinous, complete, h.19.7cm., Mus. Palermo. Poma 2009, p.236, no.28. Dewailly names the variants of the type: B XXI a, b and c. Pendants, hairstyle and the different chairs are the main differences. There are 109 figurines from this type produced at Selinous. She writes that the archetype might be Akragantine. Dewailly 1992, p.117-120.

No.110

‣ *Museum and Inventory number:* Mus. Agrigento 9000 (121)
‣ *Findspot and context:* Southern city wall
‣ *Publications:* Albertocchi 2004, p.74, no.1248; De Miro 2000, p.163, no.405, tav.LXIV
‣ *Dimensions in cm:* h.6.9
‣ *Material:* Terracotta.
‣ *Techniques:* Front moulded.
‣ *Colour:* Pink 7.5 YR 7/4
‣ *Date:* The third decade of the 5th century BCE
‣ *Workshop:* Unknown
‣ *Typology:* Veiled head group: 3b
‣ *Short description:* Head and upper right part of female figurine. The head seems a bit further forward. Round face. Eyes placed high in their sockets, close to the edge of the eyebrows. She has a large nose and a slightly curving, wide mouth with thin lips. Wavy bands of hair on the forehead are topped with a veil, quite tight around the head and straight along the sides of the neck. Sturdy neck. Simple body, with slight bending at the knees. Thin arms attached to the body, hands with thumb to the front, outstretched at the height of the bending. She wears an undergarment, of which small folds are visible on her chest, indicated by vertical ridges. On the upper part of the apron, a crescent in the middle is flanked by a disc and probably a seed-shaped pendant. The latter is very indistinct. Straight back.
‣ *Comparable objects:* **111** is probably from the same mould and **114** from the same series.

No.111

‣ *Museum and Inventory number:* Mus. Agrigento 8987
‣ *Findspot and context:* Workshop/ sanctuary near Gate V
‣ *Publications:* De Miro 2000, p.171, no.486
‣ *Dimensions in cm:* h.6.6.
‣ *Material:* Terracotta.
‣ *Techniques:* Front moulded. Slab of clay attached for the back. Pressed from the inside with fore and middle finger of the right hand. A piece of wood was in the mould when the figurine was made. Lighter coloured slip layer(?).
‣ *Colour:* Pink 5 YR 7/4
‣ *Date:* The third decade of the 5th century BCE
‣ *Workshop:* Unknown
‣ *Typology:* Veiled head group: 3b
‣ *Short description:* Head and back of figurine, damaged. Round face with large nose. Double line of wavy hair on forehead. She wears a veil, running down next to her neck. Rounded shoulders, possibly with round fibulae.
‣ *Comparable objects:* **110** is probably from the same mould and **114** from the same series.

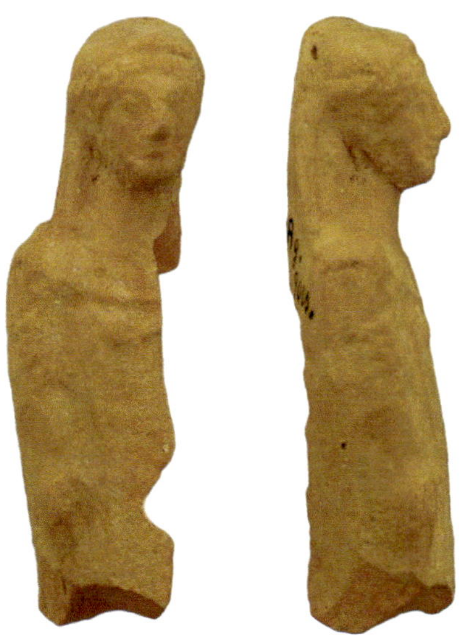

No. 110; Scale 1:1 (Museo Archeologico Regionale "Pietro Griffo", Agrigento).

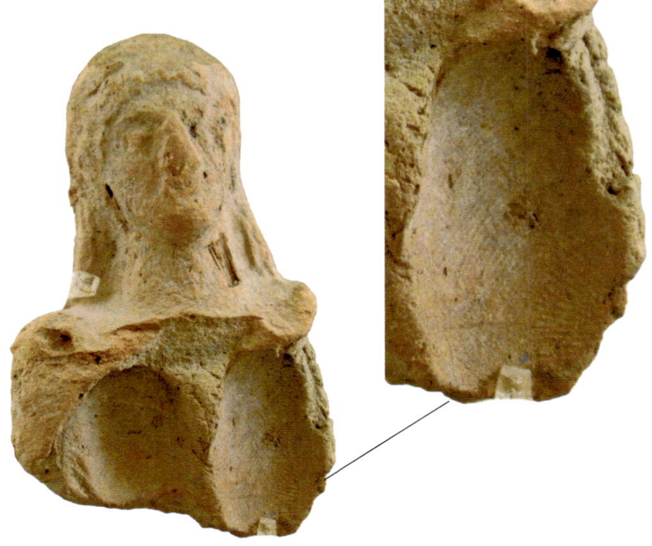

No. 111; Scale 1:1 (Museo Archeologico Regionale "Pietro Griffo", Agrigento).

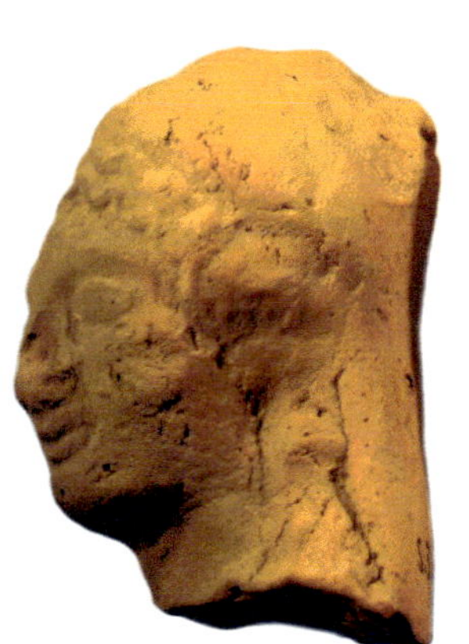
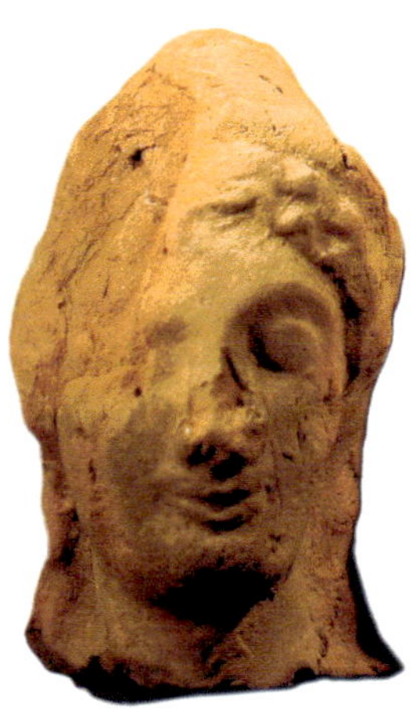

No. 112; Scale 1:1 (Museo Archeologico Regionale "Pietro Griffo", Agrigento).

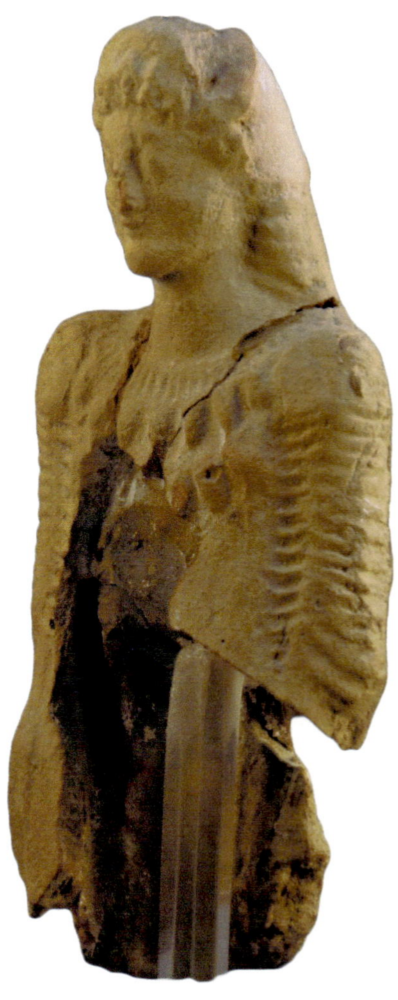

No. 113; Scale 1:1 (Museo Archeologico Regionale "Pietro Griffo", Agrigento); continued on next page.

No.112

- *Museum and Inventory number:* Mus. Agrigento S362
- *Findspot and context:* City Sanctuary
- *Publications:* -
- *Dimensions in cm:* h.5.7
- *Material:* Terracotta
- *Techniques:* Front moulded. Coarsely produced, with many small holes and folds in the clay. The face, in particular the nose, has been distorted and bent, probably when the figurine was taken out of the mould.
- *Colour:* Pink 5 YR 7/4
- *Date:* The third decade of the 5th century BCE
- *Workshop:* Unknown
- *Typology:* Veiled head group: 3b
- *Short description:* Head of a figurine, right side of head and nose heavily damaged. From a relatively new mould. She has an oval face, slightly flaring towards the forehead. Her eyes are large and deep, just below the arching eyebrows. Her cheeks are flat, but her chin is pronounced. Her upwards-curving mouth with quite thick lips is placed directly above the chin and under the nose. She has scalloped wavy hair in two lines with a veil. Along the sides of her neck, her hair falls in irregular waves. The outline of her ears is placed in front of her hair, where the waves of hair from the forehead end. The back is cut off straight.
- *Comparable objects:* From the same mould series as **114**, but of an earlier generation, because the head is larger.

No.113

- *Museum and Inventory number:* Mus. Agrigento S388
- *Findspot and context:* Akragas
- *Publications:* Albertocchi 2004, p.72, no.1240
- *Dimensions in cm:* h.12.9
- *Material:* Terracotta
- *Techniques:* Front moulded. Straightened back.
- *Colour:* Pink 7.5 YR 7/4

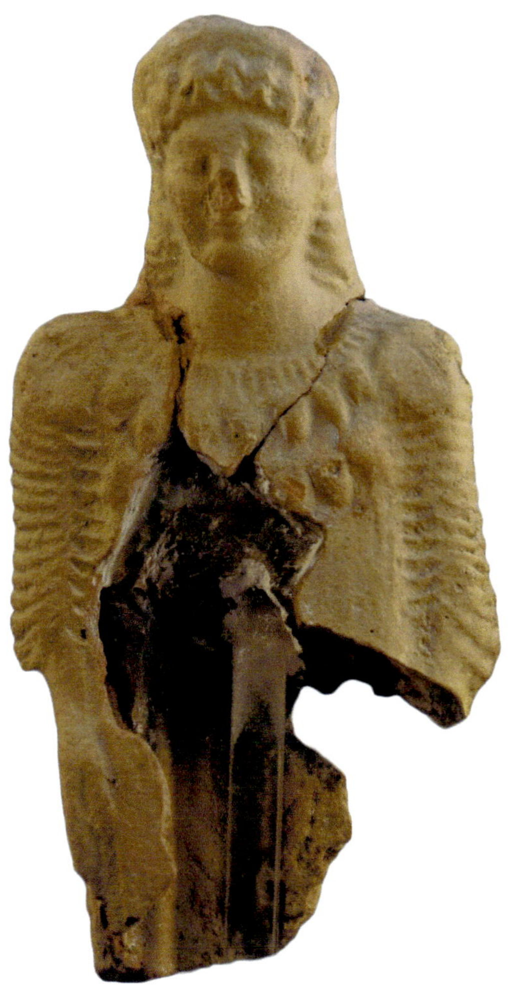

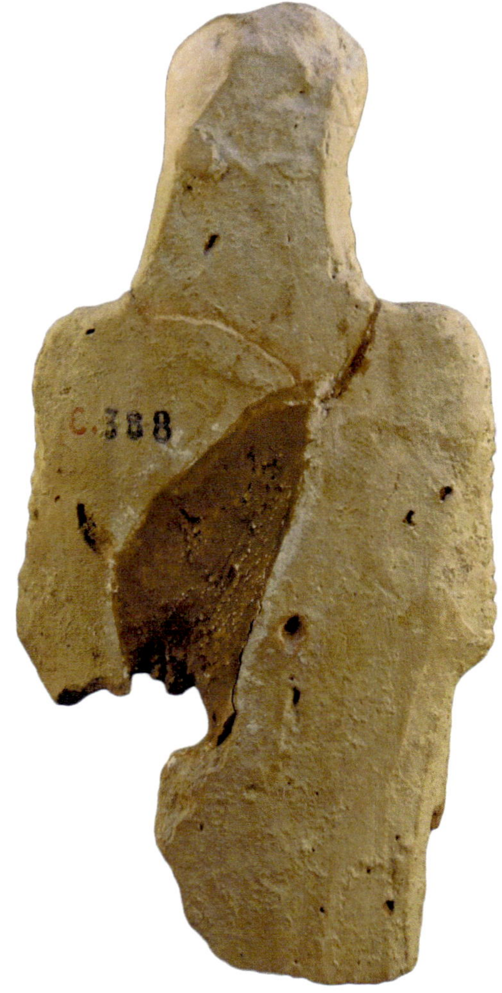

‣ *Date:* The third decade of the 5th century BCE
‣ *Workshop:* The Workshop of Straight Reworking
‣ *Typology:* Veiled head group: 3b
‣ *Short description:* Upper part of a figurine, in several pieces; restored. Nose, middle and lower part of the body heavily damaged or broken off. Fine and detailed female figurine. Glued to its stand. She has a round face, large eyes, a sizeable nose, in particular the bridge to her nose, and a smiling narrow mouth. Her chin is pronounced and the dimples on the sides, and the part between mouth and chin is deep. She has high cheekbones and fleshy cheeks. She has scalloped wavy hair in two rows. She wears a veil on top of her head. Along the sides of her neck, her hair is marked with horizontal lines. The outline of her ear (just on the right?) is placed in front of her hair, where the hair of the forehead ends. She wears a chiton with wavy folds on the chest and larger folds on her arm. The sleeve has a seam in the middle and starts from under the large round fibulae, placed on the shoulder. The sleeves end halfway down her arms, where they bend slightly. She holds her arms close to her body, the long hands with outstretched and separate thumbs running along her upper garment. She wears on top of this, two rows with pectoral pendants in seed shape, some thicker than others.
‣ *Comparable objects:* Very similar, except for the pectoral pendants, to **114**. No. **111** might be from the same mould series. The hairstyle in two rows of waves and some facial features are reminiscent of **107**.

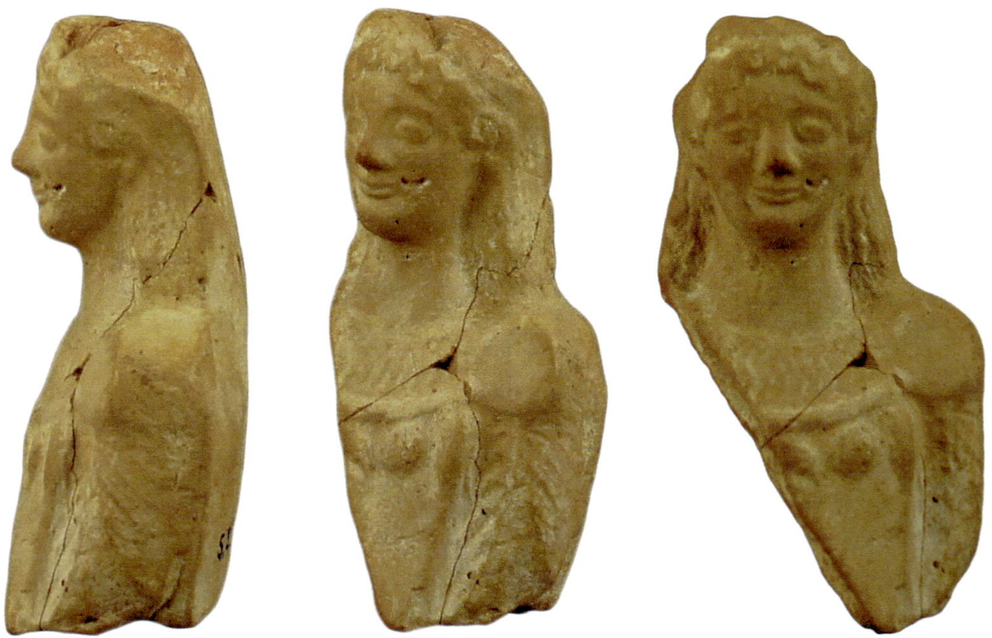

No. 114; Scale 1:1 (Museo Archeologico Regionale "Pietro Griffo", Agrigento).

No.114

- *Museum and Inventory number:* Mus. Agrigento S299
- *Findspot and context:* City Sanctuary
- *Publications:* -
- *Dimensions in cm:* h.8.3
- *Material:* Terracotta
- *Techniques:* Front moulded
- *Colour:* Pink 7.5 YR 7/4
- *Date:* The third decade of the 5th century BCE
- *Workshop:* Unknown
- *Typology:* Veiled head group: 3b
- *Short description:* Upper part and left side of a figurine in four fragments. Fine and detailed female figurine. Museum infill inside. She has a round face, eyes with eyelids, large nose and an upwards-curving mouth. She has scalloped wavy hair in two lines with a veil. Along the sides of her neck, her hair falls down in waves also. The outline of her ears is placed in front of her hair, where the hair of the forehead ends. She wears a chiton with wavy folds on the chest and larger folds on her arm. The sleeve has a seam in the middle and starts from under the large round fibulae, placed on the shoulder. She holds her arms close to her body, along her apron. She wears on top of it one row with chest pendants. A crescent with the points down in the middle flanked (probably) by a disc and a seed-shaped pendant, the latter next to the arm on the edge of the apron.
- *Comparable objects:* The same body and pendants as on **60**, though that figurine is probably older, because it does not have arms nor the folded chiton.

110 and **111** might be from the same mould series.

Type J: A patterned polos (115-137)

This group is typical of Akragantine production and was very popular. A large number belong to the Mould II series, but there are several variations and imitations. The patterned polos, three rows of pectoral pendants, and rectangular fibulae are characteristic of this type.

No.115

- *Museum and Inventory number:* Mus. Agrigento 1142
- *Findspot and context:* City Sanctuary. At the base of the southwest wall of the sanctuary
- *Publications:* Albertocchi 2004, p.17, no.28; De Miro 2000, p.130-1, no.35, tav.LXIII
- *Dimensions in cm:* h.27.1
- *Material:* Terracotta
- *Techniques:* Front moulded, reworked with sharp tool, first in Mould II series
- *Colour:* Pale Brown 2.5 Y 7/4
- *Date:* The second decade of the 5th century BCE
- *Workshop:* Workshop of 'the one pendant necklace' Mould IIa
- *Typology:* Square-and-disc patterned polos group: 3a
- *Short description:* Complete figurine. Head and left shoulder broken, restored. Film of dirt.

Seated female figurine with an oval face, wide jaws, big slightly bulging eyes, thick lips, but small mouth. Her nose is long and thin. Hair in vertical bulbs, smaller towards the middle, creating a triangular, high forehead. Whether hair along the sides of the neck is indicated is not clear, as it is very flat. On top of this part, connected with the fringe of hair on the forehead are large earrings in the form of an ear stud with a pendant-ring in the shape of a boat and a connected pendant, similar to the pendants on the chest. She wears a tall and straight decorated polos with disc-in-square pattern, with a pearl-rim and rounded edges at the top. On her flat neck, she wears a

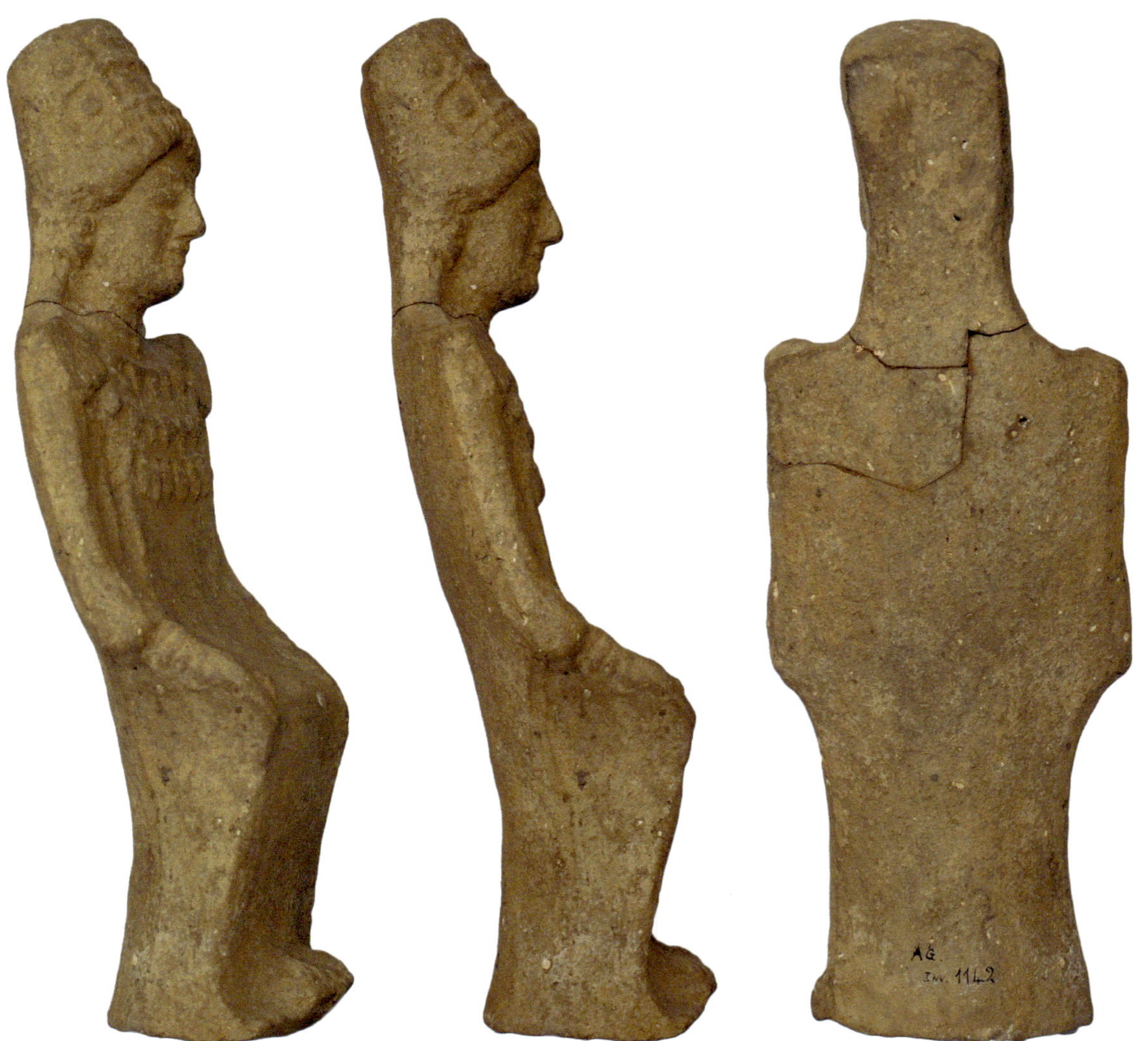

No. 115; Scale 1:2 (Museo Archeologico Regionale "Pietro Griffo", Agrigento).

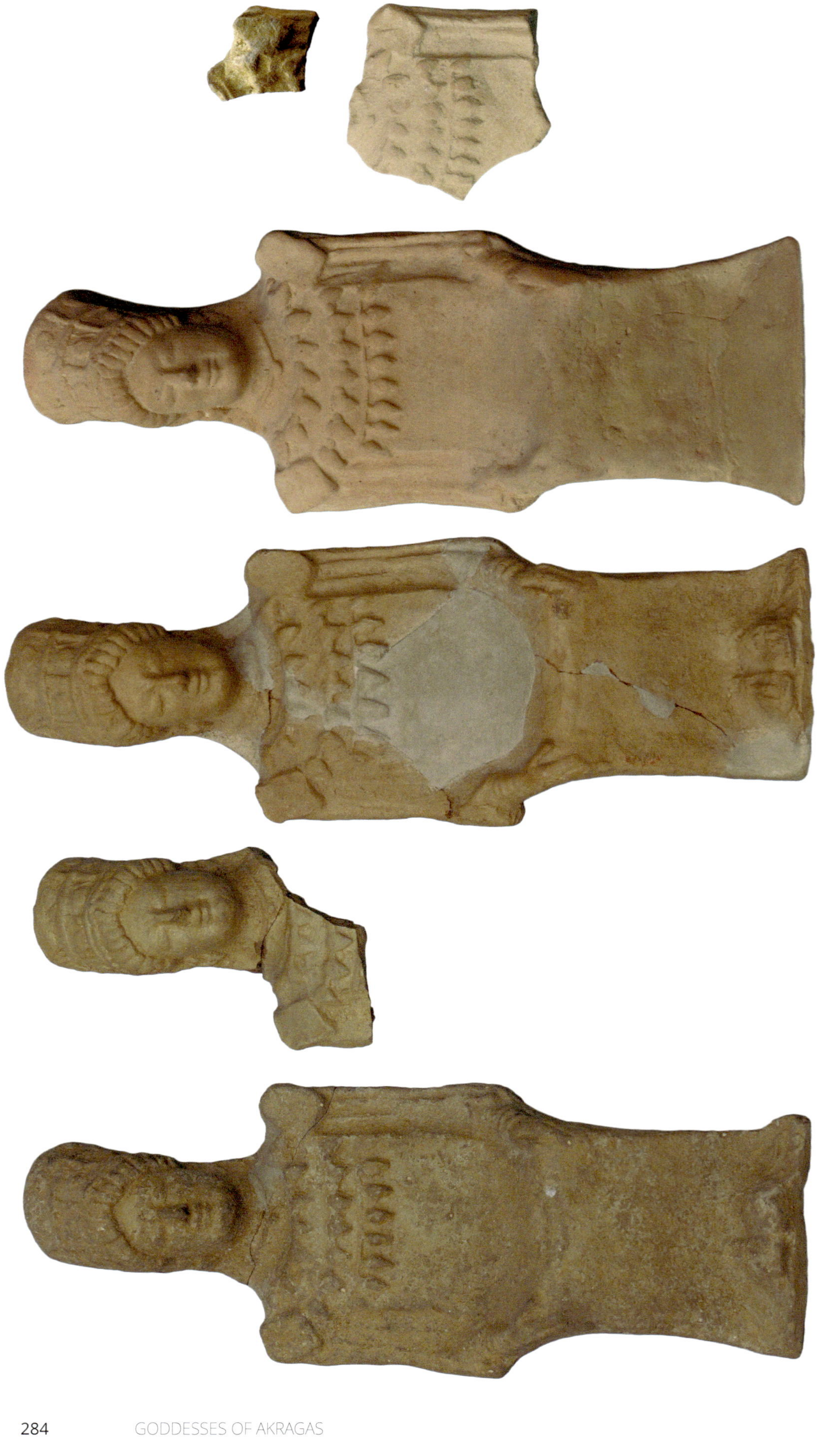

115 116 117 118 119 120

Figure 11; Overview of the Mould II figurines and fragments; Scale 1:2 (Museo Archeologico Regionale "Pietro Griffo", Agrigento).

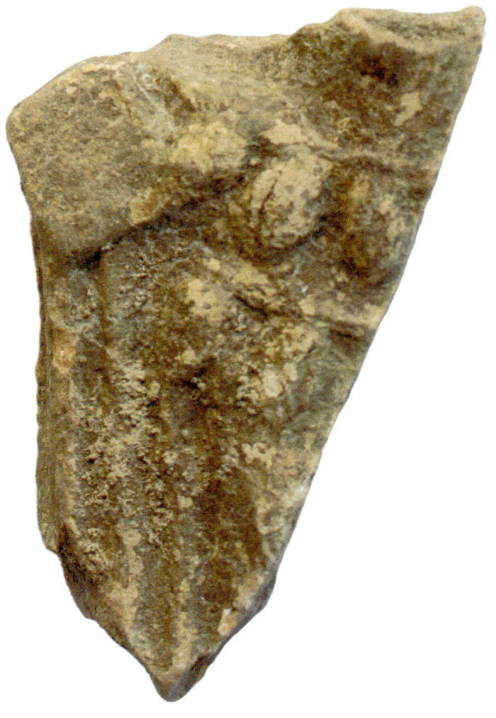

Figure 12; Part of the right shoulder and arm of a figurine belonging to the Mould II series, from S. Anna, Akragas. Scale 1:1.

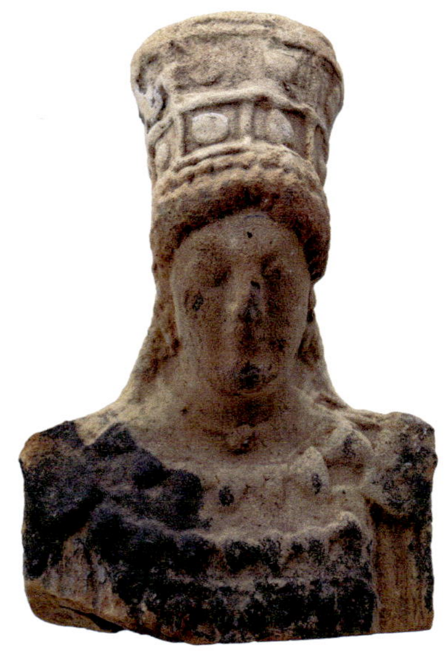

Figure 13; Upper part of a figurine, possibly from Akragas, from the Mould II series. Mus. Moscow Inv. no.2673. Scale 1:2, Photo Mus. Moscow.

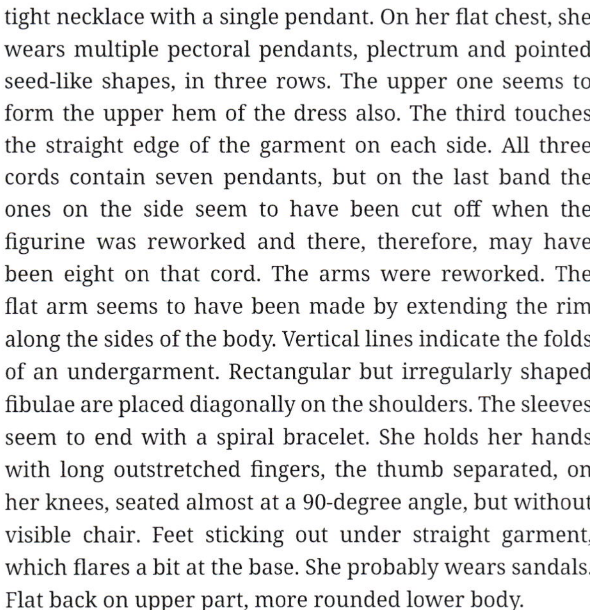

tight necklace with a single pendant. On her flat chest, she wears multiple pectoral pendants, plectrum and pointed seed-like shapes, in three rows. The upper one seems to form the upper hem of the dress also. The third touches the straight edge of the garment on each side. All three cords contain seven pendants, but on the last band the ones on the side seem to have been cut off when the figurine was reworked and there, therefore, may have been eight on that cord. The arms were reworked. The flat arm seems to have been made by extending the rim along the sides of the body. Vertical lines indicate the folds of an undergarment. Rectangular but irregularly shaped fibulae are placed diagonally on the shoulders. The sleeves seem to end with a spiral bracelet. She holds her hands with long outstretched fingers, the thumb separated, on her knees, seated almost at a 90-degree angle, but without visible chair. Feet sticking out under straight garment, which flares a bit at the base. She probably wears sandals. Flat back on upper part, more rounded lower body.

‣ ***Comparable objects:*** From the same mould as **116** and **117**, which has exactly the same measurements, the same degree of sharpness and is even broken at the same spot: on the left side of the neck. Heads **126** and **127** are from the same mould also. Comparable with three Selinuntine figurines: N.I. 7: Complete figurine, h.29cm in sitting position with her hands on her knees. Plain dress on top of peplos, of which the folds are visible as vertical lines on her arms. Decorated with three rows of fruit-shaped pendants on the chest, rectangular fibulae, bracelets and earrings. She wears a decorated polos with squares filled with discs. She sits on a bench. Feet broken off.

Mus. Palermo Inv. no.SM Pal T8748: The left shoulder, 9.3cm. The fibula seems more oval, the outline of a double palmette shape, and the pendants seem smaller. Mus. Palermo SM pal T1772: head with decorated polos, 10.2cm. Albertocchi 2004, p.20, no.78-80; Dewailly 1992, p.101-4, fig.61, 62 and 63. A similar 7.4cm high head from the same mould series is Inv. no.265. Mus. Catania. It is dated to the end of the sixth/beginning of the fifth century BCE. Pautasso 1996, p.71, no.83, tav.X. **118 -120** might be from the same mould or a generation later, Mould IIa or b. **122**, **128** and **129** are from a later generation, Mould IIb. Several fragments of figurines were excavated in 2016 at S. Anna. Two sherds with a fibula in Schnitt A Us 17 Fb 390 are clearly related to the Mould II series. However, the pendants are more ovoid and rounded, not pointed, and the cord is completely visible. The placement of the fibula is slightly different also (fig.12, h.9.3cm). Another head and upper part of the body is clearly from the same mould series also, but possibly from a later generation, Inv. no.2673, h.14.6cm Mus. Moscow. The eyes are probably reworked and look larger. The polos is narrow, but flaring at the top (fig.13). **123-125** are earlier variants of the Mould II series. These heads show some variations.

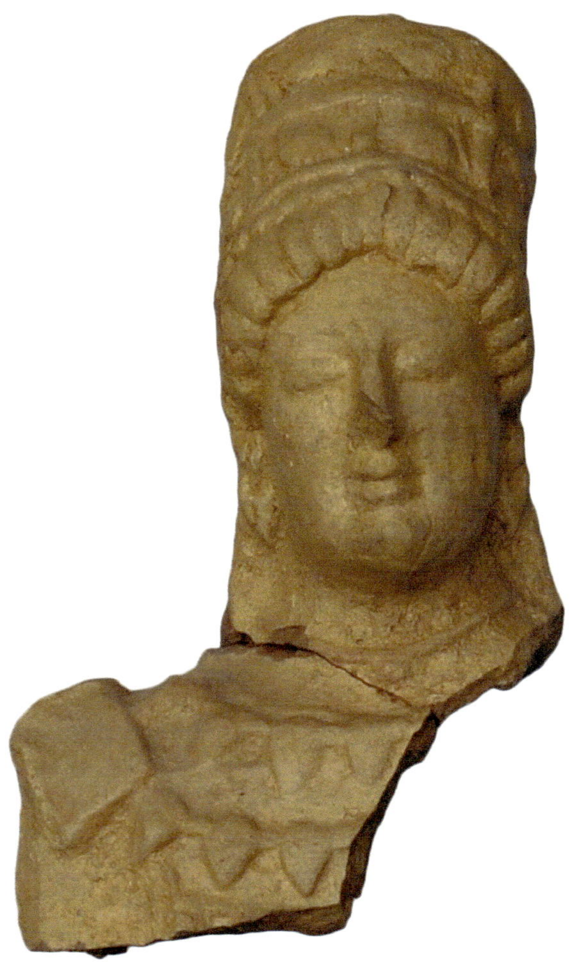

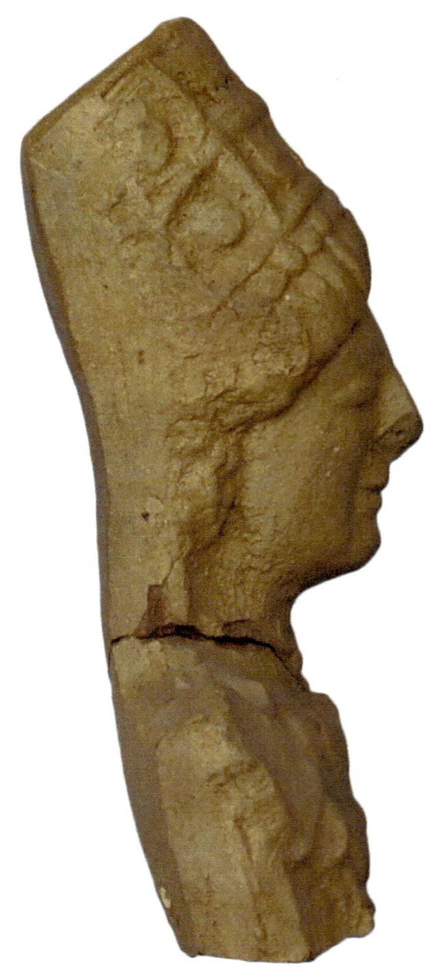

No. 116; Scale 1:1 (Museo Archeologico Regionale "Pietro Griffo", Agrigento); continued on next page.

No.116

- *Museum and Inventory number:* Mus. Agrigento 1144
- *Findspot and context:* City Sanctuary. At the base of the southwest wall of the sanctuary
- *Publications:* Albertocchi 2004, p.17, no.29; De Miro 2000, p.131, no.37
- *Dimensions in cm:* h.12.4
- *Material:* Terracotta
- *Techniques:* Front moulded, reworked with a sharp tool, second in Mould II series
- *Colour:* Light Yellowish Brown 2.5 Y 6/3
- *Date:* The second decade of the 5th century BCE
- *Workshop:* Workshop of 'the one pendant necklace' Mould IIa
- *Typology:* Square-and-disc patterned polos group: 3a
- *Short description:* Head and right shoulder of a female figurine. Oval face, wide jaws, big eyes, small mouth with thick lips. Hair in bulbs, smaller towards the middle, with smaller bulbs left of the middle. Patterned polos. Pectoral pendants, plectrum shaped, in several rows. Roughly rectangular fibula with higher edges. Short necklace with single pendant. Earrings with a triangular pendant.
- *Comparable objects:* From the same mould as **115** and **117**, which has exactly the same measurements, the same sharpness and is even broken in the same place: on the left side of the neck. Heads **126** and **127** are from the same mould also. See for other comparisons **115**.

.117

- *Museum and Inventory number:* Mus. Agrigento 1143
- *Findspot and context:* City Sanctuary. At the base of the southwest wall of the sanctuary
- *Publications:* Albertocchi 2004, p.17, no.30; De Miro 2000, p.131, no.36
- *Dimensions in cm:* h.27.2
- *Material:* Terracotta.
- *Techniques:* Front moulded. Straightened back and sides with sharp tool and a stick. Impression of a stick on the right side of her face.

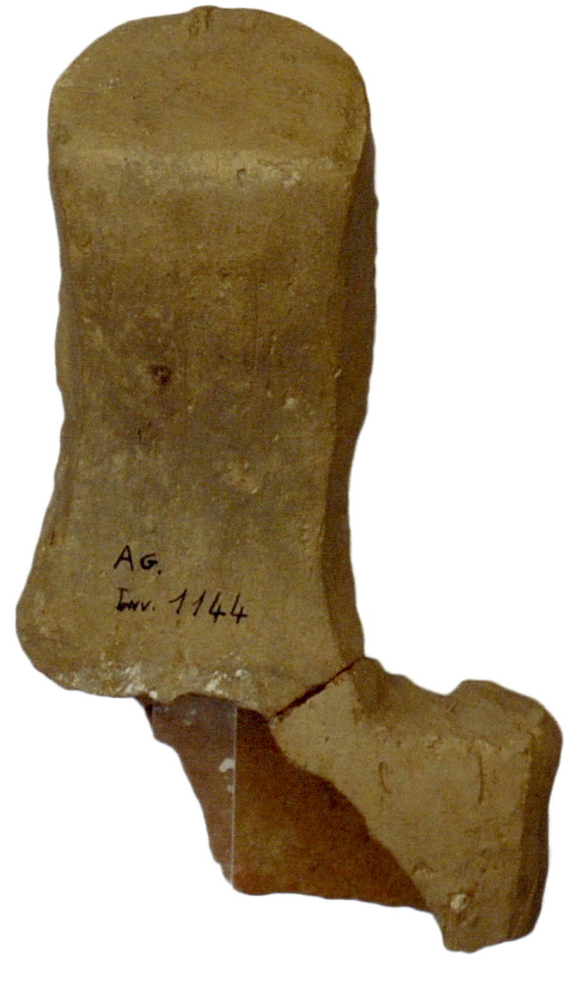

‣ *Colour:* Light yellowish brown 10 YR 6/4
‣ *Date:* The second decade of the 5th century BCE
‣ *Workshop:* Workshop of 'the one pendant necklace' Mould IIa
‣ *Typology:* Square-and-disc patterned polos group: 3a
‣ *Short description:* Nearly complete figurine. In several fragments, restored with considerable infill on the front, upper body, small amount of infill on the lower body and at the base. Larger infill at the back. For the description, see **115**.
‣ *Comparable objects:* This figurine is the most sharp in the Mould IIa group, but has a distinctive reworking on the back that is not seen on the others. See for other comparisons 115.

.118

‣ *Museum and Inventory number:* Mus. Agrigento S901
‣ *Findspot and context:* City Sanctuary
‣ *Publications:* Albertocchi 2004, p.16, no.18
‣ *Dimensions in cm:* h.26.3
‣ *Material:* Terracotta
‣ *Techniques:* Front moulded, reworked with sharp tool. Smoothed front: hands fade. Probably a lighter coloured slip layer.
‣ *Colour:* Pink 7.5YR 7/4
‣ *Date:* The second decade of the 5th century BCE
‣ *Workshop:* Workshop of 'the one pendant necklace' Mould IIb(?)
‣ *Typology:* Square-and-disc patterned polos group: 3a
‣ *Short description:* Complete figurine. Infill on the feet. Very sharp. For description, see **115**. The polos is different, flaring at the top.
‣ *Comparable objects:* This figurine has slightly different proportions than **115**-**117**. The face is of the same width, but 2mm shorter, which might have been caused by its method of production or the use of a different clay-mixture. The figurine as a whole is also less tall, but very sharp. These are arguments for the use of Mould IIb. Originally from Akragas also and probably from the same mould series as this figurine, that of Mould IIb, is a remarkably sharp figurine Mus. Moscow AT 3392 (713) h.24.5cm, fig.20, formerly Inv. no.TC 3519 from Berlin. Akimova 2013; Albertocchi 2004, p.18, no.41; Blinkenberg 1917, p.30-1, fig.6; Winter 1903, p.126, no.2; Kekulé von Stradonitz 1884, tav.II, 1. The figurine is seated on a handmade wide bench, with typically decorated sides. As common in Akragas, the bench is somewhat curling up and has a winged-back with horizontally projecting 'ears.' The chair is different from that of **135**. It has no cushion. The place of the fibulae is reworked, and it is clear that separately added fibulae belonged here. The 'lion paws,' otherwise uncommon in Akragas, are curious. The figurine was reworked after moulding, and the thicker, incised parts at the base represent lion paws. Part of the horizontally lined hair is visible behind the earrings next to the sides of the neck, while on figurines **115**-**118** this is not the case. It has been smoothed or cut away. In the same way, parts of a sort of outline rim on the sides of the head were not removed from a head from Akragas Mus. Agrigento Inv. no.S7129. h.6cm, Albertocchi 2004, p.17, no.34; De Miro 2000, p.241, no.1420, tav.LXX. The horizontally lined hair is visible in a mould from Akragas, part of the head, Mus. Agrigento Inv. no.AGS 7269 h.10cm, De Miro 2000, p.173, no.508, tav.CX. There are no earrings visible, but the polos is patterned. A head and left shoulder from Gelas could be from the same mould British Mus. Inv. no.1863,0728.287, h.12.1cm, Higgins 1954, no.302, no.1104, See museum website. See for other comparisons **115**.

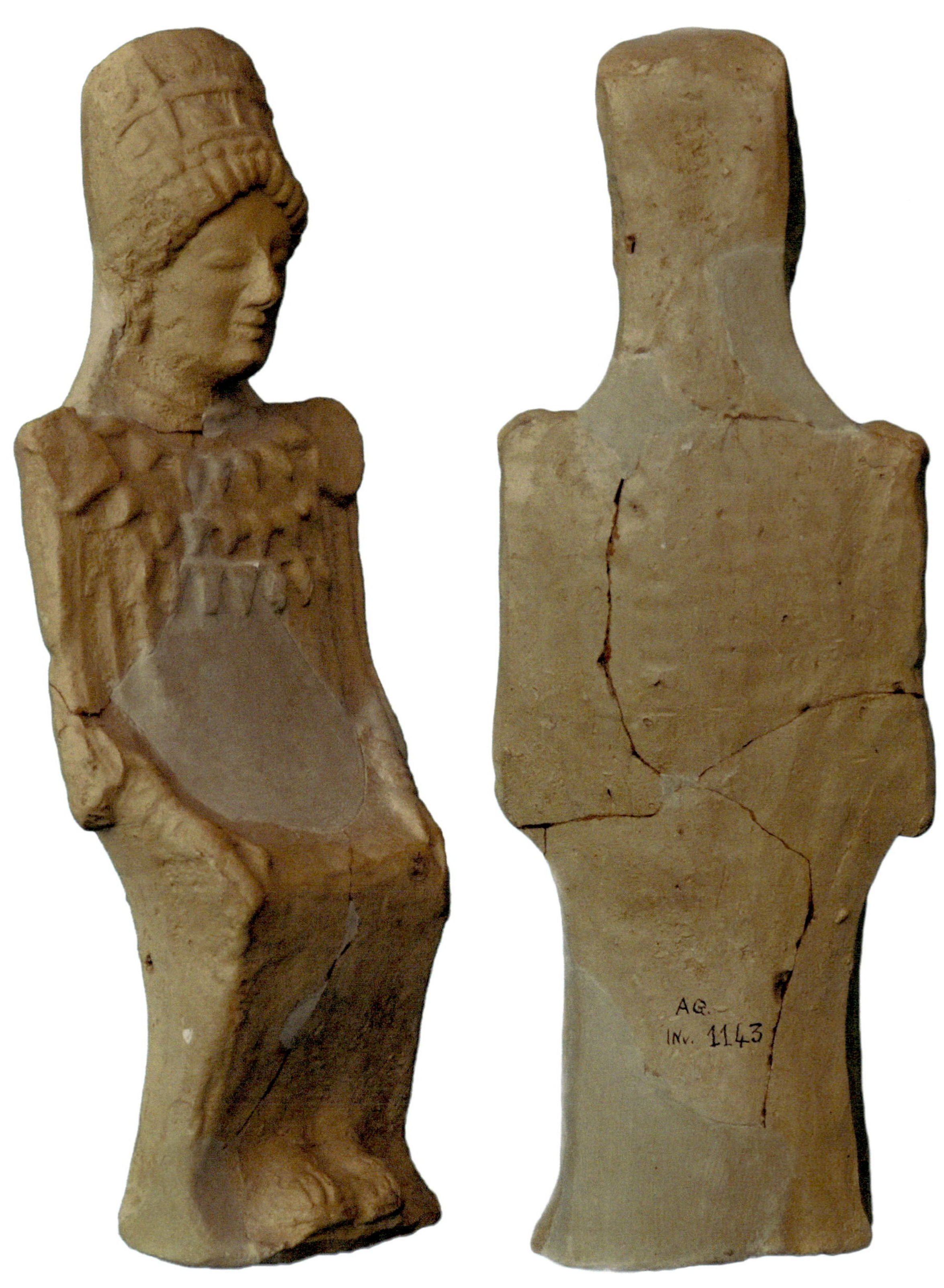

No. 117; Scale 1:1½ (Museo Archeologico Regionale "Pietro Griffo", Agrigento).

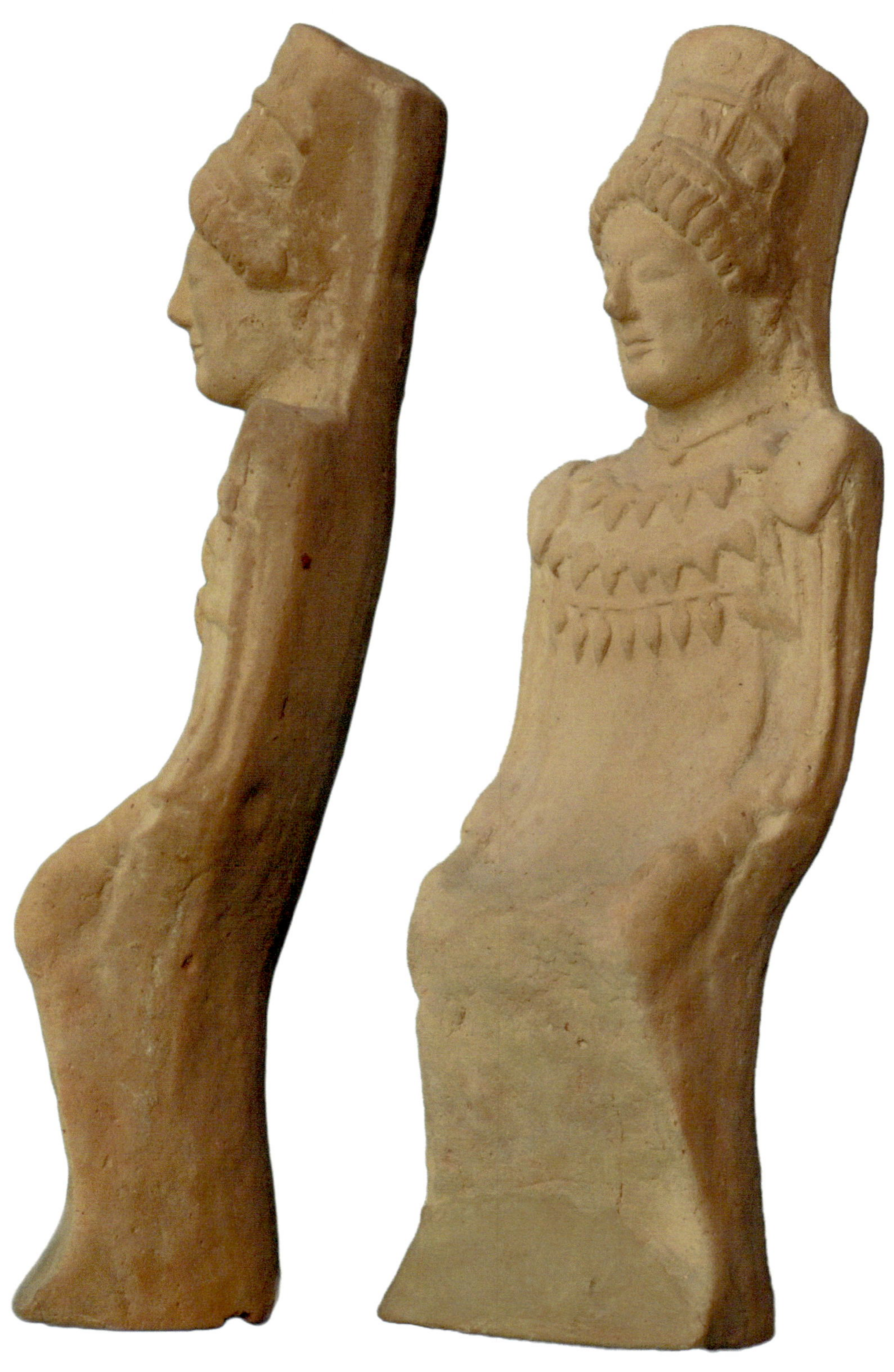

No. 118; Scale 1:1½ (Museo Archeologico Regionale "Pietro Griffo", Agrigento).

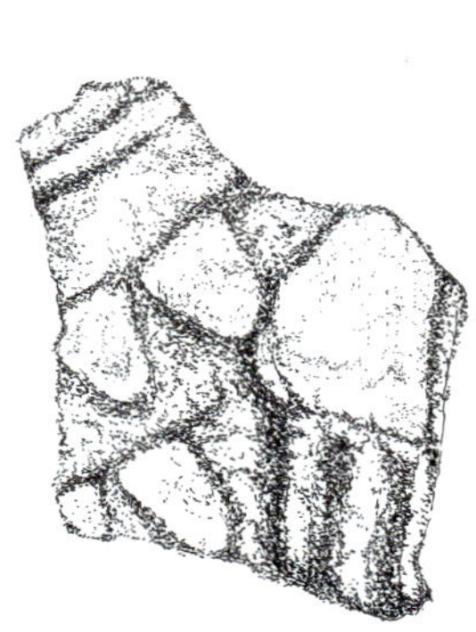

No. 119; Scale 1:1; Drawing of SA/G1: A small piece with the left fibula, some pendants, part of the necklace and upper arm. Drawing by E. van Rooijen.

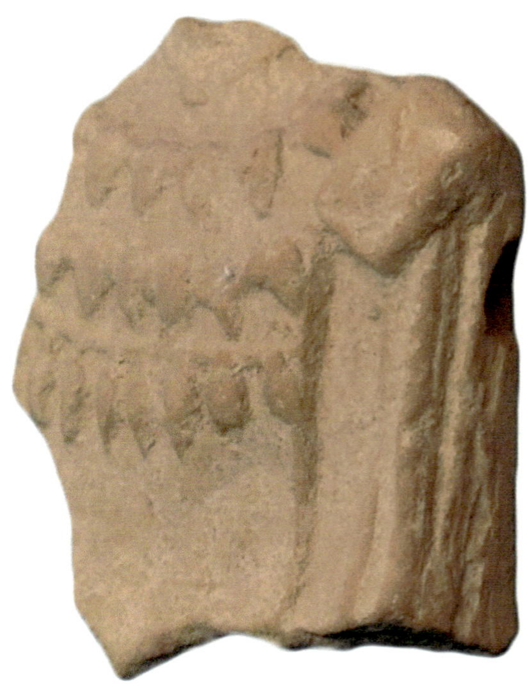

No. 120; Scale 1:1 (Museo Archeologico Regionale "Pietro Griffo", Agrigento).

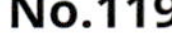

No.119

- *Museum and Inventory number:* Mus. Agrigento SA/G1
- *Findspot and context:* S. Anna Corr. G30
- *Publications:* -
- *Dimensions in cm:* h.4.0
- *Material:* terracotta
- *Techniques:* Front moulded. Lighter colour slip layer
- *Colour:* Pinkish
- *Date:* The second decade of the 5th century BCE
- *Workshop:* Workshop of 'the one pendant necklace' Mould IIa or b(?)
- *Typology:* Square-and-disc patterned polos group: 3a
- *Short description:* Left shoulder of the front of a figurine. On her neck, she wears a tight thin necklace. On her chest, just below her neck, she wears multiple pectoral pendants, plectrum and pointed seed-like shapes, in two rows. The upper one seems to form the upper hem of the dress also and is placed above the fibula. The flat and deeper arm looks to have been made by extending the rim along the sides of the body. Three vertical lines indicate the folds of an undergarment. An originally rectangular but irregularly shaped fibula is placed diagonally on the shoulder. One corner of this fibula seems to have been broken off at an earlier stage.
- *Comparable objects:* The fragment is from the Mould II series, like **115-118**. See for other comparisons **115**. Both size and sharpness indicate it is from a later generation. However, because it is so small, comparison is difficult.

More pieces from this mould series were found at the excavation of S. Anna, particularly in 2016.

No.120

- *Museum and Inventory number:* Mus. Agrigento 20396
- *Findspot and context:* City Sanctuary
- *Publications:* Albertocchi 2004, p.16, no.17
- *Dimensions in cm:* h.8.6
- *Material:* terracotta
- *Techniques:* Front moulded
- *Colour:* Very pale brown 10 YR 7.3
- *Date:* The second decade of the 5th century BCE
- *Workshop:* Workshop of 'the one pendant necklace' Mould IIa or b(?)
- *Typology:* Square-and-disc patterned polos group: 3a
- *Short description:* Sherd of neck, chest and upper left arm. For the description, see **115**.
- *Comparable objects:* The fragment is from the Mould II series, like **115-118**.

See for other comparisons **115**.

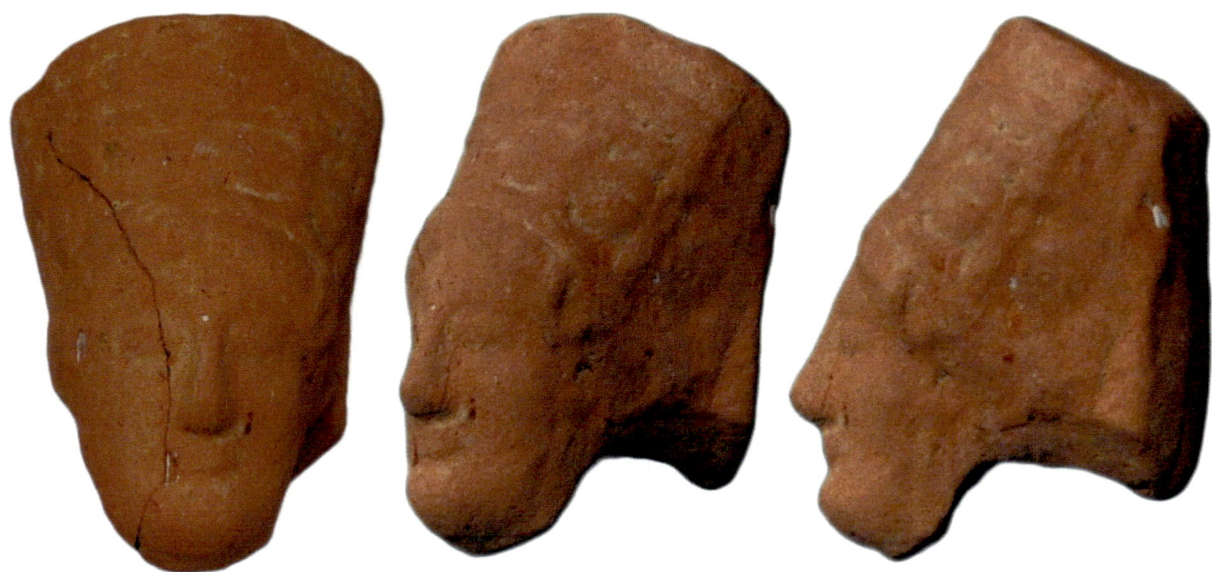

No. 121; Scale 1:1 (Museo Archeologico Regionale "Pietro Griffo", Agrigento).

No.121

‣ *Museum and Inventory number:* Mus. Agrigento 1158(?)

‣ *Findspot and context:* City Sanctuary. At the base of the southwest wall of the sanctuary

‣ *Publications:* -

‣ *Dimensions in cm:* h.7.2

‣ *Material:* Terracotta

‣ *Techniques:* Front moulded.

‣ *Colour:* Reddish-yellow 5 YR 6/6

‣ *Date:* The second decade of the 5th century BCE

‣ *Workshop:* Workshop of 'the one pendant necklace' Mould IIb

‣ *Typology:* Square-and-disc patterned polos group: 3a

‣ *Short description:* Head of a figurine, in three pieces, restored. Female face, quite indistinct, with an oval face, big, slightly bulging eyes, thick lips, but small mouth. Her nose is long and thin. Hair in vertical bulbs, smaller towards the middle, creating a triangular high forehead. She wears a tall and straight decorated polos with disc-in-square pattern.

‣ *Comparable objects:* This head might be from a parallel series, a variation on the Mould II series. The polos seems slightly different: the discs are larger and a pearl-rim is missing, like on **123** and **124**. Comparable to the head AG 9185 Albertocchi 2004, p.17, no.27; De Miro 2000, p.165, no.430, tav.LXX.

See for other comparisons **115**.

No.122

‣ *Museum and Inventory number:* Mus. Agrigento S275

‣ *Findspot and context:* City Sanctuary

‣ *Publications:* -

‣ *Dimensions in cm:* h.19

‣ *Material:* Terracotta

‣ *Techniques:* Front moulded. Cutting marks vertical and sharp, also with smaller, diagonal incisions on the back.

‣ *Colour:* Pink 7.5 YR 8/3

‣ *Date:* The second decade of the 5th century BCE

‣ *Workshop:* Workshop of 'the one pendant necklace' Mould IIb

‣ *Typology:* Square-and-disc patterned polos group: 3a

‣ *Short description:* Lower part and right shoulder of a figurine, right hand damaged. Seated figurine. For description, see **115**.

‣ *Comparable objects:* This body might belong to a later generation, as well as the head of **121**: Mould IIb.

See for other comparisons **115**.

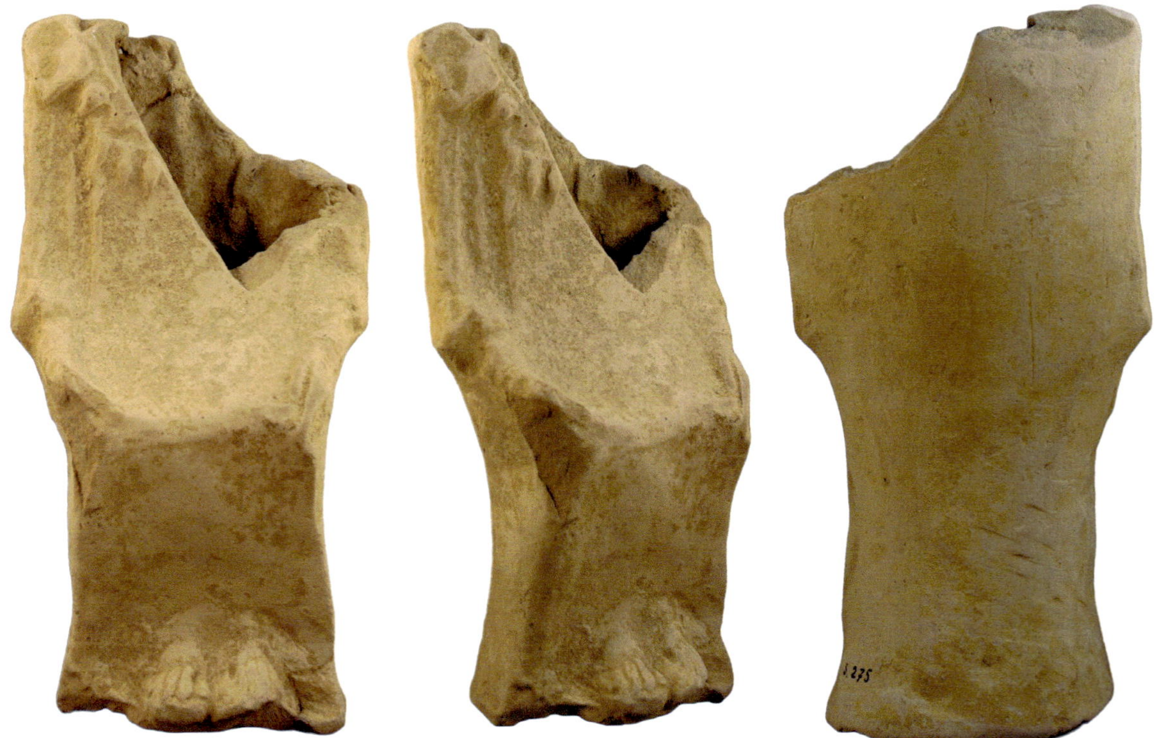

No. 122; Scale 1:2 (Museo Archeologico Regionale "Pietro Griffo", Agrigento).

No.123

- *Museum and Inventory number:* Mus. Agrigento S335
- *Findspot and context:* City Sanctuary
- *Publications:* -
- *Dimensions in cm:* h.7.6
- *Material:* Terracotta
- *Techniques:* Front moulded.
- *Colour:* Reddish-yellow 5 YR 7/6
- *Date:* The second decade of the 5th century BCE
- *Workshop:* Workshop of 'the one pendant necklace'(?)
- *Typology:* Square-and-disc patterned polos group: 3a
- *Short description:* Head of a figurine, right side broken off. Female face, quite indistinct, with an oval chubby face, big slightly bulging eyes, thick lips, but small mouth. Her nose is long and thin. Hair in vertical bulbs, smaller towards the middle, creating a triangular, high forehead. She wears a tall and straight polos decorated with disc-in-square pattern. The discs fill the squares.
- *Comparable objects:* From the same mould as **124**. **121** might be a generation later in the same series. This head seems to be a variation on the Mould II series. The polos seems slightly different, the discs are larger and the pearl-rim is lacking. The size of the face is larger than the faces of other figurines of the Mould II series. The head is similar to Inv. no.9214 from Vassallagi, which is sharper, and nearly complete h.31.9cm Albertocchi 2004, p.20, no.83, tav.II,d. The figurine wears a one pendant necklace. For its body, see comparisons at **137**. The hairstyle is comparable to a protome from Gelas, but originally from Granmichele. Uhlenbrock 1988, p.52-3 Pl. 8a, b.

No.124

- *Museum and Inventory number:* Mus. Agrigento S105
- *Findspot and context:* City Sanctuary
- *Publications:* Albertocchi 2004, p.16, no.19; Marconi 1933, p.61, tav.X.2
- *Dimensions in cm:* h.9.1
- *Material:* Terracotta
- *Techniques:* Front moulded.
- *Colour:* Very pale brown 10 YR 7/2
- *Date:* The first or second decade of the 5th century BCE
- *Workshop:* Workshop of 'the one pendant necklace'(?)
- *Typology:* Square-and-disc patterned polos group: 3a
- *Short description:* Head of a figurine in several pieces. Female face, quite indistinct, with an oval chubby face. Her jaw is wide, and her chin pronounced. She has big, slightly bulging eyes, very thick lips, but small mouth, set in a deeper part. The dimples next to the mouth make the cheeks more pronounced. Her nose is sizeable. Hair in vertical bulbs, smaller towards the middle, creating a triangular high forehead. Her hair on the sides of her face is divided into horizontal parts. There is a slightly bulging part, but earrings seem not to be depicted. She wears a tall and straight decorated polos with disc-in-square pattern. The discs, six on each row, fill the squares. Straight back.
- *Comparable objects:* From the same mould as **123**. See there. **121** might be a generation later in the same series.

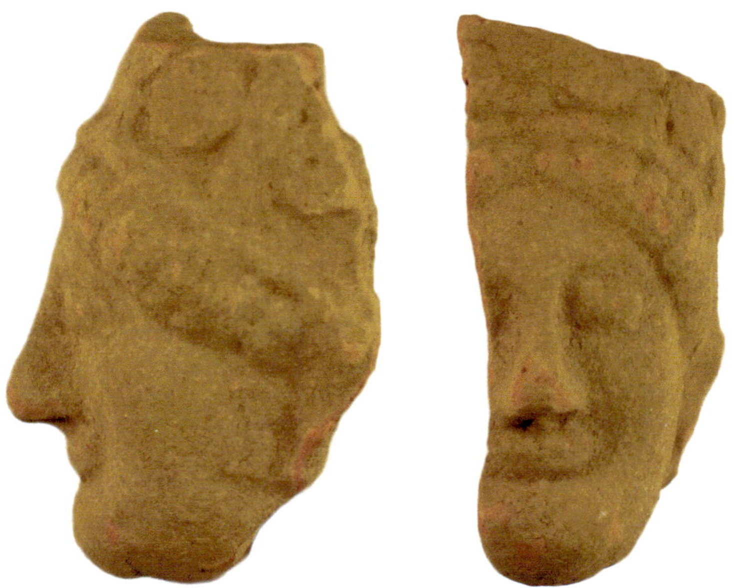

No. 123; Scale 1:1 (Museo Archeologico Regionale "Pietro Griffo", Agrigento).

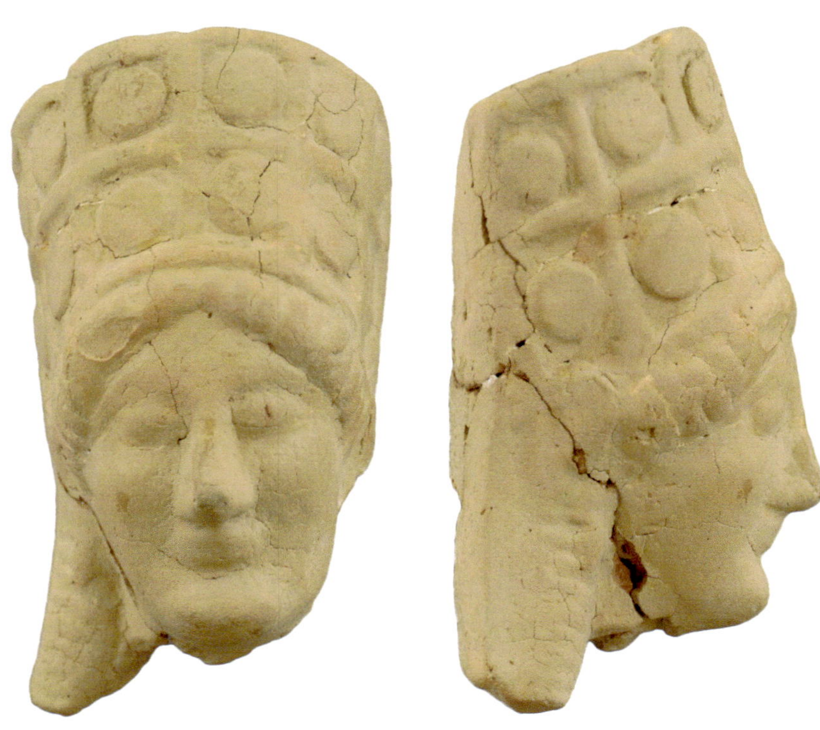

No. 124; Scale 1:1 (Museo Archeologico Regionale "Pietro Griffo", Agrigento).

No.125

‣ *Museum and Inventory number:* Mus. Agrigento S22
‣ *Findspot and context:* Sanctuary near Villa Aurea
‣ *Publications:* Albertocchi 2004, p.17, no.31; Bovio Marconi 1930, p.82, fig.14
‣ *Dimensions in cm:* h.6.8
‣ *Material:* Terracotta.
‣ *Techniques:* Front moulded. Nose flattened, probably with its removal from the mould or reworking. The horizontal lines on the hair might be handmade after moulding.
‣ *Colour:* Very pale brown 10 YR 7/4
‣ *Date:* The second decade of the 5th century BCE
‣ *Workshop:* Workshop of 'the one pendant necklace'(?)
‣ *Typology:* Square-and-disc patterned polos group: 3a
‣ *Short description:* Head and neck. Female head with oval fleshy face and triangular forehead. Her eyes are large. Her chin is protruding, cheeks and jaw are chubby. Her mouth curls up slightly and has a thinner upper lip with a thicker lower lip. Her hair is shaped in a fringe on the forehead with vertical bulbs, shorter in the middle of the forehead. This gives the impression of parted hair. Along the sides of her neck, her hair is marked by horizontal lines. Where the two strands of hair come together, the outline of an ear is visible. She wears earrings: a thick ring with a large pendant is clearly visible on her right side, but very indistinct on the left. Her polos is decorated with the square-and disc pattern in two rows, each with six squares. She wears a necklace high on her neck. The back is straight and also part of the sides near to the neck.
‣ *Comparable objects:* This seems a variation of the Mould II series. She wears a tight necklace, but without pendant. The polos is the version with medium-sized discs, not as large as those on **123** and **124**, but the pearl-rim is lacking. The size of the face is larger than the faces of other figurines of the Mould II series.

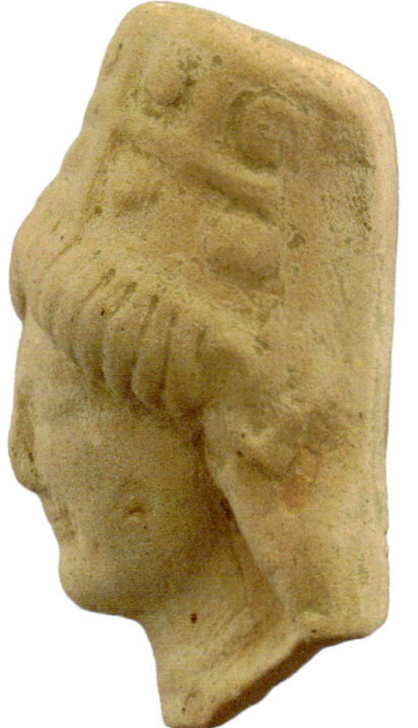
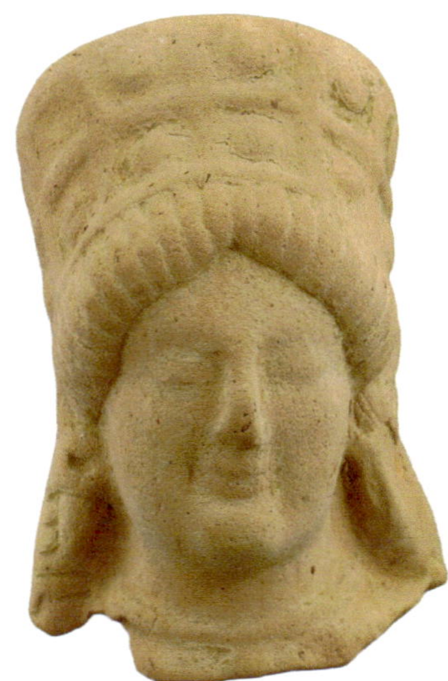

No. 125; Scale 1:1 (Museo Archeologico Regionale "Pietro Griffo", Agrigento).

No.126

‣ *Museum and Inventory number:* Mus. Agrigento S330
‣ *Findspot and context:* City Sanctuary
‣ *Publications:* -
‣ *Dimensions in cm:* h.8.6
‣ *Material:* Terracotta. Many insertions.
‣ *Techniques:* Front moulded. Slip layer in a lighter colour.
‣ *Colour:* Light red 2.5 YR 7/6
‣ *Date:* The second decade of the 5th century BCE
‣ *Workshop:* Workshop of 'the one pendant necklace'(?) Mould IIa
‣ *Typology:* Square-and-disc patterned polos group: 3a
‣ *Short description:* Head and neck of figurine.

Female head with oval fleshy face and triangular forehead. Her eyes are large. Her chin is protruding, cheeks and jaw are chubby. Her mouth is small with very thick lips. Her hair is shaped in a fringe on the forehead with vertical bulbs, shorter in the middle of the forehead. This gives the impression of parted hair. Just above the fringe and below the headgear there is a pearl-rim. The separate parts are rather indistinct. She wears earrings with a large pendant. Her polos is decorated with the square-and disc pattern in two rows, each with six squares. Thin impressed lines on the back of the head.
‣ *Comparable objects:* Probably from the same mould as **127**. The height of the face is the same as that of **115**-**117**, but it is almost a centimetre wider. It might be a parallel head or just the result of technically different handling after moulding. See for other comparisons **115**.

No.127 (not illustrated)

‣ *Museum and Inventory number:* Mus. Agrigento S336
‣ *Findspot and context:* City Sanctuary
‣ *Publications:* -
‣ *Dimensions in cm:* h.7.1
‣ *Material:* Terracotta. Many insertions.
‣ *Techniques:* Front moulded. Slip layer in a lighter colour.
‣ *Colour:* Pinkish white 7.5 YR 8/2
‣ *Date:* The second decade of the 5th century BCE
‣ *Workshop:* Workshop of 'the one pendant necklace'(?) Mould IIa
‣ *Typology:* Square-and-disc patterned polos group: 3a
‣ *Short description:* Forehead with hair and polos.

Female head. Lower part of the face missing, also as back. Her hair is shaped in a fringe on the forehead with vertical bulbs, rhizomes, shorter in the middle of the forehead. This gives the impression of parted hair.

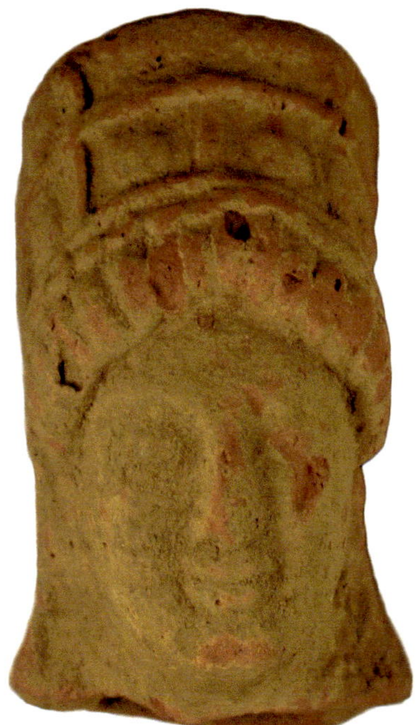
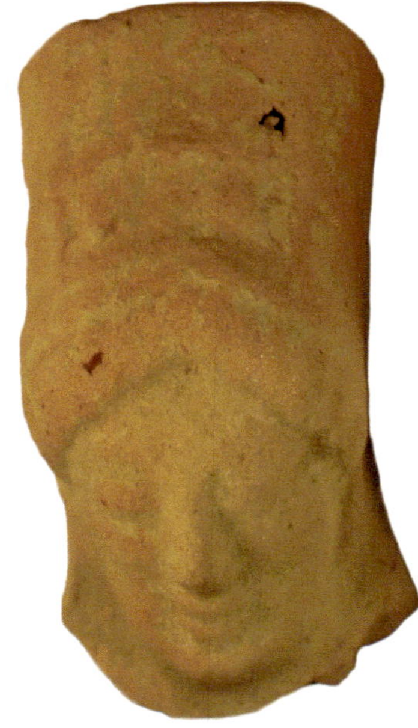
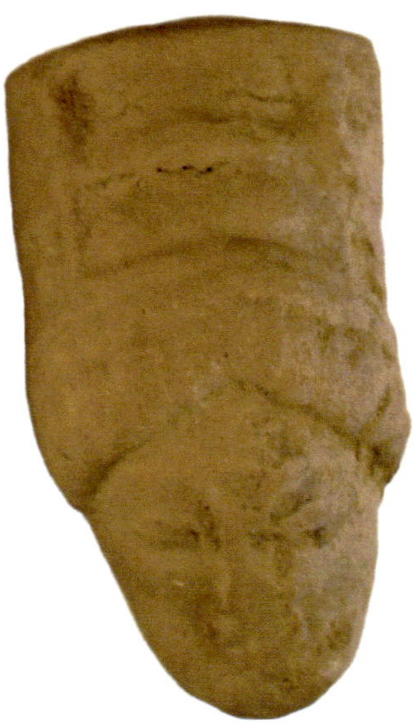

No. 126, 128, 129; Scale 1:1 (Museo Archeologico Regionale "Pietro Griffo", Agrigento).

Just above the fringe and below the headgear there is a pearl-rim. Her polos is decorated with the square-and disc pattern in two rows, each with six squares. Thin impressed lines on the back of the head.

‣ *Comparable objects:* This one is more weathered but the upper edge of the polos is sharper and more complete than **126**. The clay is much whiter. See for other comparisons **115**, which is, with **116** and **117**, probably from the same mould.

No.128

‣ *Museum and Inventory number:* Mus. Agrigento S332
‣ *Findspot and context:* City Sanctuary
‣ *Publications:* -
‣ *Dimensions in cm:* h.7.9
‣ *Material:* Terracotta. Many insertions.
‣ *Techniques:* Front moulded. Slip layer in a lighter colour.
‣ *Colour:* Pink 5 YR 7/4
‣ *Date:* The second decade of the 5th century BCE
‣ *Workshop:* Workshop of 'the one pendant necklace'(?) Mould IIb
‣ *Typology:* Square-and-disc patterned polos group: 3a
‣ *Short description:* Head and neck of figurine.

Female head with oval fleshy face and triangular forehead. Her eyes are large. Her chin is protruding, cheeks and jaw are chubby. Her mouth is small and slightly upwards-curving. Her hair is shaped into a band on the forehead with vertical bulbs, shorter in the middle of the forehead. This gives the impression of parted hair. Just above the fringe and below the headgear there is a pearl-rim. This and the earrings have become very indistinct in this generation. The tall polos is decorated with the square-and disc pattern in two rows, each with six squares.

‣ *Comparable objects:* Probably from the same mould as **129**. See for other comparisons **115**.

No.129

‣ *Museum and Inventory number:* Mus. Agrigento S333
‣ *Findspot and context:* City Sanctuary
‣ *Publications:* -
‣ *Dimensions in cm:* h.7.1
‣ *Material:* Terracotta. Many insertions.
‣ *Techniques:* Front moulded. Slip layer in a lighter colour. Dried clay caused cracks. Face damaged, probably when the figurine was taken out of the mould.
‣ *Colour:* Pink 5 YR 7/4
‣ *Date:* The second decade of the 5th century BCE
‣ *Workshop:* Workshop of 'the one pendant necklace'(?) Mould IIb
‣ *Typology:* Square-and-disc patterned polos group: 3a
‣ *Short description:* Head of figurine. Back broken off.

Female head with oval fleshy face and triangular forehead. Her eyes are large. Her chin is protruding, cheeks and jaw are chubby. Her nose is flattened. Her hair is shaped into a band on the forehead with vertical bulbs, shorter in the middle of the forehead. This gives the impression of parted hair. Just above the fringe and below the headgear there is a pearl-rim. This has become very indistinct in this generation. The polos is decorated with the square-and disc pattern in two rows, each with six squares.

‣ *Comparable objects:* Probably from the same mould as **129**. See for other comparisons **115**.

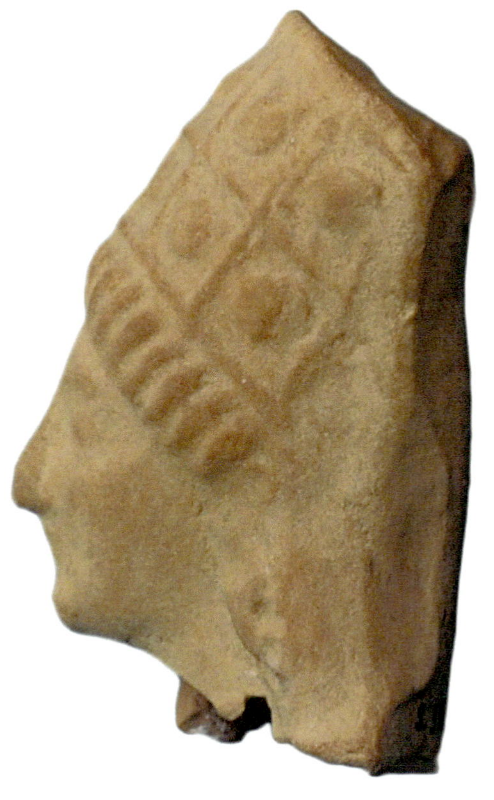
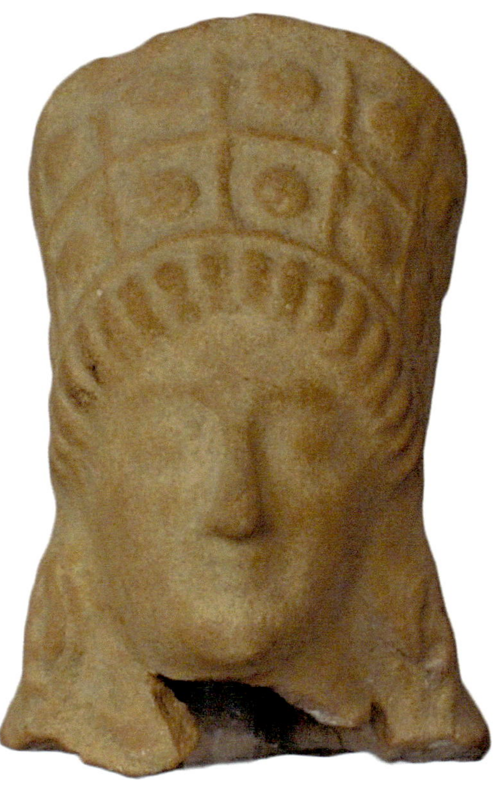

No. 130; Scale 1:1 (Museo Archeologico Regionale "Pietro Griffo", Agrigento).

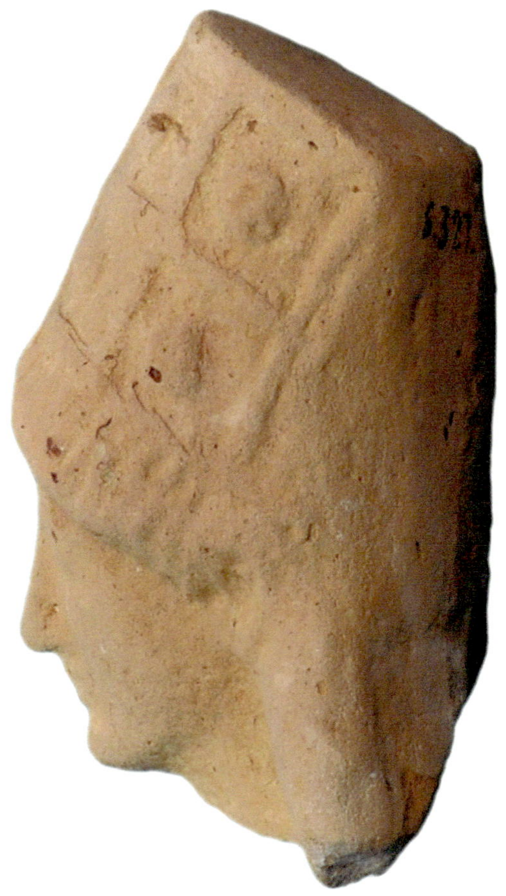
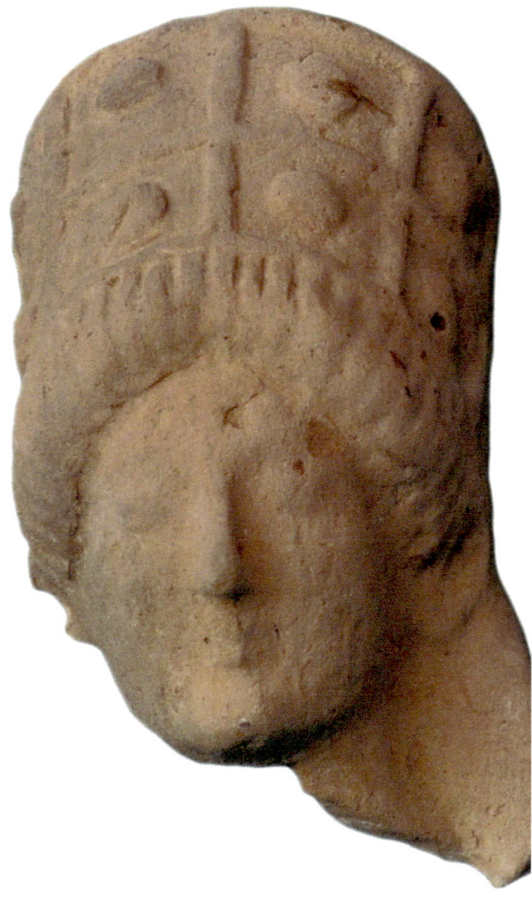

No. 131; Scale 1:1 (Museo Archeologico Regionale "Pietro Griffo", Agrigento).

No.130

‣ *Museum and Inventory number:* Mus. Agrigento S326
‣ *Findspot and context:* City Sanctuary
‣ *Publications:* Albertocchi 2004, p.17, no.23
‣ *Dimensions in cm:* h.10.1
‣ *Material:* Terracotta
‣ *Techniques:* Front moulded.
‣ *Colour:* Pink 7.5 YR 7/3
‣ *Date:* The second decade of the 5th century BCE
‣ *Workshop:* Unknown
‣ *Typology:* Square-and-disc patterned polos group: 3a
‣ *Short description:* Head of a figurine. Female face with a pointed chin, bulging eyes, but a bit indistinct. She has a narrow, long nose and a small mouth, slightly curling up. Hair in vertical bulbs, slightly smaller towards the middle, creating a rounded triangular forehead. Whether hair along the sides of the neck is indicated is not clear; it is very flat. On top, at the end of the fringe of hair on the forehead, there is the outline of small ears with large lobes and large earrings with a triangular pendant. She wears a tall polos slightly widening to the top decorated with disc-in-square pattern with two rows, each with six squares. The discs are rather flat.
‣ *Comparable objects:* Facial features are reminiscent of Mould II. The polos has a similar pattern but is not exactly the same.

No.131

‣ *Museum and Inventory number:* Mus. Agrigento S327
‣ *Findspot and context:* City Sanctuary
‣ *Publications:* Albertocchi 2004, p.17, no.22
‣ *Dimensions in cm:* h.11.6
‣ *Material:* Terracotta
‣ *Techniques:* Front moulded.
‣ *Colour:* Pink 7.5 YR 7/3
‣ *Date:* The second decade of the 5th century BCE
‣ *Workshop:* Unknown
‣ *Typology:* Square-and-disc patterned polos group: 3a
‣ *Short description:* Head of a figurine. Female face with a pointed chin, bulging eyes. She has a narrow, long nose and a slightly curling mouth. Hair in a thick band of vertical long bulbs slightly smaller towards the middle, creating a triangular forehead. Whether hair along the sides of the neck is indicated is not clear: it is very flat to the front but rounded on the side. On top, at the end of the fringe of hair on the forehead, there is the outline of a small ear, without earring. She wears a tall straight polos decorated with disc-in-square pattern with two rows, each with six squares. The discs are convex, and not always placed in the exact middle.
‣ *Comparable objects:* From the same mould series as **132**, but earlier, as the sizes indicate.

This head is known from the same mould series as that of a standing figurine from Montelusa (complete h.34.9cm). For the body see **90**: Langlotz and Hirmer 1963, p.60, no.20 left. Also, placed on a standing figurine from Selinous, complete 23.4cm, Inv. no.5909. Museo Nazionale di Palermo. Poma 2009, p.235, no.26.

No.132 (not illustrated)

‣ *Museum and Inventory number:* Mus. Agrigento S331
‣ *Findspot and context:* City Sanctuary
‣ *Publications:* -
‣ *Dimensions in cm:* h.8.6
‣ *Material:* Terracotta
‣ *Techniques:* Front moulded.
‣ *Colour:* Pink 7.5 YR 7/4
‣ *Date:* The second decade of the 5th century BCE
‣ *Workshop:* Unknown
‣ *Typology:* Square-and-disc patterned polos group: 3a
‣ *Short description:* Head of a figurine. Broken off under the chin and on the sides of the face only the left ear. The face is indistinct. She has bulging eyes, a narrow, long nose and a slightly curling mouth. Hair in a thick band of vertical long bulbs. She wears a tall straight polos decorated with disc-in-square pattern with two rows, each with six squares.
‣ *Comparable objects:* From the same mould series as **131**, but later, as the sizes indicate.

See **131**.

No.133

‣ *Museum and Inventory number:* Mus. Agrigento S106
‣ *Findspot and context:* City Sanctuary
‣ *Publications:* Albertocchi 2004, p.22, no.91
‣ *Dimensions in cm:* h.11.8
‣ *Material:* Terracotta.
‣ *Techniques:* Front moulded. Lighter coloured slip layer.
‣ *Colour:* Very pale brown 10 YR 7/3
‣ *Date:* The second decade of the 5th century BCE
‣ *Workshop:* Unknown
‣ *Typology:* Square-and-disc patterned polos group: 3a
‣ *Short description:* Head of a female figurine. Polos, left side of the face and back of the head broken off. Oval face with slanted eyes, bulging between the eyelids. Sharp-edged eyebrows. The nose is thin, and the nostrils are very small, but the tip is rounded and larger. The mouth has the same width as the nose and has a thicker upper lip and a thinner lower lip. The chin is relatively large. Her hair curls zigzag on her forehead, topped by a pearl-rim and the polos, which has a pattern with squares and small discs. Along the neck, her hair has uneven horizontal lines. The zigzag band is closed by a knob-like earring with a ring and a large pendant. The pendant has a column shape ending in a point and is covered with notches placed more or less in a line. Around her sturdy neck, she wears a ring-shaped necklace.
‣ *Comparable objects:* Head **134** is possibly from the same mould but later, because it is smaller. Very similar to

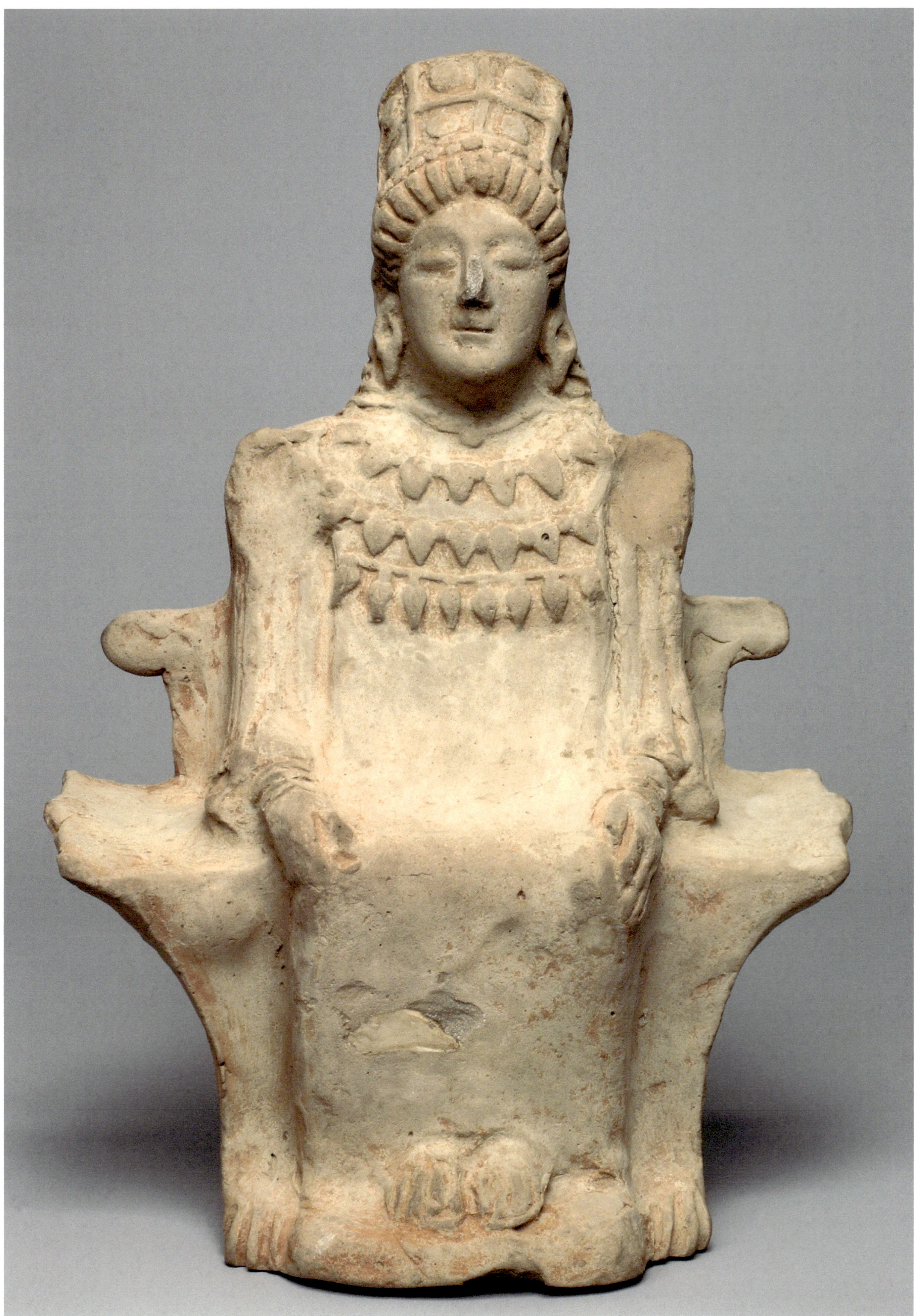

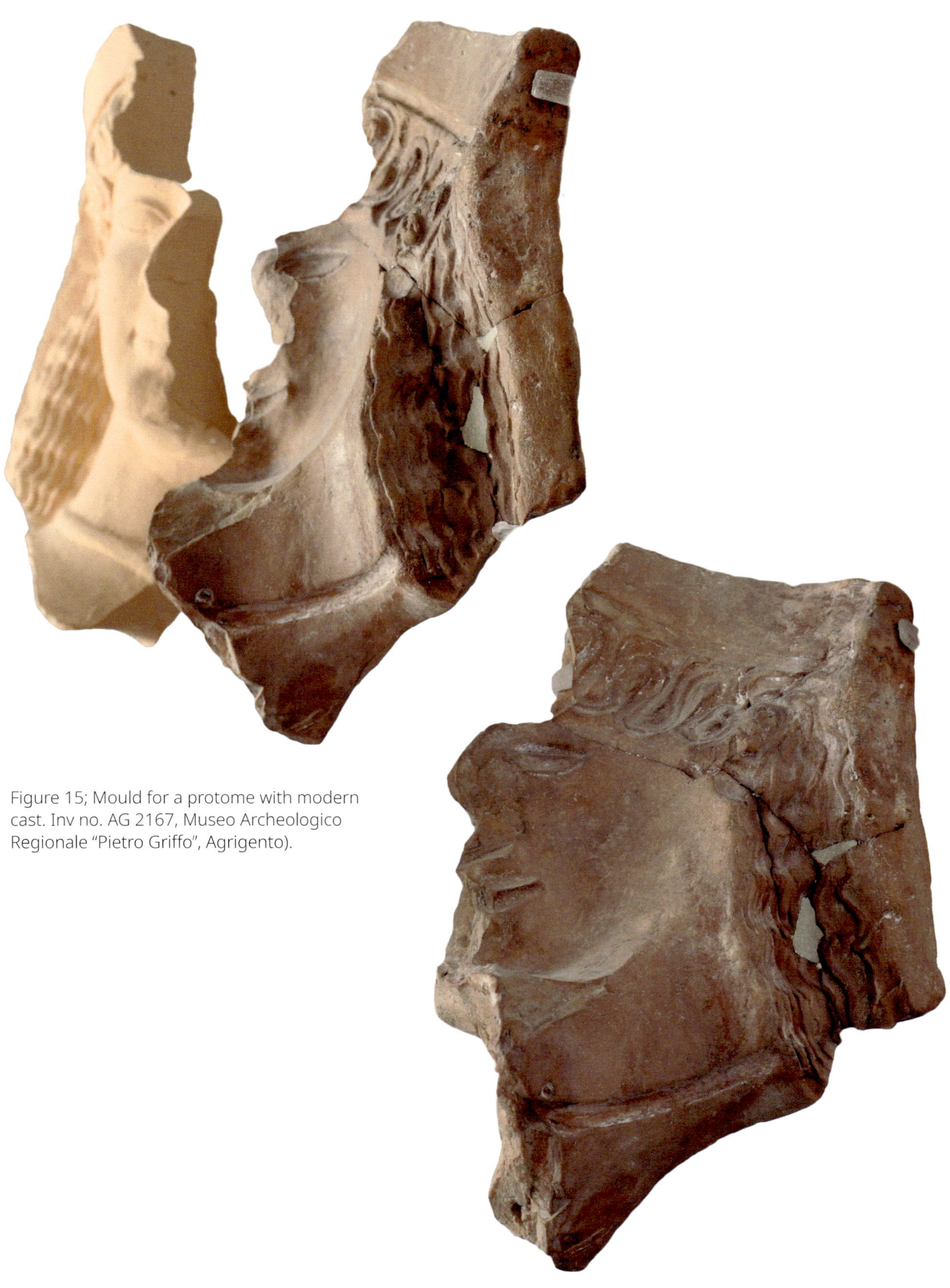

Figure 15; Mould for a protome with modern cast. Inv no. AG 2167, Museo Archeologico Regionale "Pietro Griffo", Agrigento).

Figure 14 (left page); Figurine probably from Akragas, AT 3392 (713) Mus. Moscow, h.24.5cm. Photo Mus. Moscow. Scale 1:1.

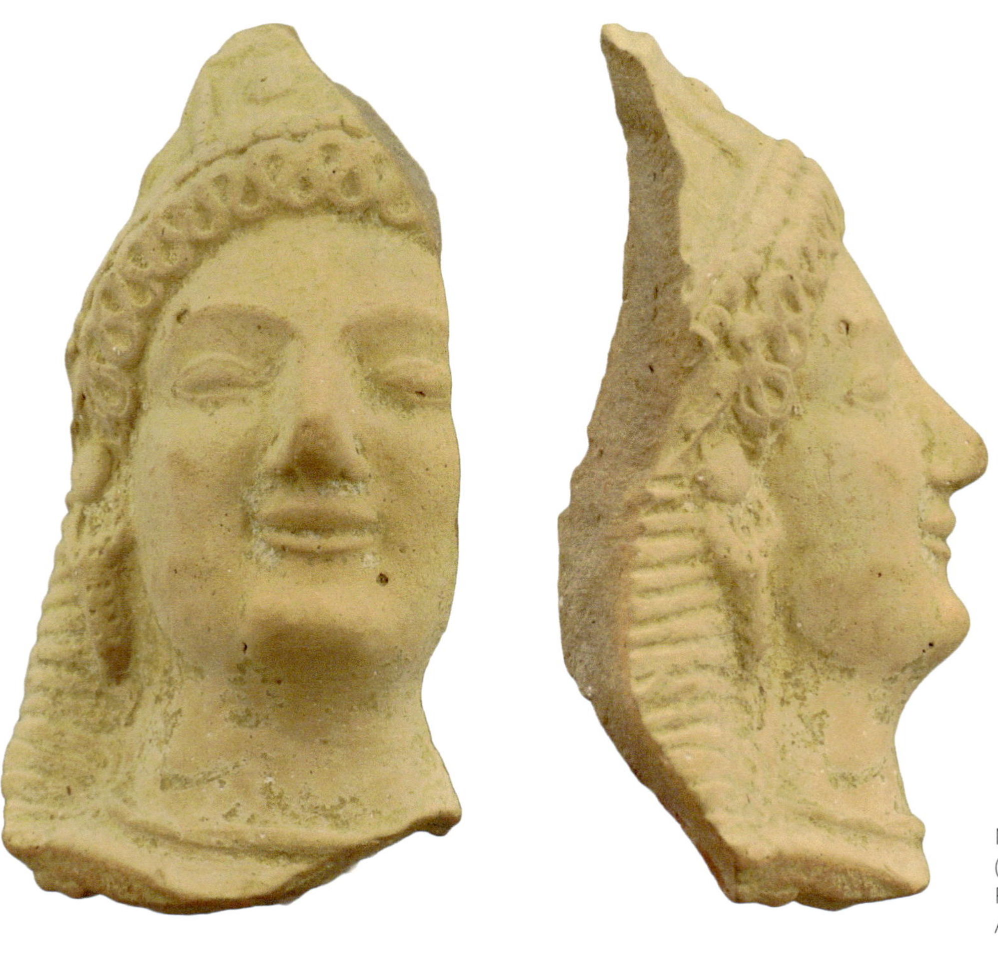

No. 133; Scale 1:1 (Museo Archeologico Regionale "Pietro Griffo", Agrigento).

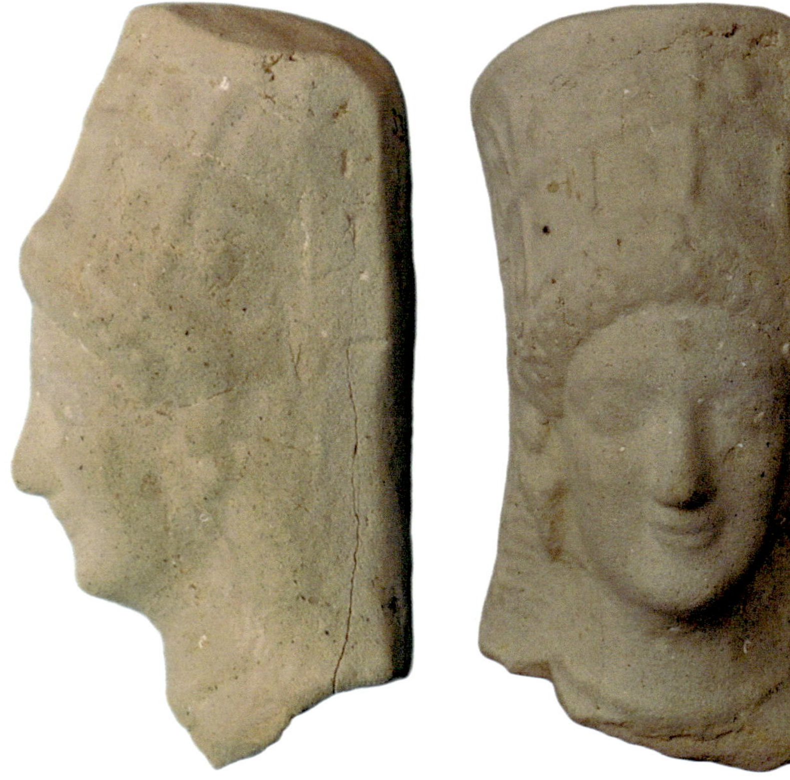

No. 134; Scale 1:1 (Museo Archeologico Regionale "Pietro Griffo", Agrigento).

Marconi 1933, p.61, tav.X, 1. **161** and **162** are probably a variation on this head. The polos is different in these three instances. This figurine is larger and has more details, such as the hair on the sides. A third(?) generation of this figurine was produced in Selinous and several figurines are found at the Malophoros Sanctuary. It is very likely this mould series originates in Akragas. Dewailly 1992, p.65. The zigzag band, facial features and necklace are similar to protome AG2167 (fig.15) and S26. The earrings are comparable with the ones of AG9187. (fig.24)

No.134

‣ *Museum and Inventory number:* Mus. Agrigento S328
‣ *Findspot and context:* City Sanctuary
‣ *Publications:* Albertocchi 2004, p.22, no.90
‣ *Dimensions in cm:* h.10.1
‣ *Material:* Terracotta.
‣ *Techniques:* Front moulded. Straightened back and sides with sharp tool.
‣ *Colour:* Pale Yellow 2.5 Y 8/2
‣ *Date:* The first or second decade of the 5th century BCE
‣ *Workshop:* Unknown
‣ *Typology:* Square-and-disc patterned polos group: 3a
‣ *Short description:* Head and neck. Female head with oval face, slightly widening towards the forehead. Her eyes are large. Her chin is a bit pointed. Her mouth is slightly curving up. Her hair is shaped in a band on the forehead with zigzag line. Along the sides of her neck, her hair is marked by horizontal lines. Where the two parts of hair join, a large knob with triangular pendant is visible. Her polos is decorated with the square-and disc pattern in two rows, each with ten squares. She wears a necklace high on her neck. The back is straight and part of the sides, near to the back also.
‣ *Comparable objects:* From the same mould series as **133**. See there for more comparable objects. Similar also to another head from Akragas, h.14.6cm, Mus. Syracuse Inv. no.20142. (fig.16) Albertocchi 2004, p.22, no.92

Similar facial features and hairstyle, but with a smooth polos on a head from Akragas: Mus. Agrigento Inv. no.9204, h.8.5cm, De Miro 2000, p.221, no.1184, tav.XCIV. The facial features are reminiscent of a head from Akragas, but the fringe of hair and the polos are different. Breitenstein 1945, p.125, fig.12 Nat. Mus. Copenhagen.

No.135

‣ *Museum and Inventory number:* Mus. Agrigento 22579
‣ *Findspot and context:* Necropolis di Contrada Pezzino Tomb 834, together with a miniature lekythos and a Corinthian skyphos (fig.17).
‣ *Publications:* Albertocchi 2004, p.22, no.87; Veder Greco: le necrópolis di Agrigento 1988, p.324; De Miro 1989, p.50, tav.XXXVIII
‣ *Dimensions in cm:* h.20.2

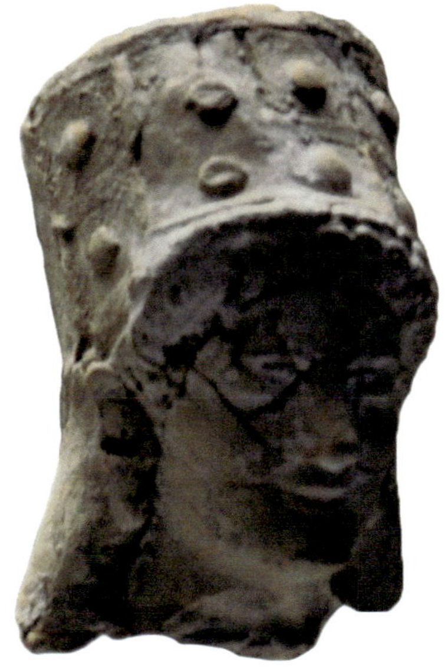

Figure 16: Head from Akragas. Inv. no.20142 (Museo Archeologico Regionale "Paolo Orsi", Syracuse).

‣ *Material:* Terracotta
‣ *Techniques:* Front moulded. Lighter coloured slip layer. Straightened back with sharp tool. This bench has been added by hand, there is a crack on the attachment corner, as well as several other cracks in the back and on the neck.
‣ *Colour:* White 2.5 Y 8/1 The statue has a lighter slip, the clay itself is redder.
‣ *Date:* The second decade of the 5th century BCE
‣ *Workshop:* Workshop of 'straight reworking', similar to Mould II
‣ *Typology:* Tall polos-wearing head: 3a
‣ *Short description:* Complete, hands are infill. Seated figurine with oval chubby face with large nose and upwards-curving mouth with thin lips. Her hair in thin bulbs is divided in the middle, creating a triangular forehead. She wears a large and slightly flaring polos with a rim. Next to her head and neck, her hair is bulging. She wears the necklace with one round pendant, and rectangular fibulae, placed as if rotated slightly, and two cords with pointed seed-shaped pendants, seven on each row. Her pose is seated, with her arms tight to her body, stretching her hands on her knees. She wears an apron, the outline of which is marked on the lower part of the body. The arms are covered with a folded garment. The three folds run vertically straight. Between the sleeve, ending below the elbow, and the hand, placed on the knee, there are several bracelets or a spiral bracelet. She sits on an upwards-curving bench with a cushion. Her feet, covered, are placed on a small podium. The back is flat on the upper part and round on the lower part to guarantee stability.

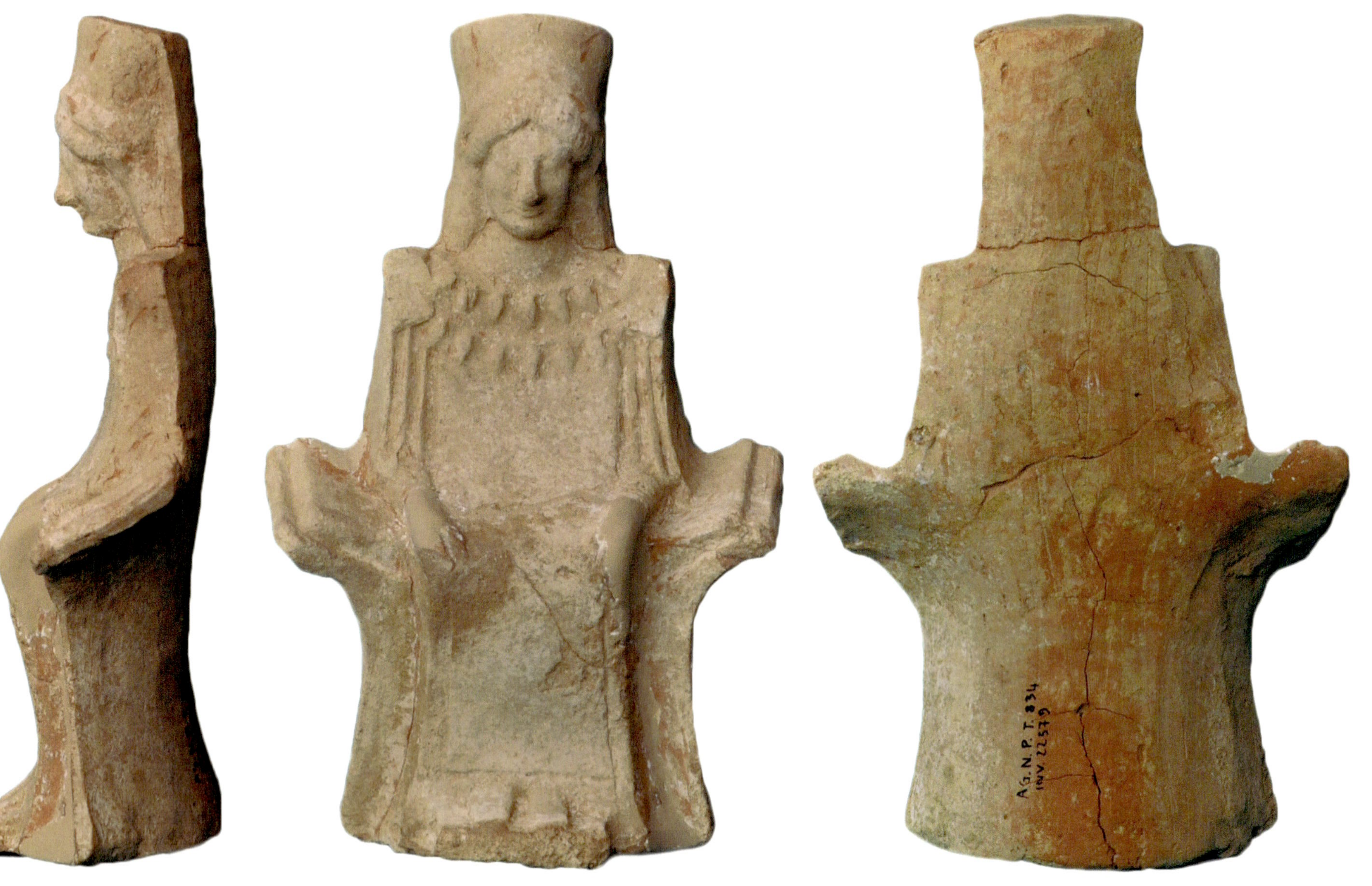

No. 135; Scale 1:1½ (Museo Archeologico Regionale "Pietro Griffo", Agrigento).

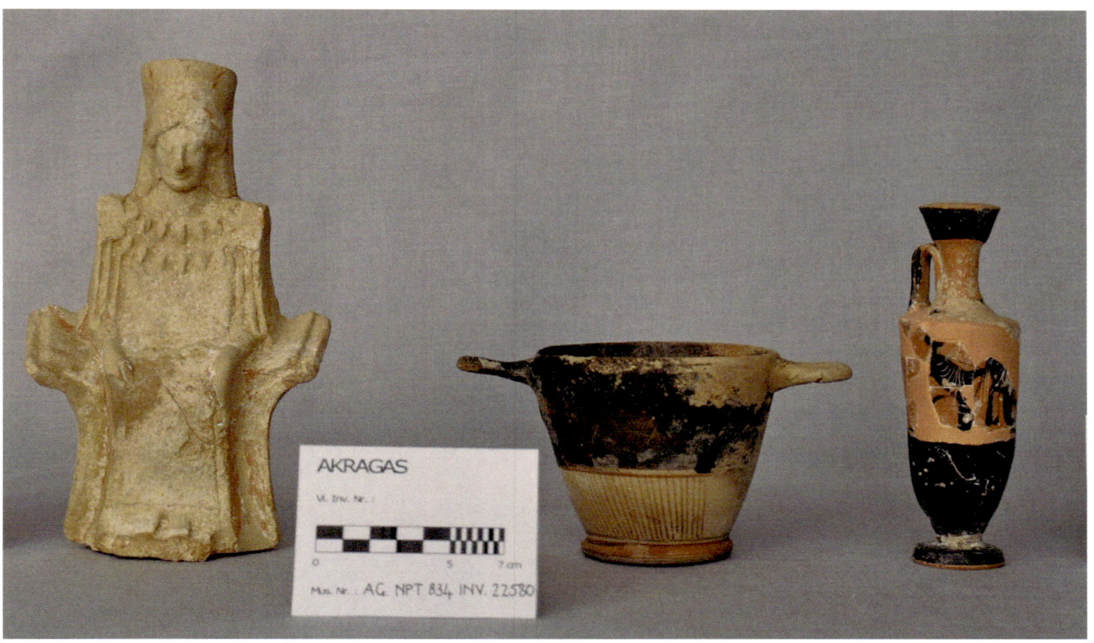

Figure 17: Context of no.135 with miniature Corinthian skyphos and Attic lekythos. Scale 1:3 (Museo Archeologico Regionale "Pietro Griffo", Agrigento).

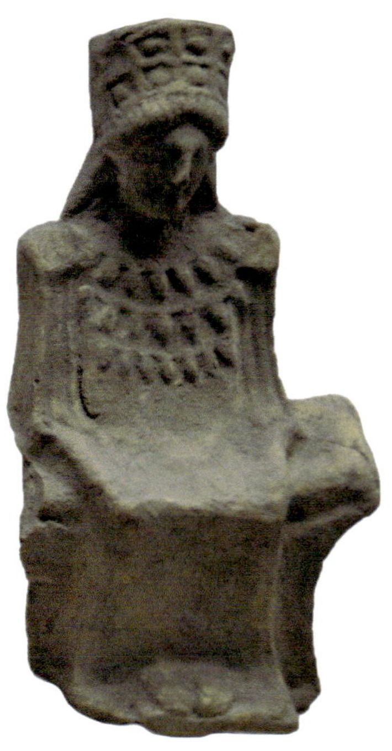

Figure 18: Figurine from Grammichele, Inv. no.14143, Scale 1:3 (Museo Archeologico Regionale "Paolo Orsi", Syracuse).

‣ ***Comparable objects:*** The body is similar to that of Mould II; later in time, but possibly partly from the same mould series. Though the facial expression is very similar, the hairstyle and polos are different. On the body, the third row with pendants on the chest is removed and the apron is lined out. The pendants overlapping the arm mark the difference between this object and the ones of Mould II. Like figurines **136** and **137**, it is a variation on the iconographic theme. The body, except for the missing third line of pendants, is very similar to Inv. no.31336 from Gelas, complete h.24.9cm. Albertocchi 2004, p.18, no.52, tav.II c; Orlandini 1966, p.21, tav.XI, fig.3. It might be from the same mould, because this one is standing on a podium and has a different head. A very similar figurine, just the lower part and right shoulder, from the Sanctuary of Predio Sola, Gela, is placed on a podium to increase its size Ismaelli 2013 129, no.661, tav.XIII. 3.

Again very close in likeness, except for a third band of pectoral pendants is a figurine from Gelas (1891,694 Ashmolean Museum, h.20.6cm, Blinkenberg 1917, p.30, fig.5; Zuntz 1971, p.124, n. 5, Pl. 16a.

It is similar also to a figurine from Grammichele: Mus. Syracuse Inv. no.14143 h.25.7cm, (fig.18) She wears a patterned polos and has three rows with pectoral pendants. Albertocchi 2004, p.40, no.613.

A very similar figurine, just the lower part and right shoulder, from the Sanctuary of Predio Sola, Gela, is placed on a podium to increase its size Ismaelli 2013, p.129, no.661, tav.XIII. 3. A figurine (fig.19) is probably from Akragas and forms a striking variation, because it has not only a wide bench and eight pendants on the upper pectoral cord, but also an outline rim from the top of the seat to the polos, complete, h.23.5cm, Louvre Inv. no.S2218. Albertocchi 2004, p.18, no.40; Mollard Besques 1954, p.78, tav.LI, B549. The rim is made like figurines 145-151.

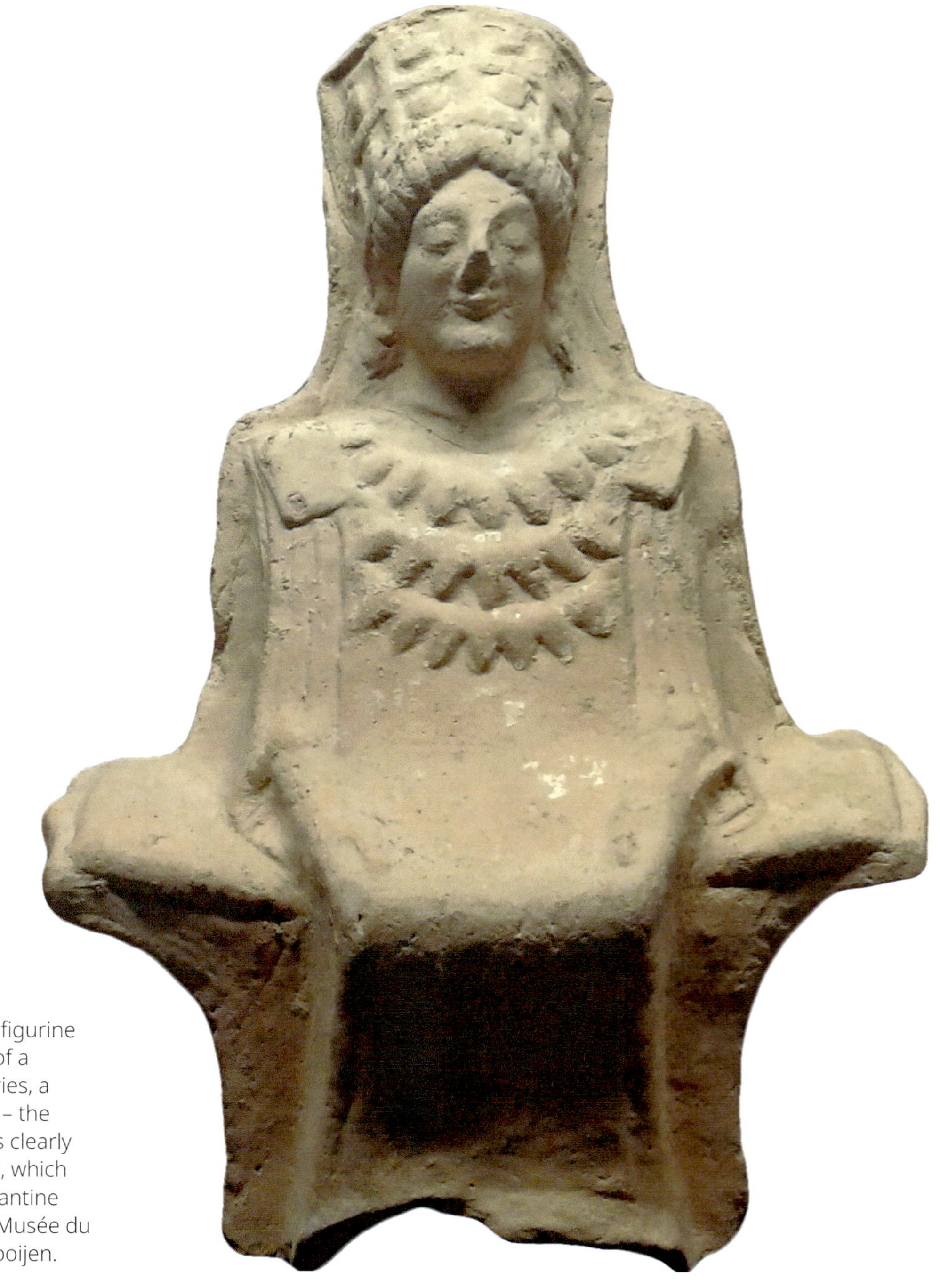

Figure 19: Scale 1:1½; This figurine forms an interesting case of a body from the Mould II series, a new patterned polos head – the seam below the necklace is clearly visible – and an outline rim, which is known from other Akragantine figurines. (Inv. no. S 2218, Musée du Louvre). Photo by B. van Rooijen.

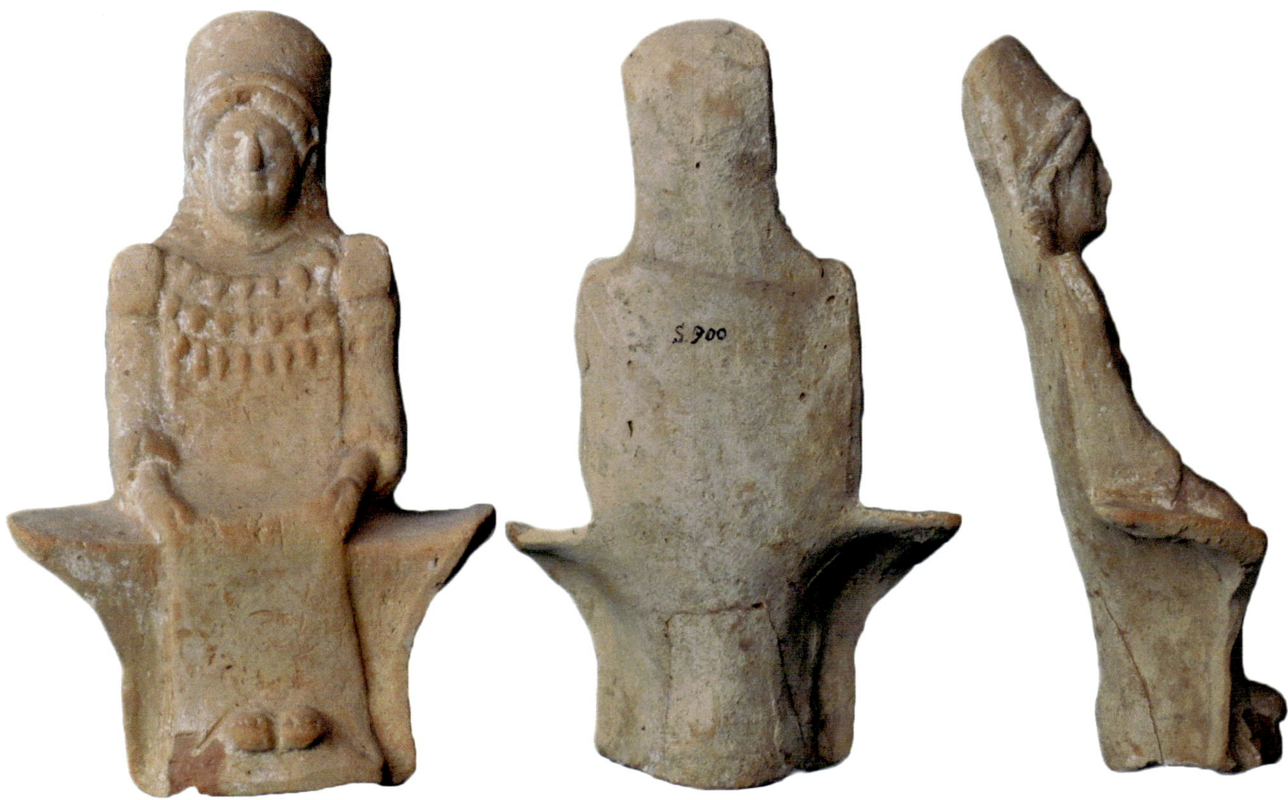

No. 136; Scale 1:2 (Museo Archeologico Regionale "Pietro Griffo", Agrigento).

No.136

- *Museum and Inventory number:* Mus. Agrigento S900
- *Findspot and context:* City Sanctuary
- *Publications:* Albertocchi 2004, p.27, no.521
- *Dimensions in cm:* h.20.9
- *Material:* terracotta
- *Techniques:* Front moulded. Handmade chair. Lighter toned slip layer. Painted white. Straightened back and sides with sharp tool.
- *Colour:* Reddish-yellow 5 YR 7/6. Lighter coloured slip layer.
- *Date:* The second decade of the 5th century BCE
- *Workshop:* Workshop of 'straight reworking', body similar to Mould II
- *Typology:* 3a
- *Short description:* Complete, small parts chipped off in places. Seated figurine with chubby face, wide jaws, and a pointed round chin. She has large rounded eyes and a small mouth with thick lips. Her fringe in a small band on the forehead consists of bulbs that are smaller in the middle, creating a triangular forehead. On the finials, her ears (?) are depicted. She wears a wide, but straight polos with a rim. Next to her head and neck, her hair has horizontal lining. She wears a necklace, but without pendant, and rectangular fibulae with rounded corners, placed straight on the upper part of arm and shoulder. Her pose is seated, with her arms tight to her body, stretching her hands on her knees. She wears three cords with pointed seed-shaped pendants, seven on the first two, eight on the third. She wears a garment that covers her whole body, draped over her feet. The sleeves end just below the elbow in a thicker part. She wears three bracelets or a spiral bracelet on each arm. She sits on a straight bench, of which the front curves down in a quarter of a circle. The part of the bench on her right is higher than the left part. Her feet, covered, are placed on a small podium. The back is very flat on the upper part and round on the lower part to guarantee stability.
- *Comparable objects:* The body is similar to that of Mould II, and one of the variations on the iconographic theme, like **135** and **137**. It shares technical aspects with **135** and is probably a variation made by someone who took a figurine from the Mould II series as a direct example. The chest could very well be from a mould of this type. The flat arms are replaced by more natural ones. Based on its small size, the body might be from the fifth or sixth generation.

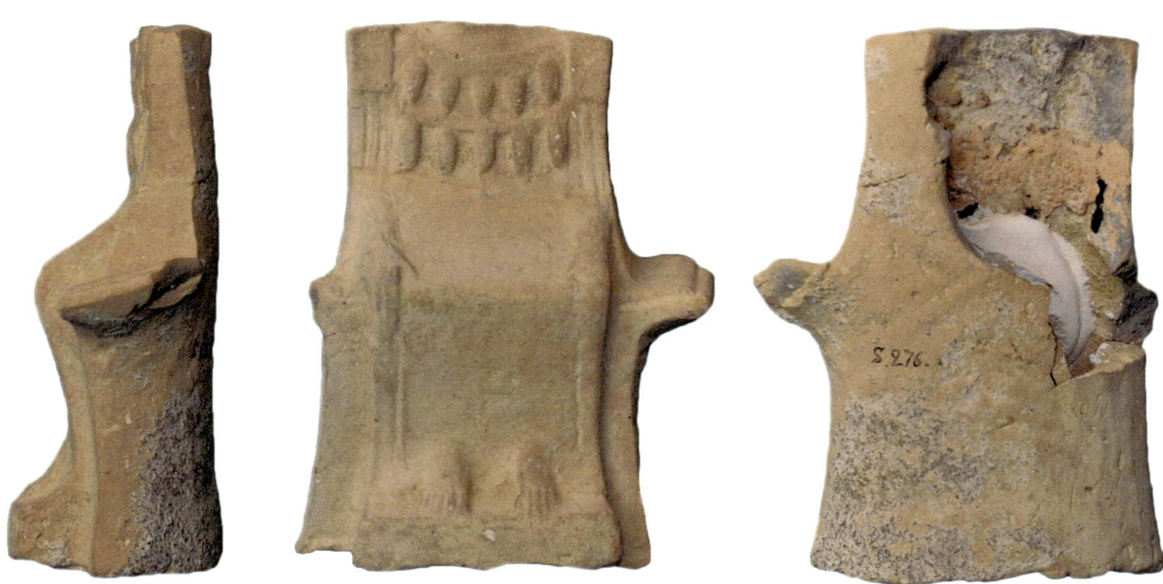

No. 137; Scale 1:2 (Museo Archeologico Regionale "Pietro Griffo", Agrigento).

No.137

‣ *Museum and Inventory number:* Mus. Agrigento S276

‣ *Findspot and context:* City Sanctuary

‣ *Publications:* -

‣ *Dimensions in cm:* h.14.7

‣ *Material:* Terracotta

‣ *Techniques:* Front moulded. Fingers reworked and front part of chair probably handmade. Back slab flattened by rolling with stick in different directions.

‣ *Colour:* Very pale brown 10 YR 8/3

‣ *Date:* The second decade of the 5th century BCE

‣ *Workshop:* Unknown, body similar to Mould II

‣ *Typology:* 3a

‣ *Short description:* Headless figurine. Seated figurines with the arms placed tight along the body, reaching her knees with her hands. Both hands and feet have finger indicated. She wears a chiton, which has three folds on each side along the body next to the apron. They do not appear, however, on the bottom on the left. The feet are placed apart from each other on a wide footstool, though they seem to hang above it. She sits on a wide bench with a cushion, which is a bit smaller than the seat itself. She wears rectangular fibulae with two cords in between. On the cords there are five relatively large shaped pendants of the seed shape each, some thicker and others more pointed.

‣ *Comparable objects:* The pose, fibulae and pendants are reminiscent of the Mould II series. The pendants are, however, larger and fewer. The fibulae are placed straight instead of diagonally. The additional chair is not seen on the figurines of Mould II. Figurine **135** and **137** are also variations on the Mould II type but none of them are from the same mould genealogies. A figurine with similar rectangular and straight placed fibulae is mentioned by Bovio Marconi. Bovio Marconi 1930 81 fig.12. Its rigidness and detailed fingers are reminiscent of figurine Inv. no.9214 from Vassallagi, which is not from the same mould but was inspired by it or made by the same coroplast, nearly complete h.31.9cm, Albertocchi 2004, p.20, no.83, tav.II, d. The figurine has three rows of pendants and a patterned polos.

Albertocchi interprets another figurine in this mould series, a derivative of the Mould II series. Albertocchi 2004, p.33, no.522. This 16.5cm tall figurine wears no shoulder clasps and the pectorals run in three rounded rows, like on the figurines from group 3b. It should be therefore dated to the second or third decade of the fifth century BCE. Mus. Karlsruhe inv. no.B 418. Schürmann 1989, p.90, no.307, tav.52. The head, however, of this figurine is much older and probably from the same mould series as **19**. The original head would have lost all details in this late generation.

Type K: The outlined-throne throne group and some similar figurines (no.138-153)

This group of figurines is characterised by increasing levels of detail on the dress and throne. A variation with an outline, the leftover clay from outside the mould, is unique to a certain mould series.

No.138

- *Museum and Inventory number:* Mus. Agrigento S402
- *Findspot and context:* Akragas
- *Publications:* -
- *Dimensions in cm:* h.9.4
- *Material:* Terracotta.
- *Techniques:* Front moulded. Slighter coloured slip layer.
- *Colour:* Very pale brown 10 YR 8/3
- *Date:* The third decade of the 5th century BCE
- *Workshop:* Unknown
- *Typology:* Rectangular fibulae group: 3b
- *Short description:* Head and left shoulder of a figurine. She has an oval face with large eyes, high arching eyebrows, a long narrow nose and a smiling mouth with a thicker upper lip. She has a pronounced chin. The fringe of hair on her forehead is divided into bulbs, the hair next to her neck plain and slightly bulging. She wears a tall slightly flaring polos on her head. On her left shoulder, she wears a rectangular fibula. She wears a high band on her chest, and a second one over her shoulder. On the first cord, some small irregularly shaped pendants(?) are visible. Straight back.
- *Comparable objects:* The rectangular fibula indicates in which part of the iconographic development this figurine should be placed. Like **139**, **140** and 152, which are not from the Mould II series, nor the outlined-body group, but shares some characteristics with those figurines.

No.139

- *Museum and Inventory number:* Mus. Agrigento 9075 (176)
- *Findspot and context:* Workshop/ sanctuary near Gate V
- *Publications:* Albertocchi 2004, p.15, no.12; De Miro 2000, p.24, no.1414, tav.LXV
- *Dimensions in cm:* h.15
- *Material:* Terracotta. Several instances of lime-spalling
- *Techniques:* Front moulded. Face is separately moulded or pressed into with a separate piece of clay.
- *Colour:* Very pale brown 10 YR 8/3 Lighter coloured slip layer.
- *Date:* The third decade of the 5th century BCE
- *Workshop:* Unknown
- *Typology:* Rectangular fibulae group: 3b
- *Short description:* Upper part with chest and right side with bench of a figurine. Nose broken off. Enthroned female figurine. She has an elongated oval face. Her lips are thick, and the mouth is horizontal, not smiling. The eyes seem to have been reworked to make them sharper. Around her forehead, she has a fringe of hair, below the polos in long thin bulbs, placed vertically, shorter in the middle and lengthening towards the sides. Along the sides of her neck, some hair with thin irregular waves hangs down. She wears a tall straight polos, with a thin

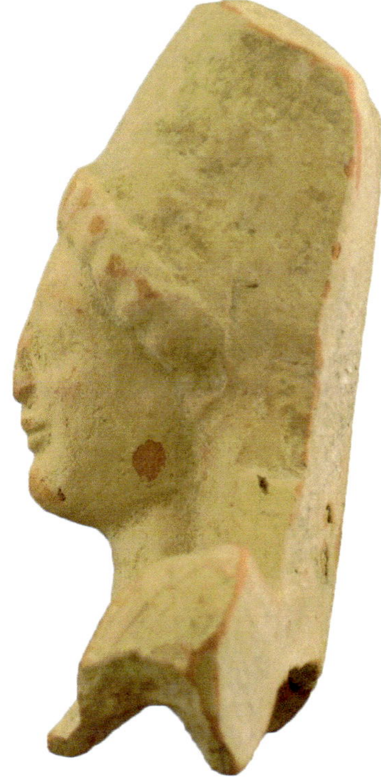

No. 138; Scale 1:1 (Museo Archeologico Regionale "Pietro Griffo", Agrigento).

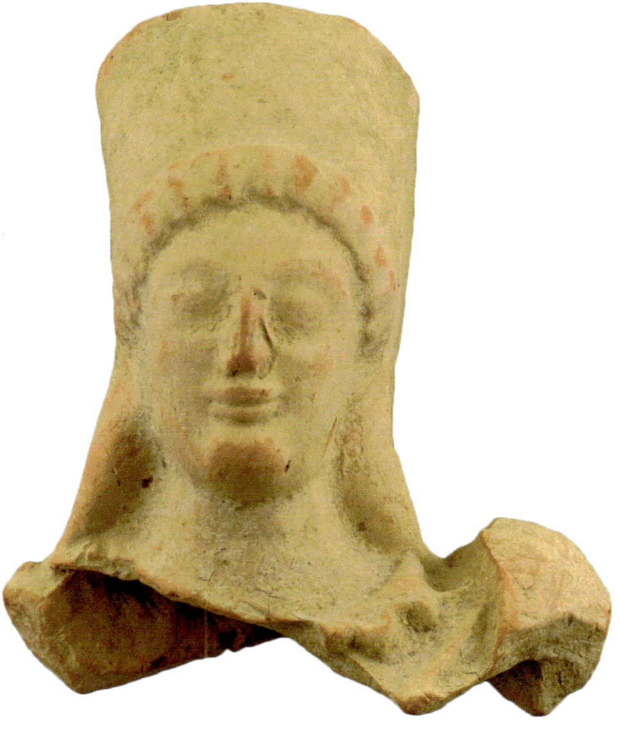

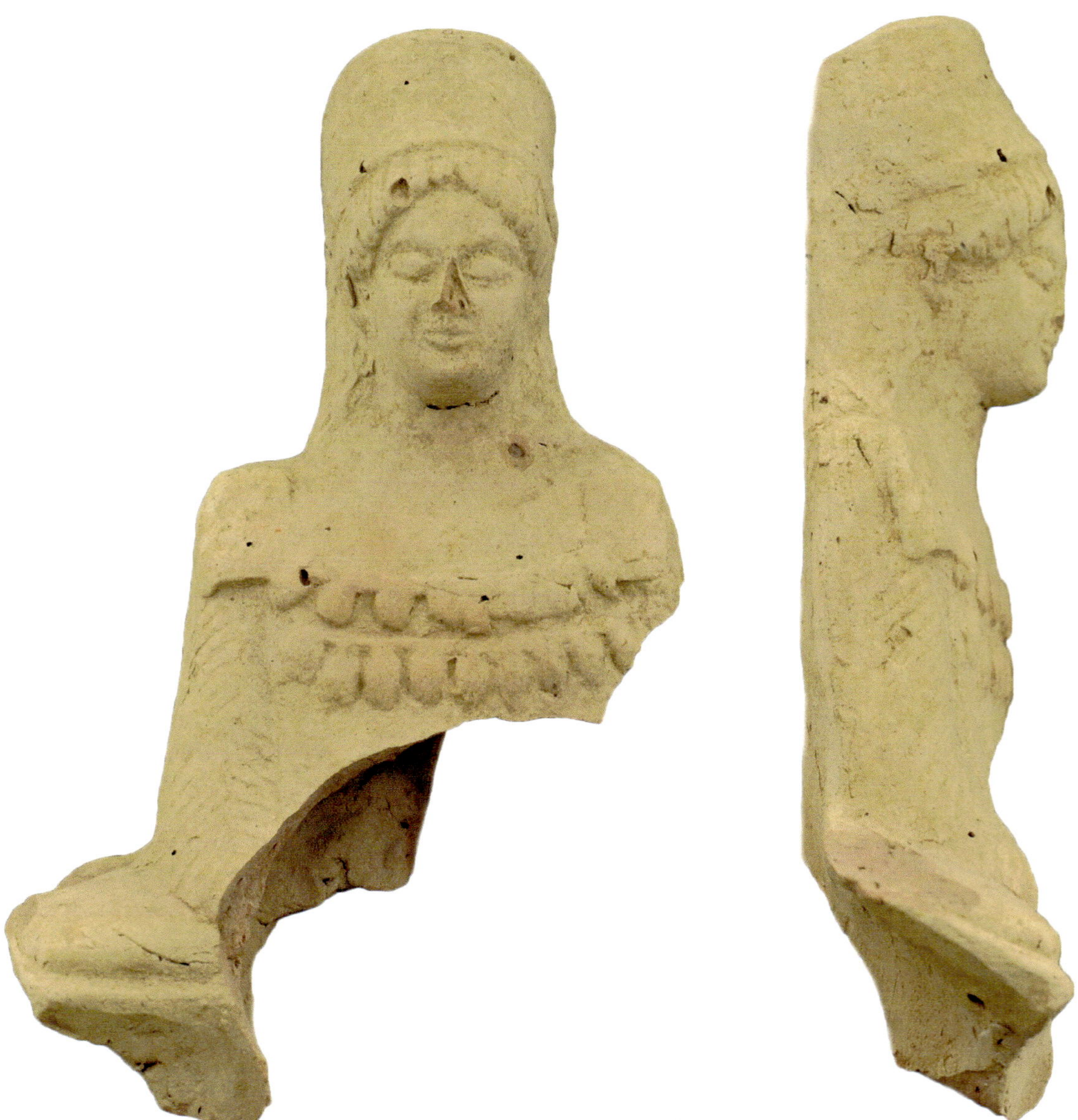

No. 139; Scale 1:1 (Museo Archeologico Regionale “Pietro Griffo”, Agrigento).

rim just above the hair. She wears an apron over an undergarment. The outer rim of this chiton is visible in the neck and the sleeve has thin folds and a seam in the middle. She wears rectangular fibulae. Her pose is seated, with her arms close to her body. She sits on a bench with a rounded side and a cushion on it. She wears multiple pendants on the chest in two rows. On the upper cord, hanging down between the fibulae are eight ovoid and disc-shaped pendants. On the lower cord, there are nine slightly thicker ovoid pendants.

‣ ***Comparable objects:*** Is reminiscent of figurines with the ‘outlined-throne model: face A’. It is also reminiscent of figurine **152**, which has a similar iconographic scheme.

No.140

‣ ***Museum and Inventory number:*** Mus. Agrigento C386
‣ ***Findspot and context:*** Akragas
‣ ***Publications:*** -
‣ ***Dimensions in cm:*** h.12.7
‣ ***Material:*** Terracotta
‣ ***Techniques:*** Front moulded. The one pendant necklace mould could be from another mould. It looks like the left earring was taken with it and therefore differs from that on the right side. The odd reworking points to such a solution also.
‣ ***Colour:*** Pink 5 YR 7/4
‣ ***Date:*** The third decade of the 5th century BCE

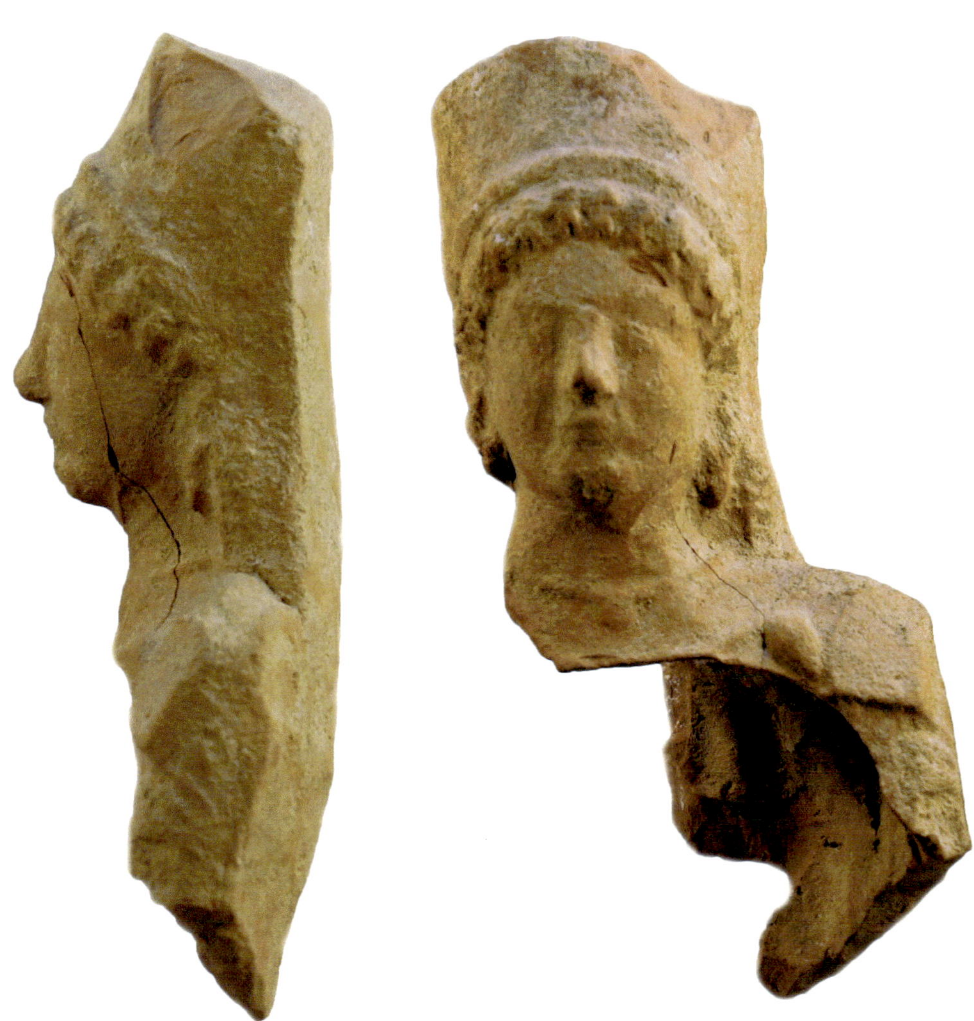

No. 140; Scale 1:1 (Museo Archeologico Regionale "Pietro Griffo", Agrigento).

- ***Workshop:*** Unknown
- ***Typology:*** Rectangular fibulae group: 3b
- ***Short description:*** Head and left shoulder of a figurine. Two fragments. Female figurine with an oval face with a high forehead and a pronounced chin. Though indistinct, her eyes seem to slant. The nose is sizeable but not too broad. She has a small mouth. Her hair is placed around her forehead in two lines of wavy curls and along the side of the neck, behind the earring depicted also with structure. She wears a low polos with a rim. Her earrings are large but not clearly visible: a ring with a pendant. On her right side, the ring seems elongated, on the left more boat-shaped. She wears a tight necklace with one round pendant. One pectoral band with a pointed ovoid pendant is visible, next to an irregularly shaped rectangular fibula. Back has been smoothed with wetted fingers. Clear traces.
- ***Comparable objects:*** The body, though only a small part is visible, might be comparable with Mould II: the rectangular fibula, the pointed ovoid pendant on a thin band, the one pendant tight necklace and the large earrings they have in common. The earring on the right side is more similar to **153**. The hairstyle is reminiscent of **156** and **157**, which also have the fringe shaped into two wavy layers. From some generations earlier, the upper part of a figurine from Akragas: Mus. Agrigento Inv. No.S 6811, upper part, h.21cm, De Miro 2000, p.283, no.1911, tav.LXVI.

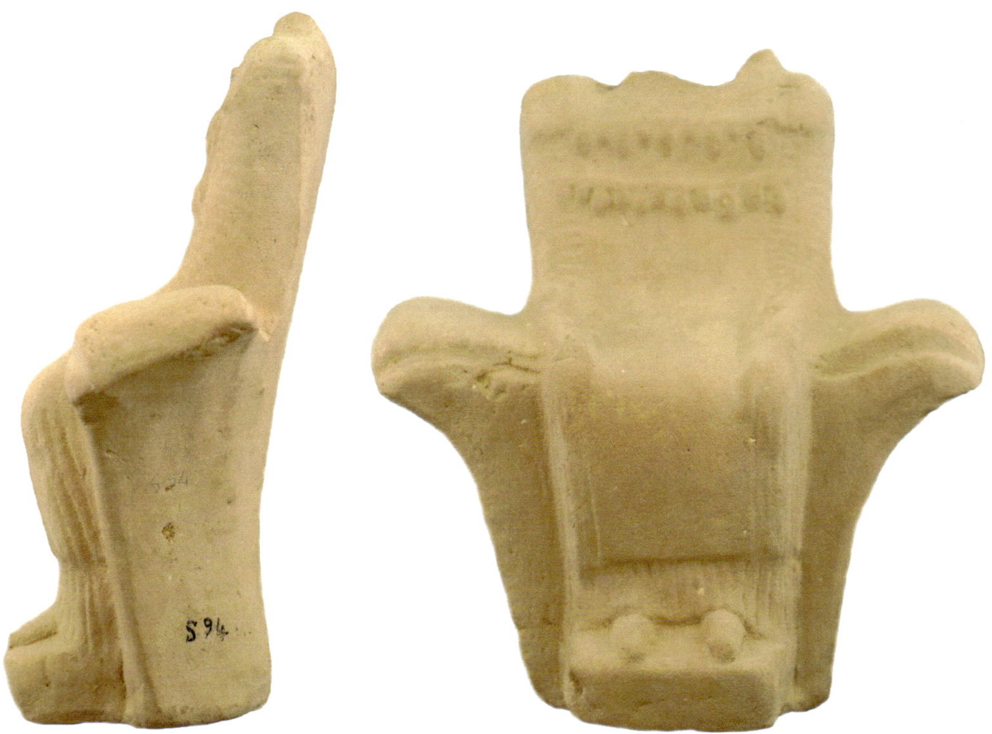

No. 141; Scale 1:2 (Museo Archeologico Regionale "Pietro Griffo", Agrigento).

No.141

‣ *Museum and Inventory number:* Mus. Agrigento S94
‣ *Findspot and context:* City Sanctuary
‣ *Publications:* Albertocchi 2004, p.15, no.11; Marconi 1933, p.57 fig.35.2
‣ *Dimensions in cm:* h.18.1
‣ *Material:* Terracotta.
‣ *Techniques:* Front moulded
‣ *Colour:* Very pale brown 10 YR 7.3
‣ *Date:* The third decade of the 5th century BCE
‣ *Workshop:* Unknown
‣ *Typology:* Rectangular fibulae group: 3b
‣ *Short description:* Body and lower part of a figurine. Head broken off. From a worn mould. The body is slightly flaring towards the shoulders on which rectangular fibulae are placed. Seated on a wide round curving bench with a cushion, the body has a rigid pose, with the arms following the sides and reaching the knees. She wears a chiton with small folds, visible on the sleeves. Vertical thin folds are visible from above the feet and next to the apron on the lower part of the body. The pectoral pendants in two distinct straight horizontal lines consist of many small and irregular shaped pendants: smaller round pendants are alternated with larger ovoid or seed-shaped ones on the first line, which comprises in total nine pendants. On the second chain, there are eleven pendants, which seem also to alternate between larger and smaller seed-shaped pendants. Her feet are placed apart from each other in shoes on a block-shaped footstool. The back is rounded on the lower part and flat on the thinner upper part.
‣ *Comparable objects:* Similar in the considerable number of pectoral pendants and according to Albertocchi from the same mould series are **238** and a mould from Akragas: Mus. Agrigento Inv. no.AG8943. Albertocchi 2004, p.no.13; De Miro 2000, p.251, no.1534, tav.CIX. On the latter, the fibula is oval, and the pectoral chain is shaped like a pearl rim.

No.142

‣ *Museum and Inventory number:* Mus. Agrigento S288
‣ *Findspot and context:* City Sanctuary
‣ *Publications:* Albertocchi 2004, p.25, no.110
‣ *Dimensions in cm:* h.21.3
‣ *Material:* Terracotta.
‣ *Techniques:* Front moulded. Clay on the edges on the back. Painted white?
‣ *Colour:* Pink 7.5 YR 7/4 The upper part is redder.
‣ *Date:* The third decade of the 5th century BCE
‣ *Workshop:* Workshop of 'straight reworking'
‣ *Typology:* Outlined-throne model: without rim, 'old face': 3b
‣ *Short description:* Upper part of a figurine. The lower part of throne and feet are broken off. Cracks on the side of the head. Worn mould. Female, seated figurine. The face is oval, with a thin nose and a very small mouth. Details of the face are indistinct. Her hair in a band on her forehead has very fine lines and is parted and thinner in the middle. The two parts hang down like a curtain. On the finials of

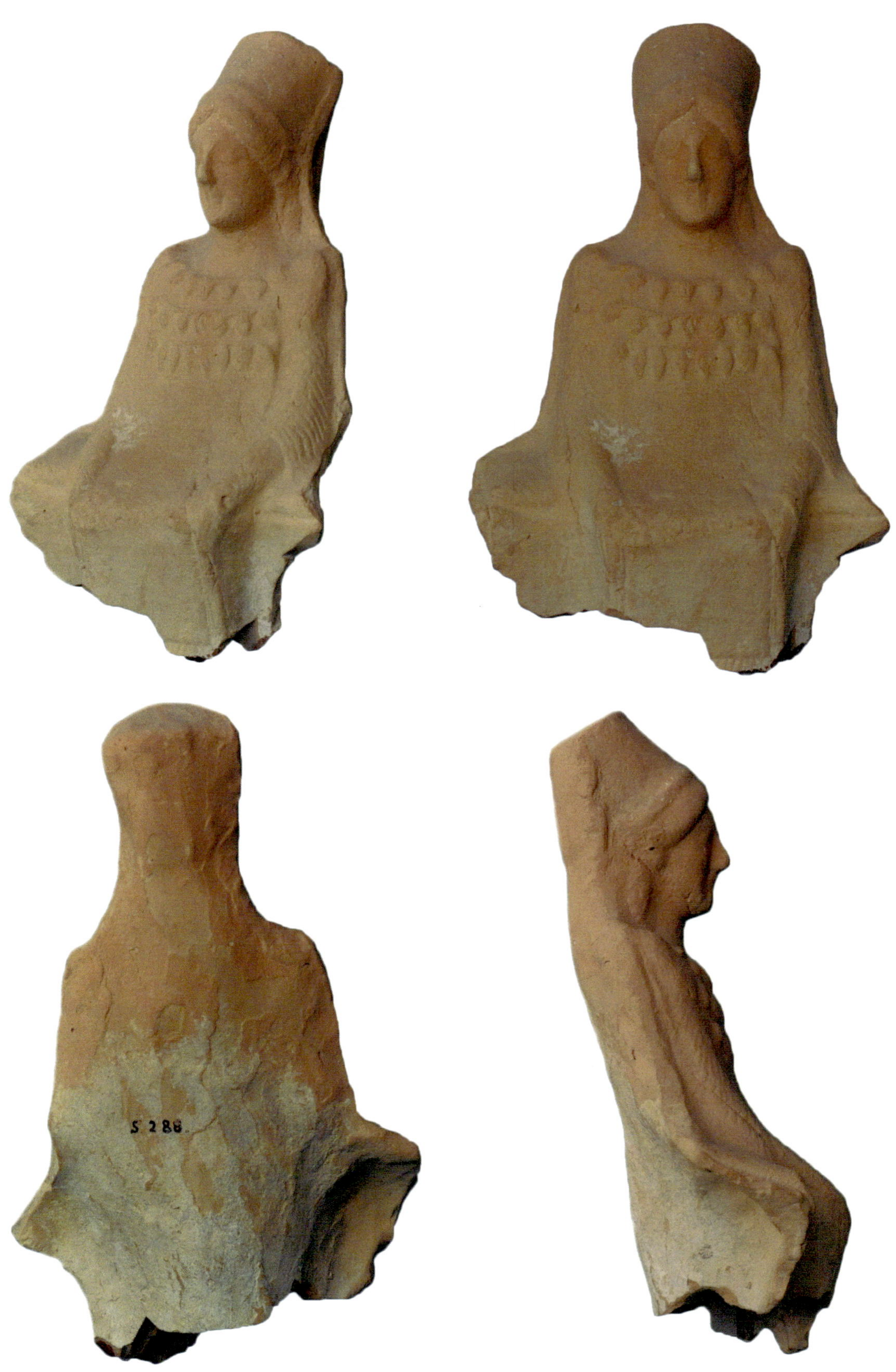

No. 142; Scale 1:2 (Museo Archeologico Regionale "Pietro Griffo", Agrigento).

this fringe, the outline of ears is placed on top. She wears a tall polos with a rim, just above the hair. Next to the sides of her neck, her hair is bulging. She seems to wear a thin necklace without pendant. She is seated upright on a wide bench, slightly curving upwards and a bit higher on the right side, topped with a thin cushion. She holds her arms tight to her body and reaches to her knees with her outstretched hand. Her fingers are indicated with a separate thumb. Her upper body runs down diagonally and the bend at the height of the bench indicates her knees. From there, the lower part of the body is straight. Her fibulae are oval, but the details are indistinct. She wears a chiton with sleeves until just below her elbows, that shows fine folds in a regular manner, with a seam in the middle. They are wide because they are draped over the arm, touching the seat. She wears an apron also, of which the edges are visible on the lower part of her body. The undergarment with fine folds appears just below the hem of the apron and on the sides. She wears three cords with pointed seed-shaped pendants, seven on the first two, eight thinner and pointier ones on the third. Sides straightened, rounded back, smoothed with soft clay. Outer rim of the back slab visible behind hair in the neck, polos and arms.

‣ *Comparable objects:* **143-151** are from the same mould series. Because of their size, they are probably from the fourth generation. Albertocchi mentions 417 figurines in total and 17 of them from Akragas – of which **142** is from the third generation – and 396 in total from Selinous. The latter objects are discussed by Dewailly, type B XV (Dewailly 1992, p.84-101). The face is reminiscent of **91**. Similar to a figurine from Ibiza: Mus. Barcelona Inv. no.8550, complete, h.20.5cm, Albertocchi 1999, p.359, fig.8; Albertocchi 2004, p.26, no.119. Three heads are mentioned, of which the last two might actually be from other moulds, as their hairstyle and polos differs significantly. Another head from Akragas seems closer to the face and hairstyle: Mus. Agrigento Inv. no.S 6821, h.6.3cm, De Miro, no.2117, tav.LXIX. This particular hairstyle is most clear on some heads from Selinous. Dewailly 1992, p.89, fig.53. The following heads from the same mould series are also in Akragas, Mus. Agrigento Inv. no.S112, h.11cm, Albertocchi 2004, p.25, no.113. AG6821, h.6.3cm, Albertocchi 2004, p.25, no.118; De Miro 2000, p.298, no.2117, tav.LXIX; AG6823, h.9.4cm, Albertocchi 2004, p.25, no.116; De Miro 2000, p.282-3, no.1910, tav.LXIX. And part of a chest: Mus. Agrigento Inv. no.AG6816, h.8.5cm, Albertocchi 2004, p.25, no.115; De Miro 2000, p.140, no.144 LXVII.

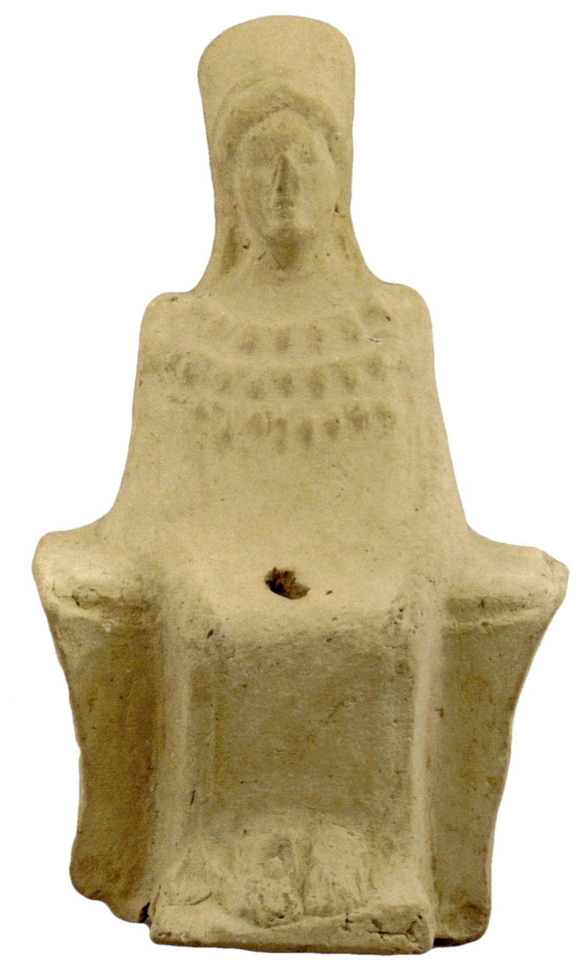

No. 143; Scale 1:1½ (Museo Archeologico Regionale "Pietro Griffo", Agrigento); continued on next page.

No.143

‣ *Museum and Inventory number:* Mus. Agrigento S899

‣ *Findspot and context:* City Sanctuary

‣ *Publications:* Albertocchi 2004, p.25, no.108

‣ *Dimensions in cm:* h.16.6

‣ *Material:* Terracotta. Many shell fragments.

‣ *Techniques:* Front moulded. There is a protruding line from the right side of the throne over the arm and the lap, which might indicate a crack in the mould or that the patrix had a protruding line already. The toes are marked on the feet with a sharp tool.

‣ *Colour:* Very pale brown 10 YR 8/4

‣ *Date:* The third decade of the 5th century BCE

‣ *Workshop:* Separate face moulded

‣ *Typology:* Outlined-throne model: without rim, 'old face': 3b

‣ *Short description:* For a further description, see **142**.

The back is rather rough, smoothed just with a sharp tool on some spots.

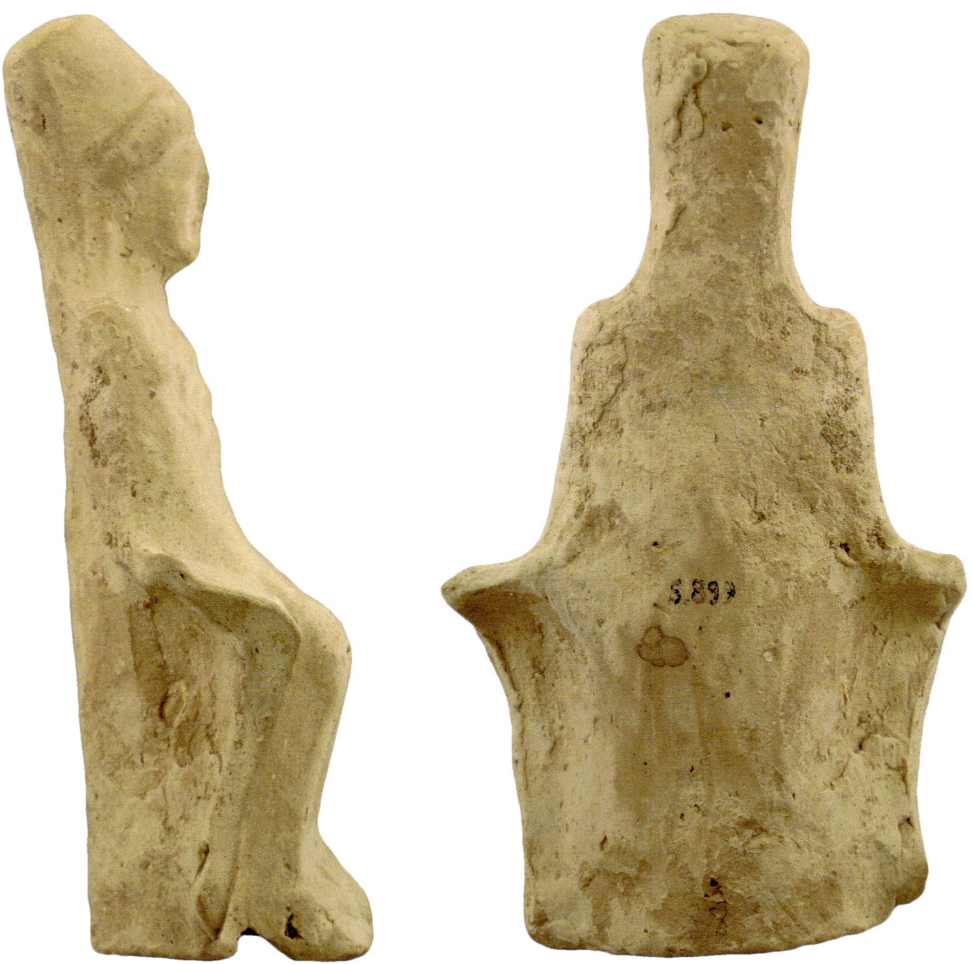

‣ *Comparable objects:* **142**, **144-151** are from the same mould series. See **142**. The protruding line on the lap appears also on **147**, which is maybe from the same mould though **147** is about 2cm taller and **143** slightly sharper. The larger podium on **147**, more reworking or a different sort of clay has caused these differences. The rim, which is absent on **143**, seems part of the mould on **147**. These problematic characteristics might indicate that there was a sort of parallel mould genealogy, in which a preceding figurine or mould caused the protruding line. Two moulds could have been made from the same patrix or two figurines from the same mould could have been used as patrices for two moulds: one with a rim and one without.

No.144

‣ *Museum and Inventory number:* Mus. Agrigento S898
‣ *Findspot and context:* City Sanctuary
‣ *Publications:* Albertocchi 2004, p.25, no.107
‣ *Dimensions in cm:* h.24.2
‣ *Material:* Terracotta. Many shell fragments. Large lime-spalling holes.
‣ *Techniques:* Front moulded. The sides have been reworked straight, which resulted in bulging clay on the edge of the back.
‣ *Colour:* Very pale brown 10 YR 7/4
‣ *Date:* The third decade of the 5th century BCE
‣ *Workshop:* From the same workshop as **145**.
‣ *Typology:* Outlined-throne model: without rim, but an alternative backrest of the throne, 'old face': 3b
‣ *Short description:* Nearly complete figurine. Parts of the handmade throne on the left are broken off. Enthroned female figurine. She has an oval face. Her lips are thick, but the mouth small. Around her forehead, she has a smooth fringe of hair, divided in the middle. Along the sides of her neck, some hair, undefined, hangs down. In the corner of these two parts of the hairstyle, she wears ovoid earrings. She wears a tall slightly flaring polos with a rim just above the hair. The polos seems a bit roughly reworked. She wears an apron over an undergarment, under which her feet stick out, placed on a footstool. The folds of the chiton are indicated near her feet, with vertical lines on her sleeves and a seam in the middle, ending in a v-shape. She might

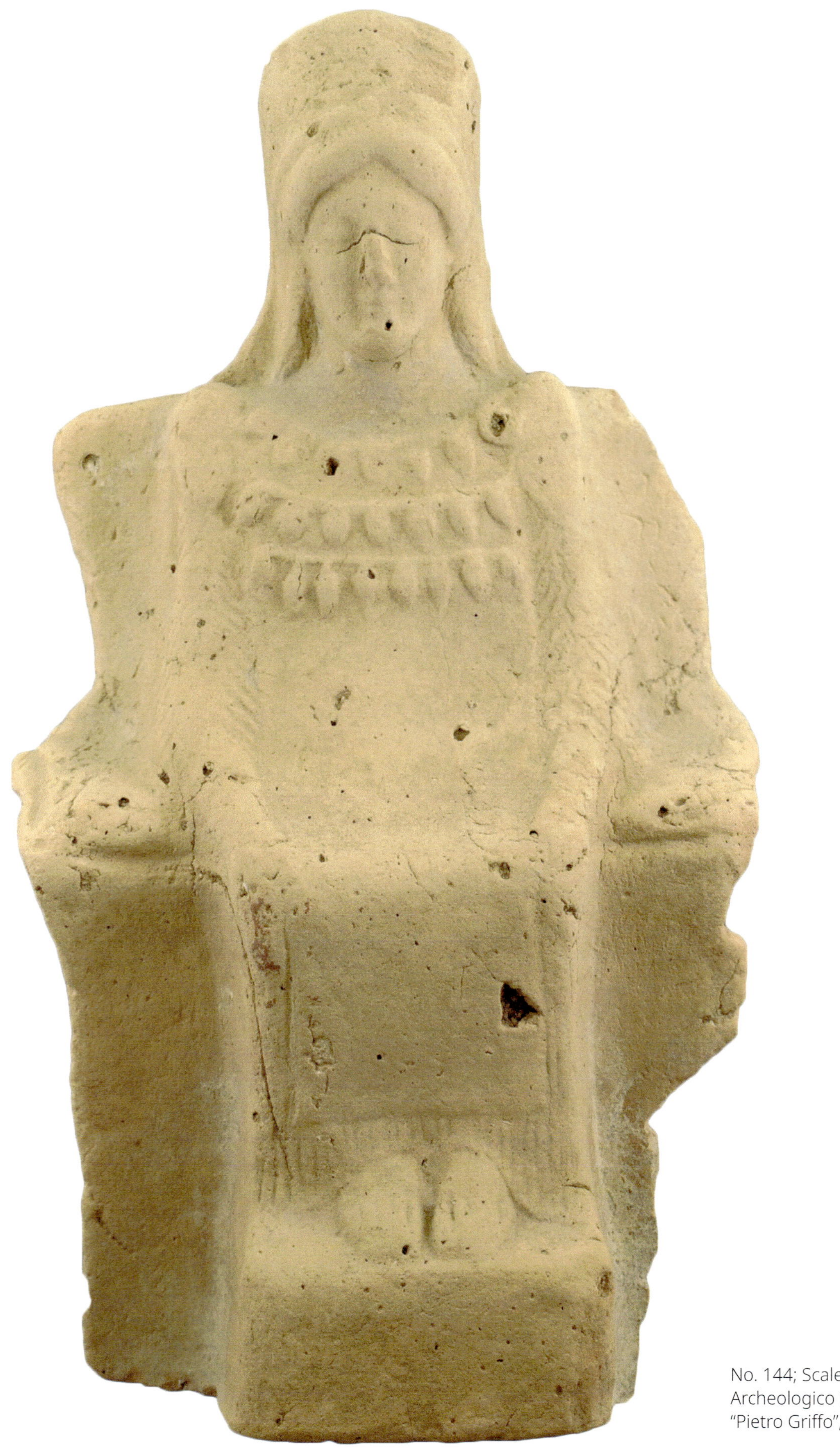

No. 144; Scale 1:1 (Museo Archeologico Regionale "Pietro Griffo", Agrigento).

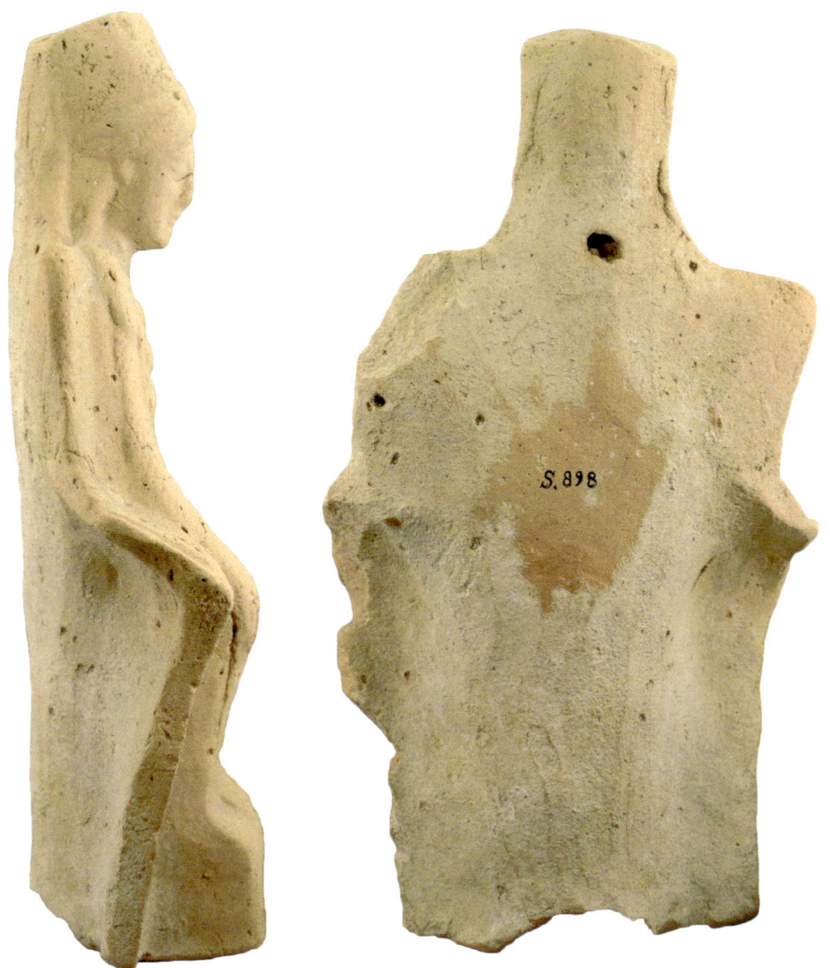

No. 144; Scale 1:2 (Museo Archeologico Regionale "Pietro Griffo", Agrigento).

wear bracelets. Her pose is seated, with her arms close to her body, reaching her knees with her outstretched hands. She sits on a wide straight bench with a cushion on it. Between the double oval (?) shaped fibulae, she wears multiple pendants on the chest in three rows. On the upper two cords, hanging down from the fibulae are seven ovoid, some more pointed, pendants. On the third cord, there are eight slightly more elongated and pointed pendants. The outline rim is reworked into a backrest with protruding rounded corners and the neck is supported with a small part outlined next to the hair and neck. The back was smoothed with a sharp tool, leaving vertical traces.

‣ ***Comparable objects:*** **142**, **143**, **145-151** are from the same mould series. See **142**.

Possibly from the same mould is a nearly complete figurine dated to the first quarter of the 5th century BCE.: Mus. Amsterdam Inv. no.APM 1419, h.24cm (fig.20) See museum website. Lunsingh Scheurleer 1986, no.41. The reworking of the rim is different; the rim is completed up to the polos, as on **145-148**. The rim has been worked into round shapes with a sharp tool, leaving the whole cushion on the throne visible and following the curves of the shoulder in the same way as on figurine 19634 R 2000 from Selinous (fig.21). This means that the mould has travelled. Where the starting point was and where the destination is unclear.

No.145

‣ ***Museum and Inventory number:*** Mus. Agrigento S897

‣ ***Findspot and context:*** City Sanctuary

‣ ***Publications:*** Albertocchi 2004, p.25, no.106

‣ ***Dimensions in cm:*** h.18.7

‣ ***Material:*** Terracotta. Many holes, probably caused by lime-spalling.

‣ ***Techniques:*** Front moulded. The clay for the head has been pressed into the mould separately.

‣ ***Colour:*** Yellow 10 YR 7/6

‣ ***Date:*** The third decade of the 5th century BCE

‣ ***Workshop:*** From the same workshop as **144**.

‣ ***Typology:*** Outlined-throne model: with rim, 'old face': 3b

‣ ***Short description:*** Nearly complete figurine. Part on knee chipped off. Enthroned female figurine. She has an oval chubby face, with pronounced cheeks and chin. The nose is quite large but flattened. Her lips are thick slightly smiling. The eyes, though indistinct, are large. Around her forehead, she has a smooth fringe of hair, divided

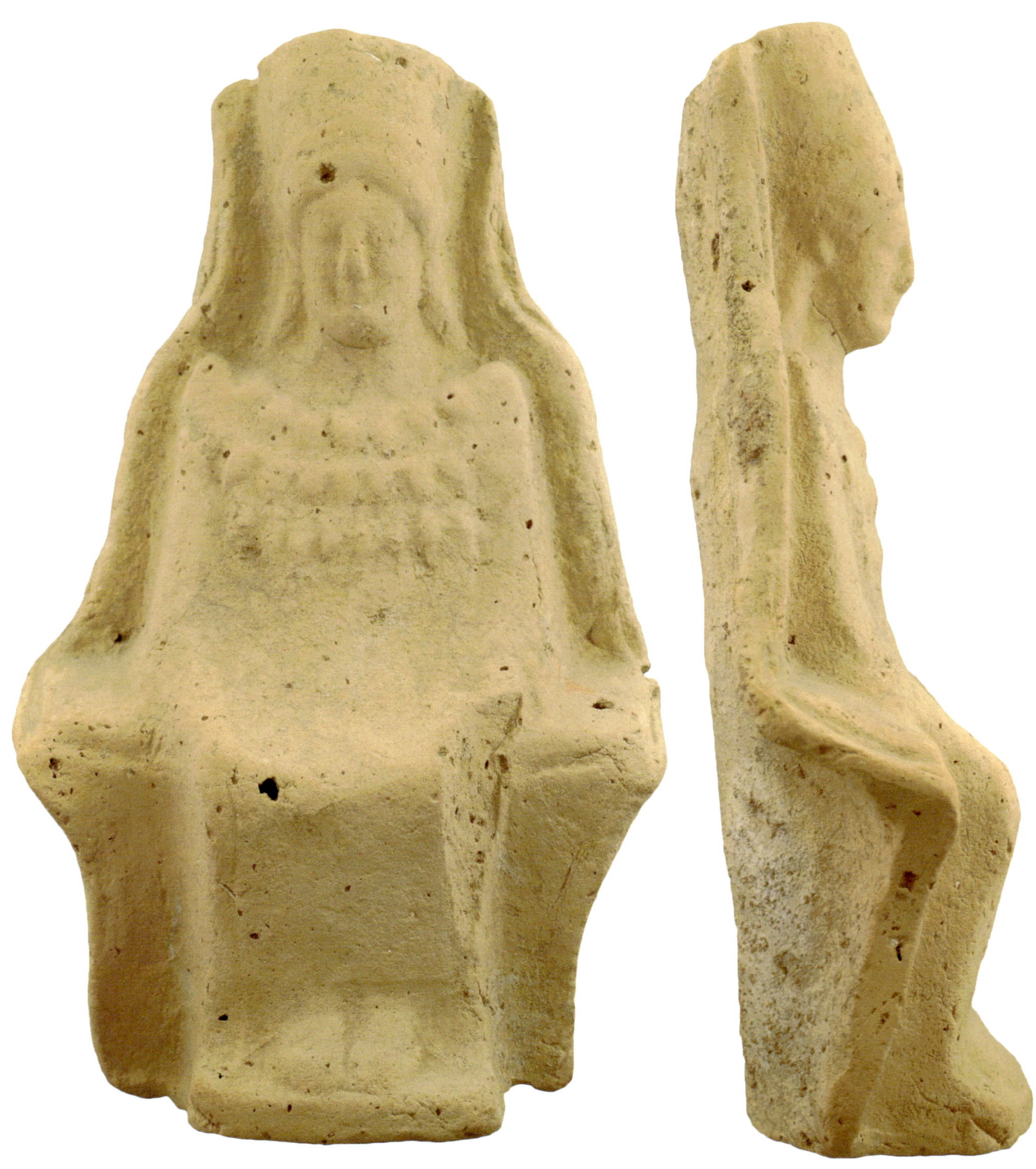

No. 145; Scale 1:1 (Museo Archeologico Regionale “Pietro Griffo”, Agrigento).

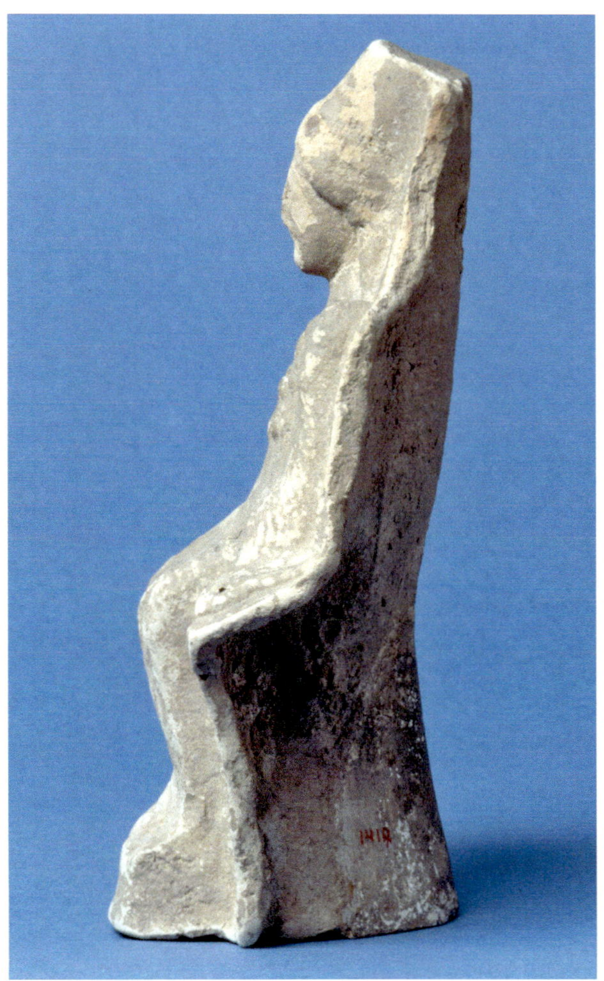

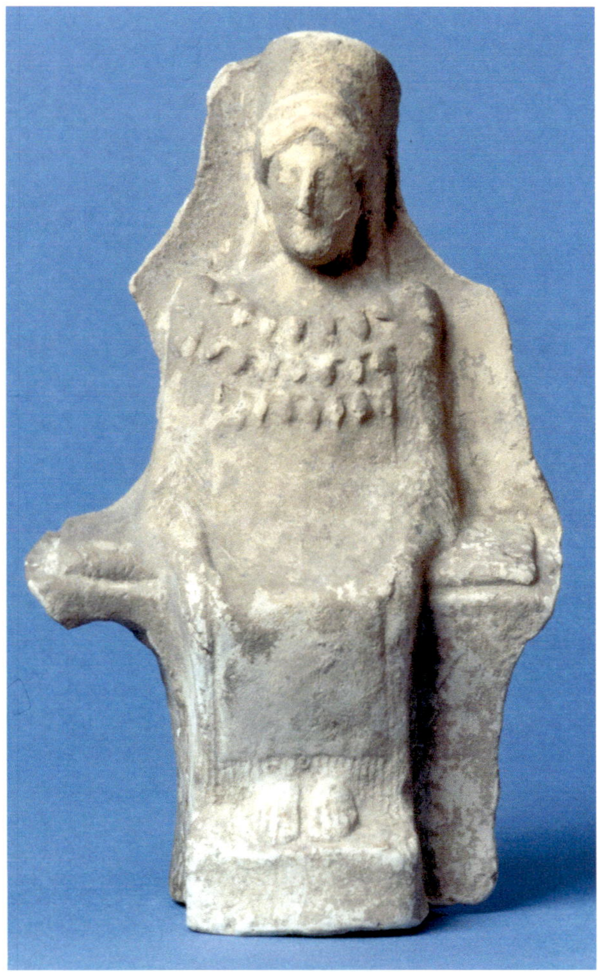

Figure 20: Inv. no. APM 1419 is probably from the same mould as 144. (Photo Allard Pierson Museum, Universiteit van Amsterdam).

in the middle. Along the sides of her neck, some hair, undefined, hanging down. The pendant on the connection between these two parts of the hair suggests an earring. She wears a tall straight polos with a rim just above the hair. She wears an apron over an undergarment, under which her feet stick out, placed on a footstool. The outline of her fibulae suggests that the double palmette was the original shape: it is oval, but long. Her pose is seated, with her arms close to her body, reaching her knees with her hand. She sits on a wide upwards-curving bench with a cushion on it. An extra rim outlines the statuette from the bench up to the polos. Though very indistinct, the v-shape of her sleeves, just below the elbow are visible. She wears multiple pendants on the chest in three rows. On the upper two cords, hanging down from the fibulae are seven ovoid, some more pointed, pendants. On the third cord, there are eight slightly more elongated and pointed pendants.

‣ ***Comparable objects:*** No.**142-144** and **146-151** are from the same mould series. See **142**.

No.146

‣ ***Museum and Inventory number:*** Mus. Agrigento S283

‣ ***Findspot and context:*** City Sanctuary

‣ ***Publications:*** -

‣ ***Dimensions in cm:*** h.19.5

‣ ***Material:*** terracotta

‣ ***Techniques:*** Front moulded. The clay for the head has been pressed into the mould separately. Clay on hair and polos scratched before figurine was fired. Handmade bench: down front part.

‣ ***Colour:*** Very pale Brown 10 YR 7.4

‣ ***Date:*** The third decade of the 5th century BCE

‣ ***Workshop:*** Separate face moulded

‣ ***Typology:*** Outlined-throne model: with rim, 'old face': 3b

‣ ***Short description:*** Nearly complete figurine. Part of base broken off. Enthroned female figurine. She has an elongated oval face. The nose is quite large. Her mouth is small, very indistinct. The eyes, though indistinct, are large. Around her forehead, she has a thick fringe of hair,

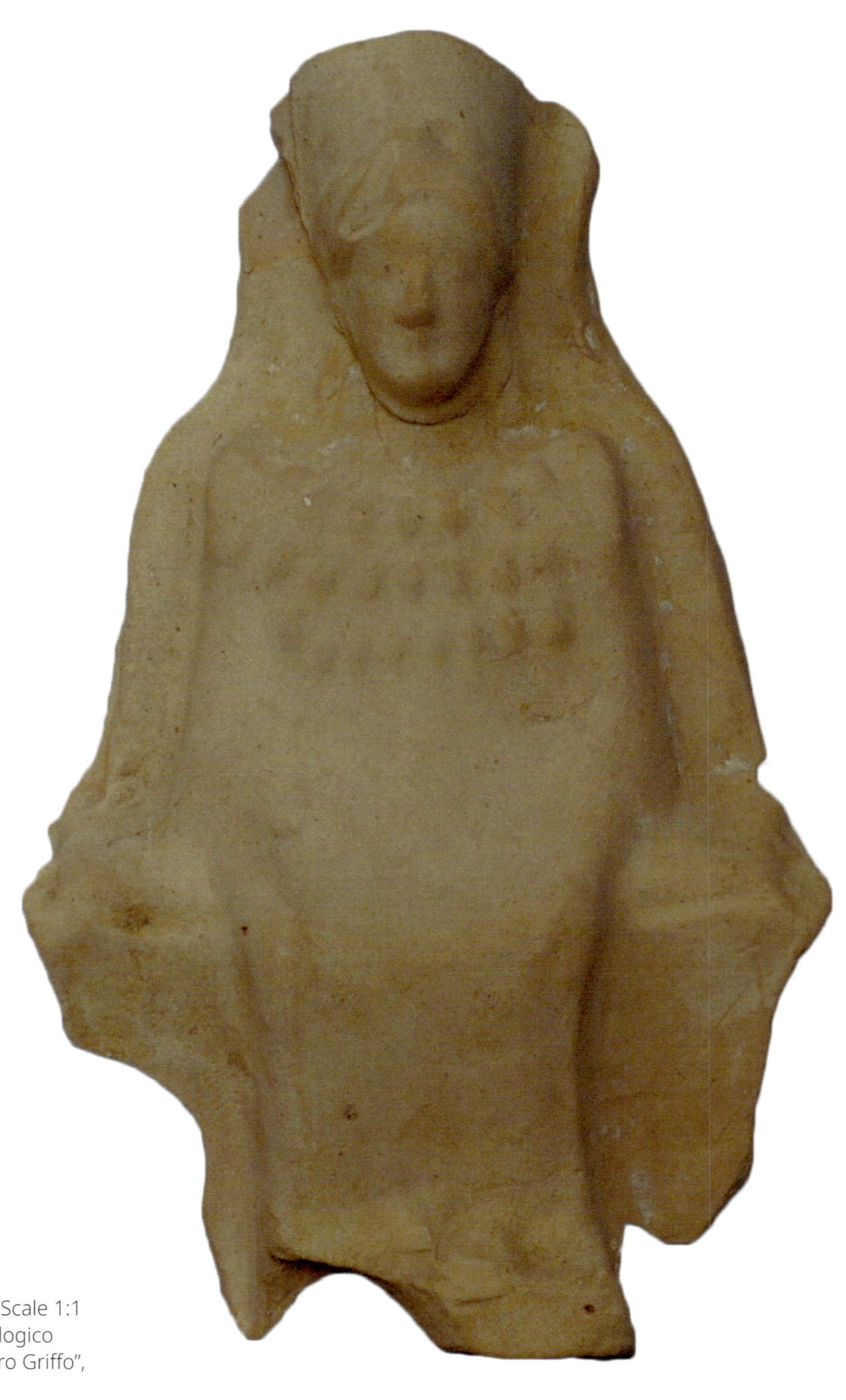

No. 146; Front, Scale 1:1 (Museo Archeologico Regionale "Pietro Griffo", Agrigento).

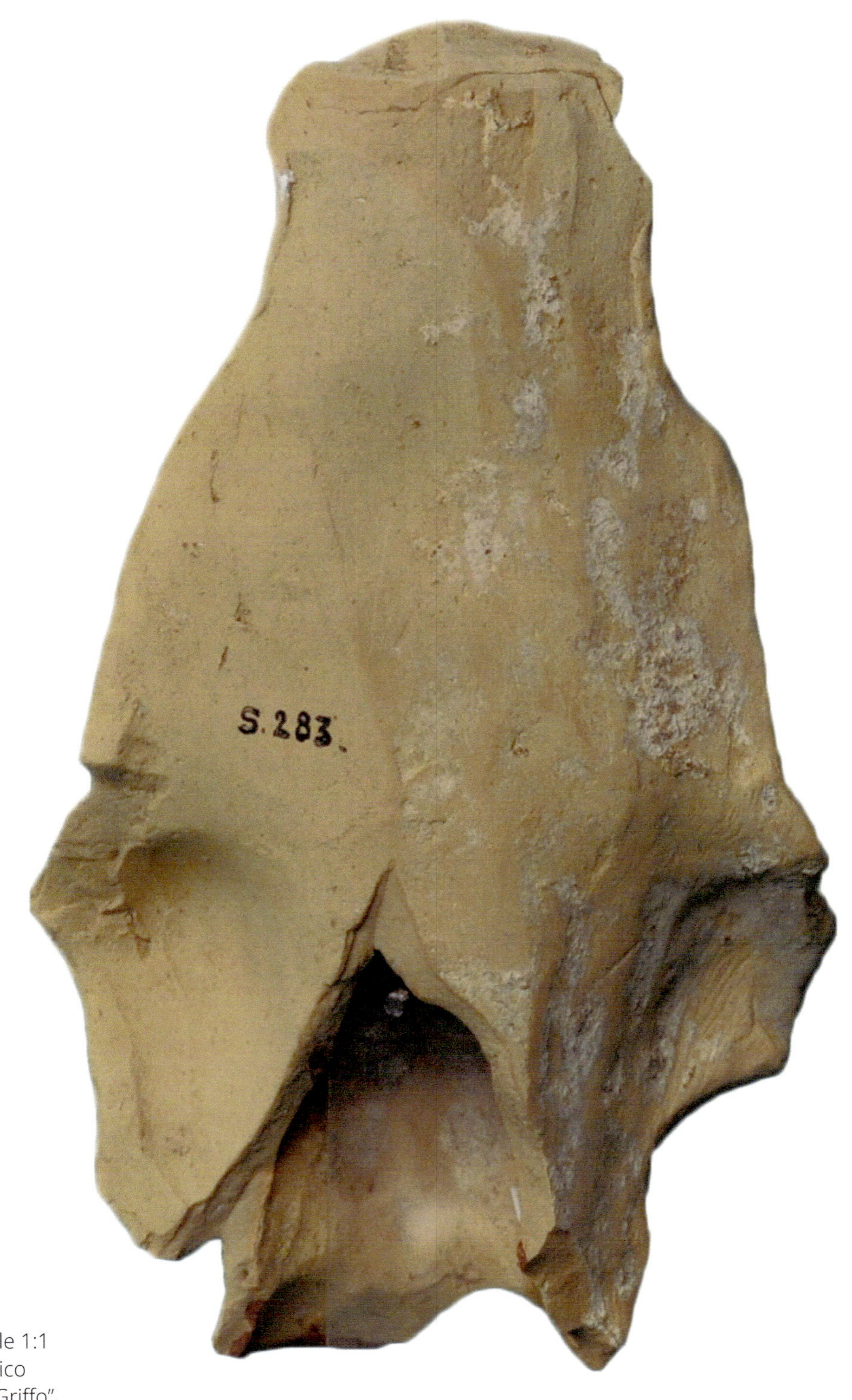

No. 146; Back, Scale 1:1 (Museo Archeologico Regionale "Pietro Griffo", Agrigento).

which is undefined or just too indistinct to see the details. She wears a sizeable polos, slightly flaring to the top with a rim just above the hair. She wears an apron over an undergarment, under which her feet stick out, placed on a small podium. The outline of her fibulae suggests that the double palmette was the original shape. Her pose is seated, with her arms close to her body, reaching her knees with her hand. She sits on a wide bench with a cushion on it. An extra rim outlines the statuette from the chair up to the polos. Though very indistinct, the v-shape of her sleeves, just below the elbow, and possibly bracelets, are visible. She wears multiple pendants on the chest in three rows. On the upper two cords, hanging down from the fibulae, are seven ovoids, and some more pointed, pendants. On the third cord, there are eight slightly more elongated and pointed pendants.

‣ *Comparable objects:* **142**-**145** and **147**-**151** are from the same mould series. See **142**.

This figurine, with its large rim, is comparable with a figurine from Selinous: 19634 and 18373 R 2000 US003, storage room Selinous: Terrakotten II. On first sight, it seems from the same mould series, but it has large ears. In addition, typical for Selinuntine figurines, a small round opening in the back. The body might be from the same mould series (fig.21).

Another figurine from Selinous, Mus. Palermo: Inv. no.5873, nearly complete h.18.8cm is comparable, but too weathered to see the details. Poma 2009, p.236, no.27. This is a very extensive mould series in Selinous, with several variants and hundreds of figurines, originally from Akragas: Type B XV. Dewailly 1992, p.84-101.

No.147

‣ *Museum and Inventory number:* Mus. Agrigento S896

‣ *Findspot and context:* City Sanctuary

‣ *Publications:* Albertocchi 2004, p.25, no.105

‣ *Dimensions in cm:* h.18.7

‣ *Material:* Terracotta. Shell fragments on the front of the polos and (with imprint) on the top of the polos, on the lower right arm and with imprint on the left of the footstool.

‣ *Techniques:* Front moulded, overlapping the rim. There is a protruding line from the right side of the throne over the arm and the lap, which might indicate a crack in the mould. A sharp tool was used to rework sides and back. On the back, some incised straight lines.

‣ *Colour:* Very pale brown 10 YR 8/4

‣ *Date:* The third decade of the 5th century BCE

‣ *Workshop:* Separate face moulded

‣ *Typology:* Outlined-throne model: with rim, 'old face': 3b

‣ *Short description:* Complete figurine. Part of knee chipped off. Enthroned female figurine. Worn mould, details have faded. She has an oval chubby face, with pronounced cheeks and chin. The nose is quite large, with a rounded tip. Her lips are thick. Eyes are not very clear. Around her forehead, she has a smooth fringe of hair, divided in the middle. Along the sides of her neck, some hair, undefined, hangs down. She wears a tall straight polos with a rim just above the hair. She wears an apron over an undergarment, under which her feet, roughly shaped, stick out, placed on a thin podium. Oval small fibulae. Her pose is seated, with her arms close to her body, reaching her knees with her hand. She sits on a wide upwards-curving bench with a cushion on it. An extra rim outlines the statuette from the bench up to the polos. Her sleeves, reaching to just below the elbow, are visible. She wears multiple pendants on the chest in three rows. On the upper two cords, hanging down from the fibulae are seven ovoid, some more pointed, pendants. On the third cord, there are eight slightly more elongated and pointed pendants. Sides are cut off with a sharp tool, next to the round rim of the outline. The clay is rounded on the edge of the rim, as if it was part of the mould. The figurine itself, but not the sides of the throne are placed on a thin podium.

‣ *Comparable objects:* **142**-**146** and **148**-**151** are from the same mould series. See **142**.

The protruding line could possibly indicate that **143** is from a parallel mould. See **143**.

No.148

‣ *Museum and Inventory number:* Mus. Agrigento S895

‣ *Findspot and context:* City Sanctuary

‣ *Publications:* Albertocchi 2004, p.24, no.104

‣ *Dimensions in cm:* h.18.4

‣ *Material:* Terracotta. Several instances of lime-spalling.

‣ *Techniques:* Front moulded. Fine vertical lines on the back could indicate the clay was rolled with a stick. The rim ('necklaces') in the neck mark the lines where a new face has been added. The parts were not completely adjusted in height. The bench on the right side has been pressed into later than the arm. The 'seam' is well visible.

‣ *Colour:* Reddish-yellow 5 YR 7/6

‣ *Date:* The third decade of the 5th century BCE

‣ *Workshop:* Separate face moulded

‣ *Typology:* Outlined-throne model: with rim, 'old face': 3b

‣ *Short description:* Nearly complete figurine. Many cracks. Worn mould. Enthroned female figurine. She has an elongated oval face. The nose is quite large. Her lips are thick, and the mouth is horizontal and small, not smiling. The eyes, though indistinct, are large. Her chin is protruding. Around her forehead, she has a thick smooth fringe of hair. Along the sides of her neck, some hair, undefined, hangs down. She wears a sizeable polos, slightly flaring to the top with a rim just above the hair. She wears an apron over an undergarment. She wears small oval fibulae, which are very indistinct. Her pose is seated, with her arms close to her body, reaching her knees with her hands. She sits on a wide upwards-curving bench with

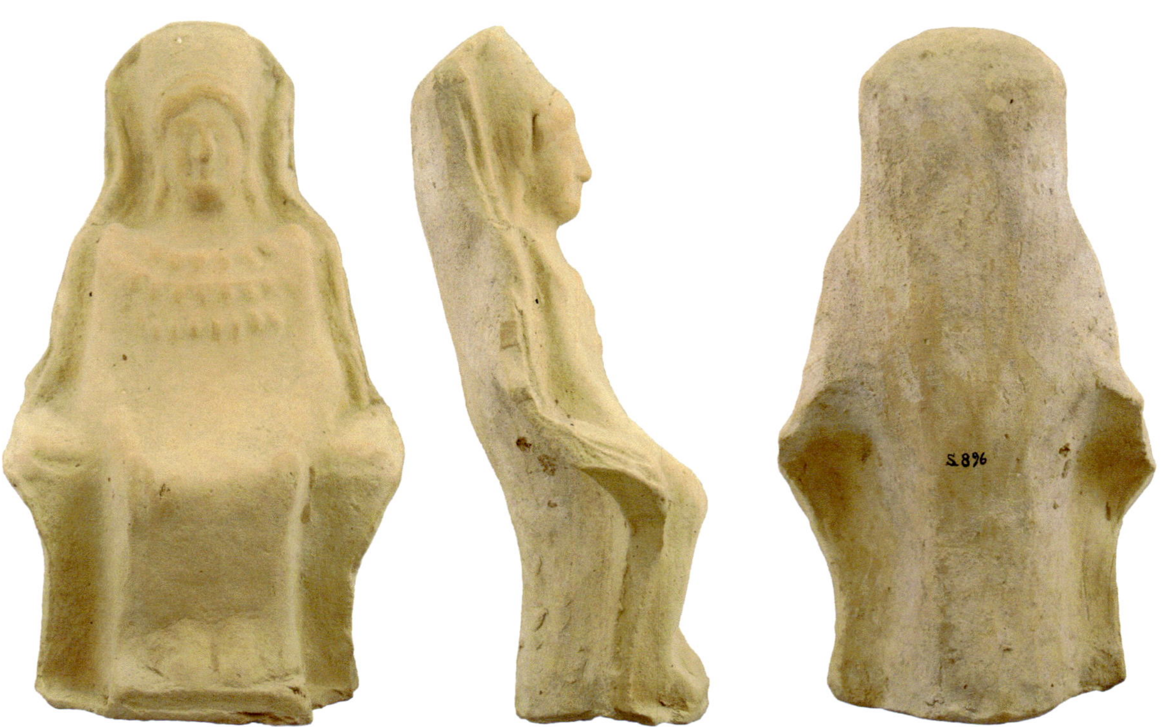

No. 147; Scale 1:2 (Museo Archeologico Regionale "Pietro Griffo", Agrigento).

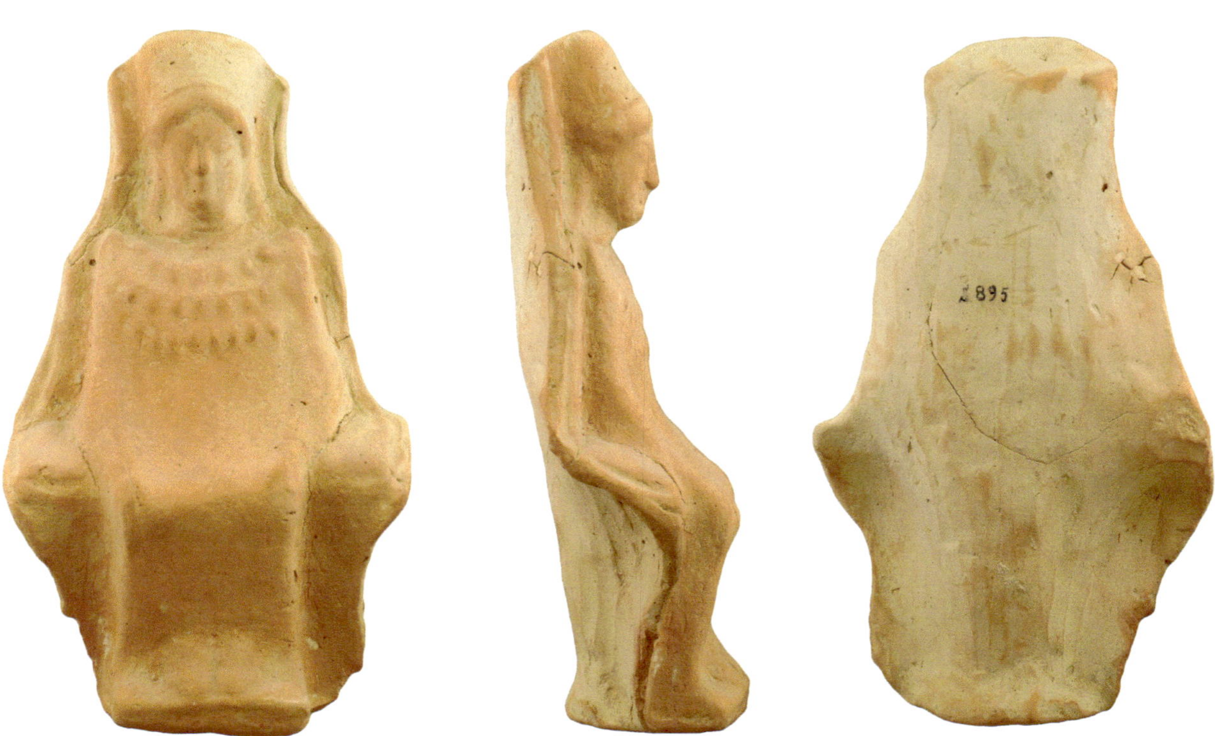

No. 148; Scale 1:2 (Museo Archeologico Regionale "Pietro Griffo", Agrigento).

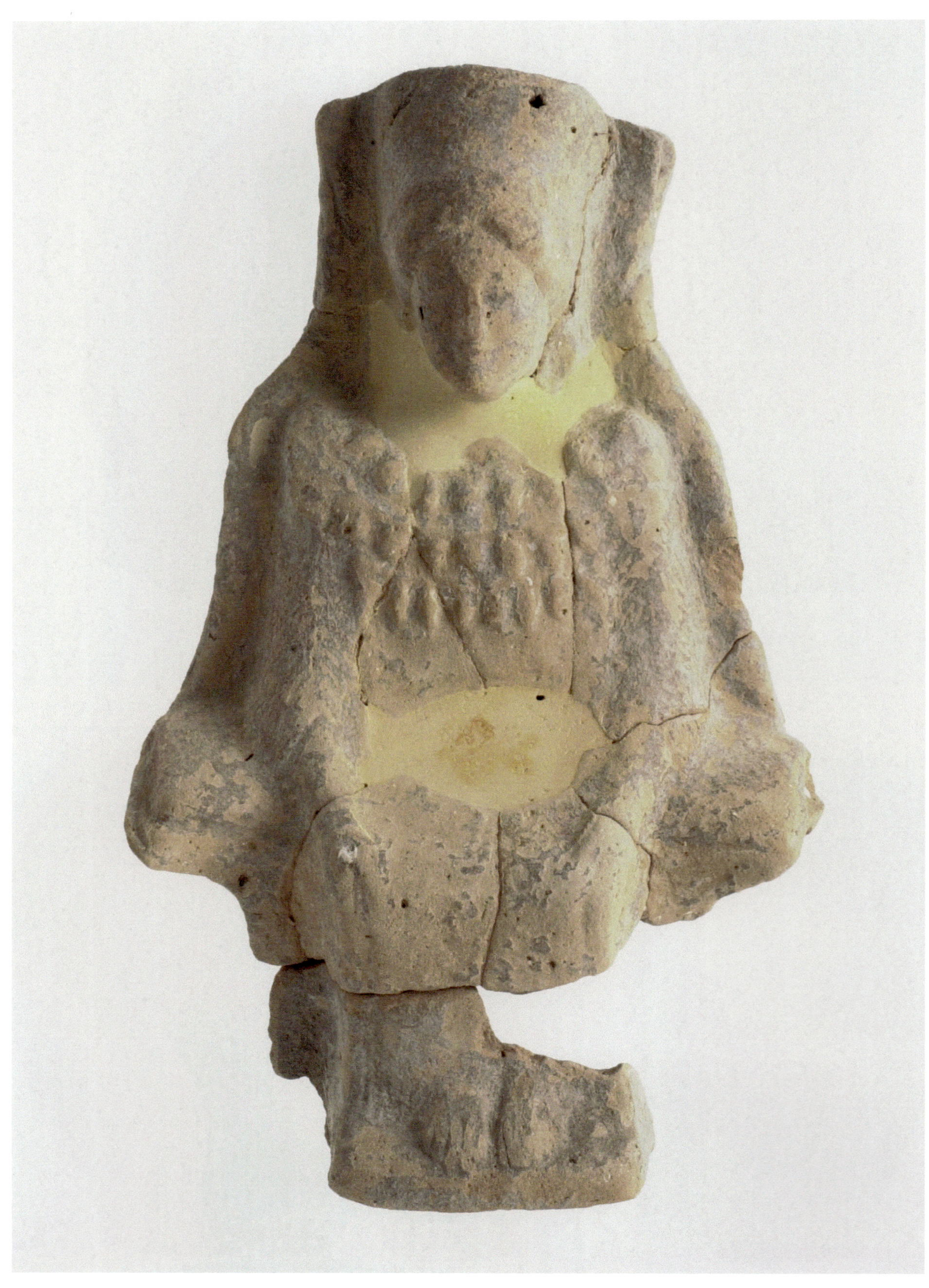

Figure 21: Selinuntine figurine with similar rim, Inv no. 19634 R 2000. (Photo Deutsches Archäologisches Institut, Rome).

a cushion on it. An extra rim outlines the statuette from the seat up to the polos. The sides are sometimes rounded, forming a second rim along the figurine, such as on the left side of the head. She wears multiple pendants on the chest in three rows. On the upper two cords, hanging down from the fibulae are seven ovoid, some more pointed, pendants. On the third cord, there are eight slightly more elongated and pointed pendants. The back has been smoothed with a sharp tool. The vertical cutting marks are visible.

‣ *Comparable objects:* **142-147** and **149-151** are from the same mould series. See **142**.

The clay colour, without slip, is comparable to **150** and **151**.

No.149

‣ *Museum and Inventory number:* Mus. Agrigento S893

‣ *Findspot and context:* City Sanctuary

‣ *Publications:* Albertocchi 2004, p.25, no.111

‣ *Dimensions in cm:* h.18.1

‣ *Material:* Terracotta.

‣ *Techniques:* Front moulded. Lighter coloured slip layer. Handmade bench, down front part.

‣ *Colour:* Pink 7.5 YR 7/4

‣ *Date:* The third decade of the 5th century BCE

‣ *Workshop:* Separate face moulded

‣ *Typology:* Outlined-throne model: with rim, 'new face': 3b

‣ *Short description:* Nearly complete figurine. Infill on right foot. Enthroned female figurine. She has an elongated oval face. The nose is quite large. Her lips are thick, and the mouth is horizontal, not smiling. The eyes are large. Around her forehead, she has a thick fringe of hair in long thin bulbs, placed vertically. Along the sides of her neck, some hair, undefined, hangs down. She wears a sizeable polos, slightly flaring to the top with a rim just above the hair. She wears an apron over an undergarment, under which her feet stick out, placed on a low podium. The outline of her fibulae suggests that the double palmette was the original shape. Her pose is seated, with her arms close to her body, reaching her knees with her hands. She sits on a wide upwards-curving bench with a cushion on it. A flat back, curving with the body, outlines the statuette from chair up to the polos. Though very indistinct, the v-shape of her sleeves, just below the elbow and possibly bracelets are visible. She wears multiple pendants on the chest in three rows. On the upper two cords, hanging down from the fibulae are seven ovoid, some more pointed, pendants. On the third cord, there are eight slightly more elongated and pointed pendants.

‣ *Comparable objects:* No.**142-148** and **150-151** are from the same mould series. See **142**.

Very similar to **150** and **151**. The first is likely from the same mould and is similar in clay also. Both have a hole in the back, while **149** has not.

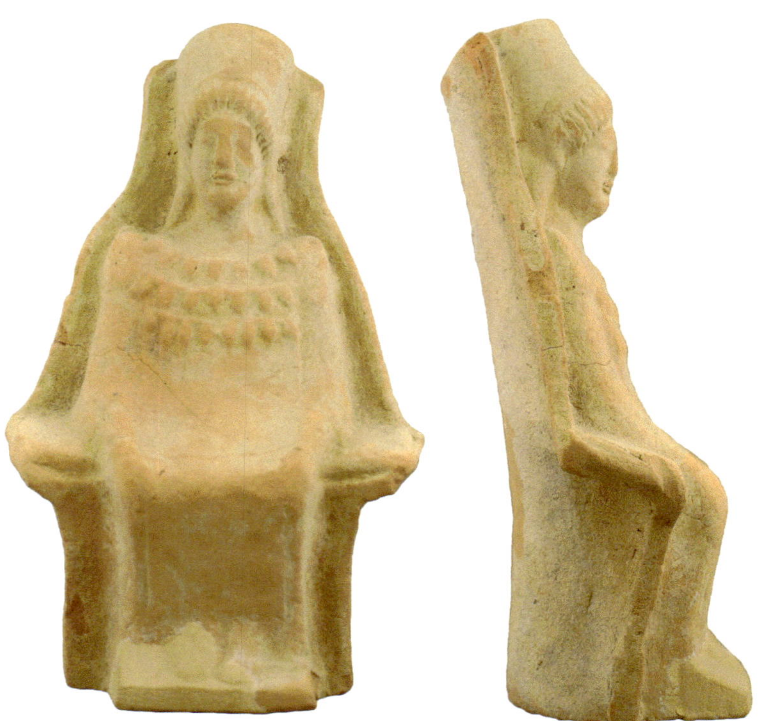

No. 149; Scale 1:2 (Museo Archeologico Regionale "Pietro Griffo", Agrigento).

No.150

‣ *Museum and Inventory number:* Mus. Agrigento S281

‣ *Findspot and context:* City Sanctuary

‣ *Publications:* Albertocchi 2004, p.25, no.109

‣ *Dimensions in cm:* h.19.8

‣ *Material:* Terracotta. Lighter colour slip layer

‣ *Techniques:* Front moulded. Lighter coloured slip layer. Vent hole in the back.

‣ *Colour:* Very pale brown 10 YR 8/4

‣ *Date:* The third decade of the 5th century BCE

‣ *Workshop:* Separate face moulded

‣ *Typology:* Outlined-throne model: with rim, 'new face': 3b

‣ *Short description:* Nearly complete figurine. Part of feet and throne on the left side, outline-rim and throne on the left side broken off. Enthroned female figurine. She has an elongated oval face. The nose is quite long and sharp. Her lips are thick, in particular the upper one, and the mouth is horizontal, not smiling. The eyes, though indistinct, are large. Around her forehead, she has a thick fringe of hair in long thin bulbs, placed vertically. Along the sides of her neck, some hair, undefined, hangs down. She wears a sizeable polos, slightly flaring to the top with a rim just above the hair. She wears an apron over an undergarment. She wears small oval fibulae. Her pose is seated, with her arms close to her body, reaching her knees with her hand. She sits on a wide upwards-curving bench with a cushion on it. A flat back, rounded and triangular, outlines the statuette from the chair up to the polos. Though very indistinct, the v-shape of her sleeves, just below the elbow, and possibly bracelets, are visible. She wears multiple pendants on the chest in three rows. On the upper two cords, hanging down from the fibulae are seven ovoid, some more pointed, pendants. On the third cord, there are eight slightly more elongated and pointed pendants. The back is rounded and has a small hole in the middle.

‣ *Comparable objects:* **142-149** and **151** are from the same mould series and from the same mould as **151**. See **142**. The opening in the back is similar to **151**. The clay colour, without slip, is comparable to **148**.

No.151

‣ *Museum and Inventory number:* Mus. Agrigento S894

‣ *Findspot and context:* City Sanctuary

‣ *Publications:* Albertocchi 2004, p.25, no.112

‣ *Dimensions in cm:* h.19.8

‣ *Material:* Terracotta. In the neck, on the polos, lap and back, some slip or white paint is left.

‣ *Techniques:* Front moulded. Fine vertical lines on the back. Opening in the back.

‣ *Colour:* Reddish-yellow 5 YR 6/8

‣ *Date:* The third decade of the 5th century BCE

‣ *Workshop:* Separate face moulded

‣ *Typology:* Outlined-throne model: with rim, 'new face': 3b

‣ *Short description:* Nearly complete figurine. Infill on the feet. Very smoothed. Enthroned female figurine. She has an elongated oval face. The nose is quite large. Her lips are thick, and the mouth is horizontal, not smiling. The eyes, though indistinct, are large. Around her forehead, she has a thick fringe of hair in long thin bulbs, placed vertically. Along the sides of her neck, some hair, undefined, hangs down. She wears a sizeable polos, slightly flaring to the top with a rim just above the hair. She wears an apron over an undergarment. She wears small oval fibulae. Her pose is seated, with her arms close to her body, reaching her knees with her hand. She sits on a wide upwards-curving bench with a cushion on it. A flat triangular backrest outlines the statuette from chair up to the polos. Though very indistinct, the v-shape of her sleeves, just below the elbow, and possibly bracelets, are visible. She wears multiple pendants in three rows on the chest. On the upper two cords, hanging down from the fibulae, are seven ovoid, some more pointed, pendants. On the third cord, there are eight slightly more elongated and pointed pendants.

‣ *Comparable objects:* **142-150** are from the same mould series and from the same mould as **150**. See **142**. The opening in the back is similar to **150**. The clay colour, without slip, is comparable to **148**.

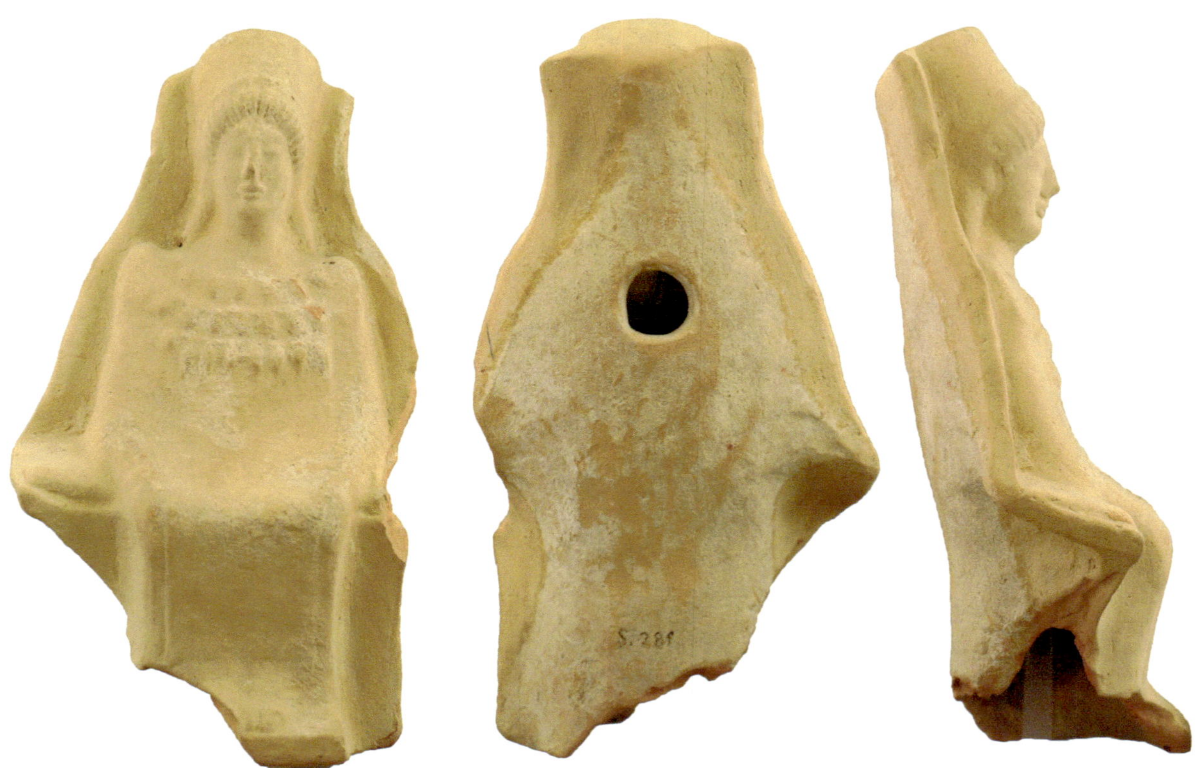

No. 150; Scale 1:2 (Museo Archeologico Regionale "Pietro Griffo", Agrigento).

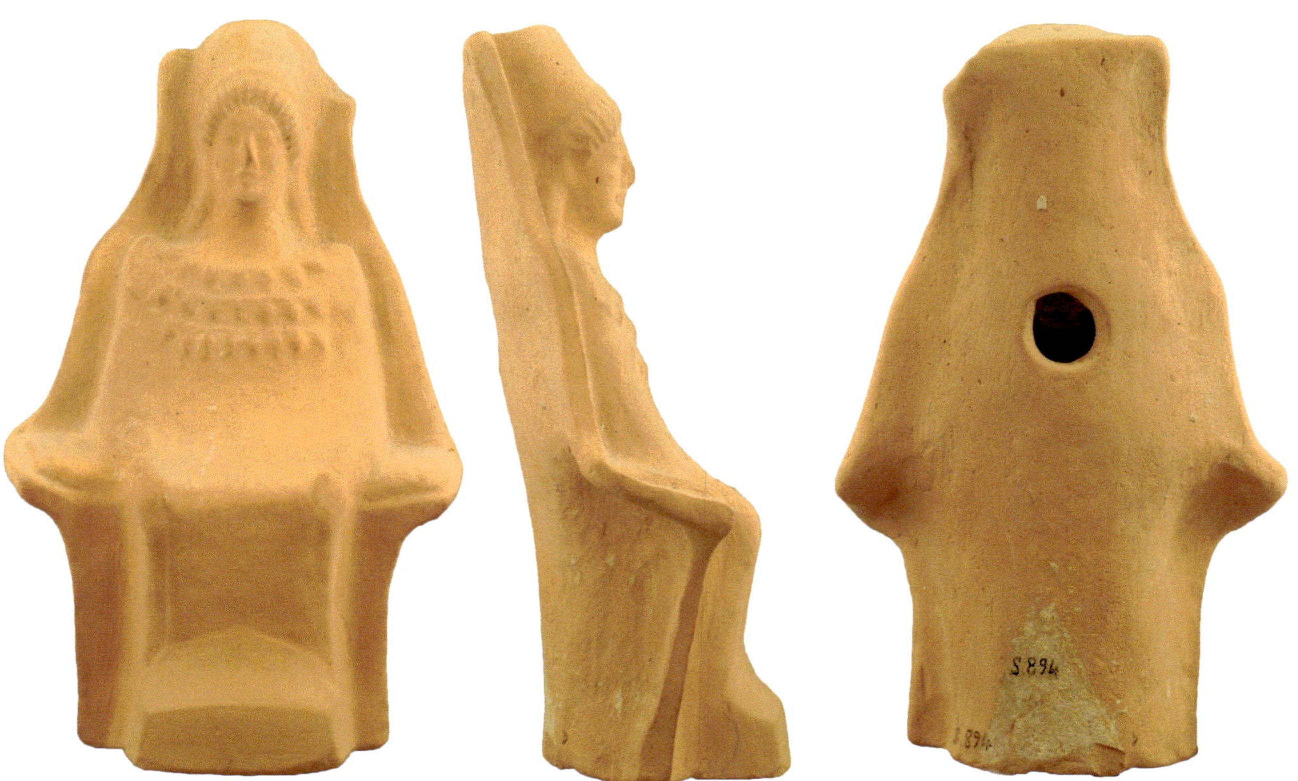

No. 151; Scale 1:2 (Museo Archeologico Regionale "Pietro Griffo", Agrigento).

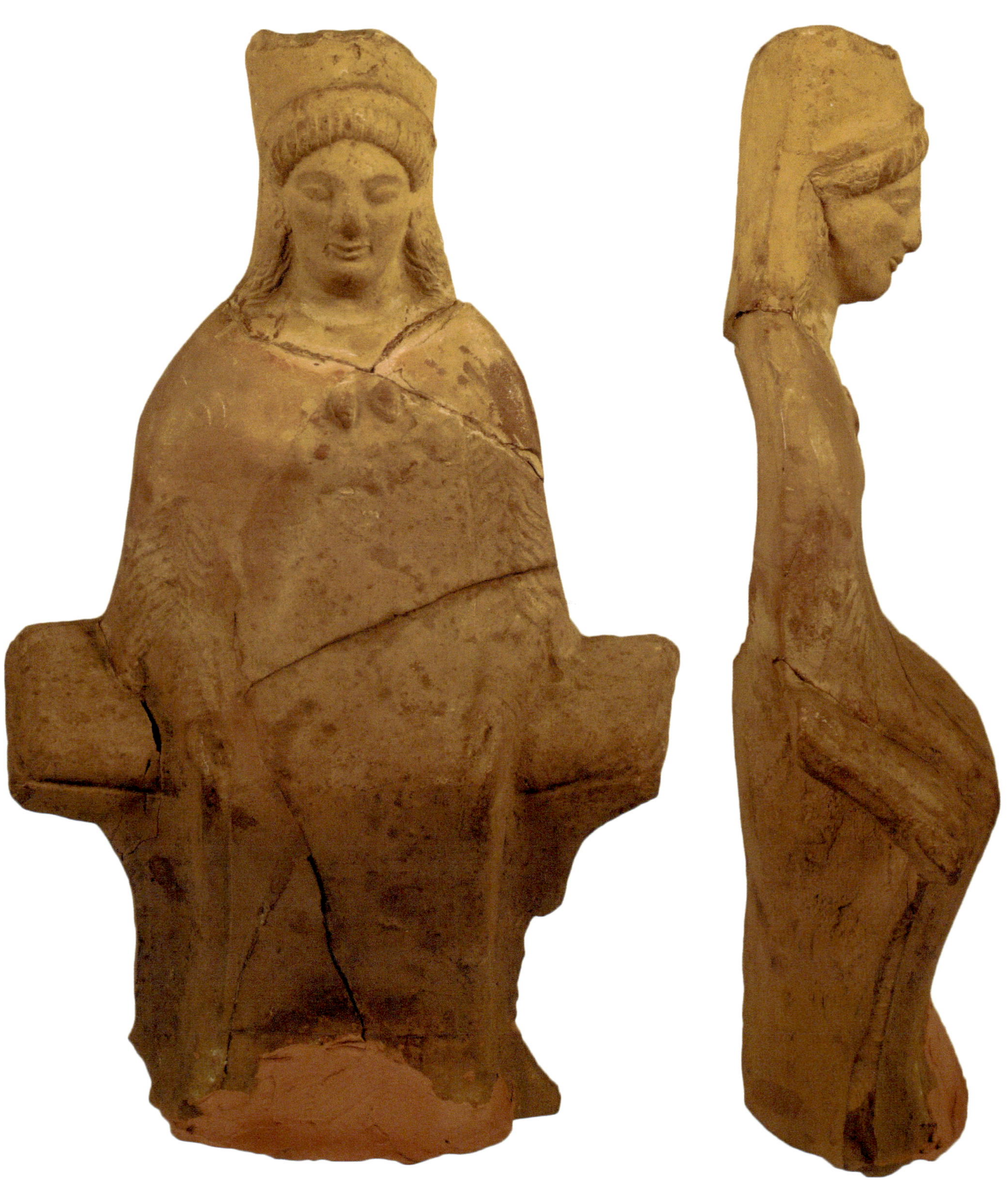

No. 152; Scale 1:1½ (Staatlichen Antikensammlungen München).

No.152

‣ *Museum and Inventory number:* Mus. Munich 6801
‣ *Findspot and context:* Agrigento
‣ *Publications:* Hamdorf 2014, p.97 C 214
‣ *Dimensions in cm:* h.26.2
‣ *Material:* Terracotta.
‣ *Techniques:* Front moulded. Smoothed inside front mould.
‣ *Colour:* Very pale brown 10 YR 7/3
‣ *Date:* The third decade of the 5th century BCE
‣ *Workshop:* Unknown
‣ *Typology:* Naturalistic-hair-group: 3b
‣ *Short description:* Thin figurine, heavily restored. Head and body glued together. The object is broken in a very strange way below the opening on the back. Sherds are glued together and there is infill on the right shoulder and feet.

The oval face of this female figurine is very sharp. The chin is small. Her eyes are slightly slanted, diagonally placed and a bit bulging. The sharp edge of her eyebrows arches high above her eyes. Her nose is pronounced and has a wide bridge and a thick tip. Her mouth curves up slightly and has sharp thin lips. The endings and the connection to the chin are deeper. The hair is placed in a band in long sharp bulbs on the forehead. Hair on the sides is reworked with thin messy lines. She wears a tall polos with a thick rim. She seems to wear a necklace, but it is scratched and smoothed away. This band could have marked the upper seam of her chiton also. Folds are, however, not visible. She is seated upright on a wide bench with a cushion. The diagonal seat of this bench makes her position half seated and leaning. Her upper body runs down diagonally and the bend at the height of the bench indicates her knees. From there, the lower part of the body is straight. Her arms are loosely attached to her body and with her hand, the thumb separated, she reaches the bend in her legs. She wears a chiton with sleeves to halfway down her lower arms that display fine folds in a regular manner, with a seam in the middle. She wears an apron also, of which the edges are visible on the lower part of her body. She wears two rows with pendants on her chest, of which the second is very indistinct. The bands themselves or the attachment is not indicated. On the first, there are two round pointed shapes visible, like droplets with the point down or seeds. On the second row, there is, in the middle, a crescent with the points down and on each side two small discs. Sides straightened, and rounded back with firing hole. It is as if the head and body do not belong together. The head is much sharper. The smooth left shoulder does not fit the finely detailed left arm. It might be that the coroplast decided to combine these two parts. The 'necklace', which is lower than the more usually tight necklace with one pendant, could be an indication of that also. The shoulder might have been used for attachment of the two parts and lost its details, because of the reworking and smoothing afterwards.
‣ *Comparable objects:* **153** is probably from the same mould series, one generation later.

Iconographic characteristics such as the dress and technical aspects such as the large firing hole on the back are reminiscent of the outlined-throne model. The different earrings, thick rim on the polos, the wavy hair along the sides of the short neck are all indications of changes to that iconographic scheme. The indistinctness of the second cord might indicate that this part is 'borrowed', and that another mould was used for this part. Albertocchi considers both groups to belong to the Type A VIII, which brings the total of this type from Agrigento to 17 figurines, including two 'other versions.' Albertocchi 2004, p.24-7. A similar figurine is probably from the same mould but reworked. A third row has been added below the other two; the hands are reworked to be clearer; the chair has been made differently; the size has also been increased by adding a podium and folds in the chiton next to the feet. These all indicate a later date. Headless, h.25.7cm. Allegro 1972, p.46 F, II, tav.XXIII.1. Inv. no.H71.728. The earrings are relatively small, compared with other figurines wearing the same type of earrings. They are also slightly different in shape: the ring is stretched vertically. On **152**, the left one is more visible, on **153**, the right one.

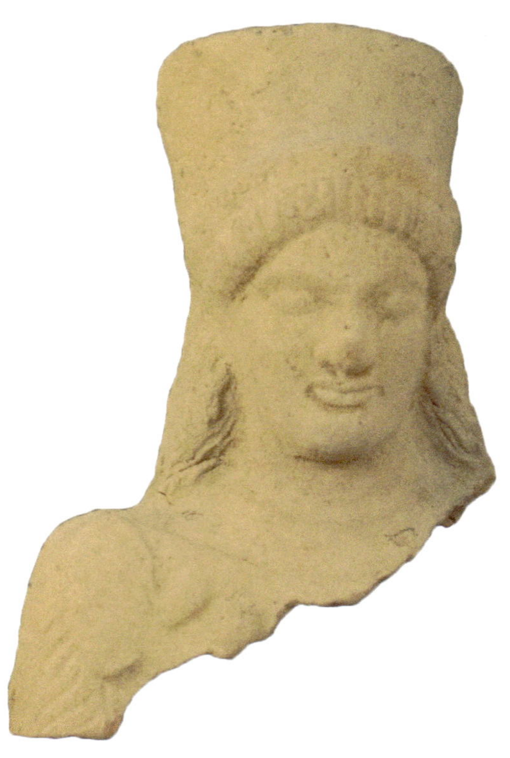
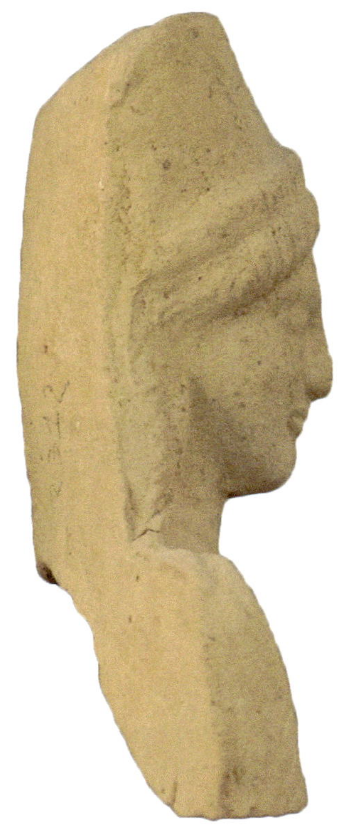

No. 153; Scale 1:2 (Museo Archeologico Regionale "Pietro Griffo", Agrigento).

No. 153

- ***Museum and Inventory number:*** Mus. Agrigento 15.1354 (2312)
- ***Findspot and context:*** West Archaic sanctuary underlying the bouleuterion
- ***Publications:*** Albertocchi 2004, p.25, no.114
- ***Dimensions in cm:*** h.9.5
- ***Material:*** Terracotta.
- ***Techniques:*** Front moulded. Head is probably separately moulded, creating a 'necklace'.
- ***Colour:*** Pink 7.5 YR 7/4
- ***Date:*** The third decade of the 5th century BCE
- ***Workshop:*** Unknown
- ***Typology:*** Naturalistic-hair-group: 3b

Short description: Upper part with chest and right shoulder of a figurine. Female figurine. She has a fleshy oval face with a sizeable nose. Her mouth is wide and slightly curving up, but not smiling. Around her forehead, she has a fringe of hair, below the polos in thin vertical bulbs. Along the sides of her neck, some hair with thin irregular waves hangs down. In front of her hair, relatively small boat-shaped earrings are hanging down: the ring is more stretched, not completely round with oval pendants on it. She wears a tall slightly flaring polos, with a thick rim just above the hair. She wears a thicker dress over an undergarment. The outer hem of this chiton is visible in the neck and the sleeve has wavy folds. She has a thick and indistinct necklace(?), which could have been caused by separate moulding of the head. She wears oval fibulae. One of the droplet-shaped pectoral pendants is visible. It is ovoid but with a slightly pointed bottom. Smoothed back. Straightened with a tool, causing clay accumulation on the edge.

- ***Comparable objects:*** Possibly from the same mould series as **152**. See **152**.

Type L: other polos-wearing heads (154-170)

This group contains only heads in a variety of sizes and with different iconography.

No.154

- *Museum and Inventory number:* Mus. Agrigento S112
- *Findspot and context:* Unknown
- *Publications:* Marconi 1933, tav.X.3
- *Dimensions in cm:* h.10.8
- *Material:* Terracotta. Very large, dark red inclusion on the top right of the back, shell fragment next to it. Small colour differences.
- *Techniques:* Front moulded. Above the rim of the polos scratches from a sharp tool.
- *Colour:* Pink 7.5 YR 7/3
- *Date:* Last quarter of the sixth century BCE
- *Workshop:* Unknown
- *Typology:* Polos-wearing head: 2a
- *Short description:* Head of a figurine. Face tapering towards the chin. Clearly marked mouth with a thicker upper lip, slightly curving but not completely smiling. Very large undefined eyes under low arching eyebrows. A thin straight nose and slightly bulging cheeks. Triangular forehead. Thick fringe of hair in vertical bulbs, smaller towards the middle. On the endings, the outline of an ear. Hair smooth next to the neck. Tall straight polos with a thick and edged rim.
- *Comparable objects:* A head from the same mould series is half the size and clearly deformed through the generations: Mus. Agrigento Inv. no.AG 1177, h.5.5cm, Museo "Griffo", De Miro 2000, p.132, no.55, tav.XCIV.
- *Other notes:* Hole drilled on the top, not all the way through. Inside filled with plaster. These might have been done in order to exhibit the object on a stand.

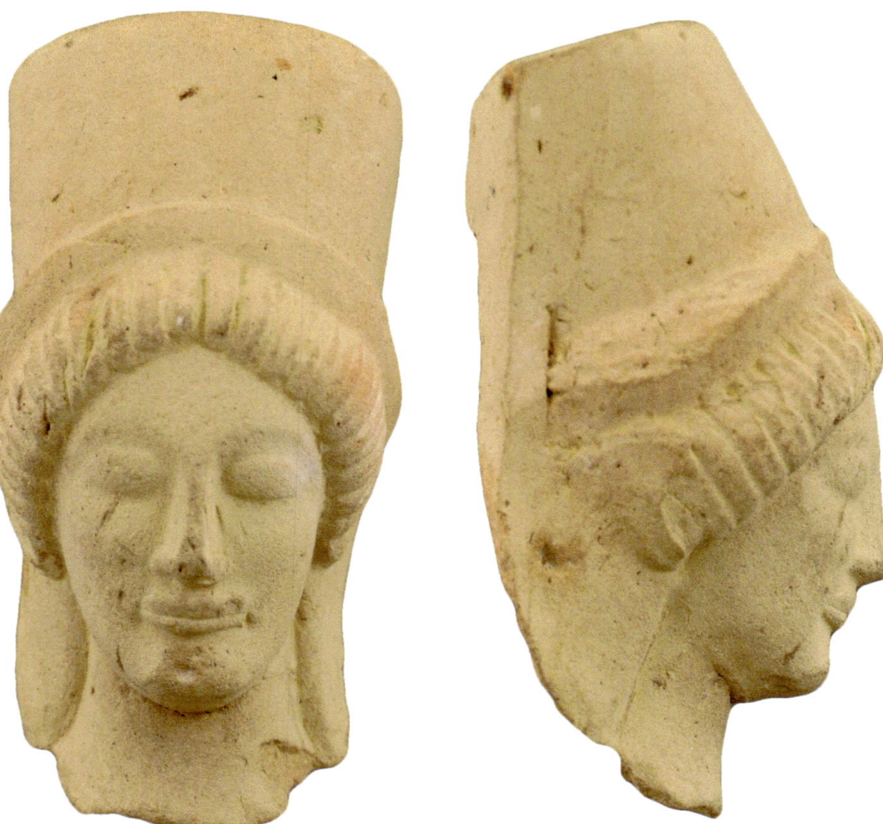

No. 154; Scale 1:1 (Museo Archeologico Regionale "Pietro Griffo", Agrigento).

No.155

‣ *Museum and Inventory number:* Mus. Agrigento S109
‣ *Findspot and context:* City Sanctuary
‣ *Publications:* Marconi 1933, tav.VIII.10
‣ *Dimensions in cm:* h.8.4
‣ *Material:* Terracotta. Shell fragment in the back. Several small holes.
‣ *Techniques:* Front moulded.
‣ *Colour:* Very pale brown 10 YR 7/4
‣ *Date:* Last quarter of the sixth to beginning of the fifth century BCE
‣ *Workshop:* Unknown
‣ *Typology:* Polos-wearing head: 2a
‣ *Short description:* Head of a figurine, back broken; in five fragments, restored. Rounded oval face with pronounced chin. Large undefined eyes under low arching eyebrows. Sizeable nose with thick tip. Smiling mouth with and dimples. High cheekbones. Triangular forehead. Thick round fringe of hair in vertical bulbs, larger towards the sides. Hair next to the neck with horizontal marks. Low straight polos with thin rim, just above the fringe.
‣ *Comparable objects:* **170** might be from the same mould series, one of two generations later.

Comparable to **95** in both facial features and iconographic scheme. Similar facial features to **156**.
‣ *Other notes:* The head has been damaged after Marconi's publication (Marconi 1933, tav.VIII.10).

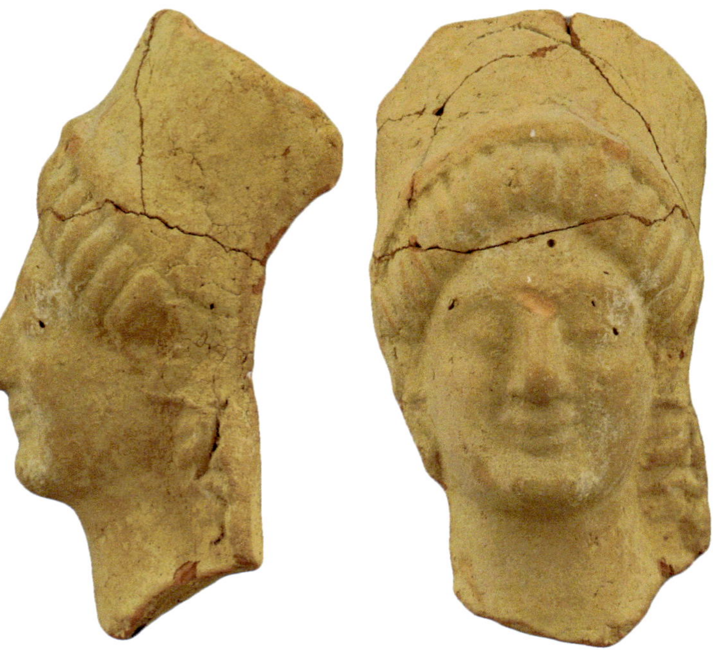

No. 155; Scale 1:1 (Museo Archeologico Regionale "Pietro Griffo", Agrigento).

No.156

‣ *Museum and Inventory number:* Mus. Agrigento C403
‣ *Findspot and context:* Akragas
‣ *Publications:* -
‣ *Dimensions in cm:* h.8.4
‣ *Material:* Terracotta. Lighter coloured slip layer.
‣ *Techniques:* Front moulded.
‣ *Colour:* Pink 5 YR 7/4
‣ *Date:* First quarter of the fifth century BCE
‣ *Workshop:* Unknown
‣ *Typology:* Polos-wearing head: 2a
‣ *Short description:* Head of a figurine. Oval face with pronounced cheeks and chin. Large eyes with eyelids and a narrow nose with a big tip. A small mouth with relatively thin lips and dimples on the ends. A fringe of wavy, scalloped hair in two rows on the forehead. The ear is placed in front of the part where the fringe ends. On the sides of the neck bulging hair. She wears a straight tall polos, with a small rim just on top of her fringe.
‣ *Comparable objects:* Probably from the same mould series as heads **157** and **158**, in three generations, possibly also of the same series as **159**, which would form the earliest generation and brings the total to four.
‣ *Other notes:* Glued to its stand.

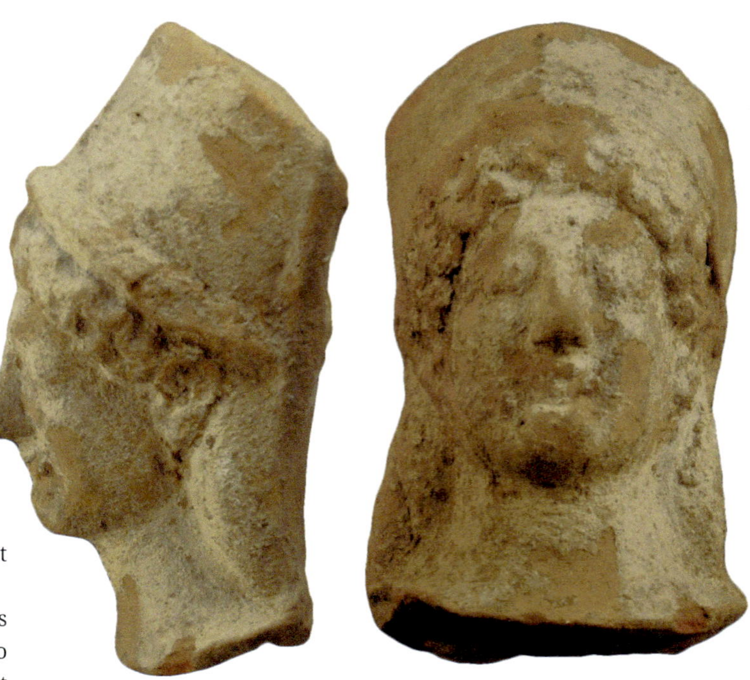

No. 156; Scale 1:1 (Museo Archeologico Regionale "Pietro Griffo", Agrigento).

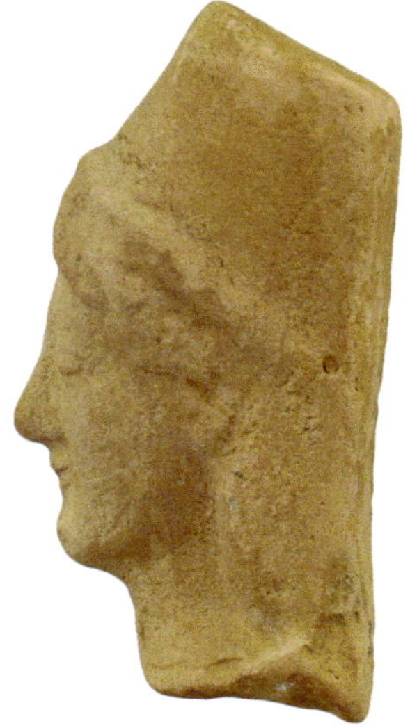
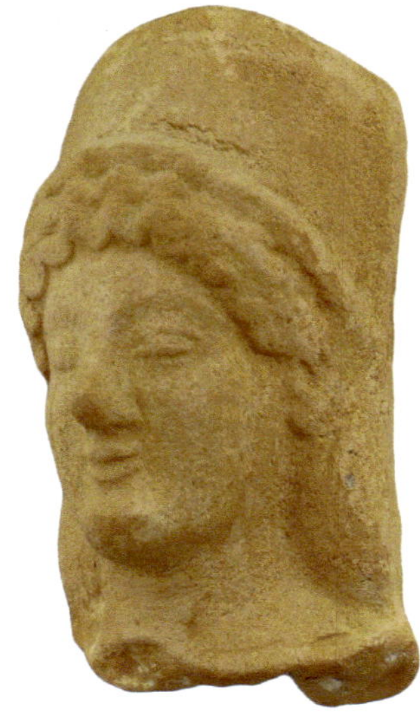
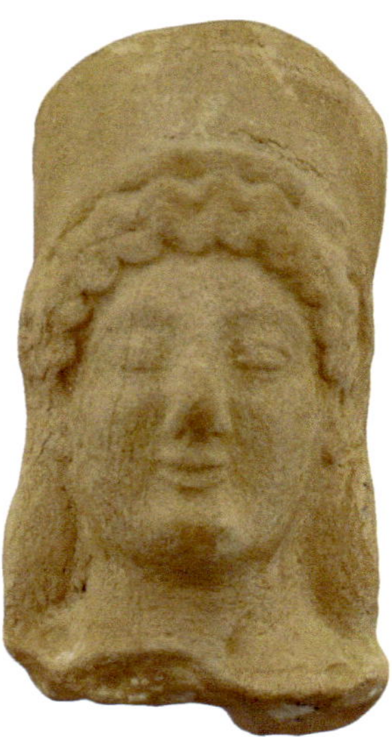

No. 157; Scale 1:1 (Museo Archeologico Regionale "Pietro Griffo", Agrigento).

No.157

- *Museum and Inventory number:* Mus. Agrigento S108
- *Findspot and context:* City Sanctuary
- *Publications:* Marconi 1933, tav.VIII.8
- *Dimensions in cm:* h.6.9
- *Material:* Terracotta. Lime-spalling.
- *Techniques:* Front moulded.
- *Colour:* Light yellowish brown 10 YR 6/4
- *Date:* First quarter of the fifth century BCE
- *Workshop:* Unknown
- *Typology:* Polos-wearing head: 2a
- *Short description:* Head of a figurine. Oval face with pronounced cheeks and chin. Large eyes with eyelids and a narrow nose with a big tip. A small mouth, not wider than the nose, with dimples on the ends. A fringe of wavy, scalloped hair in two rows on the forehead. The ear is placed in front of the part where the fringe ends. On the sides of the neck, bulging hair. She wears a straight tall polos, with a small rim just on top of her fringe.
- *Comparable objects:* Probably from the same mould series as heads **156** and **158**, in three generations, possibly also of the same series as **159**, which would form the earliest generation and brings the total to four. Possibly from the same mould series is a figurine: Mus. Agrigento Inv. no.AG 13406, head h.8.1cm, De Miro 2000, p.266, no.1703, tav.LXIX.

No.158

- *Museum and Inventory number:* Mus. Agrigento S382
- *Findspot and context:* City Sanctuary
- *Publications:* -
- *Dimensions in cm:* h.8.5
- *Material:* Terracotta. Lime-spalling.
- *Techniques:* Front moulded. The clay is impressed on the chin and the hair, probably coincidently. Small bullets of clay have become attached to the back.
- *Colour:* Pink 5 YR 7/4
- *Date:* First quarter of the fifth century BCE
- *Workshop:* Unknown
- *Typology:* Polos-wearing head: 2a
- *Short description:* Head of a figurine. Oval face with wide jaw. Large eyes with eyelids and sizeable but narrow nose. A small mouth. Wavy, scalloped hair in two rows on the forehead. On the sides of the neck, bulging hair with fine ver-tical lines. She has large ears of which the outline covers the connection between the two parts of the hair. She wears a polos, widening at the top and with a small rim just on top of the fringe.
- *Comparable objects:* Probably from the same mould series as heads **156** and **157**, in three generations, possibly also from the same series as **159**, which would form the earliest generation and brings the total to four.

No.159

- *Museum and Inventory number:* Mus. Agrigento S107
- *Findspot and context:* City Sanctuary
- *Publications:* Marconi 1933, tav.VIII.9
- *Dimensions in cm:* h.13.2
- *Material:* Terracotta
- *Techniques:* Front moulded.
- *Colour:* Very pale brown 10 YR 8/3
- *Date:* First quarter of the fifth century BCE
- *Workshop:* Unknown
- *Typology:* Polos-wearing head: 2a

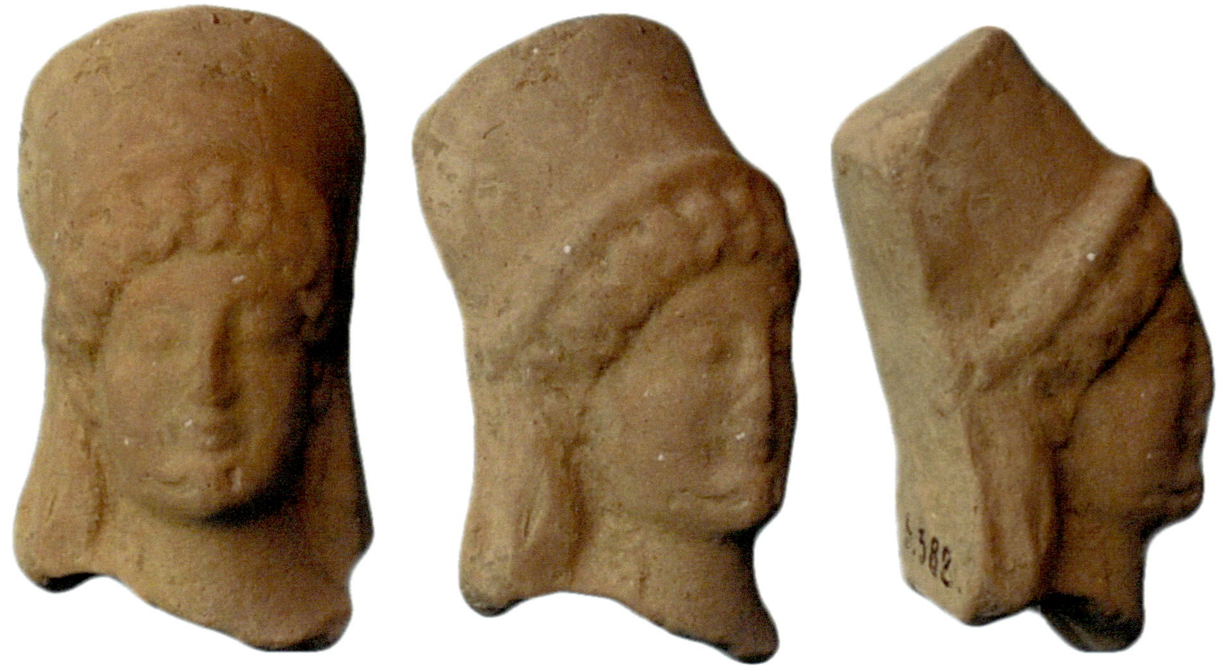

No. 158; Scale 1:1 (Museo Archeologico Regionale "Pietro Griffo", Agrigento).

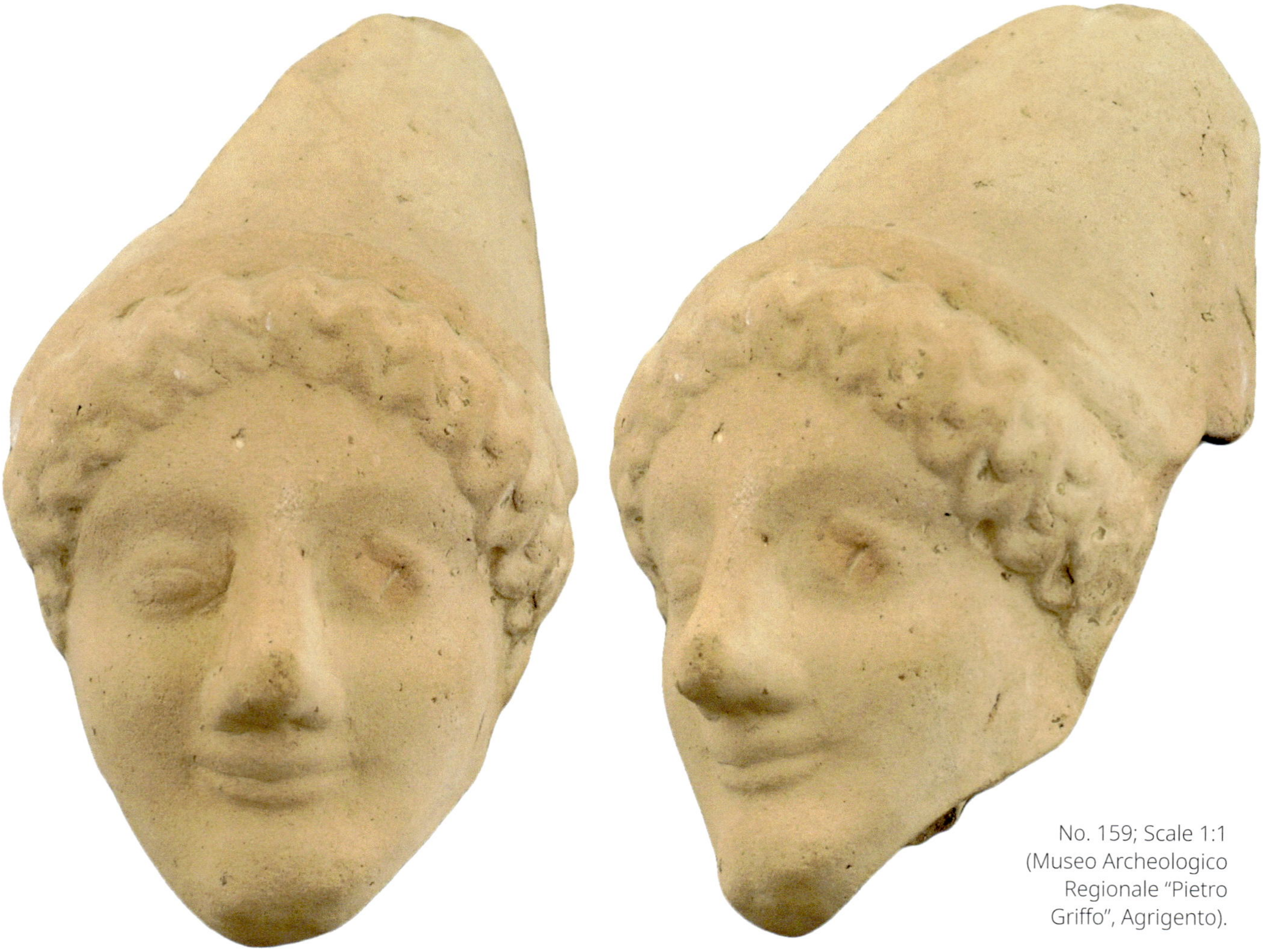

No. 159; Scale 1:1 (Museo Archeologico Regionale "Pietro Griffo", Agrigento).

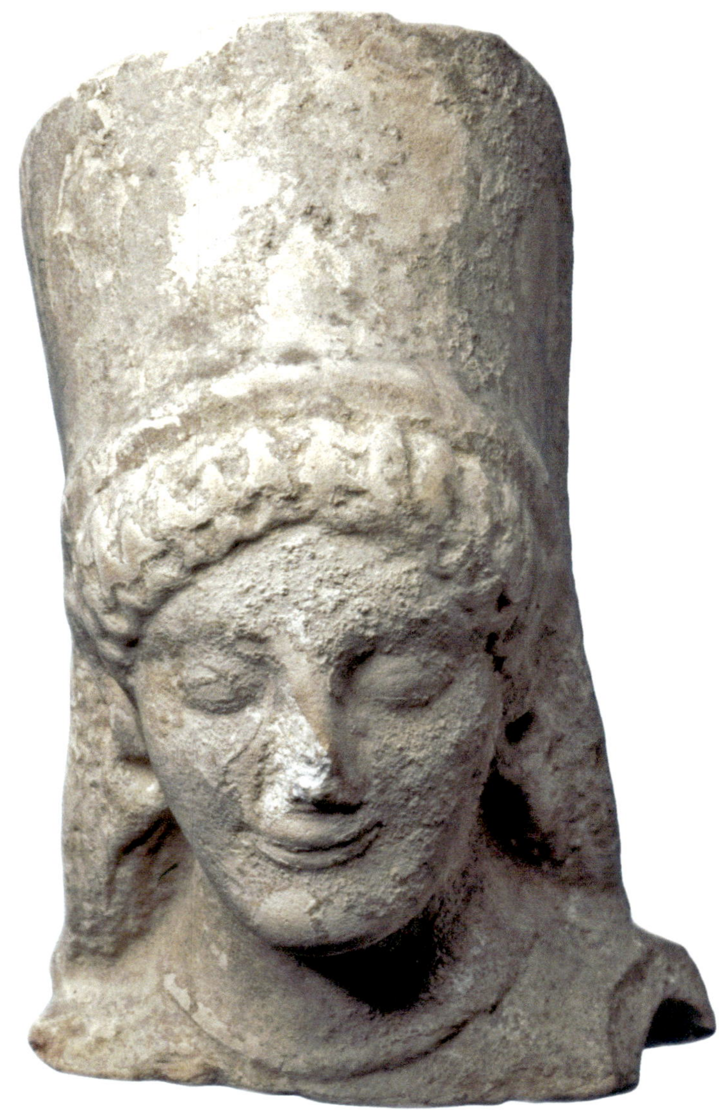

Figure 22 This head is probably from Akragas and has a similar hairstyle to figurines 156-160. Inv. no APM 4554; Scale 1:1. Photo Allard Pierson Museum, Universiteit van Amsterdam.

‣ ***Short description:*** Head of a figurine. Part of the polos, neck and sides are broken off; left eye damaged. Oval face with pronounced cheeks and chin. Large eyes with sharply marked eyelids and a sizeable nose with a big tip. A smiling mouth with thin lips and small dimples on the ends. A fringe of wavy, scalloped hair in three rows on the forehead. She wears a tall polos, with a small rim just on top of the hair.
‣ ***Comparable objects:*** Possibly, from the same mould series as heads **156**, **157** and **158**. This would be the earliest of the four generations. Similar to Mus. Agrigento Inv. no.AG 6888, head h.10cm, De Miro 2000, p.280-1, no.1892, tav.L. Similar hairstyle to **107**-**109** and two heads from Akragas and Gelas, both from the same mould, but 8 and 7cm, British Mus. Inv. no.1931,0513.3 and 1863,0728.309. Higgins 1954, p.303, no.1105 and 1106 pl. 151. See museum website.

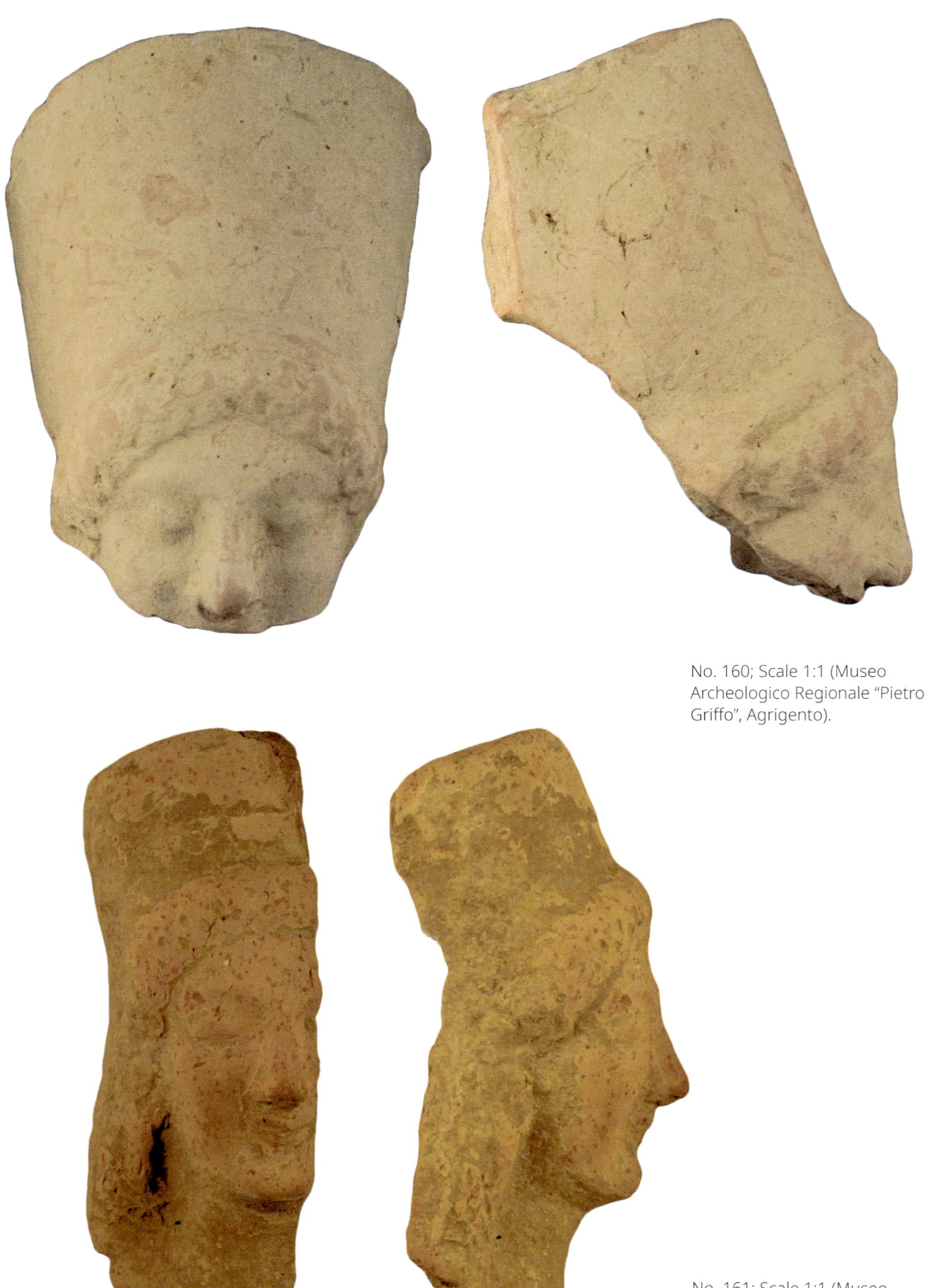

No. 160; Scale 1:1 (Museo Archeologico Regionale "Pietro Griffo", Agrigento).

No. 161; Scale 1:1 (Museo Archeologico Regionale "Pietro Griffo", Agrigento).

No.160

- *Museum and Inventory number:* Mus. Agrigento 15.1352 (2308)
- *Findspot and context:* West Archaic sanctuary underlying the bouleuterion
- *Publications:* -
- *Dimensions in cm:* h.10.8
- *Material:* Terracotta
- *Techniques:* Front moulded.
- *Colour:* Pink 7.5 YR 7/3
- *Date:* Last quarter of the sixth to beginning of the fifth century BCE
- *Workshop:* Unknown
- *Typology:* Polos-wearing head: 2a
- *Short description:* Upper part of a face and polos. Large but indistinct and undefined eyes and a long narrow nose. A fringe of wavy, scalloped hair in three(?) rows on the forehead. She wears a very tall flaring polos, with a thick round rim just above the hair.
- *Comparable objects:* Comparable to the hairstyle and polos of **159**. Similar in hairstyle to figurine S6811 from Akragas, upper part, h.21cm, De Miro 2000, p.283, no.1911, tav.LXVI. Similar in hairstyle, with the three rows of wavy hair, is a head from Akragas, dated to around 500 BCE: Mus. Amsterdam Inv. no.APM 4554, h.14.4cm. Lunsingh Scheurleer 1986, no.43.

No.161

- *Museum and Inventory number:* Mus. Agrigento S329
- *Findspot and context:* City Sanctuary
- *Publications:* -
- *Dimensions in cm:* h.11
- *Material:* Terracotta.
- *Techniques:* Front moulded.
- *Colour:* Pink 5 Y 7/4
- *Date:* The second decade of the 5th century BCE
- *Workshop:* Unknown
- *Typology:* Tall polos-wearing head: 3a
- *Short description:* Head and neck. Left side and back broken off.

  Female head with oval face, slightly widening towards the forehead. Her eyes are large. Her chin is a bit pointed. Her mouth is slightly curving up and has a thinner upper lip with a thicker lower lip. Her cheeks are protruding, accentuated by the dimples next to the mouth. Her hair is shaped in a band on the forehead with zigzag line. Along the sides of her neck, her hair is left smooth, falling down on or behind her shoulders. At the connection between the two parts of hair, a large knob with ring and a thick pendant is visible. Her polos is tall and slightly widens towards the top.
- *Comparable objects:* From the same mould series, but with slightly differently shaped and smoothed polos and probably from different generations are **133**, **134** and **162**. Those heads have a decorated polos but feature the same zigzag hair and the large earrings with pendant. This head doesn't have a necklace. The polos of **162** is shaped slightly differently. The face and hairstyle are reminiscent of a similar head from the Sanctuary of Malophoros, but the shape of the mouth and necklace are different. Gabrici 1927, tav.LVIII. Comparable also to protome AG2167 (see fig. 15), also like another head, inv. no.20142, h.14.6cm from Agrigento in the Archaeological Museum of Syracuse. (see fig. 16).

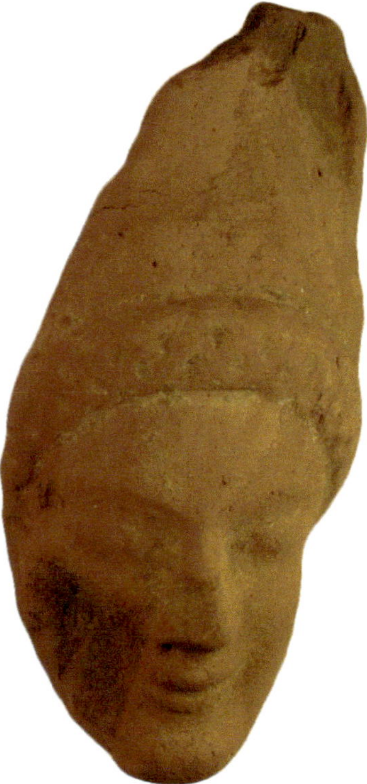

No. 162; Scale 1:1 (Museo Archeologico Regionale "Pietro Griffo", Agrigento).

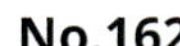

No.162

- *Museum and Inventory number:* Mus. Agrigento S375
- *Findspot and context:* City Sanctuary
- *Publications:* -
- *Dimensions in cm:* h.9.6
- *Material:* Terracotta.
- *Techniques:* Front moulded.

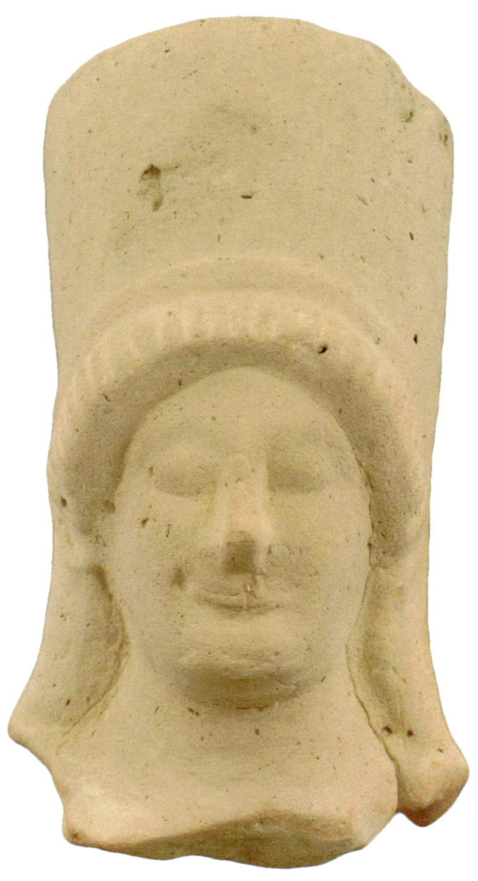
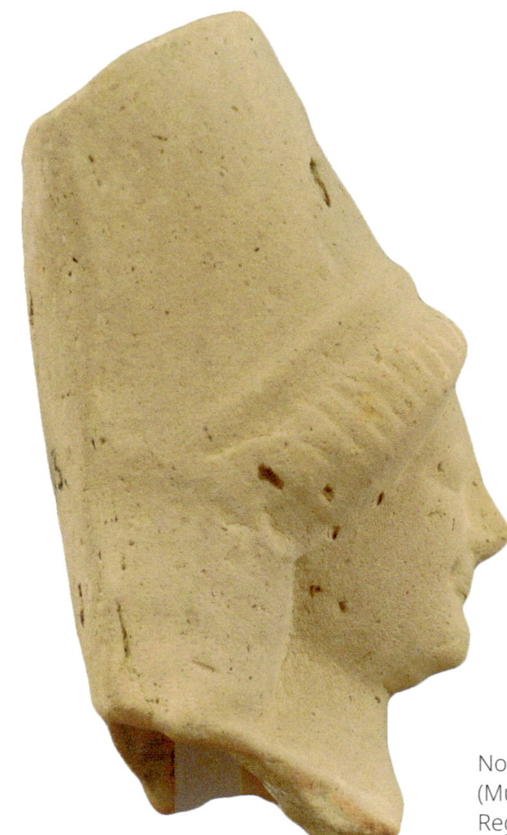

No. 163; Scale 1:1 (Museo Archeologico Regionale "Pietro Griffo", Agrigento).

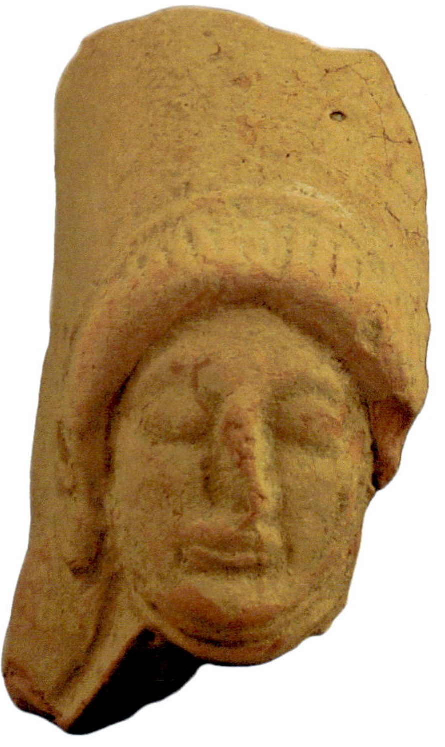
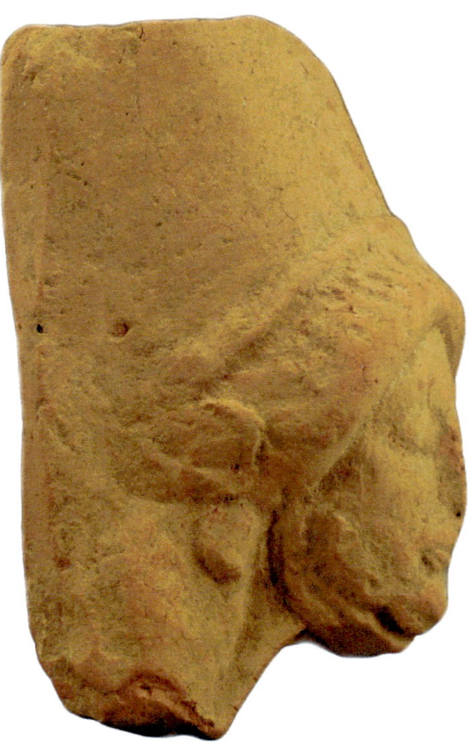

No. 164; Scale 1:1 (Museo Archeologico Regionale "Pietro Griffo", Agrigento).

- *Colour:* Pink 7.5 Y 7/4s
- *Date:* The second decade of the 5th century BCE
- *Workshop:* Unknown
- *Typology:* Tall polos-wearing head: 3a
- *Short description:* Head and part of polos. Right side of polos, neck and back broken off.

Female head with oval face, slightly widening towards the forehead. Her eyes are slightly bulging. Her chin is a bit pointed. Her mouth curves upwards. Her cheeks protrude, accentuated by the dimples next to the mouth. Her fringe of hair is shaped into a band on the forehead with zigzag line. Her polos is tall and slightly widens towards the top.

- *Comparable objects:* From the same mould series, but with slightly differently shaped poloi and probably from different generations, are **133**, **134** and **161**. See **161** for other comparable objects.

No.163

- *Museum and Inventory number:* Mus. Agrigento S103
- *Findspot and context:* City Sanctuary
- *Publications:* Marconi 1933, tav.VIII.4
- *Dimensions in cm:* h.11.3
- *Material:* Terracotta. Numerous small holes, probably caused by lime-spalling.
- *Techniques:* Front moulded. The lines in the neck might indicate that the mould for the face was added to another mould for the body.
- *Colour:* Pink 7.5 YR 7/3
- *Date:* Last quarter of the sixth century BCE
- *Workshop:* Unknown
- *Typology:* Polos-wearing head: 2a
- *Short description:* Head of a figurine. Rounded oval face with pronounced chin. Very large undefined eyes. Sizeable nose with big tip and wide bridge to the nose. Indistinct smiling mouth with thin lips. Thick-edged fringe of hair in vertical bulbs, slightly larger towards the sides. Outline of ears (?). Hair next to the neck smooth and slightly bulging. Tall straight polos with thin rim.
- *Comparable objects:* **164** is from the same mould series, probably a generation later. The clay type might indicate it is made by the same workshop. Facial features are reminiscent of **165**.

No.164

- *Museum and Inventory number:* Mus. Agrigento S373
- *Findspot and context:* City Sanctuary
- *Publications:* -
- *Dimensions in cm:* h.9.6
- *Material:* Terracotta. Numerous small holes, probably caused by lime-spalling.
- *Techniques:* Front moulded. The lines in the neck might indicate that the mould for the face was added to another mould for the body. Clay residues on chin and on the right side.
- *Colour:* Pink 7.5 YR 7/4
- *Date:* Last quarter of the sixth century BCE
- *Workshop:* Workshop with the edged fringe
- *Typology:* Polos-wearing head: 2a
- *Short description:* Head of a figurine. Nose damaged, left side broken off. Rounded oval face with pronounced chin. Very large undefined eyes. Sizeable nose. Straight mouth with thick lips. Thick-edged fringe of hair in vertical bulbs, slightly larger towards the sides. Outline of ear on the right side. Hair next to the neck smooth and slightly bulging. Tall straight polos with thin rim.
- *Comparable objects:* **163** is from the same mould series, probably a generation earlier. The mouth seems different, but the line in the neck and the characteristic fringe of hair make it clear. The clay type could indicate it is made by the same workshop. Facial features are reminiscent of **165**.

No.165

- *Museum and Inventory number:* Mus. Munich 7143
- *Findspot and context:* Akragas
- *Publications:* Hamdorf 2014, p.99, no.C 219
- *Dimensions in cm:* h.8.5
- *Material:* Terracotta.
- *Techniques:* Front moulded. Straightened back and sides with sharp tool.
- *Colour:* Pale Yellow 2.5 Y 8/2
- *Date:* Last quarter of the sixth century BCE
- *Workshop:* Unknown
- *Typology:* Polos-wearing head: 2a
- *Short description:* Head and neck. Nose partly broken off.

Female head with triangular face, widening towards the forehead. Her eyes are large, but undefined and quite indistinct. Her mouth curves upwards slightly and she has thin lips. Her hair is shaped into a smooth thick fringe on the forehead. Along the sides of her neck, horizontal lines mark her hair. She wears a very tall straight polos with a thin rim just above the hair. She wears a necklace high on her neck, but this is very indistinct. The back is straight and part of the sides, near to the back, also.

- *Comparable objects:* Similar to the appearance of the heavy and large polos of **163** and **164**, but not from the same series.

No.166

- *Museum and Inventory number:* Mus. Agrigento S386
- *Findspot and context:* City Sanctuary
- *Publications:* -
- *Dimensions in cm:* h.6.2
- *Material:* Terracotta. Many insertions. Dried clay caused cracks. Fingerprints on back.
- *Techniques:* Front moulded. She has a flattened nose, which probably happened when the figurine was taken out of the mould.
- *Colour:* Very pale brown 10 YR 7/4
- *Date:* The second decade of the 5th century BCE

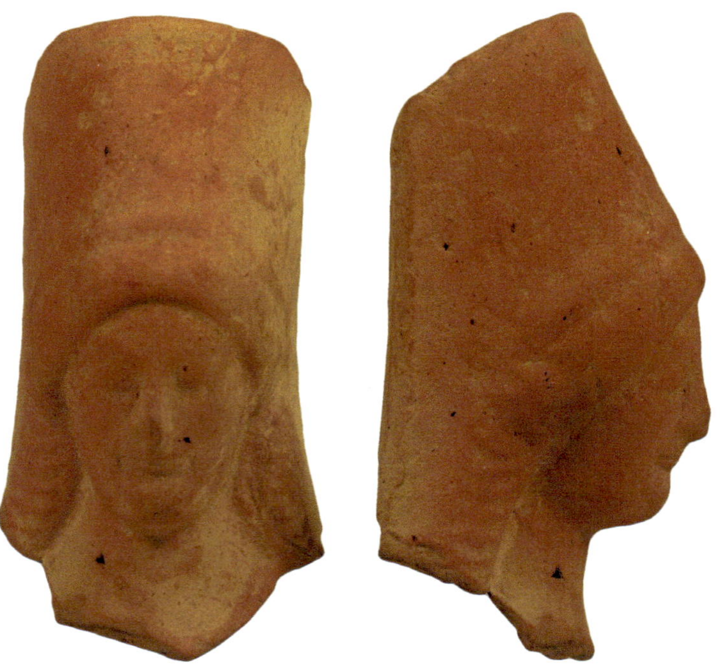

No. 165; Scale 1:1 (Staatlichen Antikensammlungen München).

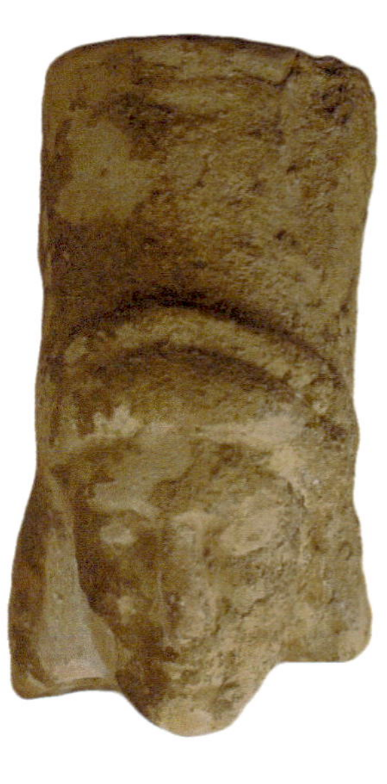

No. 167; Scale 1:1 (Museo Archeologico Regionale "Pietro Griffo", Agrigento).

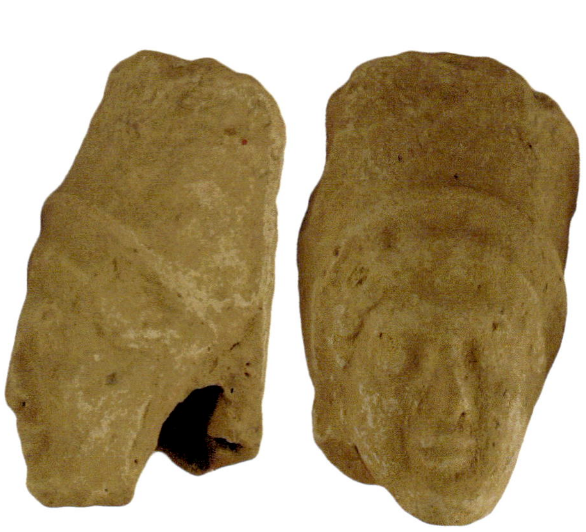

No. 166; Scale 1:1 (Museo Archeologico Regionale "Pietro Griffo", Agrigento).

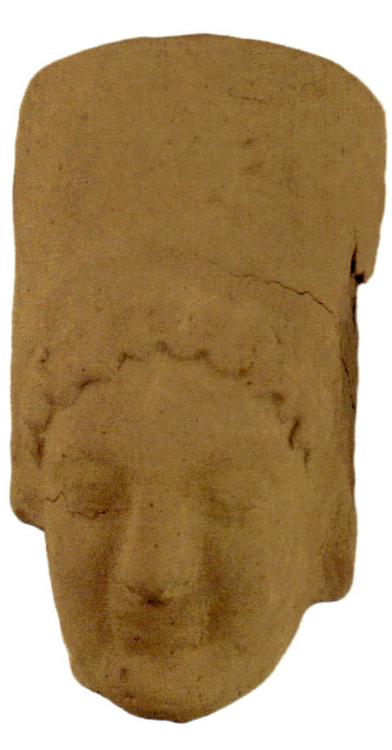

No. 168; Scale 1:1 (Museo Archeologico Regionale "Pietro Griffo", Agrigento).

‣ *Workshop:* Unknown
‣ *Typology:* Tall polos-wearing head: 3a
‣ *Short description:* Head of figurine. Female head with oval fleshy face. Her eyes are large. Her chin is protruding, cheeks and jaw are chubby. Her mouth is small with very thick lips and dimples next to it. Her fringe of hair is shaped into a band on the forehead with round bulbs in two rows. Just above the fringe and below the headgear there is a pearl-rim. This and the earrings have become very indistinct in this generation. The polos is straight and tall with a rim. Straight back.
‣ *Comparable objects:* From the same mould as S387, but with a higher polos. S388 seems also to be from the same mould genealogy, but a generation earlier. S389 is likely the next in line. These comprise three generations, which, based on their numbers, were found close together at the City Sanctuary. The facial features are similar to heads of the Mould II series. See **126** and **167**.

No.167

‣ *Museum and Inventory number:* Mus. Agrigento C394
‣ *Findspot and context:* Akragas
‣ *Publications:* -
‣ *Dimensions in cm:* h.6.8
‣ *Material:* Terracotta.
‣ *Techniques:* Front moulded. The object is relatively deep, with a relatively thick back slab.
‣ *Colour:* Pink 5 YR 8/3
‣ *Date:* The second decade of the 5th century BCE
‣ *Workshop:* Unknown
‣ *Typology:* Tall polos-wearing head: 3a
‣ *Short description:* Head in two fragments. Very worn. Film of dirt. Narrow face with large eyes, big nose and narrow mouth. Around her forehead, she has a thick fringe of hair in vertical bulbs. Alongside her face, her hair falls down. She wears a high polos with rim. Earring on the left(?).
‣ *Comparable objects:* The facial features and high polos are reminiscent of figurines from the Mould II series, like **166**.

No.168

‣ *Museum and Inventory number:* Mus. Agrigento S400
‣ *Findspot and context:* City Sanctuary
‣ *Publications:* -
‣ *Dimensions in cm:* h.7.6
‣ *Material:* Terracotta. Lighter coloured slip layer
‣ *Techniques:* Front moulded. Layers of clay have been placed in the mould first to create a sharp impression.
‣ *Colour:* Pink 7.5 YR 7/4
‣ *Date:* The second decade of the 5th century BCE
‣ *Workshop:* Unknown, but probably the same as of **169**
‣ *Typology:* Tall polos-wearing head: 3a
‣ *Short description:* Head of figurine. Back and parts on the side (veil?) broken off. Cracks and layers broken off. Female head with oval fleshy face and high forehead. Her eyes are large with eyelids under arching eyebrows. Her chin, cheeks and jaw are chubby. Her nose is sizeable with a wide bridge to her nose. Her mouth is wide, in a soft smile with thick lips, accentuated by the deep dimples next to mouth and nose. Her hair is shaped into a fringe on the forehead with scalloped hair, stylised waves in a layer. The waves are regular. She wears a tall straight polos with an indistinct rim. A veil was originally draped over the polos.
‣ *Comparable objects:* From the same mould as **169**(?). Except for the slip layer, the clay is similar. From the same mould series is a figurine from Akragas Mus. Agrigento Inv. no.6844, h.8.1cm, De Miro 2000, p.268, no.1719, tav.XCV.
‣ *Other notes:* Iron wire and gypsum are attached on the inside.

No.169 (not illustrated)

‣ *Museum and Inventory number:* Mus. Agrigento S401
‣ *Findspot and context:* City Sanctuary
‣ *Publications:* -
‣ *Dimensions in cm:* h.9.2
‣ *Material:* Terracotta. Lighter coloured slip layer on bright red base.
‣ *Techniques:* Front moulded.
‣ *Colour:* Pinkish white 7.5 YR /2
‣ *Date:* The second decade of the 5th century BCE
‣ *Workshop:* Unknown, but likely the same as of **168**
‣ *Typology:* Tall polos-wearing head: 3a
‣ *Short description:* Head of figurine. Part of the back broken off. Female head with oval fleshy face and high forehead. Her eyes are large with eyelids under arching eyebrows. Her chin, cheeks and jaw are chubby. Her nose is sizeable with a wide bridge to her nose. Her mouth is wide in a soft smile with thick lips, accentuated by the deep dimples next to mouth and nose. Her hair is shaped into a fringe on the forehead with wavy hair. The waves are regular. Next to the sides of her neck, her hair hangs down and is smooth. She wears a tall straight polos with indistinct rim. Back straight.
‣ *Comparable objects:* From the same mould as **168**. Details are less clear, possibly because of the slip layer. Except for the slip layer, the clay is similar.

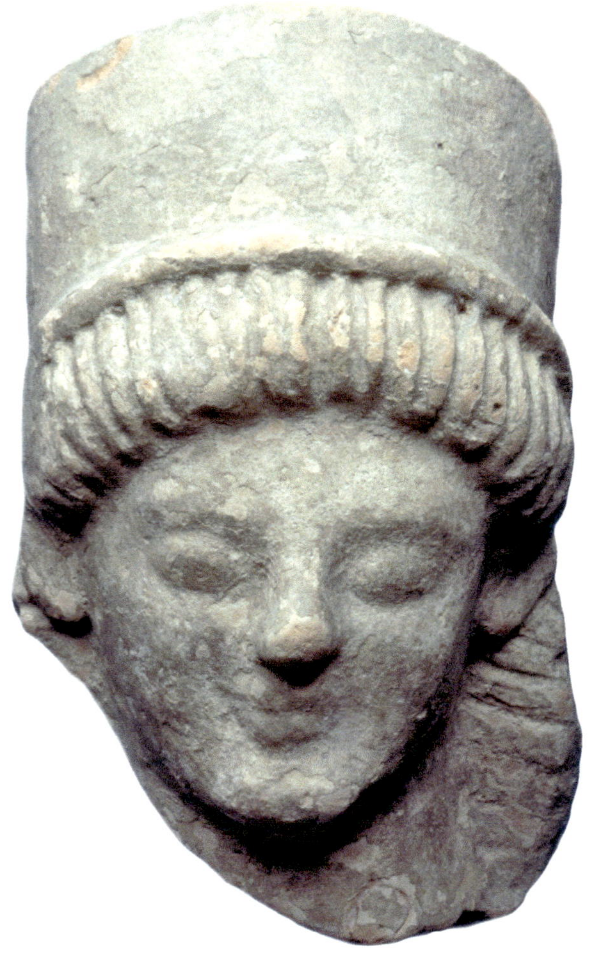

Figure 23: Very similar, but much larger head than 170. Inv. No. APM 1825. Scale 1:1 Photo Allard Pierson Museum, Universiteit van Amsterdam.

No.170

‣ ***Museum and Inventory number:*** Mus. Agrigento C400
‣ ***Findspot and context:*** Akragas
‣ ***Publications:*** -
‣ ***Dimensions in cm:*** h.5.7
‣ ***Material:*** Terracotta.
‣ ***Techniques:*** Front moulded. White slip layer?
‣ ***Colour:*** Light red 2.5 YR 7/6
‣ ***Date:*** Last quarter of the sixth century BCE
‣ ***Workshop:*** Unknown
‣ ***Typology:*** Polos-wearing head: 2a
‣ ***Short description:*** Head. Small face with large eyes, mouth a bit wider than nose, smiling. Hair in thick band with vertical bulbs. Medium-sized polos with a rim.
‣ ***Comparable objects:*** **155** might be from the same mould series, one or two generations earlier.

From the same mould, probably, as C396 (Arch. Mus. Agrigento). The face is reminiscent of **149**. Similar, possibly an earlier generation, though with a different polos is **130**. Possibly from the same mould is a figurine dated to the beginning of the 5th century BCE.: Mus. Amsterdam Inv. no.APM 1825, h.12.5cm. Lunsingh Scheurleer 1986, no.44.

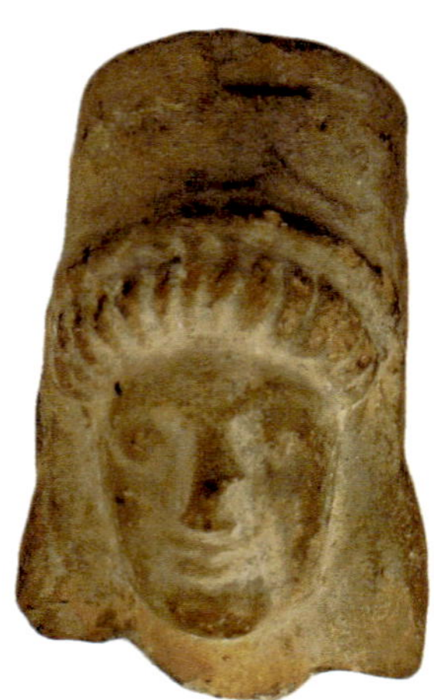

No. 170; Scale 1:1 (Museo Archeologico Regionale "Pietro Griffo", Agrigento).

Type M: The chubby face (171-184)

This group contains a specific series, Mould I, and its variations. The figurines wear figurative pendants and the short necklace is introduced with this series. Its facial characteristic, a fleshy face with pronounced cheeks, is shared by some other figurines. A seated and a standing figure appears as a variation of the type.

No.171

- *Museum and Inventory number:* Mus. Agrigento 1141
- *Findspot and context:* City Sanctuary. At the base of the southwest wall of the sanctuary
- *Publications:* Albertocchi 2004, p.13, no.1; Griffo 1955 109-10, no.1453 fig.18; De Miro 2000, p.130, no.34, tav.LXII
- *Dimensions in cm:* h.30.5
- *Material:* terracotta
- *Techniques:* Front moulded. Sides and back straightened with sharp tool. The outline of the apron is accentuated with a tool, following the reworking of the sides, feet, footstool, veil and angle of the body.
- *Colour:* Pink 7.5 YR 7.4
- *Date:* 490-470 BCE
- *Workshop:* Workshop of 'the one pendant necklace'
- *Typology:* Chubby face group: 2d
- *Short description:* Nearly complete. Piece of veil broken off, ears of throne, left hand broken. The female figure has a round face with a low forehead. Her rounded and chubby cheeks protrude, with dimples next to the mouth. The chin is large. The large nose with a wide bridge is placed high on the face. Her mouth is smiles slightly and has a thinner upper and a thicker lower lip. Her eyes are large, but the large eyelids over the bulging eye reduce this effect. The contours of the eyebrows are broad and seem to continue to the sides of the face. On her forehead, a fringe of hair runs around from halfway on one side of her face to the other. The bulbs each contain a long and narrow oval shape. She wears a low polos with a rim and a veil draped over it. The veil hangs down on the sides and places the head in a cave-like form. Below this veil, it is messy, but large earrings, boat-shaped with a smaller pendant, can be seen. Tight around her neck, she wears a necklace with one small round pendant in the middle. On her otherwise flat chest, she wears three bands with pectoral pendants. The bands themselves are thick and smooth and seem not to be directly attached to the pendants, particularly on the second row. The upper band, which seems to be attached to the palmette-shaped fibulae on the shoulders, contains five closely spaced, hanging protomes of a calf. The heads of the calves are very detailed. Their head

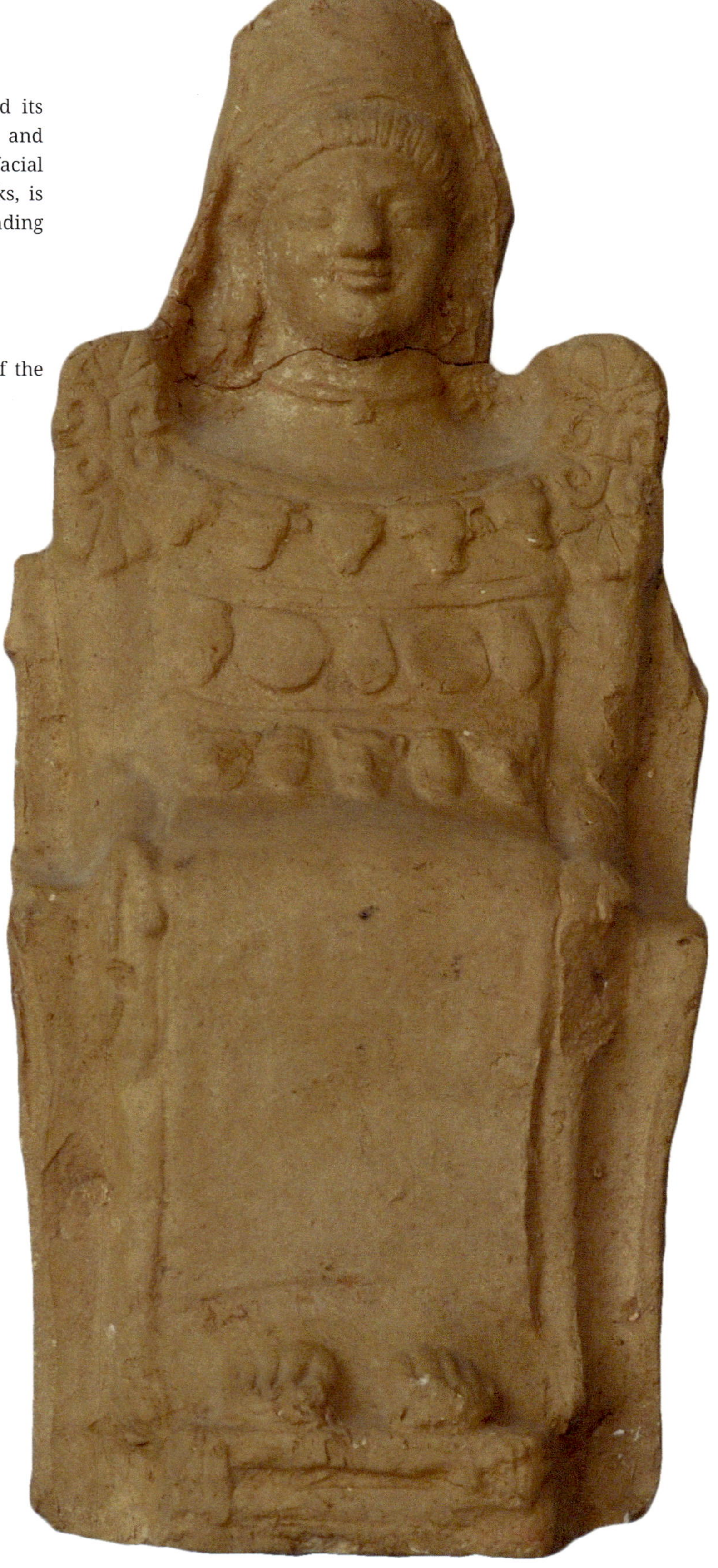

No. 171; Scale 1:1½ (Museo Archeologico Regionale "Pietro Griffo", Agrigento).

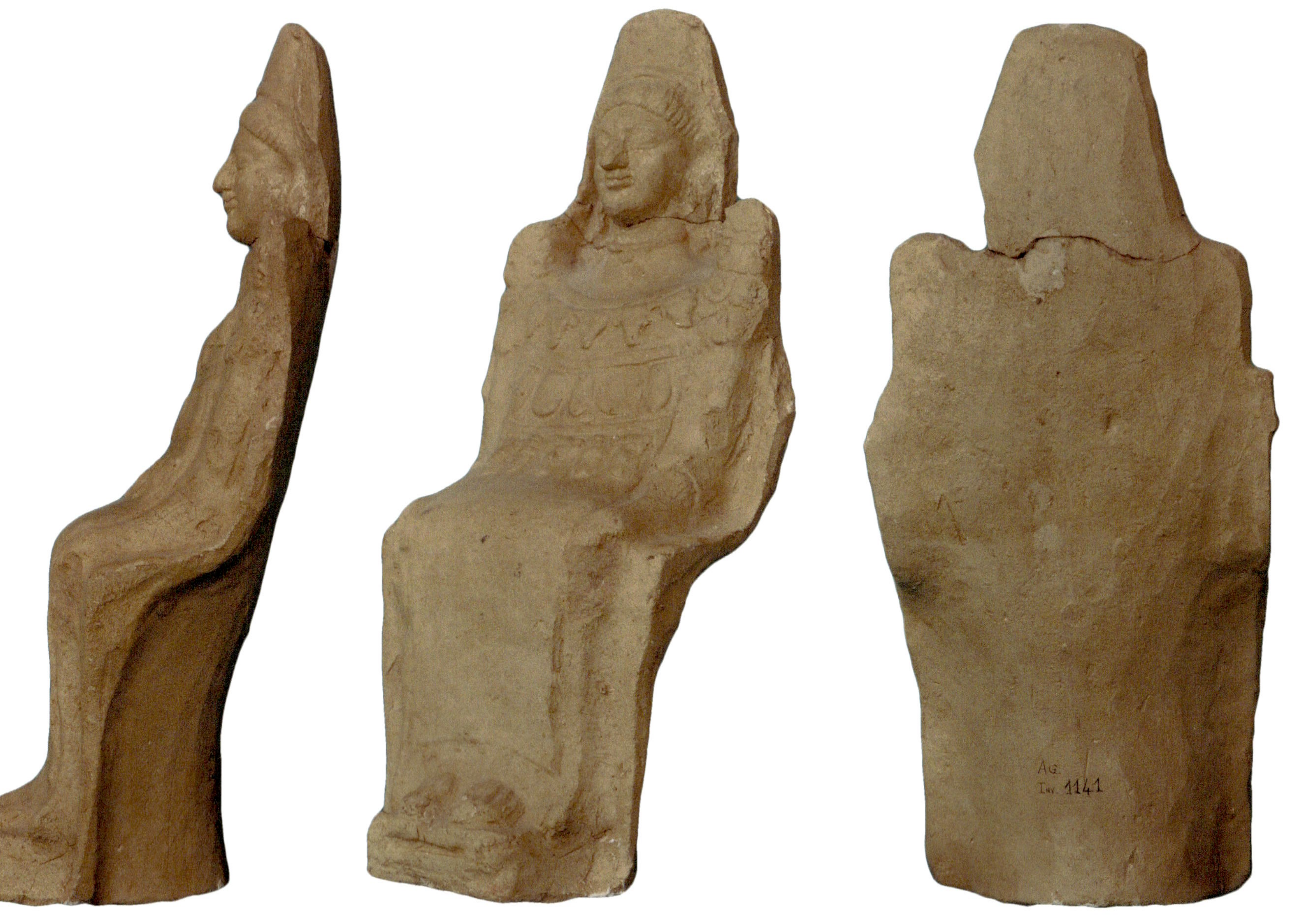

No. 171; Scale 1:2 (Museo Archeologico Regionale "Pietro Griffo", Agrigento).

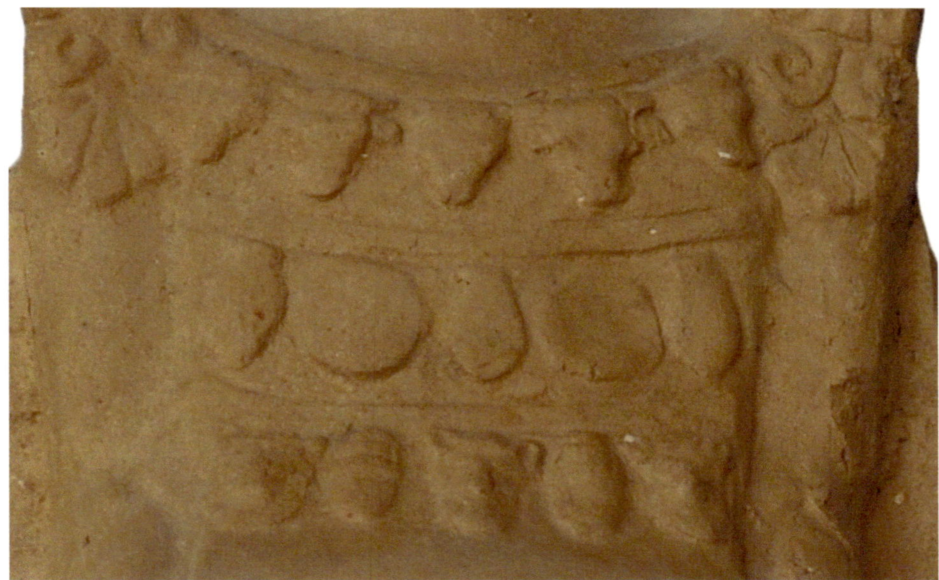

No. 171; Scale 1:1
Detail of chest (Museo Archeologico Regionale "Pietro Griffo", Agrigento).

shape, nose, ears and small horns depicted naturally, though the details are slightly faded. On the second row, there are five alternating pendants of vaselets and discs. The three vaselets have a rounded base and are ovoid but have a wider rim at the top. The two discs are flat and lack a part for attachment. On the third line, three satyr heads alternate with two acorns. These are also details but faded. The large nose and upright ears of the bearded satyrs however is clear. The acorns too are ovoid, with a larger, structured upper half. The figurine is properly seated, at an almost ninety-degree angle on a throne which is just a bit wider than her body and originally had a round part, 'an ear,' sticking out horizontally on each side. The figurine holds her round arms tight to the sides of her body, resting on the throne. The sleeves end just below the elbow. She bends her lower arms parallel to her lap, reaching her knees with her hands. Her long hands with a thick thumb are outstretched. The fingers are not separately depicted, unlike the toes. Her feet stick out from under an undergarment. The outlines of an apron are visible on the lower part of the body and follow the vertical lines of the outline and throne. Above the feet, the horizontal hem curves around the feet. Her feet, with five long toes and even nails, are placed a little apart, resting on a footstool. She seems to wear sandals, as the sole is indicated. The low footstool has a horizontal part to strengthen it. A rounded back at the base ensures the figurine stays upright.

‣ ***Comparable objects:*** From the same mould as **173** and **174**. From the same mould series are **172**, which is earlier, and **175**, a fibula from this series. The sharpest impression is that of **172**, the earliest of these figurines. **176** is another variation on the series and dates from before the seated versions of **171**, **173** and **174**, but later than **172**. Mould **177** and head **178** have a similar Ionian face. The mould might be from a following generation, after **171**. A part of a shoulder is from the same mould series also: Mus. Agrigento Inv. no.AG 13417, h.8.2cm, Albertocchi 2004, p.64, no.1056; De Miro 2000, p.265, no.1697, tav.LXV. The facial features and the earrings are reminiscent of Mus. Agrigento Inv. no.AG 9187, h.6.1cm, Albertocchi 2004, p.64, no.1057; De Miro 2000, p.163, no.400. (fig.24). The facial features and the veil draped over the polos are reminiscent of a head from Himera, h.6.7cm, Inv. no.H71.948, 1 Allegro 1972 45 D, I 2tav.XXV.1. The bearded men's heads are reminiscent of a mould for a satyr with a similar face: Mus. Agrigento Inv. no.AG 8941.

No.172

- *Museum and Inventory number:* Mus. Munich 8922 (ex 9599)
- *Findspot and context:* Akragas
- *Publications:* Hamdorf 2014, p.98, no.C 216
- *Dimensions in cm:* h.7.2; The disc measures 23mm in diameter.
- *Material:* Terracotta. A thick layer was probably put in the mould first. This layer has a different colour.
- *Techniques:* Front moulded.
- *Colour:* Very pale brown 10 YR 7/3; Inside: light red 2.5 YR 6/8
- *Date:* 500-480 BCE
- *Workshop:* Unknown
- *Typology:* Chubby face group: 2d
- *Short description:* Sherd of the chest on which two chains with pendants are still visible. On the upper row, a disc next to an aryballos with wide rim. On the second row, the beads are very clearly visible. There seem to be alternating round larger beads and smaller beads. On the band, there are five pendants attached with three silenoi or satyr-like heads/protomes with a protruding nose and a big mouth, alternating with acorns. The upper part of the fruit is divided into a squared pattern.
- *Comparable objects:* This is the sharpest and largest of the mould series, with the most depth. The pendants of the 'third row' seem to be much closer together than those on **171**. The details of the band and the three-dimensionality of the aryballoi pendants on the second row are smoothed away on the other figurines of this series, like **171**. The difference with **176** concerns the 'third row' also: there are only two satyr heads and three acorns. The heads are not just sharper, but also different, in particular the part of the ears. Those are unlikely to be from the same mould. See **171** for other comparable objects.

No.173

- *Museum and Inventory number:* Mus. Agrigento 23113
- *Findspot and context:* Necropolis di Contrada Mosè. See for the context fig.25. The deposit pit contained three terracotta heads, miniature pottery, oil lamps and figurines **21**, **54** and **83**.
- *Publications:* Veder Greco: le necrópolis di Agrigento 1988, p.271; Albertocchi 2004, p.13, no.2
- *Dimensions in cm:* h.23.3
- *Material:* terracotta
- *Techniques:* Front moulded. Sides and back straightened with sharp tool.
- *Colour:* Pink 7.5 YR 8/3
- *Date:* 490-470 BCE
- *Workshop:* Workshop of 'the one pendant necklace'
- *Typology:* Chubby face group: 2d
- *Short description:* Headless figurine, in several pieces, restored with considerable infill on the lap, right side, left foot and back. Please see **171** for an extensive description. This impression is sharper than **171**. Some details are more visible, such as the v-shaped end of the sleeve and the thick legs of the footstool. The 'ears' of the throne might have been decorated with rosettes, but it is a bit indistinct.
- *Comparable objects:* From the same mould as **171** and **174**. See **171**.

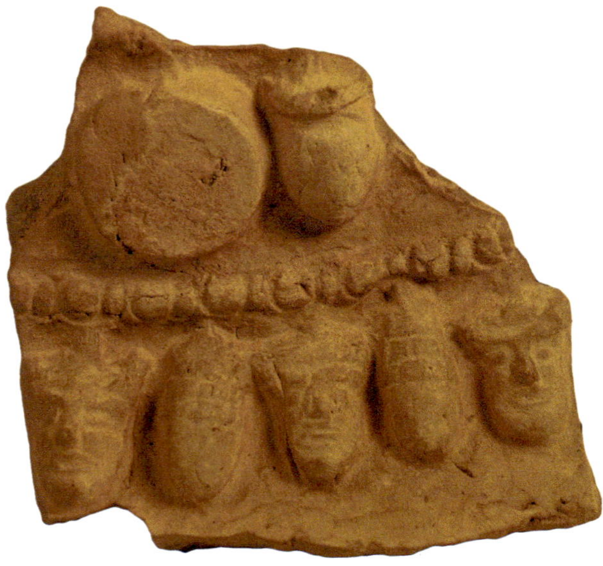

No. 172; Scale 1:1 (Staatlichen Antikensammlungen München).

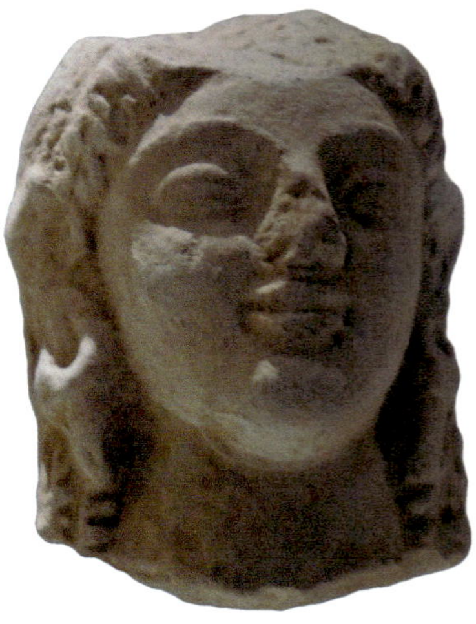

Figure 24; Scale 1:1 Head comparable with head of no. 171. Inv. no. AG9187 (Museo Archeologico Regionale "Pietro Griffo", Agrigento).

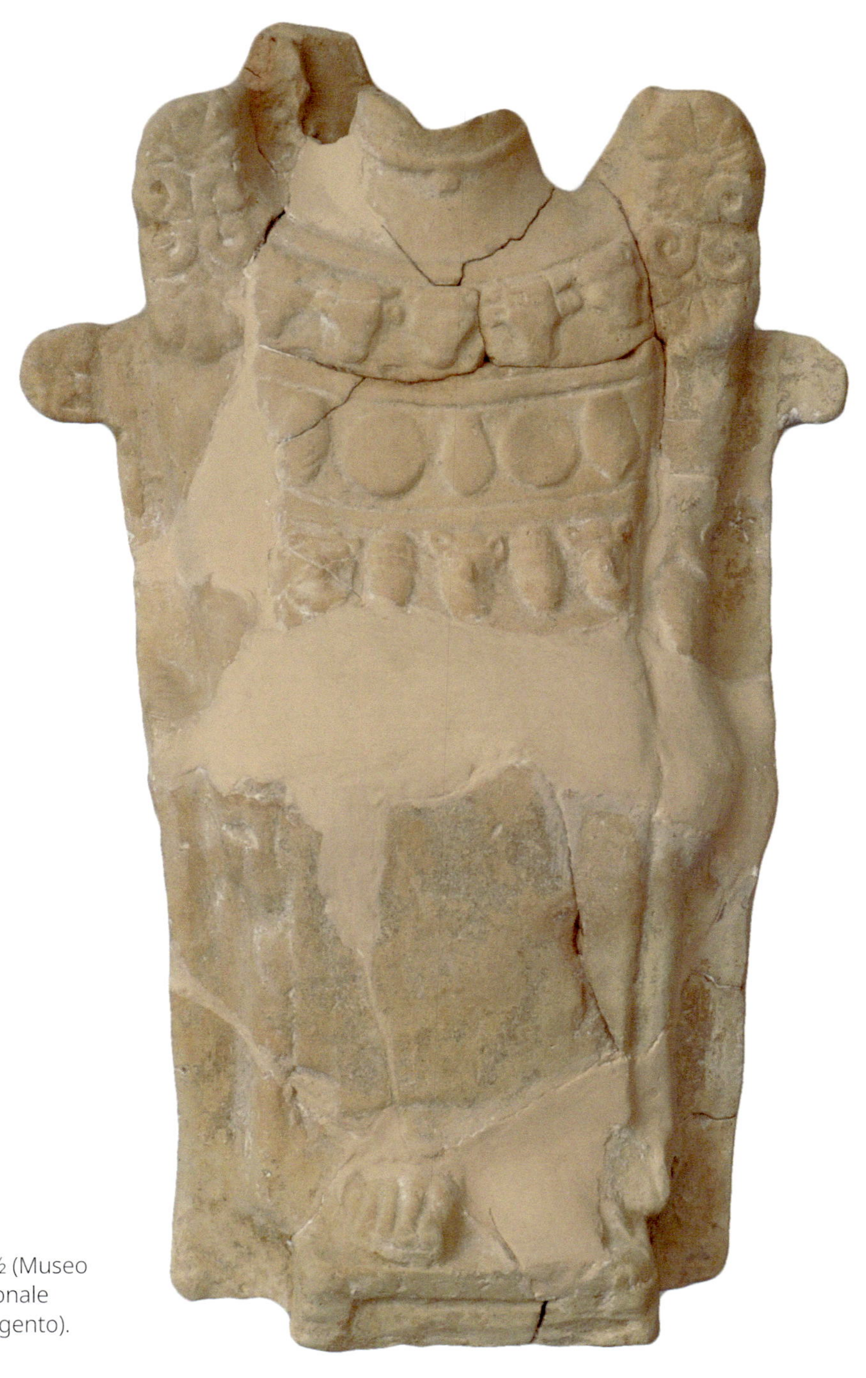

No. 173; Scale 1:1½ (Museo Archeologico Regionale "Pietro Griffo", Agrigento).

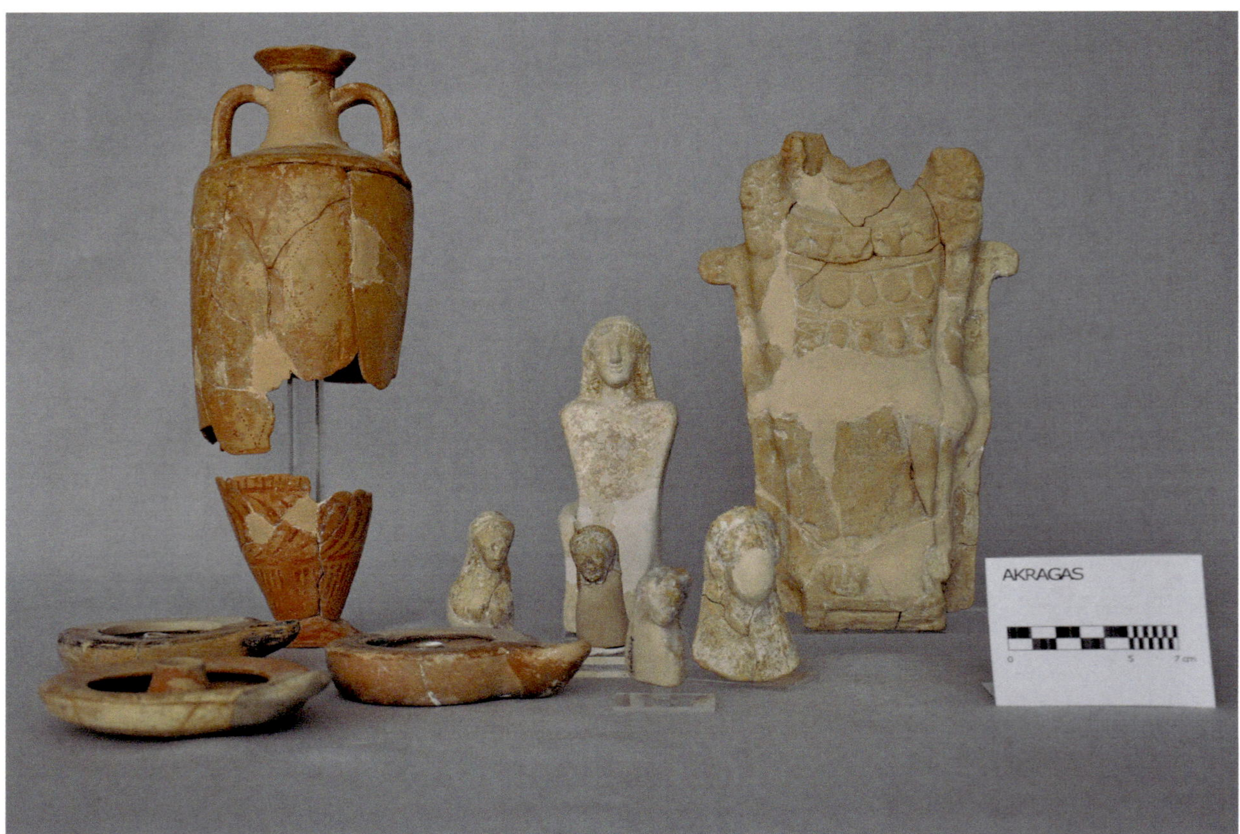

Figure 25; Some of the content of a deposit pit at the Necropolis di Contrada Mosè. Context of no.21, 54, 83 and 173. See for other items figure 4 (Museo Archeologico Regionale "Pietro Griffo", Agrigento).

No.174

- *Museum and Inventory number:* Mus. Agrigento S311
- *Findspot and context:* City Sanctuary
- *Publications:* Albertocchi 2004, p.13, no.3
- *Dimensions in cm:* h.18.5
- *Material:* Terracotta
- *Techniques:* Front moulded. Sides and back straightened with sharp tool. Painted white.
- *Colour:* Pink 7.5 YR 7/4
- *Date:* 490-470 BCE
- *Workshop:* Workshop of 'the one pendant necklace'
- *Typology:* Chubby face group: 2d
- *Short description:* Headless figurine, lower part of body broken off. This impression is less sharp than the one of **171** or **173**. Please see **171** for an extensive description.
- *Comparable objects:* From the same mould as **171** and **173**. See **171**.

No.175

- *Museum and Inventory number:* Mus. Agrigento S312
- *Findspot and context:* City Sanctuary
- *Publications:* -
- *Dimensions in cm:* h.5.8
- *Material:* Terracotta.
- *Techniques:* Front moulded. To decrease its thickness, the back is impressed and hollowed out.
- *Colour:* Very pale brown 10 YR 7/4
- *Date:* 490-470 BCE
- *Workshop:* Workshop of 'the one pendant necklace'(?)
- *Typology:* Chubby face group: 2d(?)
- *Short description:* Fibula in the shape of a large double palmette from the left shoulder. A fountain-shaped spiral motif is topped by a half rosette with a knob in the middle. This as a whole is mirrored. There are seven petals on the top and five on the bottom. The calf's head next to it is partly visible.
- *Comparable objects:* See **171**. It seems the number of petals is higher on this fibula than on **171**, **173** and **174**, which have 5 petal leaves. Because the space is relatively the same, the leaves are narrower. **177** also has seven petals on both parts of the fibula. It is likely that this belongs to another generation in which this part was reworked.

No. 174; Scale 1:1 (Museo Archeologico Regionale "Pietro Griffo", Agrigento).

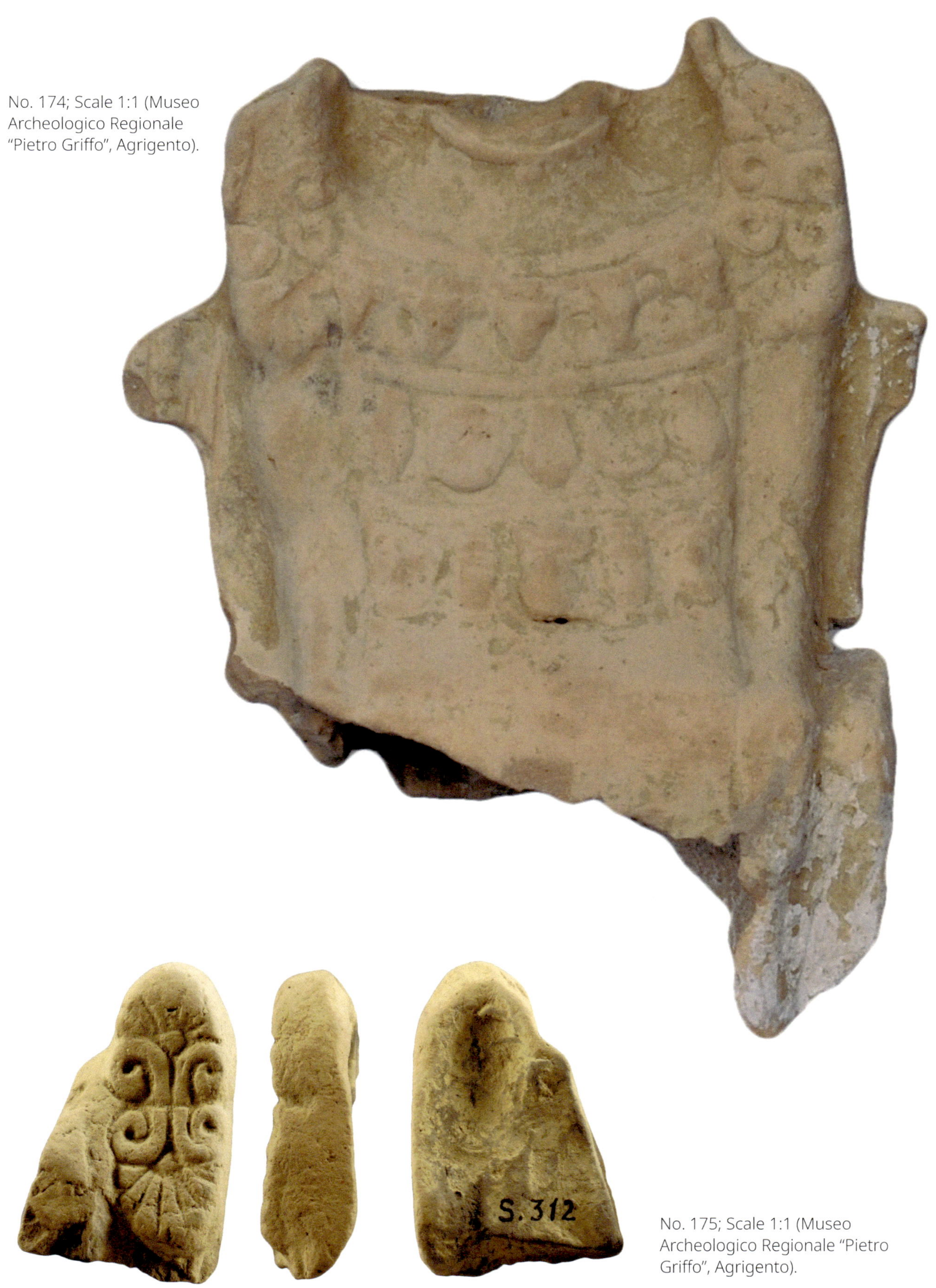

No. 175; Scale 1:1 (Museo Archeologico Regionale "Pietro Griffo", Agrigento).

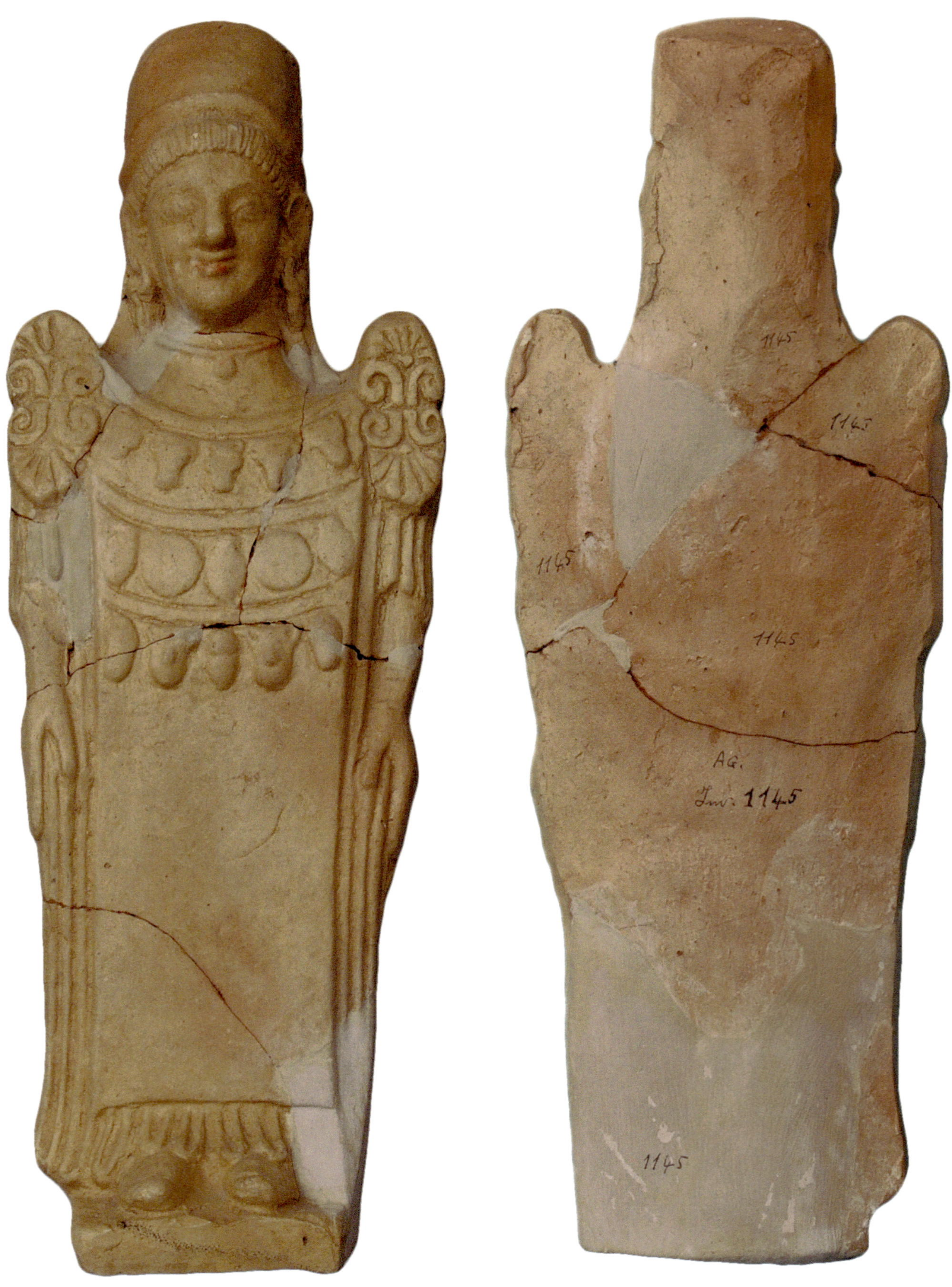

No. 176; Scale 1:1½ (Museo Archeologico Regionale "Pietro Griffo", Agrigento); continued on next page.

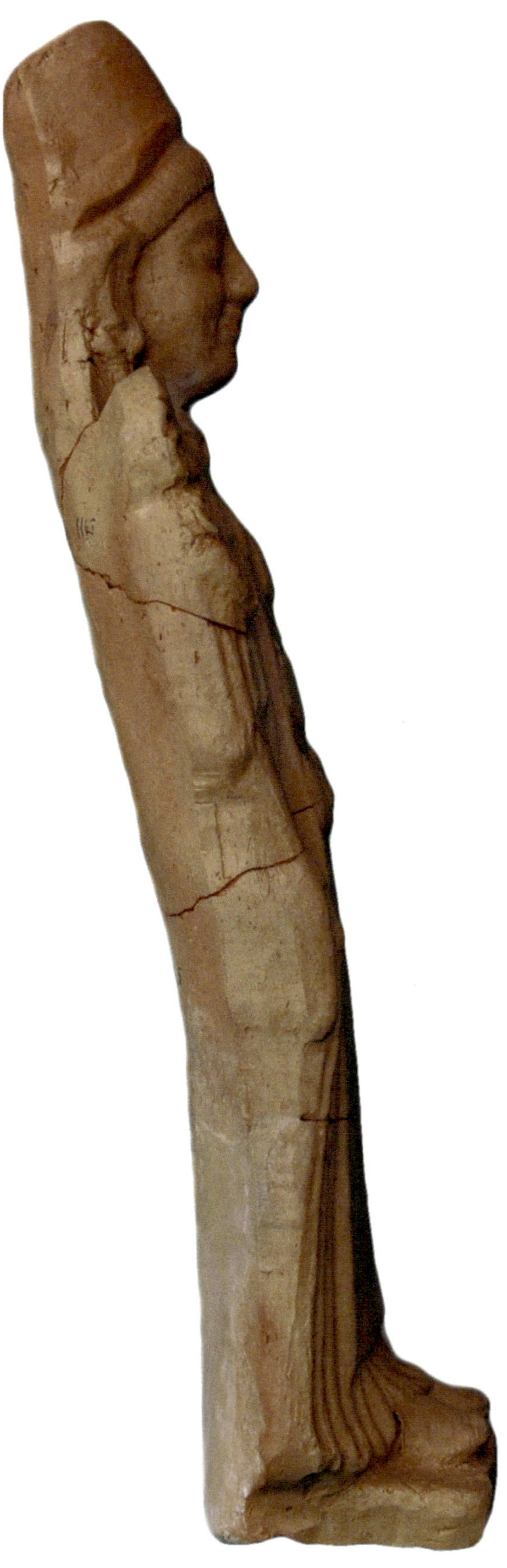

No.176

‣ ***Museum and Inventory number:*** Mus. Agrigento 1145

‣ ***Findspot and context:*** City Sanctuary. At the base of the southwest wall of the sanctuary

‣ ***Publications:*** Albertocchi 2004, p.64, no.1055, tav.XX.a; De Miro 2000, p.130, no.33, tav.LXII; Langlotz and Hirmer 1963, p.264 fig.20 right.

‣ ***Dimensions in cm:*** h.29.5

‣ ***Material:*** Terracotta. Red paint on lips, necklace and pendants.

‣ ***Techniques:*** Front moulded. Sides straightened with sharp tool. Bands on chest deepened with tool. On both sides next to the neck, an extra rim is left, on which the bulging clay reveals the use of a mould for the earring or even the complete ear.

‣ ***Colour:*** Pink 7.5 YR 7/3

‣ ***Date:*** 490-470 BCE

‣ ***Workshop:*** Workshop of 'the one pendant necklace'

‣ ***Typology:*** Chubby face group: 2d

‣ ***Short description:*** Nearly complete figurine in several pieces. Restored with minor infill on front and back. The female figurine seems from the front to be standing but can stay upright by itself because it leans backwards. She has a round face with a low forehead, a sizeable jaw and a slightly protruding chin. The large nose with a wide bridge is placed high on the face, like her mouth. Her mouth, painted bright red, is slightly smiling, and has a thinner upper and a thicker lower lip. Her eyes are large, but the large eyelids partly covering the bulging eye, reduce this effect. On her forehead, a wide rim with hair runs around from behind her ears on one side of her face to the other. The loops are each made with a long and narrow oval shape. She wears a low polos with a rim. She has large round ears on top of the hair, but without details. A ring is directly attached to the earlobe. It is boat-shaped with a large oval pendant that reaches her necklace on one side. Tight around her neck, she wears a necklace with one small round pendant on it, in the middle. On her otherwise flat chest, she wears three thick, smooth cords with pectoral pendants. The upper band, which seems to be attached to the palmette-shaped fibulae on the shoulders, contains five calf's heads. The heads have lost details. On the second row, five vassette and disc-shaped pendants alternate. The vaselets, of which there are three, are ovoid, but seem smaller at the opening. On the third line, three acorns alternate with two satyr heads. The large nose and upright ears of the satyrs can be recognised, but their faces and the details on the ovoid acorns have faded. The figurine leans and holds her arms tight to the thin sides of her body. Her outstretched hands, of which the thumb is separate from the fingers, seem to hold her undergarment. There is a small edge, like a fold in the garment, next to her arm, which is only visible on the left and runs continuously along the side. Sleeves with three folds end halfway down her arm. An elbow or bend is not indicated. The same undergarment is again visible

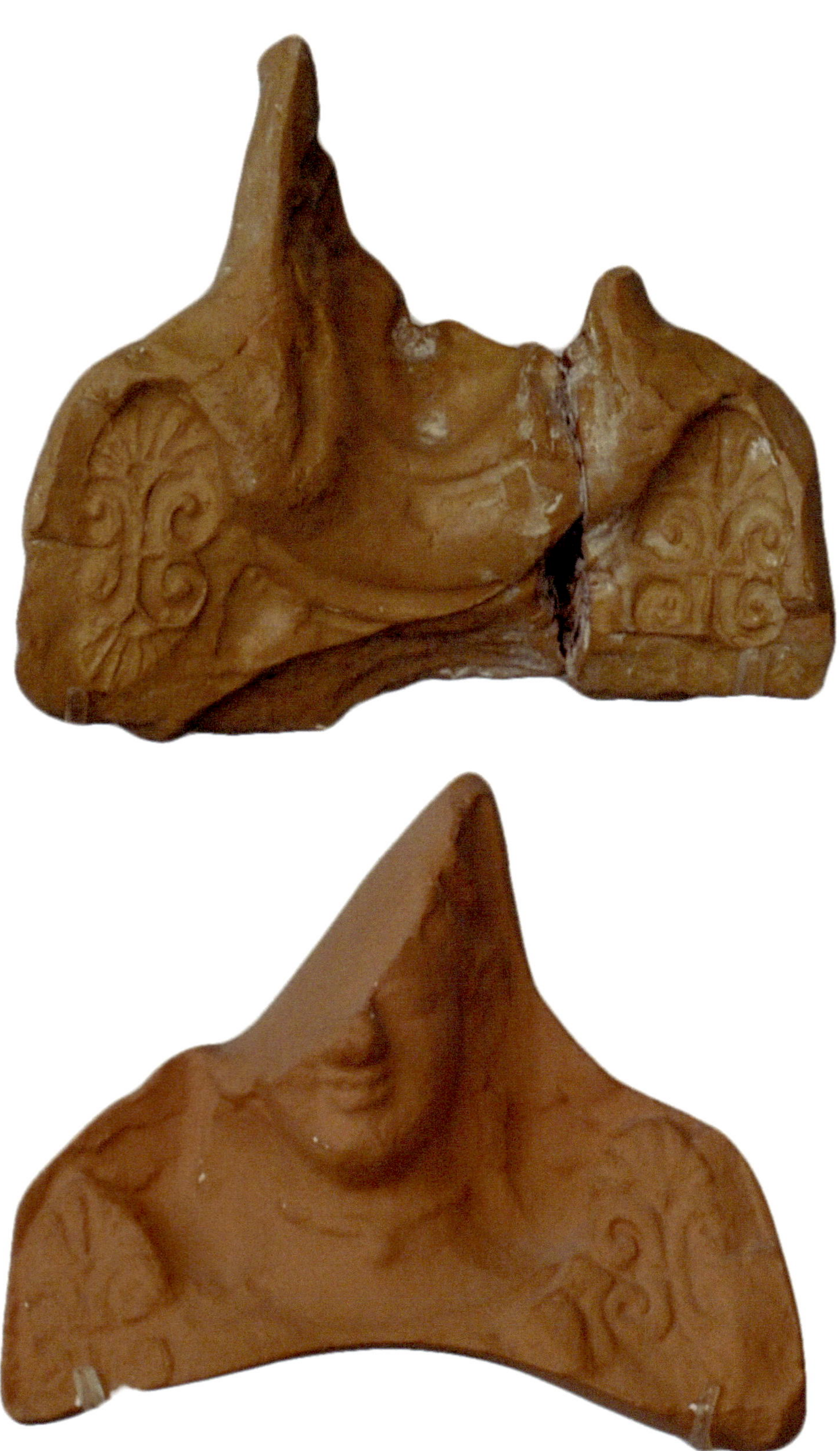

No. 177; Scale 1:1
with modern gypsum
cast below (Museo
Archeologico Regionale
“Pietro Griffo”, Agrigento).

next to the flat, straight apron. On the part above her feet, the undergarment ends in loops, which recall her hairstyle. Her feet in shoes stick out from under her garment and are placed on a small footstool. Straight back. The straightening of the sides left heaping of clay at the fibulae and head on the back, left side.

‣ *Comparable objects:* **171**, **173** and **174** are partly from the same mould series, but larger and therefore likely of earlier generations. Unlike those, she does not wear a veil. This makes her ears and earrings clearer. On the third line, acorns and satyrs have exchanged places. The details have faded and are sometimes reworked. For the fibulae, the new mould **177**, is used, which is clear and has six or seven petals on each side. The Ionian face is comparable to **179** with the same height, just 3mm less in width.

The feet on a podium with the loop-shaped chiton are probably from the same mould series. Inv. no.AGS 6839 Mus. Agrigento. De Miro 2000, p.283, no.1916, tav.LXXX.

No.177

‣ *Museum and Inventory number:* Mus. Agrigento 8946
‣ *Findspot and context:* City Sanctuary
‣ *Publications:* Albertocchi 2004, p.13, no.5; De Miro 2000, p.251, no.1533, tav.CIX
‣ *Dimensions in cm:* h.10.3
‣ *Material:* Terracotta.
‣ *Techniques:* Imprint from an object, the patrix.
‣ *Colour:* Reddish-yellow 7.5 YR 6/6
‣ *Date:* 490-470 BCE
‣ *Workshop:* Workshop of 'the one pendant necklace'
‣ *Typology:* Chubby face group: 2d
‣ *Short description:* Mould of part of the head, neck and fibulae of a figurine. The right side had been broken off, restored. The female figure has a round face. The chin protrudes slightly, and the jaw seems wide. The nose is large, and the mouth is slightly smiling, with a thinner upper and a thicker lower lip. Her eyes have eyelids. She wears a tight thin necklace with one round pendant. The fibulae are double palmette-shaped with a half rosette springing from it on the upper and lower parts. Her ears are large, but just the upper part and the large pendant of the earring are clear. On her upper chest band, one calf's head is visible.
‣ *Comparable objects:* This could have been the mould of **176** and its generation, because of the size. **176** is slightly smaller; and the fibula on the right side, with one more petal. For other comparable objects, see **171**.
‣ *Other notes:* The whitish residue inside might be a leftover from restoration or the moulding of the gypsum example figurine (in the photograph twice on the left).

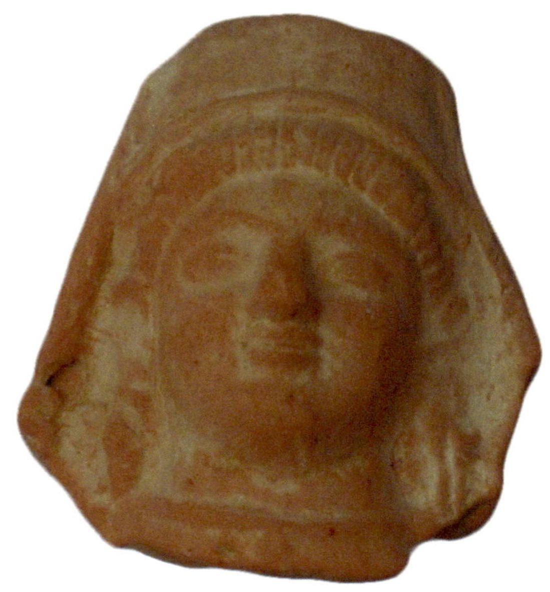

No. 178; Scale 1:1 (Museo Archeologico Regionale "Pietro Griffo", Agrigento).

No.178

‣ *Museum and Inventory number:* Mus. Agrigento S88
‣ *Findspot and context:* Akragas
‣ *Publications:* Marconi 1933, tav.VII 9
‣ *Dimensions in cm:* h.7.5
‣ *Material:* terracotta
‣ *Techniques:* Front moulded. The veil is made from the clay left on the edge or out of the mould. Worn mould. Lighter coloured slip layer.
‣ *Colour:* Reddish-yellow 5 YR 6/6
‣ *Date:* 490-470 BCE
‣ *Workshop:* Workshop of 'the one pendant necklace'
‣ *Typology:* Chubby face group: 2d
‣ *Short description:* Head. The female figure has a round face with a low forehead. Her rounded and chubby cheeks protrude from the deeper area next to the mouth. The chin is large, and the large nose with a wide bridge is placed high on the face. Her mouth is slightly smiling, and she has thick lips, no wider than the nose. Her eyes are also large. The contours of the eyebrows are broad. On her forehead, a thick fringe of hair with long and narrow oval bulbs arches across her face. She wears a low polos with a rim and a veil draped over it. The veil is protruding and bulging and has a thicker rim on the right side. Below this, there are large earrings: knob and boat-ring shaped with a large triangular pendant. They reach her necklace. On her right side, this is more visible. She wears a tight necklace with one small round pendant on it, in the middle.
‣ *Comparable objects:* The polos of **171** is a bit higher and the face slightly smaller. It is probably a generation later but made by the same workshop. See **171** for other comparable figurines.

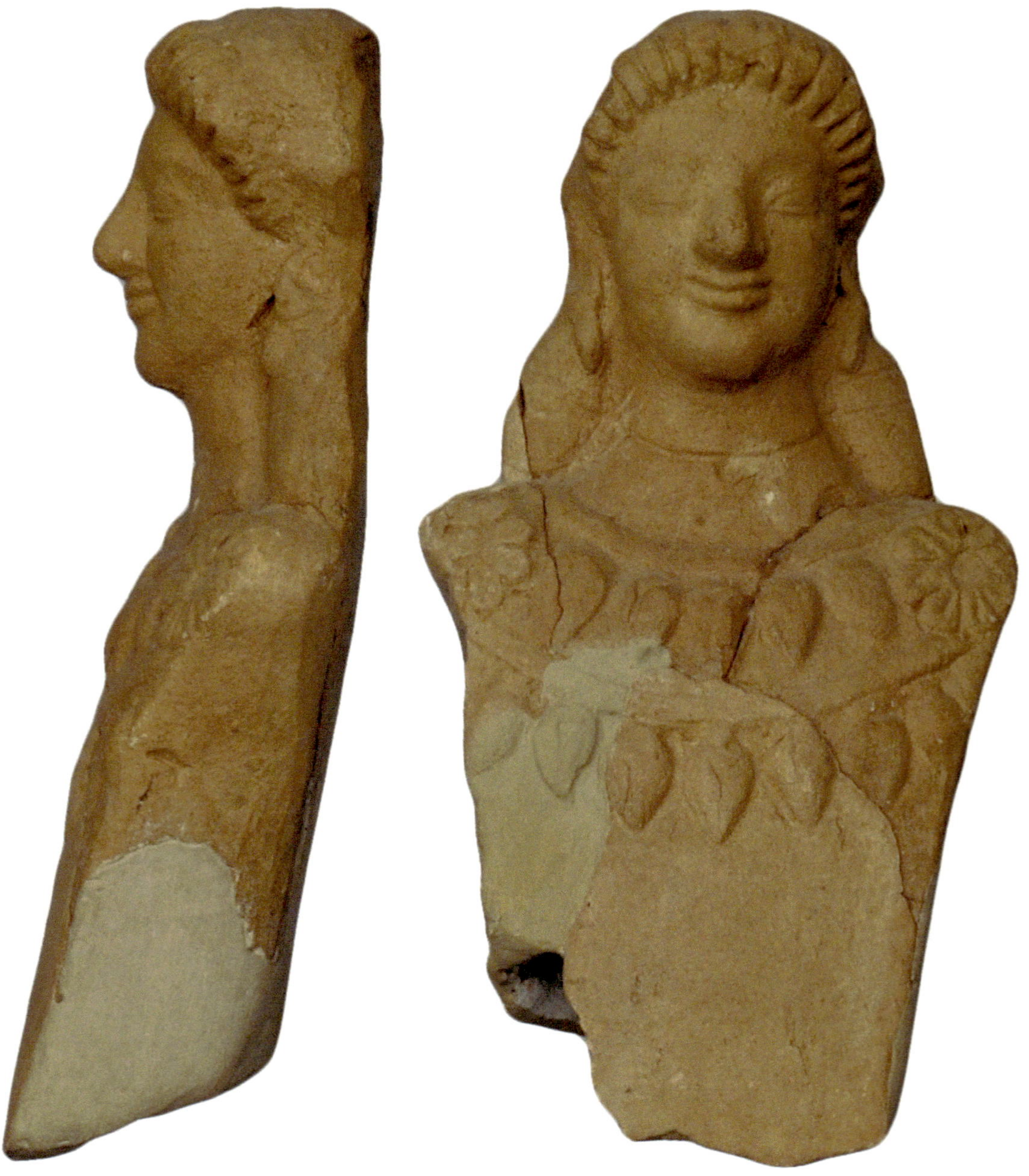

No.179

‣ *Museum and Inventory number:* Mus. Agrigento 1157

‣ *Findspot and context:* City Sanctuary. At the base of the southwest wall of the sanctuary

‣ *Publications:* Albertocchi 2004, p.85, no.1328; De Miro 2000, p.129, no.22, tav LXIV

‣ *Dimensions in cm:* h.16.2

‣ *Material:* Terracotta

‣ *Techniques:* Front moulded. A necklace with pendant was incised after moulding, as well as two horizontal lines on the hair along the sides of the neck. The pectoral pendants are reworked to make them more pointed and elongated. The fold in the clay, might indicate that they were moulded separately and applied later. Next to the pendants in the middle on the second band, lines made with a sharp tool are visible.

‣ *Colour:* Light Brown 7.5 YR 6/3

‣ *Date:* Early 5th century BCE Though with new head and adapted fibulae, the block-shaped body seems to indicate an older mould for the body. The Ionian face though is

No. 179; Scale 1:1 (Museo Archeologico Regionale "Pietro Griffo", Agrigento).

Right page; Reconstruction of no. 179 and 180; Scale 1:1 (Museo Archeologico Regionale "Pietro Griffo", Agrigento).

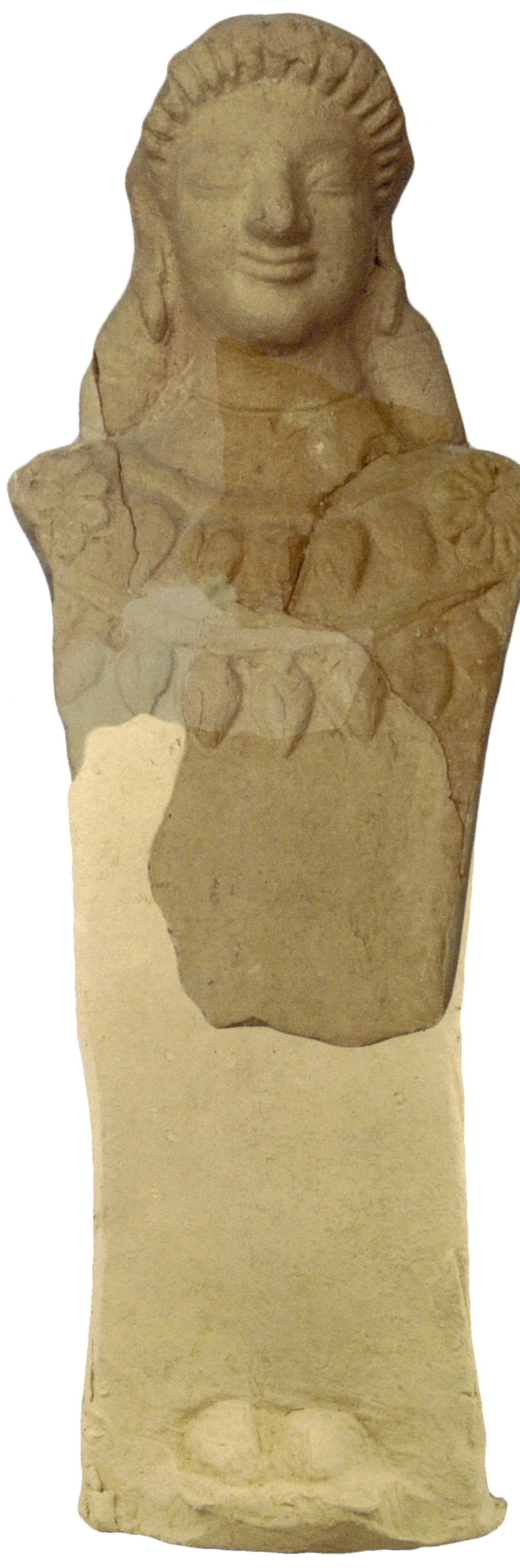

very similar to other figurines of later date and therefore the whole figurine is likely to be from 490-470 BCE.

‣ *Workshop:* Workshop of 'the one pendant necklace'

‣ *Typology:* Chubby face group: 2d

‣ *Short description:* Upper part of a figurine. Female figurine with Ionian face, very large nose, eyes with eyelids. Incised line and pendant as necklace. Very big nose. Large ears, depicted on the hair, with earrings: ring with pointed pendant. Hair in vertical bulbs. Two horizontal lines on the hair, which is bulging on each side of the neck. Veil on top of the head (?) Simple body without dress, flaring towards the shoulders with eight-petal flower or rosette fibulae. The pendants on two relatively thick and smooth cords sometimes have a line and look like shells, but the general shape is that of a flower bud. The bands contained originally five and seven(?) pendants.

‣ *Comparable objects:* From the same mould series as **180**, which forms the original body. The pendants here are reworked. Head from the same mould series AG 1169, h.7.4cm, Museo "Griffo": the necklace with pendant is not incised. Marconi 2000, no.38. Figurine from the same mould- series AG 20384, left side, h.16cm, De Miro 2000, p.129, no.23. The face is similar to the faces of Mould I, but with thicker cheeks and less rounded as a whole than **171**.

A head with neck and right fibula from Akragas is from the same mould series. It is less sharp, but no smaller than this figurine. The difference might have been caused by the type of clay that was used. The incised lines on the hair and the necklace are the same. British Mus. Inv. no.1956,0216.62, 9cm, See museum website. It is very similar to the body of an Akragantine figurine: Louvre Inv. no.C 5122, coll. Campana 178. See **104** fig 9. It has a similar outline and pendants on the first row, but a different head, fibulae and pendants on the second row. Mollard Besques 1963, p.79, B 555, pl. LII. The head is from the same mould series as **104**.

No.180

‣ *Museum and Inventory number:* Mus. Agrigento 9089 (170)

‣ *Findspot and context:* Southern city wall

‣ *Publications:* Albertocchi 2004, p.85, no.1329; De Miro 2000, p.163, no.402, tav.LXIV

‣ *Dimensions in cm:* h.18.8

‣ *Material:* Terracotta

‣ *Techniques:* Front moulded. A necklace with pendant was incised after moulding. Feet and base look a bit messy, as if reworked or even handmade.

‣ *Colour:* Light grey 10 YR 7/2

‣ *Date:* 490-470 BCE

‣ *Workshop:* Workshop of 'the one pendant necklace'

‣ *Typology:* Chubby face group: 2d

‣ *Short description:* Headless figurine, right shoulder broken off, in four fragments, restored. Simple body with slight bending at the knees. Fibulae with eight-petal flower

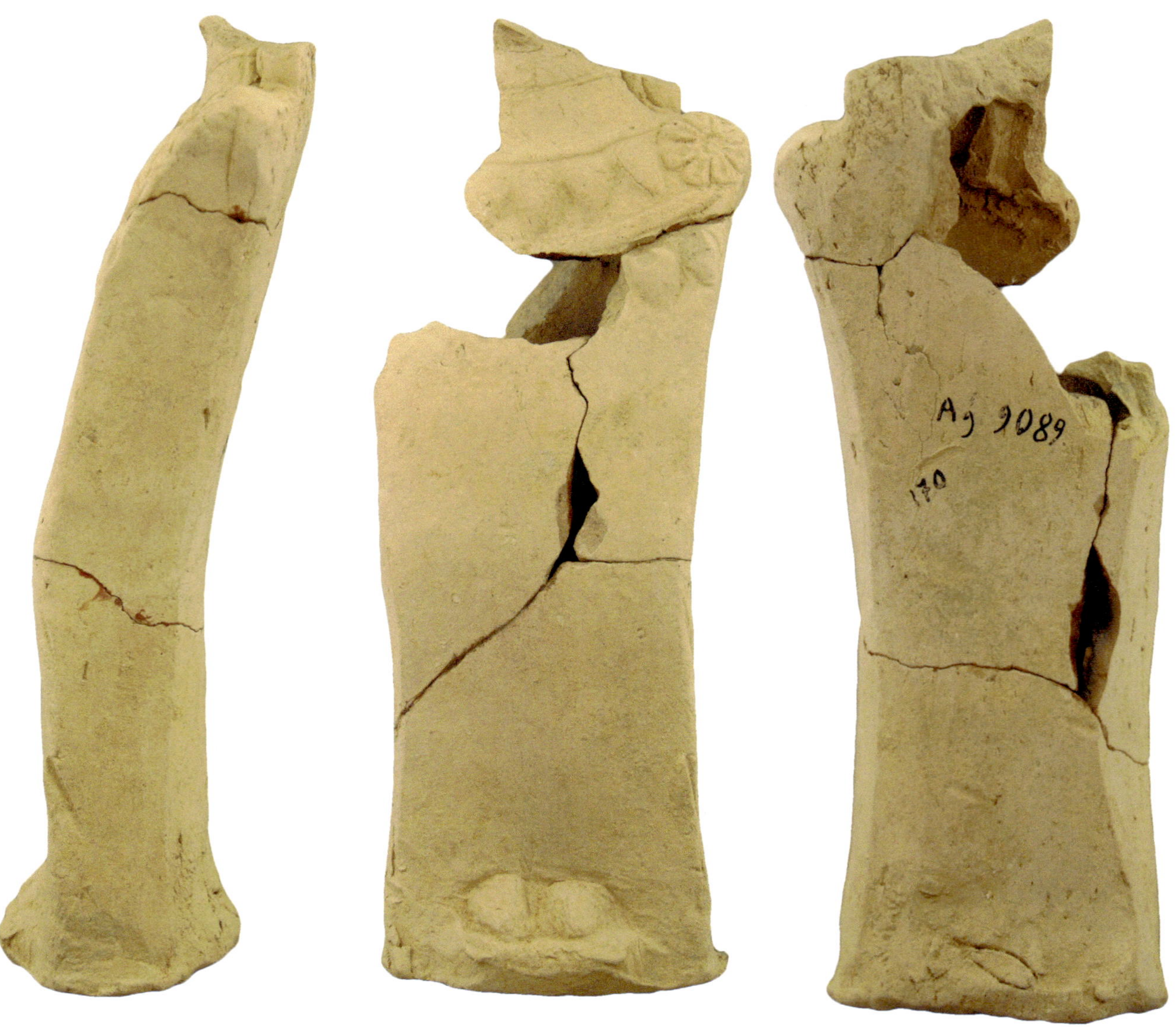

No. 180; Scale 1:1½ (Museo Archeologico Regionale "Pietro Griffo", Agrigento).

or rosette. Two bands attached with bulging rounded triangles with the point down. Dress draped over feet, sticking out on a footstool. The whole object is placed on a podium, flaring a bit.

- *Comparable objects:* From the same mould as **179**. See **179** for other comparable objects.

No.181

- *Museum and Inventory number:* Mus. Agrigento 2166
- *Findspot and context:* Temple of Zeus
- *Publications:* De Miro 1963, p.161 fig.77-8
- *Dimensions in cm:* h.10.3
- *Material:* Terracotta
- *Techniques:* Imprint from an object, the patrix
- *Colour:* Light yellowish brown 2.5 Y 6/3
- *Date:* End of the 6th century BCE (De Miro 1963, p.161)
- *Workshop:* Unknown
- *Typology:* Unknown
- *Short description:* Mould of a figurine. Part of the face and upper part of the body left. Female body, chubby face, wide and with a very broad, short nose with clear wide nostrils. The chin and jaw are rounded; the cheeks are pronounced. The broad mouth with thick lips is smiling, creating dimples at the corners. She has thin almond-shaped eyes with thick eyelids. The eyes are placed diagonally. Her hair, divided in strands, falls down next to her face over her chest to the front, curving with her breasts. On each side, three parts of the horizontally block-shaped hair, consist of two strands. It looks like she wears a kind of band around her head. She wears a multi-pleated garment with a high neck and loose parts on the arm with a decorative band along the hem. The dress has numerous

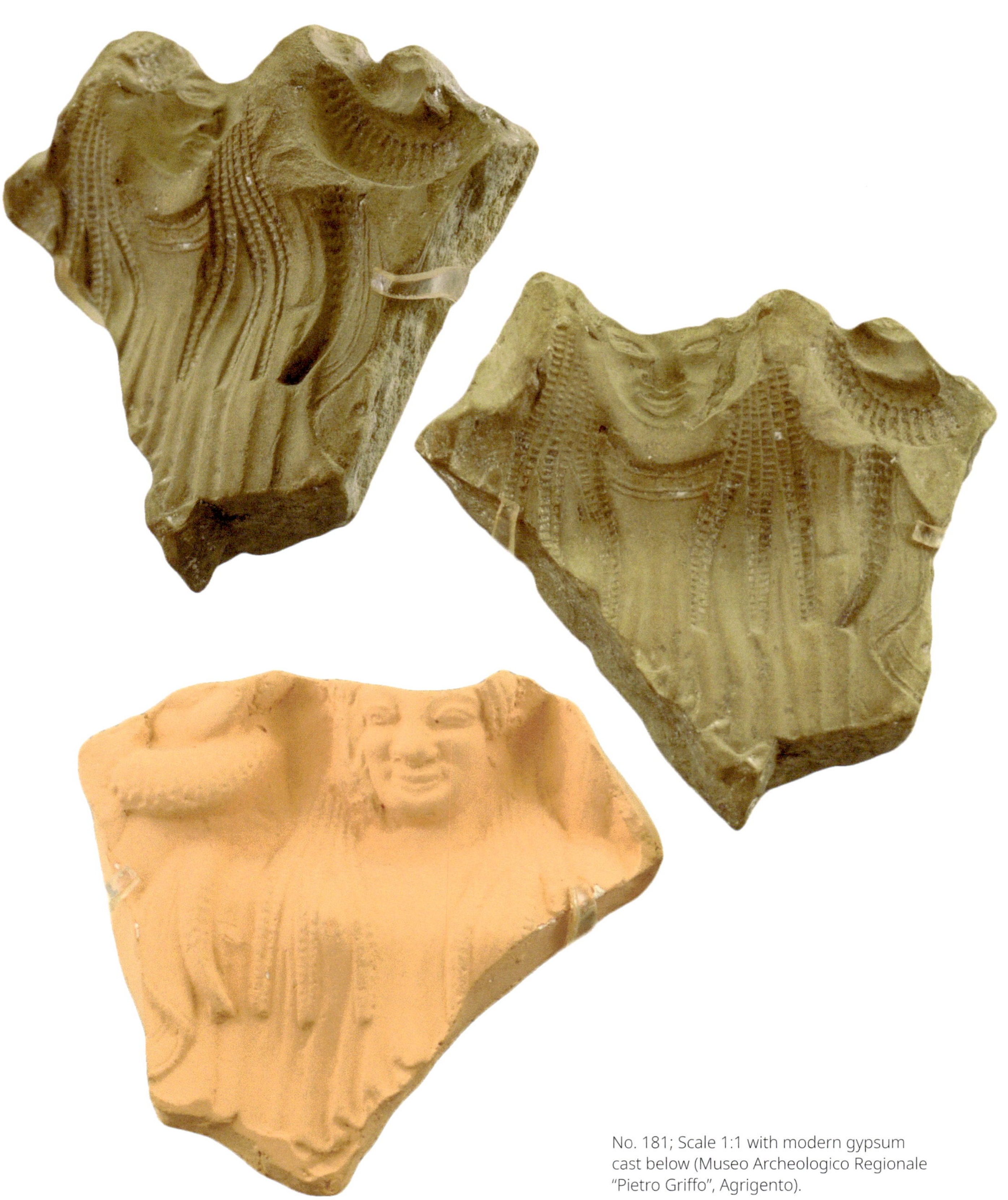

No. 181; Scale 1:1 with modern gypsum cast below (Museo Archeologico Regionale "Pietro Griffo", Agrigento).

vertical folds, falling down naturally but in a decorative manner over her broad chest. She holds her right arm up, lifting her hand, open to the viewer, next to her head, holding a thick snake curled around her wrist. The tapering tail of the snake falls down next to the hair, in the same way and to the same point. The snake has scales in vertical rows. The back of the mould is flat.

‣ *Other notes:* Fingerprint, between snake and head. Snakes in general can point to a chthonic aspect, a so-called Potnia Theron or another goddess like Hera, to whom terracotta snakes were dedicated, and this figurine is interpreted likewise. De Miro 1963, p.161. The snake on its own or the Erichthonios in particular on the aegis, around the head of Medusa, or hidden behind a shield, is associated with the goddess Athena. Though on the figurine here, the snake is not part of her aegis and much larger, it is reminiscent of the statue from the pediment of the temple of the Peisistratidai in the Gigantomachy group, around 520 BCE. Mus. Athens Inv. no.631. She also holds the snake in her left hand. Another possibility is the connection with Zeus Meilichios. This mould was found near the Temple of Zeus. The female figurine would, in that case, be interpreted as Demeter Malophoros and the snake as Zeus Meilichios. These two deities are associated and linked to each other at Selinous. This remains speculative however, as it is based on a single object.

No.182

‣ *Museum and Inventory number:* Mus. Agrigento S87

‣ *Findspot and context:* City Sanctuary

‣ *Publications:* Marconi 1930, tav.VII.9 (less damaged than now)

‣ *Dimensions in cm:* h.7

‣ *Material:* Terracotta.

‣ *Techniques:* Front moulded. A thin layer has come off the face and hair, indicating that the mould was filled first with a finer layer of clay in order to make a sharper impression.

‣ *Colour:* Very pale brown 10 YR 7/4

‣ *Date:* 490-470 BCE

‣ *Workshop:* Unknown

‣ *Typology:* Chubby face group: 2d

‣ *Short description:* Face. The face is rounded and oval. Slanted eyes with eyelids. Thick cheeks. The mouth is as wide as the nostrils and has fleshy lips. A pronounced chin and a big nose, high on the face. Hair in rhizomes with fine lines, around a low forehead.

‣ *Comparable objects:* From the same mould series as **183**, which is one generation earlier, because it is a bit larger. Similar to chubby face with the mouth placed directly under the nose from Rhodes. Nat. Mus. Copenhagen Inv. no.2511, photo 4454 below right, See museum website. A head from Akragas shows very similar facial features and seems to be male (fig.26). He wears his hair or headgear in such a way that a band occurs on the forehead, which is reminiscent of the common fringe of hair on many male figurines. The main difference is that the figurine is made in the round. The ears are on the side and the head continues to the back, which is naturally shaped also. Mus. Agrigento S81, 5.5cm, Marconi 1933, p.53, tav.VI, 8 and 10.

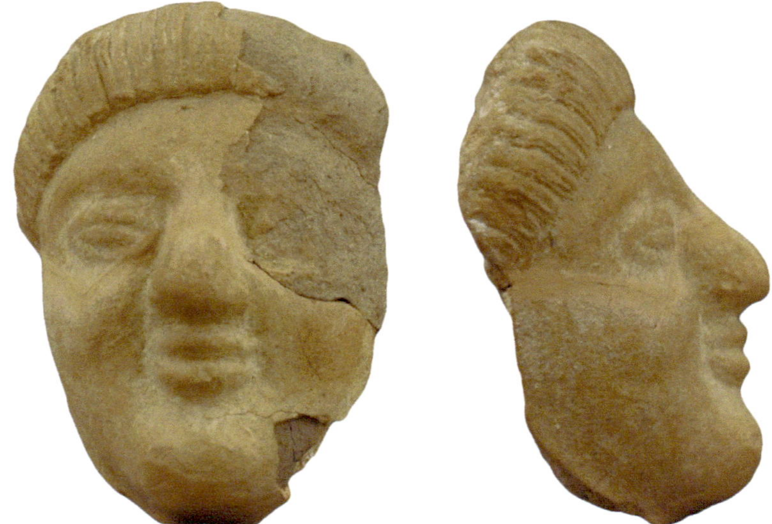

No. 182; Scale 1:1 (Museo Archeologico Regionale "Pietro Griffo", Agrigento).

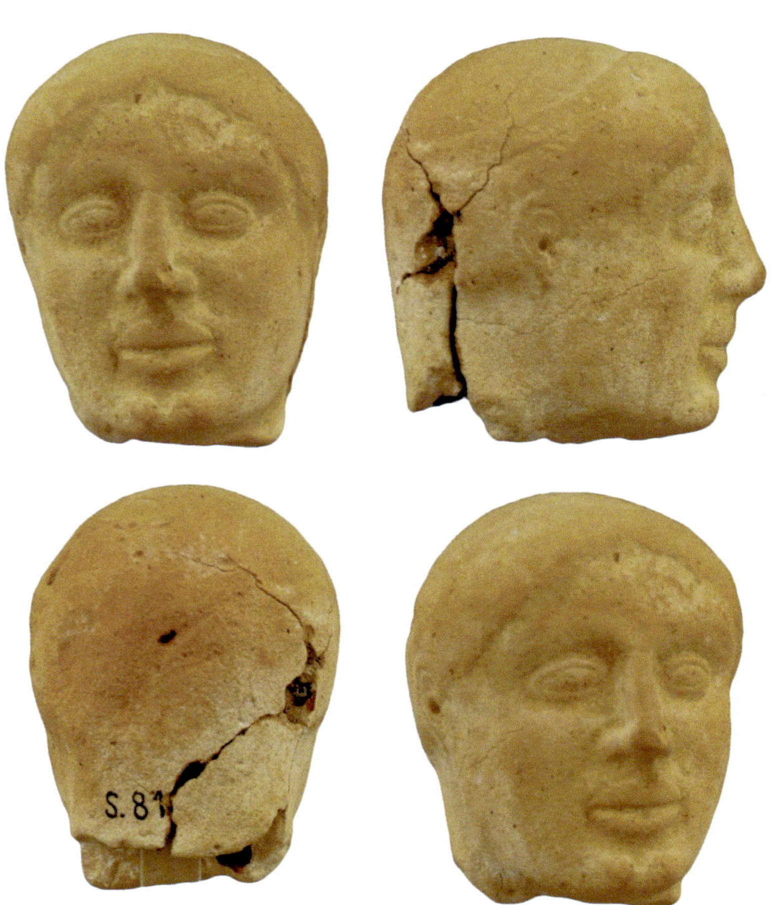

Figure 26: Head of a male from Akragas, S81; Scale 1:1 (Museo Archeologico Regionale "Pietro Griffo", Agrigento).

No.183

- *Museum and Inventory number:* Mus. Agrigento S349
- *Findspot and context:* City Sanctuary
- *Publications:* -
- *Dimensions in cm:* h.7.6
- *Material:* Terracotta. Black paint on the left side or black from burning
- *Techniques:* Front moulded.
- *Colour:* Very pale brown 10 YR 7/4
- *Date:* 490-470 BCE
- *Workshop:* Unknown
- *Typology:* Chubby face group: 2d
- *Short description:* Face. The face is rounded and oval. Slanted eyes with eyelids. Thick cheeks. The mouth is as wide as the nostrils and has fleshy lips. A pronounced chin and a big nose, high on the face. Hair in rhizomes with fine lines around a low forehead.
- *Comparable objects:* From the same mould series as **182**, which is one generation later, because it is a bit smaller.

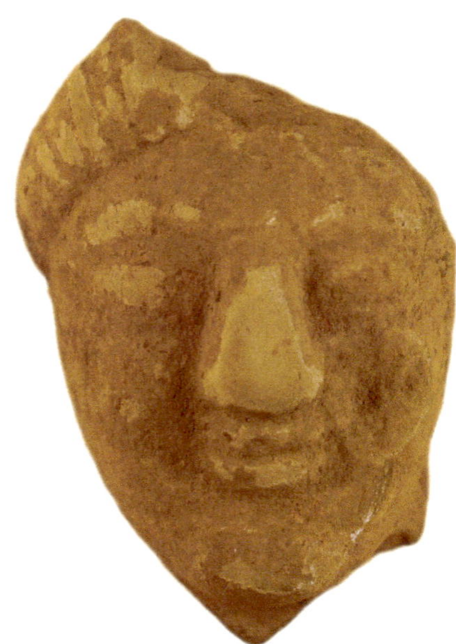

No. 183; Scale 1:1 (Museo Archeologico Regionale "Pietro Griffo", Agrigento).

No.184

- *Museum and Inventory number:* Mus. Agrigento 20539
- *Findspot and context:* Temple A
- *Publications:* -
- *Dimensions in cm:* h.4.1
- *Material:* Terracotta.
- *Techniques:* Front moulded. Solid. Suspension hole (?) on the back, at the top, through the whole head.
- *Colour:* Very pale brown 10 YR 7/3
- *Date:* 490 BCE
- *Workshop:* Unknown
- *Typology:* Unknown
- *Short description:* Head. Round face, small chin, narrow mouth with thick lips. Polos, straight and smaller than the head, placed high on the head. Hair in blocks on each side of the neck and in rounded bulbs as a rim on the forehead. Ear or earring in front of hair.
- *Comparable objects:* The face is characteristic, and the sort of polos and hairstyle are uncommon. The round face with large eyes and small mouth with thick lips, however, are reminiscent of the facial features discussed above. It shows some similar features to the head S81 discussed above (as a comparable object to **182**) which raises the question of whether these characteristics are not just an influence from Ionia but reflect also some local facial features.

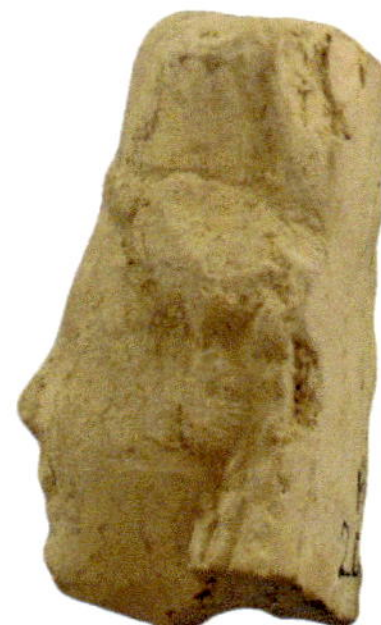

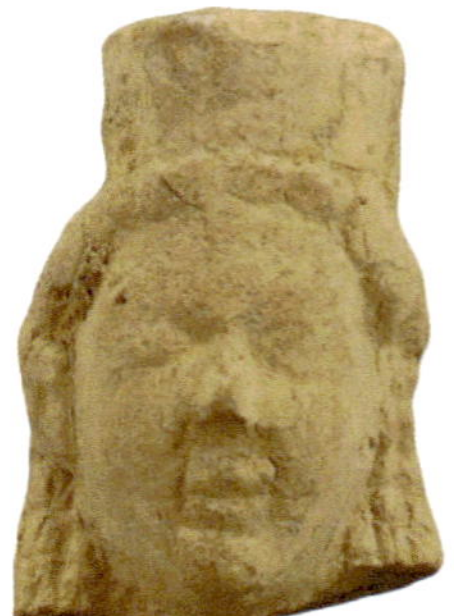

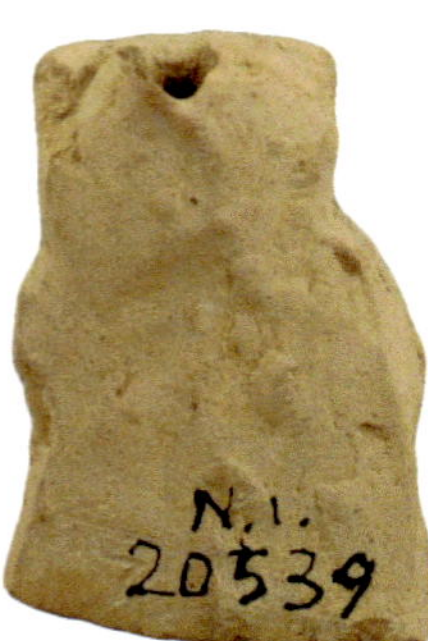

No. 184; Scale 1:1 (Museo Archeologico Regionale "Pietro Griffo", Agrigento).

Type N: A new hairstyle and widened polos (185-197)

This category coincides with group 4. The figurines are probably divided into standing dedicants and seated deities. The wide low polos is typical of this type for both figurines.

No.185

- *Museum and Inventory number:* Mus. Agrigento 8591
- *Findspot and context:* Temple of Zeus
- *Publications:* Fiertler 2001, p.58, no.37; Albertocchi 2004, p.80, no.1308
- *Dimensions in cm:* h.16.9
- *Material:* Terracotta. Painted white.
- *Techniques:* Front moulded
- *Colour:* Light Grey 10 YR 7/2
- *Date:* The third and fourth decade of the 5th century BCE
- *Workshop:* Unknown
- *Typology:* Broad-polos group: 4
- *Short description:* Front part of a standing female figurine. Worn mould. Lower part broken off. Rounded face, with pointed chin, small mouth but pronounced nose. Thick fringe of hair is unequally divided and thicker on the sides of the temples. On top of this, she wears a polos with a thin rim. Next to the sides of her sturdy neck, the hair is bulging slightly. Her pose is fully standing. She holds her arms close to her flat, thin body, reaching halfway with her outstretched hands. She wears an undergarment with

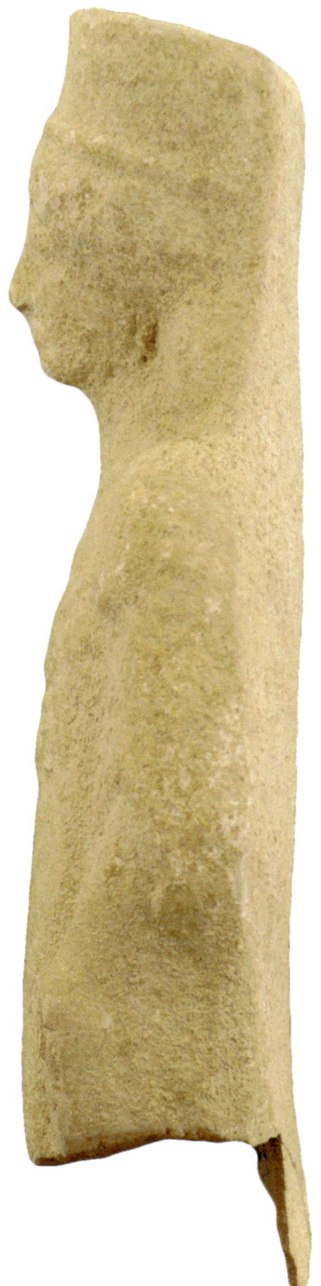

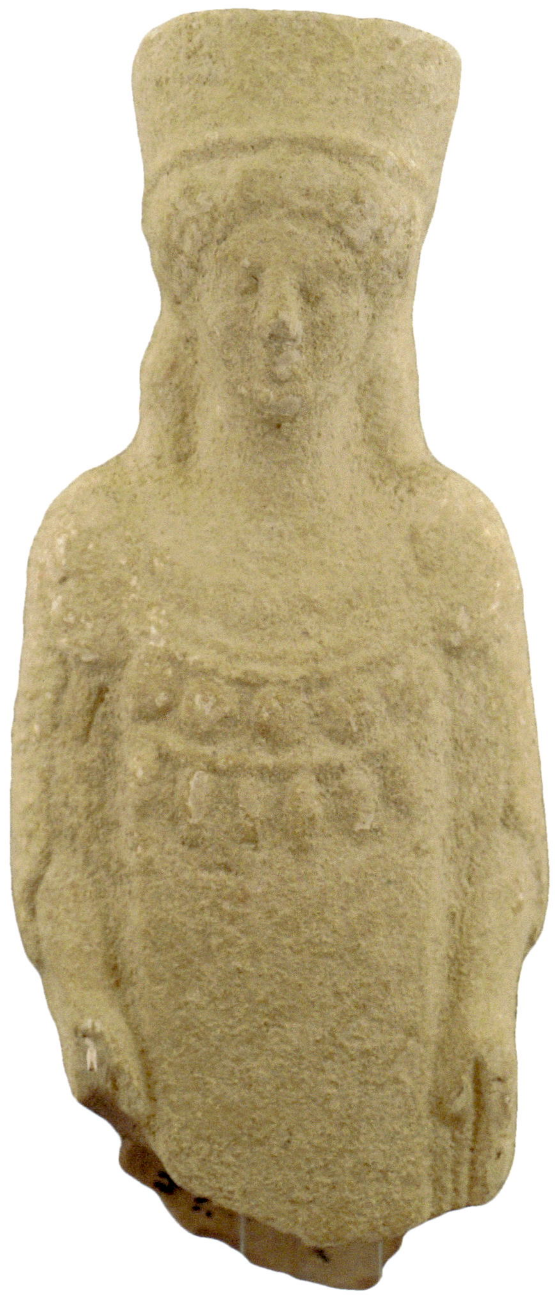

No. 185; Scale 1:1 (Museo Archeologico Regionale "Pietro Griffo", Agrigento).

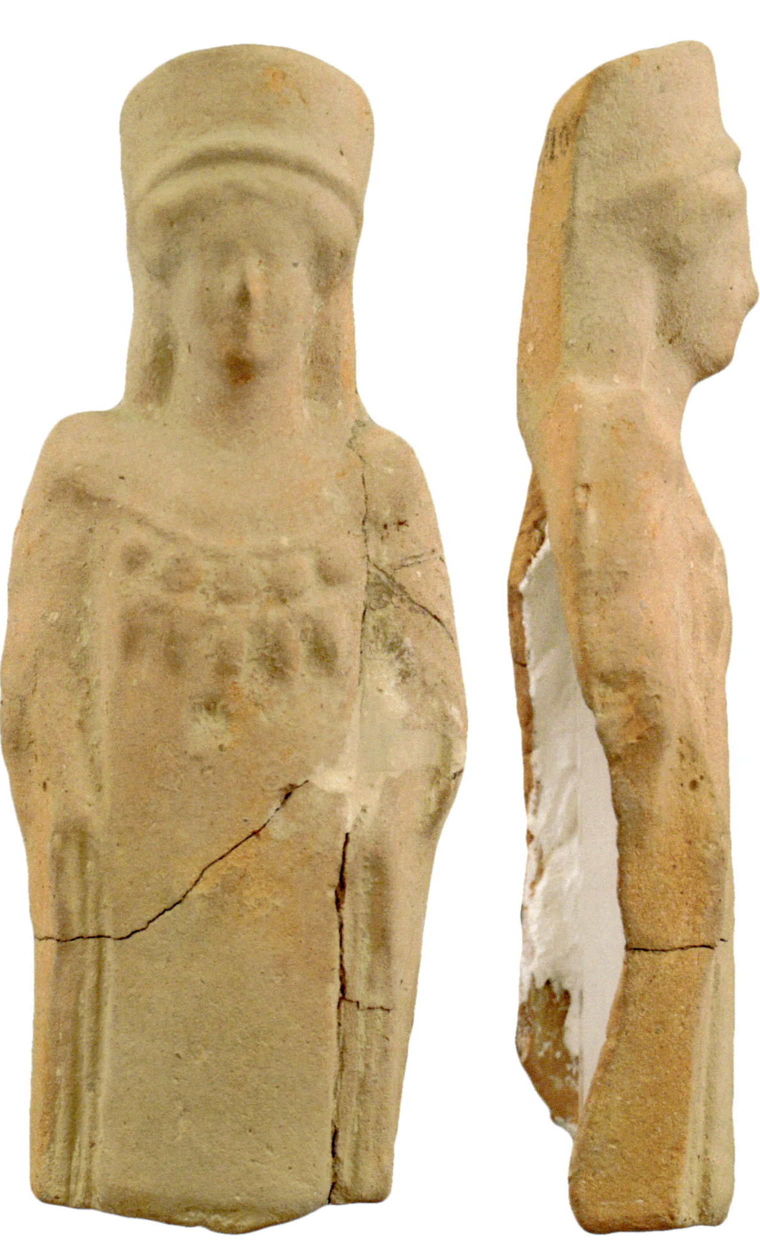

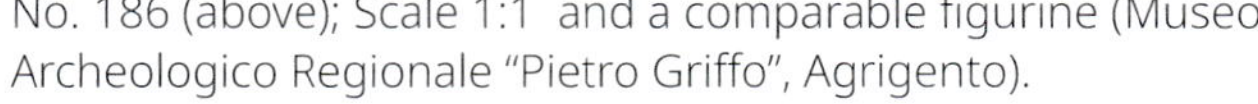

No. 186 (above); Scale 1:1 and a comparable figurine (Museo Archeologico Regionale "Pietro Griffo", Agrigento).

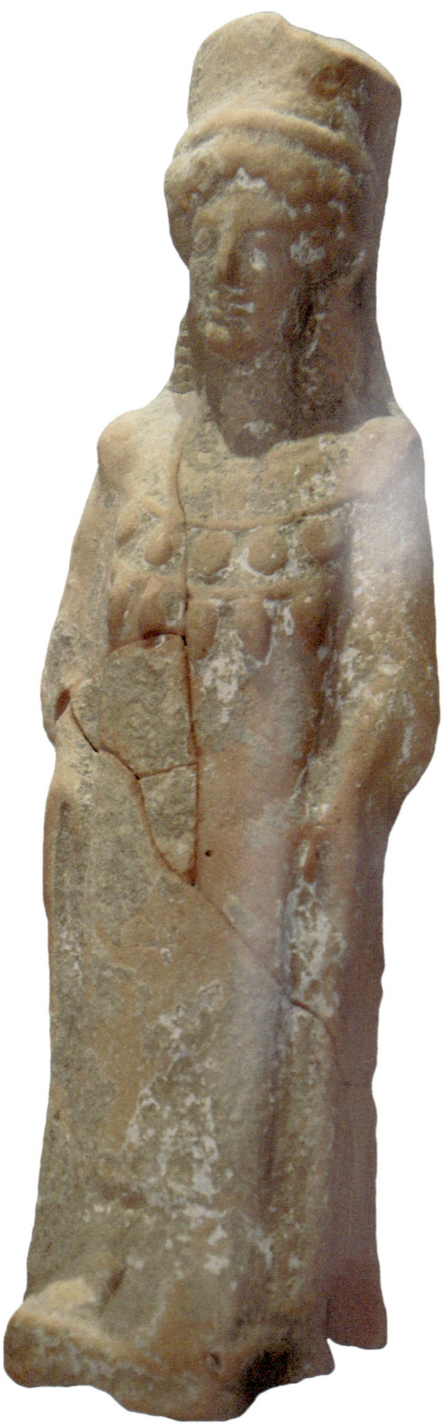

Figure 27 (right): The body of no. 186 resembles this complete figurine (Museo Archeologico Regionale "Pietro Griffo", Agrigento).

v-shaped sleeves, small folds on the chest and larger ones on the sides of the apron, below the hands. She has small round fibulae with a chord in between. Five small round pendants are attached to the cord. On a second cord, there are five seed-shaped pendants.

‣ *Comparable objects:* The figurine is possibly from the same mould series as **186**, probably a generation earlier. There is a small difference: this one has more seed-like pendants on the second row. It is reminiscent of another standing figurine, **188**, which has again six pendants on the second row. The latter has more fine detail and was painted white but is much smaller.

Though not from the same mould series, the iconographic scheme and the sort of head and pectoral pendants are comparable to a figurine from Akragas. Nat. Mus. Copenhagen Inv. no.8023, h.14.9cm, See museum website. Breitenstein 1941, p.24, no.234, tav.24.

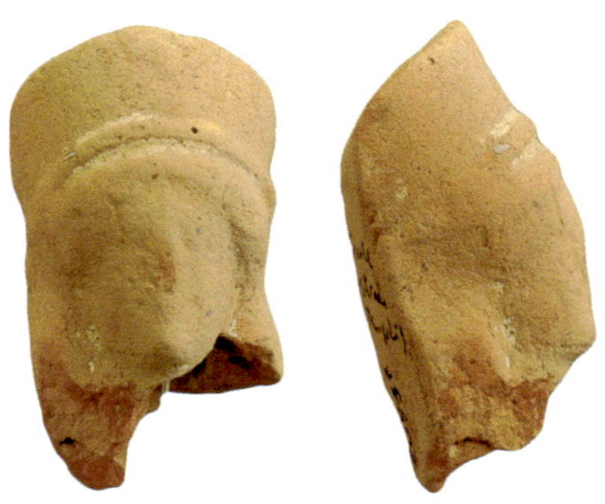

No. 187; Scale 1:1 (Museo Archeologico Regionale "Pietro Griffo", Agrigento).

No.186

‣ *Museum and Inventory number:* Mus. Agrigento S320
‣ *Findspot and context:* City Sanctuary
‣ *Publications:* Albertocchi 2004, p.80, no.1306; Marconi 1933, p.57 fig.34
‣ *Dimensions in cm:* h.15.7
‣ *Material:* Terracotta
‣ *Techniques:* Front moulded
‣ *Colour:* Reddish-yellow 5 YR 6/6
‣ *Date:* The third and fourth decade of the 5th century BCE
‣ *Workshop:* Unknown
‣ *Typology:* Broad-polos group: 4
‣ *Short description:* Front part of a standing female figurine. Worn mould. Lower part broken off. In several pieces, restored with minor infill. Rounded face, with pointed chin, small mouth but pronounced nose. Thick fringe of hair is unequally divided and thicker on the sides of the temples. On top of this she wears a wide polos with a thin rim. Next to the sides of her sturdy neck, the hair is bulging slightly. Her pose is fully standing. She holds her arms close to her flat, thin body, reaching halfway with her outstretched hands. She wears an undergarment with v-shaped sleeves, small folds on the chest and larger ones on the sides of the apron, below the hands. She has small round fibulae with a chord in between. Five small round pendants are attached to this cord. On a second cord, there are five seed-shaped pendants.
‣ *Comparable objects:* The figurine is from the same mould series as **185**, probably a generation later. Head **187** is probably from the same mould series also. The body looks very similar to that of a figurine from showcase 59, Mus. Agrigento (fig.27). While the body seems the same, the head appears to be from a later period. See the head of De Miro 2000, p.447, tav.LXXXII. Such heads are more common on figurines carrying a piglet.

No.187

‣ *Museum and Inventory number:* Mus. Agrigento 20540
‣ *Findspot and context:* Temple A
‣ *Publications:* -
‣ *Dimensions in cm:* h.4.5
‣ *Material:* Terracotta. Painted white
‣ *Techniques:* Front moulded.
‣ *Colour:* Pink 7.5 YR 7/4
‣ *Date:* The third and fourth decade of the 5th century BCE
‣ *Workshop:* Unknown
‣ *Typology:* Broad-polos group: 4
‣ *Short description:* Head. Face indistinct. Pointed chin. Wide polos with rim on top of fringe of hair. Bulging hair on the sides of the face.
‣ *Comparable objects:* Probably from the same mould series as **185** or **186**. This head is slightly larger. It might be from a generation earlier than **185**, but the weathering is surprising.

No.188

‣ *Museum and Inventory number:* Mus. Agrigento S321
‣ *Findspot and context:* City Sanctuary
‣ *Publications:* -
‣ *Dimensions in cm:* h.12.2
‣ *Material:* terracotta
‣ *Techniques:* Front moulded. Painted white.
‣ *Colour:* Very pale brown 10 YR 7/4
‣ *Date:* The third and fourth decade of the 5th century BCE
‣ *Workshop:* Unknown
‣ *Typology:* Broad-polos group: 4
‣ *Short description:* Upper part of a figurine. Small triangular face with a thin nose and a small mouth. Eyes are placed close to the nose and are rounded. Her large hairstyle consists of several rows with small bulbs as curls. Along the sides of the neck, plain hair

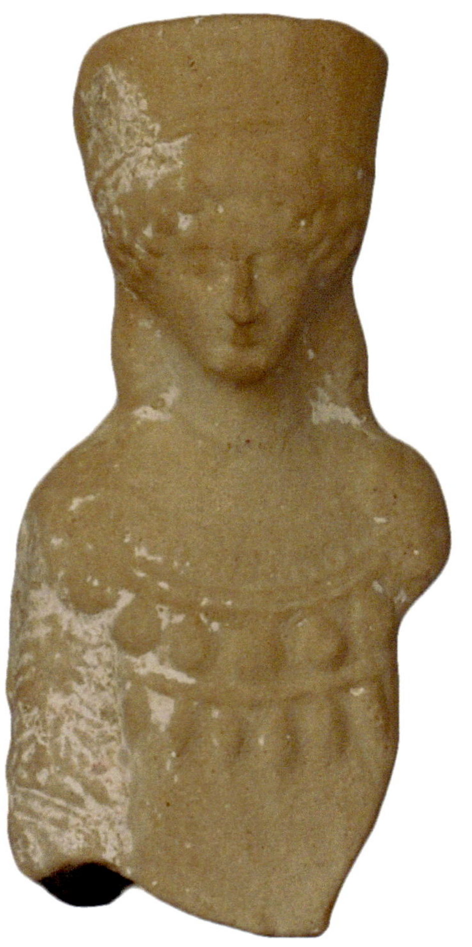
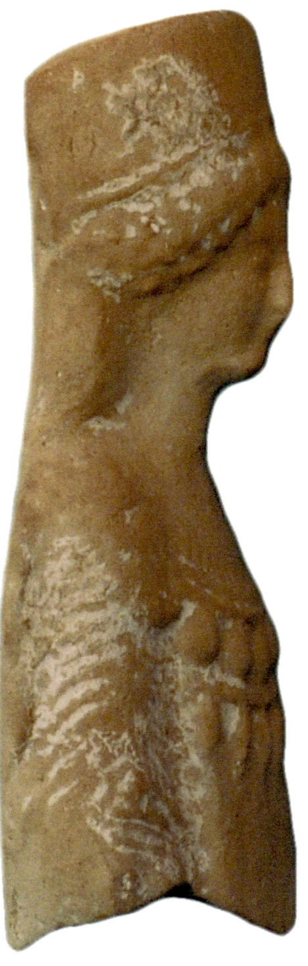

No. 188; Scale 1:1 (Museo Archeologico Regionale "Pietro Griffo", Agrigento).

is bulging. She wears a wide low polos with a thin rim. Her body is straight. Her arms are attached to her body, but the shoulders and arms are rounded. She wears an undergarment with very fine wavy folds, visible on the chest and her arms. The sleeve has a seam in the middle. On her chest, a rim might indicate the hem of her apron. This could also be a tight necklace. Low on her chest, she wears two cords with pendants. The first row, which overlaps her arm, contains of five or six discs, the one on the right shoulder seems differently shaped, as if it was impressed twice. The second has six seed-like pendants, some thicker than others.

‣ *Comparable objects:* The body is not from the same mould series but comparable in its icono-graphic scheme to **185** and **186**. The head is reminiscent of the head of 189, which has an elaborate hairstyle also.

No.189

‣ *Museum and Inventory number:* Mus. Agrigento S323
‣ *Findspot and context:* City Sanctuary
‣ *Publications:* -
‣ *Dimensions in cm:* h.11.6 (upper part)
‣ *Material:* Terracotta. White paint
‣ *Techniques:* Front moulded. The outer rim of clay when filling the mould has been used to create a rim along the body and neck, visible from the front.
‣ *Colour:* Pink 7.5 YR 7/3
‣ *Date:* The third and fourth decade of the 5th century BCE
‣ *Workshop:* Unknown
‣ *Typology:* Broad-polos group: 4
‣ *Short description:* Upper left part of a figurine with head and part of chest. Worn mould.

Her oval face has a wide jaw and a sizeable nose. Her mouth is small. The eyes are indistinct. Because of the very large crown of hair, the face looks very small. The thick round band with hair has indications of scalloped shapes in four rows. Her large polos widens to the top and has a rim. Like the hair, it creates a partial ring around her head. Along the sides of her neck, her hair falls down in waves, running irregularly and diagonally.

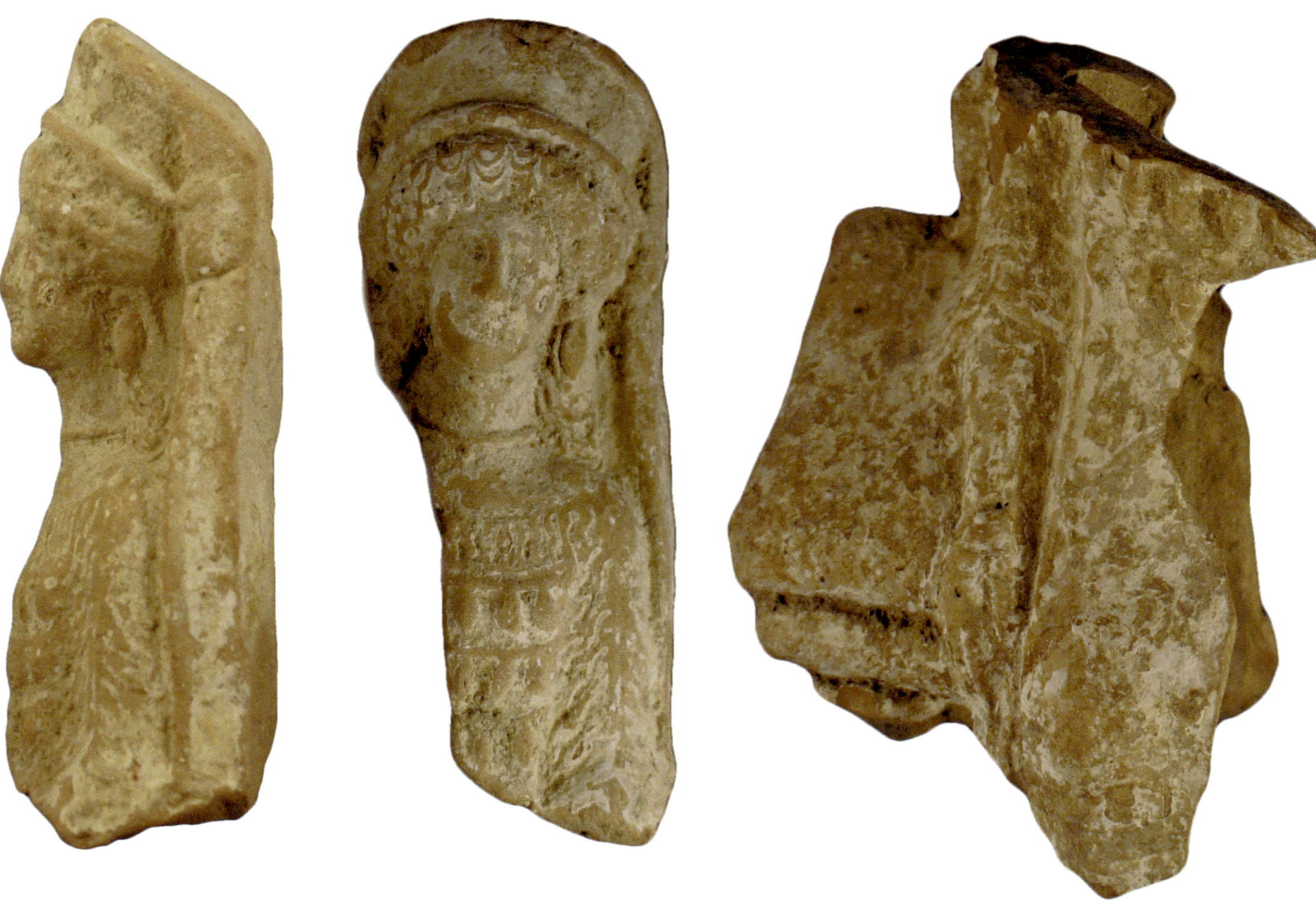

No. 189; Scale 1:1 (Museo Archeologico Regionale "Pietro Griffo", Agrigento).

In front of her hair, an elongated pendant is placed as an earring. She wears a thin necklace with one pendant, high on her neck. She is seated and an outer rim along the sides of her neck and body protrudes. Her arms are placed tight to the body and bent at the elbow. The body seems relatively small compared to the size of the hair and polos. She wears a chiton with fine wavy lines, visible on her chest and her arm. The sleeve has a seam in the middle. Three rows with thin ovoid pendants, probably in total seven on each line. These pectoral pendants are placed rather low on the chest. The back is straight, made out of a plank of clay and connected with the outer rim on the front.

The figurine has been painted white completely.

- *Comparable objects:* Comparable in iconography to **188**.

Similar to Type A XXVII. Albertocchi 2004, p.42ff.

Parts of the right and left side of the statuette (S314 and S315; h.10.5cm, and 9.2cm; Mus. Agrigento): the lower arms, the seat with cushion and on the right part some pectoral pendants. These two parts are probably from a figurine that was one generation later than **189**, but from the same mould series.

Possibly from the same series as **194-196** but different generations. No.**194** could be one generation later, because it is smaller.

- *Other notes:* Photograph together with S314 from Mus. Agrigento.

No.190

- *Museum and Inventory number:* Mus. Agrigento 20554
- *Findspot and context:* Temple A
- *Publications:* -
- *Dimensions in cm:* h.7.8
- *Material:* Terracotta.
- *Techniques:* Front moulded.
- *Colour:* Very pale brown 10 YR 8/2
- *Date:* The third and fourth decade of the 5th century BCE
- *Workshop:* Unknown
- *Typology:* Broad-polos group: 4

‣ *Short description:* Head. Nose broken off. Small flat face. Large eyes with eyelids. A straight mouth with thick lips. She has a fringe of hair, parted in the middle, with regular waves. On the sides of the neck, the hair falls down with similar waves. She wears a wide, but very low polos with a rim. The upper hem of the dress seems to be marked but is indistinct. Around her neck, she wears a necklace, thicker towards the front.
‣ *Comparable objects:* Hairstyle similar to **191** and **192**, though on their fringe it is not parted in the middle. On the sides, the hair run down further, diagonally on **191** diagonal and smoothed on **192**.

No.191

‣ *Museum and Inventory number:* Mus. Agrigento 8593
‣ *Findspot and context:* South of the Temple of Zeus
‣ *Publications:* -
‣ *Dimensions in cm:* h.8.4
‣ *Material:* Terracotta
‣ *Techniques:* Front moulded.
‣ *Colour:* Reddish-yellow 5 YR 7/8
‣ *Date:* The third and fourth decade of the 5th century BCE
‣ *Workshop:* Unknown
‣ *Typology:* Broad-polos group: 4
‣ *Short description:* Head, damaged nose. Round fleshy face. Smiling, slightly opened mouth with deep dimples next to it. Her eyes have clear eyelids. Fringe of hair with irregular waves. Hair on the sides of the neck marked with diagonal lines running outwards and parallel to each other. She wears a wide polos. Rounded back, rounded edge from the top of the polos to the back.
‣ *Comparable objects:* Comparable to the style of **190** and **193**. Similar also to Marconi 1933, tav.XII.11.

No.192

‣ *Museum and Inventory number:* Mus. Agrigento 20538
‣ *Findspot and context:* Temple of Hercules
‣ *Publications:* -
‣ *Dimensions in cm:* h.7.0
‣ *Material:* Terracotta. Painted white
‣ *Techniques:* Front moulded.
‣ *Colour:* Pinkish grey 7.5 YR 8/2
‣ *Date:* The third and fourth decade of the 5th century BCE
‣ *Workshop:* Unknown
‣ *Typology:* Broad-polos group: 4
‣ *Short description:* Head. Face with wide jaw and short but wide nose. Fringe of hair with fine regular waves, on top of which she wears a wide polos with rim and curl on one side, the other might have been broken off. She has a sturdy neck with bulging hair next to it.
‣ *Comparable objects:* **190**, **191** and **193** have a similar polos with rim, but without a sort of inwards curling tip at the back. In the middle, an upwards-curving part shows that part has been broken off. It is very likely that this was the lophos of a Corinthian helmet. Under the influence of the iconography of Athena, the figurines are altered. Other than the helmet of Athena, some figurines probably had a spear in their hand. Parisi 2017 79, n. 124; Albertocchi 2004, p.131. These figurines have been connected also to Athena Ergane. Consoli V. 2011, 9-28. Not exactly the same, but very similar in regard of facial and hair features and headgear are two figurines from Gelas. These are nearly complete and sit on thrones similar to **195**. They are wearing three rows, each with seven seed-shaped pectoral pendants. Panvini 1998 73 Inv. 36003-36004; h.23 and 20cm.

A similar polos with broken lophos is worn by a figurine from Akragas. Nat. Mus. Copenhagen Inv. no.8582, h.15.5cm, Breitenstein 1941, no.458.

No.193

‣ *Museum and Inventory number:* Mus. Agrigento 8597
‣ *Findspot and context:* South of the Temple of Zeus
‣ *Publications:* -
‣ *Dimensions in cm:* h.8.6
‣ *Material:* Terracotta
‣ *Techniques:* Front moulded.
‣ *Colour:* Reddish-yellow 5 YR 6/6
‣ *Date:* The third and fourth decade of the 5th century BCE
‣ *Workshop:* Unknown
‣ *Typology:* Broad-polos group: 4
‣ *Short description:* Head. Round face with large eyes and low arching eyebrows. She has a small mouth with thick lips. Fringe of hair with irregular waves. On the sides, her hair runs diagonally. She wears a wide polos with a thin rim. Straight back.
‣ *Comparable objects:* Hair on the sides of the face is similar to **191**.

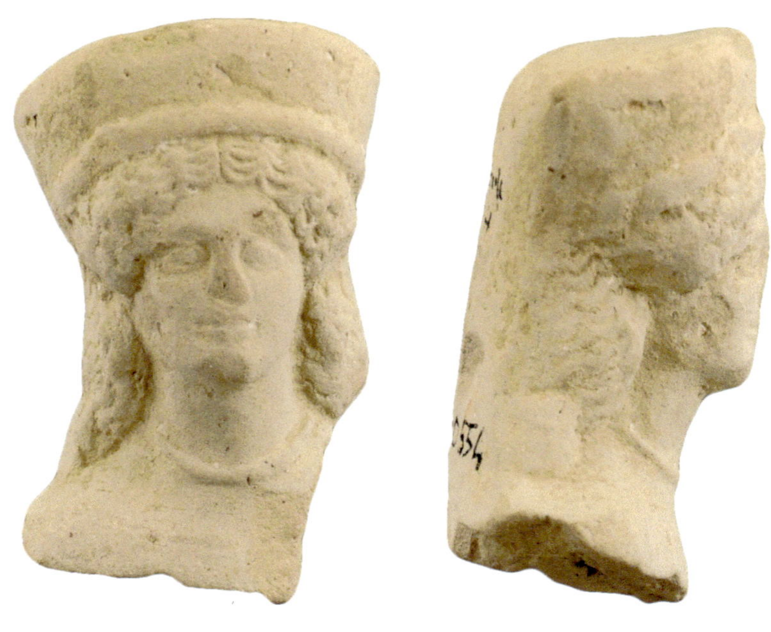

No. 190; Scale 1:1 (Museo Archeologico Regionale "Pietro Griffo", Agrigento).

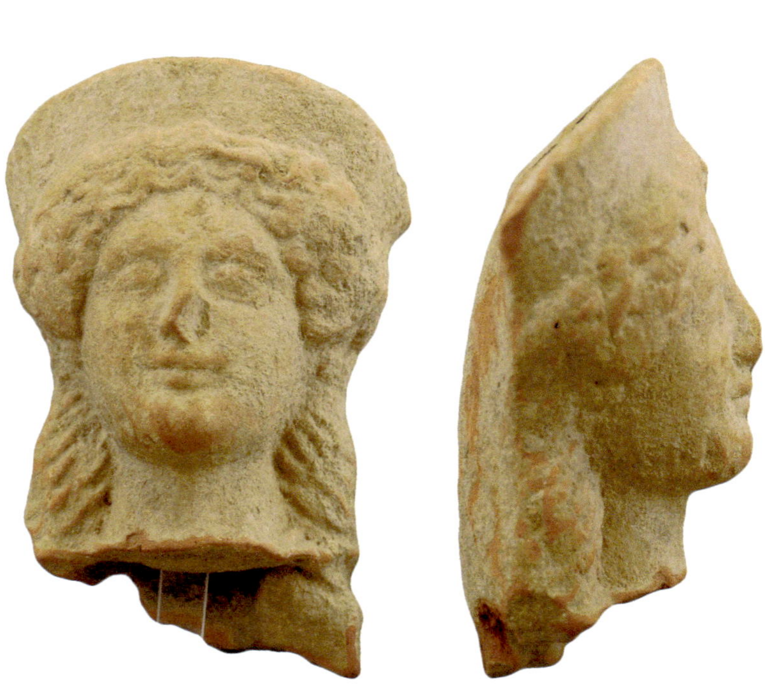

No. 191; Scale 1:1 (Museo Archeologico Regionale "Pietro Griffo", Agrigento).

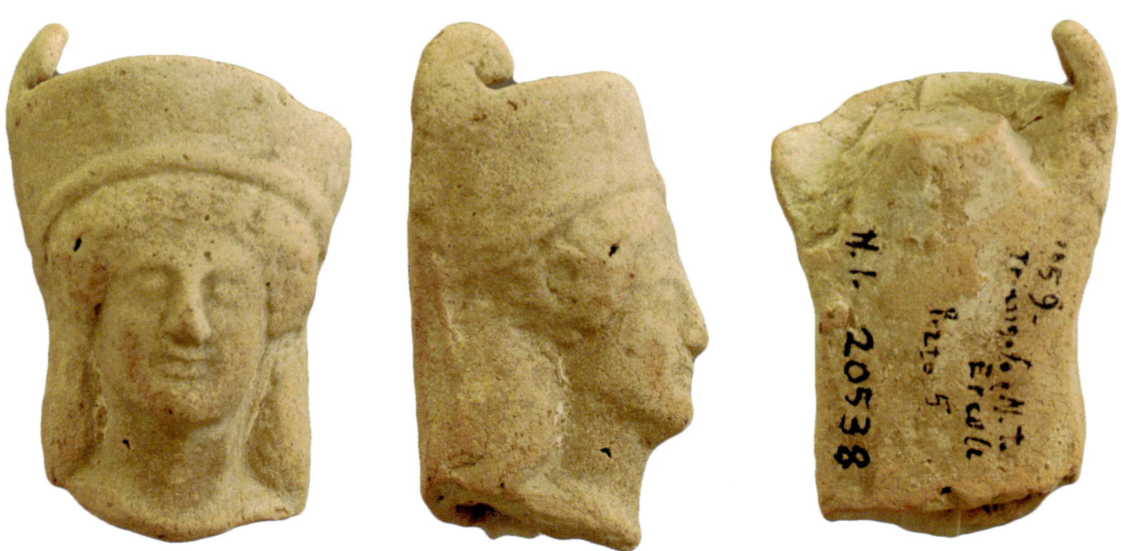

No. 192; Scale 1:1 (Museo Archeologico Regionale "Pietro Griffo", Agrigento).

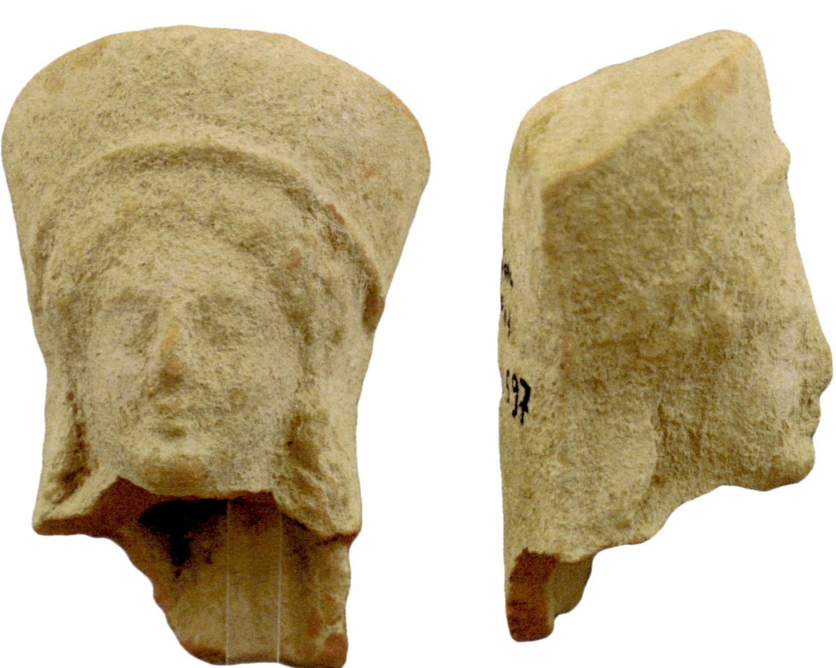

No. 193; Scale 1:1 (Museo Archeologico Regionale "Pietro Griffo", Agrigento).

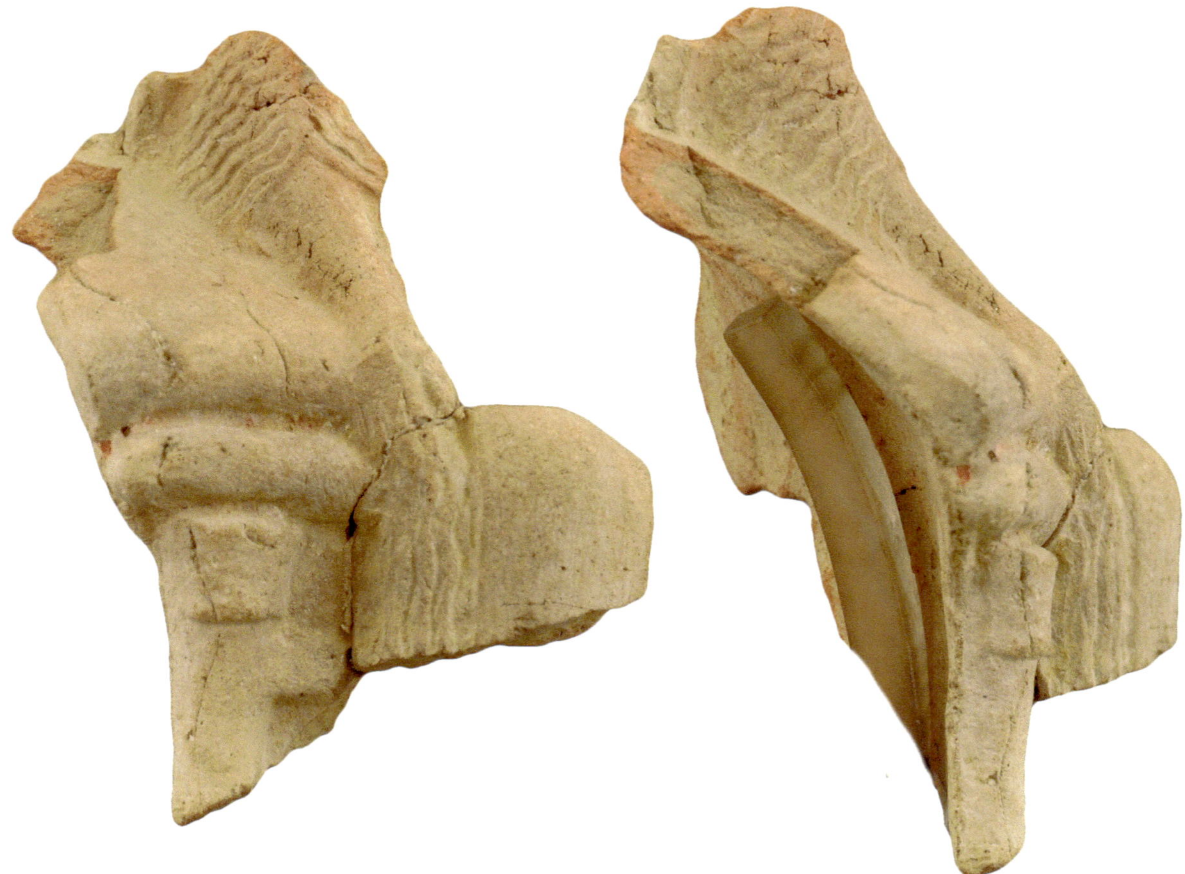

No. 194; Scale 1:1 (Museo Archeologico Regionale "Pietro Griffo", Agrigento).

No.194

- *Museum and Inventory number:* Mus. Agrigento 2597
- *Findspot and context:* Akragas
- *Publications:* Albertocchi 2004, p.42, no.621
- *Dimensions in cm:* h.11.5
- *Material:* Terracotta
- *Techniques:* Front moulded.
- *Colour:* Pink 7.5 YR 7/3
- *Date:* The third and fourth decade of the 5th century BCE
- *Workshop:* Unknown
- *Typology:* Elaborate throne group: 4
- *Short description:* Part of a seated figurine. Right part of the throne, with arm and lap of a figure. She wears a chiton: her upper arm is covered by a sleeve with a seam in the middle, creating a v-shape just below the elbow. Next to the apron, vertical slightly wavy folds indicate the undergarment. Her hand reaches her knee. She sits on a particular throne. The upper part of the leg has a flaring cylindrical part on top, which supports the seat with a horizontal stretcher. The straight seat is topped with a thick cushion.
- *Comparable objects:* Similar to **195** and in the style S314 (photograph together with **189**). There are several objects of this series from Gelas, also as moulds from Camarina. Albertocchi 2004, p.42-4.

No.195

- *Museum and Inventory number:* Mus. Agrigento S313 and S317
- *Findspot and context:* City Sanctuary
- *Publications:* -
- *Dimensions in cm:* h.17.5 (larger part)
- *Material:* Terracotta. Lighter coloured slip layer.
- *Techniques:* Front moulded.
- *Colour:* Pink 5 YR 7/4
- *Date:* The third and fourth decade of the 5th century BCE
- *Workshop:* Unknown
- *Typology:* Elaborate throne group: 4
- *Short description:* Left lower part of a figurine without head and part of chest. Broken and restored. Together with a small part of the chair with right hand. From a fresh mould. Seated figurine, with the arm along the body. Her hand reaches to just above her knee and has fine lines indicating the fingers. The thumb is a bit separated, and it seems as if the hand is about to hold the chiton up. Meanwhile the lower arms rest on the thick cushions of the seat. She is dressed in an undergarment with wavy lines in a roughly regular way, draped over her feet. Her sleeves have similar waves and a seam in the middle. It reaches to just below the elbow. On top, she wears an apron, which leaves the chiton on the sides and around her ankles

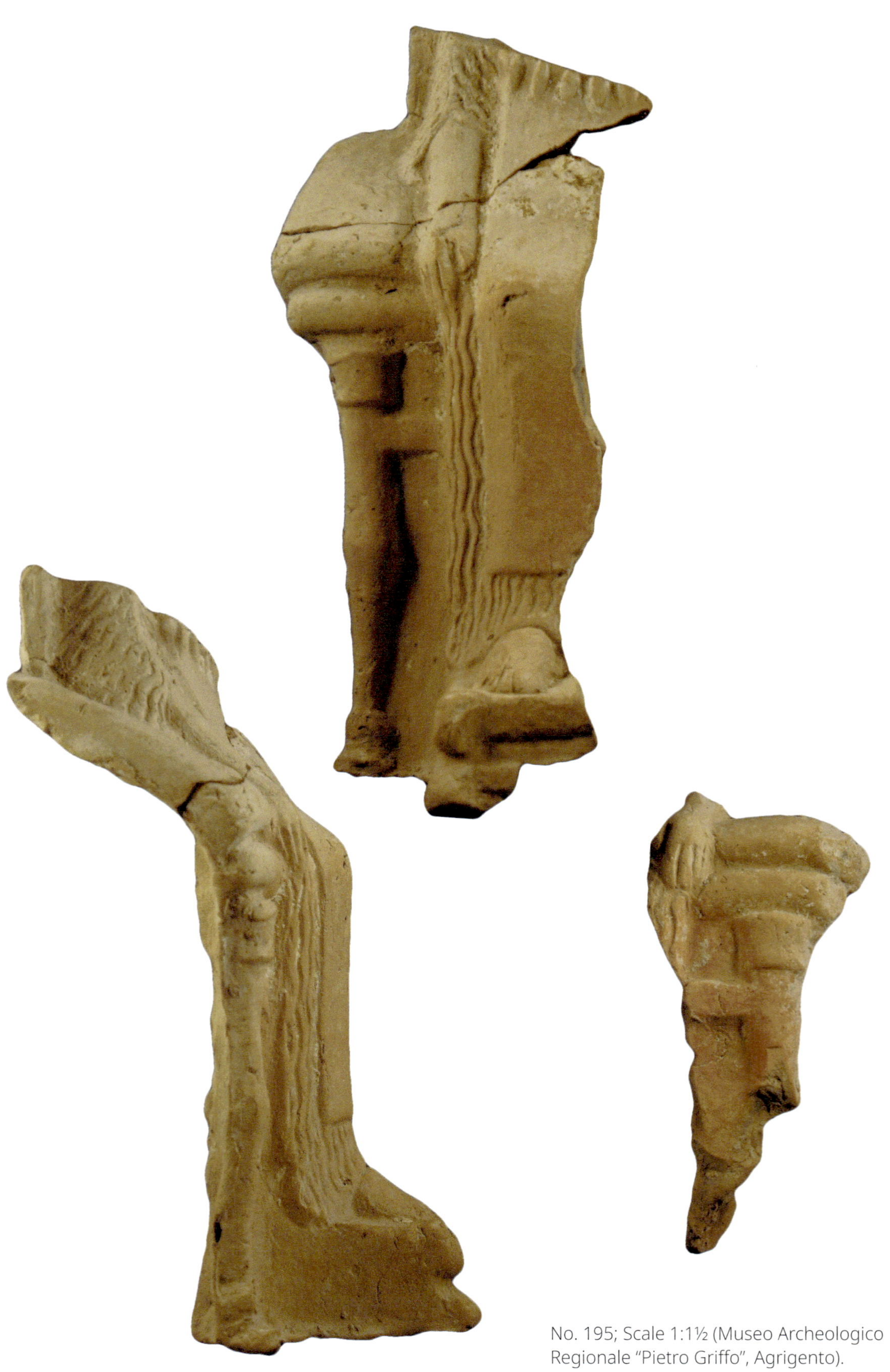

No. 195; Scale 1:1½ (Museo Archeologico Regionale "Pietro Griffo", Agrigento).

uncovered. A small part on her chest shows that she was probably wearing multiple pectoral cords with numerous seed-shaped pendants. Six of them are visible. The total number of pendants on one cord might have been eleven. She is seated on a detailed piece of furniture. The legs of the chair have a thicker part at the foot, like hooves, also as a base, which could imitate a horseshoe. Together with the joint in the middle, it is clear that a horse leg is imitated here. Almost at the top of the leg, there is a horizontal stretcher. The seat itself, however, is supported by short flaring parts, like column capitals. A cushion as thick as the front rail itself is placed on top. This part is not straight, but runs down, as if the aim were to lean, rather than sit. The area between body and chair leg, and also between the seat and the stretcher, is deeper and left empty.

Her bare feet are placed on a low rectangular footstool. Though broken, it is clear that it had one stretcher at the front. The foot and the corner are thicker, and semi-circular shaped. The sides of the footstool are smooth and closed.

- *Comparable objects:* **196** is from the same mould.

Similar 'leg' of the throne, inspired by a horse leg, is seen on a figurine from Gelas. Panvini 1998, p.54, Inv. no.35692. Though the 'capital' on top of the leg is absent on that figurine and placed directly supporting the seat. Another figurine from Gelas has such cylindrical parts on top, like **194**. Panvini 1998, p.55, Inv. no.10692.

No.196

- *Museum and Inventory number:* Mus. Agrigento S316
- *Findspot and context:* City Sanctuary
- *Publications:* -
- *Dimensions in cm:* h.8.8

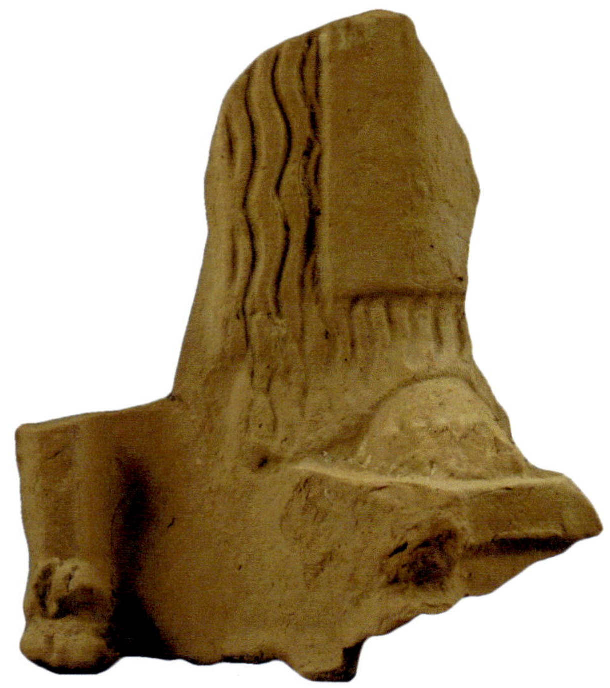

No. 196; Scale 1:1 (Museo Archeologico Regionale "Pietro Griffo", Agrigento).

- *Material:* Terracotta
- *Techniques:* Front moulded.
- *Colour:* Pink 5 YR 7/4
- *Date:* The third and fourth decade of the 5th century BCE
- *Workshop:* Unknown
- *Typology:* Elaborate throne group: 4
- *Short description:* Fragment of a seated figurine: right foot on footstool. From a fresh mould. The figure is dressed in an undergarment with wavy lines in a roughly regular way, draped over her feet. On top, she wears an apron, which leaves the chiton on the sides and around her ankles uncovered. The lower part of the leg of the chair is visible. It has a thicker part at its base, which seems, possibly accidentally, to be incised vertically. Her bare foot rests on a low rectangular footstool. Though broken, it is clear that it protrudes at the front. The corner of the seat is thicker and semi-circular shaped. The sides of the footstool are just smooth and 'closed.'
- *Comparable objects:* **196** is from the same mould.

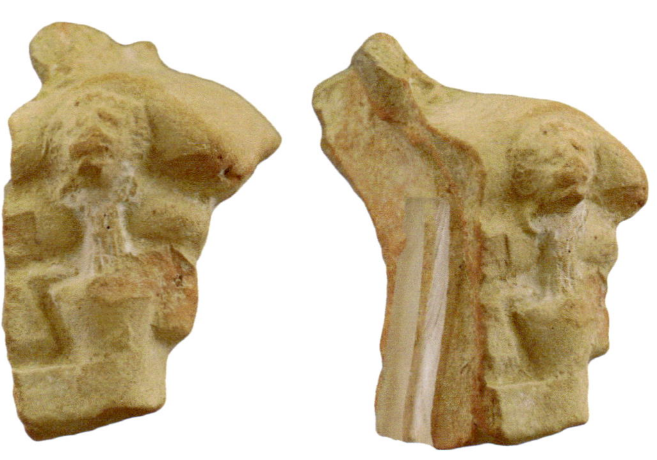

No. 197; Scale 1:1 (Museo Archeologico Regionale "Pietro Griffo", Agrigento).

No.197

- *Museum and Inventory number:* Mus. Agrigento 8612
- *Findspot and context:* Temple of Zeus
- *Publications:* -
- *Dimensions in cm:* h.5.5
- *Material:* Terracotta
- *Techniques:* Front moulded.
- *Colour:* Pink 7.5 YR 8/3
- *Date:* The third and fourth decade of the 5th century BCE
- *Workshop:* Unknown
- *Typology:* Elaborate throne group: 4
- *Short description:* Part of a figurine, which was seated. Part of the elaborately detailed throne. The upper part of the leg with above it the seat with a thick cushion. Above the leg and from under the cushion, a lion decoration. It seems to hold a ring on which four threads are connected with the construction below, as if it is holding it up.
- *Comparable objects:* Similar to **194**.

The lion protome as a frontal decoration of the corner of the seat appears on Locrian pinakes, together with the lion paws as feet and the backrest finial turned around and shaped into a head of a duck. See for example Pinax type 8/31, Zancani Montuoro 1954; Prückner 1968, p.86; Mertens-Horn 2005, p.34 Abb.24. The footstool has lion paws also on this pinax. The way the lion holds a ring and part of the construction of this figurine, however, is different.

Type O: Seated on the left shoulder (198-200)

A fragment of a plaque of a satyr with a figurine on his left shoulder and two kourotrophoi with a small version of themselves on their left shoulder.

No.198

- *Museum and Inventory number:* Mus. Agrigento S77
- *Findspot and context:* -
- *Publications:* -
- *Dimensions in cm:* h.7.7
- *Material:* Terracotta
- *Techniques:* Front moulded
- *Colour:* Pinkish grey 7.5 YR 7/2
- *Date:* 5th century BCE
- *Workshop:* -
- *Typology:* Plaque/ figurine: 6a
- *Short description:* Middle part of a figurine, in several pieces, restored. Naked ithyphallic satyr with a moustache, a large pointed beard, large ears, a belly and breasts. He holds a rectangular object in his left hand. This object has a sloping upper body and bends in the middle. The satyr holds his tail in his right hand, with his arm bent. The tail runs from the back, curling upwards. Part of his aroused penis touches the corner of the rectangular object he is carrying. The rounded back runs straight.
- *Comparable objects:* The object is very similar to a figurine and probably from the same mould series or one generation earlier: Mus. Louvre Inv. No.CA 4318, h.13.3cm (fig.28). The exemplar from Akragas is less sharp, but of the same size. From that object, the pose of the satyr, in so-called 'Knielauf', becomes clearer. He is resting on his right knee, while with his left leg he supports a figure with a block-like body. The statuette represents a female figure, seated in the typical leaning way, so common among Akragantine figurines. She wears four or five ovoid pectoral pendants. Her oval face is indistinct. She has a round smooth fringe of hair and wears a medium-high polos. Another complete similar figurine of unknown size, but comparable in sharpness, is now lost. This object and similar figures are discussed by Schneider-Herrmann 1968 and are dated to between 465 and 460 BCE. The special pose, carrying someone on the left shoulder, finds quite some similarities in

No. 198; Scale 1:1 (Museo Archeologico Regionale "Pietro Griffo", Agrigento).

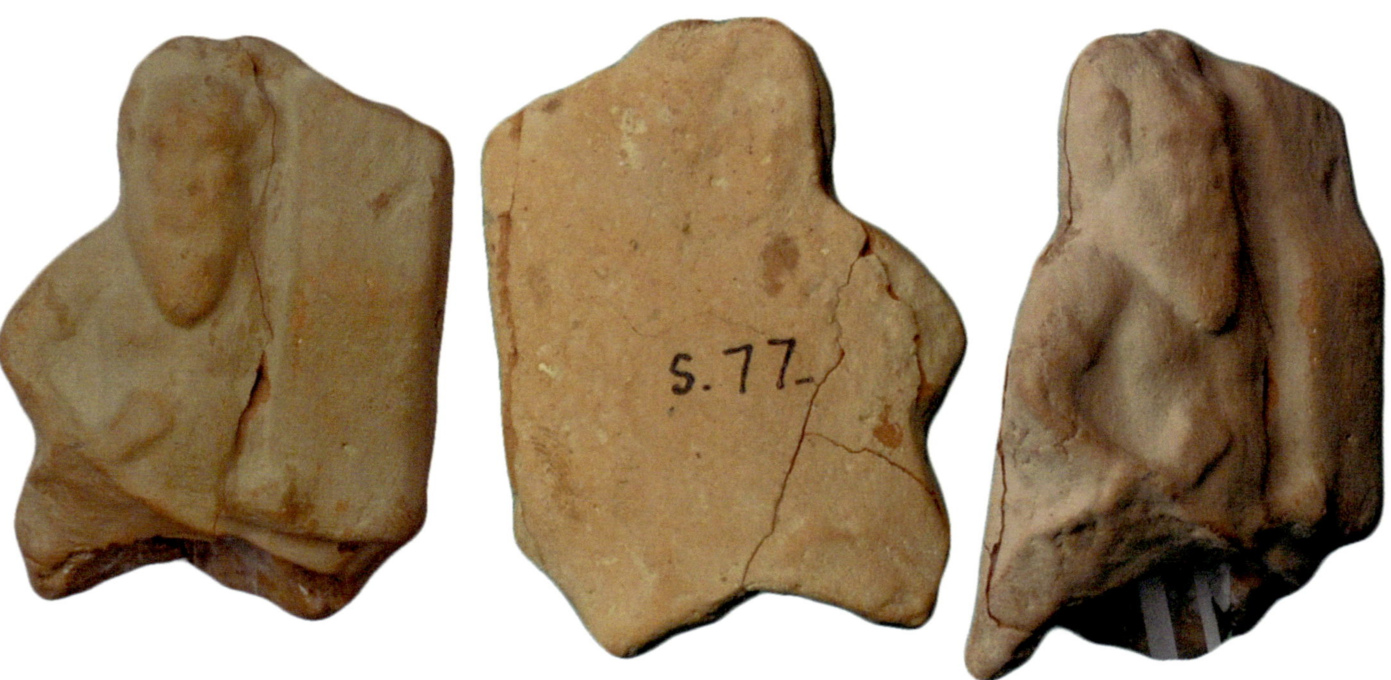

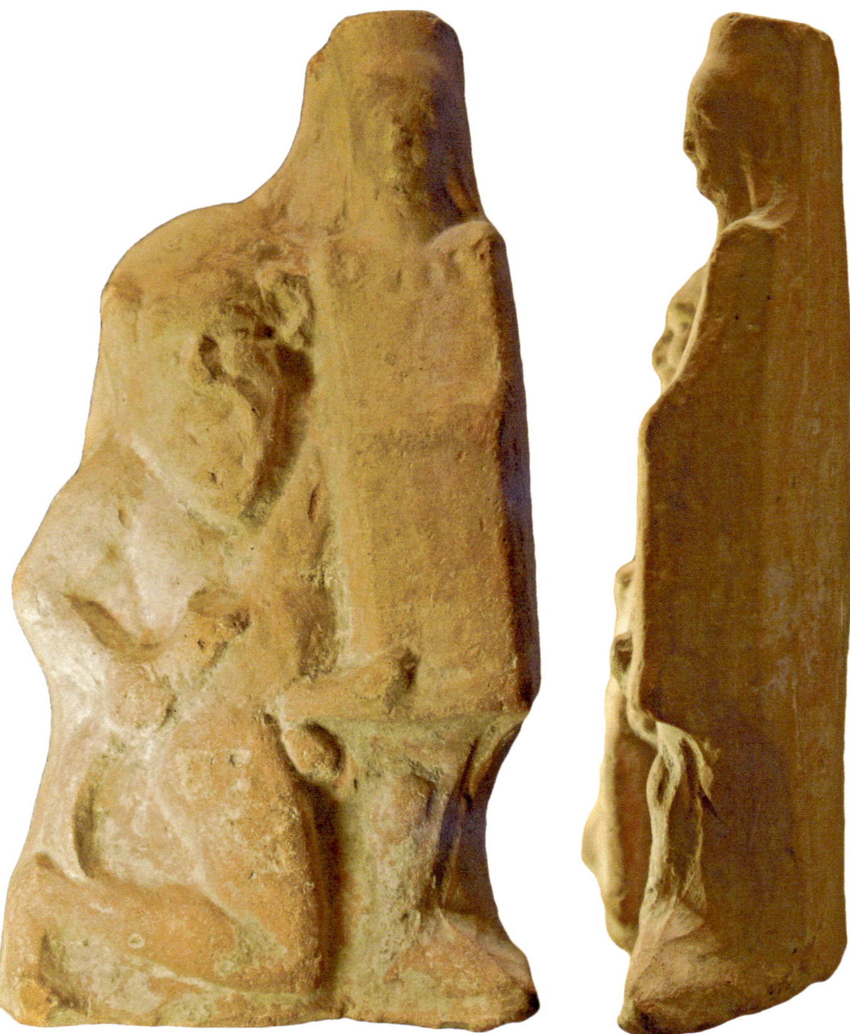

Figure 28: The front and side views of a similar figure, as exhibited in the showcase in the Louvre; Scale 1:1.

kourotrophoi figurines: a mother carrying her child on her left shoulder. See **199** and **200**. The child has the same pose and dress as the figurine. The same way of carrying a figurine is found in a statuette in the Mus. Randazzo (fig.29). A kore carries a divinity, reads the description of the 9cm tall statuette. The carrier, dressed in a fine-folded undergarment, with a coarser folded dress over the shoulder the figurine is sitting on. With her left hand he/she supports the feet of the figurine, while the right hand holds the lower legs of the figurine. The figurine itself is seated in a rather rigid pose, with the arms stretched along the body. Her face is rather worn, but it seems the hair is parted, and she wears a veil on top of it. Her ankle-length dress has folds and a belt. A cape covers her upper arms and falls down her back. Virgilio 1969, p.49, 93, photo 25, and 166.

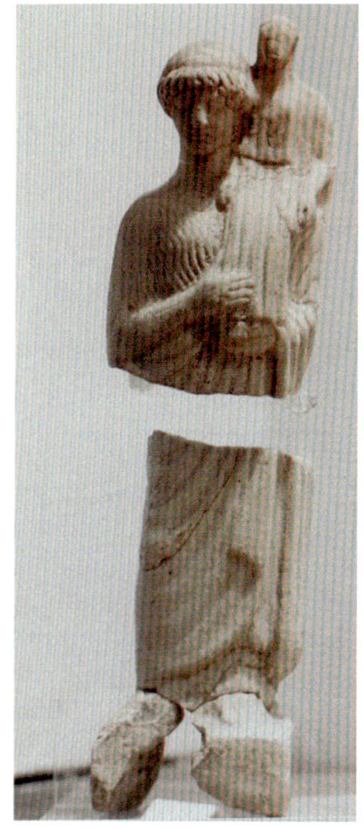

Figure 29: Figurine (h.9cm) in which a girl wears the goddess on her left shoulder, holding her with her right hand at the ankles and supporting her feet with her left hand. Mus. Randazzo. Scale 1:1.

No.199

- *Museum and Inventory number:* Mus. Agrigento C499
- *Findspot and context:* Akragas
- *Publications:* -
- *Dimensions in cm:* h.6.4
- *Material:* Terracotta
- *Techniques:* Front moulded.
- *Colour:* Pink 7.5 YR 7/3

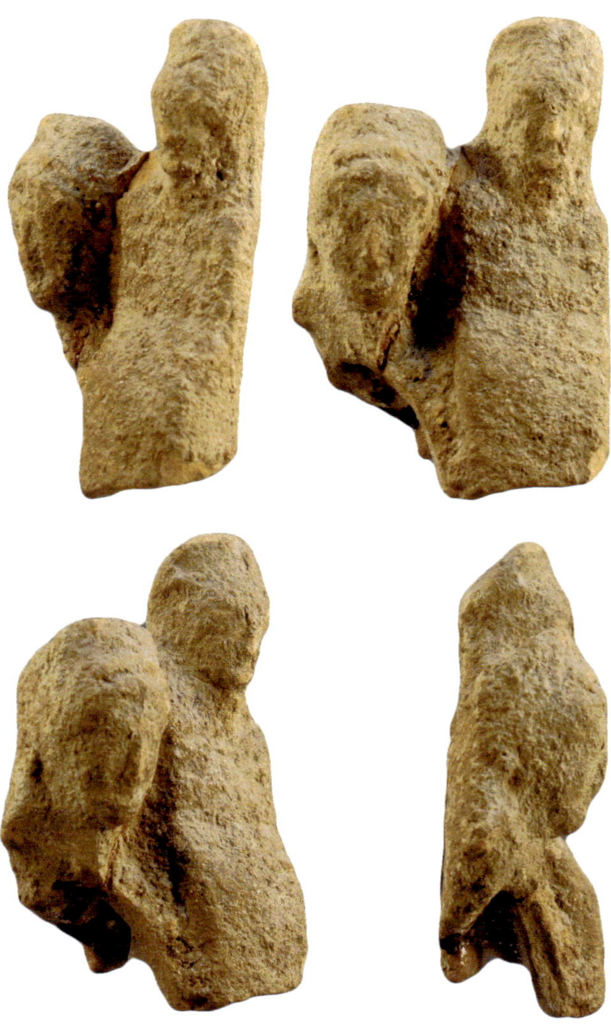

No. 199; Scale 1:1 (Museo Archeologico Regionale "Pietro Griffo", Agrigento).

- *Date:* The first half of the 5th century BCE
- *Workshop:* Unknown
- *Typology:* Female figure carrying goddess or kourotrophos: 6a
- *Short description:* Upper part of a figurine. Broken and crumbled at back. Three other fragments are glued onto the back. Very weathered.

Two similar looking figures, of which one is smaller and sitting on the larger person's shoulder. Both are wearing a polos, the one of the larger person with rim. Her head is the only part left. The smaller person just misses the feet. She has a simple body outline, dressed in a long garment; no fibulae or arms are depicted. Her knees are bulging, making her sitting position clear.

- *Comparable objects:* This object is probably a figure carrying the deity, as the Randazzo figure named above and the satyr image **198** referring to it. Another interpretation would be a kourotrophos, similar to **200**. For the latter interpretation, see a figurine, dated to around the middle of the 5th century BCE. Pautasso 1996, p.41, no.47, tav.V. The polos carried by both mother and child, in the Akragantine case, would be difficult to explain. Zuntz interprets them as Demeter and her daughter Persephone, while earlier he stated that such kourotrophoi images represent humans. Zuntz 1971, p.96 and 177. Such figurines appear in different forms, similar to the variations of the standing, leaning or sitting single figures. A figurine part from Akragas or Selinous depicts the larger head of the mother, with a child on her left shoulder. Both do not wear a polos. British Mus. Inv. no.1956,0216.21 See museum website. A similar figurine, but with the standing mother dressed in a folded chiton and a naked boy on her shoulder is found in the extra-urban sanctuary at Bitalemi, Gela Inv. no.8739., upper part 11.1cm. It is dated to the mid of the 5th century BCE. Panvini 1998 178 V17. Another comparable object is a plaque with a woman carrying a smaller figurine on her left shoulder from Carthage. The smaller person is seated in the same way and has a chest with two rows with pectoral pendants on it (?). Nat. Mus. Copenhagen Inv. no.ABb 37 h.6.1cm, Breitenstein 1941, no.759. Several kourotrophoi seated on a winged back chair, with a child on the lap, are found at the Necropoli di Contrada Pezzino, AG22608 and AG22607, h.16 and 17.5cm, Veder Greco: le necrópolis di Agrigento 1988, p.397. In addition, a comparable object might be a kourotrophos from Selinous, which looks more Rhodian and carries, according to Gabrici, a monkey on her left shoulder. The monkey appears on several Akragantine figurines in connection with toddlers but the carried person is more likely to be a child. Gabrici 1927, tav.XL.2. On a Phoenician example, the smaller figure on the shoulder wears the typical pendants also like the polos and the rounded back. Albertocchi 1999, p.362, fig.18. There are three such kourotrophoi and they date from the fourth century BCE. Albertocchi 1999, p.361. The upper part of a figurine from Carthage depicts a woman with a child on her left shoulder or arm, who seems to wear pectoral pendants (fig.30). The circle as an aureole at the back is typical for Carthaginian figurines. See Picard 1982. On one of the two Etruscan kourotrophoi amber beads, the mother seems to carry the child on her left shoulder, holding her with her arm. They are similarly dressed and veiled. Next to the mothers' feet sits a goose. The pendant is dated to between 600-550 BCE and is 8.3mm high. See museum website.

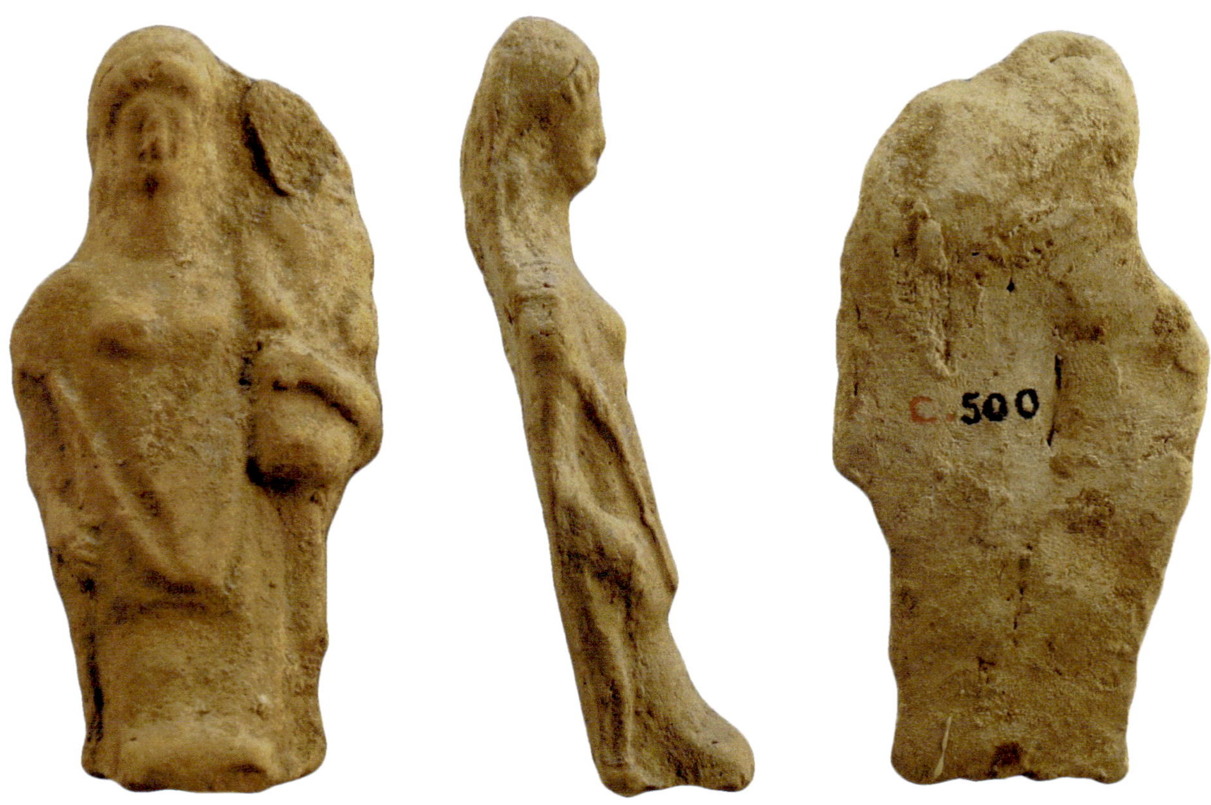

No. 200; Scale 1:1 (Museo Archeologico Regionale "Pietro Griffo", Agrigento).

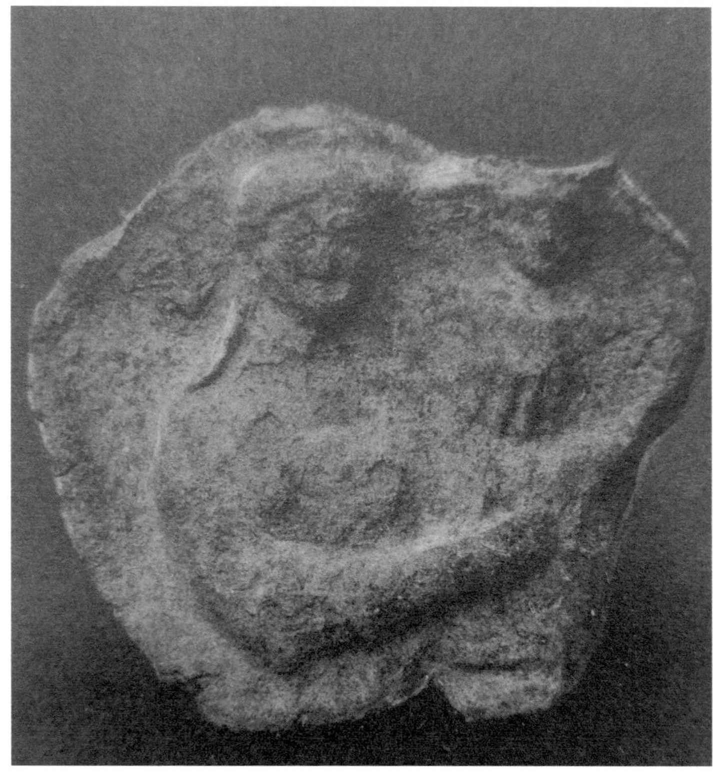

Figure 30: A smaller figure is carried on this plaque from Carthage. Photo after Breitenstein 1941, pl.90.

No.200

- *Museum and Inventory number:* Mus. Agrigento C500
- *Findspot and context:* Akragas
- *Publications:* -
- *Dimensions in cm:* h.10.2
- *Material:* Terracotta
- *Techniques:* Front moulded. Solid. Fingerprints on the back.
- *Colour:* Pink 7.5 YR 7/3
- *Date:* Fifth century BCE
- *Workshop:* Unknown
- *Typology:* Kourotrophos: 6a
- *Short description:* Nearly complete figurine of a 'kourotrophos', a mother carrying her child on her left shoulder. Head of the child is damaged. Standing, naturalistic but short-bodied female figure. She has a fine face with a very pronounced chin and large nose. It is quite indistinct. Her small round head is covered with a veil, leaving a fringe of hair visible. She has a sturdy neck, clear breasts and a wide round shoulder, her right. With her left zarm, she holds the child tight, while her right arm she holds with the fingers outstretched down her body, slightly bent, on top of her folded upper garment, which hangs from halfway down the upper arm. The child holds both arms straight down. Both figurines have no clear feet, but instead a block-like part to indicate them. Straight back.
- *Comparable objects:* This one is probably later than **199** and differs from it because it is differently dressed. The mother does not wear a polos but a veil and she wears a garment with a large fold hanging down at her knees. Her body is also more naturalistic.

  A similar figurine from a later date is from Tegea, Arcadia and dated to 440-430 BCE: Louvre Inv. no.MNB 1718, nearly complete 18cm, See museum website. The figurine is interpreted as Kore-Persephone. Mollard Besques 1963, p.34, pl. XIII.1. The digital database of the museum also suggests the figurines may be mortals.

  Also from Tegea, but very early and handmade is a figurine carrying a smaller similar styled person on her left shoulder: Mus. Athens Inv. no.4349, See museum website. Both have a 'bird' or pinched face, bullet eyes and two pectoral cords with one pendant. The style is very similar to 1 and 2. Three figurines from the necropolis of Carthage, as well as others from Ibiza and Reggio Calabria. Albertocchi 1999, p.361-3, n. 41. One of those from Cartage with the typical disc-shaped back, carries on her left shoulder a smaller female, who wears pendants and a polos. Albertocchi 1999, p.361, fig.18). A larger person in draped dress with a smaller boy (?) on her left shoulder from Rhodes. Nat. Mus. Copenhagen: photo 5389, See museum website) and another one: Inv. no.2256 probably with a male figure on her shoulder, photo 5035, See museum website.

  More on different sorts of 'kourotrophoi'. Price 1978, p.49-50, category: child held on the left.
- *Other notes:* Glued to its stand.

Type P: Earrings (201-202)

A mould for a large earring and a part of a large statue with an earring. These form comparable items with the earrings as they are represented on the figurines.

No.201

- *Museum and Inventory number:* Mus. Agrigento C272 (16A -4) (558)
- *Findspot and context:* City Sanctuary. At the base of the southwest wall of the sanctuary
- *Publications:* -
- *Dimensions in cm:* h.5.8; Inner part 4.6cm, width 15mm
- *Material:* Terracotta
- *Techniques:* Imprint from an object, the patrix
- *Colour:* Very pale brown 10 YR 6/3
- *Date:* 5th century BCE
- *Workshop:* Unknown
- *Typology:* Earring: 6b
- *Short description:* Mould of an earring. The earring consists of a knob with a rosette. From here a lyre-shaped object, suspended from the knob. This ring is thicker, boat-shaped at the bottom. In the middle of the ring and just below the knob, a very small round pendant is impressed. Three long pendants are suspended from the 'boat'. They look like they hang from a round part at the top and are widen slightly with a pointed end. The back of the earring was rounded. The edges are quite thin.
- *Other notes:* The mould is glued to its stand, the rear is not very visible.

No.202

- *Museum and Inventory number:* Mus. Agrigento S508
- *Findspot and context:* City Sanctuary
- *Publications:* -
- *Dimensions in cm:* h.10.5
- *Material:* Terracotta
- *Techniques:* Moulded
- *Colour:* Light red 2.5 YR 7/6
- *Date:* 6th century BCE
- *Workshop:* Unknown
- *Typology:* Part of hair and earring: 6b
- *Short description:* Part of life-size statue. Part of hair with earring on right side. Hair in four rows, divided into smaller block forms, like roof tiles. Earlobe with knob-shaped ear stud and sizeable boat-shaped ring. The ring is thinner at the top and thicker on the bottom. The piece has a rim on the outer side, which might have been part of a veil.
- *Comparable objects:* Very similar to the hairstyle of other large statuary. One piece was found near the Temple of Zeus 8611 Mus. Agrigento, Inv. no. 8611, h.5.4cm, (fig.31). Another piece with similar hair has been found during the recent survey and excavation at S. Anna, Agrigento, no number h.9.8cm, (fig.32), very similar and possibly from the same statue as the head found at the earlier excavation at S. Anna in a votive deposit northeast of building B. Fiorentini 1969, p.79, tav.XXXIX.2.

The hairstyle is reminiscent of that on a piece with hair arrangement in similar block-shapes from Megara Hyblaea. Gras, Tréziny and Broise 2004, p.328 fig.345. And of some large statues from Rhodes: face with part of fringe. Nat. Mus. Copenhagen Inv. no.2463; photo 5038, See museum website as well as of the arms of a statue with some parts of the same hairstyle on it from Akragas. Breitenstein 1945, p.122 fig.9, h.26.5cm, a piece found at S. Anna Inv. no.11376, See museum website. The hairstyle is reminiscent of bronze working of hair. Stibbe and Stibbe-Heldring 2006, p.188, fig.7-10.

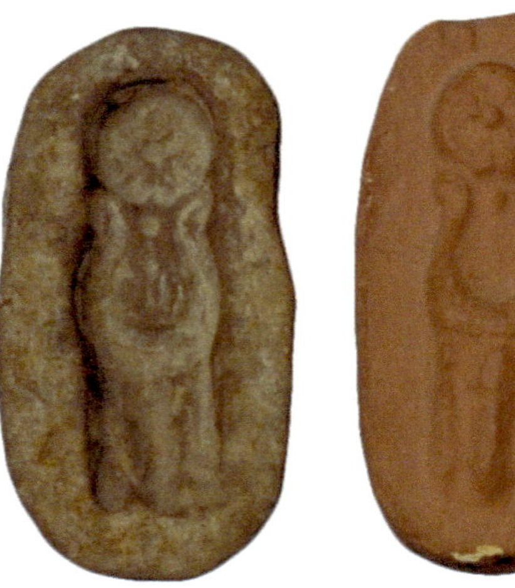
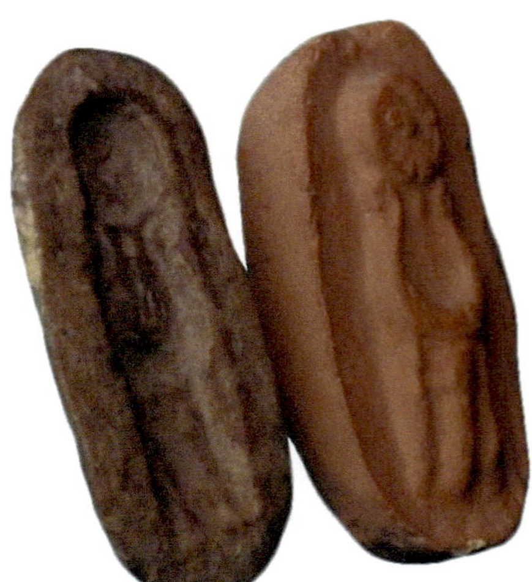

No. 201; Scale 1:1 (Museo Archeologico Regionale "Pietro Griffo", Agrigento).

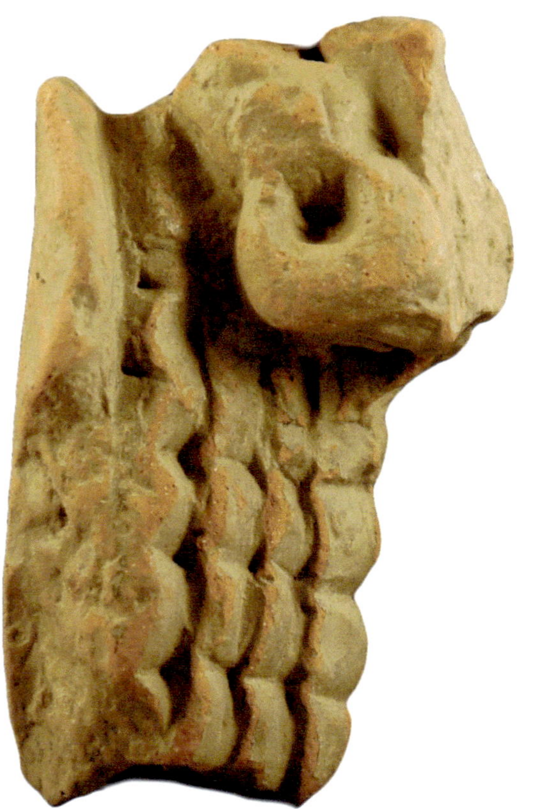

No. 202; Scale 1:1 (Museo Archeologico Regionale "Pietro Griffo", Agrigento).

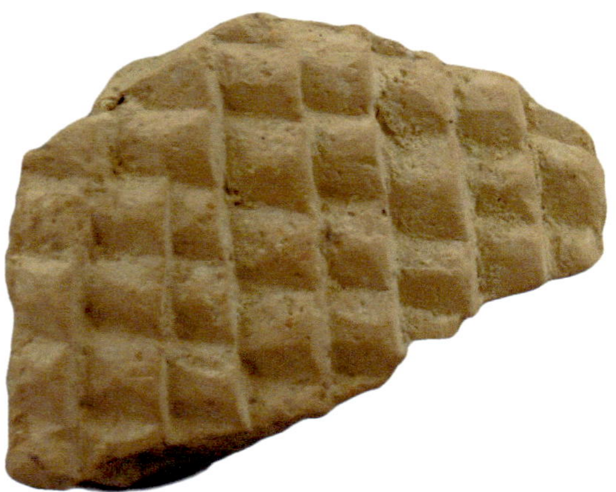

Figure 31: Part of the hair of a statue, found near the Temple of Zeus, Agrigento, AG 8611; Scale 1:1.

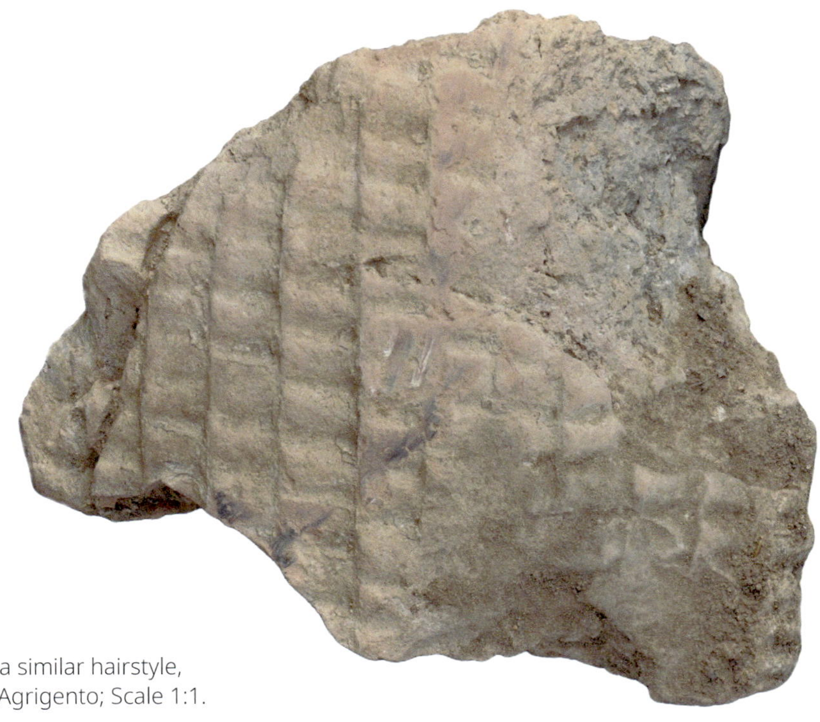

Figure 32: Part of a similar hairstyle, found at S. Anna, Agrigento; Scale 1:1.

Index

Numerical ordered inventory numbers of the musea and their corresponding numbers in the catalogue, in bold.

Mus. Munich

Mus. Amsterdam

Abstracts

English

This study of terracotta votive figurines from Akragas (Agrigento, Sicily) dating from the end of the sixth to the beginning of the fifth century BCE aims to investigate and explain their production, use and meaning as votives and grave goods. By using literature, iconography, and a chaîne opératoire approach, this study traces the cultural identities of its users, and reveals Akragas as a multicultural society in which the design and dedication of the figurines may have played a bridging role between the different inhabitants of the area.

The figurines, between 5-35 cm in height, represent a female figure, often seated and adorned with various items. Such figurines have previously been identified as 'Athena Lindia,' as they were thought to have been imported by Rhodian migrants. However, only a few of the figurines, from the second quarter of the fifth century BCE, can be positively identified as Athena as they wear a helmet. Such Athena figurines were exchanged with Gelas, Akragas' metropolis. Based on literary sources, the figurines have also been identified as Demeter and Kore/Persephone. However, there is no archaeological evidence for this identification. The figurines were produced as generic female deities, which could be adapted with the application of different attributes to represent a specific goddess. The goddess or goddesses thus signified were probably local in origin, and, despite being a popular subject for the coroplasts, their names remain unknown.

The figurines with their chubby faces, splendid furniture, and rich adornments, depict a prosperous life. The extensive jewellery on the figurines contains strikingly large fibulae appliques fastening pectoral chains with several sorts of pendants. In contrast, the body of the figurines remained armless and abstract for some time with no indication of gender. The block shaped, sloping upper body might have originated with aniconic objects, but suggests here a seated person, covered with a rectangular apron on the front. In contrast, the face is detailed, and often crowned with a specific headgear, the *polos*. The Archaic smile reveals Greek influence on its features. The jewellery on the figurines is modelled after existing items, including pectoral bands. The form of the jewellery items changed fast, influenced by different peoples and changing fashions, which show a striking resemblance with representations of jewellery and fashion on coins.

The research on the production of the figurines was partly carried out using an archaeological experiment in which figurines and moulds were reproduced. By combining data from the experiment with an analysis of their iconographic features, most of the figurines studied can be shown to have been designed and produced locally. The moulding technique, probably introduced by newcomers to the city, provided for relatively cheap and rapid production of terracotta figurines. Local clay and marl is found near to the city, and its composition was found to be very suitable, due to its plasticity, fine structure and soft tone on firing. Wooden figurines, the forerunners of the terracotta figurines, were used in the production of the moulds of their terracotta successors. The terracotta figurines evolved into more three-dimensional forms, so that they were able to stay upright unsupported. Objects and moulds were also clearly exchanged with the city of Selinous, resulting in variations of the standard figurines with finely expressed faces. Details were also sometimes reworked by hand to add or change specific features.

Designing and dedicating these votive figurines, and possibly also jewellery, to a cult statue might have acted as a unifying element for the perhaps multi-ethnic society of Akragas. By means of these anthropomorphic figurines, people gave shape to their origin and narratives, using old and new symbols such as the Phoenician crescent and the Greek satyr. Perhaps intermarriage with primarily male migrants might have accelerated social cohesion between different ethnic groups, combining and integrating cultural traits in the newly prosperous context, forging a new identity unique to Sicily. The prosperity expressed by these metal adornments, fits Diodorus Siculus' description of Akragas as a rich city.

Samenvatting (Dutch)

Dit onderzoek analyseert de terracotta beeldjes uit Akragas (Agrigento, Sicilië) van eind zesde tot begin vijfde eeuw v. Chr. Het onderzoekt hoe deze objecten werden vervaardigd en gebruikt. Dit literair, iconografisch en materieel onderzoek traceert de culturele achtergrond van de inwoners van dit gebied. De vormgeving en het gebruik van de beeldjes in religieuze context werpt een nieuw licht op Akragas als cultureel gemengde samenleving.

De beeldjes stellen een vrouwelijke figuur voor, tussen de 5-35 cm. in lengte, bijgenaamd Athena Lindia, omdat ze zouden zijn meegebracht door Rhodiërs. Deze benaming is echter niet zorgvuldig omdat slechts enkele beeldjes met een helm uit de tweede kwart van de vijfde eeuw de godin Athena voorstellen. Deze werden uitgewisseld met Akragas' moederstad, Gelas. Ook een identificatie met Demeter en Persephone/Kore wordt onterecht afgeleid uit de mythologisch literaire bronnen. De vorm was in principe generiek en de standaard een vrouw. Dit valt mede te verklaren door de productie in mallen. Het lijkt om een of meerdere lokale godinnen te gaan, waarvan we de naam niet kennen, maar die gezien de hoeveelheid votieven grote populariteit genoten.

De weldoorvoede gezichten, hun luxueuze zetels en vooral hun sieraden wekken de indruk van grote rijkdom, hetgeen overeenstemt met de vermelding van Akragas' welvarendheid door Diodorus Siculus. Het rechthoekige en armloze lichaam toont in eerste instantie geen specifiek vrouwelijke kenmerken en is wellicht afgeleid van aniconische objecten. De gebogen vorm in het rechthoekige schort suggereert een zittende houding. Dit wordt verfraaid met uitzonderlijke grote fibula-applicaties en rijk versierd met verschillende soorten borstkettingen. Het hoofd daarentegen, vaak getooid met een *polos*, een hoofddeksel, is opvallend gedetailleerd. De 'Archaïsche glimlach' toont duidelijk een Griekse oorsprong. De afgebeelde sieraden zijn gemodelleerd naar echte sieraden en volgen allerlei modetrends. De verschillende culturele invloeden nemen zowel oudere symbolen op, zoals de Fenicische halve maan, als nieuwere zoals de Griekse satyr.

Het onderzoek naar de productiewijze van de beeldjes is uitgevoerd met een archeologisch experiment, waarin mallen en beeldjes in opeenvolgende generaties werden gereproduceerd. In combinatie met de bovengenoemde kenmerken zijn de meeste beeldjes aan te wijzen als lokaal ontworpen en gemaakt en daarmee 'typisch' voor Akragas. Dit is ook af te leiden uit de productiewijze, in mallen en met lokaal gewonnen klei. Deze techniek, wellicht geïntroduceerd door de nieuwkomers op Sicilië, maakte zo een relatief goedkope en snelle productie mogelijk. De klei resulteerde gecombineerd met lokaal beschikbare mergel in soepele, matig krimpend en beige-bakkend terracotta met een fijne structuur. Houten beeldjes zijn in een vroeg stadium van deze toepassing gebruikt om mallen te maken, maar werden al snel vervangen door de meer driedimensionale blok-vorm, die rechtop kon blijven staan. Ondanks deze productiewijze is de variëteit aan modellen, mede door de uitwisseling met o.a. Selinous groot. Details werden soms handmatig of met behulp van losse mallen aangebracht.

Gezamenlijk uitgevoerde rituelen, zoals het wijden van deze votiefbeeldjes en het versieren van een cultusbeeld met sieraden, creëerden een eensgezindheid in het multi-etnische Akragas. De figuurtjes, zijn gemodelleerd naar de lokale vrouwen en geven blijk van integratie, wellicht door gemengde huwelijken. Zo werden mogelijk tradities geïntegreerd en nieuwe identiteit ontwikkeld binnen de context van het welvarende Akragas.

Sommario (Italian)

Il presente studio mira ad indagare ed illustrare il processo di produzione e l'utilizzo come oggetti funerari e votivi di statuette di terracotta datate alla fine del VI, inizio del V secolo a.C., e provenienti da Akragas (Agrigento, Sicilia). Inoltre, tramite l'impiego di fonti letterarie e studi iconografici, questa ricerca vuole ricostruire l'appartenenza culturale di coloro che furono coinvolti nella creazione e nell'utilizzo delle suddette. In tutto ciò, Akragas risulta una società multiculturale in cui la creazione e la dedica di statuette potrebbe aver giocato un ruolo importante nel connettere gli abitanti della regione.

Le statuette, la cui altezza misura circa 5-35 cm, rappresentano una figura femminile, solitamente seduta e abbellita da diversi ornamenti. Tali statuette sono state in passato identificate come rappresentazioni di Atena Lindia, provenienti da Rodi. Secondo le fonti letterarie, invece, le statuette erano identificate con Demetra e Persefone, ma non vi è alcuna prova archeologica che confermi questa affermazione. Più probabile è che le statuette venissero prodotte per rappresentare divinità femminili generiche, a cui poi potevano essere aggiunti attributi di divinità specifiche, probabilmente originarie dell'area di Akragas e il cui nome rimane purtroppo sconosciuto.

Parte di questa ricerca è stata compiuta impiegando un esperimento, attraverso cui sono stati ricostruiti gli stampi per le statuette. Incrociando i dati così ottenuti con l'analisi dell'iconografia, si è potuto dimostrare che la maggior parte della statuette furono prodotte localmente. L'innovativa tecnica di plasmatura rese il processo di produzione economico e veloce, e tale processo fu reso più semplice dalla presenza in loco di argilla dalla composizione chimica favorevole. I dettagli potevano essere cambiati in un secondo momento manualmente. Gli stampi furono plasmati tramite l'utilizzo di statuette di legno, precursori di quelle di terracotta, che si evolvettero in forme più tridimensionali e per cui fosse possibile rimanere in piedi senza supporti.

Le statuette sono il ritratto della prosperità, per mezzo dei loro visi paffuti, della raffinata mobilia, dei ricchi ornamenti. Il corpo risulta talvolta un blocco astratto coperto da un grembiule, senza braccia, e talvolta totalmente privo di indicazioni di genere. Di contro, il viso è ricco di dettagli, spesso sormontato da un particolare copricapo, detto *polos*. Il sorriso in stile Arcaico rivela l'influenza greca, mentre i gioielli, incluse le decorazioni del busto, ricordano artefatti reali. Si è inoltre registrato un rapido cambiamento nello stile dei gioielli delle statuette, strettamente collegato al cambiamento delle rappresentazioni sulle monete, e probabilmente causato da influenze esterne alla città. Sono infatti registrati scambi con Gela e Selinunte.

Creare e dedicare queste figurine votive, e spesso, in aggiunta, anche gioielli, a statue oggetto di culto fu probabilmente un elemento unificatore della società multiculturale di Akragas. Per mezzo di queste statuette antropomorfe, gli abitanti rappresentarono le loro origini, mescolando simboli antichi e nuovi, come la mezzaluna fenicia e i satiri della tradizione greca. In alcuni casi, l'unione tra donne locali e uomini provenienti da oltremare potrebbe aver accelerato la coesione sociale tra diversi gruppi etnici, mescolando e integrando diversi tratti culturali e così forgiando l'identità unica della Sicilia.

Curriculum Vitae

Gerrie van Rooijen was born on 4 March 1985 in Buren. She received her high school diploma from the Marnix Gymnasium in Rotterdam, where the foundation was laid for her later study of classical Greek and Roman texts. In the last year of high school, participating in archaeological fieldwork under the auspices of the University of Utrecht in ancient Gardara (Umm Qais, Jordan) generated a new interest in archaeological fieldwork and in material culture as a reflection of daily life in the past.

Continuing her studies in Leiden, Gerrie obtained a Bachelor's degree in Classics (Griekse en Latijnse Taal en Cultuur) concluding with a thesis on the comparison between the description by Homer of Odysseus' encounter with Circe and the depiction of the same story on vases, supervised by Dr. M. van Raalte and Dr. E. Grasman. Meanwhile, she started teaching Ancient Greek and Latin at a secondary school in Leiden, a job she continues to perform to this day, as she feels motivated to pass on her knowledge of Antiquity. Drawing on her years of experience, combined with Educational Studies at the ICLON (Leiden University) and an international Classics summer course, she has redesigned and professionalized her classes.

Following courses on Greek epigraphy and an excursion to Greece, Gerrie was encouraged to broaden her scope to include the study of material culture. She thus continued with a Master's degree in archaeology at Leiden University, specialising in ancient Near Eastern and Mediterranean archaeology. This time, it was once again the combination of text and objects that inspired her to write her thesis on the earliest Greek writing and its meaning, supervised by Prof. J.L. Bintliff. Through inspirational classes on Greek Sculpture and an excursion to Sicily, she then came into contact with Professor N. Sojc, who invited her to join a research project in Agrigento. At the archaeological museum in Agrigento, it was clear that the numerous terracotta figurines required more in-depth study, and Gerrie was encouraged to pursue doctoral research on this intriguing material. The NWO made the combination of research and working at school financially possible. She has published an article on the material aspects of her research: 'Figuring out: coroplastic art and technè in Agrigento, Sicily: the results of a coroplastic experiment.' *Analecta Praehistorica Leidensia* 47 (2017) pp. 151-161.

Through learning Italian for her research (and Persian to communicate with her in-laws), Gerrie has retained and cultivated her interest in languages and literature. She continues to study and teach the classical languages and civilization and plans to remain involved in archaeological research, continuing to scrutinise expression of identity by its representation in terracotta figurines.

Acknowledgements

Writing a PhD is a journey, long and sometimes lonely, but, at the same time, exciting and challenging. The moments of discovery, in soil, on paper or by reasoning make up for most of the hardships. Without the help and support of several people, I would have not been able to travel this route. I would therefore like to express my deep gratitude to those who walked beside me, whether professionally or personally, and sometimes both.

The latter surely applies to my promotor, Professor Natascha Sojc, who carefully read the first drafts of my texts and commented constructively on the structure and content. You were a true mentor. I am also thankful to Dennis Braekmans, co-promotor, for his comments on the material studies part of this book and the article in the Analecta. You both encouraged me and paved the way. I am thankful also to the committee members, who have read my thesis.

I would like to express my gratitude to all the museums that have kindly allowed me to work on their artifacts. *Vorrei rivolgere i miei più vivi e profondi ringraziamenti a tutte le autorità della Soprintendenza ai Beni Culturali di Agrigento e a tutte le personalità del Museo 'Pietro Griffo' di Agrigento. Un particolate ringraziamento è dovuto alle dottoresse Mangione e LaManga.*

I am grateful to Jörg Gebauer, conservator at the Staatliche Antikensammlungen in Munich for his kind assistance in studying the figurines. I am also grateful to Geralda Jurriaans-Helle, conservator at the Allard Pierson Museum in Amsterdam and Liudmila Akimova, head of the Ancient Art and Archaeology Department of the Pushkin Museum of Fine Arts in Moscow for tracing Sicilian objects and photos in the archives of the museum; and to Susan Walker, Keeper of Antiquities at the Ashmolean Museum in Oxford. The following museums have also been generous enough to allow me to use their material in this study: The Allard Pierson Museum in Amsterdam, the British Museum in London, Museo Archeologico Regionale 'Antonino Salinas', Palermo, Museo Archeologico Regionale 'Paolo Orsi', Syracuse, and Museo regionale interdisciplinare di Caltanissetta.

Guidance and assistance at the archaeological excavation in Agrigento and research in Selinunte was provided by Linda Adorno, Clemens Voigts and Agnes Henning. The German Archaeological Institute (DAI, Rome) provided me with a photograph. I would like to thank the people of the Faculty of Archaeology, Annalize Rheeder for her assistance in photography and her collegiality, Bibi Beekman for assistance with the archaeological experiment, other students who joined the work in the field and in the museum from Leiden or Augsburg University: Abel, Antonia, Alina, Charlotte, Daniela, Denis, Diederik, Erik, Fenna, Fenno, Iris, Ischa, Koos and Thomas.

Iris Daleman from Augsburg, thank you for your great hospitality and the map you drew. I also greatly appreciate the careful reviewing and editing of this text by Thurstan Robinson. *Vorrei ringraziare Valentina Alletto e la famiglia di B&B Ubriaco per l'amicizia e l'ospitalità durante la mia permanenza nell'Agrigentino.*

Elisa Perotti and Bas van Rooijen, my brother – thank you both for accepting to be my paranymphs and for being there on the day of my defence ceremony. I appreciate your support.

Nederlands

De bezielende begeleiding van Loe Jacobs bij het uitvoeren van het archeologisch experiment, alsmede bij de verslaglegging daarvan in een artikel en in dit proefschrift, heb ik heel erg op prijs gesteld. Ook Christoph Pieper en Edward Grasman ben ik dankbaar voor hun terugkoppeling op respectievelijk de literaire en kunsthistorische argumenten in mijn tekst. Het NWO ben ik zeer erkentelijk voor het toekennen van de Lerarenbeurs, David Shakouri voor het wijzen op het bestaan hiervan.

Collega's en (oud-)leerlingen van het Driestar College: Geregeld informeerden jullie naar de vorderingen van het onderzoek. Jullie betrokkenheid waardeer ik. Een speciaal woord van dank voor mijn vervanger tijdens het NWO verlof, Lydia Bouterse, aan wie ik gerust deze taken kon overlaten. De sectie klassieke talen was klein-maar-fijn. Ineke Hage verschafte helderheid in de regelgeving en ook bij mijn teamleider Bart de Jongh en de locatiedirecteur Geert Snoep staat de deur altijd open. Dank jullie wel voor het mede mogelijk maken van dit traject.

Karsten Wentink, Corné van Woerdekom en andere medewerkers van Sidestone Press wil ik bedanken voor het overleg betreffende de druk van dit boek. Fijn dat jullie me nog wat foto bewerkingstechnieken hebben willen bijbrengen!

Vele uren, die ik in de bibliotheek doorbracht, werden prettig afgewisseld met pauzes. Maita, bedankt voor je tips, je motiverende woorden, maar ook gewoon het gezellige kletsen over de sieraden van vroeger en nu. Petra Snoep, dankjewel voor je trouwe vriendschap en je luisterend oor.

Mijn ouders aan wie ik dit boek ook opdraag, ben ik dankbaar voor hun geduld en zorgzaamheid. Ook waardeer ik het zeer dat zij mij lieten kennis maken met de Oudheid. Mijn broertjes, Henk en Bas, bedankt voor jullie steun in verschillende vormen! Dat is erg gewaardeerd.

Majid, liefste, dank je wel voor je zorgzaamheid, je adviezen en je ondersteuning. Voor je liefdevolle aanwezigheid en betrokkenheid bij mijn passie ben ik je heel erg dankbaar.

Persian

همچنین از خانواده مجید بسیار سپاس گذارم بخاطر محبت ها و حمایت های همیشگی شان. امیدوارم که شما را مرتب در هلند یا در ایران ببینم.

از بر و بچ گروه خزلیخ: از شما سپاس گذارم که با آغوشی باز پذیرا و یاوری کردید. از لحظات خوبی که با هم داشتیم که باعث می شد من از فشار های کاری فراموش کنم. غذا های خوشمزه ،مهمونی های خزلیخ ، رقص و سرور و شادمانی که کمک کرد به من رقصیدن رو بهتر یاد بگیرم. ممنون از خانم های این گروه که الگوی موفقیت و استقامت برای من بودند و من رو هدایت و یاوری کردند.